August 28–31, 2012
Matsue-city, Shimane, Japan

Association for Computing Machinery

Advancing Computing as a Science & Profession

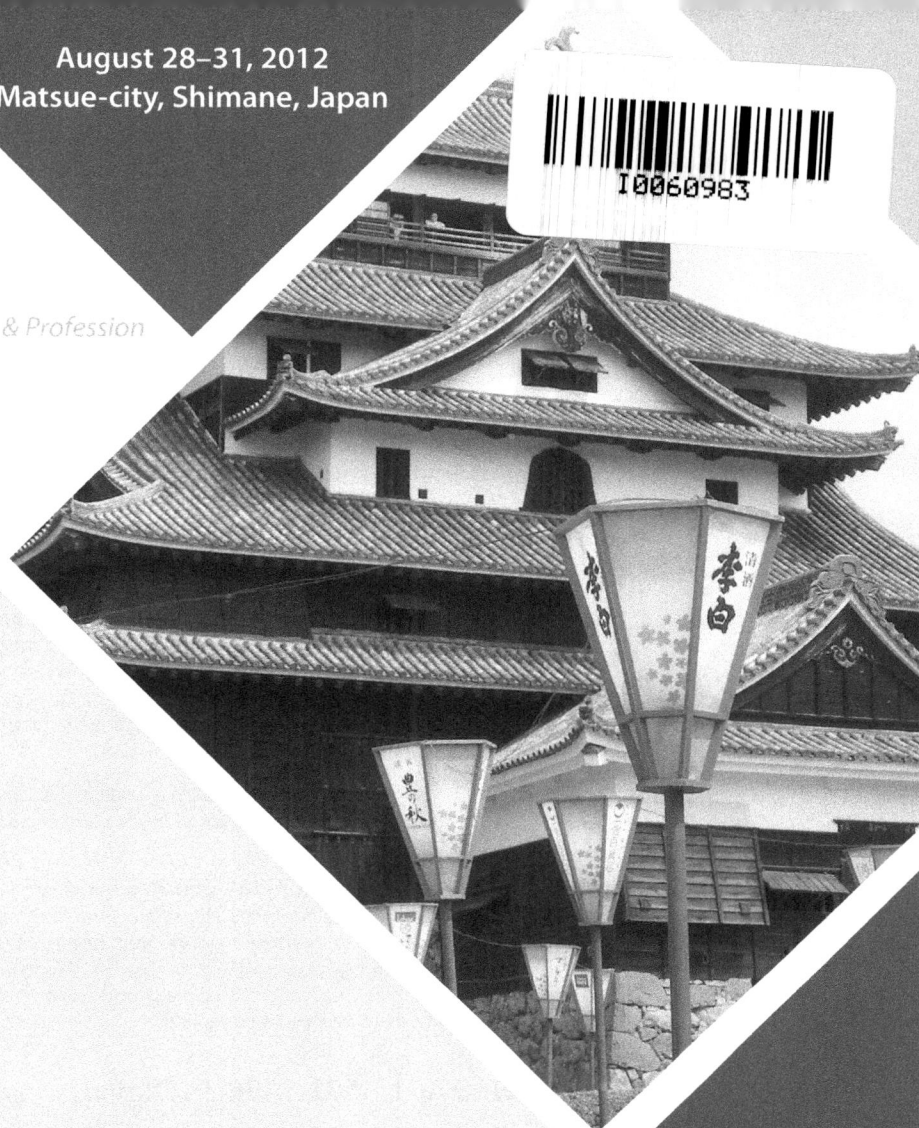

APCHI'12

Proceedings of the 2012
Asia Pacific Conference on Computer-Human Interaction

Sponsored by:
ACM SIGCHI & HCD

Supported by:
Japan Ergonomics Society, Japan Society of Kansei Engineering, Japan Society for Software Science and Technology, Human Interface Society, IPS, EiC, International Association for Universe Design, The Virtual Society of Japan, U'eyes Design Inc., Monte System Corporation, 4Assist, Namoto, Tateisi Science and Technology Foundation, & Osaka Electro-Communication University

Association for
Computing Machinery

Advancing Computing as a Science & Profession

The Association for Computing Machinery
2 Penn Plaza, Suite 701
New York, New York 10121-0701

Notice to Past Authors of ACM-Published Articles
ACM intends to create a complete electronic archive of all articles and/or other material previously published by ACM. If you have written a work that has been previously published by ACM in any journal or conference proceedings prior to 1978, or any SIG Newsletter at any time, and you do NOT want this work to appear in the ACM Digital Library, please inform permissions@acm.org, stating the title of the work, the author(s), and where and when published.

ISBN: 978-1-4503-1496-1 (Digital)

ISBN: 978-1-4503-1739-9 (Print)

Additional copies may be ordered prepaid from:

ACM Order Department
PO Box 30777
New York, NY 10087-0777, USA

Phone: 1-800-342-6626 (USA and Canada)
+1-212-626-0500 (Global)
Fax: +1-212-944-1318
E-mail: acmhelp@acm.org
Hours of Operation: 8:30 am – 4:30 pm ET

Printed in the USA

APCHI 2012 General Chairs and Program Chairs' Welcome

It is our great pleasure to welcome you to APCHI 2012, the 10th Asia–Pacific Conference on Computer–Human Interaction held on 28–31 August in Matsue-city, Shimane, Japan. Following the success of earlier APCHI conferences in Singapore (1996, 2000), Australia (1997), Japan (1998), China (2002), New Zealand (2004), Taiwan (2006), Korea (2008), and Indonesia (2010), the 10th APCHI has brought researchers and practitioners together from academia and industry and has provided an excellent opportunity to exchange ideas and information related to human–computer interaction and related areas in computer and communication technologies as well as human and social sciences. APCHI has been an important forum for scholars and practitioners in the Asia–Pacific region for the latest challenges and developments in Human–Computer Interaction (HCI). APCHI 2012 is co-sponsored by the Human-Centered Design organization (HCD-Net, Japan) and ACM SIGCHI.

APCHI 2012 is the memorable 10th event in the APCHI conference series. During the last 16 years, the field of HCI has been progressing at a rapid pace. Computers and communication technologies have become an indispensable part of infrastructure in our daily life. With these technologies, we share experiences with loved ones, connect with old school friends, broadcast homemade videos, and exchange personal opinions among a loosely coupled community. We learn new knowledge, create business documents, trade stocks, and buy books and music. Nevertheless, important problems remain unsolved, including the tension between usability and user experience, cutting-edge technology and universal access, enjoyment and office work, natural home settings and controlled laboratory settings, and creative work and labor. For this reason, APCHI 2012 set "Reflect, Discover and Innovate" as the conference theme. We reflect upon the past experiences in HCI, discover new findings from present activities, and innovate the quality of our future life. To discuss the theme, APCHI 2012 invited four keynote speakers: Dr. Shumin Zhai of Google Research, Professor Yuichiro Anzai of Japan Society for the Promotion of Science / Keio University, Professor Marc Hassenzahl of Folkwang University, and Professor Asako Kimura of Ritsumeikan University. We also have workshops and tutorials before the main conference.

APCHI 2012 attracted a total of 155 paper submissions. The review process involved a double blind-review with a minimum of two reviewers, a meta-reviewer from the International Associated Program Committee members, and program committee members who met in Tokyo, Japan on 26–28 April, 2012. Among the submissions, 41 papers were accepted as long talks (acceptance rate of 26.5%) and 48 papers were accepted as short talks (acceptance rate of 30%). This proceedings volume presents the 36 technical contributions as long talks, which were offered from many different countries and regions including Australia, Austria, Belgium, Canada, China, Denmark, France, Germany, Japan, Korea, Malaysia, Singapore, and the USA.

We gratefully acknowledge the wonderful support provided in the reviewing of the submissions by the Associated Program Committee members, as well as the additional reviewers who generously gave their time. We greatly appreciate the dedicated support of our strong Organizing Committee members and Program Committee members. Honorary Chairs and Steering Committee members provided technical advice to the chairs. Special thanks are extended also to the Tateishi Science and Technology Foundation.

Kentaro Go
APCHI'12 General Chair
University of Yamanashi, Japan

Mitsuhiko Karashima
APCHI'12 General Chair
Tokai University, Japan

Shin'ichi Fukuzumi
APCHI'12 Program Chair
NEC, Japan

Xiangshi Ren
APCHI'12 Program Chair
Kochi University of Technology, Japan

Table of Contents

Session 4B: Ergonomics Design

Session 4C: Robot and Agents

Session 5A: Multimodal

Session 5B: Gesture and User Experience

Session 5C: Robot and VR

Session 6A: Pen and UI Design

Session 6B: Home

Session 6C: Elderly

Session 7A: Touch

Session 7B: UI Design and Framework

Session 7C: Planning and Measuring

Session 8A: 3D

Session 8B: UX / Design

Session 8C: CMC / CSCW

APCHI 2012 Conference Organization

General Chairs: Kentaro Go *(University of Yamanashi, Japan)*
Mitsuhiko Karashima *(Tokai University, Japan)*

Program Chairs: Shin'ichi Fukuzumi *(NEC, Japan)*
Xiangshi Ren *(Kochi University of Technology, Japan)*

Organizing Chairs: Yoshifumi Kitamura *(Tohoku University, Japan)*
Yasuyuki Sumi *(Future University Hakodate, Japan)*

Treasurers: Haruhiko Urokohara *(U'eyes Design, Japan)*
Ryoji Yoshitake *(IBM, Japan)*

Local Arrangements Chair: Katsuhiko Onishi *(Osaka Electro-Communication University, Japan)*

Publicity Chair: Buntarou Shizuki *(University of Tsukuba, Japan)*

Publication Chair: Yuichiro Kinoshita *(University of Yamanashi, Japan)*

Sponsorship Chairs: Seiji Hayakawa *(Ricoh, Japan)*
Hideyuki Matsubara *(Canon, Japan)*

Website Design: Kohei Matsumura *(Japan Advanced Institute of Science & Technology, Japan)*

Design Director: Kazuhiko Yamazaki *(Chiba Institute of Technology, Japan)*

Steering Committee: Masaaki Kurosu *(The Open University of Japan, Japan)*
Kee Yong Lim *(Human Centered Analysis & Design, Singapore)*

Honorary Chairs: Yuichiro Anzai *(Keio University, Japan)*
Hiroshi Ishii *(MIT Media Lab, USA)*
Masaharu Kumashiro *(University of Occupational & Environmental Health, Japan)*
Hiroshi Yasuda *(Tokyo Denki University, Japan)*

Program Committee: Kentaro Kotani *(Kansai University, Japan)*
Mitsuru Minakuchi *(Kyoto Sangyo University, Japan)*
Hidehiko Okada *(Kyoto Sangyo University, Japan)*
Minghui Sun *(RIKEN, Japan)*
Yu Suzuki *(Kyoto Sangyo University, Japan)*
Linmi Tao *(Tsinghua University, China)*
Toshiki Yamaoka *(Wakayama University, Japan)*
Kazuhiko Yamazaki *(Chiba Institute of Technology, Japan)*

Associate Program Chairs:

Masaya Ando	Cecile Paris
Xiaojun Bi	Beryl Plimmer
Xiang Cao	Pei-Luen Patrick Rau
Tatsuru Daimon	Jun Rekimoto
Yi-Shin Deng	Eunice Sari
Henry Been-Lirn Duh	Yuanchun Shi
Kentaro Fukuchi	Hiroaki Shigemasu
Naotake Hirasawa	Buntarou Shizuki
Yukinobu Hoshino	Itiro Siio
Takeo Igarashi	Chaklam Silpasuwanchai
Pourang Irani	William Soukoreff
Yong Gu Ji	Masanori Sugimoto
Anirudha Joshi	Yasuyuki Sumi
Keiko Kasamatsu	Satoshi Suzuki
CW Khong	Hong Tan
Masatomo Kobayashi	Rong Tao
Tadashi Kobayashi	Feng Tian
Hideki Koike	Sanjay Tripathi
Geehyuk Lee	Huawei Tu
Joonhwan Lee	Chikamune Wada
Woohun Lee	Feng Wang
Chunyuan Liao	Hongan Wang
Youn-kyung Lim	Jingtao Wang
Gitte Lindgaard	Qianying Wang
Takashi Matsumoto	Yang Wang
Kevin McGee	Chui Yin Wong
Miwa Nakanishi	Yizhong Xin
Misako Nambu	Xiaolong (Luke) Zhang
Hiromi Nishiguchi	Shengdong Zhao

APCHI 2012 Sponsors & Supporters

Sponsors:

Technical Supporters:

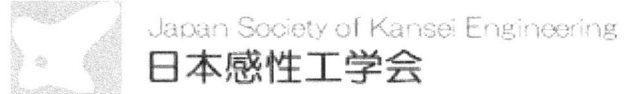

Supporters:

Institutional donor/supporters logos:

FOUNDATION • TATEISI SCIENCE AND TECHNOLOGY

O.E.C.U.
Osaka Electro-Communication University

An Investigation of the Relationship between Texture and Human Performance in Steering Tasks

Minghui Sun[1,2]
[1]Kochi Univ. of Technology
Kochi, Japan
sunmh@nagoya.riken.jp

Xiangshi Ren
Kochi Univ. of Technology
Kochi, Japan
xsren@acm.org

Shumin Zhai
Google Research
Mountain View, CA
USA
zhai@acm.org

Toshiharu Mukai
[2]RIKEN, RTC
Nagoya 463-0003
Japan
tosh@nagoya.riken.jp

ABSTRACT

Steering law is a fundamental model for steering tasks. Many researchers have investigated it according to different input devices, difficulty of task, subjective bias and scale effect etc. However, there is little study about the effect of surface environments especially on the texture of the interaction surface. In this paper, we experimentally investigated users' performances with various surface textures in steering tasks. Five common but different materials were used to supply different textures. Several potential factors of friction are considered in this study. The results showed that texture has no significant effect on movement time. Users naturally and dynamically adjust their force to suit different textures. In a limited range, the smoother the surface is, the more trajectory errors were performed. Our evaluation also proved that different textures can affect user satisfaction significantly.

Author Keywords: Texture, haptic interface, steering task, friction coefficient, human performance.

ACM Classification Keywords:
H.5.2. Information interfaces and presentation: User interfaces.

INTRODUCTION

With the development of complex computer rendering technologies, widgets and user interfaces are now often featured as multi-dimensional objects with sophisticated textures and physical properties. However, the manipulation of those objects is still constrained by the same user interfaces, making it hard for users to feel the physical features of widgets in the real world. Texture is passive haptic feedback, as described in [1, 12], with many unique properties, (e.g., roughness, hardness, stickiness, thermal conductivity). Nowadays, Input devices are changing from traditional computer mouse to pen-based devices, such as tablet PCs, PDAs, mobile phones, and touch-based devices,

such as Microsoft Surface, Apple IPhone. Many users complain that a tablet or display is too slippery for writing characters or drawing pictures on. In order to avoid such discomfort, some users put a sheet of paper on the surface of the tablet. With this additional media, users can simulate the touch of normal writing or drawing on paper. On the other hand, users may have different performances with different textures on various devices. Imagine that you walk from one place to another. Compare the movement times when you walk on ice to when you walk on an asphalt road. Obviously, the time taken to walk on ice is much longer than the time taken to walk the same distance on an asphalt road. People walk more comfortably with ground friction. However, when people walk on ice, they tend to slip since the coefficient of friction is very small, maybe even as low as zero.

Different displays or surfaces (even human skin [10]) have different textures. We can imagine that high-resolution texture displays will be designed and widely used in the near future. There are many researchers [4, 8, 9, 15, 17, 18] trying to combine the gap between the physical and digital worlds with their material qualities. Harrison and Hudson [9] used actuator to adjust the textures of six materials and proposed different texture displays. Results showed that users could recognize 2-4 different textures. Robles and Wiberg [15] applied the texture property to tangible user interface design with a case study of Icehotel. Jung and Stolterman [8] proposed preliminary studies to investigate how the subject probed and perceived the material qualities of objects and discussed how to apply user preferences to the design of interaction techniques.

In this study, we asked how texture affects steering task performance. Although pen gestures [2, 3, 13, 14] have long been investigated by researchers and users had different experiences writing characters with different texture surfaces, no study reports an investigation into the relationship between texture and user performance and satisfaction. In this paper, we try to provide insight into this question and design an experimental study to investigate this relationship.

RELATED WORK

Steering law is derived from crossing law whose recursion is the same as the Fitts' Law [7], that is $MT = a + b \log_2 (A/W + 1)$, where MT is the movement time to cross through the tunnel, a and b are constants depending on devices, A is the path amplitude and W is the path width. Accot and Zhai [1] divided a tunnel into N parts. The steering task is composed of N parts of crossing tasks when N tends to infinity. Steering law $MT=a+b(A/W)$ was proposed in that study.

There are several studies that include force factors into the steering law. Yang et al. [19] proposed a new haptic-steering model $MT=a+b(A/(W+\eta \times S))$, where η is a constant determined by the intensity of guiding force, to predict movement time for steering tasks with guiding force. Results showed that the model was more accurate than the traditional one for predicting performance times with force. The effects of stiffness and control gain on user performance were investigated for elastic devices by Casiez and Vogel [5]. Results showed that control gain affected error rate and movement time significantly but there was no significant effect for stiffness on user performance. There has not been any study that investigated texture effect in steering tasks.

EXPERIMENT

Participants

12 right-handed university volunteers (9 males, 3 females, aged from 23 to 34 years) participated in the experiment. All participants had normal or corrected to normal vision. All of them had previous experience using a stylus and had medium to expert level computer experience.

Apparatus

The purpose of the experiment was to simulate how the texture affects the trajectory, movement time and error rate when subjects performed the task. Hollins et al. [11] chose 17 tactile stimuli to show how subjects mapped their judgments of texture into the perceptual dimension. According to that paper and also the input requirement, we selected several materials. Furthermore, even for the same material, different objects may have different textures. In this study, we compared five materials, A4 paper on top of the Wacom tablet (Paper), a hard plastic cover on top of the Wacom tablet (Hard cover), sandwiching several A4 papers between a soft plastic sheet and the Wacom tablet (Soft plastic), a thin plastic sheet on top of the Wacom tablet (Plastic), and a bare Wacom tablet surface (Tablet) (See Figure1).

The experiment was conducted on a 2.13GHz Intel Core2 CPU PC with Windows XP. A 17-inch 1024×768 monitor and Wacom inuos3 PTZ-431W connected to the PC. This Wacom tablet can detect the pressure (by force) with 1024 different levels corresponding to 0 - 4 Newton. The experimental software was developed with Java 6.0. In order to evaluate whether these five materials affected the accuracy and response time on the Wacom tablet, we did a pilot study before the experiment. In this pilot study, a tracing task was designed to evaluate accuracy and a pointing task was used to test response time. Results

showed that both accuracy and response time were not affected by these materials.

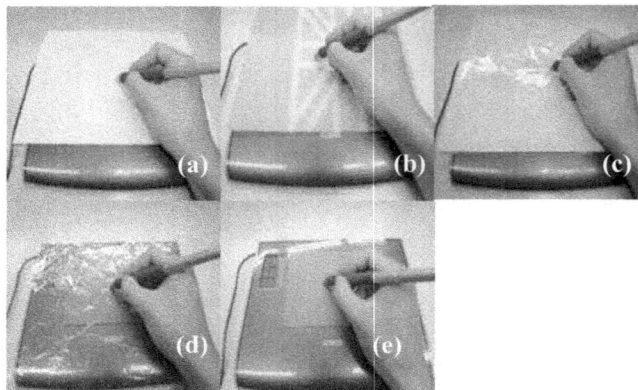

Figure 1. (a) Paper (b) Hard cover (c) Soft plastic (d) Plastic (e) Tablet.

Measurement of Coefficients of Friction
Since dynamic friction played a major role in the whole process of the steering task, we used the weight ratio method, which is the normal method used to measure the dynamic friction of all materials. The coefficients of dynamic friction are shown in Table 1.

Materials	Hard cover	Plastic	Tablet	Soft plastic	Paper
Coefficient of friction	0.081	0.126	0.153	0.233	0.295

Table 1. The coefficients of dynamic friction

Subjective Evaluation before the Experiment
There are also several factors which affect friction such as softness, pressure, speed, subjective factors and so on. The purpose of this measurement is to explore whether subjects can distinguish different textures among these five materials with a stylus. Participants with normal touch sense were seated in front of a desk. The subjects were asked to complete the experiment with their hand in a box to prevent participants using visual feedback to distinguish the different materials. Each subject estimated the roughness and smoothness of five surfaces with the stylus. We used the Thurstone paired comparison method [16] and designed the experiment to compare pairs of materials in each trial. There were 10 trials in this experiment.

After each trial, each participant was asked, "Which material was smoother?" and "Which material was softer?" If they could not distinguish the materials from each other, they were to answer, "Same". The results produced a sequence from the smoothest to the roughest as follows: plastic, tablet, hard cover, soft plastic and paper. The sequence from the softest to the hardest was: soft plastic, paper, plastic, hard cover and tablet. The sequence of actual smoothness was not the same as in the subjective evaluation. The reason for this may be that the difference is too small and the coefficient value is not significant enough to the user, thus causing them to consistently perceive it differently.

Task & Procedure

A circular steering task (Figure 2) was used in this study. The direction of the circular steering task was always clockwise. Each experimental trial started after the cursor crossed the start line and ended by crossing the end line. Both start line and end line must be successfully crossed otherwise the trial failed. Participants were asked to move the cursor inside the tunnel and to finish the task as quickly and accurately as possible. If the cursor was out of the tunnel, an error feedback via a color change in the trajectory was triggered to warn participants. *MT* (movement time taken to move from the start line to the end line), *SD* (standard deviation of the distances between trajectory points and the center of the circular tunnel) and average pressure from the stylus' tip (detected by Wacom stylus) were measured in each trial. Before the experiment, the task was explained to the participants and they were asked to perform some warm-up trials until they were familiar with both the steering task and the different material types. They were asked to have a rest between blocks.

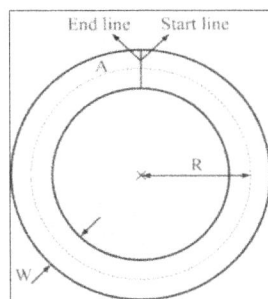

Figure 2. Experimental task

Design

We used a fully crossed within-subject factorial design. The independent variables were: *tunnel width W* (15, 30, 45 and 60 pixels), *tunnel amplitude A* (300, 450, 600, and 750 pixels), and *material type* (Paper, Hard cover, Plastic, Soft plastic and Tablet), *3 blocks*. The presentation orders of the material types were counterbalanced across participants. The five different materials were taped on the top of Wacom tablet.

All participants conducted the experiment in sitting postures. Within each *material type*, the participants performed all combinations of *tunnel widths* and *tunnel amplitudes* presented in random order, each for 3 trials.

In summary, the experiment consisted of:

8 participants ×

5 material types ×
4 tunnel widths ×
3 trials ×
4 tunnel amplitudes ×
3 blocks
= 5760 times in total.

The experiment took approximately 40 minutes per participant. After the experiment, participants completed a questionnaire to rate their subjective preferences for the material types.

Hypotheses

H1. Different material type affects movement time significantly.

H2. Under the same amount of movement time in a steering task, the lower the coefficient of friction, the more errors users perform.

RESULTS

After analyzing the data, we found when the index of difficulty (*ID= A/W*) was higher, some participants could not finish the task correctly. Based on Accot and Zhai [1], if the cursor was out of the tunnel, the task was not considered to be the steering task any more. Therefore, we removed that part from the data. 88% of trials were successful. Finally, 8 participants' data were used for analysis in this study.

Movement Time (MT)

In contrast to H1, a repeated-measure ANOVA showed that there was no significant main effect for material types ($F_{4, 28}$ = 2.296, p = 0.084). This meant that the average speed that users took to perform the task was almost the same. As shown in Figure 3, the overall average movement time was 2051 ms.

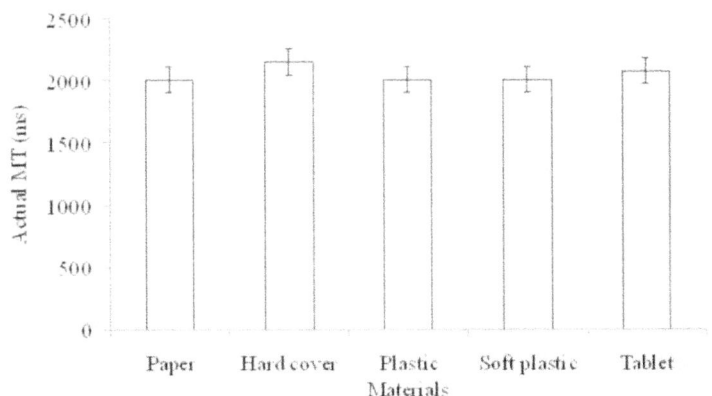

Figure 3. Mean MT by different material types (Error bars represent 95% confidence interval).

3

Standard Deviation (SD)

A repeated-measure ANOVA showed there was a significant main effect for material types ($F_{4, 28} = 8.859$, $p = <0.001$). As Figure 4 illustrated, the sequence from the biggest SD to shortest SD was plastic, tablet, hard cover, paper and Soft plastic, thus confirming hypothesis H2. An interesting phenomenon was that the subjective smoothness sequence was almost the same as this SD sequence (except the soft plastic). It showed that, within the range of coefficients of friction, the smoother the surface is, the more error trajectory user performs.

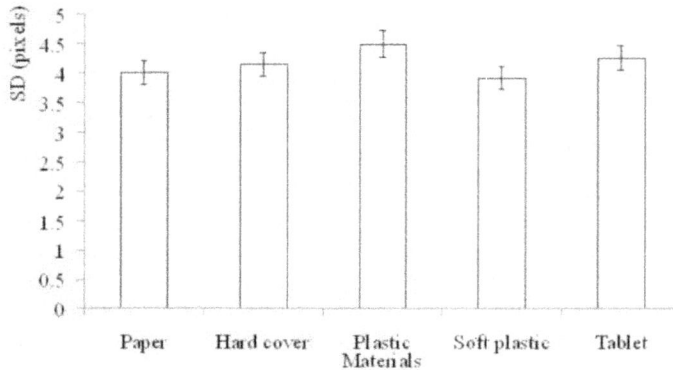

Figure 4. Mean SD by different material types (Error bars represent 95% confidence interval).

Pressure

A repeated-measure ANOVA showed there was a significant main effect for material types ($F_{4, 28} = 3.681$, $p=.016$). As Figure 5 illustrated, the sequence from the biggest pressure to lightest pressure was hard cover, paper, tablet, soft plastic and plastic. This showed another interesting phenomenon that each participant may use different forces to do steering task. It can be explained as such: each participant has a different comprehension of the task demand [21] which they should finish task as fast and accurately as possible. When there were several different textures, participants tried to keep the speed and accuracy as they thought. So they dynamically adjusted their behavior and their forces to suit the texture. Subjective bias played a role in it and covered the effect of texture. This also maybe the reason why there was no significant effect on from material types on MT.

Fitts' Law Analysis

A linear regression of MT by ID for each material was summarized in Table 2. The results of linear regression for each materials suggested the information capabilities (described by $1/b$) [20] of same devices with different texture surfaces were almost the same.

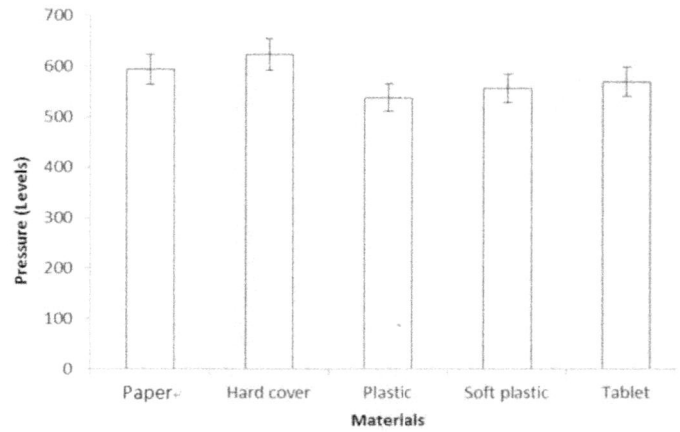

Figure 5. Mean pressure by different material types (Error bars represent 95% confidence interval).

Materials	a (ms)	b(ms/bit)	r^2
Paper	23.85	125.54	0.992
Hard cover	152.65	126.97	0.994
Plastic	132.23	125.37	0.996
Soft plastic	140.87	119.47	0.991
Tablet	123.27	128.58	0.997

Table 2. Steering Law regression values for material types.

Subjective Evaluation

We used two dimensions which were ease-of-use and accuracy to evaluate the five materials subjectively. Participants were asked to rate these materials using a 7 – point Likert scale (7 for best, and 1 for worst). As shown in Figure 6, most participants liked paper and disliked plastic. Most of them reported "It is comfortable to steer on the paper" and it is the most "natural" material and most suitable for a stylus. One participant said that "plastic is too slippery for me and I can't have precise control over the stylus".

CONCLUSION & FUTURE WORK

Haptics is one of the people's modalities that has been investigated and exploited in human-computer interaction. Due to the limitation of hardware that produces haptic feedback, most haptic feedback is vibration (supplied by a motor) and force feedback (supplied by Phantom and CyberGlove). Texture reveals the status of the target and increases the interaction information. This factor plays a significant role in pen-based interfaces. This study is an initial contribution to the investigation of the effect of texture in steering tasks.

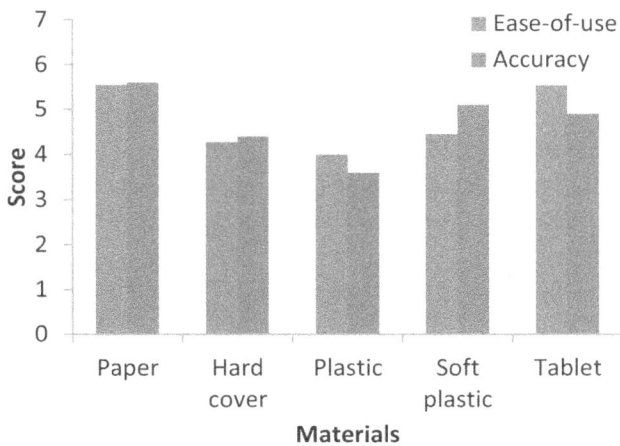

Figure 6. Subjective evaluation of ease-of-use and accuracy.

The movement time results indicated that texture did not affect the time significantly as expected in hypothesis 1. One of the potential reasons is that the circle steering task is not sensitive enough to detect the relationship between movement time and the friction of materials. In further work, we will use different tasks to explore the effect of texture. Another potential reason is that users dynamically changed the force they applied to suit the different textures according to the task demand that they should perform the task as quickly and accurately as possible. In order to get the larger anti-friction force to assist movement, users have to apply greater force to the tablet surface and therefore the delay of movement is overcome.

The accuracy results show that texture had a significant main effect on standard deviation which was a symbol of accuracy. Under the same amount of movement time in a steering task, the lower the coefficient of friction, the more errors users performed. Considering pressure and subjective evaluation together, the more the user applies force, the more accurately they performed. For the rough material, users controlled the pen actively applying greater force. However, for the slippery material, users had to reduce the force to reduce uncontrolled slippage. The movement of the pen was much more affected by rough the material than by the slippery material. Therefore, the trajectory achieved with the rough surface was much more accurate.

All results from the experiments show that the relationship between MT and ID obeyed the steering law. The changes of constant *a* and *b* revealed adjustments when using different materials. Subjective evaluation showed that most users preferred paper and disliked plastic. We observed that, in the pilot study of subjective evaluations, the sequence from the smoothest to the roughest was: plastic, tablet, hard cover, soft plastic and paper. This means that most users preferred rough material but disliked slippery material. It can be stated as follows: users can control the movement of a pen tip fluently with greater force on a rough surface.

Another potential reason is that paper has long been familiar to users. This long experience and natural knowledge makes this result likely.

This research investigates the effect of texture in steering tasks. As information communicating between humans and computers increase, it is critical that we explore and apply different modalities of the human being into interactive interfaces. This work gives a basic understanding of this kind of haptic feedback. Our findings are the more significant because they demonstrate that the common glass surface of most tablet surfaces is not the best kind of surface for optimum accuracy or for user satisfaction. It suggests that user should change different textures to get natural and realistic haptic feedback according to the different tasks and personal preferences. In the future, we also want to use gesture tasks to investigate the effect of different textures.

ACKNOWLEDGMENTS
This study has been partially supported by Grant-in-Aid for Scientific Research (No. 23300048) in Japan. We wish to thank the members of Ren Lab in Kochi University of Technology.

REFERENCES
1. Accot, J. and Zhai, S., Beyond Fitts' Law: Models for trajectory-based HCI tasks. In *Proc. CHI 1997*, ACM Press (1997), 295-302.

2. Appert, C. and Zhai, S. Using strokes as command shortcuts: cognitivebenefits and toolkit support. In *Proc. CHI 2009*, ACM Press (2009), 2289-2298.

3. Bau, O. and Mackay, W. E. OctoPocus: a dynamic guide for learning gesture-based command sets. In *Proc. UIST 2008*, ACM Press (2008), 37-46.

4. Brownell, B. Transmaterial: A Catalog of Materials That Redefine our Physical Environment. Princeton Architectural Press, *Princeton*, NJ, USA, 2006.

5. Casiez, G. and Vogel, D. The effect of spring stiffness and control gain with an elastic rate control pointing device. In *Proc. CHI2008*, ACM Press (2008), 1709-1718.

6. Cholewiak, R., Collins, A. Sensory and physiological bases of touch, *The psychology of touch*, M. Heller and W. Schiff, Ed. Lawrence Erlbaum (1991), 23-60.

7. Fitts, P.M. The information capacity of the human motor system in controlling the amplitude of movement. *Journal of Experimental Psychology* (1954), 47. p. 381-391.

8. Jung, H. and Stolterman, E. Material probe: exploring materiality of digital artifacts. *Proceedings of the fourth international conference on Tangible, embedded, and embodied interaction*, 2011, 153-156.

9. Harrison, C. and Hudson, S. F. Texture displays: a passive approach to tactile presentation. In *Proc. CHI 2009*, ACM Press (2009), 2261-2264.

10. Harrison, C., Tan, D. Morris, D. 2010. Skinput: Appropriating the Body as an Input Surface. In *Proc. CHI 2010*, ACM Press (2010), 453-462.

11. Hollins, M., Faldowski, R., Rao, S., and Young, F. Perceptual dimensions of tactile surface texture: A multidimensional scaling analysis. *Perception and Psychophysics*, (1993), 54, 697-705.

12. Klatzky, R., and Lederman, S. Tactile roughness perception with a rigid link interposed between skin and surface. *Perception and Psychophysics* (1999), 61, 591-607.

13. Kurtenbach, G., Sellen, A. and Buxton, W. An empirical evaluation of some articulatory and cognitive aspects of "marking menus". *Human Computer Interaction*, 8, 1 (1993), 1-23.

14. Long, A.C., Landay, J.A., Rowe, L.A. and Michiels, J. Visual similarity of pen gestures. In *Proc. CHI 2000*, ACM Press (2000), 360-367.

15. Robles, E. and Wiberg, M. Texturing the "material turn" in interaction design, In *Proceedings of the fourth international conference on Tangible, embedded, and embodied interaction*, January 24-27, 2010, Cambridge, Massachusetts, USA.

16. Thurstone, L. L. The Method of Paired Comparison for Social Values. *Journal of Abnormal and Social Psychology* (1927), 21, 384-400.

17. Vallgårda, A. and Sokoler, T. A material focus: exploring properties of computational composites. In *Ext. Abstracts CHI 2009*, ACM Press (2009).

18. Vallgårda, A. and Redstrom, J. (2007). Computational composites. In *Proc. CHI 2007*, ACM Press (2007).

19. Yang, X. D., Irani, P., Boulanger, P. and Bischof, W. F. A Model for Steering with Haptic-Force Guidance. In *Proc. INTERACT 2009*, 465-478.

20. Zhai, S. Characterizing computer input with Fitts' law parameters: the information and non-information aspects of pointing. *International Journal Human-Computer Studies*, (2004), 61(6), 791-809.

21. Zhou, X. and Ren, X. An Investigation of Subjective Operational Biases in Steering Tasks Evaluation. *Behaviour & Information Technology*, (2010), 29, 125-135.

Enhancing Collaboration in Tabletop Board Game

Taoshuai Zhang, Jie Liu, Yuanchun Shi

Department of Computer Science and Technology, Tsinghua University, Beijing, China

{thcescuu, liujiejesse}@gmail.com

shiyc@tsinghua.edu.cn

ABSTRACT

Through combination of tabletop and mobile phones, we introduce a mechanism containing private, public and group workspaces for computer-mediated tabletop board game. It can sustain the important sociality between players while ensuring privacy and enhancing visual effect. Based on the popular board game *Monopoly*, we design *Copoly* on a multi-touch tabletop and mobile phones where players can form groups to collaborate. A qualitative and quantitative user study was conducted to explore the pattern of collaboration and its effect on tabletop game experience. The results indicated that social bonding did play an important role on the frequency and pattern of collaboration in tabletop games, and players gained a more joyful experience through competition and collaboration.

Author Keywords

Tabletop games; Board game; Sociality; Collaboration; Group workspace; Game experience.

ACM Classification Keywords

H.5.3 [Information interfaces and presentation]: Group and Organization Interfaces - computer-supported cooperative work.

INTRODUCTION

Board game is a popular game in which players gather together to play by managing and playing tangible items (e.g. counters, pieces, dices or cards) around customized-designed surface called *board*. One of the most exciting parts of board game is the all-round face-to-face interaction. Players are usually co-located, therefore spoken languages and emotionally relevant communication signals like body gestures, facial expression and even the frequency of breathing can become useful information with regards to collaboration and competition. These factors could enhance the sociality in board game.

On the other hand, physical board games can be costly with their rapid developments recently. Newcomers have to spend lots of time reading complicated game rules to get familiar with new games. The number of game tools and

items are also greatly increased. It's not always pleased to store and carry such massive and heavy things. A common solution is to transform board games into traditional online-game mode. Each user launches a separate client in personal devices like PC, which renders all data on it. All of operations are done there, and the metadata of status would be transmitted among remote servers and other clients for computation and synchronization. Player would only focus on his/her terminal during the game, thus depriving significant sociality of board games. Though some Massively Multiplayer Online RPG also encourage social interaction in both specific virtual game locations and offline real world [3], important human factors like personality and ability of communication have no direct relationships with game playing.

In the sense of gathering many people together to play board game, tabletop promises to be a natural interaction substrate. By inheriting the richness of visual and audial effects provided by computers, tabletops can illustrate and express the scenes of board game clearly no matter how many tools the game requires and how complex the game rule is. Tabletops also provide natural motion interaction to make players' action more comfortable and clear to others. Moreover, tabletops can also serve as a central role to support group activities: players sit around the shared display, and then those social activities and information are visible to others, which still work to enhance entertainment.

One obvious problem in the tabletop games is that private information, like the cards in each player's hand in physical card games, goes public since all the game data appear on shared tabletop. Some solutions come forward. Simply a shielding gesture [1] can establish a physical barrier around the playing cards to prevent the cards' visibility to other players. Small-screen devices, like PDAs or mobile phones, are exploited to hold private information as a general approach, such as STARS [4] and Poker Surface [7].

Meanwhile, in order to take fully advantage of social interactions between users, we introduced the concept of *group collaboration*. It allows part of players who might share a joint purpose and common interests at a time to form a group where they can trade and reach some agreements, and it won't be known by others outside group. On the other hand, such collaborations also mean competitions among different intersecting groups in the game, thus making the players important elements too.

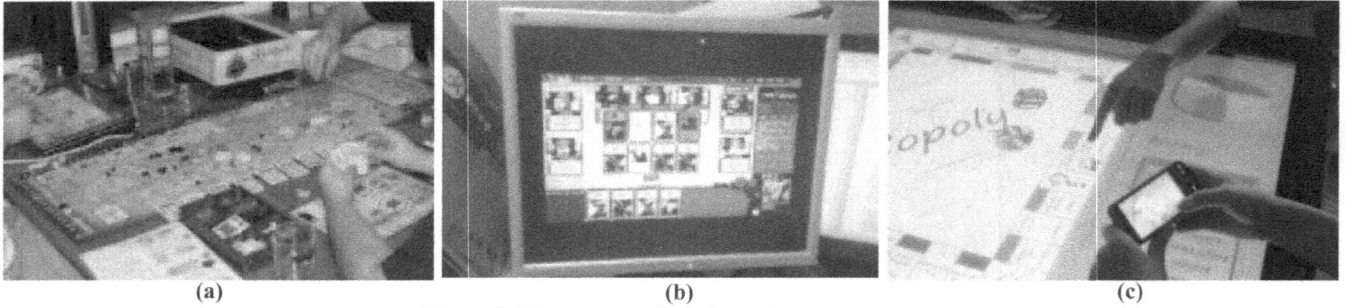

Figure 1. Three ways of implement board games:
(a) Physical Board game: Shogun, (b) Online-game mode Board game: Sanguosha OL and (c) Tabletop game: Copoly

Generally speaking, we divide our system into three different genres of workspace to meet such requirements: 1) *Private workspace* deployed on mobile phone each player holds, and then private data and necessary private operations are displayed and handled only on it and won't get exposed to others. 2) *Public workspace* which clearly illustrates the whole board and public information to all players with visual and audial richness on the tabletop, as well as providing interface for players to take public actions such as specifying the target on the board. 3) *Group workspace* that enables valid group collaboration. Such group relationship might vary as the game proceeds, and the diplomacy strategy to other players act as an essential part to win. These workspaces can ensure the fairness and visual effects in tabletop games and enough encourage collaboration between users.

We designed a tabletop game named *Copoly* based on a famous board game called *Monopoly* [5]. We utilize these three genres of workspaces and allocate each workspace some relevant functions in the game to try to sustain improving the collaboration. A user study on exploring how users competed between groups and collaborated within groups is introduced later.

GAME DESIGN AND IMPLEMENTATION
In Copoly, players take turns to roll the dice to traverse the board randomly, during which they make trade and manage their properties. Bankrupted players would be eliminated from the game, and the last stander wins the game. The tabletop displays the world map and supports multi-touch interactions. Quantity of money and list of owned properties are privately shown on phones for users to manage. Figure 2 shows a scenario of playing Copoly.

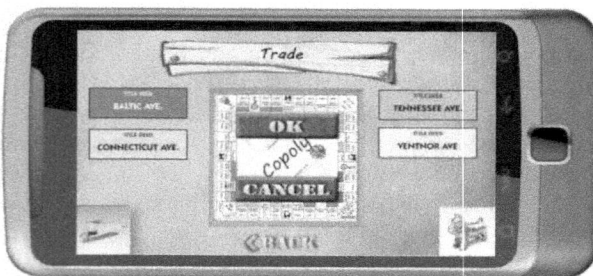

Figure 2. Trading within group workspace on mobile phones (the player is deciding whether to accept the trading)

In group workspace, we set two kinds of collaborative activities. *Transaction of properties* lets player trade with others for properties with a desired color, so that s/he tries to get properties in the same specific color. The other activity is *money lending*. Group mates may lend money to allies who are almost bankrupted to avoid confiscation by opponents. As we mentioned above, the alliances between groups are flexible. Players can join or quit temporary groups anytime when all of members approve the request. When a player wants to take group activities, for example trading with his playmate, he chooses the playmate's avatar, properties he provides and properties he wants on his mobile phone. The playmate would receive a notification and will see the UI in Figure 2. Then he can touch the button *OK* to accept this trading or the button *CANCEL* to decline it. The detail of the trading won't be exposed to others out of the group.

We use the multi-touch tabletop uTable [6]. It can not only provide public display and multi-touch input, but also has a server computer to maintain data and message. Each player surrounding the table is equipped with a HTC Android smartphone. It holds private data, and provides communication between players. Mobile phones communicate with each other and with uTable via a wireless network under TUIO network protocol [8]. The system on the part of uTable is developed using a software toolkit, uTableSDK [9].

USER STUDY ON COLLABORATION
As the first step, we proposed an experiment under our mechanism proposed above. We wonder whether the social relationships between players would take effect on one of the most important activities – collaboration. A qualitative and quantitative user study to test the pattern and frequency of collaboration in Copoly and its impact on the game experience is conducted then.

Participants Setup
We recruited 40 participants, including 26 males and 14 females. Their ages range between 10 and 55 years old (mean = 23.5). We classified their relationships with each other into 3 categories: (C1) close friends and relatives, (C2) acquaintances such as colleagues and classmates, (C3) strangers. According to their relationships, we divided them into 10 teams of 4 people each, represented by T1 to T10.

As a comparison, we disabled the group workspace and make all related functions public to form a non-grop collaborative Copoly game called *Mopoly* temporarily. The request and response of Transaction of properties and Money leading between plays can be seen by everyone.

Before the test, we described the basic operations of Copoly and let them read the rules and watch the tutorial on the tabletop. The preparation took about 20 minutes. During the user test, half of teams played Copoly first and then Mopoly, while the rest did the opposite so as to counter balance the order of these two games. Each session took 0.5-2 hours, and game was sentenced to end if time exceeds 2 hours.

Measures

Copoly records every action players performed. We count the frequency of collaboration between players.

To measure the game experience, we adopted a self-report measure, the Social Presence in Gaming Questionnaire (SPGQ) [2]. SPGQ is based on focus group interviews and a social presence scale. It is applied to measure the game experience of digital games. It comprises Psychological Involvement Empathy (PIE), Psychological Involvement Negative feelings (PIN) and Behavioral Engagement (BE). Empathy means that players empathize with others, feel connected and admire others. Negative feelings include revenge, malicious delight, jealousness, envy and so forth. Behavioral Engagement means players' actions are interdependent and they pay close attention to others. Participants filled in questionnaires by rating these three subscales after playing the game. We hypothesized that collaboration would increase PIE and BE, while decrease PIN.

In front of each participant, there was a camera with a microphone inside to record their oral communication and facial expression in the game process with consent. The times of oral communication and eye contact were counted. With log data, questionnaire results and video records, we held an informal interview with each team to learn about their game experience.

Log Analysis

Inspired by the research of Xu et al. [10], where they plotted each participant's egocentric network [3] of other players to reveal the interaction pattern, we use a network graph to show the pattern of collaboration. Figure 3. visualizes the pattern of collaboration in each team. A node represents a player. Numbers along the link and the thickness of link represent the frequency of collaboration between two players. The ellipse indicates players inside form a "permanent" group that never sever during the game.

The first row was made up of close friends and relatives. The frequency is relatively high. Collaboration inside the group is much more frequent than that between groups. Acquaintances comprised T4-T7. The frequencies of collaboration in them are slightly less than the first row, while the topologies of interactive connection are similar. Some players also had strong collaborations and formed de facto "permanent" groups. Participants in T8-T10 were strangers mutually. Connections are fewer among them. Notice that collaboration was much more frequent in T8, and the players told us they were all satisfied with the trial collaboration.

From the analysis above, we can see some features of collaboration. 1) Social bonding influences the frequency and pattern of collaboration greatly. Participants tend to collaborate with someone who was familiar with. 2) There are more collaboration happened within "permanent" group.

Questionnaire

After taking Copoly and Mopoly, participants filled in the same questionnaire proposed in SPGQ [2] and rated their agreement with each statement. The points are anchored at not at all (0), slightly (1), moderately (2), fairly (3) and extremely (4).

We put all participants into three categories according to their social bonding. T1-T3 are in tight-bonding C1, T4-T7 in average-bonding C2 and T8-T10 in weak-bonding C3. The means and standard error of means are shown in Figure 4. Besides, we used two-way ANOVA in SPSS to analyze both the collaboration and social bonding which may affect the game experience.

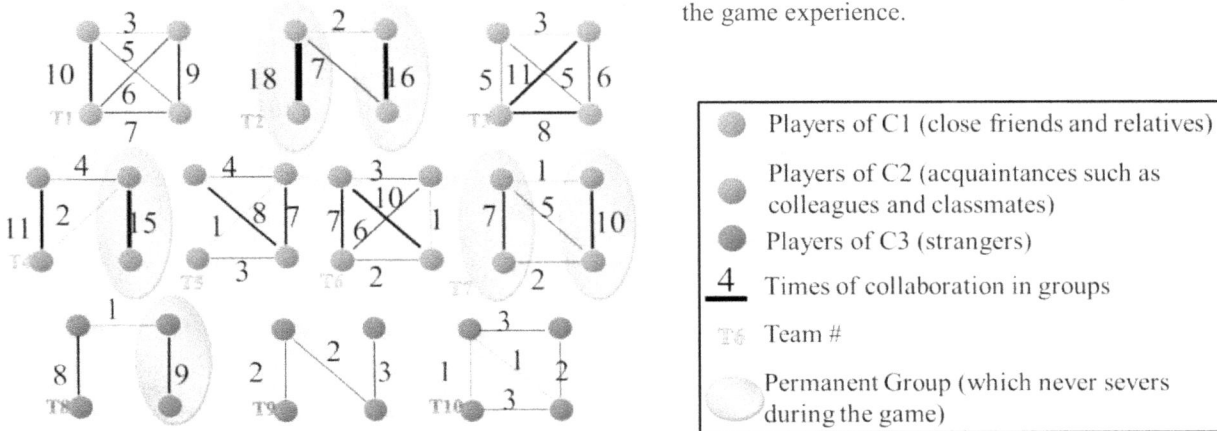

Figure 3. Collaboration in each team

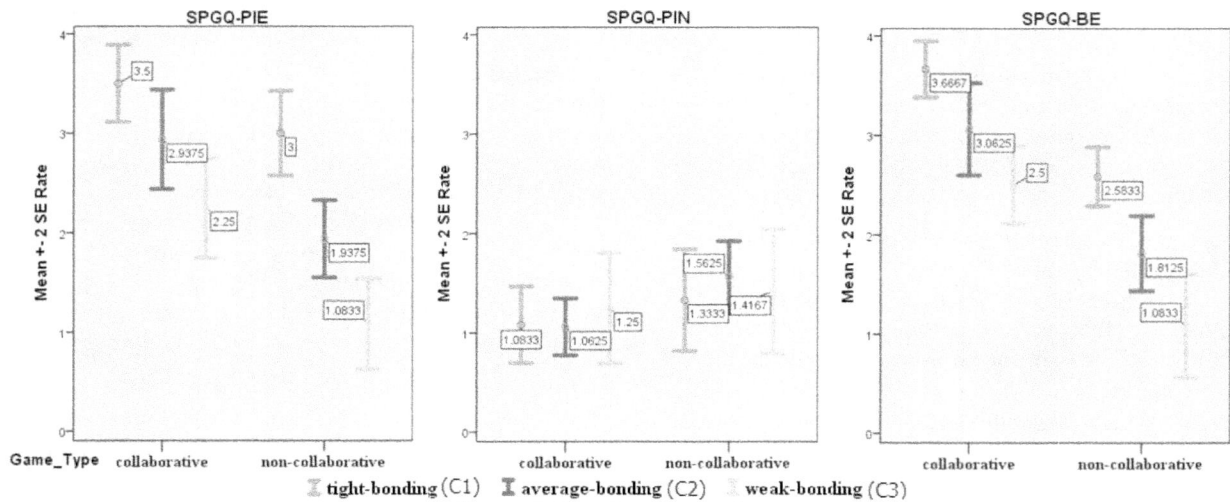

Figure 4. Questionnaire results

In general, empathy and behavioral engagement was significantly higher in Copoly (PIE: mean=2.9, SD=.831; BE: mean=3.08, SD=.748) than in non-collaborative Mopoly (PIE: mean=1.95, SD=1.048; BE: mean=1.83, SD=.918). But the negative feelings were similar in different social bonding and slightly higher in Mopoly (Copoly: mean=1.13, SD=.722; Mopoly: mean=1.45, SD=.875).

Collaboration increases empathy in all kinds of social bonding with the relatedness $F(1,34)=18.20, p=.001$. Collaboration also increases behavioral engagement ($F(1,34)=17.38$, $p<.001$). This means participants in the Copoly interacted more frequently with others. Since trade and help are activities involving two parts, what one participant did affect the other did and vice versa. They were more dependent with others and paid more attention to their group mates.

As with negative feelings (PIN), the difference between Copoly and Mopoly tests are not statistically significant, $F(1.34)=1.25$, $p=.058$. Some participants said that when they were seated face-to-face, they felt closely with each other. So negative feelings, such as envy or revenge is slight thanks to the inherent quality of tabletop games.

Figure 4. also reveals that social bonding has an impact on empathy and behavioral engagement (PIE: $F(2,34)=20.23, p<.001$; BE: $F(2,34)=15.70$, $p<.001$). This conforms to the results of log analysis.

By analysis of the video record, we observed participants' reaction in both tests. While playing Copoly, the frequency of oral communication (OC) and eye contact (EC) was significantly higher (OC: 38.5, EC: 42.1 on average per team) than that in Mopoly (OC: 13.6, EC: 27.0 on average per team). Participants' attention in Mopoly was mainly on the tabletop and mobile phones while less on group mates.

CONCLUSION AND FUTURE WORK
Copoly exploits game rules to guide players to collaborate. Through collaboration in group workspace, players improve empathy and behavioral engagement, and at the same time

have less negative feelings. The results shed light on that collaboration improve game experience in augmented tabletop games. This paper focuses on the influence in tabletop game experience that collaboration exerts. The methods about how to integrate collaboration in different kinds of games needs further research. Besides collaboration and social bonding, other factors, such as number of players and audience, should be investigated to find their connections with game experience.

REFERENCES
1. Dang, C.T., Andre, E. Surface-Poker: Multimodality in Tabletop Games. *In Proc. ITS 2010*, pp. 251-252.

2. de Kort, Y. A. W., IJsselsteijn, W., Poels, K. Digital Games as Social Presence Technology: Development of the Social Presence in Gaming Questionnaire. *In Proc. PRESENCE 2007*, pp. 195-203.

3. Ducheneaut, N., Moore, R. The social side of gaming: a study of interaction patterns in a massively multiplayer online game. *In Proc. CSCW 2004*, pp. 360-369.

4. Magerkurth, C., Memisoglu, M., Engelke, T., Streitz, N. Towards the Next Generation of Tabletop Gaming Experiences. *In Proc. GI 2004*, pp. 73-80.

5. Monopoly *http://www.hasbro.com/monopoly/en_US*

6. Qin, Y., Yu, C., Jiang, H., Wu, C., Shi. Y. pPen: Enabling Authenticated Pen and Touch Interaction on Tabletop Surfaces. *In Proc. ITS 2010*. pp. 283-284.

7. Shirazi, A.S., Döring, T., Parvahan, P., Ahrens, B., Schmidt, A. Poker Surface: Combining a Multi-Touch Table and Mobile Phones in Interactive Card Games. *In Proc. MobileHCI 2009*, pp. 1-2.

8. TUIO Network Protocol. *http://www.tuio.org/*

9. uTableSDK *http://utablesdk.codeplex.com/*

10. Xu, Y.. Cao, X., Sellen, A., Herbrich, R., Graepel, T. Sociable Killers: Understanding Social Relationships in an Online First-Person Shooter Game. *In Proc. CSCW 2011*, pp. 197-206.

The Influence of Cooperative Game Design Patterns for Remote Play on Player Experience

Anastasiia Beznosyk, Peter Quax, Karin Coninx, Wim Lamotte
Hasselt University — tUL — IBBT
Expertise Centre for Digital Media
Wetenschapspark 2, B-3590 Diepenbeek (Belgium)
{anastasiia.beznosyk, peter.quax, karin.coninx, wim.lamotte}@uhasselt.be

ABSTRACT

The collaborative nature of many modern multiplayer games raises a lot of questions in cooperative game design. We address one of them in this paper by analyzing cooperative game patterns in remote gameplay in order to define benefits and drawbacks for each one. With the help of a user experiment, we analyzed player experience in a set of existing cooperative patterns for games played remotely without communication. By comparing patterns, supporting closely- and loosely-coupled collaboration, we discovered that the first type provided a more enjoyable experience but introduced additional challenges in case of a lack of communication. By analyzing patterns for both closely- and loosely-coupled interaction, we determined the most beneficial pattern within each type. We concluded with the results of a pattern comparison in co-located and remote setups.

Author Keywords

Cooperative game patterns; remote gameplay; communication; closely-coupled collaboration; loosely-coupled collaboration; player experience.

ACM Classification Keywords

H.5.2 Information Interfaces and presentation: User Interfaces; H.5.3 Group and Organization Interfaces: Evaluation/methodology.

INTRODUCTION

Integrating collaboration in some genres of multiplayer games has increased their popularity. Such games encourage players to team up and work together towards common goals whilst emphasizing group interest versus personal stakes. When creating a collaborative game, one has to motivate players to interact with each other in an effective manner. One possible solution is to incorporate different forms of interaction based on the coupling between players, either

closely-coupled or loosely-coupled. While the first one implies one player's actions to be directly influenced by the others, the second form of interaction leaves more independence for the players.

Since collaboration has evolved from merely an additional element to a core component of a game, cooperative design has become an integral part of game design. Many game designers are currently exploring different ways of the integration and evaluation of cooperative activities within their games [6]. In doing so, one of the open issues remains the discovery and analysis of cooperative patterns that could improve interaction between players in multiplayer games with a collaborative nature. Additionally, as gaming occurs under a variety of circumstances (players can be located next to each other or play remotely, be able or not to hear and/or see partner, communicate through text chat,...), these varying conditions may directly or indirectly affect the player's experience. The same type of interaction could, therefore, result in a completely different player perception and influence his/her choice to play the game in the future. Most likely, the conditions a game is played in, affects closely-coupled interaction more due to a high dependency between players. Although a lot of cooperative games on the market are based on close coupling between players, most of them are designed for a co-located setup (e.g. Wii games[1]) or have facilities for rich communication. When it is not easy or even not possible to have this kind of continuous communication between players, closely-coupled interaction can suffer more from these setup conditions and, as a result, decrease player engagement with the game.

We investigate cooperative game patterns where gameplay occurs over a distance and players are not able to communicate in any form. We have performed a comparative analysis of several cooperative patterns. Although modern games usually apply a combination of patterns, in our study we look at separate patterns to define those best suitable for given conditions. Using different criteria, each pattern was graded based on its influence on player experience, revealing the drawbacks and benefits of each pattern. Six popular patterns were chosen [6, 10] based on their high frequency of occurrence in modern multiplayer cooperative games. Based on these findings, we define the best performing patterns separately for closely- and loosely-coupled collaboration. Finally, we illus-

---

[1] www.nintendo.com/wii

trate the differences between the evaluation of the same patterns in both situations: when they are used remotely and co-located.

RELATED WORK

Game design patterns have been in focus for many years. Game patterns are descriptions of reoccurring interaction, that depict how game components are used by players to affect various aspects of gameplay [2]. In [2], the authors have identified a large amount of patterns by analyzing existing games, some of them being classified as the cooperative patterns with different possibilities and incentives for the players to achieve things together. In the last decades, cooperation has developed from an additional feature into a full-grown game component, motivating more and more players to join a game. Although several works attempted to address the question of cooperative game design patterns [1, 4, 6, 7, 9, 10, 11], it remains open in the research community.

In [9], the cooperative nature of interaction between players is classified by the order in which actions may be taken: turn-taking and simultaneous games. Zagal et al. [11] explore cooperative patterns based on board games. Interaction patterns in massive multiplayer games (based on the example of Star War Galaxies) are investigated by Ducheneaut et al. in [4], but here the authors focus on the social aspect of interaction (verbal and non-verbal communication between players). Cooperation in educative applications is studied by Holzinger et al. [8] and Ebner et al. [5]. Other studies [1, 7] investigate cooperative game design as a motivational factor for special target groups (e.g. people with disabilities) and focus on such patterns as enforced collaboration, sequentially-dependent roles, etc.

More elaborated research in the area of cooperative design patterns is performed in [6, 10]. Following the same approach presented in [2], in [10], Rocha et al. define several cooperative design patterns by analyzing numerous commercial games, that support some form of collaboration between players. This list is considerably extended by El-Nasr et al. [6]. Here, the authors not only introduce a more complete series of cooperative game patterns, but also describe a methodology to evaluate the cooperative nature of games – Cooperative Performance Metrics (CPMs). Using this methodology, they analyze which pattern triggers which event during the shared gameplay (e.g. laughing, strategy discussion, etc.). The aim of the analysis was to investigate connections between the CPMs and the cooperative design patterns discussed in their study resulting in building better cooperative games.

The evaluation described in [6] was performed for several existing cooperative games that were played on a shared screen, and players could easily and naturally communicate with each other. The analysis of cooperative design patterns in a remote setup without communication has not yet been performed. To our knowledge, most cooperative games allow at least basic communication with the help of text chat, while some of them provide players with the ability to hear and see their partners. Nowadays, only a few games are available on the market where cooperation between players is supported without the ability to communicate in any form (e.g. Journey[2]). Therefore, we find it crucial to investigate how interaction between players can be improved based on introducing different cooperative patterns in order to compensate a possible negative effect due to a lack of communication.

EXPERIMENT

Our work evaluates cooperative game design patterns from the perspective of a remote setup where interaction between players happens without the possibility of directly communicating with one another. A user experiment was conducted, where players had to evaluate six custom games, each based on one of the cooperative patterns. For purposes of the experiment, a selection of patterns (selected from the list presented in [6]) was made based on their popularity and the frequency of appearance in existing multiplayer games. The goal of our study is two-fold. First, we analyze to what extent each cooperative pattern is appropriate for remote play without communication depending on a variety of criteria. Here, based on the coupling between players, we group the selected patterns either in a closely- or loosely-coupled type of interaction, in order to define the most benefiting patterns for each group. Secondly, a comparative analysis is performed between the same patterns when they are evaluated in co-located and remote setups.

Participants

Thirty-six unpaid subjects (thirty-one males and five females) participated in the experiment. Their average age was 28 years old, ranging between 21 and 38. Most of them had a computer science background and were recruited among university staff and students. Based on self evaluation, the average player experience with multiplayer games was 3.42 on a scale from 1 (never played) to 5 (played a lot).

Setup

During the experiment two players were located in neighboring rooms separated by a hallway. Each player used a 15.4" laptop connected over a LAN. One of the laptops was a HP Compaq 8510p (Intel Core 2 Duo T8100, 2.1 GHz, 3 GB with ATI Mobile Radeon HD2600 graphic adapter) and the other was a Dell Latitude E6510 (Intel Core i3 M370, 2.4 GHz, 2 GB with NVIDIA NVS 3100M). A separate external keyboard was attached to each laptop for a more comfortable input. There was no communication possible between the two players. To avoid any chance of hearing each other, music was played in the background.

Procedure

Eighteen pairs of participants consecutively played six different collaborative games, described in detail in the following section. During each game the player had to collaborate with his/her partner who was located in a different room. Players were coupled anonymously and, therefore, did not know who their partner was. Any form of communication (voice chat, text chat, pop-up messages, etc.) was avoided. Pop-up windows were used only in one game to support some basic level of awareness between two players. Several days before

---

[2]www.thatgamecompany.com/games/journey

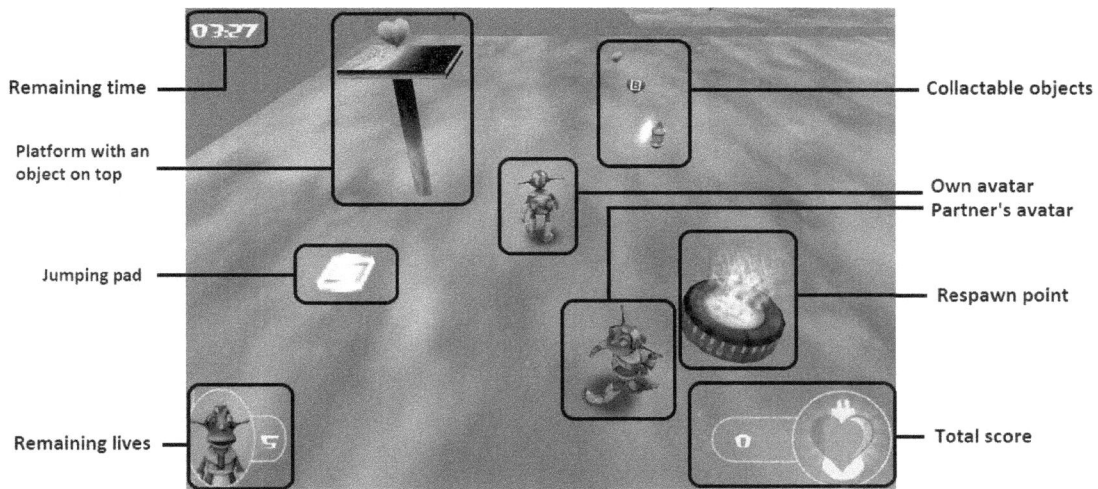

Figure 1. The gaming environment.

the actual experiment, a pilot test was performed to check the playability of every game.

Before the experiment, participants read a brief introduction and conducted a five minute trial to familiarize themselves with the gaming environment and controls. In addition, written rules were given, in which both the goal and the way of interacting with the partner were explained. After each game, players were asked to evaluate the subjective perception of their experience. In particular, they were asked to quantify the following aspects of collaboration:

- the necessity to discuss the game (strategy, ask your partner for help, etc.);
- level of collaboration with the partner;
- the amount of waiting for the other player during the game;
- level of awareness of the partner's actions;
- negative impact on the efficiency caused by the absence of communication, the physical distance, the necessity to wait for the other player, the actions of the other player;
- negative impact on the enjoyment caused by the absence of communication, the physical distance, the necessity to wait for the other player, the actions of the other player.

For evaluation purposes, a visual analogue scale (VAS) [3] was used. The participants marked on the 10 cm line the point that they felt represented their perception of the current state from *not at all* to *very much*. Additionally, the players ranked the six games based on the level of their enjoyment. It took approximately 60 minutes for each pair to complete the actual experiment.

Games

Six custom games were created for the experiment, each adopting one of the selected cooperative game patterns (Table 1). Based on the coupling between players, we classified each game into one of two categories: closely- or loosely-coupled. If a game required a lot of waiting or if the actions

of one player directly affected the other player, it was categorized as the first type. The games that did not require tight collaboration between players and allowed more independent performance were assigned to the second type.

For every game, a similar 3D virtual environment was developed, which consists of several islands (a rectangular area, on which all game elements are located). Players are represented by alien-like avatars used from Unity 3D tutorial[3]. To distinguish the two avatars in the virtual environment, one is colored in a light blue color, while the other avatar is brown. Players are able to navigate freely in the environment and are not forced to stay together. They have to collect different objects by running over them. Some of the objects are located on higher platforms not directly reachable by the players. Therefore, they have to use the jumping pads that help a player to jump higher to collect certain items. In order to get on a different island players need to jump across the abyss. If one of the players falls off the island the team loses one life. After the fall, the player reappears at one of the respawn points. A group score is calculated and analyzed to measure the successfulness of the game completion. The game continues until one of the following conditions is met: (1) players collected all required objects; (2) players lost all their lives; (3) the time ran out. An example of the environment with all gaming elements is shown on Figure 1.

For closely-coupled **Game 1**, a *limited resources* pattern is adopted. Two players have to collect items, but are able to store a maximum of 10 items at the same time. Once both players reach the maximum amount of items, they can collect the following 10 objects. If one of the players collects 10 objects he/she has to wait for the other player and cannot pick up new items in the meantime.

In closely-coupled **Game 2**, a *complementary* pattern is used, which implies that players have a different role to complement each others' activities within the game. During this

---

[3]available online at http://unity3d.com/support/resources/tutorials/3d-platform-game

Nr	Design pattern	Closely- or loosely-coupled	Amount of islands	Amount of lives	Total amount of objects	Necessary to pick up	Object type	Time, min
1	Limited resources	Closely-coupled	5	5	100	75	hearts	7
2	Complementary	Closely-coupled	5	5	100	75	hearts	7
3	Interaction with the same object	Closely-coupled	4	5	100	75	hearts	7
4	Shared puzzles	Loosely-coupled	5	5	200	10	letters	5
5	Abilities that can be used on other players	Loosely-coupled	4	5	200	150	hearts weapons	5
6	Shared goals	Loosely-coupled	5	3	150	115	hearts	5

Table 1. Cooperative games used during the experiment.

game two roles are introduced. One player moves the jumping pad around the island while not being able to jump, and the other player uses it for jumping to reach objects located on higher platforms. There is only one jumping pad on each island. The roles are assigned randomly when players start the game.

Closely-coupled **Game 3** follows an *interaction with the same object* pattern. In this game players have to move the jumping pad simultaneously. As soon as one of the players selects the jumping pad to move, the other player receives a message on his/her screen that the pad is selected and he/she is needed to help moving it. However, it does not indicate the location where the player has to be in order to help his/her teammate. When selected by two players, the jumping pad can be moved when both players walk in the same direction. Both players can use it for jumping. Similar to game 2, there is only one jumping pad on each island.

Loosely-coupled **Game 4** utilizes a *shared puzzles* pattern. Here, the focus is to collect 10 special objects: each contains a heart with a letter on one side. Once all 10 special objects and therefore ten letters are found, players need to use them to formulate a word containing all the letters, and put them in a designated window. The game succeeds when the word is entered correctly. Players do not see what words are entered by their partners while guessing. Once the correct solution is given by one player, the other one can also see it in his/her window.

An *abilities that can be used on other players* pattern is used in loosely-coupled **Game 5**. In this game, players have to collect two types of objects: hearts and weapons. Each one is assigned to one player. They can see only one type which is randomly assigned on starting the game. Every time a player collects his/her 10 items, he/she gets the ability to see the partner's objects for about twenty seconds, and is able to collect them as well. The goal of the game is not only to collect enough objects as a team. Individual results of each player also need to exceed a certain amount of items of both types.

Loosely-coupled **Game 6** utilizes a *shared goals* pattern. The collaboration is reduced to a shared goal of collecting a certain amount of objects while acting independent from the partner.

Design

During the experiment, a within-subject design was used. The independent variable was the game type with six conditions. All participants, in pairs, had to complete six sessions testing every game type. The order of the conditions was counterbalanced using a balanced Latin square design. The dependent variables were: task completion time, player score, total group score and amount of lives lost. A subjective evaluation of each game type was collected through a self-developed post-experiment questionnaire.

RESULTS

This section presents the results of our study. As mentioned earlier, the main goal of the experiment was to analyze the most popular cooperative game design patterns in a remote setup with no communication. We aimed to investigate which patterns, if any, were affected more than the others by the conditions they were played in. First, we present an overview of player performance and preference. Secondly, we report results that reflect an impact of the remote setup on the player experience (absence of communication and physical distance). Finally, the patterns are compared from the perspective of collaboration between players. Here, we also investigate if any relation between player performance and his/her partner's evaluation exists. Throughout this section, we name games by the corresponding number. For detailed information on each game we refer to Table 1.

Player Performance and Preference

Table 2 summarizes the results of player performance (game completion rate and mean player efficiency) and preference (enjoyment and player decision upon games' suitability).

Performance

For every game, players had to collect a certain amount of objects within a certain time limit in order to successfully complete it. In order to compare three closely-coupled games, they all had equal conditions: players had to pick up 75 objects within 7 minutes (Table 1). Conditions of loosely-coupled games varied due to differences in game design for these patterns. Due to the different ways of interacting between players, some games were found to be more difficult to finish within a given period. Analysis of the game completion rate has revealed that the majority of players managed to finish only two games in time: the ones with the limited resources and shared goals patterns (Table 2). As can be seen,

#	Completion rate, %	Average amount of collected objects	Efficiency, obj/min	Enjoy-ment*	Not suitable rate, %**
1	88.89	74.22	8.54	2	11.11
2	11.11	56.06	4.04	5	16.67
3	0	54.61	3.93	6	19.44
4	16.67	109.28	11.10	3	19.44
5	38.89	144.56	16.40	4	11.11
6	83.33	111.94	16.41	1	13.89

* 1 - lowest, 6 - highest
** 27.78% of participants found all games suitable

Table 2. Player performance and preference.

the difference between the average amount of collected objects and the necessary amount of objects for games 2 and 3 was higher than in the other games.

Due to our decision to design games with equal conditions, in most cases the games were not completed successfully but finished because of a lack of time. In these conditions it was hardly possible to compare game completion time. Therefore, as an alternative measurement of performance, we calculated the efficiency of the players for every game. It was defined as the amount of objects collected by each player in one minute. Repeated measures ANOVA has shown a significant difference across six patterns ($F(2.73, 95.37) = 105.37$, $p < 0.01$). A Bonferroni post-hoc test has demonstrated a significantly lower efficiency in two of the closely-coupled games, games 2 and 3, than in any other game ($p < 0.01$). At the same time, no significant difference was found between the three loosely-coupled games, all of them sharing a high level of player efficiency.

Preference
The participants were asked to rank the six games according to the level of their enjoyment. They were explicitly asked to judge each game based on the way in which players interact and not take into account other gaming elements (e.g. design of the environment, look of the avatar, etc.). We have analyzed how many times each game appeared on the first, second, etc. and last places, in order to define the most preferred games. Game 3 has been found to be the most enjoyable, followed by games 2, 5, 4 and 1. Game 6 has been indicated as the least enjoyable due to its total independence between players while working towards a shared goal. In this game, the other player was often considered as a non-player character or competitor than a team member. From Table 2 we observe that the low efficiency in closely-coupled games (games 2, 3) did not decrease player enjoyment.

Finally, we asked players to define if there were any game patterns that are not suitable for playing remotely without communication. Participants were free to indicate which game(s), to their opinion, they would prefer not to play under the same circumstances. It was also allowed to leave the question unanswered if they found them all suitable. Although we have observed that participants found games 3 and 4 to be the least suitable (possible reasons for that will be shown further throughout the Results section), a high percentage of participants indicated all games to be playable, even when there was no communication.

Impact of the Remote setup on Player Experience
Once the level of player performance and enjoyment for each game was evaluated, we aimed to estimate to what extent they were affected by the setup conditions (the absence of communication and physical distance).

Absence of Communication
First of all, we asked players to evaluate to what extent they felt a necessity to discuss the game. We considered any type of topic that could improve gameplay, e.g. strategy discussion, asking for help, etc. Our findings (Figure 2(a)) tend to confirm the general expectation that loosely-coupled games require less communication. Most of them have been evaluated significantly lower by the participants than closely-coupled games. Repeated measures ANOVA has shown a significant difference between six games ($F(5,175) = 11.45$, $p < 0.01$). A Bonferroni post-hoc test has demonstrated that game 6 required significantly less communication ($p < 0.01$) than all other games (except game 5). It has been also discovered that games 2 and 3 required more discussion than game 5. At the same time, there was no difference between closely-coupled games.

Observing these necessity ratings (indicating an eagerness to communicate within certain games), it is important to see how the lack of communication affects player enjoyment and efficiency. As can be seen from Figure 2(b), for all games players indicated a perceived negative impact of communication on their enjoyment as relatively low (on average for every game, it did not exceed 5 on the 0 to 10 scale). A repeated measures ANOVA has shown a significant difference across the games ($F(5,175) = 6.13$, $p < 0.01$), but a Bonferroni post-hoc test has indicated that this difference in fact only existed between game 2 and games 5 and 6.

Finally, we analyzed whether or not a lack of communication decreased player efficiency. Figure 2(b) shows that games 2 and 3 are most affected. Players indicated that they felt they could be more efficient if they were able to discuss the strategy. Repeated measures ANOVA ($F(5,175) = 14.82$, $p < 0.01$) and a follow-up Bonferroni post-hoc test ($p < 0.01$) confirmed that this difference was significant. Moreover, we found that even among loosely-coupled games game 4 was rated significantly worse ($p < 0.01$). For this particular game, players found communication important as it would improve the word guessing assignment if they would be able to discuss the possible options with a partner.

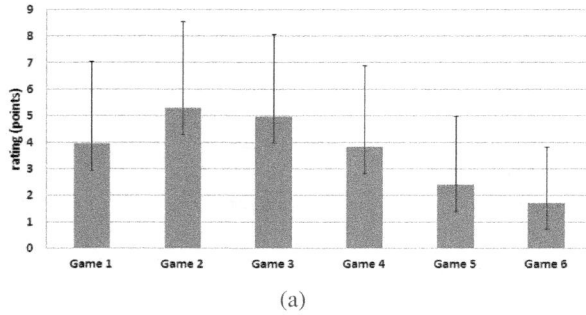

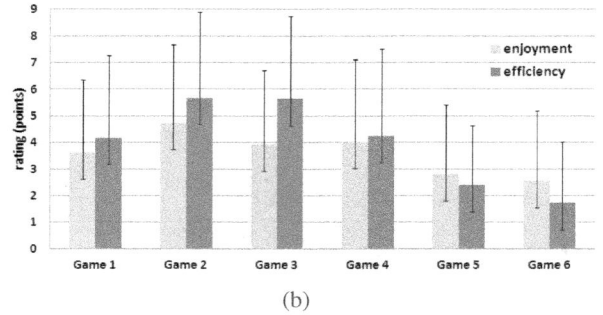

Figure 2. Necessity to discuss the game (a) and its influence on player enjoyment (yellow) and efficiency (blue) (b).

Physical Distance

Furthermore, we evaluated the negative impact caused by the physical distance between players. For both enjoyment and efficiency, players indicated that the physical distance had a rather low negative effect (Figure 3). For its impact on player enjoyment, we did not find any significant difference between the six games ($F(3.33, 116.41) = 2.48$, $p > 0.05$), indicating that all games were equally enjoyable when played over distance. When analyzing the influence on player efficiency, we found a significant difference ($F(3.71, 129.96) = 3.7$, $p < 0.01$). Further post-hoc testing showed that these difference existed only between games 3 and 6 ($p = 0.021$). No difference between games within the closely-coupled and loosely-coupled groups was found.

Impact of the Type of Collaboration on Player Experience

The final part of the analysis is focused on the collaborative aspects of each game. Every game was developed in such a way that it follows a certain cooperative design pattern. Although all patterns are assumed to support team work, the level of collaboration in every game may be perceived differently among players.

Level of Collaboration

When creating multiplayer games, in some cases game designers try to insert tasks that require a high level of collaboration between players in order to enhance their gaming experience. Analyzing the six patterns presented in this paper, our findings confirmed that closely-coupled games tended to provide a higher level of collaboration than loosely-coupled. All games (except game 5) were significantly more collaborative

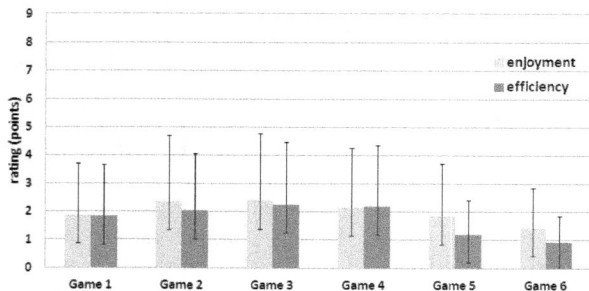

than game 6 ($F(3.47, 121.58) = 77.09$, $p < 0.01$), with games 2 and 3 showing the highest level of collaboration (Figure 4). Therefore, we can state that among both closely-coupled and loosely-coupled games, some patterns can be more efficient when it comes to providing high level of collaboration between players.

Additionally, we wanted to check for which types of games a higher level of collaboration will result in a higher gaming enjoyment. We found a positive correlation between collaboration and level of player enjoyment for games 1 ($R = 0.39$, $p = 0.019$), 2 ($R = 0.36$, $p = 0.031$) and 4 ($R = 0.39$, $p = 0.018$). Although game 3 had one of the highest levels of collaboration, it did not show an increase in player enjoyment. One possible explanation for this is that the other factors (e.g. way of interacting between players during the game) influenced player preference towards this game more than the level of collaboration.

Waiting for Others

One of the characteristics, typical for team work, is the amount of time players have to wait for each other before being able to continue. The waiting time is caused by a variety of reasons: player skills, occupation with different in-game tasks, etc. Therefore, we wanted to investigate how often it was necessary to wait for the partner in each game. As we did not allow communication between players, we expected closely-coupled games to introduce more waiting time. This assumption was confirmed by further analysis. We asked players to estimate the necessity to wait for each other in every game. Figure 5(a) represents the amount of waiting between six test conditions. A significant difference

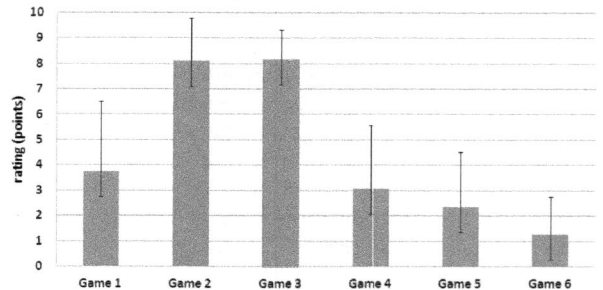

Figure 3. Influence of physical distance on player enjoyment (yellow) and efficiency (blue).

Figure 4. Level of collaboration.

16

between them was found ($F(5,175) = 37.79$, $p < 0.01$). A post-hoc analysis has shown that during any of the closely-coupled games, players spent significantly more time waiting for their partners than during the loosely-coupled gaming sessions. We observed that this was mainly due to the amount of collaboration required in closely-coupled games, although a difference in the experience level of players could also increase waiting time. At the same time no difference within the group of both closely- and loosely-coupled games was found.

As waiting time is a factor that can decrease player enjoyment and performance, we analyzed how their enjoyment and efficiency were affected (Figure 5(b)). Results of repeated measures ANOVA followed by a post-hoc test showed that player experience in closely-coupled games suffered significantly more from the necessity to wait ($F(3.09, 108.21) = 16.85$, $p < 0.01$ for enjoyment and $F(3.24, 113.44) = 26.43$, $p < 0.01$ for efficiency).

Based on the subjective measurements, the necessity to wait decreased player efficiency and enjoyment. However, we still wanted to see whether or not the waiting time affected the player experience objectively, based on the actual performance. This is especially important in case of closely-coupled games as they introduce lots of waiting into the play. Surprisingly, the additional waiting in closely-coupled games did not affect players' efficiency, as no correlation was found. The same result was obtained for loosely-coupled games.

Additionally, we checked if there was any negative impact of waiting on the level of collaboration. A significant negative correlation between collaboration and amount of waiting time for game 3 was found ($R = -0.33$, $p = 0.047$), making it weaker among other closely-coupled games when it comes to providing high level of collaboration, as this game required quite a lot of waiting between players (players may move away from each other but need to combine their efforts in order to move the jumping pad).

Influence of Partner's Actions

In multiplayer games, the actions of one player often directly or indirectly affect the gaming experience of others. Here, we present results regarding the extent of the influence of the partner's action and behavior on the player's own performance and enjoyment. We expect that, when tightly collab-orating, players notice other players actions more, and therefore, are more affected by them.

One of our initial assumptions was that partner performance greatly affects player enjoyment, especially in closely-coupled games where two players are almost always working together. Repeated measures ANOVA rejected our assumption, indicating that the partner's actions did not decrease player enjoyment in certain games more than the others ($F(3.60, 125.83) = 2.63$, $p > 0.05$). Also, the values for negative effect of partner's action on player enjoyment provided by participants, remained very low (on average for every game, they did not exceed 3.5 on the 0 to 10 scale).

At the same time, it was not the case when comparing the influence of partner's actions on player efficiency. We found that closely-coupled games were affected more than loosely-coupled games ($F(3.77, 131.8) = 14.95$, $p < 0.01$). As before, we have also checked the correlation between this influence and player enjoyment. No game showed a relation, indicating all games to be enjoyable even when the player efficiency was affected by the actions of the partner.

Finally, we wanted to see if the actual player contribution had an influence on the evaluation of the partner. We estimated player contribution to be based on the amount of objects he/she and his/her partner collected (total amount of objects collected by a team is considered as 100%). Here, we confronted the player evaluation with the objective contribution of the partner to see if any correlation between those two existed. Such correlation existed only for games 2 and 3 (Table 3). In case of game 2, we found that higher partner's contribution reduced the negative effect of lack of communication on player enjoyment. In case of game 3, both player enjoyment and performance were related to the partner's contribution. The higher the contribution, the more it reduced a negative impact on player experience that existed due to the gaming conditions (i.e. lack of communication, physical distance and waiting). This allows us to conclude that tasks triggering a higher player performance may improve the outcome of team work. Based on the obtained results, we can, for instance, see that a higher player contribution can compensate for the negative effect caused by the setup conditions.

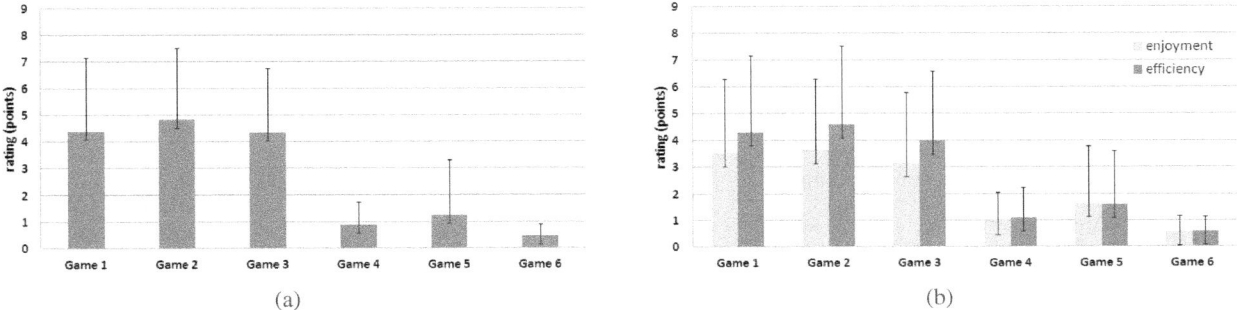

Figure 5. Necessity to wait for the partner (a) and its influence on player enjoyment (yellow) and efficiency (blue) (b).

	Partner's contribution & enjoyment decreased by lack of communication	Partner's contribution & effectiveness decreased by lack of communication	Partner's contribution & enjoyment decreased by physical distance	Partner's contribution & effectiveness decreased by waiting
Game 2	$R = -0.38$ $p = 0.021$			
Game 3	$R = -0.39$ $p = 0.018$	$R = -0.35$ $p = 0.039$	$R = -0.35$ $p = 0.039$	$R = -0.34$ $p = 0.046$

Table 3. Influence of partner's contribution.

DISCUSSION

To our knowledge, previous research initiatives have analyzed cooperative game patterns only when the players were present on the same location, and could naturally communicate and see each other [6]. When considering interaction over distance, especially when no communication is allowed, additional challenges are present when trying to maintain the same level of player experience. Therefore, games based on the same cooperative patterns can result in an entirely different experience when considered in a non-collocated setup. Knowing these differences may help game developers improve player interaction in collaborative multiplayer games, both for co-located and remote play.

In order to see how different patterns affect player experience under two different circumstances, we compared results obtained in our study with the evaluation of patterns provided in [6]. In their work, the authors have chosen four popular multiplayer collaborative games and defined a set of patterns that occur in each game. Then, using some self-developed Cooperative Performance Metrics (CPM), they mapped CPM elements to the cooperative patterns that caused them. Although we have not applied CPM for evaluation during our experiment, we believe some of the questions in our post-experiment questionnaire can be matched to certain CPM components. We had to eliminate game 1 from the comparison analysis as this pattern was not evaluated in [6].

The first metrics in [6] was 'laughter and excitement'. The authors reported that shared goals (in our case, game 6), shared puzzles (Game 4) and complementary (game 2) patterns provided the highest values for this metric, while abilities on other players (game 5) and interaction with shared object (Game3) caused less positive emotions. Although in our case we did not analyze laughter and excitement directly, we believe that it is comparable with the rating of games based on the player enjoyment. Oppositely to co-located play, in our case game 6 was found to be the least enjoyable, while games 2 and 3 had the highest preference. Based on our findings, we believe that such difference between remote and co-located setups is caused by the inability to talk. Some players even indicated that without communication, game 6 tended to be more competitive than collaborative, as one barely notices the other player, and tasks are performed individually.

The next CPM components were 'worked out strategies' and 'helping events'. These two patterns are directly connected with an ability to communicate between players. If you can communicate, you can easily decide upon the strategy or ask your partner for help. Therefore, we associated these two criteria with the evaluation of necessity to communicate. During the co-located condition the authors observed that patterns of shared puzzles (game 4) and goals (game 6) caused most of 'worked out strategies' and 'helping events'. These are followed by complementary (game 2) and interaction with same object (game 3) patterns. In our case, complementary and interaction with the same object patterns required the most communication between players. One of the reasons for that was players not willing to stay together in the gaming environment. As a consequence, once help was needed players could not immediately find their partner.

In their work, El-Nasr et al. analyzed the 'wait for each other' events that were caused by each pattern. In their analysis complementary (game 2) and interaction with same object (game 3) patterns did not cause waiting events at all. It is quite natural when you are together to immediately communicate what you are going to do, and whether it involves the other player. At the same time they have ascertained that shared puzzles (game 4) and goals (game 6) patterns were resulting in additional waiting. In our case due to their loosely-coupled nature games 4 and 6 required the least waiting in comparison with game 2 and 3.

The final metric used in [6] was 'got in each others' way', which is similar to the influence of partner's actions in our questionnaire. Similarly to their results we observed that shared goals pattern (game 6) had the least influence of partner's actions, while the complementary pattern (game 2) was rated highest in both studies.

CONCLUSION AND FUTURE WORK

In this paper we have presented a user experiment where different types of collaboration were analyzed in a remote setup without communication between players. Six collaborative games were developed, each following one of the cooperative game design patterns: limited resources, complementary roles, interaction with the same object, shared puzzles, abilities that can be applied on other players and shared goals. Based on the coupling between players, each pattern was referred to as either closely-coupled or loosely-coupled.

Among closely-coupled games, *complementary* and *interaction with the same object* patterns were found to be the most enjoyable and provided the highest level of collaboration among all six patterns. At the same time, they were most affected by the lack of communication between two players. The game based on *limited resources* pattern was less influenced by the absence of communication and the remote setup, but among all closely-coupled games it showed the lowest level of collaboration and enjoyment.

When comparing loosely-coupled collaboration, the *abilities that can be used on other players* pattern showed a high level of player satisfaction with a minor negative effect brought by the lack of communication. This game did not provide players with a high perception of team work, but this did not impact player enjoyment. Absence of communication affected the *shared goals* pattern the least, but the game based on this pattern introduced the lowest level of enjoyment with (almost) no collaboration.

With this study we have made the first attempt to evaluate cooperative game patterns in remote setup where any form of communication was not supported. The evaluation of each pattern was based on a single game. Although we realize that the same game patterns can be integrated and designed in multiple ways, we believe that these results can be valid for further research in cooperative game design. Results from this study revealed several interesting design lessons that can be further applied in order to build better cooperative games being played under different circumstances or certain limitations (in our case, absence of communication).

We have covered only six cooperative game patterns. Analysis of other existing patterns is still necessary. Furthermore, an effective way of combining these patterns together should be investigated under different play conditions (remote or co-located, with or without communication). Defining what patterns work best together under different circumstances could be of significant value for game designers aiming for an increasingly enjoyable player experience.

ACKNOWLEDGMENTS

The research described in this paper is directly funded by Hasselt University through the BOF framework. The authors would like to thank Tom De Weyer for his assistance with the implementation and all participants who contributed to this research by taking part in the experiment.

REFERENCES

1. Battocchi, A., Pianesi, F., Tomasini, D., Zancanaro, M., Esposito, G., Venuti, P., Ben Sasson, A., Gal, E., and Weiss, P. L. Collaborative puzzle game: a tabletop interactive game for fostering collaboration in children with autism spectrum disorders (asd). In *Proc. ITS 2009*, ACM (2009), 197–204.

2. Björk, S., and Holopainen, J. *Patterns in Game Design (Game Development Series)*. Charles River Media, Inc., 2004.

3. Crichton, N. Information point: visual analogue scale (VAS). *Clinical Nursing 10*, 5 (2001), 697 – 706.

4. Ducheneaut, N., and Moore, R. J. The social side of gaming: a study of interaction patterns in a massively multiplayer online game. In *Proc. CSCW 2004*, ACM (2004), 360–369.

5. Ebner, M., and Holzinger, A. Successful implementation of user-centered game based learning in higher education: An example from civil engineering. *Computers & Education 49*, 3 (2007), 873 – 890.

6. El-Nasr, M. S., Aghabeigi, B., Milam, D., Erfani, M., Lameman, B., Maygoli, H., and Mah, S. Understanding and evaluating cooperative games. In *Proc. CHI 2010*, ACM (2010), 253–262.

7. Goh, W.-B., Fitriani, Ting, L. G., Shou, W., Goh, C.-F., Menon, M., Tan, J., and Cohen, L. G. Potential challenges in collaborative game design for inclusive settings. In *Proc. of workshop on UI Technologies and Their Impact on Educational Pedagogy, available online at http://www.dfki.de/EducationCHI2011/* (2011).

8. Holzinger, K., Lehner, M., Fassold, M., and Holzinger, A. Archaeological scavenger hunt on mobile devices: from education to e-business: A triple adaptive mobile application for supporting experts, tourists and children. In *Proc. ICE-B 2011*, INSTICC (2011), 131–136.

9. Pape, S., Dietz, L., and Tandler, P. Single display gaming: examining collaborative games for multi-user tabletops. In *Proc. of workshop on Gaming Applications in Pervasive Computing Environments* (2003).

10. Rocha, J. B., and Mascarenhas, S. P. R. Game mechanics for cooperative games. In *ZDN Digital Game* (2008), 73–80.

11. Zagal, J. P., Rick, J., and Hsi, I. Collaborative games: lessons learned from board games. *Simul. Gaming 37*, 1 (2006), 24–40.

Novel Interaction Techniques Based on a Combination of Hand and Foot Gestures in Tabletop Environments

Nuttapol Sangsuriyachot   **Masanori Sugimoto**

Department of Electrical Engineering & Information Systems, University of Tokyo

7-3-1 Hongo Bunkyo-ku, Tokyo, 113-8656, Japan

{nuttapol, sugi}@itl.t.u-tokyo.ac.jp

ABSTRACT

Interactive tables, or tabletop devices, employ multi-finger gestures to interact with digital contents on a table's surface. Many studies have confirmed the convenience and intuitiveness of multi-finger gestures performed with the hands. However, there are still some tasks which cannot be conducted effectively by users via two-handed or multi-finger gestures. Given that feet are used occasionally in the real world to support the hands in the performance of complex tasks such as driving a car, we considered that it might be useful to combine foot gestures with hand gestures to enhance user interactions with tabletop environments.

In this study, we developed a high-resolution foot sensing platform based on multi-touch techniques known as frustrated total internal reflection and diffused illumination. We then used the device to study the effect of combining hand and foot gestures on tabletop systems by using a 3D drawing application. We conducted user evaluations to compare foot gestures and identified which gestures were most comfortable for performing a 3D model rotation task. We also compared the performance in a 3D drawing task when using only hand gestures with the performance when using hand and foot gestures together. Finally, we discussed how hand and foot gesture combination techniques could provide new user experiences in tabletop environments.

Author Keywords
Foot Gesture; Interactive Design; Multi-touch; Tabletop

ACM Classification Keywords
H.5.2 [Information interfaces and presentation]: User Interfaces - Interaction Styles.

General Terms
Design; Human Factors

INTRODUCTION
Digital tabletop systems are becoming one of the subjects of future workspaces because of their large size, interactive display, and touch sensing support. At present, user inputs on tabletops are heavily reliant on multi-finger and hand

gestures. This is probably because the hands are our main medium of interacting with environments in daily life. However, performing simultaneous tasks on tabletop systems is difficult even with a multi-touch capability. Previous studies of multi-touch systems have shown that a user typically coordinates both hands to perform a task where the dominant hand is the main controller and the nondominant hand provides support [25]. Although the simultaneous performance of two different tasks with different hands is possible, it may increase user's cognitive load and reduce task performance.

The feet are human limbs which can be used occasionally as inputs to perform tasks while the hands are occupied. Although they are not as convenient to use as the hands, the feet are used to control numerous mechanisms in various everyday machines such as car accelerator pedals or sewing machines, as well as virtual user interface environments, e.g., CAVE [5]. Many foot gestures, such as jumping, toe-tapping [2], or kicking [10], have been designed as input channels for computing devices. We believed that tabletop interactions could be enhanced by the integration of hand and foot gestures. Considering a shared, limited space around tabletops, however, we argued that subtle gestures which require less movement, such as foot rotations [23] or body weight shifting [22], are more suitable. Several hardware devices have been developed for tracking foot gestures, including sensors-embedded tiles [21] or even a usage of accelerometers inside cellphones [23]. We observed that tabletops are usually located in public spaces and are often accessed by passers-by who are uncomfortable with hardware preparation such as wearing special footwear. Base on this observation, we finally chose a camera-based approach for a foot gesture tracking system. This configuration also has an advantage in its high-resolution tracking capability which requires for subtle foot gesture tracking [2].

In this study, we developed high-resolution foot sensing floor (Figure 1) to capture fine-grained foot gestures, study the effects of hand and foot gesture combinations on tabletops, and design novel tabletop interactions. The study investigated the effect of combining hand and foot gestures when using a 3D model drawing application in a tabletop environment. We conducted two user studies. The first study aimed to identify which foot gestures are more comfortable and acceptable for users, while the second study compared a hand only gesture approach with a

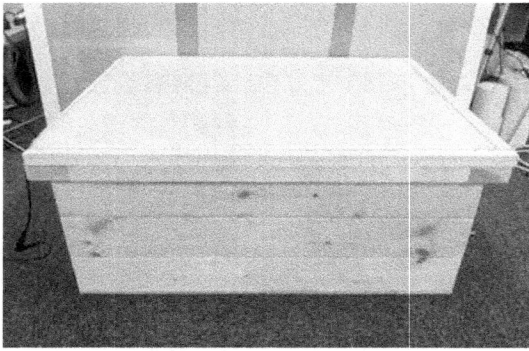

Figure 1. The developed foot hardware platform.

combined hand and foot gesture approach in 3D drawing tasks.

RELATED WORK

Foot sensing hardware

Many technologies are available for producing sensing floors, including physical actuators, sensors, and cameras. Magic carpet [18] detected the pressure and position of the feet using piezoelectric wires and two Doppler radars. Z-Tiles [21] were interlocked tiles that contained a number of force-sensitive resistor sensors. Each sensor measured continuous pressure values and the system could calculate low-resolution pressure distributions of each foot. Multitoe [2] was a high-resolution multi-touch floor system that used a combination of frustrated total internal reflection (FTIR) [9] and front diffused illumination (front DI) [6], thus allowing foot pressure images to be captured by a camera beneath an acrylic floor. The resolution of the pressure images was sufficiently high to extract accurate foot information and apply a pattern recognition algorithm (e.g., identify individual users based on the pattern of their shoe soles). However, this system focused only on foot interactions with a large multi-touch floor and did not consider hand interactions.

Combined hand and foot gestures

Supplementary foot inputs can be used occasionally when working at workstations to increase the degrees of freedom of manipulations. This allows us to perform several activities simultaneously, which can increase work productivity. Mole [19] was a foot input device that provided swinging foot pedals under a workstation desk with a cursor-positioning function. It was designed to be used as a mouse while both of the user's hands operated a keyboard, thus reducing the time required for switching between keyboard and mouse. Another study used the Wii balance board as an additional input to virtual reality applications [8]. The study also investigated the use of a foot input device with a keyboard and a mouse to provide three degrees of freedom when manipulating 3D applications such as 3D model rotation. Schöning et al. also used the Wii balance board to study the effects of a combination of multi-touch hand and foot gestures in

spatial navigation systems [22]. They found that foot gestures could reduce the difficulty of map panning tasks compared with using multi-touch hand only gestures. The use of foot gestures also facilitated simultaneous map navigation tasks such as panning and zooming in a map at the same time.

Foot gesture design

To identify foot gestures that are intuitive for users and easy to perform, we needed to observe the role of foot movements in daily life and study the effectiveness of different foot gestures. Choi et al. [4] developed walking and leaning gestures based on the data pattern received by sensors embedded in augmented shoes. Multitoe [2] used user-centered evaluations to find suitable gestures for activating buttons and menus on a multi-touch floor. It also suggested that a user's head and eye perspective could be approximated by calculating the pressure distributions of their feet. Scott et al. [23] evaluated the use of foot gestures for controlling a mobile device in eyes-free situations by identifying the most comfortable of four foot gestures, i.e., dorsiflexion (lifting the toe), plantar flexion (lifting the heel), and foot rotations while pivoting around the heel or toe. Schöning et al. [22] also suggested that foot gestures based on pressure distribution changes were intuitive and matched with users' intuition for using with the map navigation systems. Alexandar et al. [1] conducted user studies and propose suitable foot gesture patterns for controlling mobile devices.

DESIGN REQUIREMENTS

Our goal was to design a system that allowed a user to efficiently use hand and foot gestures to conduct simultaneous tasks on a tabletop. To achieve this, we addressed the following hardware, software, and gesture design considerations.

- According to human cognitive knowledge, the simultaneous performance of multiple activities can produce high cognitive loads and reduce task efficiency. Therefore, multimodal tasks must be divided into primary and secondary subtasks. The primary task requires the user's attention whereas the secondary task demands less attention and it should preferably be processed automatically [7]. We therefore need to consider how to divide tabletop tasks into two subtasks, where the primary task is conducted intentionally using hand gestures while the secondary task is conducted with less conscious involvement using foot gestures.

- We need to minimize a user's attention during the performance of foot gestures; such gestures should therefore be simple, easy to perform, and match users' intuition. Furthermore, the foot input device should contain no display units, as these would distract the user's attention from the main display area (i.e., the tabletop surface).

- Foot interactions are not as accurate as hand interactions [17]. Therefore, all tasks that require precise control should be assigned to hand interactions, whereas foot gestures should be related to less precise and complementary manipulations.

- To obtain high precision from foot information and detect foot gestures accurately, we need to employ a high-resolution sensing floor device at a reasonable cost.

PROTOTYPE

We developed a foot sensing floor with a high-resolution sensing capacity by adapting the multi-touch floor setup based on FTIR and front DI technologies used in Multitoe [2]. However, as we could not modify the floor to embed an infrared camera beneath the floor because of site limitations, we raised the hardware platform rather than making a hole in the floor. Our hardware was a wooden platform measuring 69 cm × 59 cm on the top surface with a height of 30 cm. We placed an FMVU-13S2C Firefly camera (resolution: 1328 × 1048) with a 2.1 mm wide-angle lens at the center of the base of a box. This tracked the activities of feet on a 40 cm × 30 cm subregion of the surface.

The platform's surface consisted of two layers of 20 mm acrylic panes that supported the user's weight. One of the acrylic layers also served as an infrared waveguide for the FTIR setup. To frustrate the infrared light and improve the quality of the pressure images, we created a compliant surface by applying a thin layer of silicone to a tracing paper sheet using Tinkerman's method [24] and placed it on top of the acrylic panes. Finally, we covered the entire surface with a thin plastic sheet to protect the hardware system from dust and stains. The structure of the surface is shown in Figure 2. As the light sources for the front DI technique, we surrounded the platform with four infrared lamps. No display device or projector was embedded into the foot platform.

By using the combination of FTIR and front DI technologies, the foot pressure images and shapes of soles were captured. This enabled the platform to be able to recognize foot gestures performed by users who might or

might not wear shoes. We adapted algorithms used for capturing feet movements from [2]. Grayscale pressure images were captured by the camera to extract information related to the feet (e.g., pressure distribution, foot positions, and foot angles). This information was processed and a foot gesture recognition module was implemented using the Java version of OpenCV [16] image processing library known as JavaCV [13].

For the tabletop system, we used a rear-projection DI tabletop developed by Mi et al. [14]. The tabletop system measured 105 cm × 108 cm × 90 cm and it had a 90 cm × 70 cm interactive touch screen area. Finger gesture recognition was managed using the reacTIVision toolkit [20] and the graphical user interface on the tabletop was developed using the MT4J framework [15]. Figure 3 shows a subject simultaneously using the tabletop and foot platform to perform hand and foot gesture interactions.

INTERACTION DESIGN

We used a 3D drawing application to investigate the efficiency of simultaneous hand and foot gesture interactions, where a user could manipulate a 3D model in 3D space and draw free-form lines on its surface. As the drawing task required precise control, we assigned the task to hand gestures and the 3D model manipulation task to foot gestures. This allowed the user to simultaneously draw and manipulate a 3D model using a combination of hand and foot gestures. We limited the manipulation to two degrees of freedom to reduce the complexity of the 3D model manipulation, i.e., rotating around the x-axis (Figure 4 (c) and (d)) and y-axis (Figure 4 (a) and (b)). We used a simple 3D cube as the test model so the user could easily distinguish the angle and direction of rotation.

Through observations on users using a tabletop system, we found that a space for their foot gestures around the system was limited. Thus, foot gestures for tabletops should be designed as small movements as possible. Studying prior works on foot gesture design, we chose the following three foot movements for our exploratory studies; (i) pressure distribution changes, (ii) foot rotations, and (iii) foot

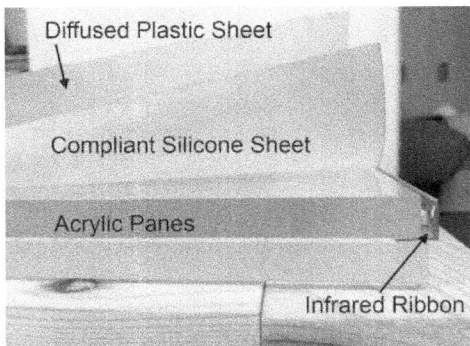

Figure 2. The foot platform has two layers of 20 mm acrylic panes, a custom-made silicone compliant surface, and a thin sheet of plastic.

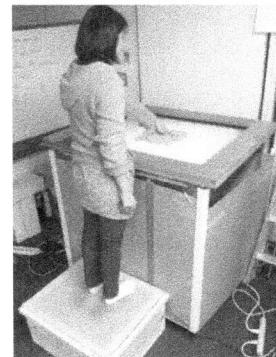

Figure 3. A user simultaneously performs hand and foot gestures using our tabletop and foot platform system.

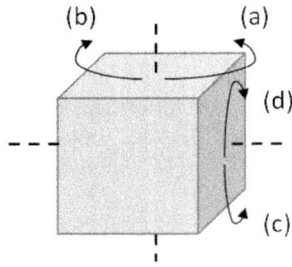

Figure 4. 3D model rotation. (a) Left rotation, (b) right rotation, (c) upward rotation, and (d) downward rotation.

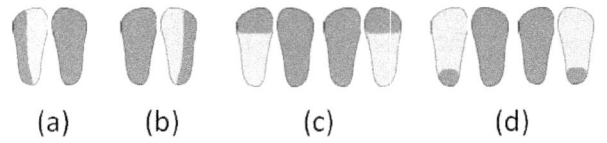

Figure 5. Pressure distribution change gestures. (a) Left rotation, (b) right rotation, (c) upward rotation, and (d) downward rotation.

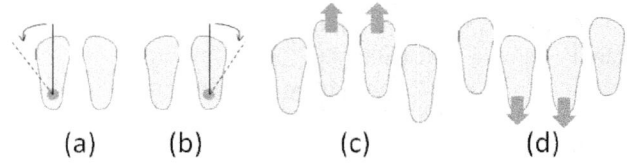

Figure 6. Foot rotation and transition gestures. (a) Left rotation, (b) right rotation, (c) upward rotation, and (d) downward rotation.

transitions. We designed these movements based on body angles and perspective-changing responses, e.g., people turn their bodies to the left or right to observe left or right edges of the 3D model, and they crane their necks and step forward to see its upper edge. To find out the comfortable foot gestures, we categorized the gestures into two groups:

- **Pressure distribution changes:** The foot gestures are shown in Figure 5. A user puts pressures on the red area of each foot to perform each gesture, for example, a user puts pressures at the left side of the left foot while fully standing on the right foot to perform the left rotation gesture.

- **Foot rotation and transition:** The foot gestures are shown in Figure 6. The left and right rotation gestures are performed by externally rotating left or right feet while pivoting the rotation on the heel. These gestures were reported in [23] as the most comfortable foot rotation gestures. The upward and downward rotations are performed by translating feet to the front or back respectively.

There was also a dominant-side issue with upward and downward rotation gestures in both groups, which could be performed using the left or right foot. As a previous study indicated that the dominant foot provides more effective input than the nondominant foot [12], the foot gestures used for upward and downward rotations should be selected on an individual basis depending on the user's dominant foot. Note that the rotation directions are on the opposite face of the cube that is shown to the user after rotation and we refer to the manipulation based on this notation, i.e., a left rotation gesture will rotate the cube to the right side and reveal its left face, whereas an upward gesture will rotate the cube downward and show its upper face.

The high-resolution pressure images generated by the FTIR setup allowed us to detect the direction and number of pressure distribution changes by counting the number of bright pixels in the areas of each foot, which were translated into pseudo-pressure values. However, to avoid unintentional gesture detection due to a small weight shift, we set the minimum thresholds of the pressure values and a user had to press harder than the values to perform the

gestures. Since users had different foot pressure values, we allowed them to set their own threshold values by asking them to rotate a 3D model in each direction. Their personal thresholds were recorded by the system to identify whether the gestures were intentional. Following Scott's work on heel gestures [23], we also limited the rotation angle within ±40 degrees because this was reported to be the comfortable range for users.

We also facilitated more responsive foot interactions by mapping the magnitude of foot gestures (i.e., the pressure value, the rotated angle, and the distance of the foot transition) to the rotation speed, which allowed users to rotate a model more slowly or rapidly.

EXPERIMENT 1: IDENTIFYING SUITABLE GESTURES

The goal of this experiment was to identify the foot gestures that were comfortable for users. We compared the performance of two groups of foot gestures for the 3D model rotation task, i.e., the left, right, upward, and downward rotations. This will ensure that the foot gestures are intuitive enough to support simultaneous task performances with hand gestures.

Task

Each participant performed two groups of foot gestures to rotate a 3D cube model: pressure distribution changes (Figure 5), and foot rotations and transitions (Figure 6). The order of the groups tested by users was counterbalanced. In each group, participants performed 10 sets of four gestures where the order of the gestures in each set was random but no two similar gestures were performed consecutively. Each participant was told to perform each gesture until the cube was completely rotated to the next face (no other faces but one were shown to the user) before conducting the next gesture. Note that we asked users to calibrate their threshold forces before conducting the first gesture group. Each participant was given one minute for trying foot gestures before doing the real experiments. The experiments were designed to be finished within three minutes. After users had performed the gestures in each group, we measured their overall task performance time and asked each of them to complete a questionnaire rating each gesture from 1 to 9 in terms of ease and user satisfaction using a Likert scale. Note that these questions were selected from a Questionnaire for User Interaction Satisfaction (QUIS) [3].

Participants

Eight volunteers (two male and six female; 23–30 years old) participated. All were right-footed. Participants confirmed that they had no prior experience of using foot input devices or tabletop systems in their daily life.

Results

Figure 7 shows the mean execution time for the cube rotation task using two foot gesture groups. The mean time for the pressure distribution change group was 13 s less than for the rotation and transition group. This difference was significant (paired samples t-test: $t(7) = -5.88$, $p < 0.005$). The ease and satisfaction of four foot gestures in each gesture group are shown in Figures 8 and 9. All foot gestures in the pressure distribution change group had higher scores in terms of ease compared with the gestures in the foot rotation and transition group. (Wilcoxon signed-rank test: $p < 0.05$ for all gestures). The user satisfaction for all gestures in the pressure distribution change group was also significantly higher than for the rotation and transition group (Wilcoxon signed-rank test: $p < 0.05$ for all gestures). Since we did not implement a function to snap the 3D model into a right angle when the rotation to another face was nearly done, users needed to control the rotation speed of the model by themselves through foot gestures. However, because the rotation speed used in this study was not very fast, the errors of rotation degree were negligible.

Discussion

The results showed that foot gestures in the pressure distribution change group were more acceptable to users than foot gestures in the foot rotations and transitions group in the cube rotation tasks. Some users also reported that the foot transition gestures (Figure 6 (c) and (d)) required more force and attention, which made them uncomfortable. This suggests that foot gestures should not include large foot movements (foot transitions). Rather, foot gestures should be small movements that a user can perform with small parts of the foot (e.g., toe tapping) or no movement (pressure distribution changes).

EXPERIMENT 2: EVALUATION OF THE COMBINED HAND AND FOOT GESTURE METHOD

The goal of this experiment was to compare the performances of the hand only method and the combined hand and foot method during multiple tasks on the tabletop. We used a 3D drawing task as the evaluation task. In this experiment, foot gestures were based on pressure distribution changes according to the previous experimental

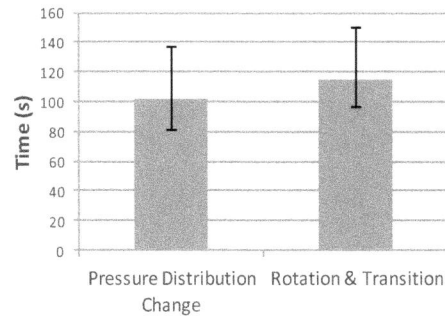

Figure 7. Average execution time for the cube rotation task for each foot gesture group.

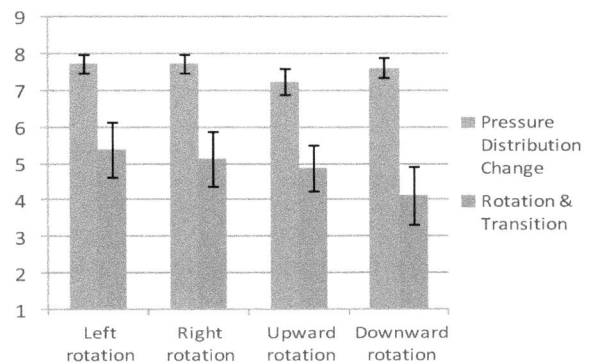

Figure 8. Ease of foot gestures for each gesture group rated from 1 (hard) to 9 (easy).

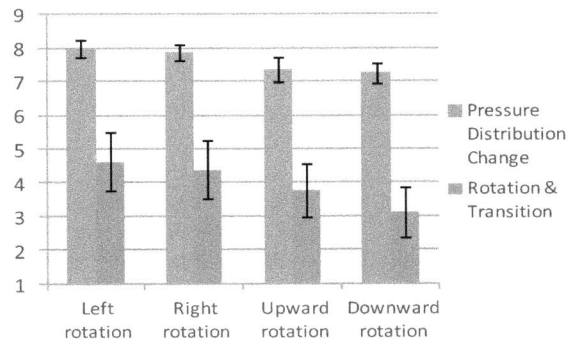

Figure 9. User satisfaction with foot gestures in each gesture group rated from 1 (frustrating) to 9 (satisfying).

results. This was to ensure that the movements were easy to perform and intuitive for users.

Task

The 3D drawing task consisted of two subtasks, i.e., drawing and rotating. Each participant used the following two methods to conduct these tasks.

- *Hand only method*: With this method, the participants used one-finger drag gestures to draw free-form lines on the model surface and two-finger drag gestures to rotate the model (Figure 10(a)).

- *Hand and foot method*: With this method, the participants used one-finger drag gestures to draw lines on the model surface, but used foot gestures based on pressure distribution changes to rotate the model (Figure 10(b)).

The order of the two methods was counterbalanced. Participants completed five trials for each method. In each trial, participants drew a simple circle on the first face of the cube before rotating it to the next face. These two activities were alternated until circles had been drawn on all of the cube's faces. The order of rotation manipulations was fixed to avoid the side effect of the user preferences (for example, one might feel more comfortable and conduct tasks only with the left and upward rotation gestures, while another preferred the right and downward rotation gestures). Each trial was designed to be finished within one minute. Each participant was given one minute for trying hand and foot gestures before doing the real experiments. We measured the time for each trial with both methods. Finally, all participants answered the questionnaire to rate their overall reactions to each method. The questions were chosen from QUIS to compare satisfaction, stimulation, and the ease of each method.

Participants
Eight volunteers (two male and six female; 23–30 years old) participated. All were right-footed. All participants confirmed that they had no prior experience of using foot input devices or tabletop systems in their daily life.

Results
Figure 11 shows the mean time taken to complete the 3D drawing task for each of the two methods. The average time with the hand only method was slightly longer (1.6 s) than with the combined hand and foot method (paired samples t-test: $t(7) = 5.348$, $p < 0.002$). The mean user ratings for satisfaction, stimulation, and ease for each method are shown in Figure 12. The results show that the score for satisfaction with the combined hand and foot method was slightly higher than for the hand only method, whereas the ease rating for the hand only method was slightly higher than for the combined hand and foot method, although the differences were not statistically significant. However, we found that the rating for stimulation was significantly higher for the combined hand and foot method compared with the hand only method (Wilcoxon signed-rank test: $z = -2.539$, $p < 0.05$).

Discussion
This experiment showed that novice users could combine hand and foot gestures to perform multiple tasks on a tabletop system and these tasks took approximately the same amount of time as when the hand only method was used. Although we did not demonstrate that our proposed

method was more satisfactory or easier than a hand only method, our system stimulated users to interact more with tabletop systems using their feet, which enhanced the user experience during tabletop interactions. Many participants

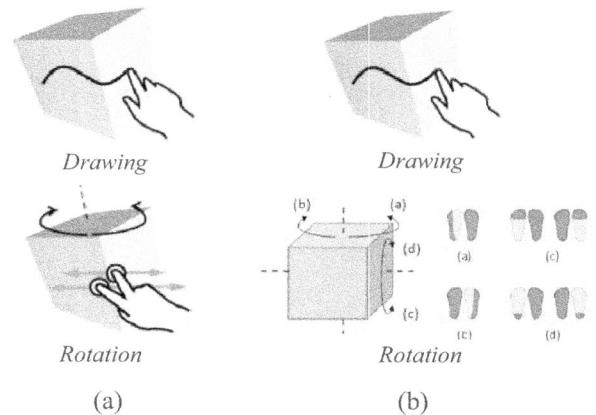

Figure 10. Hand and foot gestures used for the drawing and rotation tasks with each method. (a) hand only method, (b) combined hand and foot method.

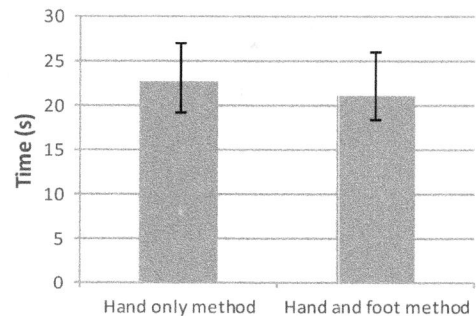

Figure 11. Average time required for 3D drawing tasks using each method.

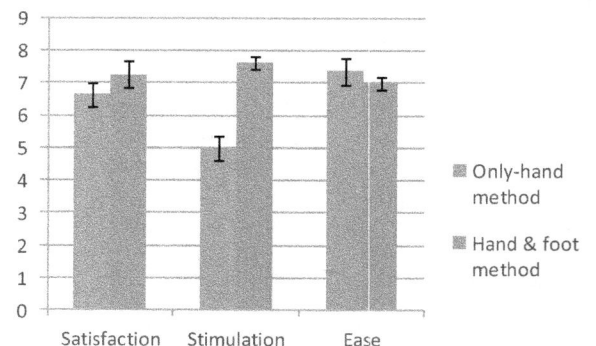

Figure 12. Mean overall ratings for each method rated from 1 (worst) to 9 (best).

commented that the use of foot gestures to perform supporting tasks was helpful because it could reduce the number of tasks that required the hands so they could perform more tasks overall. Several participants also reported that using the feet as a controller was fun and it made boring tasks more interesting. Comprehensive, long-term investigations are required to evaluate the effects of supplementary foot gesture inputs.

LIMITATION OF THE CURRENT SYSTEM

There are some issues that need to be considered for practical implementations of a system integrating hand and foot gestures. In our study the users stood still during the experiments and did not move around the tabletop, which would not always happen in normal tabletop usages. Also in a tabletop system with a large surface, there are chances that users will try to touch out-of-reach objects, which may cause side effects to the feet pressure distribution and make the system misinterpret the foot gestures. These issues can be solved in a couple of ways. It is possible to predict some extreme movement patterns, such as detecting too much pressure in the front of soles, and temporarily stop gesture tracking. We can also implement an on-off feature to enable foot gesture tracking at users' will. For example, a user can perform double toe-tapping gestures to enable or disable the gesture tracking.

Another issue is the lack of the foot gesture studies in the sitting situations. In many recent tabletop systems, their heights are short and they are designed to be used by seated users. We believe that the fatigue due to continuous standing and the loss of balance caused by weight shifting gestures are two major factors that degrade the foot gesture performance. In addition, we observed that users' feet are more relaxed and are likely to have fewer movements while sitting, which will decrease recognition errors due to unintentional foot movements. In order to confirm our ideas, we need to implement a low-height multi-touch surface with an empty space under the table so that users can put legs while sitting. This can be implemented by using planar sensors such as scanning range finders [11] instead of FTIR or DI techniques. We also need to reduce the height of the foot sensing platform, for example, installing all platform hardware under the floor.

CONCLUSIONS AND FUTURE WORK

In this study, we proposed the combination of hand and foot gesture interactions to perform multiple tasks on tabletop systems. We identified suitable foot gestures that could be combined with hand gestures by conducting a user study experiment where we compared two sets of foot gestures that were based on foot pressure distribution changes, foot rotation, and transition. After selecting acceptable foot gestures, we compared the performance of a combined hand and foot method with a hand only method in completing a 3D model drawing task, which requires two subtasks, i.e., drawing and rotating. We found that the combination of hand and foot gestures was intuitive for novice users. The combined method required the same amount of time as the hand only method while it could speed up multiple task performance on occasion. The combined method also encouraged users to employ both their hands and feet to

control a tabletop system, which enhanced the user experience during tabletop interactions.

The limitations of our hardware setup prevented us from investigating the performance of foot gestures when a user was *sitting*. In addition, the height of the current platform (30 cm) was too high for normal tabletop systems. We need to consider alternative high-resolution floor sensing technologies to reduce this height or embed a camera beneath the floor. Finally, we plan to study the effect of conducting two different tasks on a tabletop *simultaneously* using a combination of hand and foot gestures. We hope that this will reduce the task execution time and provide users with a better experience compared with hand only gesture systems.

ACKNOWLEDGEMENT

This work is supported by JSPS Grant-in-Aid Scientific Research (Grant Number: 22300279).

REFERENCES

1. Alexander, J., Han, T., Judd, W., Irani, P. and Subramanian, S. Putting Your Best Foot Forward: Investigating Real-World Mappings for Foot-based Gestures. In *Proc. CHI'12*, 1229-1238.

2. Augsten T., Kaefer, K., Meusel, R., Fetzer, C., Kanitz, D., Stoff, T., Becker, T., Holz, C., and Baudisch, P. Multitoe: high-precision interaction with back-projected floors based on high-resolution multi-touch input. In *Proc. UIST '10*, 209-218.

3. Chin, J. P., Diehl, V. A., and Norman, K. L. Development of an instrument measuring user satisfaction of the human-computer interface. In *Proc. CHI '88*, 213-218.

4. Choi, I., Ricci, C. Foot-mounted gesture detection and its application in virtual environments. *IEEE International Conference on Systems, Man and Cybernetics. '97*, 4248-4253.

5. Cruz-Neira, C., Sandin, D. J., DeFanti, T. A., Kenyon, R. V., and Hart, J. C. The CAVE: audio visual experience automatic virtual environment. *Commun. ACM 35, 6* (June 1992), 64-72.

6. Diffused Illumination. http://wiki.nuigroup.com/Diffused_Illumination.

7. Eyesenck, M. W. and Keane, M. T. *Cognitive Psychology: A Student's Handbook, 3rd edition*, Lawrence Erlbaum Associates (1995), 107 – 116.

8. Haan, G., Griffith, E. J., and Post, F. H. 2008. Using the Wii Balance Board™ as a low-cost VR interaction device. In *Proc. VRST '08*, 289-290.

9. Han, J. Y. Low-cost multi-touch sensing through frustrated total internal reflection. *In Proc. UIST '05*, 115-118.

10. Han, T., Alexander, J., Karnik, A., Irani, P., and Subramanian, S. Kick: investigating the use of kick

gestures for mobile interactions. In *Proc. MobileHCI '11*, 29-32.

11. Hirai, S. and Shima, K. Multi-touch wall display system using multiple laser range scanners. In *Proc. ITS '11*, 266-267.

12. Hoffmann, E. R. A Comparison of Hand and Foot Movement Times. *Ergonomics 34, 4* (1991), 397 – 416.

13. JavaCv. http://code.google.com/p/javacv/.

14. Mi, H., Krzywinski, A., Fujita, T., and Sugimoto, M. 2012. RoboTable: An Infrastructure for Intuitive Interaction with Mobile Robots in a Mixed Reality Environment, *Journal of Advances in Human-Computer Interaction*. Volume 2012, Article ID 301608.

15. MT4j - Multitouch for Java. http://mt4j.org/.

16. OpenCV. http://opencv.willowgarage.com/.

17. Pakkanen, T., and Raisamo, R. Appropriateness of foot interaction for non-accurate spatial tasks. In *Proc. CHI '04*, 1123–1126.

18. Paradiso, J., Abler, C., Hsiao, K., and Reynolds, M. The magic carpet: physical sensing for immersive environments. *Ext. Abstracts CHI '97*, 277-278.

19. Pearson, G. and Weiser, M. 1986. Of moles and men: the design of foot controls for workstations. In *Proc. CHI '86*, 333-339.

20. reacTIVision - a toolkit for tangible multi-touch surfaces. http://reactivision.sourceforge.net/.

21. Richardson, B., Leydon, K., Fernstrom, M., and Paradiso, J. A. Z-Tiles: building blocks for modular, pressure-sensing floorspaces. *Ext. Abstracts CHI '04*, 1529-1532.

22. Schöning, J., Daiber, F., Krüger, A., and Rohs, M. 2009. Using hands and feet to navigate and manipulate spatial data. *Ext. Abstracts CHI '09*, 4663-4668.

23. Scott, J., Dearman, D., Yatani, K. and Truong, K. N. Sensing foot gestures from the pocket. In *Proc. UIST '10*, 199-208.

24. Tinkerman's method - Casting Textured Silcone. http://nuigroup.com/forums/viewthread/2383/.

25. Yee, K. Two-handed interaction on a tablet display. *Ext. Abstracts CHI '04*, 1493-1496.

A Comparison of Flick and Ring Document Scrolling in Touch-based Mobile Phones

Huawei Tu[1], **Feng Wang**[2], **Feng Tian**[3] and **Xiangshi Ren**[1]

[1]Kochi University of Technology, Kochi, Japan, ren.xiangshi@kochi-tech.ac.jp

[2]Kunming University of Science and Technology, Yunan, China, wf@cnlab.net

[3]Institute of Software, Chinese Academy of Sciences, Beijing, China, tf@iel.iscas.ac.cn

ABSTRACT

This study quantitatively analyzed the performance of two scrolling techniques (flick and ring) for document navigation in touch-based mobile phones by means of three input methods (index finger, pen and thumb). Our findings were as follows: (1) overall, for the three input methods, flick resulted in shorter movement time and fewer numbers of crossings than ring, suggesting that flick is superior to ring for document navigation in touch-based mobile phones; (2) regarding pen and thumb input, there were interaction effects between scrolling technique and target distance. Ring led to shorter movement time than flick for large target distance. This finding indicated that ring has a potential interaction advantage, which should be deeply explored for future scrolling technique design; (3) both flick and ring document scrolling in touch-based mobile phones can be modeled by the Anderson model [2]. We believe these findings offer several insights for scrolling technique design for document navigation in touch-based mobile phones.

Author Keywords

Flick scrolling, ring scrolling, document navigation, touch-based mobile phones

ACM Classification Keywords

H.5.2 Information Interfaces and Presentation: User Interfaces—*Interaction techniques*

INTRODUCTION

Advances in processing speed and memory allow mobile phones to support a number of applications such as text view and edit. However, the small screen area of mobile phones restricts the size of displayed text. Therefore, the user has to interact more fluently with the device to get to the desired location in the text. Thus scrolling is important for the support of many document related tasks in mobile phones.

As two commonly employed techniques for document and list navigation, flick and ring are present in a wide range of electronic devices including touch-based mobile phones and portable media players. In flick gesture a finger slides in a line along the screen. As an intuitive and natural form, flick has been commonly employed in touch-based mobile phones such as the iPhone. On the other hand, ring is used to effect document scrolling by means of the user's circular strokes. Ring serves as an efficient scrolling technique in mobile devices such as the Apple iPod.

For efficient interaction with digital devices for scrolling documents, much research in recent years has focused on the design and analysis of flick and ring techniques [1, 3, 6, 8, 9, 10]. For example, Aliakseyeu et al. [1] systematically investigated the effectiveness of multi-flick in pen-based interface by designing several flick-based scrolling techniques and comparing their performance with that of a scrollbar. In the study, multi-flick technique achieved as good a performance as the scrollbar. Inspired by the hardware scrolling rings like the one in the Apple iPod, Moscovich and Hughes [6] proposed a technique for scrolling through documents by means of a virtual scroll ring.

However, to the best of our knowledge, the performances of these two techniques in touch-based mobile phones have never been directly compared in a formal evaluation. The widespread use of flick and ring for document scrolling in touch-based mobile devices signified the importance of these two scrolling techniques. An open question is which scrolling technique performs better in the context of document navigation tasks. Finding the advantages and disadvantages of each scrolling technique can expedite the design of scrolling techniques and result in significant benefits to users.

The present paper described an experiment in which we examined the performance of flick and ring scrolling for document navigation in touch-based mobile phones using three input methods (index finger, thumb, and pen). In index finger input, the non-dominant hand holds the device and the index finger of the dominant hand is used for gesturing. In thumb input, the dominant hand holds the device and the thumb of the dominant hand is used for gesturing. Although pen input is not prevalent in touch-based mobile phones, it can be an alternative to finger input in some cases such as when users operate small targets in mobile phones [7]. Hence, we also compared the performance of flick and ring with pen input. A variant of Fitts' reciprocal tapping task, which is similar to that used by Hinckley et al. [4] was used to thoroughly compare flick scrolling and ring scrolling.

This paper begins a review of related work, covering literature on flick scrolling, ring scrolling and movement time models for scrolling. This is followed by a description of the experiment design. Then we discuss the experiment results and provide several guidelines for the design of scrolling techniques in mobile phones.

RELATED WORK
This work builds upon three areas of previous research, most of which focused on pen-based interaction. The first refers to the flick scrolling technique. The second is a body of work on the ring scrolling technique. The last is movement time model for scrolling. We review each in turn.

Flick Scrolling Technique
Flick scrolling is an intuitive and natural scrolling method for mobile touch devices such as the iPhone. Aliakseyeu et al. [1] designed four flick-based scrolling (multi-flick) techniques and compared them with the traditional scrollbar for navigating lists and documents on different devices (PDA, tablet PC, large table). In the study, multi-flick technique achieved as good a performance as the scrollbar. Yin and Ren [11] used pen pressure to improve the performance of flick-based and ring-based scrolling techniques. Experimental results indicated that the techniques with pressure information performed better than those without pressure information. However, they did not compare of flick and ring techniques.

Ring Scrolling Technique
Ring gesture is a circular motion. The rotating scroll wheels is one of the most widely adopted scrolling techniques in devices such as the iPod. Earlier work by Wherry [10] investigated the performance of a touchpad scroll ring, a mouse scroll wheel and touchpad scroll zone in a variant of Fitts' tapping task; the scroll ring performed faster with fewer errors. To improve list selection performance, Diehl et al. [3] designed a novel scroll ring with pressure sensitivity.

Inspired by the hardware scrolling ring such as that in the Apple iPod, Moscovich and Hughes [6] proposed a technique for scrolling through documents by means of a virtual scroll ring. The technique used the amplitude and frequency of repetitive circular movement, rather than the angle and radius, to better support ring document scrolling. Results showed that VSR performed at least as well as a mouse wheel for medium and long distances, and was preferred by users.

In order to better support scrolling on touch displays, Smith and Schraefel [9] designed a radial scroll widget: the scrolling time for the scroll widget was shorter than that for the traditional scrollbar for short scrolling distance. However, the scroll widget suffered a drawback which was that the user

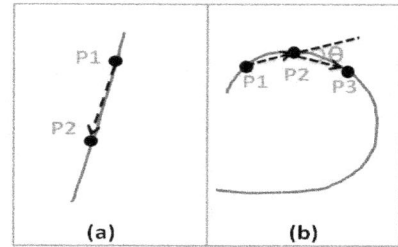

Figure 1. The illustration of (a) flick scrolling and (b) ring scrolling.

must maintain visual focus on it. Curve dial [8] can support eyes-free parameter entry for document scrolling, as it tracked the curvature arc rather than the center. Radial scroll tool and curve dial selected a minimum of three points to determine the angle of curvature, which inspired the ring technique design in our study.

Movement Time Model for Scrolling
A quantitative human performance model would facilitate the design and evaluation of scrolling techniques by quantitatively predicting their efficiency before running extensive user studies. In an early study, Zhai et al. [12] investigated the performance of three input methods (mouse with isometric joystick, mouse with a track wheel, and two handed joystick and mouse) in a task that involved both scrolling and pointing. The results showed that a mouse with a finger wheel did not improve user performance while the other input methods significantly improved user performance. In a noteworthy analytical study, Hinckley et al. [4] have shown that Fitts' law can model certain scrolling patterns. In the study, participants were asked to perform a variant of Fitts' reciprocal tapping task by means of an IBM ScrollPoint and an IntelliMouse Wheel. However, the study did not examine the applicability of Fitts' law for ring and flick document scrolling in touch-based mobile phones. Another movement time model for scrolling was proposed by Andersen [2](Andersen model), taking into account that Fitts' law was developed for "aimed" movement, however, for scrolling tasks the target position is usually not known. The study indicated that movement time was linearly dependent on the target distance. In our study, we further examined the effectiveness of Fitts' Law and Andersen's model for the prediction of movement time with ring and flick document scrolling in touch-based mobile phones.

METHOD
Flick and Ring Techniques
The flick technique used here was designed based on the method proposed in [11]. As illustrated in Figure 1a, p2(x2, y2) and p1(x1, y1) respectively denote the current and previous points in a gesture trajectory. The document scrolling distance is equal to the absolute value of (y2 - y1). The document scrolling direction is determined by the sign of (y2 - y1): if the sign is negative, the document will scroll forward. Otherwise, the document will scroll backward.

On the other hand, for ring technique, we utilized a method similar to that used in [8, 9, 11]. As illustrated in Figure

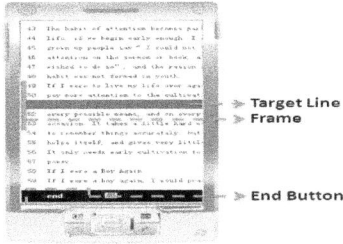

Figure 2. Experimental interface.

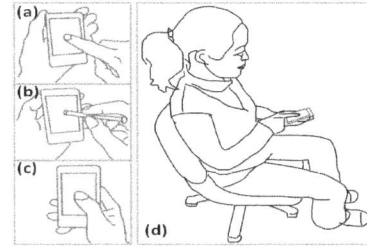

Figure 3. (a) Index finger input. (b) Pen input. (c) Thumb input. (d)Participant in the experimental environment.

1b, there are a minimum of three points p1, p2 and p3 (p1 is a previous point of p2, and p2 is a previous point of p3) in a gesture trajectory. θ denotes the angle that rotates from the vector (p1, p2) to the vector (p2, p3). The document scrolling distance is equal to $\theta \times R/2\pi$ (R is a constant with a value of 220 pixels). The scrolling direction is determined by the sign of the dot product of the vector (p1, p2) and the vector (p2, p3): if the sign is positive, the document will scroll forward. Otherwise, the document will scroll backward. Scrolling by angle indicates that fast and small circles can cause fast scrolling, while slow and large circles can cause slow scrolling.

Reciprocal Framing Task for Scrolling

The experimental task was similar to [4], which was a variant of Fitts' reciprocal tapping task. In the experiment, participants were instructed to scroll down and up, moving back and forth between two target lines in a document using the flick or the ring technique. As illustrated in Figure 2, a document which consisted of 288 lines with a line height of 21 pixels (0.30 cm) was used. We assigned every line a unique number, starting at 1 for the first line and incrementing by 1 for each successive line. We expected that these numbers would help participants find the target lines easily. The initial target line appeared with red and the second one was marked by blue. A frame was placed at the left of the task window and always centered on the screen. Participants were asked to scroll the target line toward the range of the screen identified by the frame. Once the target line fully entered the identified screen range, participants were asked to press the end button in order to complete the current scrolling task and continue to the next scrolling task; meanwhile, the target line disappears. If participants pressed the end button without the target line fully entering the identified screen range, a warning beep tone would sound, but we asked them to continue to scroll toward the next target i.e., not to repeat the failed task.

Participants

Ten participants, 9 males and 1 female, from 20 to 27 years of age, took part in this experiment. All of them were right-handed and had prior experience with bare finger operation on touch screen devices such as iPhone. Six of them had prior experience operating digital screens with digital styli.

Apparatus

The study was conducted on an HTC Touch HD mini smart phone equipped a capacitive touch screen with HVGA res-

olution. The screen size is 3.2 inches and its resolution was 320×480 pixels. The platform is Windows Mobile 6.5 Professional with HTC Sense. The experimental program was designed in the C# environment.

Task and Procedure

When performing the experimental task, participants were asked to sit in a chair (see Figure 3d). The experiment used a $3 \times 2 \times 4 \times 3$ within-factor design with a variety of planned comparisons. The independent variables were input method (index finger, pen and thumb, see Figure 3a, b,c respectively), scrolling technique (flick and ring), target distance (20, 60, 120 and 200 lines), and frame width (3, 6 and 12 lines). A (partially-balanced) Latin-square was used to counterbalance the order of the presentation of the input method and scrolling technique. For each input method and scrolling technique, the order of the 4 target distances for the 3 frame widths was randomized. For each target distance and frame width, the participants completed 7 individual target acquisitions (phase). The participants took 60 minutes on average to complete the experiment. In summary, experiment data collection consisted of:

10 subjects $\times$
3 input methods $\times$
2 scrolling techniques $\times$
4 target distances $\times$
3 frame widths $\times$
7 phases
= 5040 scrolling trials

At the end of the experiment, a questionnaire was administrated to gather subjective opinions. Participants were asked to rate flick and ring for each input method on 7-point Likert Scales regarding *movement speed, easy to position target line* and *hand fatigue* (7 for highest preference, and 1 for lowest preference).

RESULTS

Learning Effects

Recall that for each target distance and frame width, each participant performed 7 phases. In order to ensure data stability, we first checked the learning effect on movement time over the 7 phases to see if the data we collected had reached a level of stability. Movement time is defined as the duration from the moment the pen or finger touches the screen to the

31

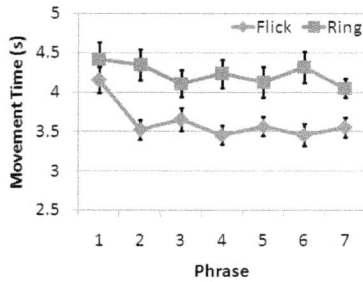

Figure 4. Mean movement time for each phase and scrolling technique.

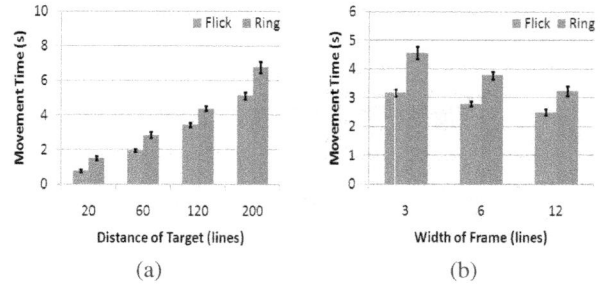

Figure 5. Regarding index finger input, mean movement time for two scrolling techniques for each (a) target distance and (b) frame width. Error bars represent 0.95 confidence interval.

moment the target line last enters the region specified by the frame before the "end" button is pressed.

As shown in Figure 4, for flick technique, repeated measures ANOVA showed that phase had a significant main effect on movement time ($F_{6,54} = 12.43$, $p < 0.001$). Post-hoc comparisons revealed that the first phase had a significant longer movement time than the other phases ($p < 0.05$). Therefore, we excluded the data for the first phase for the rest of our analysis. On the other hand, with respect to ring technique, although no significant main effect was found on movement time for phase ($F_{6,54} = 2.06$, $p = 0.07$), it was found that the first phase resulted in a significantly longer movement time than the third, fifth and seventh phases ($p < 0.05$ for all); in these four phases, the experimental tasks were the same: moving the red target line into the region specified by the frame. Hence, the data from the first phase was excluded from the rest of our analysis.

Number of Crossings (NC)

When moving the target line into the screen region specified by the frame, participants sometimes crossed the frame more than once. The number of crossings is defined as the number of times the target line enters or leaves the specified frame region for a particular trial with one target distance and frame width, minus 1.

Regarding index finger input, a repeated measures ANOVA analysis showed a significant main effect on NC for scrolling technique ($F_{1,9} = 107.37$, $p < 0.001$). The mean NC was 2.14 in the flick condition and 5.05 in the ring condition for each target distance and frame width. Other independent variables influenced NC. A significant main effect was found on NC for target distance ($F_{3,27} = 7.08$, $p < 0.01$) and frame width ($F_{2,18} = 47.49$, $p < 0.001$). Interesting, although there was no significant interaction effect on NC for frame width, there was an interaction between scrolling technique and target distance ($F_{3,27} = 3.76$, $p < 0.05$).

For pen input, there was a significant main effect on NC for scrolling technique ($F_{1,9} = 41.90$, $p < 0.001$). The mean NC was 1.83 in the flick condition and 5.04 in the ring condition for each target distance and frame width. There was a significant main effect on NC for target distance ($F_{3,27} = 5.88$, $p < 0.01$) and frame width ($F_{2,18} = 47.49$, $p < 0.001$). Although no significant interaction effect was found between scrolling technique and target distance, there was a strong interaction

between scrolling technique and frame width ($F_{2,18} = 4.14$, $p < 0.05$).

With respect to thumb input, a significant main effect was found on NC for scrolling technique ($F_{1,9} = 75.21$, $p < 0.001$). The mean NC was 0.73 in the flick condition and 3.08 in the ring condition for each target distance and frame width. The frame width had a significant main effect on NC ($F_{2,18} = 35.07$, $p < 0.001$). Although there was no significant interaction between scrolling technique and target distance, there was a strong interaction between scrolling technique and frame width ($F_{2,18} = 8.66$, $p < 0.05$).

Overall, for index finger, pen and thumb input, ring technique resulted in more NC than flick technique, indicating it is difficult for participants to position the target line within the frame using ring technique. More NC indicated that it would take more time to position the target line within the frame, which may yield a false measurement of the movement time for scrolling. Therefore, for the analysis of movement time, we excluded the data of the experimental trial in which NC was greater than 3.

Movement Time (MT)

Movement time, as defined in the subsection "learning effects", is another basic measure of the performance.

For index finger input, a repeated measures ANOVA analysis showed that scrolling technique had a significant main effect on MT ($F_{1,9} = 51.54$, $p < 0.001$). The mean MT was 2.82s for flick technique and 3.86s for ring technique. Other independent variables influenced MT. A significant main effect was found on MT for target distance ($F_{3,27} = 567.55$, $p < 0.001$) and frame width ($F_{2,18} = 87.23$, $p < 0.001$). There was an interaction between scrolling technique and target distance ($F_{3,27} = 6.65$, $p < 0.01$) (see Figure 5a). In addition, there was a significant interaction between scrolling technique and frame width ($F_{2,18} = 14.59$, $p < 0.001$) (see Figure 5b). The results indicated that flick performed faster than ring when users performed scrolling tasks by means of the index finger.

With respect to pen input, there was no significant main effect on MT for scrolling technique ($F_{1,9} = 2.59$, $p = 0.14$). The mean MT was 3.39s for flick technique and 3.65s for

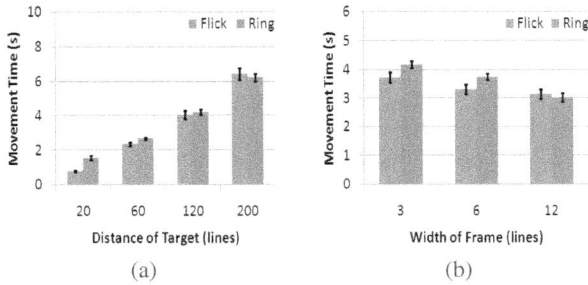

Figure 6. Regarding pen input, mean movement time for two scrolling techniques for each (a) target distance and (b) frame width.

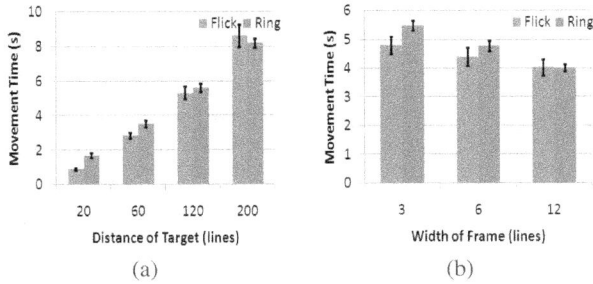

Figure 7. Regarding thumb input, mean movement time for two scrolling techniques for each (a) target distance and (b) frame width.

ring technique. There was a significant main effect on MT for target distance ($F_{3,27} = 588.87$, $p < 0.001$) and frame width ($F_{2,18} = 98.64$, p < 0.001). A significant interaction effect on movement time was found between scrolling technique and frame width ($F_{2,18} = 12.12, p < 0.001$) (see Figure 6b). Interesting, as illustrated in Figure 6a, there was also an interaction between scrolling technique and target distance ($F_{3,27} = 3.85, p < 0.05$). Ring resulted in a longer MT than flick for the target distance of 20, 60, 120 lines, but shorter MT for the target distance of 200 lines.

With regard to thumb input, there was no significant main effect on MT for scrolling technique ($F_{1,9} = 0.92, p = 0.36$). The mean MT was 4.40s in the flick condition and 4.75s in the ring condition. Other independent variables influenced MT. It was found that there was a significant main effect on MT for target distance ($F_{3,27} = 383.83, p < 0.001$) and frame width ($F_{2,18} = 71.27, p < 0.001$). There was a significant interaction between scrolling technique and frame width ($F_{2,18} = 6.69, p < 0.01$) (see Figure 7b). Additionally, an interaction effect on movement time was found between scrolling technique and target distance ($F_{3,27} = 3.11, p < 0.05$) (see Figure 7a). Ring produced a longer MT than flick for the target distance of 20, 60, 120 lines, but shorter MT for the target distance of 200 lines.

The Fit of Fitts' Law and Andersen Model
We examined the relationship between movement time and scrolling task with respect to each scrolling technique and each input method. It was found that for each scrolling technique and input method, linear regression of the movement time by ID showed low correlations with Fitts' law ($R^2 <$

0.8). However, for the Andersen model [2], regression of D against movement time for each scrolling technique and input method yielded a good fit, with regression coefficients of 0.99. The results verified the applicability of Andersen's model in flick-based and ring-based scrolling in touch-based mobile phones.

Error Rates
The error rate was defined as the percentage of target acquisition trials in which the participants pressed the "end" button but the target line was not in the range specified by the frame. It was found that for each input method and scrolling technique, the error rate was very low with a value less than 4%.

Subjective Evaluation
A repeated measures ANOVA analysis showed that for index finger input, flick was rated significantly higher than ring in terms of movement speed, ease in positioning the target line and hand fatigue ($p < 0.05$ for all). With respect to pen input and thumb input, although there was no main effect on *movement speed* and *hand fatigue* for scrolling technique, scrolling technique had a significant effect on *easy to position target line* ($p < 0.05$); flick was rated higher than ring. The subjective preference was fairly consistent with the movement time and number of crossings performance.

DISCUSSION
Advantages and Disadvantages of Flick and Ring
Flick and ring scrolling techniques were examined in the context of mobile document navigation tasks. For index finger input, flick resulted in shorter movement time than ring and was preferred by the participants, indicating that flick is a superior technique for document scrolling. The flick gesture is analogous to a throwing motion in the real world while ring gesture is a circular motion. Therefore, compared to ring gesture, flick gesture may be more natural and intuitive for index finger input.

Regarding pen and thumb input, no significant difference was found in movement time for ring and flick techniques. The interaction effects on movement time for scrolling technique may have design implications. Flick led to shorter movement time than ring for short scrolling distances (target distance $<= 120$ lines). However, when scrolling actions were longer than 200 lines, ring tended to be faster than flick. With respect to pen input, the greater degrees of freedom afforded by the pen may allow participants to use the ring technique more comfortably than the flick technique. For thumb input, the thumb's movement range on the screen may have an effect on scrolling performance; it is difficult to move the thumb up and down but easy to rotate it along a circle [5]. Overall these interaction effects suggest that ring is a promising scrolling mechanism for pen and thumb input.

Smooth Scrolling for Ring Technique
Smooth scrolling is a feature used to reduce what the user would perceive as "jumps" (discontinuous movement) of

33

a document. However, in this study, the number of crossings (NC) was larger for ring than for flick technique, indicating that the participants could not perform ring smoothly. Also, participants reported that it was more difficult with ring than with flick to position the target line within the region specified by the frame. As expected, larger NC led to longer movement times. Therefore, for more effective ring scrolling technique design, it is better to increase the smoothness of response to sample points. It should be noted that for the data analysis of movement time, data from the experimental trial in which NC was greater than 3 were excluded. We believe that even after increasing the smoothness, the experimental results would not change.

As introduced in the subsection "flick and ring techniques", the document scrolling distance was calculated according to the angle between two vectors indicating current and previous finger or pen positions on the screen. With respect to the ring scrolling mechanism, sufficiently fine control of ring was difficult to achieve and as a result(, participants could not achieve smooth scrolling). Several methods have been proposed to support smooth scrolling, including linear least-squares fit [6], and increasing the gap between sampling points selection [8]. These methods will be used in our future examination of the performance of ring scrolling.

Mapping Function for Flick and Ring techniques

Aliakseyeu et al. [1] proposed three mapping functions for flick technique and demonstrated their effectiveness in the context of document and list navigation tasks. However, we did not use those mapping functions for two reasons. First, we wanted to avoid complicating our results with different varieties of mapping functions in the preliminary investigation of the performance of flick and ring, so we designed our scrolling techniques based on a simple mapping function which performed a linear translation of the displacement of input method to the distance of document scrolling. Second, the aim of this study was to compare flick and ring scrolling techniques, so it is essential to use a mapping function which is "fair" for both scrolling techniques (i.e., one that does not prejudice either scrolling technique). As the mapping functions in [1] were designed for evaluating flick scrolling only, they may favor flick over ring. Instead, we used the linear mapping function proposed in [8, 9, 11] to provide a fundamental mechanism which was fair for both ring and flick. Future work should further explore the performance of flick and ring document scrolling in the context of different mapping functions. As a fundamental study, our study provides a methodology and some important conclusions for future study (e.g. flick is superior to ring for document navigation in touch-based mobile phones; ring has a potential interaction advantage).

For ring technique, R, a constant coefficient, plays an important role in determining scrolling speed. Hence, we conducted a pilot study to select a proper R. We designed three ring techniques, in which R was set as 110, 220 and 330 pixels respectively (R110, R220 and R330 were used to denote the three ring techniques respectively). Six participants were asked to perform these three ring techniques. The ex-

periment procedure was similar to that introduced in subsection "experiment design". As a result, R220 resulted in significantly shorter movement times than R110 but fewer NC than R330. In addition, no significant difference was found in movement time between R330 and R220. Hence, R was set as 220 pixels for our study.

CONCLUSION

This paper presented a controlled experiment, which empirically evaluated the performance of two commonly used scrolling techniques (flick and ring) for document navigation by means of index finger input, pen input and thumb input in touch-based mobile phones. It was found that flick performed better than ring for the three input methods. Also, with regard to pen input and thumb input, ring performed faster than flick for long target distance, indicating ring has a potential interaction advantage and should be deeply explored for future scrolling technique design. Additionally, both flick and ring document scrolling in touch-based mobile phones can be modeled by Anderson model [2]. These findings may be useful in improving the performance of flick and ring document scrolling in touch-based mobile phones.

ACKNOWLEDGMENTS

This study has been partially supported by Grant-in-Aid for Scientific Research (No. 23300048) in Japan and NSFC of China (No. 61063027). We wish to thank the members of Ren Lab in Kochi University of Technology for their assistance. We also thank Yuan Fu and Shinpei Iwanami for conducting the experiments for this study.

REFERENCES

1. Aliakseyeu, D., Irani, P., Lucero, A. and Subramanian, S. Multi-flick: an evaluation of flick-based scrolling techniques for pen interfaces. In *Proc. CHI 2008*, ACM Press (2008), 1689-1698.

2. Andersen, T.H. A simple movement time model for scrolling. *Ext. abstracts. CHI 2005*, ACM Press (2005), 1180-1183.

3. Diehl, J., Möllers, M. and Borchers, J. Improving list selection performance with pressure-sensitivity on a scroll ring . *Ext. abstracts. UIST 2008*, ACM Press (2008), 65-72.

4. Hinckley, K., Cutrell, E., Bathiche, S. and Muss, T. Quantitative analysis of scrolling techniques. In *Proc. CHI 2002*, ACM Press (2002), 65-72.

5. Hirotaka, N. Reassessing current cell phone designs: using thumb input effectively. *Ext. abstracts. CHI 2003*, ACM Press (2003), 938-939.

6. Moscovich, T. and Hughes, J.F. Navigating documents with the virtual scroll ring. In *Proc. UIST 2004*, ACM Press (2004), 65-72.

7. Ren, X. and Moriya, S. Improving selection performance on pen-based systems: a study of pen-based interaction for selection tasks. *TOCHI, 7,* 3(2000), 384-416.

8. Schraefel, M., Smith, G. M. and Baudisch, P. Curve dial: eyes-free parameter entry for GUIs. *Ext. abstracts. CHI 2005*, ACM Press (2005), 1146-1147.

9. Smith, G.M. and Schraefel, M.C. The radial scroll tool: scrolling support for stylus- or touch-based document navigation. In *Proc. UIST 2004*, ACM Press (2004), 53-56.

10. Wherry, E. Scroll ring performance evaluation. *Ext. abstracts. CHI 2003*, ACM Press (2003), 758-759.

11. Yin, J. and Ren, X. ZWPS and pressure scroll: two pressure-based techniques in pen-based interfaces. *IPSJ, 3*(2007), 767-778.

12. Zhai, S., Smith, B. A., and Selker, T. Improving browsing performance: A study of four input devices for scrolling and pointing tasks. In *Proc. Interact 1997*, Chapman & Hall, Ltd. Press (1997), 286-293.

Tag-based Interaction in Online and Mobile Banking: A Preliminary Study of the Effect on Usability

Rajinesh Ravendran, Ian MacColl, Michael Docherty
Queensland University of Technology
2 George Street, Brisbane, QLD 4000
{r.ravendran, i.maccoll, m.docherty}@qut.edu.au

ABSTRACT

In this paper we describe tag-based interaction afforded by a tag-based interface in online and mobile banking, and present our preliminary usability evaluation findings. We conducted a pilot usability study with a group of banking users by comparing the present 'conventional' interface and tag-based interface. The results show that participants perceive the tag-based interface as more usable in both online and mobile contexts. Participants also rated the tag-based interface better despite their unfamiliarity and perceived it as more user-friendly. Additionally, the results highlight that tag-based interaction is more effective in the mobile context especially to inexperienced mobile banking users. This in turn could have a positive effect on the adoption and acceptance of mobile banking in general and also specifically in Australia. We discuss our findings in more detail in the later sections of this paper and conclude with a discussion on future work.

Author Keywords

Tags; interaction; banking; usability; customization; user satisfaction;

ACM Classification Keywords

H.5.2 [Information Interfaces and Presentation]: User Interfaces - Interaction styles.

INTRODUCTION

Tags, also known as user-defined metadata, are a popular Web 2.0 technology, enabling users to assign keywords to Web resources (e.g., photo, video, people, etc) primarily for the purpose of personal information management. Tags are a popular and easy-to-use technology [1] that are personal, contextual and dynamic [2] and a source of knowledge about users [3]. Tags aid users to recall and retrieve information content and when represented as tag clouds they facilitate visual information retrieval [4]. Tags can also help to establish associations between like minded individuals through analysis of tags semantics [3, 5].

In the financial domain, tags are widely used particularly to aid in personal financial management via external tools such as Mint[1] and Yodlee[2]. Australian banks, as part of their efforts to increase their competitive advantage and improve user satisfaction have begun to include PFM as part of their offerings with Australia and New Zealand Bank (ANZ) pioneering the initiative through its ANZ-MoneyManager[3] service. These tools enable users to assign tags to annotate transactional data for purposes such as budgeting, expense tracking, cash flow analysis, etc. However, they only allow tags to be assigned to financial transactions at a high level as category or description, but not at a granular level for resources such as bank account, or biller. There may be compelling advantages in doing so in the online and mobile banking contexts, opening doors to tag-based interaction alongside personal financial management. The earlier mentioned characteristics of tags, particularly "personal" and "contextual" appear suitable to afford a personalized interaction, unique to every individual based on tags assigned to resources. To date, tags have yet to be studied in the banking context to afford a customized interaction. We explore this notion in online and mobile banking based on a conceptual interaction customization model put forward by Fung [6].

This study is relevant and important, particularly in the Australian context as customization in online banking is cited as imperative to user satisfaction, particularly among the younger generation of Australia [7].Tag-based interaction can help facilitate customization defined as the ability for a website to be shaped in a way that better fulfills the wants of individual users [7]. Previous studies on customization indicate a positive impact on users especially in terms of overall appeal, engagement and commitment towards a website [6, 8-11]. Also, several studies indicate that customization positively affects user satisfaction in online systems [9, 10]. Therefore, we hypothesize that tag-based interaction can improve the usability especially user satisfaction of online and mobile banking.

---

[1] http://www.mint.com
[2] http://www.yodlee.com
[3] http://www.anz.com/ANZ-moneymanager/default. asp

TAGGABLE RESOURCES

In [12, 13], we define a set of taggable resource in both online and mobile banking contexts. The resources were identified by examining the online and mobile banking websites of two of Australia's leading banks[4]. The taggable resources are account, biller, reference, application and message. Table 1 lists and briefly describes these resources.

Resource	Type / Description
Account	Personal - User owned accounts (e.g., everyday, savings, cheque, credit card, business, etc)
	Payee - Linked (personal account) or Other (third party e.g., internal, external and overseas account)
Biller	All types of registered and unregistered billers
Reference	Personal - Description of transaction for self reference
	Payee - Description of transaction for recipient's reference
Application	All types of financial products (e.g., account, credit card, loans, etc)
Message	Personal communication between customer and bank

Table 1. Taggable Resources.

INTERACTION CUSTOMIZATION TYPES

The conceptual interaction customization model based on human to human interaction proposed by Fung [6] encompasses three types:

- Remembrance-based
- Comprehension-based
- Association-based

The definition of each interaction and the application of tags to facilitate these interactions in both online and mobile banking context are discussed in the following sections.

Remembrance-based

This type is defined as interaction customization through simple remembering of user's information based on the recurrence rate of a particular action on a website [6].

Remembrance-based interaction can be fulfilled through tags assigned to resources that are presented as tag clouds. This provides a visual retrieval interface that can simplify and ease the execution of past or recurring transactions. Simply by clicking on a tag, related information about a transaction that the tag is associated with can be retrieved

---

4 Commonwealth Bank (http://www.commbank.com.au/) and Suncorp Bank (http://www.suncorp.com.au/)

and displayed. If a selected tag is associated with two or more tags then the tag cloud can be filtered to show tags which are co-occurring with the selected tag. This removes the need to navigate to a different page or perform a manual search query. This also means to carry out a past or recurring transaction, users will only need to update necessary information such as amount (if different) and possibly retain other details.

Comprehension-based

This type is defined as interaction customization through recognition of user's behaviors used to provide assistance towards fulfilling the user's needs [6].

Comprehension-based interaction can be fulfilled by inferring possible banking actions (i.e., fund transfer) based on tags selected by a user. Such inference is possible for tags with certain types of relations (e.g., account to account, account to biller). Using these relations and simple pre-defined rules (e.g., transfer from Savings account to Visa account is valid but not the other way around) possible actions can be populated. The actions may also constitute different types of services or features offered by the bank for a particular need which otherwise may not be known to the user. By providing users with relevant options, banks may be able to provide subtle suggestions to users based on their personal banking usage. For example, if a user performs two transfers to a selected payee two months in a row, then a new option suggesting the user to schedule a monthly transfer may be provided and selected by default.

Association-based

This type is defined as interaction customization through association of user's behaviors with other individuals who share similar interests or needs [6].

Association-based interaction can be fulfilled by recommending tags to users (dropdown as focus is set on field and filter as user types). Tags can be associated and recommended to users based on certain criteria such as biller name or type. For example, when users select the biller Vodafone, a mobile service provider, tags associated with this specific biller can be recommended (i.e., "phone", "mobile", etc). Tags associated with a particular resource can be either defined by users (folksonomy) or system (taxonomy), or both combined (automanual folksonomies) [1]. The relevance and appeal of recommended tags may be further improved by making sense out of the underlying meanings of tags via semantic analysis [3, 5]. This can in turn assist to form more relevant associations between like-minded individuals within a community of users primarily through discovery of semantic relationship between tags.

CONVENTIONAL INTERFACE

The current banking interface is largely based on standard html objects (dropdowns, checkboxes, tables and menus) with minimal customization. Presently, only remembrance-based interaction is offered via dropdown selection. For example, when a user selects a particular biller, the biller details are automatically populated. This prevents the user from retyping the biller details. Apart from customization, the conventional interface is distinct in terms of information display. By default the conventional interface displays detailed financial information at all times for decision making. Conversely, the tag-based interface provides information on-demand. Information displayed is kept to a minimal through tags and browser events such as 'mouseover' and 'tap' are used as triggers to fetch and display detailed information.

TAG-BASED INTERFACE

An early prototype with tag integration for a few key resources namely bank account, biller and reference was implemented. The prototype is web-based with separate versions for online and mobile. The mobile version is aimed at smart phones with touch screen input such as iPhone, HTC, etc. According to Google[5], Australia has the second highest smart phone usage in the world. More information on the design and implementation of our prototype in the online and mobile contexts can be found in our previous papers [12, 13]. In this paper, we evaluate our prototype against the present 'conventional' banking interface.

METHODOLOGY

To assess the usability and overall user satisfaction we adapted System Usability Scale (SUS) developed by Brooke [14] by replacing "system" with "website". The SUS is a 10-item questionnaire with Likert scales that gives an overview of effectiveness, efficiency and satisfaction of a software/website. Tullis & Stetson [15] compared SUS against other usability questionnaires specifically for website usability assessment, and found that SUS yielded among the most reliable results across sample sizes. To further improve SUS, we included an 11-th item on "user-friendliness" with adjective ratings equivalent to a Likert scale of 1-7 ("Worst Imaginable", "Awful", "Poor", "Ok", "Good", "Excellent", and "Best Imaginable") to inquire about the summative experience of participants. This was suggested by a study that empirically evaluated nearly 10 year's worth of SUS data collected on numerous products in all phases of the development lifecycle [16]. The study regards SUS as a highly robust and versatile tool used in more than 200 studies for usability evaluation. To further examine the actual user performance (effectiveness and efficiency), we used time spent for each task as an indicator. Users were observed while they carried out tasks and usability issues were recorded and in the end of the evaluation a short interview was conducted to gather user feedback.

---

[5] http://google-au.blogspot.com.au/2011/09/smartphones-at-dinner-table-smartphone.html

As part of the evaluation, participants were given a set of online banking tasks which required them to carry out tasks using the conventional interface and tag-based interface. The tasks were essentially made up of two primary activities: bill payment and fund transfer. The evaluation was conducted in both online and mobile contexts. Post-completion of the tasks for a specific context, the SUS was administered to all participants. To ensure the absence of any pre-meditated associations in terms of experience and brand commitment among participants, a fictional banking website was used known as 'XBANK Online Banking'. The study's goals, objectives, and banking tasks were explained in a cover letter. The evaluation procedure was explained during a briefing session.

Task No.	Task Name	Task Details
T1	Rent transfer	This task requires the participants to make a fund transfer to a recipient for amount specified.
T2	Phone bill payment	This task requires the participants to make a bill payment to a biller for amount specified.
T3	Charity contribution	This task requires the participants to make a fund transfer to a recipient for amount specified.
T4	Foreign money transfer	This task requires the participants to make a bill payment to a biller for amount specified.
T5	Rent payment (recurring)	This task requires the participants to carry out a previous fund transfer (T1).
T6	Phone bill payment (recurring)	This task requires the participants to carry out a previous bill payment (T2).

Table 2. Evaluation tasks

POPULATION AND SAMPLE

The population of interest for this study is online banking users. A total of 8 online banking users were recruited: 6 males and 2 females between the age group of 21 to 40. All of the participants had at least one active online banking account at the time of participation and were familiar with online banking with at least one year of experience. However, only half of the participants had prior experience in mobile banking. According to our pre-test questionnaire, the most common banking activity carried out by the participants through their online and mobile banking is fund transfer, bill payment, transaction history and check balance. All participants had similar levels of experience in computer and Web. Data was collected using the adapted version of Software Usability Scale (SUS) and also user activity logs. Participation was entirely voluntary and each individual consented to participate in the study.

RESULTS

The following figures 1 and 2 show the computed SUS scores and the summative experience ratings by banking context for each participant (Px). The SUS score range is 0-100 and the summative experience rating range is 1-7 (1 = Worst Imaginable, 2 = Awful, 3 = Poor, 4 = Ok, 5 = Good, 6 = Excellent, 7 = Best Imaginable).

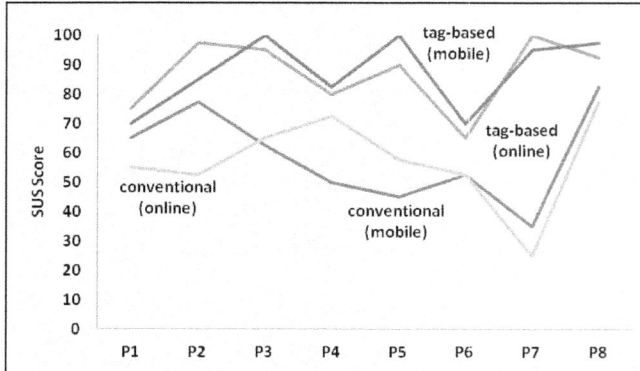

Figure 1. SUS score (online & mobile)

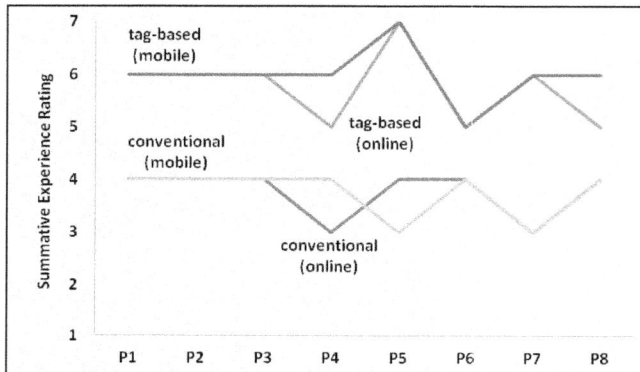

Figure 2. Experience rating (online & mobile)

Figures 1 and 2 indicate improved overall score/rating for tag-based interface compared to conventional interface in both online and mobile banking. The mean SUS score for tag-based interface is 86.9 and 87.5, and the mean summative experience rating is 6 (Excellent) for both contexts. In contrast, the mean SUS scores for conventional interface are 58.8 and 57.5, and the mean summative experience rating is 4 (Ok) for both contexts. To test the significance of the result, we conducted a paired t-test analysis with an alpha value of 0.05 (CI: 95%). The t-test analysis showed the difference in the scores is significant ($p < 0.05$) in both online (p=0.002) and mobile (p=0.001) contexts.

The following figures 3 and 4 show the mean SUS scores and summative experience ratings by familiarity with mobile banking given that not all participants of our study had prior experience in mobile banking. Participants were grouped into two basic categories: with experience and no experience.

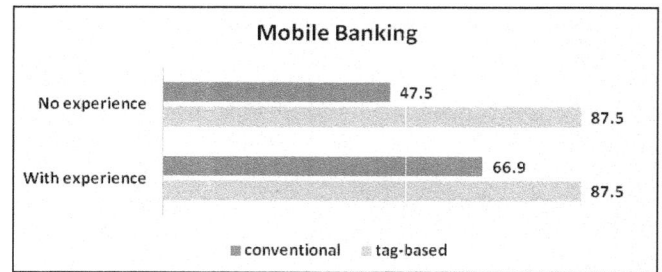

Figure 3. SUS score by familiarity

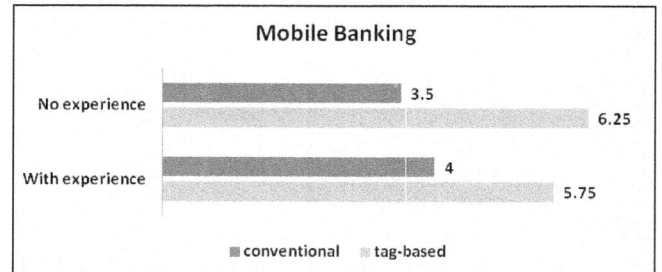

Figure 4. Experience rating by familiarity

Figure 3 shows the mean SUS scores for participants without prior experience are 47.5 and 87.5 for the conventional and tag-based interfaces, respectively. For participants with experience, the mean SUS scores are 66.9 and 87.5. This indicates that participants without prior experience in mobile banking experienced the biggest difference of 40%, while the experienced participants recorded a difference of 20.6%. Figure 3 lends support to this outcome by recording an increase of 2.75 among inexperienced participants with an overall individual rating of 3.5 and 6.25 for the conventional and tag-based interfaces, respectively. This is one rating higher compared to the increase of 1.75 seen with experienced participants with an overall individual rating of 4 and 5.75.

Task completion

The figure below shows the average time spent on each task by all participants in the online and mobile contexts.

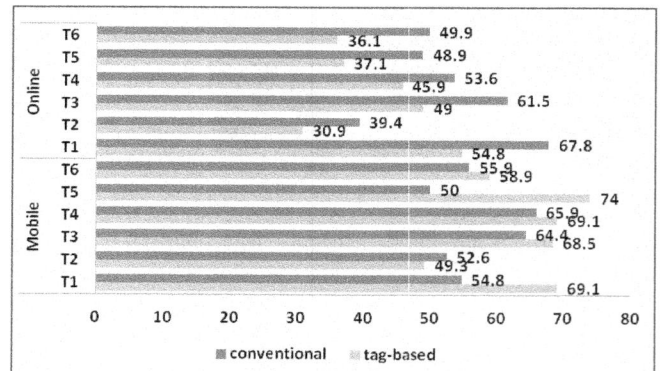

Figure 5. Task completion time

Figure 5 illustrates that participants in general completed their tasks within a shorter period of time online compared to mobile. Overall, tag-based interface yielded a higher performance online for all tasks, but was on the slower side in the mobile context. Participants are quicker on the conventional interface in mobile for just about all tasks. For tag-based interface, participants spent the most amount of time on task 5 (74s), but spent relatively less time (about 15s) for subsequent comparable task 6 (58.9s).

DISCUSSION

The results from this study support our initial hypothesis that tag-based interaction can improve usability especially user satisfaction of online and mobile banking. The observed effect of tag-based interface on usability warrants further investigation and needs to be rigorously tested for statistical significance with a larger sample.

Based on the SUS scores, participants are generally more satisfied with tag-based interface than the conventional interface. This outcome is even more evident in the mobile context compared to the online context. This is possibly due to the ability to carry out transactions by selecting tags which reduces the effort required from users on mobile devices. Participants also perceived the tag-based interface as more user-friendly (summative experience ratings) compared to the conventional interface in both contexts. This may be the case as participants find it easier and more intuitive to interact via their own tags.

Interestingly, participants with no prior experience in mobile banking are more satisfied with the tag-based interface compared to experienced participants (see Figure 3 & 4). This may have a positive impact on the adoption and acceptance of mobile banking, particularly from a usability perspective. According to Global Industry Analysts (GIA)[6], the global customer base of mobile banking is expected to reach close to one billion users by 2015. This highlights both the relevance and importance of mobile banking and the need for an interface with good usability.

As part of the study, we also inquired participants about minimal information on screen (tag-based) versus detailed information on screen (conventional). Participants preferred seeing minimal information on screen by default and being presented with detailed information when requested. This could be strongly tied to the security and privacy concerns of banking users especially those related to mobile banking [17].

The notion of providing tag suggestions on as a way to encourage the user to tag and re-use tags already present in the system was well received especially in the mobile context where many find it cumbersome to tag. Additionally, from our observations and interview with participants, it was obvious that they preferred to select suggested tags that were appropriate in their view than

---

[6]http://www.prweb.com/releases/2010/02/prweb3553494.htm

typing their own, however if they did, they expect their tags to be shown first in the list of suggested tags.

The actual user performance indicates improvements only in the online context, while participants appear to have spent more time on mobile. However, the questionnaire results for mobile do not reflect this and participants appear to be more satisfied and inclined to use the tag-based interface than the conventional interface. They perceive the tag-based interface as one that can improve their performance. One possible explanation is the unfamiliarity and lack of experience with the new tag-based interaction style, further exacerbated by smaller display. As seen with task 5, participants seem to have spent more time using tag clouds to carry out a past transaction, however they spent relatively less time for task 6, which is akin to task 5. Nevertheless, longer task completion times were anticipated for this study partly due to the way the study was carried out (see Limitation section) and our goal was to assess the overall usability of tag-based interaction.

LIMITATION

There are a few limitations to this study. Firstly, a sample size of only 8 participants was used for the study. However, being a pilot study, this is around 65% of the recommended sample size [15], and a suitable size to discover most usability problems in an interface [18].

Additionally, this study did not consider the order in which the different interfaces were introduced. Instead, a logical order was used by introducing the conventional interface first, followed by the tag-based interface.

Another limitation is the lack of experience and familiarity in using tags as a means of interaction among participants. We believe this played an important role in the actual user performance. In an effort to evaluate the usability of the prototype in a real-world setting, we did not explain how each tag-based interaction worked instead we left the participants to 'discover'. We only offered explanation in the event the participant was not able to complete a particular task. We believe this was a good way of assessing the overall usability of the prototype in the early stages to tease out design issues and making the interaction as intuitive as possible.

The result of this study is certainly influenced by the tasks which were given to the participants. Although the tasks selected were meant to be generic, inevitably, participants who had conducted similar transactions in real life to the ones given during the study might have been able to better relate to the tasks as opposed to others who did not. This would have implications on tags assigned to tasks as well as the perceived usefulness of the interface.

CONCLUSION & FUTURE WORK

In this paper we present the preliminary usability evaluation findings of tag-based interaction in both online and mobile banking. Our findings suggest improved usability especially user satisfaction with the tag-based interface compared to the conventional interface. The feedback from this pilot study is significant in that it informs future work which most of all will comprise of a larger and more representative sample to confirm our preliminary findings and to better understand the effects on usability. In addition, through this study we now better understand the impact of solutions put forward to address some of the inherent challenges related to tag-based interaction such as on-demand information display and tag suggestions on mobile devices.

Based on the feedback gathered from participants, minor modifications have been made to the prototype to improve the usability including better heading, defaulting to the appropriate keyboard type in mobile devices and improved error control. Also, for our future study we intend to explain the different interaction types to the participants through examples beforehand so that they are familiar with the interaction style. Furthermore, we will randomize the order in which the two interfaces and evaluation tasks are introduced to improve the validity of data. We are also interested in studying the impact of the proposed interaction style with online banking users who are above 40 years of age.

The knowledge from our future work will inform a set of guidelines for the design and implementation of tag-based interface in online and mobile banking. This is expected to directly benefit banking providers and other financial institutions alike. The broader goal of our work is to develop a generic tag-based interaction framework aimed at improving usability of e-commerce websites.

ACKNOWLEDGMENTS

This research work is sponsored by the Smart Services Cooperative Research Centre (CRC) of Australia. We would like to thank our colleague Ms. Claudia Murillo and the anonymous reviewers for their valuable comments and suggestions.

REFERENCES

1. Smith, G. Tagging: emerging trends. The Bulletin of the American Society for Information Science and Technology, August/September, 34, 6 (2008).

2. Marlow, C., Naaman, M., Boyd, D. and Davis, M. HT06, tagging paper, taxonomy, Flickr, academic article, to read. In *Proc. Hypertext and Hypermedia 2006*. ACM.

3. Durao, F. and Dolog, P. A personalized tag-based recommendation in social web systems. In *Proc. International Workshop on Adaptation and Personalization for Web 2.0 2009*. Citeseer.

4. Hassan-Montero, Y. and Herrero-Solana, V. Improving tag-clouds as visual information retrieval interfaces. In *Proc. Multidisciplinary Information Sciences and Technologies 2006*. Citeseer.

5. Qi Xin, M., Uddin, M. N. and Geun-Sik, J. The wordNet based semantic relationship between tags in folksonomies. In *Proc. Computer and Automation Engineering 2010*.

6. Fung, T. Banking with a personalized touch: Examining the impact of website customization on commitment. *Electronic Commerce Research*, 9, 4 (2008), 296-309.

7. Rahim, M. M. and JieYing, L. An empirical assessment of customer satisfaction with Internet Banking applications: An Australian experience. In *Proc. Computers and Information Technology 2009*.

8. Kalyanaraman, S. and Sundar, S. S. The psychological appeal of personalized content in Web Portals: Does customization affect attitude and behaviors? *Communication*, 56, 1 (2006), 110-132.

9. Horan, T. A. and Abhichandani, T. Evaluating user satisfaction in an e-government initiative: results of structural equation modeling and focus group discussions. *Information Technology Management Reviews*, XVII, 4 (2006).

10. Wang, Y. S., Wang, Y. M., Lin, H. H. and Tang, T. I. Determinants of user acceptance of Internet banking: An empirical study. *Service Industry Management*, 14, 5 (2003), 501-519.

11. Hiltunen, M., Heng, L. and Helgesen, L. Personalized Electronic Banking Services. Springer, 2004.

12. Ravendran, R., MacColl, I. and Docherty, M. Online banking customization via tag-based interaction. In *Proc. 13th IFIP TC13 International Conference Workshop on Data-Centric Interaction on the Web 2011*. CEUR-WS.

13. Ravendran, R., MacColl, I. and Docherty, M. Mobile banking customization via user-defined tags. In *Proc. Australian Computer Human Interaction 2011*. ACM.

14. Brooke, J. SUS – A quick and dirty usability scale. Taylor&Francis, London, 1996.

15. Tullis, T. S. and Stetson, J. N. A comparison of questionnaires for assessing website usability. In *Proc. Usability Professionals' Association 2004*.

16. Bangor, A., Kortum, P. T. and Miller, J. T. An Empirical Evaluation of the System Usability Scale. *Human-Computer Interaction*, 24, 6 (2008), 574-594.

17. Wessels, L., & Drennan, J. An investigation of consumer acceptance of M-banking. *Bank Marketing*, 28, 7 (2010), 547-568

18. Turner, C. W., Lewis, J. R. and Nielsen, J. Determining usability test sample size. In *International Encyclopedia of Ergonomics and Human Factors*, W. Karwowski, Ed. CRC Press, (2006), 3084–3088.

Social Life Logging: Can We Describe Our Own Personal Experience by Using Collective Intelligence?

Koh Sueda
National University of Singapore
/The University of Tokyo
21 Heng Mui Keng Terrace,
Singapore
apochang.jp@gmail.com

Henry Been-Lirn Duh
National University of Singapore
21 Heng Mui Keng Terrace,
Singapore
duhbl@acm.org

Jun Rekimoto
Sony CSL/
The University of Tokyo
7-3-1, Hongo Bunkyo-ku
Tokyo
rekimoto@acm.org

ABSTRACT

A famous Gestalt psychologist Kurt Koffka left a statement "The whole is o ther th an the su m o f its parts." Sim ilarly, collective in telligence su ch as so cial taggin g expo ses a social milieu that cannot be obtained from the descriptions of each indivi dual. Previ ous autom atic (or passive) life logging projects mainly focused on recording the individual life activ ity h owever, sometimes it is d ifficult to recollect the situ ation fro m th eir own perspective log s alone. In this project, we p ropose a soci al life logg ing system calle d "KiokuHacker" (Kioku m eans m emory in Ja panese) tha t encourages the user to describe their life activity by using a massive amount of pr ocessed ge otagged social tagging from the Internet. The result of a one year user test not only shows th at our so cial life lo gging system encourages the user's rem iniscence whic h the user cannot recollect by oneself but a lso indicates that the user e vokes t heir reminiscence which is not d irectly relat ed with to t he tags/scenes the system displayed.

Author Keywords

Social t agging, Vi sualization, Urban se nsing, R everse geocoding, AR, Social life logging

ACM Classification Keywords

H.5.m. Information interfaces and presentation (e.g., HCI): Miscellaneous.

PROJECT BACKGROUND AND ISSUES

A famous Gestalt psychologist Kurt Koffka left a statement "The whole i s ot her t han the s um of i ts pa rts." This statement comes from a the oretical fram ework "Princi pal Totality" o f Gestalt p sychology [12]. According t o t he statement, *"when the perceptual system forms a percept or gestalt, the whole thing has a reality of its own, independent of the parts"*. We can also observe this situ ation in a cit y which c onsists of many el ements among our environs. We recognize the character of t he place by passing t hrough

these elem ents. For e xample, p eople w ho liv e in Tokyo identify places as being "around Tokyo tower" (a landmark), "near Sum idagawa" (a ri ver), or "at t he front of Shibuy a station" (a node) from the elements of their environs. Kevin Lynch, an u rban planner po inted out that people bui ld a "public i mage", w hich i s t he ove rlap of many i ndividual definitions for the living environment in 1960's [15]. Lynch plotted th ese public im ages as co gnitive maps th at were based on t he res ult of i nterviewing t he resi dents a nd observing the residents' behaviors. According to 'A City Is Not a T ree' by C. Alexa nder, a city is com posed of m any factors overlapping one another, and he aimed to read these structures of the city more systematically. Alexa nder the n defined 'set' which is a small syste m th at is a part of th e structure o f the city[1]. In his work, he def ines *"A set is a collection of elements which for some reason we think of as belonging together."* For example, we percei ve an amusement park as a place that consists of a food c ourt, haunted house, and a roller c oaster (These elements can be a set of the amusement park). However, the people living in Tokyo rec ognize t he place which c onsisted of a n amusement park, a Buddhist temple, and shopping street for tourists as Asakusa district. Alexander c onsidered a city is composed of m any factors ove rlapping one an other. Thus, the stru cture of th e city is a semi-lattice fo rm, n ot a tree. Therefore, w e c an con sider "W e a re liv ing a nd are experiencing in the place while passing through these 'sets' and we b uild and sha re the im age of t he c ity through the experiences.

Alternatively, we can also find these 'sets' in a 'c ollective intelligence' such as social tagging which exposes a so cial milieu th at can not be ob tained fro m th e descriptions of each individual. For e xample, ta g clouds of that form at are useful for quickly perceiving the most prominent terms. We are ab le to grasp t he trend s of a situation from th e tag clouds w ithout r eading/watching all th e i nformation. At present, th ere are al ready over one hun dred m illion g eotagged photographs on flickr, w hich are socially tagged by their users. Users' t ag t hese p hotos with desc riptions alluding to environ ments, situations, and in terests that were relevant when t he user t ook t he p hotograph. M any web services (i ncluding flickr) ca n provide i nformation t hat i s easily u nderstood b y using th e user tags as co llective intelligence [14].

In this study, we propose a social life logging system called "KiokuHacker" that encourages the user to describe their life activity using a massive amount of processed geotagged social tagging from the Internet.

Can We Describe our Own Personal Experience by Using Collective Intelligence?

The development of a life-log computing system has fueled the hope that the human memory can be augmented. At the same time, life logs require reusability and should be easy to search (or find). The current mobile technology allows us to record life activity that contains geographical information, and this geographical information can be a strong context for our memories. Previous life logging projects focused mainly on recording of the individual life activity however, we cannot always record what we would like to recollect of our daily activities. In other words, we cannot always recollect our memories from a life log that we record ourselves [26]. On the other hand, we often recollect memories triggered by similar situations that we experienced in the past. Moreover, we sometimes recollect a memory that is triggered by another person's episode that is not our own real-life experience merely through communication with them. These traits come from our brain's memory system[2, 9].

In this paper, we exploit the traits of recollecting a memory when triggered by another's episodes to build an automatic/highly descriptive life-log ging system to augment our memory using geo-tagged social tagging. There have been many studies about meta-cognition [17]. The term of meta-cognition is defined as "cognition about cognition," or "knowing about knowing." The aim of encouraging meta-cognition is to enhance experiences including learning and memorizing by reviewing these experiences objectively. For example, Sumi et al explored a collaborative activity capturing system that encourages sharing meta-cognitive experiences [25]. In addition to the contributions of these experiences, we aim to develop social tagging for meta-cognitive collaborative activity capturing as augmented life logging on mobile environments.

RELATED WORKS

Passive/Bio-Sensed Life Logging

Sellen et al. reported that the automatic way in which the SenseCam captures these images results in cues which are as effective in triggering a memory as images which people capture on their own initiative [22]. Kalnikaite et al. showed that there are multiple types of data that we might collect about our pasts, as well as multiple ways of presenting this data [10]. The StartleCam utilizes "startle response" to capture events that are likely to get the user's attention and to be remembered [7]. These previous works intended to enhance user's memory using the life logs that were recorded by the user itself. Additionally, our approach focused on the user's environmental understanding based on their public image, which we compared with social tagging on the Internet.

Collaborative Life Logging

Sumi et al explored a collaborative activity capturing system that encourages the sharing of meta-cognitive experiences [21]. In this case, they aimed to utilize the descriptions (or aspects) of other users who have been together. Also Point-to-GeoBlog [21] utilizes (or correlated with) the nearby user generated content to support low-cost life logging. Additionally, we aim to utilize the descriptions by the general public users as a collective intelligence to promote the grasping of the trends of a situation without reading/watching all the information for life logging.

Utilizing Geotagged Social Tagging

Kennedy et al. proposed a method of classifying photographs using flickr to automatically extract places and events from the assigned tags, thus providing a visual/context based geographical information retrieval/sharing procedure [11, 19]. Sueda et al. suggested a method that enables the indication of a people-defined locative information using flickr's geotagged object [24]. Additionally, we aimed to complement and enhance the activity recording assistance by using geotagged objects for mobile user interfaces.

Summarizing Lifelog

Rekimoto et al. proposed a method of summarizing the user activities with reverse geocoding [20]. They also provided lists that are more descriptive by labeling the user descriptions of street addresses (e.g., the street address of a user's home is labeled "home"). These methods are related in terms of extracting information from people-contributed media. Moreover, our methods provide the labels that are dug out from social tagging. There are interesting applications of spatial/social context-based photograph browsing for mobile user interfaces, proposed as Mobiphos [5] and Zurfur [8]These applications were designed for browsing/sharing photographs via the Internet in a mobile environment but were not designed for continuous activity recording.

Augmented Cognition

E.chi et al. proposed social web applications that are based on the concepts of social transparency and balancing interaction costs and participation levels to enhance our Social Cognition[4]. Some concrete examples do exist. "Pensieve" provides the user context aware life activity browsing function of augmenting episodic memory[1], that facilitates the capturing of events and retrieving them later, using various relevant cues and associative browsing [18]. "Life Editing" also allows the user opportunities for discovery by using a custom-designed storytelling application in constructing meaningful lifelog summaries from third-party perspectives [3]. These previous works are

---

[1] Episodic memory is the memory of autobiographical events (times, places, associated emotions, and other contextual knowledge) that can be explicitly stated.

URL: http://en.wikipedia.org/wiki/Episodic_memory

related in terms of enhancement to the user's cognition by focusing more on the recording/displaying of descriptions of nearby environs that were generated by other users rather than providing the actual records of the user. In addition, these works utilize the nearby environs described by others as a 'set' of their life experiences to compose the context of the user's life activities. While our approach aims at describing the user's activity with a low-interaction cost lifelog function that is used in augmenting the user's memory using processed massive amounts of geotagged objects on the Internet as collective intelligence.

DESIGNING A SOCIAL LIFE LOGGING SYSTEM

Overview: In this section, we describe designing the function of our social life logging system. Our system utilizes an existing API of SNSs/Photo sharing service to develop a quick and stable recording (or retrieving) of the lifelog. Basically, our lifelog system automatically creates a timeline style record that consists of 1) nearby (by distance from the user) photographs/tags from flickr and 2) nearby hash tags from Twitter of the user.

Using Geotagged Social Tagging to Describe Experiences

In today's world, people often en use GIS (geographic information systems) or GPS (global positioning systems) on their mobile devices in their everyday lives. People have used these technologies based on latitude and longitude values for navigation and also to record people's activities as life logging. The values of latitude and longitude are not easily understood by the typical user, therefore several GIS technologies provide the corresponding street addresses using a reverse geocoding database (i.e., a database that converts latitude and longitude values into street addresses); however, users cannot always identify the spatial definition between the street address and the user's location. Generally speaking, users define their spatial understanding from their memories and personal experiences [15]. Thus, their definition of space is not the same as a street address defined by an administrative district. In this study, we utilize user tags from geotagged photographs on the flickr website (www.flickr.com). Users tag these photographs with descriptions alluding to environments, situations, and interests that were relevant when the user took the photograph. Many web services (including flickr) can provide information that is easily understood by using the user tags as collective intelligence [14]. Additionally in this study, we apply this method to collect nearby environs of the user's track.

Exploiting Non-Geotagged Objects Using Nearby Tags as Queries

Currently, we are able to describe and to share our experiences as status/photographs on web services such as Twitter, Facebook, and flickr, however many of our shared experiences do not include locative data (e.g. Only 2.5% of photographs on flickr are geotagged). To obtain more related topics, our system searches Twitter's content using nearby tags (contained geotagged flickr's photographs

taken in the user's neighborhood) collected by the system, and used as a query. Practically, our system submits the collected nearby tags to the timeline on Twitter as hash tags (see Figure. 4 on the next page).

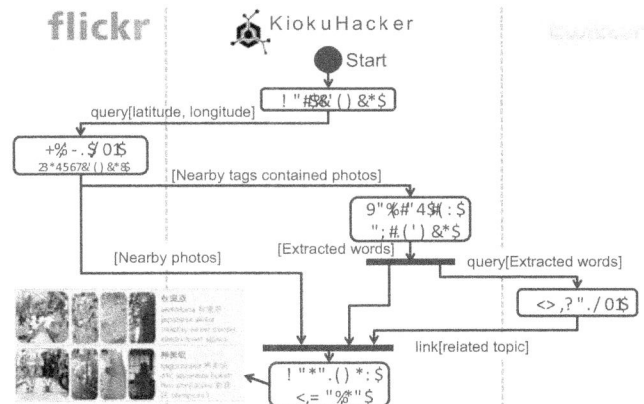

Figure 1 - Life log data activity of KiokuHacker

SYSTEM DESCRIPTION (IMPLEMENTATION)

Overview: This application is an automatic life-logging tool using social tags and Twitter, recording the user's activities as a life-log summary with photographs, and hash tags automatically on the user's Twitter's timeline based on their location (Figure.1). It also allows users to find something missed or forgotten without keeping their own manual journal. In addition, this application provides a summarizing lifelog function (time span based/keyword based) to grasp the user's life activity easily.

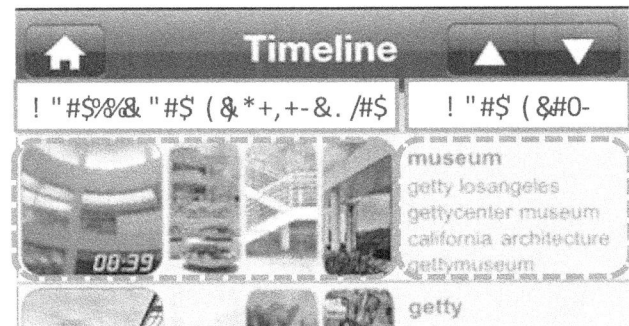

Figure 2: Shows a unit of the user's track on Kioku Hacker: Allowing the user to record temporary/spatially-interpolated life-logging automatically with nearby tags and photographs that enables the user to review their tracks periodically (from 2 to 60 minutes).

Activity Records Using Social Tagging

Kioku Hacker records the user's tracks by using nearby photographs/tags from flickr as a timeline. This user interface allows the user to record temporary/spatially-interpolated life-logging automatically by using nearby tags and photographs. The user can review their tracks periodically (maximum every 2 minutes, capturing the records triggered by the user who has moved further than 50 meters from the previous location.) and retrieve hybrid visual/verbal geographical information through the use of this system. According to the work of Kalnikaite et al., different types of memory promote the lifelog user's recollections [10]. This can be seen in figure 2 where our application indicates both nearby photos and nearby tags on a unit of record to assist the user (Figure 2). This figure is a case of a walk around the Getty Centre in Los Angeles; nearby photographs are laid out in order of the distance from a recorded point and the nearby tags are indicated in the order of the densities on the unit of the record. The user can view the image from the feature of both the sceneries (architectures) and the related words of the environs (e.g. Getty, Los Angeles, California, museum etc.). Through the use of this function, the timeline augments the stream of the user's track by using the geotagged objects.

Figure 3: Shows a sample of timelines created by a user of KiokuHacker. We can observe vivid descriptions of the users' track from nearby photographs and tags.

The Way to Getty Center (Los Angeles, CA): The user drove on the freeway from Venice Beach to Getty Center via Culver City. We can guess and observe the sceneries of the environs from these photographs/tags, a scene of Venice Beach, a freeway in Culver City, the vivid contrast of white colored architecture and the colorful botanic garden in Getty Center.

Taking a Train to have Dinner (Tokyo, Japan): The user who worked in Kagurazaka, (神楽坂) Tokyo, went to dinner travelling to his destination using multiple trains (Recorded his tracks every 10 minutes). The area of his office is an old urban area in Tokyo. As can be seen in the record there are women wearing Kimonos (many of whom are working in traditional Japanese restaurants) walking on a stone pavement lane in the area. The user transferred trains at Akihabara that is the largest electrical devices shopping area and the mecca of the Japanese pop culture, en route to Shinbashi which is a downtown area of Tokyo. Nearby this station, the area has many bars and restaurants catering for business people. Using this function, we are able to observe the atmosphere and sceneries of the user's track from the activity records on the timeline.

In addition, this application submits each of the user's track records to twitter's line of the user as hash tags and attached photographs (see the left side of Figure 3 on the following page). As shown in the figure, the user is able to access additional non-geotagged topics related to their track of various Twitter clients, which the user prefers to use simply by clicking the hash tags.

Obtaining Temporal Significant Topics from Twitter
Our system is equipped with optional functionality that shows the user the nearby trends as hash tags using twitter API (GET trends/available). Through the use of this function, the user is able to access nearby hybrid significant spatial/temporal patterns that encourages the reminiscence thereof. For instance, in the season of the Mid-autumn Festival (that is held on the 15th day of the eighth month of the Chinese calendar), a user will find plenty description of this Festival (e.g. lantern, moon cakes etc.) on the public time line (Figure 3). The user's memory of this episode would be triggered when he looks back on his timeline that combines spatial and temporal information.

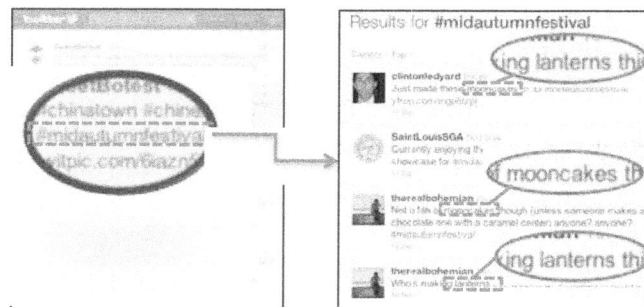

Figure 4: KiokuHacker exploits nearby tags as hash tags for obtaining non-geotagged related information

Before (Sort by time, devided each record by "|")	After (Extracting words more than score>70)
ebisu ,恵比寿, film, people, shibuya, city, dof, japanese, blue, daikanyama, tōkyō| shibuya ,渋谷, street, city, people, japanese,fashion, bw, tl |girl ,japanese ,harajuku ,fashion ,cosplay ,portrait ,people ,face ,street , はらじゅく,color ,原宿	新宿御苑, shinjuku, shinjukugyoen ,d300 ,sakura ,japanese ,新宿,サクラ,pink, japanese , shinjuku, aoyama ,新宿 |新宿 御,shinjukugyoen ,tree ,urban ,yellow	japanese ,hanami ,yasukuni ,ichigaya ,賞花, 日本国 ,花見,はなみ , 自助旅行 ,backpackers |とうきょう, 後楽園, color iidabashi ,飯田 橋|,sakura,小石川後楽園 ,koishikawa ,korakuen , 桜,urban ,japanese	shinjukugyoen japanesegirl 新宿御苑 shibuya urban koishikawa ebisu iidabashi 原宿

Table 1: Before/after of tag processing by TF-IDF

Summarizing User's Tracks by TF-IDF
In addition, we adopted the text-mining model TF-IDF[2] to indicate and summarize more semantic tags. In this case, our system (1) fetches the latest 10 records of the user's track, and then submits them to the TF-IDF algorithm

---

[2] The TF-IDF weight (frequency–inverse document frequency) is a weight often used in information retrieval and text mining.

provided by *Yahoo! API* [28] (2) The algorithm ranks the words/phrases, from the received article in order of importance (maximum value=100), and (3) then sends the listing to the submitter. Table 1 shows the before/after of the tag processing of an author's track by TF-IDF (the track was in the area of the author's home (central parts of Tokyo) to Ebisu (恵比寿: located in the Shibuya District located on the west side of Tokyo) as can be seen in Table 1, where we can observe the locative related words including "Shinjuku (新宿)" and "Shibuya (渋谷)" from the response list. We are also able to find the word "Japanese girl" on the list. The Harajuku (原宿) area is the most popular shopping area for the modern adolescents and many girls dress up to go there. On the other hand and, the more general words such as "people", "city", and "street" were excluded. In this way, we can observe that the locative terms are selected by using TF-IDF. At the same time, we are considering using not only TF-IDF but also other sorting/mining methods for the following reasons:

1) The result shows overlapping words in multiple languages such as "Shijukugyoen" and "新宿御苑". It should be sorted by the user's language.

We can observe the words such as "sakura/桜/さくら (that means cherry blossom)" and " はなみ/花見/hanami (that means cherry blossom viewing)" from the left cell of table 1 because Ichigaya (市ヶ谷) on the user's track is a famous place for cherry blossom viewing. Most of the photographs containing these words (tags) were taken in the spring (especially from March to April). A more relevant and characteristic result is indicated by sorting the each season.

These methods are not only simple but also effective ways in improving the validity of the system.

CASE STUDY
To evaluate the effect of our system, we conducted a user test for one year (1/1/2011-12/13/2011). Through the user test, we obtained valid lifelog data for a period of 189 days. It was not possible to obtain the data for the entire period due to trouble with the system or APIs of flickr/Twitter. After one month of the user testing, we conducted a recollection test that was done using the following procedures.

Procedures:

1. Counting (a) *the number of the days enabling the recollection of episodes (or scenes)* using a blank calendar (we considered the overlapping days captured as valid data) and noted the detail of these episodes each day.

2. Counting (b) *the number of days enabling one to recollect episodes (or scenes)* by watching the aided timeline created by the system. In the procedure, the subject is also able to refer to the summary of timeline like Table 1.

3. Counting (c) *the number of days that associated different episodes (or scenes) with the tags/photographs* provided the system with the day captured in procedure 1, 2.

4. Plotting a chart and graphs according to the days counted in (a), (b), (c).

Statistical Results and Findings
Figure 5 shows the overview of the result of the test. As can be seen in the figure, the recollection by referring to the lifelog described by social tagging/photos (hereinafter called "aided recollection") support the user is able to recollect nearly three times more (total: 100 days (52%)) than the recollection without referring to them (total: 35 days (18%)) (hereinafter called "unaided recollection"). This result shows that the system encourages the user's recollection four times more than an unaided recollection. As for the rest of the 54 days, the subject did not recollect anything by reviewing the timeline created by the system.

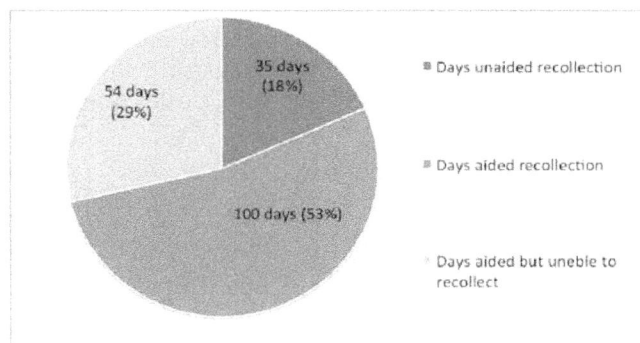

Figure 5: Shows the number of day recollection by using KiokuHacker: The system encourages the user's recollection 4 times more than an unaided recollection

Figure 6 shows the number of days associated with the different scenes/ episodes with the tags/photographs provided by the system. It means that the tags/photographs (recorded by general public) trigger the recollecting episodic memory of the user. For example, the subject associated the menu of his dinner in Chinatown, Singapore with the watching of the timeline, which showed the way from Merlion Park to Chinatown on that day, or associated the episode of another day at Chinatown or Merlion Park. As seen in the figure, the numbers of days associating different scenes/episodes are high from April to May and October to November. The reason for this result is that there were many events such as trips, and birthdays of his family during this period. Also the subject is able to describe the details of scenes/episodes he experienced when triggered by his timeline.

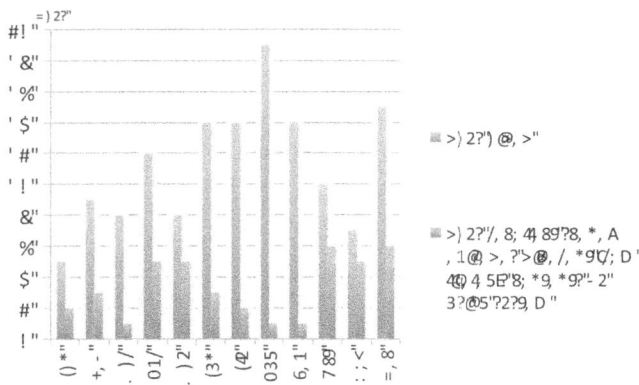

Figure 6: Shows the number of days associated different scenes/episodes with the tags/photographs provided the system.

The subject mentions (of course) he could recollect his episodic memory directly when he referred to the photographs or diary that were taken by himself. According to Kalnikaite et al., multiple types of lifelog data contribute recollection [10]. Similarly, he initially cannot recollect his episodes when reviewing his timeline. However, thereafter, he feels the scenes closer to his experience through continuously associating with the each of the scenes and tags.

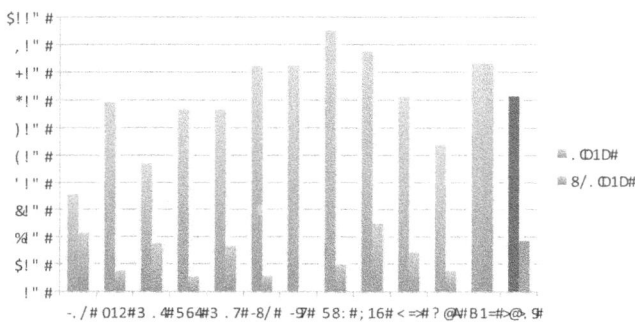

Figure 7: Shows the monthly variation of recollection rates in 2011: The case when the user is aided by the system that the recollection rate has kept rather than an unaided recollection.

Figure 7: Shows the ratio of the aided/unaided recollection of each month in 2011. We can observe the lifelog created by the social tagging/photographs contribute to the user's recollections. This result infers that the subject forgot the triggers of recollecting his episodic memory and triggered his recollections by reviewing his own timeline generated by photographs/tags of another user. Also we can observe that both aided/unaided recollection rates are the same in December 2011. This result infers that the subject still retains his episodic memories.

Association and Collocation

In the case of not being able recollect anything by unaided recollections, is thought as context-dependent forgetting. Context-dependent forgetting is a situation that cannot recall the retrieval cue when recollecting episodic memory

[6]. To avoid forgetting, we typically record events as a diary, memo, photograph, tagging, etc. however, we cannot always recollect things by reading the record. The cause of forgetting is thought to be that the records were not relevant for recollecting the events. In the case of not being able to recollect anything with aided recollections by using our system, this is thought that the photographs/tags are not relevant for recollecting for the subject.

Recalling by Using Kioku Hacker

In the case of recollection by reading photographs/diary taken by ourselves over again, we can recall the scene or episode directly in most cases. On the other hand, when recollecting by reading tags/photographs from the timeline, we cannot recollect the episodes directly. In many of these cases, recollecting supported indirectly by association and collocation through reading photographs/tags. The recollection occurs when reading multiple objects in the timeline obtained from geotagged social tagging and photos shared by others. We hereby describe an example in which the case of the subject enjoyed archery on his holiday on Bintan Island (A resort island near Singapore).

Firstly, the subject recollected the episode that he went to Bintan resort only by viewing the photographs of the beach and ethnic dishes in his timeline however he did not recollect the archery at all. After that he found a tag of "horse riding" in the timeline and at the same time, the subject associated his episode of enjoying archery because it showed the tag which has recreation amenities including a riding ground and a field for archery. In this case, the subject collocated these tags: "beach", "hotel", "horse riding and his personal experience "archery" as the set of these environmental elements.

In addition, we introduce another case study when the user recollected by the temporal significance of geotagged tag that was automatically obtained from Twitter. The subject recollected an episode that he went to a ministry to update his working pass by finding a hash tag "electionsg (Election SG (Singapore))". At first he could not recollect anything by the tags "Clark Quay" (the name of the district in which the ministry was located) only. He could not specify his activity from the date and the tag, because he sometimes went shopping there. After he found the tag "electionsg", he recollected and specified his episode completely. In the beginning of May 2011, there were many geotagged hashtag "electionsg" on Twitter, because the general election was held in Singapore May 9th 2011. At that time, he was in a curry shop and was listening to people sitting at the next table discussing the election before visiting the ministry.

Limitations

1) In this study, the user test was conducted on one subject only. It should be conducted with more subjects to obtain more findings.

46

2) As mentioned in the previous subsection in this section, photographs t aken by t he user hi mself we re st ronger and had m ore di rect recollecting epis odic m emory. Social t agging ai ded l ifelog i s not cl oser t han t he photograph/diary taken by ourselves. To improve more practical use, the ne xt sy stem can be consi dered a hybrid function t hat m erges activ e and passive life logging.

3) We shou ld not on ly use the so phisticated filtering tags function, but also u tilize a tag embedded with a v alue such as "f oursquare: venue=xxxxxx" f or use o f other locative web services. Now flick r has p lenty of these tags h owever these val ues are not readable fo r the typical use r. When we ca n expl oit these tags , our system will possess more locative descriptions by other users by using the API provided by these web services.

POTENTIAL APPLICATIONS AND FUTURE WORK

Supporting a Hybrid Active/passive Life Logging System Using Social Tagging

"Easy Ta gging Cam" is a digital im age rec ording function equipped with m ultiple shutter bu ttons (Fig ure 8)[23]. Tagging is a p owerful method to retrieve (or find) a user's records an d t o devel op a re-usable life-log. At th e sam e time, t agging is t ime consu ming. T his f unction l ets users capture and tag photographs simultaneously and also allows the use r t o be free of tagging t asks. (According t o flickr, iPhone u sers tag 2% of t heir ge otagged photos. Other non-smart mobile phone (Nokia N73) u sers t ag 0.4% of t heir photos.) Watanabe et al., also developed 'WillCam', which enables u sers t o c apture various i nformation, s uch as location, tem perature, ambient noise, and t he photographer's facial expre ssion, ai med at avoi ding spending the time and effort to carry out annotation [27].

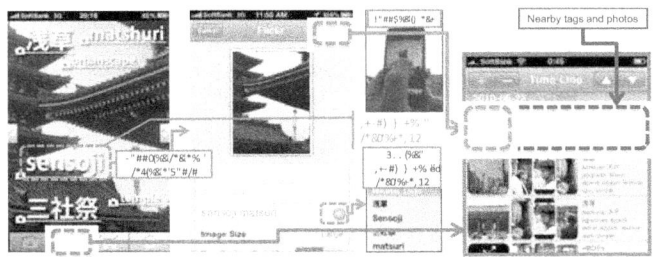

Figure 8: Hybrid active/passive life logging system using social tagging: Simultaneous photograph capture and tagging conducted by tapping the overlaid tag recommendation

In o ur case, we u tilized the system to p rovide th e recommended t ags from so cial tagg ing, i ncluding geotagged objects on m obile de vices. T he use r i s a ble t o develop a re usable l ife l og and to c ontribute in de veloping social tagging continuously. This system also utilizes a life-log system which facilitates th e easy retriev al of information.

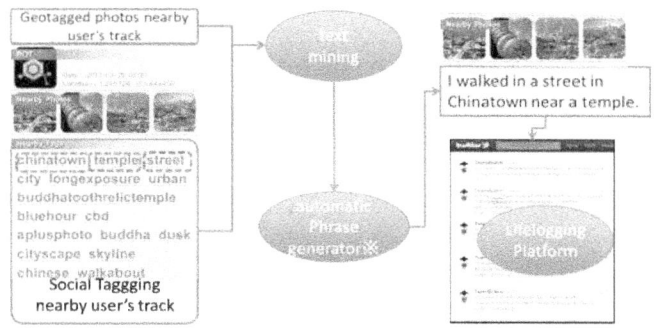

Figure 9: Image of the phrase generator using the geotagged social tagging: this function allows the user to record a context aware description about nearby environs of the user.

Story Telling Style Life Reco rd Using So cial Tagg ingIn this sectio n, we d iscuss the life lo g by a th ird person's aspects. Peesapati et al . pr oposed Pe nsieve provides a context aware l ife logging di splaying fu nction that remind the user their life activity records through use of the Internet events including emailing and Internet surfing. To promote the user's rem iniscence[18]. Life Ed iting by Byrn e et al., provide opportunities fo r th e u ser to learn and red iscover from th eir ev eryday life b y showing a story tellin g style lifelog s ummary that has naturally meaningful descriptions reconstructed/generated f rom t he part s of t he user's o wn lifelog[3]. Additionally, to g enerate a m ore n atural description of a u ser's life activity, we are d eveloping a phrase ge nerator usi ng geo tagged social tagging. This function allows th e u ser to record con text aware descriptions a bout t he nearby envi rons of the use r (Figure 9).

Collaged and Multi-Modal Life-Logging

Similar to our m ethod of e xploiting non-geotagged contents, the system enabl es the user to provide ot her user generated con tent (e.g. YouTube, d elicious, etc.) to utilize related c ontents of the user's life l og. For instance , a user who visits a bathing bea ch c ould a ugment his e xperiences with not only nearby tags (e.g. s hore, s wimming, etc.), but also m ovies (or so unds) o f t he nearby e nvirons t hat a re found by using tags as a query.

Expanding Meta-Recognition Using Collective Intelligence

In general, m onitoring an experience or de scribing our environs en courages our m eta-cognition. These activ ities are known a s "m etacognitive reflection" in cognitive science [16]. In term s of t his as pect, s ocial life loggi ng support th e user's cog nitive reflection usin g t he p eople powered description of the environs. At the same time, our result of the case study shows social tagging aided lifelog is not cl oser t han a photograph/diary t aken by ourselves. Moreover, using another's records occasionally has privacy problems. However, most of the u sers' cannot al ways take photographs or describe th eir activ ities i n their daily life. Also, privacy issues are also able to be solved by applying the context information di lution [13] to pr otect pri vacy information.

Our Future Strategy

In L ondon, t here are m ore t han four m illion cam eras all over the city and they are   cap turing a n avera ge of 15 minutes of m ovie per person l iving i n t hat area eve ry day. That m eans ev eryone liv ing i n London h as t heir own personal h istory movie o f 15 minutes p er day r ecorded by third pe rson's aspects . In o ther words, they can know a third person's aspect of their own life. Currently, we cannot access these records by others easily, in terms of costs, manpower, and privacy issues. In the future, we will be able to access (or share) more ge otagged collec tive intelligenc e including SNSs, so cial tagg ing, and d igital i mages th an before. We aim to develop an application that enhances the user's meta-cognition by showing the aspects of the general public from processed social tagging.

CONCLUSION

We pr opose an aug mented l ife-log system "K iokuHacker" that allows t he user to assis t their rem iniscence by usi ng geotagged s ocial t agging as nea rby en vironmental descriptions of th e user. Th e resu lt of t he user test sh ows that our system encourages user's recollection 4 times more than the case with recollecting organically. In add ition, the result shows that our system does not only trigger the users' reminiscence but als o indicates that the user evokes the ir episodes th at are no t related d irectly with tags/scenes t he system d isplays. Ou r fu ture asp ect will b e pursued in developing a tool t hat enh ances ou r m eta-cognition (or social cognition) by using geotagged collective intelligence for our everyday life.

REFERENCES

[1] Alexander, C. A city is not a tree. *City*. 122, 1 (1966), 58-62.

[2] Bower, G.H. et al. Selectivity of learning caused by affective states. *Journal of Experimental Psychology: General*. 110, 4 (1981), 451-473.

[3] Byrne, D. et al. Life Editing˜: Th ird-Party Perspectives on Lifelog Content. *Collections*. (2011), 1501-1510.

[4] Chi, E.H. Augmented social cognition: using social web technology to enhance the ability of groups to remember, think, and reason. *Proceedings of the 35th SIGMOD international conference on Management of data*. (2009), 973-984.

[5] Clawson, J. et al. Mobiphos: a collocated-synchronous mobile photo sharing application. *Proceedings of the 10th international conference on Human computer interaction with mobile devices and services*. (2008), 187-195.

[6] C ue-dependent forgetting: *http://en.wikipedia.org/wiki/Forgetting#Cue-dependent_forgetting*.

[7] Healey, J. and Picard, R.W. StartleCam: A Cybernetic Wearable Camera. *Digest of Papers Second International Symposium on Wearable Computers Cat No98EX215*. 468 (1998), 42-49.

[8] Hwang, A. et al. Zurfer: mobile multimedia access in spatial, social and topical context. *Proceedings of the 15th international conference on Multimedia*. (2007), 557-560.

[9] Joh nson, M.K. et al. Source monitoring. *Psychological Bulletin*. 114, 1 (1993), 3-28.

[10] Kalnikaite, V. et al. Now let me see where i was: understanding how lifelogs mediate memory. *Proceedings of the 28th international conference on Human factors in computing systems*. (2010), 2045-2054.

[11] Kennedy, L. et al. How flickr helps us make sense of the world: context and content in community-contributed media collections. *Proceedings of the 15th international conference on Multimedia*. (2007), 631-640.

[12] Ko ffka, K. *Principles of Gestalt Psychology*. Harcourt, Brace and World.

[13] K üpper, A. *Location-Based Services: Fundamentals and Operation*. Wiley.

[14] Lamere, P. Social Tagging and Music Information Retrieval. *Journal of New Music Research*. 37, 2 (2008), 101-114.

[15] Lynch, K. The Image of the City (Harvard-MIT Joint Center for Urban Studies Series). (Jun. 1960).

[16] Mazzoni, G. and Nelson, T.O. eds. *Metacognition and Cognitive Neuropsychology: Monitoring and Control Processes*. Psychology Press.

[17] Metcalfe, J.A. et al. Metacognition: Knowing About Knowing. *American Psychologist*. 34, 10 (1994), 352.

[18] Peesapati, S.T. et al. Pensieve: supporting everyday reminiscence. *Proceedings of the ACM Conference on Human Factors in Computing Systems*. (2010).

[19] Rattenbury, T. et al. Towards automatic extraction of event and place semantics from flickr tags. *Proceedings of the 30th annual international ACM SIGIR conference on Research and development in information retrieval*. (2007), 103-110.

[20] Rekimoto, J. et al. Lifetag: WiFi-based continuous location logging for life pattern analysis. *Proceedings of the 3rd international conference on Location-and context-awareness*. (2007), 35-49.

[21] Robinson, S. et al. Point-to-GeoBlog˜: Gestures and Sensors to Support User Generated Content Creation. *Human Factors*. (2008), 197-206.

[22] Sellen, A.J. et al. Do life-logging technologies support memory for the past?: an experimental study using

sensecam. *Proceedings of the SIGCHI conference on Human factors in computing systems*. (2007), 81-90.

[23] Sueda, K. et al. Easy-Tagging Cam: using social tagging to augment memory. *ACM SIGGRAPH 2010 Posters*. (2010), 36:1.

[24] Sueda, K. et al. Social Geoscape: Visualizing an Image of the City for Mobile UI Using User Generated Geo-tagged Objects. *Mobile and Ubiquitous Systems: Networking Services, MobiQuitous '11. 8th Annual International* (2011), 1-12.

[25] Sumi, Y. et al. Collaborative capturing, interpreting, and sharing of experiences. *Personal and Ubiquitous Computing*. 11, 4 (2006), 265-271.

[26] Tulving, E. and Thomson, D.M. Encoding specificity and retrieval processes in episodic memory. *Psychological Review*. 80, 5 (1973), 352-373.

[27] Watanabe, K. et al. WillCam: a digital camera visualizing users. interest. *CHI '07 extended abstracts on Human factors in computing systems*. (2007), 2747-2752.

[28] Yahoo! API: Key phrase extraction : *http://developer.yahoo.co.jp/webapi/jlp/keyphrase/v1/extract.html*.

Select Ahead: Efficient Object Selection Technique using Tendency of Recent Cursor Movements

Soonchan Park
Computer Science
Department, KAIST
291 Daehak-ro, Yuseong-gu,
Daejeon, 305-701, Korea
soonchan@cs.kaist.ac.kr

Seokyeol Kim
Computer Science
Department, KAIST
291 Daehak-ro, Yuseong-gu,
Daejeon, 305-701, Korea
puresession@kaist.ac.kr

Jinah Park
Computer Science
Department, KAIST
291 Daehak-ro, Yuseong-gu,
Daejeon, 305-701, Korea
jinah@cs.kaist.ac.kr

ABSTRACT

Virtual hand is one of the most intuitive metaphors for object selection in the virtual environment because of its natural mapping between the user action input and the cursor. However, it has a limitation of lengthy cursor manipulation for object selection task which is directly related to the level of workload of the user in performing object selection. In this paper, we propose 'Select Ahead' as a new object selection technique that improves efficiency by reducing the physical workload. Select Ahead guides the user to select the distant object along the estimated tendency of the recent cursor movements. We evaluate the relative performance of Select Ahead through the experiments in the 3D virtual environment with various object densities. The results show that Select Ahead significantly reduces the length of the cursor movements compared to those of the 3D point cursor and the 3D bubble cursor regardless of the object density. In the aspect of the total duration time for selection, Select Ahead outperforms the 3D point cursor and has no significant difference compared to that of the 3D bubble cursor.

Author Keywords

Object selection; virtual hand; 3D cursor; 3D interaction; virtual reality

ACM Classification Keywords

H.5.2 [User Interfaces]: Graphical User Interfaces, Interaction styles

INTRODUCTION

Recently, with an increase in attention to spatial input devices [6], the various interesting 3D contents are being developed not only in interactive 3D games but also in immersive virtual reality (VR) applications. Thanks to such

spatial input devices, a user is able to interact with the 3D virtual world by manipulating the diverse DOF (Degree of Freedom) input directly. Of the 3D user interaction components, 3D object selection refers to the action of explicit pointing or identifying the object in a 3D virtual world, and it is a typical user interaction required before following any other interactions such as object manipulation [3,8].

Among the 3D object selection metaphors, the virtual hand is one of the most intuitive metaphors where the user naturally controls the 3D cursor and selects an object by locating the cursor in the target object [3]. Since the cursor should travel the entire distance from its current position to the position of the target object, the virtual hand demands a relatively lengthy cursor manipulation and selection time. Due to these limitations, the user suffers from high level of workload when performing many object selection tasks with spatial input device which does not have any form of support.

To resolve the problem of virtual hand metaphor, the previous researches focused on designing non-linear mapping between the cursor and the physical input [2] or expanding the size of the cursor to expedite the contact with objects [4,11]. The non-linear mapping function scheme may shorten the interaction time, but it can damage the intuitiveness of the virtual hand. As for expanding the size of cursor, it may help the user to select an object quickly, but it has the problem of lengthy cursor manipulation.

We propose Select Ahead as an efficient object selection technique which significantly reduces the length of cursor manipulation in the environment with the virtual hand metaphor. When the user wants to select a certain object, the cursor is intentionally manipulated toward the target object. Thus, we assume that the user's intention related to object selection can be inferred by analyzing the recent cursor movements. By this assumption, Select Ahead estimates the tendency of the recent cursor movements (we dub as 'ToCM') and identifies the object the user wants to obtain while the movement of the cursor is approaching the target. Additionally, Select Ahead includes considerations to exclude cursor movements which do not have user's intention from the update process of the ToCM and to stably identify the target object by recovering the errors of the cursor manipulation. Finally, we evaluate the relative performance of Select Ahead in comparison to the existing methods (the 3D point cursor and the 3D bubble cursor). We also conducted the experiments with the various object densities in order to examine the impact of the object density on the performance.

The following section gives an overview of the previous work related to object selection with the cursor based on not only 3D interface but also 2D interface, and then next session describes the details of our design and implementation of Select Ahead. In the experiment section, the experiments for verifying the relative performances of Select Ahead are shown in comparison with the existing techniques. Lastly, we discuss our findings and the future work of Select Ahead.

RELATED WORK
In this section, we will discuss the existing object selection techniques with cursor-based metaphor in not only 3D but also 2D interface. To make a clear distinction between the virtual hand and other 3D object selection metaphor, we also mention the ray-casting metaphor at the end of this section.

Object Selection Techniques using Cursor
To improve the efficiency of object selection with the virtual hand, we need to review the existing researches based on not only the 3D virtual hand environment, but also the 2D cursor environment. In this subsection, we describe three major approaches which try to improve the efficiency of the object selection.

Designing Mapping between Cursor and Input
With non-linear mapping between the cursor and the input, the sensitivity of the cursor manipulation is adjusted. For example, when the user needs to move the cursor a great distance, the system will increase the sensitivity of the cursor's movement. Semantic pointing [2] dynamically adapt the mapping function between the cursor movement and the user. These non-linear mapping approaches can reduce the physical distance which the user has to work for, but lose the intuitiveness natural mapping of the motion applied.

Expanding Cursor Size
Expansion of a cursor size makes it easier to make contact between the cursor and objects both in the 2D and 3D interface [4,7,9]. The silk cursor [9] expands the selectable area of the cursor to a semi-transparent hexahedron volume which visualizes the relative depth information between the cursor and the objects. This study shows that the silk cursor outperforms in terms of the interaction time and the accuracy compared to the 3D point cursor. However the target is vague when the multiple objects are included in the cursor volume. The bubble cursor [4,10] is a technique

to resolve this ambiguity in the selection. The 3D bubble cursor defines the sphere-shaped selection volume, and changes its radius dynamically in order to include only one object which is closest from the cursor. As a result, the 3D bubble cursor significantly outperforms the 3D point cursor. These approaches make object selection easier by expanding the cursor range, but the cursor still needs to approach closely to the object for selection task, leading to the same problem of lengthy cursor manipulation.

Reducing Length of Cursor Manipulation for Selection
Drag-and-pop and drag-and-pick [1] are 2D interaction techniques used to reduce the lengthy motion for moving the cursor around for object selection. When the user decides the direction by dragging, the objects located along the dragging direction pop up near the current position of the cursor. Drag-and-pop and drag-and-pick outperform in terms of the interaction time in the large display interface. However, in addition to manipulating the position of the cursor, this technique asks the user to perform additional dragging interactions to select the object. Also, it is apprehended that the dragging motion will duplicate the existing metaphors such as grouping.

The object pointing [5] is another approach which reduces the length of the cursor manipulation for object selection. In the 2D interface, when the user controls the input, the cursor jumps from one object to another. By eliminating the time when the cursor roams in empty space, it reduces both the interaction time and the length of the input trace for object selection. However, banding the user from the empty space may be too much restriction for the user by limiting the possible tasks that the user may want to perform in the space.

Ray-casting Metaphor
Ray-casting metaphor is another object selection metaphor whose main concept is that the user performs the object selection by using a ray instead of a cursor in the virtual hand metaphor [7,9,10]. When the user just aims the half ray at the target object, the ray is automatically cast towards the aimed direction so that the targeted object becomes selectable. Owing to the characteristics of the ray, the ray-casting metaphor is designed to reduce the additional effort to control the cursor to move toward the remote object, and generally outperforms the virtual hand metaphor in terms of the selection time [10]. However, its degree of freedom is restricted by the angle of the motion, and it requires rather delicate manipulation for the objects that are a great distance apart as a small change in degree amplifies the radial displacement.

DESIGN AND IMPLEMENTATION
In this section, we introduce the key ideas and the implementation details of Select Ahead to reduce the length of the cursor manipulation and the selection time over the general virtual hand metaphor.

The Main Concept of Select Ahead

In the virtual hand metaphor, as we describe in the previous section, the cursor should physically approach and make contact with the target to complete the selection task. While the cursor is approaching the target, the direction of the recent cursor movements shows a tendency oriented towards the target. Thus, if we recognize that the recent cursor movements are oriented towards a specific object, we may suppose that the user has an intention to select the object.

In this perspective, 'Select Ahead' technique that we propose in this paper, allows the user to select the distant object located along the *tendency of recent cursor movements* (ToCM) and can decrease the length of the cursor manipulation and the interaction time for object selection (see Figure 1). In the following section, we describe the method to estimate the ToCM and how to implement the object selection technique based on the ToCM.

Moving Average Method

Moving average method is a popular method to estimate the tendency of values obtained in time series. To measure the current tendency of the values in time series, n of recent values are averaged. This average represents the current tendency of the values. Also, we can apply a weighting scheme to weight more on the more recent values when we compute the average, and this method is called weighted moving average (see Equation 1). When we read in the cursor positions while the cursor is in motion, we can convert the positions as a vector in unit sampling time. This series of vectors represent the cursor movement in time sequence, and the moving average model can be used to estimate its tendency, ToCM (see Equation 2).

There are two parameters in the moving average model. One is the number of frames (n) that you want to consider as recent cursor movements, and the other parameter is the weight w_i to be applied for each cursor movement. To determine n, there is a trade-off between the stability of ToCM and the sensitivity of ToCM to reflect the current cursor movement quickly. If n is high, a few of unexpected

(a) Selecting with the 3D point cursor

(b) Select Ahead

Figure 1. While the 3D point cursor requires the contact between the target object and the cursor, Select Ahead can select the distant target object located along the estimated ToCM from the cursor

$$WMA_n = \frac{1}{W} \sum_{i=N-(n-1)}^{N} w_i \cdot x_i \, , \quad where \sum_{i=N-(n-1)}^{N} w_i = W$$

Equation 1. Weighted moving average

$$ToCM_n = normalize \left(\sum_{i=CF-(n-1)}^{CF} w_i \cdot \frac{(CurPos_i - CurPos_{i-1})}{||CurPos_i - CurPos_{i-1}||} \right)$$

where, $CF = (index\ of\ current\ frame)$,
$CurPos_i = (the\ position\ of\ the\ cursor\ at\ frame\ i)$

Equation 2. ToCM by using weighted moving average

cursor movements do not dramatically affect the ToCM making it stable, but at the same time, it also lags down the cursor motion making it less sensitive to most recent changes. The tolerance can be adjusted with the weighting value w for each cursor movement. Since the more recent cursor movement is considered to be more in sync with the direction where the user wants to go, the more weight can be put on to the more recent cursor movement. This study includes the empirical setting of the parameters for the moving average model (n and w_i), because the optimal setting of them is dependent on the update frequency of the input device.

Implementation of Select Ahead

The cursor can be manipulated not only by the intention of the user to select the certain object, but also by the unintentional input changes. When we update the ToCM with input changes which do not reflect the user's intention, the estimation of the ToCM can be incorrect to represent the genuine intention of the user for object selection. In this section, we describe the implementation of the updating strategies for ToCM by classifying the user's intention by the velocity of the cursor movement. Also, methods to identify a target object by utilizing ToCM are introduced.

Update Strategies of ToCM

We have observed that the momentary velocity of the cursor can also be a cue for distinguishing the user's intention with respect to his action. Therefore, we set a threshold value to decide if the cursor movement is changing fast or slow, and define three cases of the user's action based on both the velocity of the cursor movement and the characteristics of the recent cursor movement history.

If the cursor has low velocity, two cases can be considered. The first one is that the cursor is controlled by unintentional input changes such as the noises of the input device (*CASE 1*). As these cursor movements do not reflect any intention of selecting an object, they should not be considered for the update of the ToCM. The other case of slow cursor movement occurs when the user carefully controls the cursor (*CASE 2*). In this condition, although the cursor movement is slow, the cursor movement has the user's

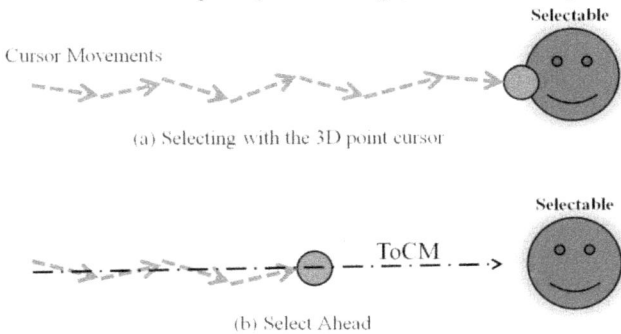

intention for object selection and it should be included to the update processes of the ToCM. To distinguish the two cases, we test the continuity and the consistency of slow cursor movements. When the user carefully controls the cursor toward the target, the cursor is kept moving slowly in a consistent direction. However, in case of unintentional input changes, in most cases, their movements are temperamental and do not generally show any consistency.

On the other hand, when the user manipulates the cursor with high velocity, we can regard the user having intention to approach an object to select it (*CASE 3*). The cursor movements in this condition should be reflected to the update of ToCM, and hence we accumulate the cursor movements and find the moving average.

To implement Select Ahead based on these considerations, the update algorithm of the ToCM has two queues to accumulate the cursor movements: *sQueue* is for slow cursor movements and *fQueue* is for fast cursor movements. The size of both queues is same as the number of cursor movements to consider in the moving average method. When the cursor is slowly manipulated, the cursor movement is enqueued to *sQueue*. After that, two tests are sequentially performed. The first test is to confirm slow cursor movement is temporary or not by checking whether *sQueue* is full. The second test is to verify consistency between the elements in *sQueue*. To check the consistency, we compute the moving average of the elements in *sQueue* and count the number of elements whose angular difference with the moving average bigger than the threshold. In this implementation, we set the threshold angle as the compensation angle (θ) which will be discussed in the next section. If the number of counted element is less than ten percent of the size of queue, we consider the elements in

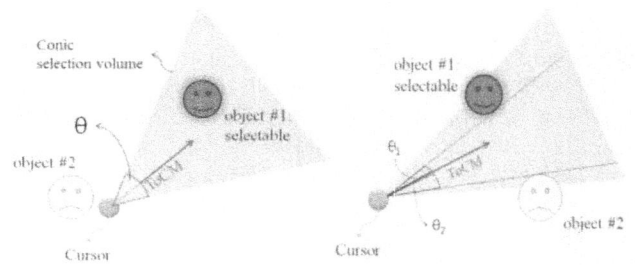

Figure 3. (left) The object #1 falls in the selection volume. (right) The object #1 has the minimum angular difference value ($\theta_1 < \theta_2$) among the objects fall in the selection volume.

sQueue to have the consistency. Only when both tests are satisfied (*CASE 2*), the ToCM is updated as the moving average of elements in *sQueue*. Otherwise, we do not update the ToCM (*CASE 1*). When the cursor is manipulated quickly(*CASE 3*), the update algorithm makes sQueue empty to initialize continuity of slow cursor movement and enqueues the cursor movement to *fQueue* and updates the ToCM as the moving average of the elements in *fQueue*. Figure 2 describes the flow chart showing update process of the ToCM based on the velocity of the cursor movement.

Object Selection Algorithm
Although the 3D virtual environment can be displayed in a stereoscopic display, the depth perception problem still exists without any extra clues such as shadow. In general, it is still difficult for the user to get accurate relative depth information of the 3D virtual environment. Owing to this fact, the cursor may not be able to accurately approach the target object. To resolve this problem, we need the additional utilization of the ToCM to enhance the usability of object selection. For that, Select Ahead considers angular compensation θ around the ToCM which means using the conic selection volume toward the ToCM [1,7,9] (see Figure 3, left). With this approach, the multiple objects can be located within the conic selection volume. In order to avoid the ambiguity, Select Ahead has two basic rules to make only one object selectable. First rule is that if the multiple objects are located in the selection volume, Select Ahead will select the object which has the minimum angular difference from the ToCM (see Figure 3, right). Second rule is that when multiple objects are accurately located along the ToCM, Select Ahead will select the object closer from the cursor.

EXPERIMENT
We implemented Select Ahead with the simple virtual hand metaphor which has one-to-one mapping between the input and the cursor. We made a virtual space match the physical work-space whose size is 14.7cm x 10.92cm x 16.8cm and distributed the selectable spheres whose diameter is 1cm. To show relative performance of Select Ahead in terms of the interaction time and the length of the cursor manipulation, we also implemented the 3D point cursor and

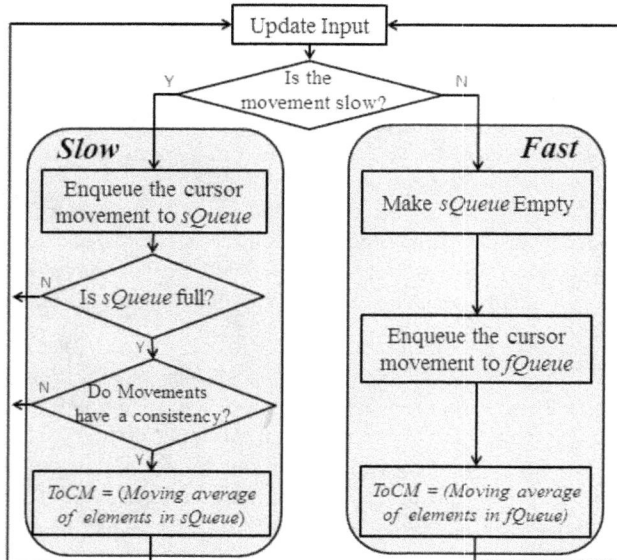

Figure 2. Flow chart of the update algorithm for ToCM utilizing the velocity of the cursor movements

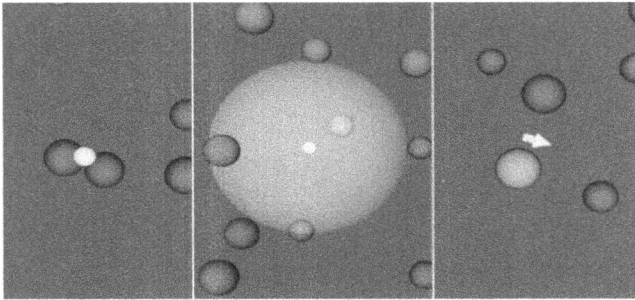

Figure 4. Visualization of 3D point cursor (left), 3D bubble cursor (middle), and Select Ahead (right)

Figure 5. The experiment apparatus

the 3D bubble cursor [3,10] as existing object selection techniques. In our implementation of the 3D bubble cursor, we set the maximum diameter of the 3D bubble cursor as 6cm to prevent visual cue of the selection volume from disturbing the interactions of the participant.

For selecting the optimal parameter values required for the moving average method, we performed a pilot experiment to evaluate various parameter settings. We made six combinations with three n (n=30, n=60, and n=90) and two types for the moving average (non-weighted and linearly weighted moving average). The condition with n=90 and weighted moving average resulted in the best performance, thus, we used these parameter settings in the main experiment. Additionally, the angular compensation θ was 50 degrees to enhance usability of Select Ahead while eliminating too compulsory selection which does not correspond to the user's intention.

In this study, we hypothesized that Select Ahead will reduce the length of the cursor manipulation in comparison with the two existing methods and this result is maintained regardless of the object density. In addition, reducing the length of cursor manipulation also makes the completion time for object selection shorter.

To provide the visual feedback during the interaction, we visualized the 3D point cursor as a small sphere, the 3D bubble cursor as a semitransparent sphere-shaped volume, and the cursor of Select Ahead which indicate the ToCM as the arrow cursor (see Figure 4).

Apparatus

We used a 23-inch LG FLATRON stereoscopic display with NVIDIA 3D vision which was made of active glasses. We rendered graphical scenes at 120Hz with stereoscopic rendering, which is equivalent to 60Hz per each eye. For the input devices, we used PHANToM Omni to manipulate the cursor, and a keyboard for selection command. PHANToM Omni was selected as an input device due to its stability and intuitiveness in controlling within 3D environment even for the participants who had never experienced any 3D input device. Only 3 DOF position value of Omni was used, and the force feedback was not provided. Omni was updated at 150Hz which was the similar frequency to that of the mouse input updated in Windows OS. Additionally, to minimize the unintentional cursor manipulation when the participant tries to push the button on the Omni, the participant pushed the button on the keyboard for selection command. Figure 5 illustrates a participant performing the object selection task in the study.

Participants

Twelve paid participants (ten males and two females, ranging in age from 22 to 25) performed the experiment. All participants were right-handed. They used Omni with their right hand, and pushed the button on the keyboard with their right hand.

Procedure

We set the object selection environment with randomly distributed the sphere-shaped objects. The case that an object completely occludes another is not considered. Each participant performed the 15 selections with the pre-defined order. To minimize the confusions regarding depth information, not only the stereoscopic scene was provided, but also the same sized object was set.

When a participant performed object selection, the given objects were highlighted to visualize the status of the participant in the virtual environment. The default color of the objects was gray. The target object which the system asked the participant to select was highlighted in green, and the object selectable was highlighted in red.

All participants were asked to locate their cursor at the starting point before performing each given task. The position of the cursor was manipulated by the Omni device, and selection command was generated by pushing buttons on a keyboard. When the participants completed the tasks, the log of the cursor manipulation from all frames, the completion time for each selection, the length of cursor trace for each selection, and the number of selection miss were automatically recorded.

Design

A repeated measures within-participant design was used. The independent variables in this experiment was object selection type *OST* (3D point cursor as *PC*, 3D bubble cursor as *BC*, and Select Ahead as *SA*), and object density

OD (10 objects, 15 objects, and 20 objects). A fully crossed design resulted in 9 combinations of OST and OD.

The experiment was divided as three sessions by the OD, and three sessions were ordered by increasing order of the object densities (session 1 has 10 objects, session 2 has 15 objects, and session 3 has 20 objects). In each session, we applied counter-balancing to the order of OST except with the 3D point cursor. The object selection task with the 3D point cursor was performed first to make the participants relatively evaluate the 3D bubble cursor and Select Ahead compared to the 3D point cursor. After performing the object selection tasks with the 3D point cursor, half of the participants performed the given task with the 3D bubble cursor first and then with Select Ahead, and the other half of the participants performed the given task in reverse order. After each session, a questionnaire was given to collect data for the qualitative evaluation for the 3D bubble cursor and for Select Ahead in comparison with the 3D point cursor. Between each session, the participants did warm-up practice to get familiar with the object selection technique and the 3D virtual environment.

Results

Completion Time (second)
In terms of the completion time for 15 selections in each session, repeated measures of analysis of variance (ANOVA) showed main effects of the object selection type, OST, ($F_{2,22}=92$) with $p<0.0001$ level, but there was no significant main effects of the object density, OD, with $p = 0.73$. There were no significant interaction effects between OST and OD with $p=0.52$.

In session 1, the average of the completion time was 27.62s for the 3D point cursor, 16.92s for the 3D bubble cursor, and 16.67s for Select Ahead. From the paired-samples t-test, Select Ahead was significantly faster than the 3D point cursor ($p<0.0001$), but there was no significant difference between the 3D bubble cursor and Select Ahead ($p=0.80$). In session 2, the average of the completion time was 26.94s for the 3D point cursor, 17.39s for the 3D bubble cursor,

and 17.72s for Select Ahead. Select Ahead was significantly faster than the 3D point cursor ($p<0.0001$), and there was no significant difference between the 3D bubble cursor and Select Ahead ($p=0.64$). In session 3, the average of the completion time was 25.37s for the 3D point cursor, 16.94s for the 3D bubble cursor, and 17.87s for Select Ahead. Again, Select Ahead was significantly faster than the 3D point cursor ($p<0.0001$), and there was no significant difference from the 3D bubble cursor ($p=0.26$). The bar chart, Figure 6, illustrates the averages of the completion time by OST in each session.

Length of Input Trace (cm)
In this section, we translate the length of cursor trace in virtual space into the length of physical input trace (centimeter).

In terms of the length of the input trace, repeated measures of ANOVA showed main effects for OST ($F_{2,22}=151$) with $p<0.0001$ level, but there was no main effects of OD with $p=0.57$. Also there were no significant interaction effects between OST and OD with $p=0.52$.

In session 1, the average of the input trace was 210.39cm for the 3D point cursor, 168.07cm for the 3D bubble cursor, and 95.44cm for Select Ahead. The length of the input trace of Select Ahead was significantly shorter than those of the other selection techniques ($p<0.0001$). In session 2, the average of the input trace was 208.84cm for the 3D point cursor, 165.21cm for the 3D bubble cursor, and 94.60cm for Select Ahead. Select Ahead had a significantly shorter length of the input trace than those of the other selection techniques ($p<0.0001$). In session 3, the average of the input trace was 199.45cm for the 3D point cursor, 152.11cm for the 3D bubble cursor, and 103.01cm for Select Ahead. Same as the results from the previous sessions, the length of the input trace of Select Ahead was significantly shorter than those of other selection techniques ($p<0.0001$).

Figure 7 illustrates the average of the length of the input trace by OST in each session.

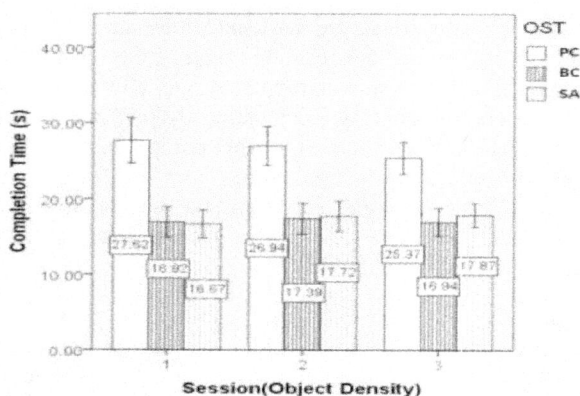

Figure 6. Completion time by the object selection types and the object densities

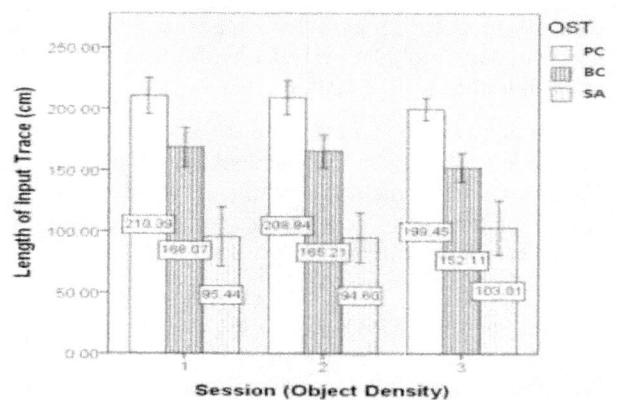

Figure 7. Length of the input trace by the object selection types and the object densities

Selection Miss Rate (%)

Selection miss means the number of triggering selection when the target object is not selectable. The miss rate in session 1 was 2% for the 3D point cursor, 0.5% for the 3D bubble cursor, 1% for Select Ahead, and 1.4% in total miss rate of session 1. The miss rate in session 2 was 2.7% for the 3D point cursor, 0.5% for the 3D bubble cursor, 2.7% for Select Ahead, and 2% in total of session 2. The miss rate in session 3 was 2.1% for the 3D point cursor, 1% for the 3D bubble cursor, 0% for Select Ahead, and 1% in total of session 3. There was no significantly difference between miss rates of each selection technique in each session.

Learning Effect

At the end of the experiment, all participants consequently performed three identical tasks (same as session 2 with 15 objects) only with Select Ahead. In the completion time, the average of each trial was 17.40s for the first trial, 18.03s for the second trial, and 16.56s for the third trial. For reference, the completion time of Select Ahead in session 2 was 17.72s and that of 3D bubble cursor in session 2 was 17.39s (see Figure 8). However, there was no significant difference between each trial with p=0.18 and also there was no significant difference between each trial

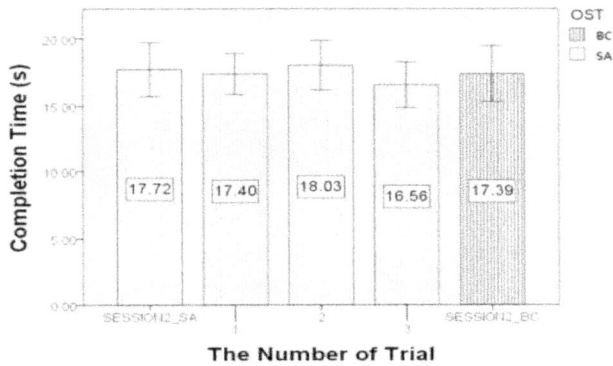

Figure 8. Completion time by the number of trial compared to previous result of Select Ahead in session 2 and that of the 3D bubble cursor in session 2

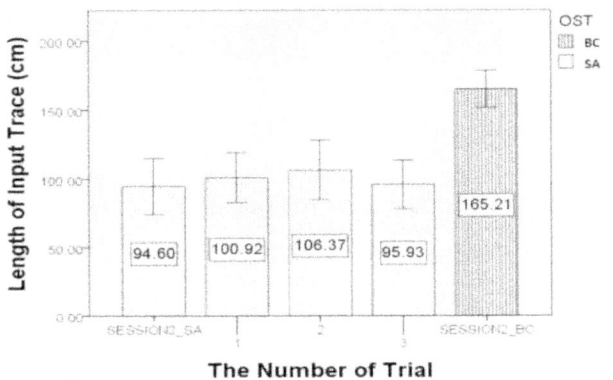

Figure 9. Length of the input trace by the number of trial compared to previous result of Select Ahead in Session 2 and that of the 3D bubble cursor in session 2

and the result of the bubble cursor in session 2 with p=0.91 for trial 1, p=0.42 for trial 2, and p=0.09 for trial 3. In terms of the length of the input trace, also there was no significant difference between each trial with p=0.16. The results from each trial are significantly smaller compared to the length of the input trace of the 3D bubble cursor in session 2 with p<0.0001(see Figure 9).

Qualitative Evaluation

The participants were given a questionnaire for qualitative evaluation of Select Ahead (see Appendix I). We asked six questions in Likert scale and one question for free comments. For the questions with Likert scale, the participants gave relative points of the 3D bubble cursor and Select Ahead compared to the 3D point cursor. Score being greater than 5 means that the selection technique is preferred over the 3D point cursor.

The overall average for Select Ahead was 6.53 for session 1, 6.27 for session 2, and 6.34 for session 3, while the 3D bubble cursor received 7.88 for session 1, 7.65 for session 2, and 7.77 for session 3. This meant Select Ahead was evaluated as more positive than the 3D point cursor (because the average score of Select Ahead is higher than 5), but less preferred than the 3D bubble cursor. Seven out of twelve participants commented about sensitivity of the ToCM in Select Ahead. They thought that the ToCM was too sensitive to control. The participants also left comments about the visualization of Select Ahead. The 3D bubble cursor had visualization of the interaction volume and it allowed the user to understand not only selection volume but also the relative position of the cursor and objects in 3D space. However, the arrow cursor showing ToCM for Select Ahead was not enough to distinguish the direction of ToCM and the relative position between the cursor and the objects.

DISCUSSION

The experimental results show that Select Ahead has reduced the length of the cursor manipulation approximately up to 55 percent and 35 percent in comparison to the 3D point cursor and the 3D bubble cursor, respectively. In the view of the selection time, Select Ahead outperforms the 3D point cursor and had no significant difference from the 3D bubble cursor. In addition, we observe the consistent performance of Select Ahead from the result of the repeated selection tasks in the experiment.

The results from the qualitative evaluation show that Select Ahead needs some improvement with respect to the robustness of pointing and the easiness to control the selection. We further analyze the causes of the difficulty in use by carefully comparing our method with the 3D bubble cursor. In case of Select Ahead which utilizes the approaching direction of the cursor to the target, the usability tends to be affected by depth perception of each participant. In order to help the user understand the depth of the 3D interface, an effective visual feedback needs to be employed. In our preliminary experiment, we provided a semi-transparent cone as a visual cue of the selection volume of Select Ahead. However, with this visual feedback, some of the users confuse Select Ahead with the ray-casting technique in that, they tried to change mostly the direction only, rather than to manipulate the cursor towards the target object. Therefore, further considerations and the user study are needed to design the visual feedback which intuitively visualizes the relationship between the objects, the cursor, and the ToCM to guide the user for precise cursor manipulations.

CONCLUSION AND FUTURE WORK

In this paper, we have introduced Select Ahead as an object selection technique which enhances the efficiency of the virtual hand scheme in 3D environment. The experimental results show that Select Ahead substantially reduces the length of the cursor manipulation for object selection compared to both the 3D point cursor and the 3D bubble cursor. The reduction in the length of cursor manipulation directly mitigates the physical workload of the users when they perform the interaction with the virtual environment. In addition, we believe that this reduction in physical workload will have a greater positive influence on a virtual environment which has much bigger work-space.

Regarding the duration of selection time, Select Ahead outperforms the 3D point cursor and has the similar performance to the 3D bubble cursor regardless of object density. The selection time reflects the efficiency related to the cognitive load. We expect that the intuitiveness of performing object selection with Select Ahead can be improved by further considerations of effective visual feedback for the technique. The future study includes the verification of the performance for Select Ahead technique in the general virtual environment.

ACKNOWLEDGMENTS

This work was supported by the IT R&D program of MKE/KEIT [KI002096, Contact-free Multipoint Realistic Interaction Technology Development].

REFERENCES

1. Baudisch, P., Cutrell, E., Robbins, D., Czerwinski, M., Tandler, P., Bederson, B., and Zierlinger, A. Drag-and-pop and drag-and-pick: Techniques for accessing remote screen content on touch- and pen-operated systems. *Proc. of Interact.,* (2003), 57-64.

2. Blanch, R., Guiard, Y., and Beaudouin-Lafon, M. Semantic pointing: improving target acquisition with control-display ratio adaptation. *ACM Conference on Human Factors in Computer Systems(CHI),* (2004), 519-526.

3. Bowman, D.A., Kruijff, E., LaViola, J.J. and Poupyrev, I. 3D User Interface: Theory and Practice. Addison-Wesley/Pearson Education(2004).

4. Grossman, T., and Balakrishnan, R. The bubble cursor: enhancing target acquisition by dynamic resizing of the cursor's activation area. *ACM Conference on Human Factors in Computing Systems(CHI),* (2005), 281-290.

5. Guiard, Y., Blanch, R., and Beaudouin-Lafon, M. Object Pointing: a complement to bitmap pointing in GUIs. Graphics Interface, (2004), 9-16.

6. LaViola, J.J. and Keefe D.F. 3D Spatial Interaction: Applications for Art, Design, and Science, *Siggraph Course Notes,* (2011).

7. Liang, J. and Green, M. JDCAD: a highly interactive 3D modeling system. *Computers & Graphics,* (1994), 18(4): 499-506.

8. Mine, M. Virtual environment interaction techniques, *University of North Carolina,* Technical Report TR95-018, (1995).

9. Mine, M. Working in a Virtual World: Interaction Techniques Used in the Chapel Hill Immersive Modeling Program. *University of North Carolina,* Technical Report TR96-029, (1996).

10. Vanacken L., Grossman T., and Coninx K. Exploring the effects of environment density and target visibility on object selection in 3D virtual environments. *In Proc. of the IEEE Symposium on 3D User Interfaces,* (2007), 115–122.

11. Zhai, S., Buxton, W., and Milgram, P. The "Silk Cursor": Investigating transparency for 3D target acquisition. *ACM Conference on Human Factors in Computing Systems(CHI),* (1994), 459-464.

APPENDIX I – The contents of the qustionnaire

Q1. How quickly does a current method detect the intended object? (0~10)

Q2. Does a current method keep aiming for the intended object robustly in spite of some trembling input? (0~10)

Q3. When the cursor points to a unintended object, can it be easily corrected? (0~10)

Q4. How easily do you complete the task with a current method? (0~10)

Q5. How quickly do you complete the task with a current method? (0~10)

Q6. How would you rate the overall interaction quality of a current method? (0~10)

Q7. Free Comments for Select Ahead technique

3D Object Selection for Hand-held Auto-stereoscopic Display

Euijai Ahn
Digital Experience Laboratory
Korea University, Seoul, Korea
saintpio@korea.ac.kr
+82-2-3290-3579

Hyunseok Yang
Digital Experience Laboratory
Korea University, Seoul, Korea
baroeye@korea.ac.kr
+82-2-3290-3579

Gerard J. Kim
Digital Experience Laboratory
Korea University, Seoul, Korea
gjkim@korea.ac.kr
+82-2-3290-3196

ABSTRACT

Interacting in a small (mobile) auto-stereoscopic display can be difficult because of the lack of accurate tracking of an interaction proxy, and having to maintain a fixed viewpoint and adapt to a different level of depth perception sensitivity. In this paper, we first propose to modify a standard stylus into a mechanical chain with joint sensors for 3D tracking. We also investigate a way to assist the user in selecting an object in the small phone space through supplementary multimodal feedback, such as sound and tactility. We have carried out an experiment comparing the effects of various combinations of multimodal feedback to object selection performance.

Author Keywords

Auto-stereoscopy, Depth perception, Mobile interaction, Multimodal interaction, Selection, 3D tracking.

ACM Classification Keywords

H.5.m [Information Interfaces and Presentation]: Miscellaneous.

INTRODUCTION

With the continuing technological innovation and recent keen public interests, stereoscopic displays are becoming more commonplace these days. They are being adopted for TVs, desktop displays and finally smart phones and hand-held devices [1, 2, 3, 4], but in most cases, still used for viewing only. An exception is for when used for special purpose virtual reality (VR) based interactive applications. In fact, 3D interaction techniques for VR (with relatively large-sized stereoscopic display) have been studied considerably [5]. However, not much attention has been paid to the problem of interacting in a relatively "small-sized" hand-held stereoscopic display such as that of a smart phone.

One of the difficulties arise from the lack of accurate and robust method for 3D tracking within the small "phone"

space (e.g. small rectangular volume right above the phone display, also see Figure 2a). Another possible source of complications is the fact that small mobile 3D displays are invariably auto-stereoscopic (e.g. parallax barrier type), limiting the user to fix and maintain one's view point to feel the 3D effect. This is undoubtedly a more difficult task with hand-held devices than with large fixed displays. In addition, it is plausible to expect some differences in workings of the human's depth perception in the significantly "small" phone space compared to the nominally sized space (e.g. human scale).

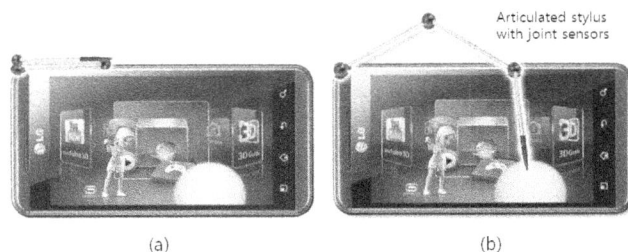

Figure 1. 3D interaction on a stereoscopic phone using an articulated stylus with joint sensors (for 3D tracking). The stylus can be folded for easy stow away (left).

Our paper thus starts with a proposal for a practical solution to 3D tracking for a mobile phone, using an articulated stylus with joint sensors (see Figure 1). Then we also propose to assist the user in selecting an object in the small phone space through supplementary multimodal feedback, such as sound and tactility to overcome the aforementioned projected difficulties. We have carried out an experiment comparing the effects of various combinations of multimodal feedback to object selection performance.

Our paper is organized as follows. First we provide a review of previous and related research. Then we describe the 3D auto-stereoscopic smart phone and newly proposed tracking system, used for the following experiment. Section 4 gives details of the experiment and results. Finally we discuss and summarize the findings from our experiments to conclude the paper.

RELATED WORK

3D interaction techniques have been studied much in depth mainly in the virtual reality community. An excellent review of the various techniques and their taxonomy are given in [5]. However, subtle difference in their performance or usability according to different types of 3D displays (e.g. auto-stereoscopic, active or passive type, head mounted display) has not been looked at much, especially for small displays [6]. One noteworthy work by [7] studied interaction for small hand-held stereoscopic (passive chromatic anaglyph) display. In this work, the interaction was indirect or gesture based realized by tracking the user's fingertip on the other side of the display using the back facing camera. To our knowledge, there has not been a research study for directly interacting with stereoscopically rendered object in 3D. This is partly due to the difficult problem of accurate tracking in the "phone" space in a self-contained way (i.e. without any third party sensor). The most prevalent approach is to use the phone camera, however, due to its limited field of view, it is not feasible for the tracking volume to cover the entire "phone" space, especially near the display surface.

The phenomenon of altered depth perception with the use of stereoscopic display also has been reported in [8, 9]. For example, humans tend to underestimate depth when head mounted display (HMD) is used [8]. Not much is known about the dynamics of depth perception for auto-stereoscopic displays that use parallax barriers or lenticular sheets, not to mention for small-sized ones. Yang et al. compensated for the depth underestimation in HMDs by manipulating its geometric field of view providing additional multimodal feedback [10]. Similarly, multimodal feedback has been regarded one way to improve 3D task performance (which must be related to depth perception) [11, 12, 13, 14, 15, 16, 17]. For example, Stephen et al. [14] used multimodal (visual and aural) feedback to help users perceive depth more accurately and carry out 3D spatial tasks. However, to date, the results are not consistent in terms of which modality combination is most helpful due to differences in the task and experimental conditions.

EXPERIMENTAL PLATFORM

3D Tracking: Articulated Stylus

In order to interact directly with 3D objects, 3D tracking is required. Our proposal is to use an articulated stylus with joint sensors as shown in Figure 1. We believe such a device can be designed almost as compact as the conventional stylus with miniaturized yet highly accurate joint encoding sensors. Such a design consideration is necessary to keep the mobile phone light and "handy" to use. The sensors and feedback devices would be directly connected into the smart phone for end-effector coordinate computation and feedback control. Note that the articulated stylus is not a haptic device, but merely a tracking one. When not in use, it can be simply be folded and stowed away.

Our actual "lab" implementation was bigger in size than the envisioned version, with four degrees of freedom articulation, and using analog potentiometers at the joints

(rather than more accurate high resolution digital encoders). Additional circuitry were needed for digital conversion and interfacing into the smart phone using Bluetooth. Lego pieces were used for the links (see Figure 2). A small vibrator and button were attached for the interaction purpose.

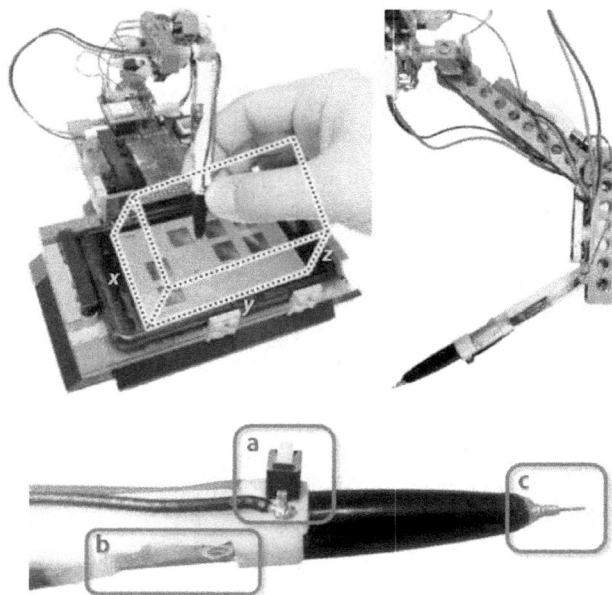

Figure 2. Actual "lab" implementation of the articulated stylus using lego pieces, potentiometers and associated circuitries. (a) button, (b) vibrator, (c) stylus tip.

As for the associated circuitry, the Arduino board [18] using the Atmega328 MCU was used and the on-board 10 bit A/D converter was used for converting the potentiometer joint angles into digital values. Based on a standard forward kinematic formulation (which we omit the details in this paper) [19], the positional coordinate of the stylus tip is easily computed. For stable output, basic low pass filtering was applied. The orientation (of the tip) was not computed nor used in this work. All the computations (for now) were carried out on the MCU and transmitted to the smart phone at a rate of approximately 35 Hz. The vibrator motor was controlled by the pulse width modulation signal output from the same board. We re-emphasize that, if professionally built with the state-of-the-art components, the stylus can be as compact and accurate as originally proposed.

Tracking Accuracy and Calibration

To measure the accuracy of our device, we built small 3D structures with Lego blocks (see Figure 3) and compared the computed coordinates of the stylus tip and the ground truth of various points in the structures. Figure 4 illustrates the accuracy of the articulated stylus in the x-y plane (ground truth: red circles, measured and computed: blue diamonds). In all three directions, the errors were on the average within about 2mm. As our focus was more with deriving an effective 3D object selection technique, no further significant effort was made to improve the accuracy. However, due to the personal variations in depth perception, we asked each user, during the experiment, to designate several 3D landmark points (similarly to calibrating a touch screen) to calibrate them against the corresponding ones in the virtual space (see Figure 5).

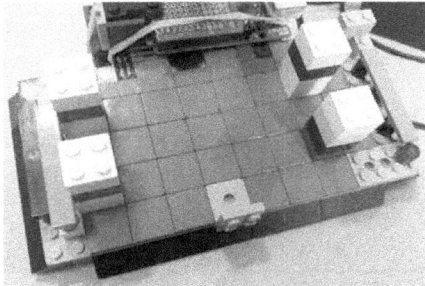

Figure 3. One of the 3D structures used for accuracy measurement.

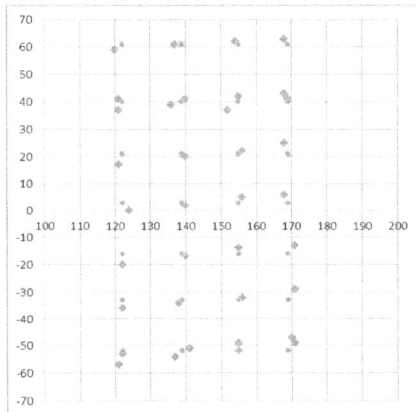

Figure 4. Accuracy in the x-y plane (units in mm). Ground truth are marked in red circles, and measured and computed in blue diamonds.

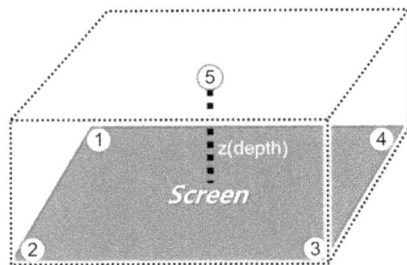

Figure 5. The "Phone" space and the five designated points for calibration to the virtual volume.

Auto-stereoscopic smart phone

The auto-stereoscopic phone used in our experiment was an LG Optimus 3D [4] with a 4.3 inch 3D (parallax barrier) LCD display (480 x 800 pixels, 16M colors). Parallax

barrier technology refers to creating the 3D effect by using a barrier (layer of material with a series of precision slits) placed on the image source (e.g. LCD) such that each sees the respective right or left image (without the need to wear special glasses, see Figure 6) [20]. A disadvantage of the technology is that the user must be positioned in a well-defined spot to experience the 3D effect. The exact spot depends on the inter-ocular distance of the user, but for this phone model, it was approximately 30cm perpendicularly above from the center of the screen. Another disadvantage is that the effective horizontal pixel count viewable for each eye is reduced by one half. The typical operational phone space was assumed be shaped as a rectangular volume with the physical dimensions of 56mm x 93mm x 40mm, as viewed from the sweet spot. Note that above figures are nominal values only; both the proper viewing position and perceived size of the phone space would be slightly different for different users.

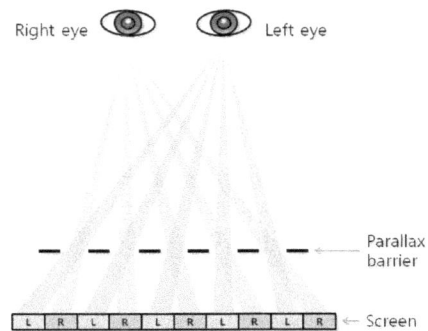

Figure 6. The parallax barrier technology used in the LG auto-stereoscopic phone.

Overall interaction architecture

Figure 7 illustrates the overall architecture combining the tracking device to the smart phone. The computed stylus tip coordinates are relayed to the smart phone which visually renders the virtual world in stereo, and other modal feedback (e.g. aural and tactile).

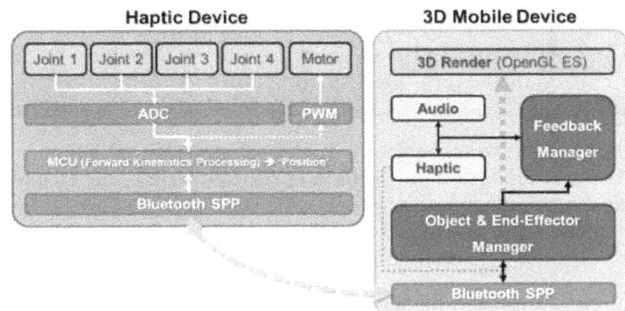

Figure 7. Overall interaction architecture: tracking module on the left and smart phone on the right.

EXPERIMENT: OBJECT SELECTION TECHNIQUE

Experiment Design

With the experimental platform in place, rudimentary object selection in the 3D phone space has become possible. Nevertheless due to the factors mentioned previously (e.g. fixed spot viewing, reduced resolution, unknown dynamics of the depth perception in small sized volume, etc.), we expect some difficulties in fluid interaction. As such, we propose to take advantage of supplementary modal feedback, namely, aural and tactile, and carry out an experiment to explore the feedback design space. We compare four different feedback conditions as an aid to making object selection. They are (1) visual only (V, the reference), (2) visual and aural (VA), (3) visual and tactile (VT), and (4) visual, aural and tactile (VAT).

Since the correct depth perception is the matter of importance in this work, as for the experimental task, we presented two objects (cubes) of similar depth and asked the user to disambiguate the depth between them. More experimental details follow in the subsequent subsections. In summary, the experiment had one factor, the type of multimodal feedback, with four levels (1 x 4 within subject repeated measure) and the task performance and usability were measured as major dependent variables. Our main hypothesis was that higher degree of multimodal feedback would generally improve the object selection or depth perception performance.

Multimodal Feedback

The visual feedback merely consisted of rendering of the cubes. To remove any external bias, we rendered the cubes with orthogonal projection and minimal lighting effects (Figure 8). It is well known that perspective projection alone is a very strong psychological depth cue. We eliminated all depth cues except for the binocular disparity.

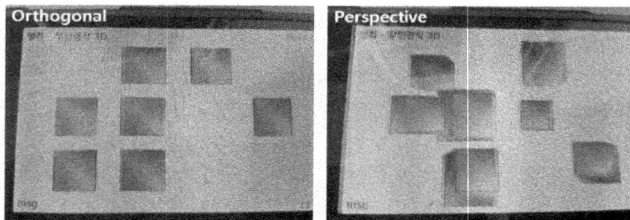

Figure 8. Orthogonal vs. perspective rendering. When the depth is similar, it is difficult to tell the difference solely from the appearance (stereoscopy needed), whereas with perspective rendering it is somewhat possible to judge the depth more correctly even without stereoscopy.

As for the aural and tactile feedback, they were generated when the 3D cursor (drawn at the tip of the articulated stylus) came into some proximal distance with a nearby object (Figure 9).

A sine tone was generated as aural feedback and the frequency was determined by the depth (or discrete depth level) of the object to whom the 3D cursor is proximal. The

higher the object was (i.e. distant from the screen, closer to the user), likewise the tone frequency. A reasonable audible frequency range was mapped to the depth range of the stereoscopic display.

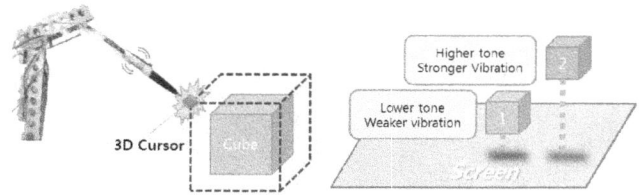

Figure 9. Indication of proximity of the 3D cursor to an object. The indication is expressed aurally and/or tactically based on their depth relative to screen.

Depth from user (cm)	Depth from screen (cm)	Tone Frequency (Aural Feedback)	Vibration Duty rate (Tactile Feedback)
29.0	1.0	730Hz	31%
28.5	1.5	1360Hz	43%
28.0	2.0	1990Hz	54%
27.5	2.5	2610Hz	66%
27.0	3.0	3240Hz	77%
26.5	3.5	3870Hz	89%
26.0	4.0	4500Hz	100%

Table 1. Stimulation parameter values used for aural and vibratory tactile feedback.

Similarly, the amplitude/frequency of the vibratory tactile feedback was inversely proportional to the depth (from the user) of the object as well. The vibration motor, when controlled by the PWM signal, varies the vibration frequency and its amplitude at the same time. Ideally, only the amplitude would be varied with a fixed vibration frequency, supposedly most perceptible by humans, for instance at around 250 Hz [21]. In this experiment, both feedback lasted for one second when generated. Table 1 shows the stimulation parameters used for the respective modal feedback.

Experimental Task

The experimental task involved the user to determine the relative depth between two cubes. The subject was to carry out a series of these depth determination tasks as fast and correctly as possible. Two cubes with different (randomly chosen) depth values appeared in the 3D phone space (but with an equal planar distance), and the user was to choose the deeper object using the articulated stylus under different treatment or feedback conditions (see Figure 10).

Figure 10. Experimental task: depth determination.

Experimental Procedure

Twenty one paid subjects (15 men and 6 women) participated in the experiment with the mean age of 24.5. After collecting one's basic background information, the subject was briefed about the purpose of the experiment and instructions for the experimental task. A short training (15 to 20 minutes) was given for the subject to get familiarized to the experimental process and using the stylus.

The subject tried out each treatment combination in a balanced order. For each treatment, the depth test was conducted five times. The task completion time and correctness data were captured and after all the treatments were tried, a general usability questionnaire was filled out (answered in 7 scale Likert scale).

RESULTS

Task Performance

ANOVA has reaffirmed the effect of the multimodal feedback. VAT exhibited the fastest task performance but with no statistical difference from VA. In addition, VT was neither differentiated from V. Thus, in our experiment, only the aural feedback was meaningfully effective (Figure 11).

Task Completion Time

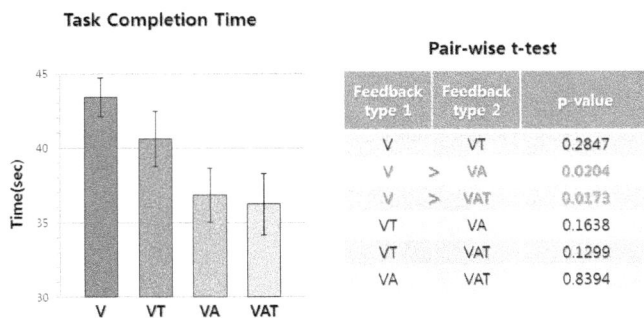

Pair-wise t-test

Feedback type 1		Feedback type 2	p value
V		VT	0.2847
V	>	VA	0.0204
V	>	VAT	0.0173
VT		VA	0.1638
VT		VAT	0.1299
VA		VAT	0.8394

Figure 11. Task completion times for the four feedback conditions.

Figure 12 shows the number of incorrect answers among the four feedback conditions. In this case, while tactile feedback was effective, it was not as effective as that by the aural (VT > V, VA > VT, VAT > V, VAT > VT).

No. of Incorrect Responses

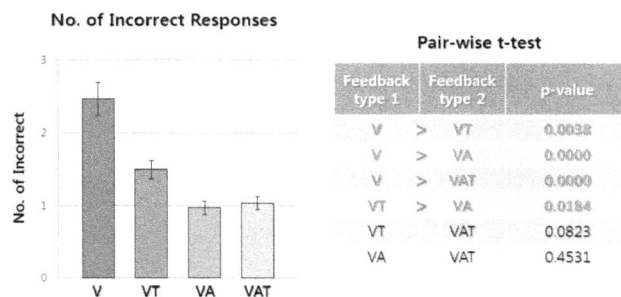

Pair-wise t-test

Feedback type 1		Feedback type 2	p-value
V	>	VT	0.0038
V	>	VA	0.0000
V	>	VAT	0.0000
VT	>	VA	0.0184
VT		VAT	0.0823
VA		VAT	0.4531

Figure 12. Number of incorrect responses for the four feedback conditions.

Usability

The usability questionnaire asked the subject to comparatively rate the four selection (or feedback) techniques in terms of ease of use, degree to which feedback was helpful in recognizing the depth, ease of learning, interaction naturalness and the level of fatigue. Figure 13 illustrates the results.

The usability results are quite consistent with that of the quantitative performance results. For instance, with multimodal feedback, the user felt the task was generally easier, and the easiest for VA and VAT, which were statistically not different, again showing the reduced role of the tactile feedback (Figure 13a). Users also responded that the aural feedback was the most helpful, and less so when only tactile feedback was present or mixed (Figure 13b). Figure 13c shows that, as we have hypothesized, that it was difficult for the users to determine depth solely from visual feedback. Again, the subjects felt the selection technique was easiest to learn, most natural and least tiring with the aural feedback only. We observe in general that when aural and tactile feedback are both presented, the usability and task performance was lower than when only aural feedback is presented. Thus there seems to be an interaction among these two elements. In fact, it is reported that redundant feedback may degrade task performance [22] and this result is also consistent with cases when object selection is carried out in larger interaction space [13]. However, it is also quite possible the vibratory tactile feedback we devised was not ideally designed to human perception.

Ease of Use

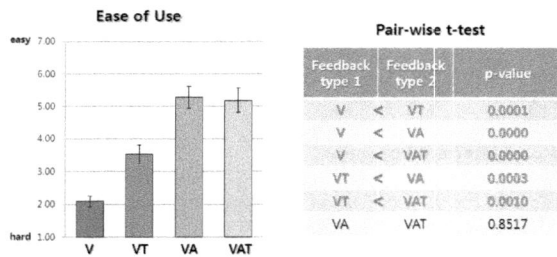

Feedback type 1		Feedback type 2	p-value
V	<	VT	0.0001
V	<	VA	0.0000
V	<	VAT	0.0000
VT	<	VA	0.0003
VT	<	VAT	0.0010
VA		VAT	0.8517

(a) Ease of use

How much feedback was helpful?

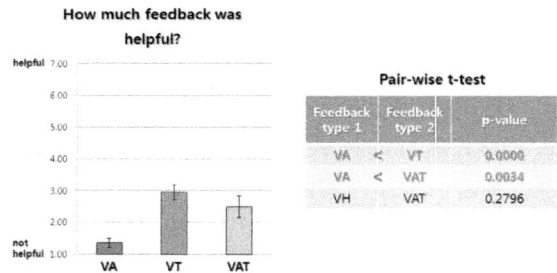

Feedback type 1		Feedback type 2	p-value
VA	<	VT	0.0000
VA	<	VAT	0.0034
VT		VAT	0.2796

(b) Feedback helpfulness

Ease of Learning

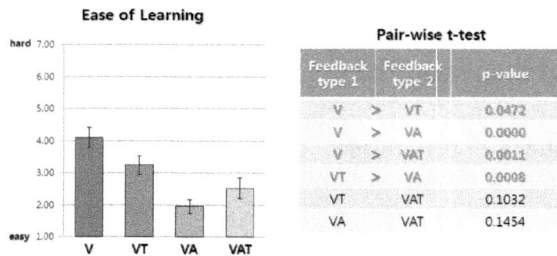

Feedback type 1		Feedback type 2	p-value
V	>	VT	0.0472
V	>	VA	0.0000
V	>	VAT	0.0011
VT	>	VA	0.0008
VT		VAT	0.1032
VA		VAT	0.1454

(c) Ease of learning

How natural?

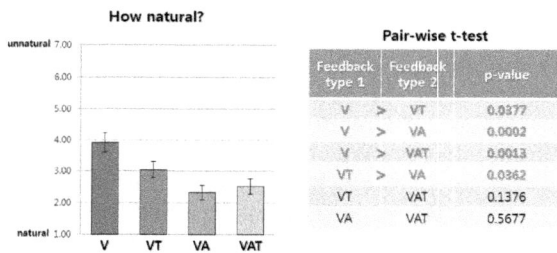

Feedback type 1		Feedback type 2	p-value
V	>	VT	0.0377
V	>	VA	0.0002
V	>	VAT	0.0013
VT	>	VA	0.0362
VT		VAT	0.1376
VA		VAT	0.5677

(d) Interaction naturalness

Fatigue

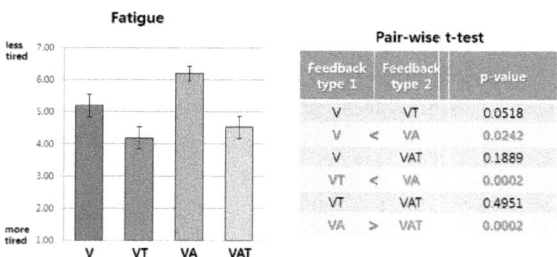

Feedback type 1		Feedback type 2	p-value
V		VT	0.0518
V	<	VA	0.0242
V		VAT	0.1889
VT	<	VA	0.0002
VT		VAT	0.4951
VA	>	VAT	0.0002

(e) Level of Fatigue

Figure 13. Usability results among the four feedback conditions.

DISCUSSION AND CONCLUSION

Based on our experiment, we reaffirmed that multimodal feedback helped users select objects better. Post-brieifing with the subjects further confirmed this deduction. Many complained of dizziness and blurred imagery in trying to perceive 3D. This was more apparent with the higher degree of negative parallax (object being felt to hover further out of the screen). Despite the possibility of non-ideally designed vibratory tactile feedback method, we converge to a conclusion that only one supplementary and aural feedback was the most effective object selection method. Many subjects indicated that they were confused when both aural and tactile feedback were given and preferred only one of the two. They also reported the difficulty to sense the depth with the "vibrating" stylus and due to the low disambiguating power (relative to the depth range) of the tactile feedback itself. Some even consciously tried to block tactile feedback when presented together with the aural feedback.

Our future work includes investigating in other interaction techniques such as object manipulation and menu selection. Other forms of aural and tactile feedback

ACKNOWLEDGMENTS

This work was supported by the National Research Foundation of Korea(NRF) grant funded by the Korea government (MEST) (No. 2011-0030079).

REFERENCES

1. Samsung, Samsung 3D TV. http://www.samsung.com/uk/3d/, (2011).

2. LG, LG 3D Notebook. http://www.lg.com/in/computer-products/notebook/LG-A520-D.jsp, (2011).

3. Nintendo, Nintendo 3DS. http://www.nitendo.com/3ds, (2011).

4. LG, LG Optimus 3D. http://www.lge.com, (2011).

5. Bowman, D., Kruijff, E., LaVioloa, J. and Poupyrev, I. 3D User Interfaces: Theory and Practie. Addison Wesley, (2004).

6. Henrysson, A., Marshally, J. and Billinghurst , M. Experiments in 3D Interaction for Mobile Phone AR, Proc GRAPHITE, ACM Press, (2007), 187-194.

7. Yousefi, S., Kondori, F. A. and Li, H. 3D Gestural Interaction for Stereoscopic Visualization on Mobile Devices. Proc. CAIP, Part II, LNCS 6855, (2011), 555-562.

8. Postka, J., Lewis, S. A., and King, D. Effects of Field of View on Judgments of Self-Location: Distortions in Distance Estimations Even When the Image Geometry Exactly Fits the Field of View, Presence: Teleoperators and Virtual Environments, (1998). 7(4), 352-369.

9. Waller, D. Factors Affecting the Perception of Inter-Object Distances in Virtual Environments, Presence:

Teleoperators and Virtual Environments, (1999), 8(6), pp.657-670.

10. Yang, U. amd Kim, G. J. Increasing the Effective Egocentric Field of View with Proprioceptive and Tactile Feedback. Proc. of IEEE Virtual Reality Conference. (2004), 27-34.

11. Bouguila, L., Ishii, M., Sato, M. Effect of Coupling Haptics and Stereopsis on Depth Perception in Virtual Environment, Proceedings of the 1st Workshop on Haptic Human Computer Interaction, (2000), 54-60.

12. Murphy, E., Moussette, C., Verron, C. and Guastavino, C. Design and Evaluation of an Audio-Haptic Interface, Proceedings of the eNTERFACE Workshop, (2008).

13. Richard, P., Burdea, G., Gomez, D. and Coiffet, P. A Comparison of Haptic, Visual and Auditiory Force Feedback for Deformable Virtual Objects, Proceedings of the Fourth International Conference on Artificial Reality and Tele-Existence, (1994), 49-62.

14. Mereu, S. and Kazman R. Audio Enhanced 3D Interfaces for Visually Impaired Users, Proc. of SIGCHI, (1996), 72-78.

15. Richard, P., Burdea, G., Gomez, D. and Coiffet, P. A Comparison of Haptic, Visual and Auditiory Force Feedback for Deformable Virtual Objects, Proceedings

of the Fourth International Conference on Artificial Reality and Tele-Existence, (1994), 49-62.

16. Chang, A. and O'Sullivan, C. An Audio-Haptic Aesthetic Framework Influenced by Visual Theory Correct, Haptic and Audio Interaction Design, Third International Workshop, (2008), 5270, 70-80.

17. Müller-Tomfelde, C. Interaction Sound Feedback in a Haptic Virtual Environment to Improve Motor Skill Acquisition, Proceedings of ICAD, (2004).

18. Arduino UNO (Atmega328) http://www.arduino.cc, (2011).

19. Denavit J. and Hartenberg, R. A Kinematic Notation for Lower-pair Mechanisms based on Matrices, Trans ASME J. Appl. Mech., (1955), 23, 215–221.

20. Parallax-barrier auto-stereoscopic display, http://en.wikipedia.org/wiki/Autostereoscopy, (2011).

21. Jung, J., and Choi, S. Perceived Magnitude and Power Consumption of Vibration Feedback in Mobile Devices, Proc. HCII, 4551, (2007), 354-363.

22. Kim, H. and Kim, G. J. Designing of Multimodal Feedback for Enhanced Multitasking Performance, Proc. of SIGCHI, (2011).

Extending "Out of the Body" Saltation to 2D Mobile Tactile Interaction

Youngsun Kim, Jaedong Lee and Gerard J. Kim
Digital Experience Laboratory, Korea University
Anam-dong 5-ga, Seongbuk-gu, Seoul, Republic of Korea
{ zyoko85@korea.ac.kr, jdlee@korea.ac.kr, gjkim@korea.ac.kr }

ABSTRACT
Funneling and saltation are two main perceptual illusion techniques for vibro-tactile feedback. They are often used to minimize the number of vibrators to be worn on the body and thereby build a less cumbersome and expensive feedback device. Recently, these techniques have been found to elicit "out of the body" experience, i.e. feeling for phantom sensations indirectly on a hand-held object. This paper explores the practical applicability of this theoretical result to mobile tactile interaction. Two psychophysical experiments were run to validate: (1) the 1D saltation effect through the hand-held smart phone, and (2) the effect of saltation based approach to 2D phantom sensation elicitation. Experimental results have first confirmed the same "out of the body" saltation effect in 1D, originally tested on a metallic ruler by Miyazaki [15], on an actual mobile device. In addition, 2D modulated phantom sensation with a resolution of 5 x 3 on a 3.5 inch display space was achieved with saltation based stimulation.

Author Keywords
Saltation, Phantom sensation, Illusory feedback, Funneling, Vibro-tactile feedback.

ACM Classification Keywords
H.5.m. Information interfaces and presentation (e.g., HCI): Miscellaneous.

INTRODUCTION
Employing vibro-tactile feedback is one inexpensive and effective way to enhance interaction experience. Tactile feedback is also often combined with other modalities to amplify its effect or produce illusory sensation. One primary illusory technique associated with vibro-tactility is saltation [8]. Saltation generates pseudo-tactile sensations by presenting two or more tactile stimuli directly to the skin with time delay, or inter-stimulus interval (ISI). The locations of the pseudo-tactile sensation can be changed by modulating the ISI. Recently, Miyazaki has discovered that

saltation could be extended to body-worn objects and to create phantom sensations from "out of the body" (see Figure 1) [15]. This result is appealing in its application possibility to mobile devices [11]. That is, there now is a potential method to make a user feel (phantom) sensations indirectly emanating from the hand-held device (e.g. middle of the display), but supplying actual vibrations only to the "natural" holding locations.

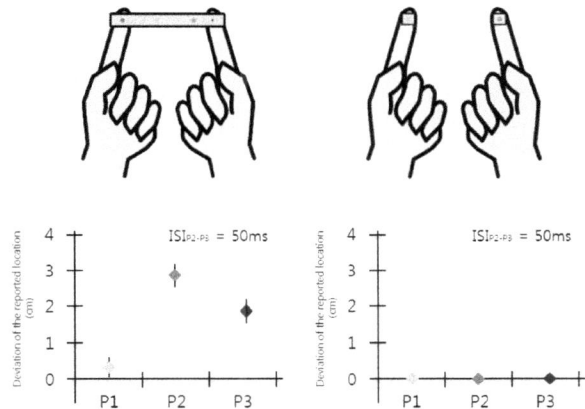

Figure 1. The concept of "out of the body" tactile experience (saltation) from a hand-held object (this figure is reproduced from [15]). When vibrations are given to the fingertips (at P1 and P3) with proper delay values, phantom tactile sensations are felt as if occurring in the middle of the hand-held ruler (at P2) (left). No such sensations were felt without the physical medium (right)

However, while the basic study regarding the "out of the body" experience had been carried out by [15] (using a small ruler), the same effect has not been verified on an actual everyday mobile device. Moreover, to be useful in mobile devices, it would be desirable to create saltation based phantom sensations in 2D (e.g. mapped to the mobile display). If verified, the results will serve as a scientific basis for realizing more flexible and inexpensive tactile/haptic feedback for mobile interfaces without using too many vibrators or actuators.

Accordingly, in this paper, we conduct two experiments (1) to validate the same out of the body experience using an actual mobile device (i.e. smart phone) and (2) assessing the effects of our newly proposed extension of 1D saltation to 2D.

In the next section, we first review previous research literatures related to phantom tactile sensations and its application to practical interaction design for mobile devices. Then, we describe the two validation experiments and report their results. Finally, we conclude the paper with a discussion and directions for future research.

RELATED WORK

Perceptual illusions can be applied to human computer interfaces to enrich user experience. For instance, a mere vibrational feedback, when combined with other modalities, can induce phantom directional haptic feedback [5]. Funneling and saltation are two major perceptual illusion techniques for vibro-tactile feedback. Funneling refers to stimulating the skin at two different locations simultaneously with different amplitudes and eliciting phantom sensations in between the two [4]. Several researchers have applied this phenomenon to human interfaces, experimenting with different ways of modulating the vibration amplitudes for detailed controlling of the target phantom sensation locations [1, 3, 17]. Mizukami has used funneling to generate phantom sensations in 2D and applied it to tactile character recognition [16].

On the other hand, in saltation, the skin is stimulated at two locations (at P1 and P3) with proper time intervals (also known as inter-stimulus interval or ISI), and with the phantom sensation felt in between (at P2) [8]. Because of the "timed" stimulation, the sensation is felt "moving" (often characterized as "hopping of a rabbit"). In the usual scheme, two weaker timed stimulations (i.e. with ISIP1-P2) are given at P1 then a stronger one at P3 (i.e. with ISIP2-P3). Saltation has been investigated further by other scientists in terms of the effects of different ISI values [7,18,23].

The 1D saltation has been applied to actual interfaces. For instance, Hoggan et al. experimented with using three vibrators on a mobile device to emulate a tactile progress bar [11]. Tan et al. applied saltation to implementing a tactile chair using a 3 x 3 tactile array for pattern recognition [22]. A similar work was done by [12]. Note that even though the tactile array was a 2D structure, 1D saltation was used. Seo et al. applied saltation to generating tactile feedback on mobile devices [20]. The difference from our work is that we apply the out-of-body saltation (described subsequently). In their work, most part of the mobile device is in contact with the whole hand, where in our case, the sensation is to be felt only through the hand/finger holding the device on the far two ends.

Recently, Miyazaki has discovered the saltation can be extended to body-worn (e.g. hand-held) objects and create "out of the body" tactile experience [15]. This form of saltation is appealing in its practical application because less direct contact would be needed between the device and users body. Thus, the main purpose of our work is to validate, for the first time, the potential of the "out of the body" saltation for tactile feedback in 2D.

EXPERIMENT I:

"OUT OF THE BODY" SLATATION ON MOBILE DEVICE

Experimental Design and Set up

In this experiment, the user experienced two types of stimulation, (1) non-saltation based and (2) saltation based as shown in Figure 2. A mobile device was attached with three vibrators in line (in equal spacing) on its back. The two vibrators on each end of the line where placed at convenient positions to be in contact with the holding hands/fingers, and the other in the middle between the two. Thus, for the non-saltation based stimulations, all three vibrators were used, while for the saltation-based stimulation, only the vibrators on the two left/right ends were used.

The experiment was designed as a psychophysical one in the form of an appearance based one alternative forced choice (1AFC). That is, "one" stimulation was given either in non-saltation form or the other, and the users were to answer in yes/no whether they felt any sensation at/from the middle position (L2). There was no correct answer and the objective was to simply compare the user behavior between non-saltation (middle vibrator used) and saltation (middle vibrator not used). The details of the way the stimulations were prescribed are described in the next subsection.

A common coin-type vibrator was used (placed on the respective fingertips) and controlled in part by an Arduino board [2] (and interfaced indirectly to the smart phone experimental program through a PC). The vibration motor used in our experiment has the same specification as reported in [13]. It is controlled by a voltage input using a pulse width modulation signal with an amplitude between 0 to 5V, which in turn produces vibrations with frequency between 0 and 250 Hz and associated amplitudes between 0 to 2G (measured in acceleration, or 0 to 18μm in position) respectively. According to [6, 10, 13, 20], these values are well above the human's normal detection threshold (about 6 ~ 45db SL).

Our hypothesis was that there would be no statistically significant difference between the effects of non-saltation and saltation based stimulations. Our hypothesis was simply due to the observation that there was not much qualitative difference (to the brain) between holding a ruler (in the fashion as tested in [15]) to the usual gripping of mobile devices in terms of extending the internal body map to external objects.

Detailed Procedure

Ten paid subjects (5 men and 5 women) participated in the experiment with the mean age of 23.6. After collecting one's basic background information, the subject was briefed about the purpose of the experiment and instructions for the experimental task. A short training was given for the subject to get familiarized to the experimental process. None of the participants were aware of the saltation phenomenon. The subjects wore ear muffs to prevent any bias from the sounds of the vibration. The ear muff was tested such that no sound could be heard for any biased effect toward the experiment results.

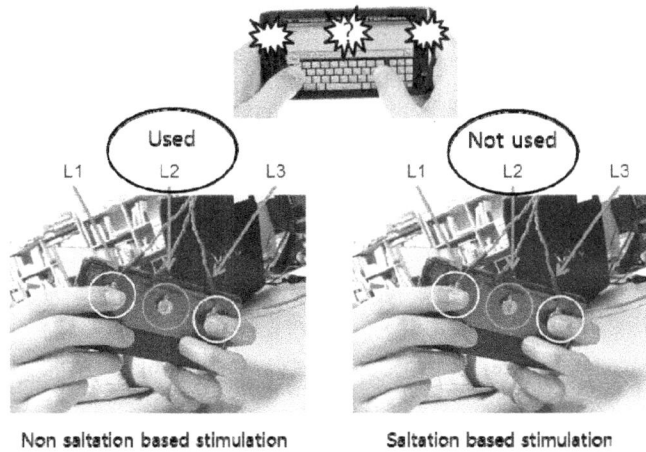

Figure 2. The experimental set up for Experiments I comparing the effects of non-saltation based stimulation to that of the saltation-based.

The non-saltation stimulation was given in the following way. For example, the first vibrator on the right end was activated (at location L1 at T1), followed by the one in the middle (at location L2 at T2) and then the left (at location L3 T3). The inter-stimulus intervals (ISI) were varied at six different levels (T1-T2: 800ms x T2-T3: 80, 100, 120, 150, 200, 300ms). The ISI's were chosen around values that were known to be successful in inducing saltation from the previous literatures [8, 15, 17, 18].

The stimulation was given in two directions, half starting from the right and vice versa. The saltation-based stimulation was given in a similar way except that the second stimulations were given at location L1 (or L3 when given from right to left). An example is illustrated in Table 1.

	Non-saltation			Saltation		
	L1	L2	L3	L1	L2	L3
T1 @ 0ms	P1			P1		
T2 @ 800ms		P2		P2		
T3 @ 880ms			P3			P3

Table 1: An example of right (L1) to left (L3) stimulation pattern example with T1-T2 = 800ms and T2-T3 = 80ms for non-saltation based and saltation based stimulations

During the actual sessions, each subject made a total of 96 trials for about 50 minutes (2 types of feedback x two directions x 6 different ISI's x 4 repetitions). Different types of stimulations were given in a balanced order and each stimulus was apart by a 10 second break. The subjects were asked to indicate by yes or no whether a sensation was felt at or near L2.

Results

The main purpose of our work was to validate that there was no significant perceptual difference between saltation/funneling driven phantom sensation and actual sensation. Thus we only applied ANOVA rather than signal detection theoretic (SDT) analysis. We felt the SDT to be more proper to derive things like "Just Noticeable Difference" and amplitude perception, whereas ANOVA, more convenient yet still valid in comparing effects of these two types of stimulations (across different stimulation intervals).

Figure 3 shows the comparative user behavior between the cases of non-saltation and saltation across the six different ISI's. While there was a trend of generally weaker response for saltation, ANOVA had revealed no statistically significant differences across all ISI's. Note that even the non-saltation based stimulation would be difficult to produce a 100% "appearance" response (e.g. always feeling for the sensation from the middle when the middle vibrator is activated) because the stimulation is still indirect (without direct touch to the middle vibrator at L2). In effect, the subjects were not able to distinguish between the case when the middle vibrator was used and when a phantom sensation was elicited without the use of the middle vibrator.

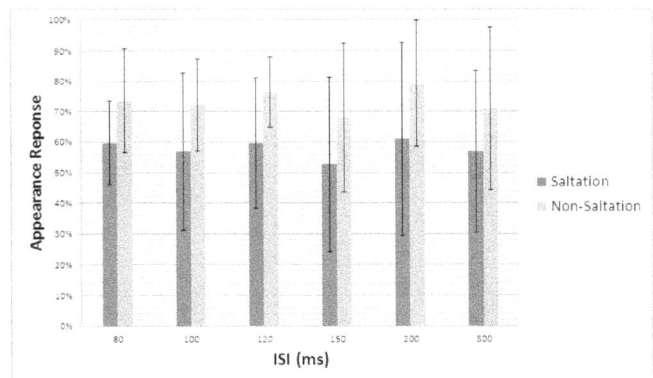

Figure 3. Comparative user behavior to non-saltation and saltation based stimulations across different ISI's. No statistically significant differences were found between the two for all ISI's

EXPERIMENT II:

EXPENDING OUT OF THE BODY SALTATION TO 2D

Experimental Design and Set up

For the second experiment, we used five vibrators attached in the four rear corners (where the fingers would be touching in a normal two handed grip) and middle of the mobile device (see Figure 4). Three types of stimulations were tested with the objective to induce indirect sensation

69

emanated from 2D display/device space: (1) "nominal" in which only one vibrator (in our case, the middle one) was used, (2) "funneling" in which simultaneous vibrations were generated from four corner vibrators with interpolated amplitudes and (3) "saltation" in which timed vibrations were generated from four corner vibrators.

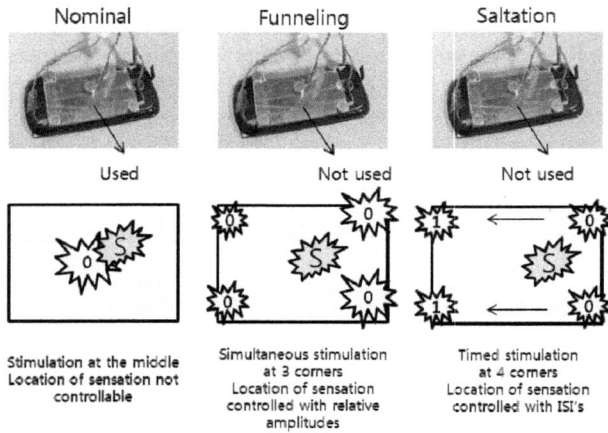

Figure 4. The experimental set up for Experiments II comparing the effects of nominal, funneling and saltation based stimulations in 2D.
Numbers indicate the timing order of the stimulation and "S" indicates the sensed location by the user.

The experiment was designed as a psychophysical one in the form of a 2 alternative forced choice (2AFC). The stimulations were given in one of the three types (either to elicit real (with nominal) or phantom (with funneling or saltation) sensations. The display space was divided into 15 (5 x 3) grid sections[1], and the subject was to make a response to the stimulation in the following way (see Figure 5). After experiencing a stimulus, two markings appeared at two grid locations. One was at the "intended target location of the real or phantom sensation" (hence abbreviated as "ITL"), and the other at a location away from the first one. The user was to tap on the display to make one's response, selecting which location marker was felt closer to the sensed location. For the sake of the argument, assuming that a correct answer means choosing the marking that coincides with the ITL, the subject has 50% (a baseline performance in a 1AFC experiment [9, 14]) of getting the "correct" answer. Note that in actuality, there is no notion of "correctness" because none of the three stimulation types guarantee fine control of the real/phantom sensation locations. Instead, we use the term "pseudo-correct" answers to reflect this aspect. The details of the way the stimulations were prescribed are described in the next subsection. Otherwise, the same vibrator and system set up was used as in Experiment I.

<hr>

[1] In the actual experiment, the display was divided into 60 grid regions (10 x 6), but every 2 x 2 region was treated as the same region (in the analysis) resulting in effectively a 5 x 3 grid. This was because most subjects complained the initial resolution was set too high.

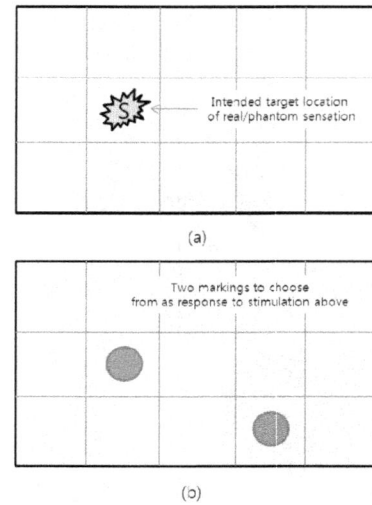

Figure 5. Making a response to a stimulus. (a) A stimulation is given with an intended target location (ITL) for phantom sensation (indicated with "S"). (b) Then the user is presented with two markings in the 5 x 3 grid and is to choose between the two. One marking coincides with the "S" location (pseudo-correct answer) and the other reasonable deviated from it.

Detailed Procedure

Ten paid subjects (5 men and 5 women) participated in the experiment with the mean age of 24.5. After collecting one's basic background information, the subject was briefed about the purpose of the experiment and instructions for the experimental task. A short training was given for the subject to get familiarized to the experimental process. None of the participants were aware of the saltation phenomenon. The subjects wore ear muffs to prevent any bias from the sounds of the vibration.

The "nominal" stimulation was given by activating the middle vibrator. The intention was to elicit sensations from a 2D position with only one vibrator similarly to how current hand-held devices operate. Obviously, it is quite expected that it would be difficult to control the location of the phantom sensation in 2D space with only one fixed vibrator.

The "funneling" stimulation was given by activating 4 vibrators simultaneously with linearly interpolated amplitudes according to the intended target location of phantom sensation. Because the display space was divided as a 5 x 3 grid, there were mainly two cases of stimulus prescription. When the ITL was on the boundary (12 regions except for B2, C2 and D2 in Figure 6), only two vibrators in the corresponding row or column was used. For instance in Figure 6, for D1, the top two vibrators were used and their amplitudes interpolated linearly in 1D. As for the three remaining regions, all four vibrators were used as shown in Figure 6 (b). The vibration amplitudes of the right/left set of vibrators are determined as was just explained, but since these locations are vertically in the middle, the amplitudes were mirrored in the vertical dimension. Each stimulation lasted for 80msec. The previous studies have used durations of 40~50ms, however, we have adjusted this value based on user feedback from pilot tests.

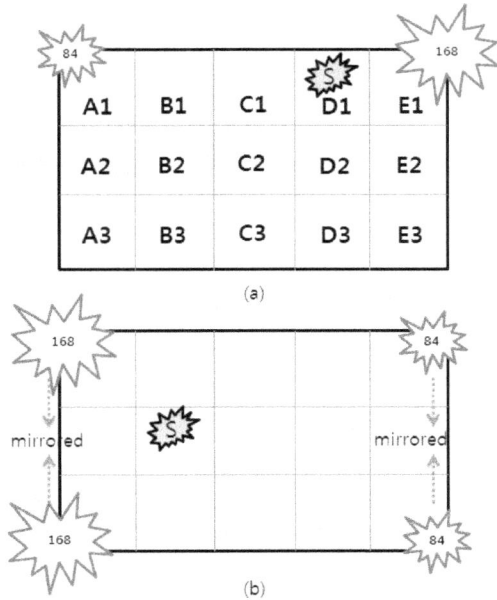

Figure 6. Funneling stimulations for the 5x3 grid display. (a) When the intended target location (ITL) is on the boundary, only two vibrators are used with interpolated amplitudes. (b) For locations B2, C2, and D2, all four are used.

Intended Target Location of Phantom Sensation (ITL)	Stimulation method
A1, A3, E1, E3 (Four corners)	Only two vibrators used. Stimulations given from the other direction with T1-T2 fixed and T2-T3 = 50ms
B1, D1, B3, D3	Only two vibrators used. Stimulations given from the other direction with T1-T2 fixed and T2-T3 = 65ms
C1, C3, A3, E2	Four vibrators used. Stimulations given from the other direction with T1-T2 fixed and T2-T3 = 50ms
B2, D2	Four vibrators used. Stimulations given from the other direction with T1-T2 fixed and T2-T3 = 65ms
C2 (Middle)	Four vibrators used. Stimulations given from the either direction with T1-T2 fixed and T2-T3 = 80ms

Table 2: Methods of stimulation for saltation case.

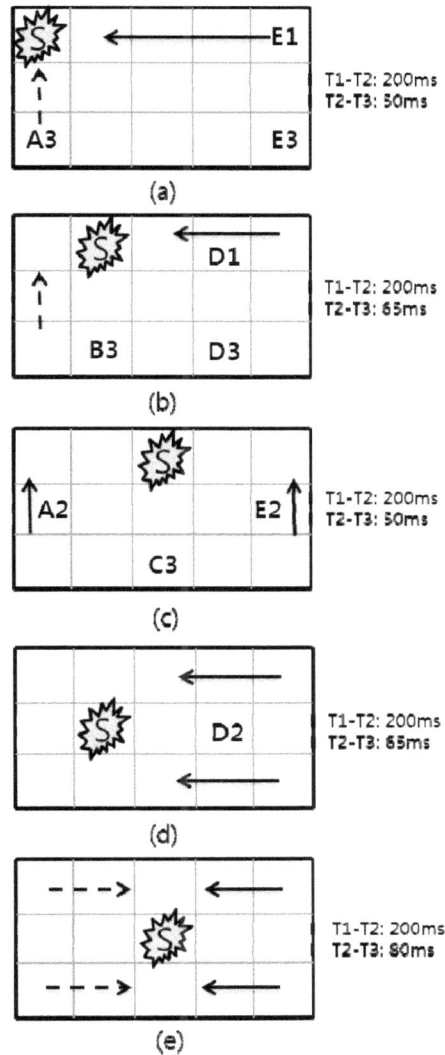

Figure 7: Five main cases of saltation based stimulation for eliciting sensations on the 2D space. Sensation locations were categorized in 5 groups according to the stimulation methods: (a) A1, A3, E1, E3 (four corners), (b) B1, B3, D1, D3, (c) C1, C3, A2, E2, (d) B2, D2, (e) C2 (middle). Arrows indicate direction of stimulation. Dashed arrows are alternative stimulation direction.

Similarly for saltation, different ISI's and vibration patterns were used to create ITL at the 15 grid positions as summarized in Table 2 and illustrated with examples in Figure 7. For instance to elicit a sensation in the corner (e.g. upper left corner, A1), the timed stimulation was given from the other direction (upper right corner) toward the upper left (A1) with T2-T3 set to 50ms. Only two vibrators were used as the corner is on the boundary of the display. 50ms is about the lower bound for a person to feel any saltation effect [8, 15, 18]. Thus for extreme corner positions (like A1), the T2-T3 ISI was set at this value (Figure 7 (a)). Note that the stimulation could be alternatively given in the bottom to top direction (and symmetrically for the other three corner cases, indicated with the dashed arrow).

Let's take another example. For location B2, four vibrators were used since it was located in the middle row. The vibration started from the right (because B2 was slightly to the left) and went toward the left direction. Since B2 was not all the way to the left, the T2-T3 ISI was set to 65ms (Figure 7 (d)).

Result

As was in the Experiment I, ANOVA was applied for analyzing the results. Figure 8 shows the statistics for the existence of the out of the body saltation effect in 2D. Namely, the graph illustrates that for the nominal condition, the pseudo-correct performance was about the 50% chance level. This is an expected result as only one vibrator is used to induce feelings for 15 different locations. Near chance performance is expected at most locations except for where the vibrator is actually located (middle, C2). As for funneling and saltation, over 75% pseudo correct responses (with collective statistically significant difference, $p < 0.000$ and $p < 0.000$ respectively) were obtained indicating a distinct psychophysically sensed event [9,14]. In other words, subjects were, to some degree, able to sense phantom sensation as modulated by the respective (funneling and saltation) methods used in this experiment.

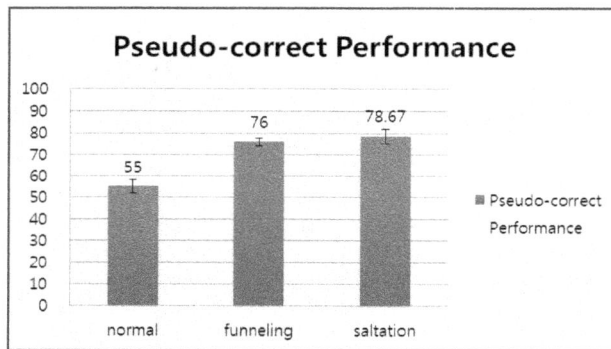

Figure 8: Subject's performance of making pseudo-correct responses from all regions. The nominal condition shows close to 50% performance whereas for funneling and saltation about 75~80% performance was obtained

When analyzed in more detail with regards to the 15 individual regions, most regions followed the trend of the whole, that is, showing a distinct and better (~75~80% correct rate) performance with funneling and saltation. Figure 9 shows two examples of such results from the region A1 and B2.

However, as for regions in the middle (C1, C2, and C3), there were no statistically significant differences found among the three conditions (Figure 10). In addition, all

three conditions showed over 75% performances (more or less). This is in line with our expectation that because the lone vibrator used for the nominal condition was located in the middle, the sensation was naturally felt from there (or near there). Thus, this is a positive result in the sense that the funneling and saltation exhibited non-differential behavior from this natural "nominal" sensation. If this statistics is subtracted from the whole, the figures of the overall performance would further improve (Figure 11).

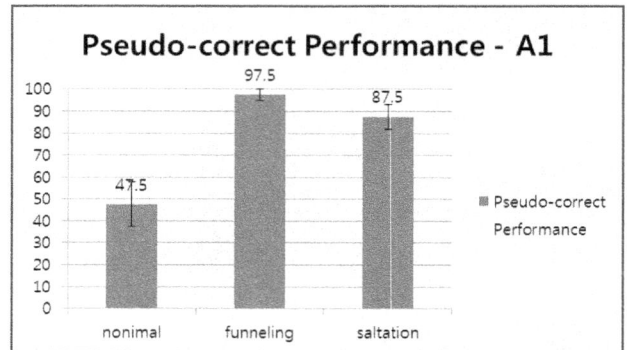

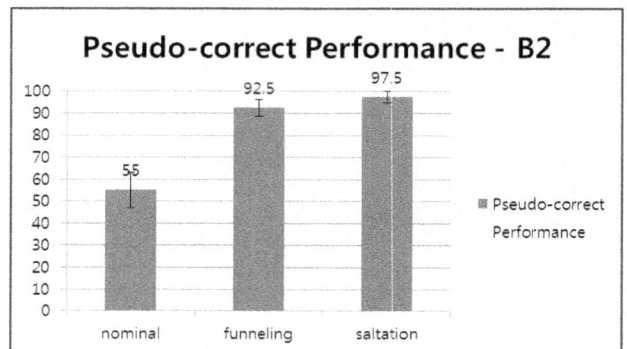

Figure 9: Subject's performances of making pseudo-correct responses from region A1 and B2. The nominal condition shows close to 50% performance whereas for funneling and saltation, over 75~80% performance is shown.

However, as for regions in the middle (C1, C2, and C3), there were no statistically significant differences found among the three conditions (Figure 10). In addition, all three conditions showed over 75% performances (more or less). This is in line with our expectation that because the lone vibrator used for the nominal condition was located in the middle, the sensation was naturally felt from there (or near there). Thus, this is a positive result in the sense that the funneling and saltation exhibited non-differential behavior from this natural "nominal" sensation. If this statistics is subtracted from the whole, the figures of the overall performance would further improve (Figure 11).

The analysis is muddled in the sense that 75% came out by adding all the figures in Figure 10, however this is at best an ad-hoc interpretation. Nevertheless it is still true there was a marked difference in performance between when the middle region is considered and not, because of the location of the middle vibrator for the nominal condition.

DISCUSSION AND CONCLUSION

In this paper, we presented two experiments in which the out of the body saltation effect was verified to exist with actual hand-held media devices and furthermore, was shown for the first time that it could be extended to 2D. Funneling, another perceptual illusion technique was also equally exhibited similar 2D "out of the body" effect. In our experiment, the extent of the controllable resolution for the phantom sensations were about 5x3 or 5x2 for 3.5 inch sized 2D display.

To be useful in practical applications, more research is needed in finding the way to more precisely modulate the location of the phantom sensation and testing with real world applications and more number of subjects. We also expect the phantom tactile sensations be even more effective when combined with other modalities.

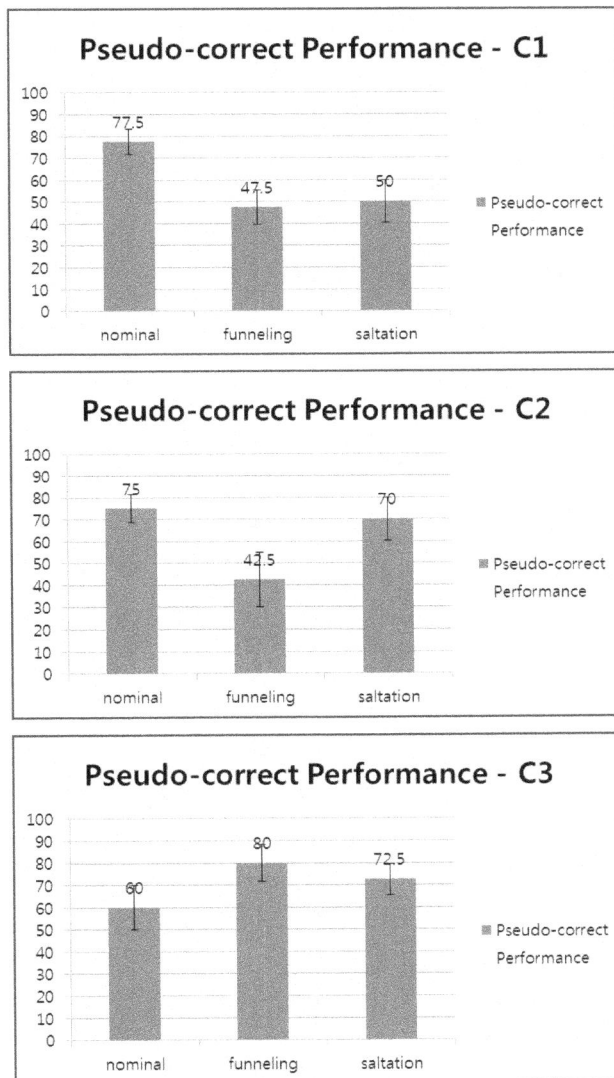

Figure 10: Subject's performance of making pseudo-correct responses from region C (C1, C2 and C3). No statistically significant differences are exhibited from funneling or saltation condition.

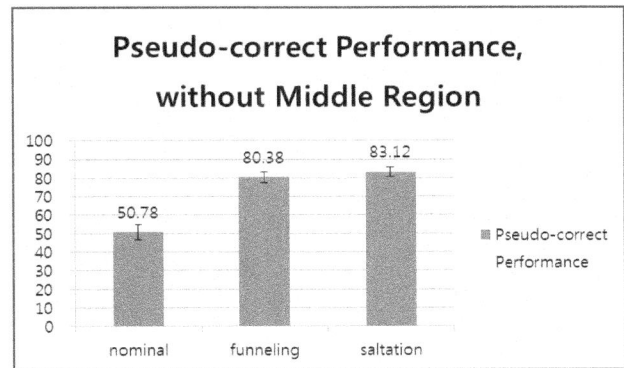

Figure 11: Subject's performance of making pseudo-correct responses from all regions without the statistics from the middle region. The nominal condition shows close to 50% performance whereas for funneling and saltation about 80~85% performance is shown.

ACKNOWEDGEMENTS

This research was supported in part by the Strategic Technology Lab. Program (Multimodal Entertainment Platform area) of MKE/KIAT and the National Research Foundation of Korea(NRF) grant funded by the Korea government (MEST) (No. 2011-0030079).

REFERENCES

1. Alles, D.S. Information transmission by phantom sensations. *IEEE Transactions on Man-Machine Systems*, (1970), 11(1), 85–91.

2. Arduino. http://www.arduino.cc/

3. Barghout, A., Kammerl, J., Jongeun, C., Steinbach, E., and El Saddik, A. Spatial resolution of vibrotactile perception on the human forearm when exploiting funneling illusion. In *Proc. IEEE International Workshop on HAVE*, (2009), 19-23.

4. Bekesy, G.V. Funneling in the nervous system and its role in loudness and sensation intensity on the skin. *The Journal of the Acoustical Society of America*, (1958), 30(5), 399–412.

5. Bouncing Ball on Nokia N900. http://bit.ly/x2-bouncingball

6. Burdea, G., and Coiffet, P. Virtual Reality Technology (2nd Ed.), (2003).

7. Cholewiak, R.W., and A.A. Collins, The generation of vibrotactile patterns on a linear array: Influences of body site, time, and presentation mode. *Attention, Perception, & Psychophysics*, (2000), 62 (6). pp. 1220-1235.

8. Geldard, F.A., and Sherrick, C.E. The cutaneous rabbit: a perceptual illusion. *Science*, (1978), 178, 178-179.

9. Geshelder, G. Psychophysics: The Fundamentals. Lawrence Erlbaum Associates, (1997).

10. Gunther, E., Davenport, G., and O'Modhrain, S. Cutaneous grooves: composing for the sense of touch. In *Proc. NIME*, (2002), 57-82.

11. Hoggan, E., Brewster, S., and Anwer, S. Mobile multi-actuator tactile displays. In *Proc. HAID*, (2007), 22-33.

12. Israr, A., and Poupyrev, I. Control space of apparent haptic motion. *IEEE World Haptics Conference*, (2011).

13. Jung, J., and Choi, S. Perceived magnitude and power consumption of vibration feedback in mobile devices. In *Proc. HCII*, (2007), 354-363.

14. Kingdom, F., and Prins, N. Psychophysics: A Practical Introduction, Elsevier-Academic Press, (2010).

15. Miyazaki, M., Hirashima, M., and Nozaki D. The "Cutaneous Rabbit" hopping out of the body. *The Journal of Neuroscience*, (2010), 30(5), 1856-1860.

16. Mizukami, Y., and Sawada, H., Tactile information transmission by apparent movement phenomenon using shape-memory alloy device. *International Journal on Disability and Human Development*, (2006), 5(3), 277–284.

17. Rahal, L., Cha, J., Kammerl, J., El Saddik, A., and Steinbach, E. Investigating the influence of temporal intensity changes on the apparent movement Phenomenon. *Proc. Int. VECIMS*, (2009), 310-313. Raisamo, J., Raisamo, R., and Surakka, V. Evaluating the effect of temporal parameters for vibrotactile saltatory patterns. In *Proc. ICMI-MLMI*, (2009), 317-326.

18. Richter, H., Hang, A., and Blaha, B. The Phantom station: Towards funneling remote tactile feedback on interactive surfaces. In *Proc. AH*, (2011).

19. Seo, J., and S. Choi. Initial study for creating linearly moving vibrotactile sensation on mobile device. In Proc. *IEEE Haptics Symposium*, (2010), 67-70.

20. Sherrick, Carl E. A scale for rate of tactual vibration. *Journal of the Acoustic Society of America*, (1985), 178-83.

21. Tan, H.Z., and Pentland, A. Tactual displays for wearable computing. In *Proc. IEEE ISWC*, (1997), 84-89.

22. Verrillo, R.T., and Gescheilder, G.G. Perception via the sense of touch. In Summers, I.R. (ed.) Tactile Aids for the Hearing Impaired, Wiley Publishers (1992), 1-36

The Groovepad:
Ergonomic Integration of Isotonic and Elastic Input for Efficient Control of Complementary Subtasks

Alexander Kulik [1]   André Kunert [1]   Anke Huckauf [2]   Bernd Froehlich [1]

[1]Bauhaus-Universität Weimar
[1]<first name>.<last name>@uni-weimar.de

[2]Universität Ulm
[2]anke.huckauf @uni-ulm.de

ABSTRACT

The Groovepad is an input device that uses the physical frame of a regular touchpad as an elastic force sensor to permit additional rate-control input. The two independent input sensors can be used separately, but facilitate frequent and fluent switching between position-controlled and rate-controlled interaction techniques.

We studied the usability of the Groovepad in pointing, panning, and dragging tasks. Our observations indicate that the use of the two input sensors for the same functionality (e.g., cursor control) can result in a decision dilemma, which adversely affects performance. As an alternative, we propose to use both sensors for complementary subtasks. For example, we performed workspace panning with the elastic frame of the Groovepad, while cursor motion was operated with the touchpad. This particular mapping possesses the compelling property that the frame of the touchpad serves as a tactile reference of the visual workspace. A user study revealed that our approach was preferred and performed significantly better than techniques that only used touchpad input.

Author Keywords

Pointing; workspace panning; position control; rate control; hybrid pointing.

ACM Classification Keywords

H.5.2. [Information Interfaces and Presentation]: User Interfaces; Input Devices and Strategies.

Introduction

Touchpads are a viable alternative to the mouse for many users. Similar to the latter, the isotonic input devices are typically operated with well-known position control, but they offer a much smaller form factor. Position control has a number of advantages over rate control for a variety of tasks. For example, position control is well suited for direct pointing, and it is easier to learn. However, rate control is ideal for smooth motions across larger distances.

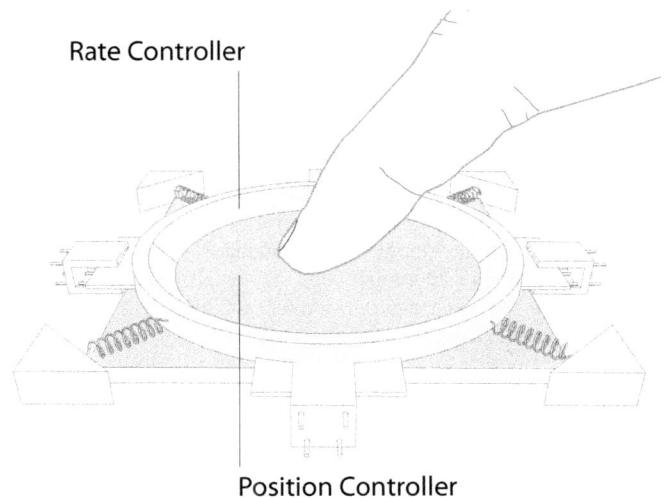

Figure 1. The center area of the Groovepad input sensor consists of a regular touchpad for position-controlled input. The elastic ring suspended around the touchpad is used for elastic rate control.

The Groovepad offers the ergonomic integration of a touchpad with the functionality of an elastic joystick, and permits users to easily switch between the two inputs, or even use both in a single coordinated action (Figure 1). The device consists of an elastic force sensor that surrounds a circular surface area for isotonic touch input. The first Groovepad prototype was used in a one-handed 3D controller [14]. In this paper we present a significantly improved desktop prototype, which provides more accurate and responsive input. We anticipated that users could benefit from the ergonomically arranged isotonic and elastic sensor combination in the context of a 2D desktop workspace.

Casiez et al. [4] used a force-feedback stylus to substantiate advantages of combined position control and rate control in the facilitation of cursor motion over large distances. They coined the term hybrid pointing for this cursor control method. As a result of their experiments, Casiez et al. proposed a touchpad extension very similar to the design of the Groovepad, however, they never presented a suitable hardware implementation. Therefore, a performance study of such a device has not been undertaken before.

We compared the usability of the Groovepad to basic touchpad functionality in common pointing, panning, and dragging tasks, which are generally available in a 2D workspace. Efficient pointer acceleration was applied in the touchpad condition to ensure a comparison under realistic conditions. The results of our studies contribute the following interesting insights on the usability of input devices that combine position control with rate control:

1. Hybrid pointing does not offer offer higher performance benefits than using only position control with appropriately adjusted pointer acceleration.

2. Performance is likely to decrease when employing two input channels for the same task as users have to continuously decide on which one to use.

3. The use of both input channels to control complementary subtasks provides performance benefits and is very compelling for the users.

These results are based on our advanced Groovepad prototype that works smoothly and responsively, as is expected from today's user interfaces. Accuracy is provided by the use of a high resolution touchpad in combination with the optically measured displacement of the touchpad frame. The key to the Groovepad's responsiveness is the embedding of a touch sensor in the elastic input sensor, which resets itself to the neutral position when it is not in use. This feature prevents the need of any thresholds for the rate-controlled manipulation.

Related Work

In 1987, Card et al. [2] compared step keys and continuous motion input devices for text selection. Although the mouse performed better than the rate-controlled isometric joystick, both continuous devices still allowed for more efficient interaction than keystroke input. Later studies expanded the knowledge on the usability of various input devices for 2D pointing tasks (e.g. [6, 8, 10, 16]). Common observations from the various studies are that isotonic devices such as touchscreens, tablets and mice perform best and that position control is superior to rate control.

These observations conflict with an in depth analysis of 3D tasks carried out by Shumin Zhai [18]. Zhai proved that position control used with isotonic devices and rate control used with isometric or elastic devices can result in similar performance. He discovered that the main difference between the two conditions is that rate control requires more training time. The question thus arises, as to why rate control never reaches position control performance in studies on 2D pointing tasks. In some cases, subjects might not have trained enough to achieve the best performance with rate control, but at least [2] and [8] reported that they ensured sufficient training.

In addition to visual feedback, position control provides proprioceptive cues, which are not available for rate control. This advantage was not visible in the results of Zhai et al. [18]. However, for a similar 6-DOF docking task, Kunert et al. [15] found that position control used with isotonic devices leads to a better performance than elastic rate control, if the distances to be covered do not exceed the available manipulation range of the human hand-arm system. In the case of larger distances, position control forces users to clutch. Kunert et al. observed that in this case, rate control may catch up with position control performance.

Casiez et al. [4] and Hinckley et al. [12] reported similar observations. Hinckley et al. compared the two input techniques in the context of a text scrolling task. The isotonic mouse wheel used with position control resulted in shorter task completion times for short distances, and the isometric joystick used with rate control resulted in shorter task completion times for long distances. In terms of Fitts' Law [9], these outcomes reveal that the regression line of pointing performance with rate control generally has a larger intercept (a) but also a lower slope (b) compared to position controlled input. Hinckley et al. further demonstrated that non-linear acceleration techniques - like those employed for the mouse pointer in most operating systems - have the potential to stretch the range of distance, which can be covered efficiently with position control.

Andersen [1] argued that the scrolling rate, instead of the next document position is the relevant factor to efficiently scan a document, if the target position is not known beforehand. For such situations, Andersen found a linear relationship between target distance and task completion time. Therefore, rate control may be more suitable for this kind of visual exploration.

In summary, rate control appears to be the best method when covering large distances, especially during visual scanning tasks. Position control on the other hand works better for short motion input. Users may benefit from these different characteristics, if the interface offers both modalities in a sensible combination. A good example of such a hybrid interface is the "Bubble" technique developed by Dominjon et al. [7]. The "Bubble" technique uses a force-feedback device to simulate isotonic position control in the center of the device's workspace and elastic rate control towards the boundaries. This interface for 3D manipulation is an efficient alternative to clutching with a bulky device in a large virtual interaction space.

Casiez et al. [4] used a similar system based on a force feedback stylus to show benefits of hybrid motion input to master large distance pointing in 2D workspaces. From their observations, Casiez et al. derived models for distant pointing with two input strategies. The first strategy involved frequent clutching as required with low-gain position control, and the second strategy combined input of rate and position control. As a result of their findings, Casiez et al. suggested the RubberEdge input device. Similar to the Groovepad, RubberEdge consists of an elastic circular frame surrounding a touch-sensitive area, but it is applied as a purely mechanical overlay for conventional touchpads.

The idea that an unfinished movement can be continued with rate control when the position control input reaches the physical borders of the tracking range has been adapted to other applications. Cirio et al. [5] suggested the Magic Barrier Tape to combine rate controlled navigation with physical locomotion through virtual environments. Tsandilas et al. [17] explored the idea to extend the range of distant pointing with rate control when the user reaches the physical limits of their limb's mobility. Tsandilas et al. revealed the benefits of this combination under the condition of low input resolution that would, otherwise, not provide sufficient accuracy.

The Groovepad

The Groovepad is an input device that consists of two separate sensors each providing two degrees of freedom: a touchpad and an elastically suspended ring surrounding the touch-sensitive area. Due to the isotonic nature of the touchpad it should be used with position-control techniques while the elastic ring affords rate control [18]. Our design enables rapid switching between both input modalities and facilitates the assignment of subtasks to the most appropriate controller.

Using two separate controllers has the advantage that each sensor has the appropriate resolution. Using just the boundary area of the touchpad for rate control input as with EdgeMotion™ or GlideExtend™ the resolution is limited and haptic feedback for switching between the two modes cannot be provided. Adding only haptic feedback as suggested with the RubberEdge design [4] is also insufficient. During the development of our device we found that responsive and accurate tracking of the user's elastic input cannot be granted when relying solely on the fingertip's position on the touchpad.

The first prototype of the Groovepad device was used for a one-handed 3D controller called TWO-4-SIX [14]. We developed the sensor combination to support the user's thumb with more than the common two degrees of freedom of a joystick. The touchpad was used to operate view orientation in a virtual world, while the elastic ring was used for rate-controlled viewpoint motion. Both tasks could thus be controlled by one finger without causing interferences between both inputs. The prototype (Figure 2) presented in this paper is desktop based and operated with the index finger. It consists of a partially covered touchpad (Cirque TSM9925) with a resolution of $40\frac{counts}{mm}$. The remaining circular input area has a diameter of $35\,mm$. The surrounding mask is elastically suspended and allows a deviation of $\pm 3mm$ at a maximum input force of $1.5\,N$. Its displacement is measured by optical position sensors. An optical mask, moving between a luminance

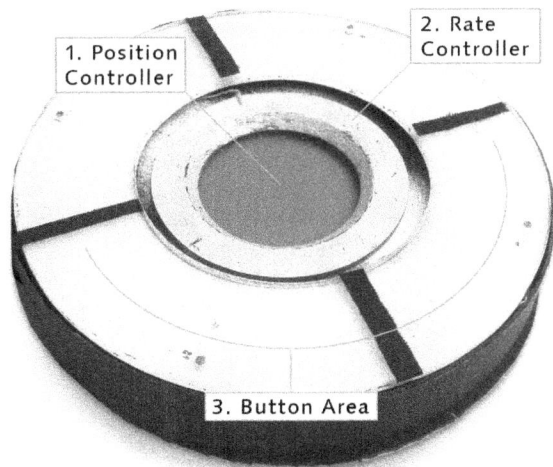

Figure 2. The Groovepad desktop prototype: The center area consists of a regular touchpad for position-controlled input. The elastically suspended ring around the touchpad is used for rate control.

pended and allows a deviation of $\pm 3mm$ at a maximum input force of $1.5\,N$. Its displacement is measured by optical position sensors. An optical mask, moving between a luminance sensor (e.g., photo resistor) and a light source (LED), causes luminance differences reported by the more or less obscured sensor. We achieve a resolution of $160\frac{counts}{mm}$.

The elastic input sensor cannot return to a precise zero position due to the partially plastic deformation of the springs. Thus, without any thresholding, the reported input values would cause drifting of rate-controlled objects. We use a touch sensor connected to the ring, which informs us if the ring is actually touched or not. Hinckley and Sinclair [13] reported the idea of such implicit user input already in 1999. Here we use this approach to avoid drifting without reducing the input range as it would happen with a simple threshold. This implicit resetting of the device and its use without any threshold creates a very sensitive and direct input device.

Hybrid Pointing

Casiez et al. [4] concluded that a hybrid pointing device offering isotonic position control and elastic rate control simultaneously can be beneficial. Their results demonstrate clear advantages if position control requires excessive clutching to reach distant targets. They also observed that for short target distances as they occur during the closed-loop phases of a pointing action, position control is preferable – even if that involves a few clutching actions. Although the tests had been performed with a bulky force-feedback device only, they suggested the application of hybrid pointing to touchpads.

Due to many differences, it was unclear whether their results can be extrapolated to the suggested application. With target distances of up to 688 mm and low C/D gains their test setup was deliberately designed to demand frequent clutching. Such large pointing distances do not occur with laptop computers, where touchpads are incorporated. Also, the force-feedback device used in their experiments involves more friction and inertia, which makes clutching particularly difficult. The most important difference to the envisioned touchpad application was that users could not choose the most appropriate input method for each situation as the input device did not allow for clutching in the hybrid input condition. Finally, they applied a one-dimensional pointing task in their experiments which facilitated continuous activity planning on a level that cannot be realized during common computer usage.

Pointer acceleration is another technique that facilitates rapid cursor motion over large distances with a minimum of clutching actions while maintaining or even improving accuracy [3]. During informal tests we felt that this well-established technique has the potential to improve pointing performance with a touchpad comparably well, as hybrid pointing does. We observed in the latter case that cognitive operations may impede the input performance. Having two options at hand to solve the same task requires frequent decision-making.

Towards a better understanding of these issues we performed two formal user studies comparing hybrid pointing with the Groovepad to regular touchpad functionality with fine-tuned pointer acceleration. Firstly, we analyzed the benefits and drawbacks of adding rate-control to the touchpad without further adaptations of the isotonic input device. The results revealed that such a secondary input option is rather disadvantageous. As a consequence we tuned the characteristics of both transfer functions for position control and rate control in order to increase their complementarity. While we observed that these adaptations improved the usability of hybrid pointing, our results demonstrate that hybrid pointing still cannot compete with pointer acceleration in the context of touchpad input. Below is a detailed analysis of both studies.

Experiment I

Both pointing techniques were tested with the same hardware as well as with the same C/D gain functions. In a pilot study with three participants, the gain functions were optimized for position control and rate control individually. Position input always used smooth pointer acceleration with a high slope. The transfer function was combined from a power function to improve accuracy of slow motion input and a logarithmic function confining the C/D gain to a maximum level of 22. It was possible to cover the whole screen width with one single stroke on the touchpad, while pointing at targets of one single pixel was still achievable. For rate control we used a sine function that was parameterized to map zero input force to its minimum (corresponding to zero pointer velocity) and the maximum deviation of the elastic ring to its maximum (corresponding to a pointer velocity of $0.5\frac{m}{s}$).

Users were seated about 80 cm in front of a 30" LCD screen with the input device within a comfortable range for their hands. They were encouraged to interact as fast as possible, as the test had been organized as a competition. Nevertheless, each target had to be selected accurately before moving on to the next trial. Selection errors were counted when users pressed a button or tapped an event when the mouse pointer was not accurately positioned above the target position.

After an introduction and a 5 minute training session, eight *repetitions* of 32 successive trials in one set were performed with both pointing *techniques* one after the other. After every *repetition* users were required to take a break. One *repetition* consisted of four *distances* (85 mm, 170 mm, 255 mm, 340 mm) between start and target in the eight cardinal directions. Other than the mouse pointer only the next target (a red circle with 10 mm in diameter) was visible on a light gray background. The sequence of input conditions was balanced between users.

We recorded task completion times, selection errors and the number of clutching operations. After completion of all 16 *repetitions*, a questionnaire was filled out by the participants asking them to rate both tested conditions on a five-point Likert scale (-2, -1, 0, +1, +2).

Participants

Six female and six male users aged between 19 and 30 years participated in this study. All were right handed and all had extensive experience with WIMP computer interfaces. Seven reported that they use touchpads regularly. Four among them had prior experience with rate controlled pointer interfaces like the isotonic joystick found on some notebook computers.

Hypotheses

Based on our literature review and informal observations we had two opposing hypotheses:

H1: Since the *Groovepad* condition only offers rate control as an additional option, the performance in both conditions should not differ greatly, except for large distances where users can benefit from continuous rate control.

H2: The choice of two redundant input channels in the *Groovepad* condition increases cognitive load that becomes apparent in longer tasks completion times independent of the factor *distance*.

Results

Data was collapsed and entered into a 2 (*devices*) × 4 (*distances*) × 8 (*repetitions*) analysis of variance with Bonferroni adjustment of alpha for pairwise comparisons.

Regarding task completion times we found significant main effects for *technique* ($F_{(1,11)} = 13.252, p < .01$), *repetition* ($F_{(7,77)} = 5.514, p < .01$) and *distance* ($F_{(3,33)} = 110.254, p < .01$), as well as a significant interaction of *technique* with *repetition* ($F_{(7,77)} = 4.148, p = .001$).

Mean task completion times were significantly longer in the *Groovepad* condition (2.43 s, SE=0.96) than with the *touchpad* (2.00 s, SE=0.59). This time difference of nearly half a second remained almost constant over all *distance* conditions (Figure 3). Obviously, our test users could not take advantage of rate control for large distances, so we must reject H1. Instead, user performance seems to suffer from the decision between both input options, as predicted by H2.

Generally, larger distances required longer acquisition times. Interestingly, no significant difference could be found between 170 and 255 mm (Figure 3). The difference between these two distances seems to be whether the ballistic phase results in an overshoot (for the shorter one) or an undershoot (for the larger one). In both cases the remaining distance for the final target acquisition was similar.

The effect of *repetitions* indicates a general effect of learning the task, but with respect to the interaction between *technique* and *repetition* this effect should be analyzed independently for both *techniques*. Post-hoc comparisons (Tuckey) confirm a significant learning effect only in the *Groovepad* condition between the first set of trials (Mean=2.77 s, SE=0.06) and all further *repetitions* (Mean=2.38 s, SE=0.17). In the *touchpad* condition task completion times remained almost constant over all repetitions (Mean=2.00 s, SE=0.11).

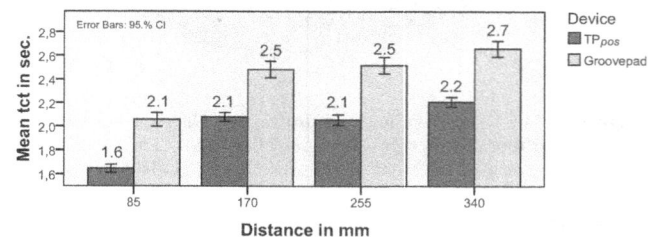

Figure 3. Mean task completion times in s for the hybrid pointing task.

Concerning the error rate we only found a significant main effect of *technique* ($F_{(1,11)} = 6.723$, $p < .05$). We observed that less selection errors occurred in the *Groovepad* condition (Mean=0.1, SE=0.02) as compared to pointing with the *touchpad* (Mean=0.15, SE=0.03). Apparently, the additional option of rate controlled motion input in the *Groovepad* condition influenced the users' interaction strategy. While operating slower with the *Groovepad* they achieved a higher pointing accuracy.

We analyzed the number of clutching operations during the tests and found significant main effects for the factors *technique* ($F_{(1,11)} = 18.520$, $p < .01$) and *distance* ($F_{(3,33)} = 70.920$, $p < .01$). Also, the interaction between both factors was significant ($F_{(3,33)} = 14.182$, $p < .01$). We observed that more clutching operations were required to master large distances and that the *Groovepad* required less clutching (Mean=2.4, SE=.133) than the *touchpad* (Mean=3.3 SE=.15). As indicated by the interaction effect, this difference between both *techniques* was more pronounced for larger distances. However, compared to the results of Casiez et al. [4] we observed a relatively low number of clutching operations in both conditions. The users' subjective ratings reflect our quantitative results. The Groovepad received a mean score of 0.67 (SE=0.19), and the touchpad of 1.08 (SE=0.26). Three users preferred the Groovepad, three evaluated both techniques as comparable, while four users preferred the regular touchpad.

Observations

Our results show advantages of the *Groovepad* in terms of pointing accuracy that are accompanied by largely decreased interaction rapidity. Therefore, additional input options as provided through hybrid pointing with the *Groovepad* is not necessarily beneficial. Demanding frequent decisions for one of both input options can even impede effective interaction. Our observations show that it is not always intuitively clear to the user which sensor to employ for the next action.

After undershooting the target, for example, one might make another step with the elastic controller or perform a clutch on the touchpad to finish the task. Clutching is generally the better alternative in this situation, since accurate pointing is difficult with the elastic ring. Overshooting and undershooting, which permanently occur during pointing tasks require frequent changes of motion direction during the closed loop phase. These small movements in varying directions cannot efficiently be mastered with the ring-shaped input device. Isotonic pointer control on the touchpad seems to be better suited for the final phase of acquiring a target.

Using the Groovepad with pointer acceleration that enables high C/D-gains, results in a similar dilemma also at the start of a pointing task. Users must decide whether to make a fast stroke on the touchpad or use the elastic ring for coarse target approximation during the ballistic phase.

Improving Hybrid Pointing

We tried to improve the Groovepad's performance by addressing these issues. Both input channels of the Groovepad were tuned in correspondence to different pointing subtasks. For coarse error reduction during the ballistic phase the rate

control function now enabled higher acceleration, so that pushing against the elastic ring of the Groovepad felt more like throwing the cursor. This increased acceleration came at the expense of accuracy. For improved accuracy during the closed-loop phase, the input gain for position control was decreased, but still maintained a moderate acceleration.

Experiment II

We conducted a follow-up study with these adapted transfer functions for the *Groovepad* condition. The transfer function for the *touchpad* remained the same. Other parameters of the pointing experiment were adapted as follows:

We introduced three different target *diameters* as a factor, since we expected benefits of the improved accuracy of position control in the *Groovepad* condition to become visible only for small targets. With each *repetition* of the 32 different trials the target *diameter* changed from 10 mm to 5 mm and then to 2 mm. This procedure was repeated three times in this order.

For the best possible exploitation of the hybrid pointing benefits, our participants were instructed to use the elastic ring for coarse target approximation only and perform the final pointing with the touchpad. Three test *sessions* on three consecutive days ensured sufficient training for proficient interaction with both input conditions.

Participants

Three female and seven male users aged between 23 and 32 years participated in this second study. All but one were right handed and all of them had extensive experience with WIMP computer interfaces. Four of them reported to use touchpads regularly. Three of them had prior experience with rate controlled pointing interfaces.

Hypothesis

We expected that the adaptations to the transfer functions would improve the performance of hybrid pointing. Our explicit instructions on how to use rate rate control for coarse approximation and position control for the final phase of target acquisition was meant to further eliminate the decision problem. From the reduced C/D gain for position control we expected additional benefits for the acquisition of small targets. Therefore, we adapted our Hypothesis H1 from the first experiment as follows:

H3: While both input *techniques* will perform on a comparable level for large targets, hybrid pointing allows for more accurate input and thus results in shorter task completion times and less errors for the acquisition of small targets.

Results

Data was collapsed and entered into a 2 (*techniques*) × 4 (*distances*) × 3 (*diameters*) × 3 (*sessions*) analysis of variance with Bonferroni adjustment of alpha for pairwise comparisons.

We found significant main effects of all factors on task completion times. *Diameter* had the largest effect ($F_{(2,18)} = 332.554$, $p < .01$), followed by *distance* ($F_{(3,27)} = 165.105$,

$p < .01$), and *session* ($F_{(2,18)} = 37.542$, $p < .01$). The difference between both tested *techniques* was also significant ($F_{(1,9)} = 8.091$, $p < .05$).

Each smaller target diameter resulted in longer task completion times ($p < .01$). Larger distances also required more time to be covered. As in the previous study we could not find a significant difference between both intermediate distances (Figure 4). Our test users achieved significantly shorter task completion times with each of the performed sessions ($p < .05$). Interactions of *session* with *diameter* ($F_{(4,36)} = 5.632$, $p < .01$) and also *distance* ($F_{(6,54)} = 3.789$, $p < .01$) indicate that learning was slightly stronger for higher indexes of difficulty.

Despite improved performance in the *Groovepad* condition with adapted transfer functions (Mean=2,71 s, SE=0.09), touchpad interaction was still significantly faster (Mean=2.55 s, SE=0.08). Interaction with distance ($F_{(3,27)} = 4.988$, $p < .01$) indicates, that the dependency of performance and distance is slightly different for both *techniques*, but a post-hoc test (Tuckey) revealed, that the competitive edge for the touchpad remains significant for all distances (all $p < .05$). Therefore, we must reject H3. With respect to the interaction effect of *technique* with *diameter* ($F_{(2,18)} = 11.516$, $p < .01$), we performed a post-hoc analysis (Tuckey). We found significant difference between both *techniques* for all ($p < .05$), except the smallest target *diameter* of 2 mm (Figure 5).

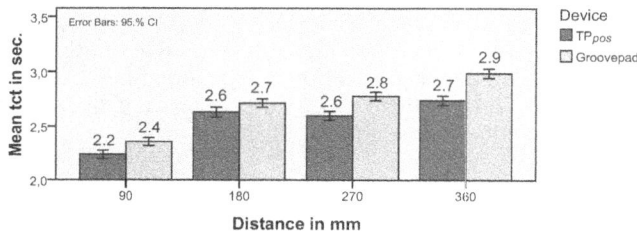

Figure 4. Mean task completion times in s for the hybrid pointing task, sorted by distance.

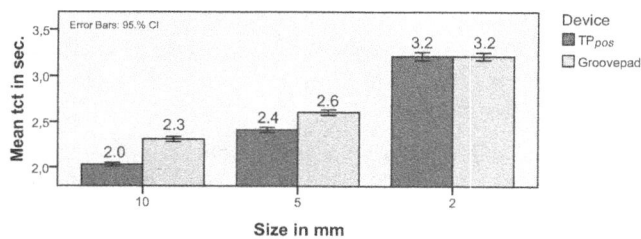

Figure 5. Mean task completion times in s for the hybrid pointing task, sorted by size

Selection errors in this second experiment were more balanced between the *touchpad* (Mean=0.144, SE=0.029) and the *Groovepad* condition (Mean=0.126, SE=0.027). We obtained a significant main effect for *session* ($F_{(2,18)} = 5.369$, $p < .05$). Training over subsequent days enabled users to slightly reduce selection errors from 0.170 (SE=0.033) to 0.114 (SE=0.026). *Diameter* had a stronger effect on the error

rate ($F_{(2,18)} = 23.874$, $p < .01$). We recorded mean selection errors of 0.089 for 10 mm target diameter (SE=0.023), 0.106 for 5 mm target diameter (SE=0.022) and 0.210 for 2 mm target diameter (SE=0.038).

The MANOVA on selection errors also revealed a significant interaction between *technique* and *size* ($F_{(2,18)} = 5.883$, $p < .05$). Post-hoc comparisons (Tuckey) between *techniques* in all three *size* conditions reveal significantly improved accuracy for the *Groovepad* but only for the targets of 2 mm in diameter ($p < .05$). While the error rate of the *touchpad* increased to a mean of 0.236 (SE=0.045) for the smallest target size in our tests, we recorded a mean error rate of 0.165 (SE=0.026) for the *Groovepad*. In all other manifestations of *size* the difference between error rates was only marginal.

Also the number of clutches was more balanced between both devices in our second experiment. An effect of *technique* on the number of clutching operations could not be found, but we obtained significant effects of *size* ($F_{(2,18)} = 20.696$, $p < .01$) and *distance* ($F_{(3,27)} = 74.399$, $p < .01$). Smaller target sizes as well as larger distances (all $p < .01$) resulted in an increased number of clutching operations. Similar to tasks completion times the difference between both intermediate distances 170 mm (Mean=3.422, SE=0.242) and 255 mm (Mean=3.583, SE=0.256) was negligible.

The user feedback clearly tended toward the *Groovepad* in this second study. Apparently, users liked the frequent alternation between both input modalities. The *Groovepad* received a mean score of 0.6 (SE=0.27), and the touchpad of 0.2 (SE=0.33). Six users preferred the Groovepad, two evaluated both techniques as comparable, and two users preferred the regular touchpad.

Discussion

The results of the first experiment revealed substantial disadvantages for hybrid pointing. We believe that the additional time required for completing the tasks evolved from the frequent demand to decide for one of both motion control methods. Bearing in mind, the *Groovepad* condition only offered an additional input option, without any adaptation to the basic touchpad functionality.

The results of the second experiment show that our adaptations to the transfer functions of position control and rate control in the *Groovepad* condition improved the performance of hybrid pointing. Nevertheless, regular touchpad input remains to be more effective - although the disadvantage could be reduced from about 18% to approximately 6%. In all conditions, we observed a nearly constant disadvantage of 158 ms for the *Groovepad* condition. Only when acquiring the smallest involved targets did both methods perform on a comparable level.

With data from pointing at four different target distances and three different target sizes, we analyzed Fitts' Law regression fitness for the pointing performance of both input *techniques*. Unlike Casiez et al. [4] we found a robust match for both tested devices to Fitts' Law (Touchpad: $a = 0.25$, $b = 0.42$, $r^2 = .875$, Groovepad: $a = 0.59$, $b = 0.38$, $r^2 = 0.96$).

The shallower slope of the Groovepad indicates that hybrid pointing may indeed outperform pointer acceleration at some point. However, based on our data we could expect this only at ID's of 9 and larger. With a common target width of 10 mm this corresponds to a target distance of 5.5 m (while seated less than 1 m in front of the screen). We conclude that hybrid pointing is rarely useful in common application scenarios for touchpads. The availability of two input options to perform the same operation caused additional cognitive load in our studies. Consequently, we suggest to use such ergonomically arranged input channels as provided by the Groovepad for complementary tasks.

Complementary Input

The elastic frame of the Groovepad can be regarded as a tangible correspondence to the window frames of a graphical user interface. Following this metaphor, it affords panning operations in active windows. Force induced against the physical border moves the view across the workspace.

In current user interfaces panning is often controlled with software tools like the hand metaphor to grab and move the workspace with the mouse pointer. An obvious disadvantage of this concept is that the mouse pointer cannot be used for anything else while panning is performed. This fact provokes additional mode changes to allow for long distance dragging and area selection across the whole workspace. Toggling between cursor control and workspace panning is generally achieved by pressing modifier keys or based on the number of involved fingers in the case of multi-touch input.

Many user interfaces also offer implicit panning techniques. If only one window is active, panning can be triggered automatically when the mouse pointer reaches the border of this window. In the simplest case, the position-controlled pointer is used to push the graphical window frame in the desired direction, which results in inverse motion of the workspace. However, more popular is to activate automatic workspace motion in reverse direction when the pointer reaches the window frame. Some implementations allow adjustment of the motion rate by the distance of the cursor to the application window.

While other techniques offer more versatility, these implicit panning techniques are arguably most efficient if only one window is active. Thus, we compared these two basic touchpad panning techniques, employing position-controlled panning or alternatively rate-controlled panning to our new device that offers an additional input sensor for workspace panning.

Experimental Setup

We used the same physical setup as in the studies on hybrid pointing. The task involved scanning a graphical workspace for a circular item, selecting it and then dragging it to a target position. Searching the item and subsequently the target position required panning.

On the left hand side of the screen a circular application window of 32 cm in diameter, surrounded with a semi-transparent border of 3 cm was displayed. The pointer was displayed

within this window. Regular pointer interaction was limited to the application window. The background showed abstract graphics, that allowed to visually perceive workspace panning motion without the graphics being recognizable as anything in particular (Figure 6).

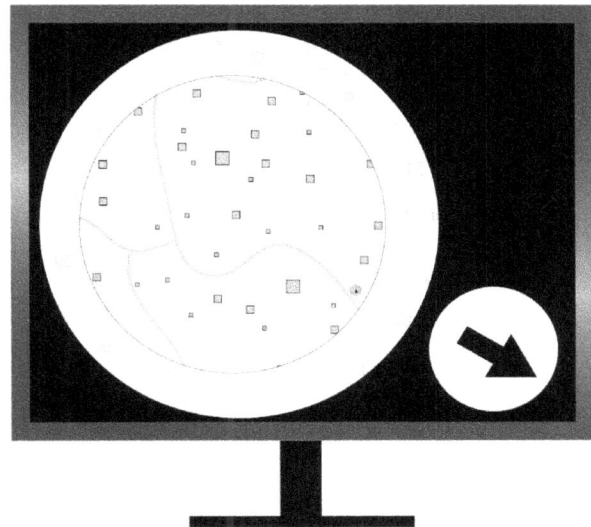

Figure 6. The panning test setup.

Dragging items were visualized as circular red icons of 10 mm diameter. Target areas for docking the dragged icons were of the same shape, but colored in blue. Dragging items were only visible when in range. In the lower right corner of the screen an arrow pointed toward the next item to be picked up for dragging or the next target area respectively. Due to the arrow, users knew in which direction they had to search, but did not know the distance to find the next target. Users could only find targets by scanning the graphics in the circular application window while moving accordingly to the indicated direction. This meant performing a visual search task which resembles a common situation of users interacting with geographical maps or known graphic documents.

In rectangular application windows, techniques employing the window border to control panning only allow for motion in eight major directions: along the vertical and horizontal axis as well as along both diagonals of the window. However, tasks like navigation on geographical maps and image editing require not only movement along the cardinal axes. The Groovepad offers panning control in arbitrary directions. In order to compare our new device to common panning techniques, we decided to use a circular window, which ensured that all techniques were tested under comparable conditions.

We compared three panning techniques. With the touchpad using position control for panning (TP_{pos}), users had to push the pointer against the border of the application window to move the workspace. Using rate control with the touchpad (TP_{rate}), the pointer was enabled to move inside the window's semi-transparent border, and panning velocity was controlled by the penetration depth. A line, drawn from the boundary of the window to the current pointer position, visualized the velocity (Figure 7). With the Groovepad, panning was unaffected by pointer input since its elastic rate controller was used for this subtask.

All three input techniques were tested with the same hardware device. Position input always used the same pointer acceleration as applied for the *touchpad* condition during the hybrid pointing study. Rate control, used the same parameterized sine function as in the first experiment on hybrid pointing. The range was based either on the maximal displacement of the elastic ring or the extent of the semi-transparent border. Dragging operations had to be performed with the button on the device kept pressed by the thumb.

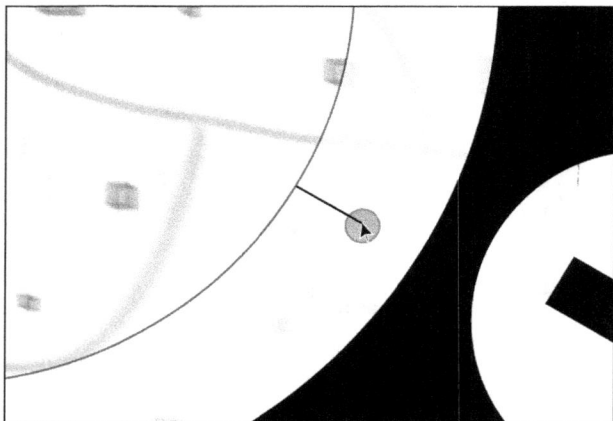

Figure 7. Graphical interface for rate-controlled panning with touchpad input.

Design and Procedure

Users participated in an initial training session of five minutes to accommodate to the actual interface condition before starting a test session. Thereafter, five *repetitions* of 12 trials were performed. Each set of trials began with the presentation of a starting point (red circular icon) in the center of the application window. Once selected, it disappeared and the counter for task completion time started. The users had to find dragging items and move them to specified target locations. Only the next dragging item or target location was displayed on the workspace. 12 trials of picking one item (referred to as pointing) and dragging it to the target position (referred to as dragging) were performed within one set. Displaying the average completion times for pointing and dragging created a break between *repetitions*. Each *repetition* consisted of two distances between start and target location (60 cm and 120 cm) in six directions (according to an equilateral triangle). The sequence of directions and *distances* was randomized.

After performing five *repetitions* of trials, users took a break of 15 minutes and then continued with the next interaction technique. The sequence of *techniques* was fully balanced between subjects. After the trials the participants were given a questionnaire to fill in. It consisted of items assessing previous experiences with GUI's and touchpads, and items evaluating each *technique* on a five-point Likert scale.

Participants

Seven female and eleven male users aged between 22 and 32 years participated in this study. Two were left handed and one claimed to be ambidextrous. All but three had extensive experience with WIMP computer interfaces. All users reported to have used touchpads, five of them regularly. Nine of them had prior experience with rate-controlled pointer interfaces.

Results

Since pointing and dragging might be differently affected by the interaction technique at issue, we distinguished between both subtasks. Pointing was calculated from the first movement of the cursor until the red icon was selected, and dragging time was counted from taking that object until the task was finished. Data was collapsed and entered into a 2 (*subtasks*) × 3 (*techniques*) × 2 (*distances*) × 5 (*repetitions*) analysis of variance with Bonferroni adjustment of alpha for pairwise comparisons.

We found significant main effects on task completion times for all involved factors: subtask ($F_{(1,17)} = 939.431$, $p < .01$), technique ($F_{(2,34)} = 36.723$, $p < .01$), repetition ($F_{(4,68)} = 27.399$, $p < .01$), and distance ($F_{(1,17)} = 411.320$, $p < .01$).

All techniques differed significantly (all $p < .01$) from each other (Figure 8). The *Groovepad* condition performed best (Mean=5.37 s, SE=0.14), closely followed by TP_{pos} (Mean=5.91 s, SE=0.13). The popular technique to control a panning rate with the isotonic controller at the window border (TP_{rate}) produced the worst results (Mean=6.99 s, SE=0.25). *Distance* and *subtask* produced main effects, in that larger distances and the more difficult *dragging* task resulted in longer task completion times. Both factors also interacted significantly with *technique* ($F_{(2,34)} = 3.679$, $p = .036$). Figure 8 and 9 illustrate that for the more difficult panning subtasks as well as for short distances, the performance difference between TP_{pos} and the *Groovepad* becomes negligible. A post-hoc test (Tuckey), reveals significant differences between all *techniques* ($p < .05$), except TP_{pos} and panning with the *Groovepad* in these two cases.

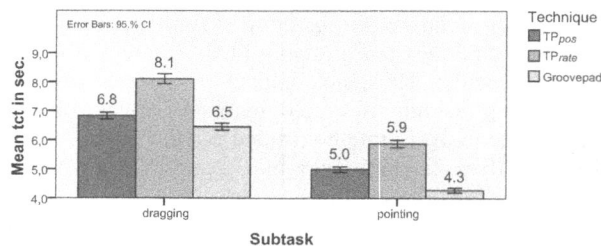

Figure 8. Mean task completion times in s for the three techniques the panning experiment, sorted by subtask

Rate control does not require clutching to cover large distances. However, it has been shown that employing rate control with an isotonic device, as in the TP_{rate} condition of our test, results in a significantly higher number of clutches than using elastic rate control [11]. Similarly, we observed that users tend to interrupt their actions when losing control.

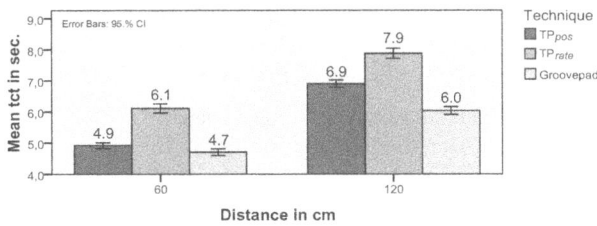

Figure 9. Mean task completion times in s for the three techniques the panning experiment, sorted by distance

Figure 10 shows sections of representative velocity-time diagrams of the panning operations and pointer movements for the different conditions in the panning study. It clearly shows that the position-controlled panning with the touchpad results in short motion bursts of the pointer and the workspace, which are interrupted by clutching operations. Using the touchpad with rate-controlled panning results in fewer clutching operations, however, the panning velocity seems difficult to control. The Groovepad enables smooth and continuous panning motion and requires only a little cursor motion at the end of the task.

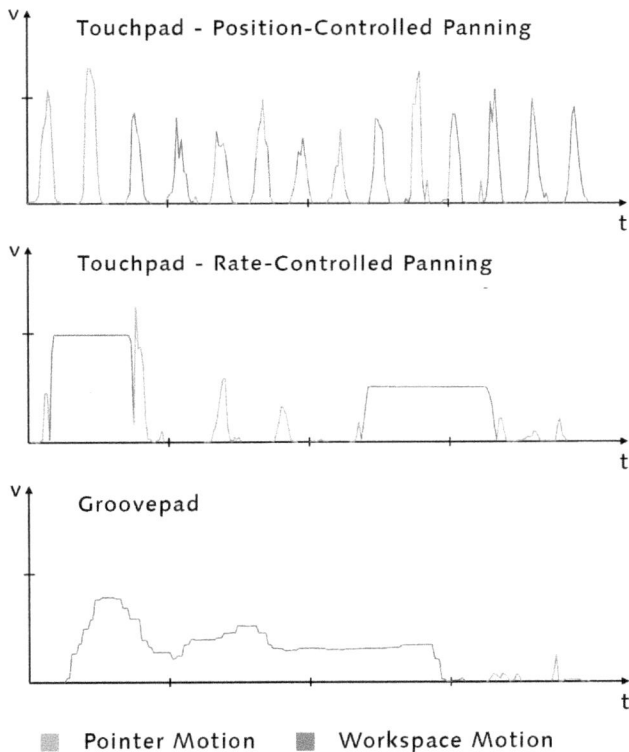

Figure 10. Motion diagrams for the different conditions

Similar to task completion times, the number of clutches is affected by the *subtask* ($F_{(1,17)} = 235.205$ as well as by *distance* ($F_{(1,17)} = 249.632$, $p < .01$). The further the target is away and the more difficult the subtask is, the more clutches occur during operations. *Technique* also reveals a significant

main effect ($F_{(2,34)} = 200.126$, $p < .01$). All techniques differ significantly ($p < .01$) from each other. The mean number of clutching operations is 12.66 for TP_{pos} (SE=0.497), 10.76 for TP_{rate} (SE=0.537), and 4.07 for the Groovepad (SE=0.16).

Furthermore we found significant interaction effects of *technique* with *distance* ($F_{(2,34)} = 181.599$, $p < .01$) as well as with *repetition* ($F_{(8,136)} = 5.764$, $p < .01$). As expected, the number of clutching operations depends on the distance. A large difference was observed for the touchpad, using position-controlled panning (60 cm: 10.04 (SE=0.384), 120 cm: 15.278 (SE=0.63))

Users strongly preferred the Groovepad with 1.61 (SE=0.14) over the regular touchpad using rate-controlled panning(-0.06, SE=0.17) or position-controlled panning (-0.17, SE=0.22).

Taken together, the results provide evidence that panning performance over large distances is superior when using the Groovepad instead of touchpads with software interfaces for panning. For tasks requiring pointing or dragging while moving the window, the Groovepad offers an appreciable improvement over regular touchpad input.

Discussion

We found that isotonic position control and elastic rate control may perform comparably well for pointing and dragging in a compound task involving panning, whereas touchpad-based isotonic rate control is hard to control and results in a much lower performance. This reflects the findings of Zhai [18]. Paradoxically, many applications offer rate control instead of position control for pointer-actuated workspace panning during dragging operations for tasks such as text selection across window boundaries.

We also found a strong user preference for rate control if supported with adequate elastic feedback. Most users complained about jerky movements caused by position-controlled input. This is especially disturbing if it affects motion of the whole surrounding workspace. Employing a proper input device for rate-controlled panning operations seems to be the most sensible choice if frequent workspace navigation is necessary.

Conclusions and Future Work

The primary idea of the Groovepad is to surround touch-sensitive input areas operated with position control with an elastic rate controller. This allows the user to quickly switch between position control and rate control. We showed that this can be very efficient for tasks requiring complementary input, e.g., pointing with the touchpad and panning with the elastic ring. Hybrid pointing on the other hand seems to increase cognitive load as the users must continuously choose between both controllers. This is the case even if both input channels are tuned to serve a particular subtask of pointing. Consequentially, we conclude that it is better to employ the two sensors for different tasks, which are related to each other.

We are convinced that the Groovepad is a worthy extension to the current touchpad. It allows users to quickly switch back and forth between position-controlled and rate-controlled input whenever it is beneficial. In particular, the increasingly popular zoomable user interfaces are a promising application domain for the Groovepad, since they require pointing, panning, and zooming as inherent operations. Pointing and panning is directly supported by the Groovepad, and smooth circular gestures along the Groovepad ring can be used to specify the zoom factor.

Besides augmenting touchpads with rate-control input, touchscreens are another application area for this idea. In particular, small touch devices such as mobile phones, music players, or PDAs can benefit from this idea, since the limited screen space often enforces panning operations.

Acknowledgments
This work was supported by the German Federal Ministry of Education and Research (BMBF) under grant 03IP704 (project Intelligentes Lernen). We thank the participants of our studies and the members and students of the Virtual Reality Systems group at Bauhaus-Universität Weimar (http://www.uni-weimar.de/medien/vr) for their support.

REFERENCES
1. Andersen, T. H. A simple movement time model for scrolling. In *Proc. CHI 2005*, ACM Press (2005), 1180–1183.

2. Card, S. K., English, W. K., and Burr, B. J. Evaluation of mouse, rate-controlled isometric joystick, step keys, and text keys, for text selection on a crt. *Human-computer interaction: a multidisciplinary approach* (1987), 386–392.

3. Casiez, G., Vogel, D., Balakrishnan, R., and Cockburn, A. The impact of control-display gain on user performance in pointing tasks. *Human-Computer Interaction 23*, 3 (2008), 215–250.

4. Casiez, G., Vogel, D., Pan, Q., and Chaillou, C. Rubberedge: reducing clutching by combining position and rate control with elastic feedback. In *Proc. UIST 2007*, ACM Press (New York, NY, USA, 2007), 129–138.

5. Cirio, G., Marchal, M., Regia-Corte, T., and Lécuyer, A. The magic barrier tape: a novel metaphor for infinite navigation in virtual worlds with a restricted walking workspace. In *Proc. VRST 2009*, ACM Press (2009), 155–162.

6. Cohen, O., Meyer, S., and Nilsen, E. Studying the movement of high-tech rodentia: pointing and dragging. In *Proc. CHI 1993*, ACM Press (1993), 135–136.

7. Dominjon, L., Lecuyer, A., Burkhardt, J.-M., Andrade-Barroso, G., and Richir, S. The "bubble" technique: interacting with large virtual environments using haptic devices with limited workspace. In *Proc. Eurohaptics 2005*, IEEE (2005), 639–640.

8. Douglas, S. A., Kirkpatrick, A. E., and MacKenzie, I. S. Testing pointing device performance and user assessment with the iso 9241, part 9 standard. In *Proc. CHI 1999*, ACM Press (1999), 215–222.

9. Fitts, P. The information capacity of the human motor system in controlling the amplitude of movement. In *Journal of Experimental Psychology 47* (1954), 381–391.

10. Gillan, D. J., Holden, K., Adam, S., Rudisill, M., and Magee, L. How does fitts' law fit pointing and dragging? In *Proc. CHI 1990*, ACM Press (1990), 227–234.

11. Hachet, M., and Kulik, A. Elastic control for navigation tasks on pen-based handheld computers. In *Proc. 3DUI 2008*, IEEE (2008), 91–96.

12. Hinckley, K., Cutrell, E., Bathiche, S., and Muss, T. Quantitative analysis of scrolling techniques. In *Proc CHI 2002*, ACM Press (2002), 65–72.

13. Hinckley, K., and Sinclair, M. Touch-sensing input devices. In *Proc. CHI 1999*, ACM Press (1999), 223–230.

14. Kulik, A., Blach, R., and Fröhlich, B. "two-4-six" - a handheld device for 3d-presentations. In *Proc. 3DUI 2006*, IEEE (2006), 167–170.

15. Kunert, A., Kulik, A., Huckauf, A., and Fröhlich, B. A comparision of tracking- and controller-based input for complex bimanual interaction in virtual environments. In *Proc. IPT-EGVE 2007* (2007), 43–52.

16. MacKenzie, I. S., Sellen, A., and Buxton, W. A. S. A comparison of input devices in element pointing and dragging tasks. In *Proc. CHI 1991*, ACM Press (1991), 161–166.

17. Tsandilas, T., Dubois, E., and Raynal, M. Free-space pointing with constrained hand movements. In *Ext. Abstracts CHI 2010*, ACM Press (2010), 3451–3456.

18. Zhai, S. User performance in relation to 3d input device design. *SIGGRAPH Comput. Graph. 32*, 4 (1998), 50–54.

Pygmy: A Ring-shaped Robotic Device that Promotes the Presence of an Agent on Human Hand

Masa Ogata[1], Yuta Sugiura[2], Hirotaka Osawa[1], Michita Imai[1]

[1] Graduate School of Science and Technology,
Keio University,
3-14-1 Hiyoshi, Kohoku,
Yokohama, 223-8522 Japan
{ogata, osawa, michita}@ayu.ics.keio.ac.jp

[2] Graduate School of Media Design,
Keio University,
4-1-1 Hiyoshi, Kohoku,
Yokohama, 223-8526 Japan
y-sugiura@kmd.keio.ac.jp

ABSTRACT

The human hand is an appropriate part to attach an agent robot. Pygmy is an anthropomorphic device that produces a presence on a human hand by magnifying the finger expressions. This device is in trial to develop an interaction model of an agent on the hand. It is based on the concept of hand anthropomorphism and uses finger movements to create the anthropomorphic effect. Wearing the device is similar to having eyes and a mouth on the hand; the wearer's hand spontaneously expresses the agent's presence with the emotions conveyed by the eyes and mouth. Interactive manipulation by controllers and sensors make the hand look animated. We observed that the character animated with the device provided user collaboration and interaction as though there were a living thing on the user's hand. Further, the users play with the device by representing characters animated with Pygmy as their doubles.

Author Keywords

Device art; hand gesture; anthropomorphism; wearable robot; ubiquitous computing;

ACM Classification Keywords

H.5.m [Information Interfaces and Presentation]: Miscellaneous.

INTRODUCTION

Hands not only express emotions through gestures but have also been used in performance, communication, and art [1, 2] throughout human history. Shadow puppetry, sign language [3], and hand paintings [4] prove that human hands are highly expressive. In particular, a shadow puppet requires finger expression because the hand acts as the character. The human hand has the ability to act as a living thing. For example, anthropomorphism can be realized by hand postures and movements such as bipedal locomotion by two fingers on a desk and a fox by keeping the little

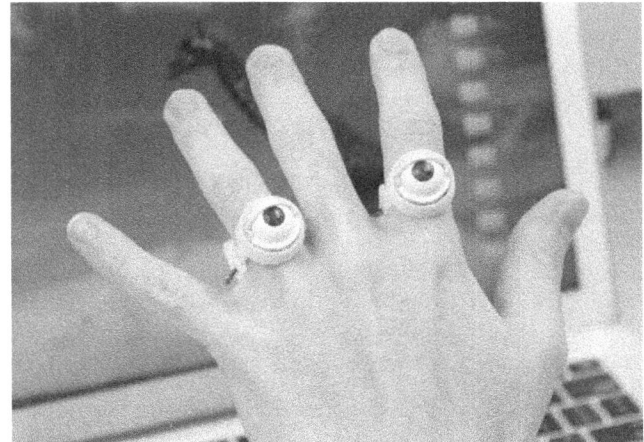

Figure 1. Pygmy worn on the hand

finger and the forefinger up with the other fingers close together. This could be because of the flexibility and reflexibility of the hand. This high flexibility of the human hand can be attributed to the fact that it has many joints. Reflexibility refers to the ability of the hand to reflect a human's intentions and to easily operate interface devices such as keyboards and touchpads.

We have simulated the characteristic of "finger expression" that can be enhanced by appending an anthropomorphic device that produces the presence of an agent robot on the human hand. We have invented Pygmy to function as an agent robot that possesses easy-to-wear features for performances, communication, and storytelling. It is a ring-shaped anthropomorphic device that complements hand gestures. Pygmy is a ring embedded with certain face parts such as the eyes and the mouth. A user can generate various facial expressions by configuring the devices worn on his fingers. The presence simulated by Pygmy is required to play a performance role to impress the audience and the user.

RELATED WORK

Research pertaining to wearable robots, interfaces the use of hand metaphors, and anthropomorphization have much in common. To begin with, in wearable robots, there are some agent and avatar robots. These include (a) the accessory-type robot [5], which is worn as a necklace to aprouse personal information and (b) the shoulder-mounted robot known as Telecommunicator [6], which provides the telepresence function as a wearable robot. These robots have a body and help reduce the physical distance involved in human–robot interactions. Pygmy is robotic, but it directly collaborates with the human body by exploiting human expressions and flexibility in a novel manner. Moreover, there is no skeleton required for the ordinal robots; the advantage of Pygmy is that it consists only of body parts without bones and motors to move itself. In this context, Parasitic Humanoid [7] shares the concept of a robot by using the human body as its skeleton.

Finger expressions are attractive because of their use in the entertainment industry. They also provide intuitive input methods for robot and CG characters. Whadget [8] makes it possible for users to control CG character motion on a tabletop computer by using only two fingers. This is achieved by mimicking bipedal walking. Walky [9] is a robot that can walk and play soccer on the basis of instructions given to it from a touchpad mobile device with a registered finger gesture. This is a finger-based interface method wherein fingers are considered to be a metaphor of human expressions. Pygmy also exploits finger postures and movements, but the finger behaves as an agent independently.

Trials are being conducted for anthropomorphizing day-to-day objects. DisplayRobot [10] is an attachable robotic device with minimal facial features. It works as an agent describing the object to which it is attached. Although the Pygmy's viewpoint of reconfiguring the device to build an agent system is similar to that of DisplayRobot, it focuses on enhancing the body performance by attaching devices on the human hand. Nikodama [11] is also an anthropomorphizing object; it has only two eyes. The fact that Pygmy is an interactive device manipulated by a controller or a sensor device and animates the human hand by using finger expressions makes it different from the other anthropomorphic devices.

DESIGN
We have designed Pygmy in the shape of a ring to make it a standalone device. Pygmy must be designed for several applications such as a wearable robot, a robot agent on a human hand, and an anthropomorphic device. To achieve this design, we follow the policy given below:

- **Flexibility.** Each finger remains in contact with the device when it is worn. We designed the device structure such that it does not interfere with the up-and-down finger movements. In addition, because each person's finger size is different, we have designed the ring such that it can be removed for size adjustments.

- **Reconfigurability.** The ring-shaped design makes it easy for users to wear the device and remove it from their

body quickly, and it enables the user to customize the device to generate various patterns of facial and animal expressions. Reconfigurability helps users simulate the agent in various forms with anthropomorphic parts.

- **Scalability.** To diversify the pattern, the device arrangement can be changed freely according to the finger posture. The device can be added dynamically by the user. It can also be extended using Bluetooth modules for wireless communication.

- **Human likeness.** This policy must be considered strongly because impressions made by an appearance of the robot device are crucial for simulating the user's feeling of the presence generated by the agent device. The eyes and mouth were chosen as the minimal parts forming the human face. Although we also considered the design of a realistic eyeball and a mouth, these features were only painted on the device to avoid giving it a weird appearance. The eyelids of the eye module were painted in light orange; the eyeballs were painted in two colors, black and white. The mouth was also painted in light orange, and the inside was red.

- **Safety.** We needed to design the device so that it could be used by children as well. Because of the need to attach the device to the body, we ensured that the microcontroller board and the battery were fixed inside a plastic case. The motor portion was connected with a vinyl lead so that it could not be touched and could not fall out of the device.

- **Responsiveness.** This is an important factor for interactions. The developed device guarantees fast response. We designed the entire system without a perceivable delay.

- **Miniaturization.** Miniaturization of the ring device is

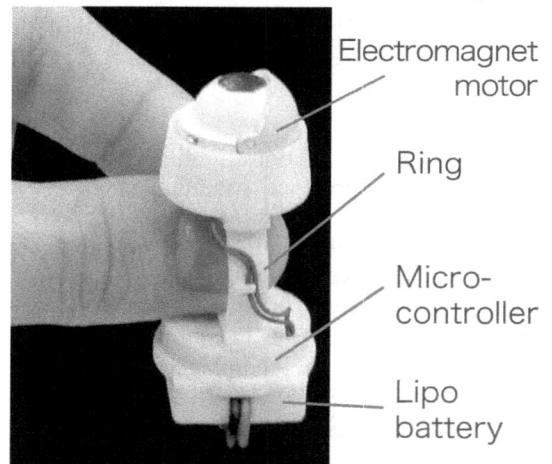

Figure 2. Device detail

indispensable for better implementation to achieve flexibility, reconfigurability, and human likeness. We designed a small microcontroller circuit and structure within the device. The size of the device is crucial for the quality of agent experience because the proportion of the device size to the human hand should be the same as that of the eye size to the face.

PYGMY

Pygmy consists of a ring-shaped anthropomorphic device that includes a face and mouth item, a ring-shaped sensor device, and a controller for the user to manipulate the ring device. The ring device and the controller are connected to a host computer with wireless transmission, via Bluetooth and XBee.

Miniature Implementation

Miniaturization was indispensable in designing Pygmy. The ring device consists of face parts simulated using a motor, microcontroller, and battery made from polycarbonate. A motor driver IC on the circuit board controls the motor in pulse-width modulation (PWM). The face parts can be moved at a great speed. We designed a circuit board to embed the small motor and battery within the device. The device is controlled by Bluetooth (Figure 2).

Ring device

A ring part is designed such that it can be separated from the ring device. The finger size is different for different people and depends on the finger position; hence, it is necessary that the ring be customized so that it fits on a finger. We prepared the ring part to be 14 mm to 20 mm by 1 mm (diameter).

Interaction with sensors and a controller

We developed a ring-shaped sensor containing an

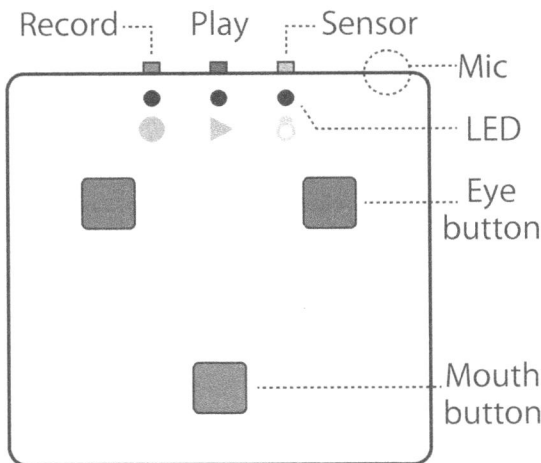

Figure 3. Controller

accelerometer so that its movements could be passed to the open level of the eye ring. In the same way, the microphone passes its volume level to the mouth ring. The user can control the face parts by moving the finger with the accelerometer or by talking to it. We built controller for

intuitive operations; this controller contained buttons that resembled the eyes and a mouth (Figure 3). Three buttons were arranged at the top of the controller for functions such as record, play, and input sensor change. By changing the input, we could select operations (from the controller) and inputs (from the sensor). Further, this controller can store the operation history generated by the first controller and by the sensor for 1 min.

USABILITY STUDY

In order to evaluate the device, we observed the spontaneous interactions between users. The subjects were divided in two-person pairs. All the ten subjects who participated in this study were computer science majors. Instructions were provided by controllers and sensors, and the motions were recorded. At the end of the experiment, the subjects completed a questionnaire.

We gave the subjects the following instructions after describing how to use the device and the controller.

1. Control the device with the controller

2. One subject manipulates the device on the other's hand

3. Use accelerometer and mic sensors

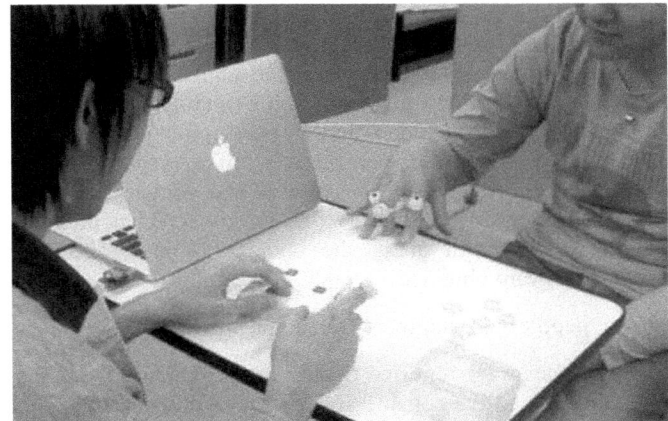

Figure 4. Usability study

4. Use record and play functions

5. Express animal and human motion by hand

6. Talk while moving the hand

7. Play freely

The subjects were also interviewed about the device's impression and their experience with the device (Figure 4). The questions in the questionnaire are shown in Table 1 and were evaluated using the 7-scale Likert scale method. Further, in this table, there are three columns that provide the mean, standard deviation, and positive response (written as "%," is a rate of who answered higher than the center value).

Question	Mean	SD	%
1. Ease of operation	4.4	6.3	100
2. Ease of motion generation	4.5	3.1	90
3. Ease of controller	6.4	0.66	100
4. Excitement because of the device working	6.1	0.94	100
5. Ease of expressing characters	4.3	1.79	70
6. Feeling as though the user's hand were another living thing	5.7	1.00	90
7. Ability of playing by changing finger postures	6.0	1.48	90
8. Feeling excited when you speak while synchronizing with the device motion	6.1	1.37	80

Table 1. Questionnaire on device operation.

RESULT

Usability

Items 1 to 3 in Table 1 represent the evaluation of the usability of the ring device and the controller. From the positive response and the mean value obtained through the evaluation, we concluded that Pygmy could provide user satisfaction from the perspectives of physical design, communication between the devices, and cooperation with the controller. Moreover, for the question "What did you think was difficult about the operation?" the following responses were obtained:

- 2 people said that there was no problem;

- 2 issues were reported regarding the preparation of the device and the considerable time taken for establishing the wireless communication with the host computer;

- 2 issues were reported regarding the delay of the device from controller operation;

- 1 issue regarding the lack of appropriate correspondence of the movement of the eye part to the up-and-down movement by the accelerometer was reported; and

- 1 issue was reported regarding the difficulty of deciding the direction of the hand when the user wore the device on his finger.

Character generation

Users enjoyed making faces and characters using their hands. We found that users could generate several expressions by attaching the device on the palm and the back of the hand. For example, they showed a face looking down by bending their entire hand forward. To show an angry or a troubled face, the degree of the eyelid was changed by turning the fingers wearing the face parts (Figure 5). Some users changed the arrangement of the face parts freely to display a human face or an animal. By interviewing the subjects, we were able to list the different types of gestures observed in the usability study (Figure 7). For one gesture, only the index finger was equipped with the mouth ring; the rest of the expressions were provided by the other fingers that did not have any rings on them (Figure 6).

Collaboration

It was observed that the users used facial expressions to query one another when they gestured in cooperation (Figure 5). While controlling face parts on the other person's fingers, the users coordinated the timing of pushing the button with the motion of the other person's fingers. The users were also instructed to speak along with the operation; we watched the users talk to the other person while controlling the device of that person.

Question	Mean	SD	%
1. Do you want to wear the wearable robot?	4.4	2.01	60
1'. The same question after the study.	4.6	1.62	80
2. Do you want wear the device if it is ring shaped?	4.8	1.47	50
2'. The same question after the study.	5.3	1.85	80
3. Do you feel that the wearing robot is an obstacle? (positive response value reversed)	5.4	1.2	20
3'. The same question after the study.	4.0	1.1	30

Table 2. Contrast of impression of the wearable robot.

User experience

Item 4 in Table 1 denotes the positive evaluation from all subjects about interactions carried out using the sensing device and the controller and the communication and play in a pair task when they used the ring device. Further, the users evaluated the experience positively based on factors such as

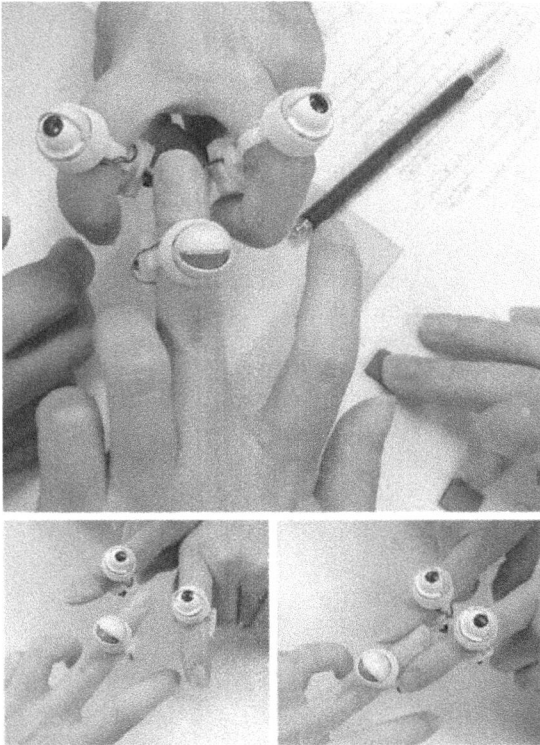

Figure 5. Collaboration and trial for making facial expressions

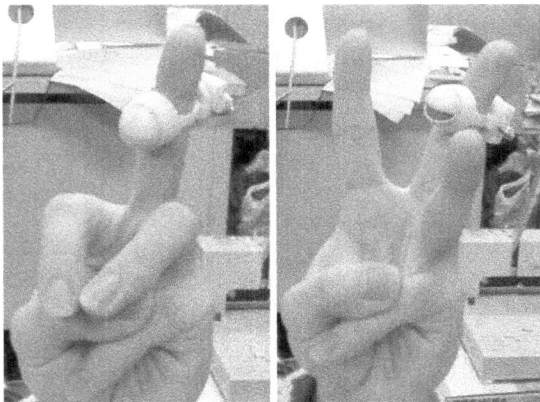

Figure 6. Human expressions

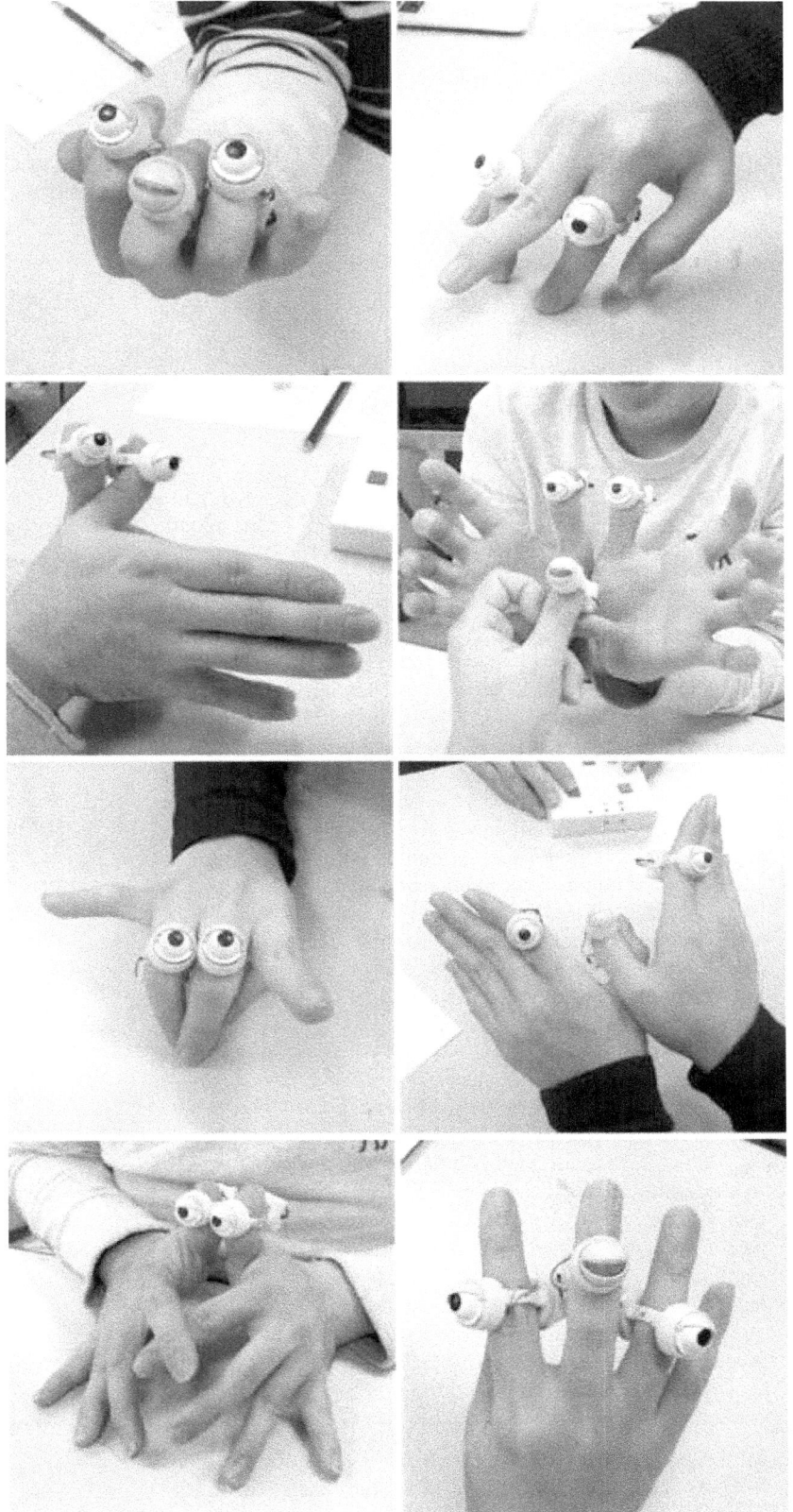

Figure 7. Different gestures for animals: a face, an elephant, a bird, a crab, a fox, a butterfly, an octopus, and a giraffe

- the option of arranging face parts;

- the ease of expressing a wink and surprise;

- the ability to communicate in ways other than a conversation;

- the ability to make various facial expressions using a combination of devices;

- minimal changes in arrangement; and

- a feeling that the face is one's own hand.

On the other hand, the negative feedback was based on a number of factors such as

- difficulty in animating characters because of few previous experiences of displaying expressions using hands;

- the inability to imagine a performing character; and

- boredom due to the monotonous motion of the mouth part.

Impression to wearable robot

We carried out one more questionnaire study on the impression of the device as a wearable robot. Table 2 shows the contrast of items that consists of questions asked before and after the usability study. The first objective of this study was to make a small wearable robot because some of the wearable robots that have already been presented are difficult to wear on the user's body. This questionnaire study revealed the small robot device could be potentially accepted in situations such as human–robot interactions or human–agent interactions. Item 3 of Table 2 denotes that at least the ring-shaped robotic device was better than the other wearable robots. In this questionnaire study, we first described what wearable robots are or they are already known through certain related works.

Agent presence

Some users reported that they felt that the device was a living thing, as shown by Item 6 Table 1. This shows that there is a possibility of making the device an agent robot on the body. The human hand is a part of the body that is used for accessing objects in the world; hence, the agent on the user's hand will act as an information interface to the real world. In a future work, we intend to propose some of the agent applications that Pygmy will realize. On the other hand, in Table 2, we also presented the responses to questions on the use of Pygmy as an agent robot and its presence. These responses indicated that Pygmy was accepted as an agent device; this impression improved the evaluation for Pygmy as a wearable robot.

Further, we observed that when users talked with other subjects in the collaboration task, the users made the character's face and spoke while performing with the

Pygmy mimicking their own or their friends. The result revealed that Pygmy could act as a double of its user.

DISCUSSION

Validity of design policy

A considerable amount of feedback on the policy of the original design was obtained from the user study. On the basis of this feedback, each policy was reconsidered and is listed below:

- **Flexibility.** It was difficult to stabilize and equip the device in every position of a finger because of the structure of the ring device. Depending on the position of the equipment, the face part could appear to be swinging and convey an odd expression. Moreover, since the case of a microcomputer board and battery was large, it was thought that the operation in the state where the finger was bent and grasped the hand was difficult.

- **Scalability.** The ring type was effective from the perspective of simplicity of attachment and detachment. However, looking for the right size of the ring according to the size of the user's finger for the first time of use was inconvenient, and there were users who found it difficult to remove the device because their finger joint was thick. Hence, it is necessary to devise a universal structure suitable for fingers of various sizes or forms.

- **Reconfigurability.** Since the ease of rearranging the device was guaranteed, the user could create and direct expressions freely. However, as there was some discomfort caused by the device size, further miniaturization is required for attaching two or more devices to one finger.

- **Responsiveness.** The responsiveness of the device can be improved by the addition of wireless communication, which requires rebooting because of the problem caused by the server program. Further, the communication distance was restricted to approximately 1 m since the Bluetooth antenna approaches the microcomputer.

- **Responsiveness and safety.** Although the power supply of the ring device was acquired from the battery, the power supply was turned on and off by taking out and inserting the battery terminal. The indication to turn the device on and off was received from the user for the sake of safety or convenience. Moreover, since the battery capacity was low, it device operation was limited to 20–30 min; hence, it is necessary to improve the battery capacity for long use.

- **Human likeness.** Although the design of the personification of a simple structure was adopted, we checked the device for a complete extension of the anthropomorphism of the human hand. Although only hands and fingers were used for the personification, the users stated that powerful animation and presence were realized by adding eyes and a mouth to the personification.

Significance of physical device

The personification device could be moved by a motor in the eyelid and jaw of the personified part. The animation of the body part such as a hand or a finger, which is not anthropomorphized usually, could be significantly realized because this part could be moved physically. For example, when an LED was used as the face part, although expressions could not be recognized by the direction of the finger because of the plane structure of the display or the CG of the eyes or mouth projects on the finger, it was possible to not adapt oneself to the surrounding finger or hand. This led to the physical vibration observed at the time of the rotation of an eyelid across the hand, for example, and the subject memorized the interactive feeling by using a device and adopting a physical mechanism.

Limitation

It is clear that a user's imagination is crucial for exploiting hand expressions. It is successful in extending and directing the likeness to a living thing. In order to use Pygmy as a communication tool, it is necessary to improve the lack of function for practical use from the perspective of design or function. Moreover, certain users could not create certain forms without instructions because their understanding and methodology was different. However, user trials, which included different finger positions, helped achieve various types of expressions. Certain specific emotions seemed impossible to express because of the size limitation related to the embedding of one more motor. Therefore, it is important to design systems and devices that can incorporate results from the user trials. In the future, it is necessary to improve the user instructions and sensing for increased interactivity.

Applicable research field

From the results of the usability study, we concluded that the subjects used Pygmy as their double, which suggested that Pygmy had the ability to act as an agent on the hand. Further, Pygmy can be used as a telecommunication robot device and a security robot for preventing children from interacting with strangers. Furthermore, by acting as an agent on a hand, Pygmy will provide a new interaction model because this type of agent is comparatively close to the user and can be worn on the user's body. Pygmy can be used as a wearable intelligent agent that can provide advice related to shopping and traveling.

FUTURE WORKS

We showed that Pygmy not only is a small robotic device but can also behave as an anthropomorphic agent for the user and another person around the user. Pygmy can function as a communication device such as a telepresence robot and toy for establishing a relationship between a baby and its parents. With the embedding of sensors such as an accelerometer and a touch sensor, Pygmy will act along the user's finger motion. Moreover, an intelligent system to recognize the finger posture for performance generation will achieve automatic operation without the use of a controller. Further, as a wearable agent, Pygmy will interactively provide information about what the user watched or touched.

CONCLUSION

By using a ring-shaped anthropomorphic device that enhances hand expressions by incorporating posture and motion, we could produce a character, a facial expression, an emotion, and the sense of an animal. Pygmy also established its presence as an agent robot on the user's hand. In the usability study, the users understood the concept of hand anthropomorphism and performed it with the device; they were able to converse while using the device. We also found that the user could resolve device limitations by collaboration. The impression of Pygmy as a wearable robot was improved by the goodness of usability and presence magnified by the anthropomorphic appearance.

REFERENCES

1. Desmond Morris: Bodytalk: The Meaning of Human Gestures. Crown, 1995.

2. David McNeill: Hand and Mind, Univ of Chicago Press, 1992.

3. Liddell, S. K. Spatial representations in discourse: comparing spoken and signed language. Lingua 98, pp. 145-167, 1996.

4. Hand painting, Guido Daniele, retrieved from http://www.guidodaniele.com/

5. Kostov, V., Ozawa, J., Matsuura, S., Wearable accessory robot for context aware apprise of personal information. In Proc. RO-MAN 2004, pp. 595-600.

6. Tsumaki, Y., Fujita, Y., Kasai, A., Sato, C., Nenchev, D.N., Uchiyama, M., Telecommunicator: a novel robot system for human communications. In Proc. RO-MAN 2002, pp. 35-40.

7. Maeda, T., Ando, H., Sugimoto, M., Watanabe, J., Wearable robotics as a behavioral interface –The study of the parasitic humanoid–. In Proc. ISWC 2002, pp. 145-151.

8. Nagao, Y., Yamaguchi, H., Harada, K., Omura, K., Inakage, M., Whadget: Interactive Animation using Personification Gesture Expression of Hand. SIGGRAPH 2008 Posters.

9. Sugiura, Y., Fernando, C.L., Withana, A.I., Kakehi, G., Sakamoto, D., Sugimoto, M., Inami, M., Igarashi, T., Inakage, M., An operating method for a bipedal walking

robot for entertainment. ACM SIGGRAPH Asia 2009 Emerging Technologies, pp. 79-79.

10. Osawa, H., Mukai, J., Imai, M., "Display Robot" - Interaction between humans and anthropomorphized objects. In Proc. RO-MAN 2007, pp. 451-456.

11. Nikodama, Ryota Kuwakubo, retrieved from http://www.mediascot.org/lefttomyowndevices/ryotaku wakubo/

Motion Design of an Interactive Small Humanoid Robot with Visual Illusion

Hidenobu Sumioka[1], Takashi Minato[1], Kurima Sakai[2], Shuichi Nishio[1], and Hiroshi Ishiguro[1,2]
[1]Hiroshi Ishiguro Laboratory, ATR
2-2-2 Hikaridai, Keihanna Science City, Kyoto 619-0288, Japan
[2]Graduate School of Eng. Science, Osaka Univ.
Machikaneyamacho 1–3, Toyonaka-shi, Osaka, 560–0043 Japan
sumioka@atr.jp
minato@atr.jp
nishio@ieee.org
sakai.kurima@irl.sys.es.osaka-u.ac.jp
ishiguro@is.sys.es.osaka-u.ac.jp

ABSTRACT

We propose a method that enables users to convey nonverbal information, especially their gestures, through portable robot avatar based on illusory motion. The illusory motion of head nodding is realized with blinking lights for a human-like mobile phone called Elfoid. Two blinking patterns of LEDs are designed based on biological motion and illusory motion from shadows. The patterns are compared to select an appropriate pattern for the illusion of motion in terms of the naturalness of movements and quick perception. The result shows that illusory motions show better performance than biological motion. We also test whether the illusory motion of head nodding provides a positive effect compared with just blinking lights. In experiments, subjects, who are engaged in role-playing game, are asked to complain to Elfoids about their unpleasant situation. The results show that the subject frustration is eased by Elfoid's illusory head nodding.

Author Keywords

telecommunication; nonverbal communication; portable robot avatar; visual illusion of motion

ACM Classification Keywords

H.5.2 Information Interfaces and Presentation (e.g. HCI): User Interfaces

Recent telecommunication technology progress has enabled us to convey not only voices or text messages but also images to people in distant places with small portable devices. This allows us to communicate with distant people anytime and anywhere. However, telecommunication remains different from face-to-face communication because we can not feel people in distant places even when we see their images. It is still difficult to carry presence of distant people in portable devices.

One critical problem is that the current portable devices fail to convey enough nonverbal information of distant people for us to feel their presence. Many studies have reported the importance on smooth communication of nonverbal information, including not only gestures but also space sharing (e.g., [16]). With emphasis on physical interaction, recent studies in robotics have explored the reasonable degree of personal telepresence that allows humans to interact in a useful manner with distant humans [15]. Several studies have focused on portable physical avatars that are teleoperated to convey the nonverbal information of their operators to remote places [1, 22]. However, such avatars often lack portability due to the need of several heavy motors for changing posture. Furthermore, less attention has been paid to their appearance, even though many studies on very human-like robots called androids [3] have shown the importance of the agent's appearance as well as its motion so that humans respond to it as they interact with humans [19].

In this context, "Elfoid" (Figure 1) has been developed as a simplified human-like portable avatar aiming at telepresence. It is designed to transfer a speaker's voice using cellphone networks to talk to others. Since it has human-like head and arms, the speakers expect to teleoperate its body synchronized with their motions to express their presence. However, no actuator is implemented due to its small body.

To solve this problem, we exploit the fact that humans perceive the movement of objects due to the distortion of human senses, even when the objects do not actually move. Such distortion, called illusory motion, provides a different implementation from using actuators; if Elfoid makes users perceive the illusory motion of its body by light, it can support natural interaction without embedding actuators for moving its body.

This paper proposes a method to give the illusion of gestures by Elfoid by blinking LEDs embedded in its body. We focus on a head-nodding motion because it is an important component in communication for the activation of conversation [10] and to ease frustration [11]. Two blinking patterns of LEDs, which are designed based on biological motion [4] and illusory motion from shadows [5], are implemented with point light sources or diffused ones. The patterns are compared

Figure 1. Cellphone-type teleoperated android robot: Elfoid

to select an appropriate pattern for the illusion of motion in terms of the naturalness of movements and quick perception. We test whether the appropriate pattern of illusory-nodding motion shows an effect that resembles actual nodding motion. Experiment results with grumbling about difficult customers to Elfoid shows that human subjects are more affected by illusory-nodding motion than a simply blinking LED, although they need short training to perceive the illusion.

RELATED WORK

In telepresence research on robotics, studies on teleoperation systems for communication are receiving much attention. Tachi *et al.* proposed TELEsarPHONE as a conceptual prototype for a mutual telexistence system that conveys the multisensory information of a robot in distant places to its operator whose images are projected onto the robot's screen. Due to the operator images, the operator and humans communicating with the operator through the robot can feel their mutual presence [21, 18]. Some studies have developed a teleoperation system with an android that resembles a living person instead of an operator's image to investigate what information we need to feel the person's presence by focusing on personality traits [17, 13].

While these studies need robots with highly multiple degrees of freedom and large operation systems, other studies have proposed highly portable teleoperation systems that enable telecommunication anywhere and anytime. Adalgeirsson and Breazeal developed a telepresence robot that allows social expressions to a communication partner in face-to-face interaction [1]. Their robot has a physical body to express gestures and a display to project the operator's facial image. They showed that such robots are more engaging and likable than static ones. Some studies developed shoulder-mounted robots that allow us to share attention with their operators [22]. Although these robots can exploit nonverbal information including gestures and gaze direction for communication with distant humans, their portability is spoiled by the weight of the actuators. Conveying nonverbal information with fewer actuators is an important problem for portable avatars. We tackle it using illusory motion. To the best of our knowledge, so far no studies have used not actuators but illusory motion to convey nonverbal information of operators.

Another solution to maintain portability is to associate the meaning of nonverbal information with another symbol. Komatsu *et al.* proposed the concept of artificial subtle expression (ASE), which argues that simple expressions including blinking LEDs and beeps are enough for humans to estimate the internal states of artificial agents [8]. They showed that the expression of the processing state from a robot by blinking LEDs during conversation tasks enables us to smoothly

take turns. Furthermore, they reported that such expression of the robot's internal state produces positive impressions [6]. Although ASE seems to express the internal states of artificial agents well, teleoperated avatars should express nonverbal information as humans do to intuitively convey the intention of operators. For example, if you express your anger against people communicating with you through a robot, a blinking light on the robot face might make the people underestimate the intensity of your anger.

The influence of nodding motions has been investigated in face-to-face interaction. Matarazzo *et al.* [9] showed that the head nodding of interviewers significantly increases the duration of interviewee's speech. Analysis on the relationship between voice and body movement has revealed that the head nodding of human listeners has a strong relation with their body movement [23]. Some studies with artificial agents have reported the effectiveness of nodding movements on collaboration in virtual space [14] and in the real world [20]. Matsubara and Ueda showed that head nodding by a robot eases the frustration of humans who complain to the robot [11]. In this paper, the effect of the illusory nodding motion on human impressions is evaluated for how it eases subject frustration.

ROBOTIC PLATFORM: ELFOID

Elfoid has been developed as a cellular phone that conveys operator presence (Figure 2). Its main feature is its human-like shape: human-like head, arms, and legs but no hands and feet. Its skin is fashioned from silicon and resembles and feels like human skin. It has a communication module inside that is covered with a plastic case to enable us to talk with other persons. Instead of an actual Elfoid system, in this paper, we used a full-scale blown-molded mock-up model made of polyvinyl chloride (PVC) to embed the LEDs.

DESIGN OF ILLUSORY MOTION WITH BLINKING LIGHTS

Multiple white LEDs are embedded in Elfoid's body to illuminate the surface of the body parts from the inside. The blinks of LEDs are remotely controlled through the control box, which is set up outside Elfoid. We induce a perception of illusory head motions by sequentially changing the illumination.

Two different illumination patterns are considered as possible implementation based on human cognition: biological motion and illusion of motion from shadow. Studies of biological motion [4] have revealed that humans perceive a human's motion in a display of the movement of structured point lights. A

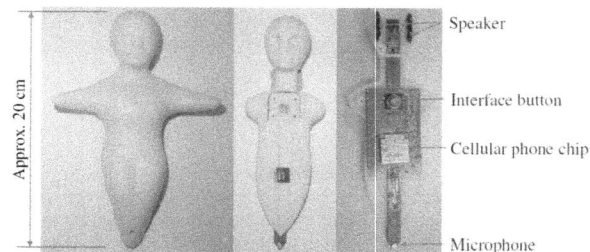

Figure 2. Elfoid: skin (left), plastic case (center), and communication module (right)

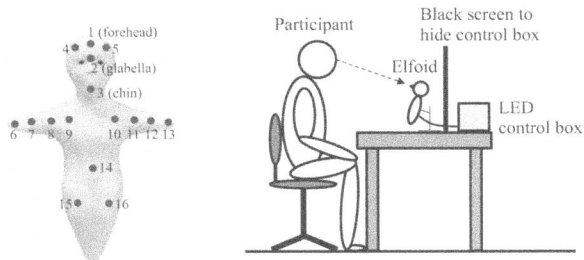

Figure 3. Experimental setup: designs of LED locations (left) and experimental scene (right)

biological motion expressed by embedded LEDs might provide an illusion of motion since Elfoid has a human-like body. Studies of the visual illusion of motion have reported that humans perceive a movement of a still object when its shadow moves [5]. This might be applicable for human gestures because human movement changes the shaded areas of human body; for example, the shade on the lower part of the face appears and disappears when nodding. By controlling the shift of the shaded parts of Elfoid's body with blinking LEDs, we might be able to evoke illusory motions of its head.

In this paper we focus on a head-nodding motion of Elfoid and designed the illumination patterns of the LEDs embedded in its body to express illusory head-nodding motions. Figure 3 shows the location of the embedded LEDs. We designed the following patterns.

- Pattern BP (Figure 4(a)): LEDs 1 and 2 are lit in the sequence of 1(i) - 2(ii) - 1(i) to express the biological motion (i.e., a motion of point lights) of the forehead. This motion takes about 500 msec. Other LEDs (3, 6, 9, 10, 13, 14, 15, 16) are also lit during the nodding motion to express human body shape (iii). Every LED expresses a point light.

- Pattern SD (Figure 4(b)): LEDs 1 to 5 are lit at first (i). LEDs 2 and 3 are gradually turned off (ii) and then gradually lit again (i). The motion takes about 500 msec. To widen the shadow area, diffusion filters are attached to all LEDs. This pattern expresses the shadow shift when looking down and up; the shadow on the lower part of the face appears (ii) and disappears (i). Other LEDs (6, 7, 8, 11, 12, 13) are also lit during the nodding motion to illuminate the body parts as well as Pattern BP. In this pattern the upper body part is highlighted and the lower body part is shaded.

In addition, we designed two patterns by switching the diffused and point lights.

- Pattern BD (Figure 4(c)): This is the same as Pattern BP except that diffused lights are used.

- Pattern SP (Figure 4(d)): This is the same as Pattern SD except that point lights are used.

EVALUATION OF THE DESIGNED PATTERNS
We conducted subjective experiments to find the patterns that participants perceive as illusory-nodding motions more naturally and more quickly among all patterns.

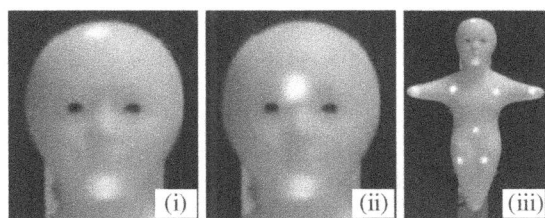

(a) Biological motion based pattern with point lights (Pattern BP)

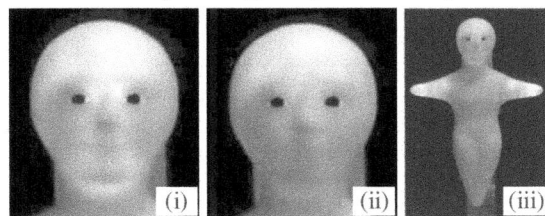

(b) Shadow motion based pattern with diffused lights (Pattern SD)

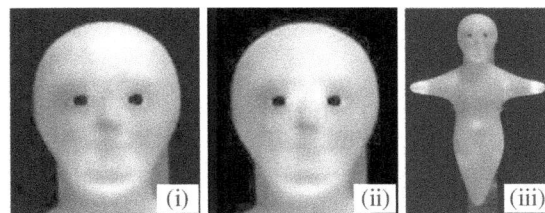

(c) Biological motion based pattern with diffused lights (Pattern BD)

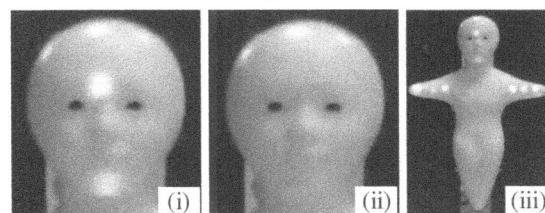

(d) Shadow motion based pattern with point lights (Pattern SP)

Figure 4. Designed illumination patterns

Procedures of experiment
First we evaluated the ease for perceiving the illusory-nodding motion (experiment 1). Before the experiment, we told the participants that Elfoid's blinking LED denotes its nodding motion. Twenty-three people (fourteen men and nine women) who had never interacted with Elfoid participated in the experiments. The average age of all participants was 21.4 (SD=2.2). They observed the blinking patterns of Elfoid, which was fixed on a table (the right figure in Figure 3). They adjusted the height of the chair to see Elfoid's face from the front. We maintained the illumination condition in the room throughout experiments 1 and 2. We continuously repeated the blinking pattern and exposed it to participants until they perceived the illusion of nodding. They were asked to subjectively decide their perception of the illusion and to notify the experimenter when they perceived it.

We measured the length of time before they perceived the illusion. If they did not perceive it within five minutes, the measurements were stopped. Participants tried four patterns in random order.

We then evaluated the subjective impression of the perceived illusory motions (experiment 2). Fifteen of all the participants (nine males and six females) in experiment 1 took part in experiment 2 (average age=21.7, SD=2.4). They were asked paired comparisons for the subjective naturalness of the illusory nodding motion (total six pairs). For each pair, they separately observed two stimuli (one stimulus consisted of two consecutive noddings of one blinking pattern) and answered which nodding pattern was more natural. Note that they don't need to observe Elfoid blinking LEDs before the experiment because they have already recognized illusory head nodding in the experiment 1. They were allowed to repeatedly observe the nodding patterns. When they failed to observe a difference in the naturalness or did not perceive the illusory-nodding motion, they answered no difference. The order of the pairs was randomly changed for every participant.

Results

Figure 5 shows the length of time before subjects perceived the illusory-nodding motion measured in experiment 1. When a participant did not perceive it, no data were plotted. The measured values vary widely. Analysis of the time difference with ANOVA revealed that there was no significant difference between the patterns. However, it can be seen that the participants tended to perceive the illusory motion of pattern SD quicker than the other patterns. Therefore, we also tested the time difference between SD and the others using a Wilcoxon signed rank test since their normality cannot be assumed by the Shapiro-Wilk test. In this test, the case of no paired data was omitted from the test. It showed that the SD time is significantly smaller than BD ($T(n = 16) = 0, p < 0.01$), SP ($T(n = 12) = 14, p < 0.05$), and BP ($T(n = 9) = 0, p < 0.01$).

Table 1 shows the paired comparison results of experiment 2. The pattern which was more natural than the other are presented in each box. When there was no difference, we put "=". Scheffe's paired comparisons test with Nakaya's modified model [12] showed a significant effect of the blinking patterns ($F(3, 42) = 32.3, p < 0.01$). Figure 6 shows the scale value to express the subjective impression of naturalness obtained by the yardstick method. SD is significantly more natural than BD, SP, or BP ($p < 0.01$), and BD is significantly more natural than BP ($p < 0.01$).

These results suggest that the pattern SD makes us perceive illusory motion of head nodding more naturally and more quickly. Therefore, we use the pattern SD as illusory motion pattern in later experiment.

EVALUATION OF EFFECT OF ILLUSORY HEAD NODDING

Since we selected a model that shows the best nodding performance in terms of naturalness of the motion and time to perceive the illusion, we tested whether the model gives an impression that resembles actual head nodding.

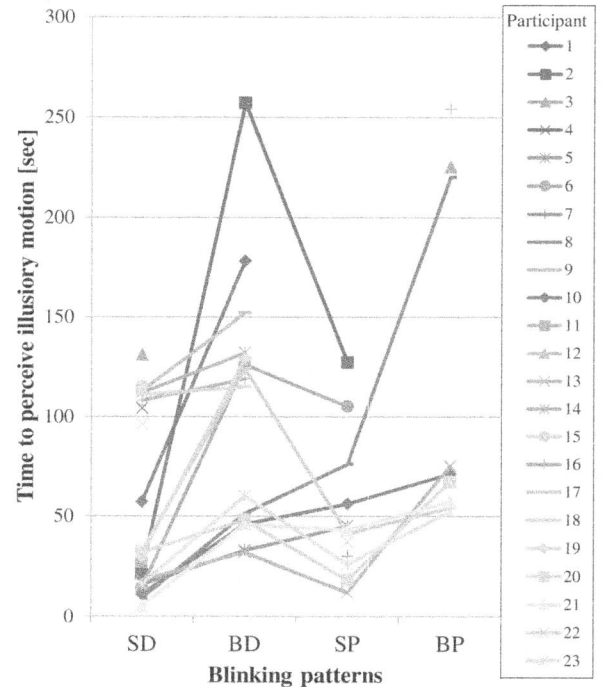

Figure 5. Time to perceive illusory-nodding motion

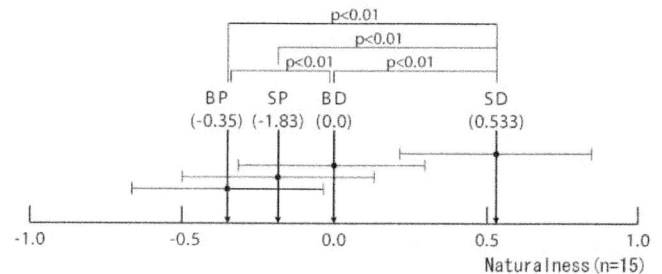

Figure 6. Scale value of subjective naturalness of blinking patterns (yardstick test, 99% confidence interval $Y(4, 42, 0.01) = 0.316$).

Working hypothesis

Recent studies revealed that when a user complains to a robot the satisfaction rating improved by increasing the frequency of the robot nods [11]. Although this result suggests the advantage of the head-nodding behavior of robots, perhaps illusory head nodding could be replaced with a LED that blinks simply, as described in the concept of ASE [8]. Therefore, we hypothesize that the frustration of subjects who complain to Elfoid will be eased more if Elfoid presents illusory head nodding than an Elfoid whose LEDs blink simply. We evaluated the performance of illusory head nodding with grumbling situations where the subjects complained about difficult customer. The performances of different blinking LEDs were measured by rating the ease of frustration based on a previous study [11].

The design of blinking pattern

We used the pattern SD as a pattern to create illusory motion of head nodding. All configuration was the same as the

Participant	SD - BD	SD - SP	SD - BP	BD - SP	BD - BP	SP - BP
1	BD	SD	SD	BD	BD	BP
2	=	SD	SD	BD	=	SP
3	SD	SD	SD	SP	BD	BP
4	=	=	=	=	=	=
5	SD	SD	SD	SP	BD	BP
6	SD	SD	SD	BD	BD	SP
7	SD	SD	SD	SP	=	SP
8	SD	SD	SD	SP	=	=
9	SD	SD	SD	BD	=	=
10	SD	SD	SD	SP	BD	SP
11	=	=	SD	=	=	=
12	=	SD	SD	BD	BD	=
13	SD	SD	SD	=	BD	=
14	BD	=	=	BD	BD	BP
15	SD	SD	SD	SP	BP	BP

Table 1. Paired comparison of naturalness of nodding motions expressed by blinking patterns. more natural pattern is shown in each box. Symbol "=" stands for no difference between the pair.

first and second experiments except that LEDs on the body (6,7,8,11,12,13) were turned off in this experiment to direct subject's attention to the Elfoid's head. For comparison, we designed a simple blinking model that is not supposed to create the illusory motions (see Figure 7). The blinking pattern was realized with diffused lights that were symmetrically placed on the left and right sides of Elfoid's head. We call the pattern SD the illusion model and the simply blinking pattern the no-illusion model. The other configurations, such as number of LEDs, blinking frequency, and light intensity, are the same among all the models.

Experimental procedure

Sixteen people (nine men and seven women) participated in the experiment. Their average age was 21.4 (SD = 2.4). First they looked at the blinking patterns of the illusion and no-illusion models (Figure 8(a)). Each pattern was repeated for three minutes [1]. The subjects were informed that the blinking pattern gives the illusion of head nodding for the illusion model while for the no-illusion model the blinking pattern expresses the internal state of the operator. This explanation was needed so that the subjects clearly perceived the illusion. These patterns was presented in random order.

Next, the subjects had a three-minute conversation on a given topic with an experimenter through Elfoid to become accustomed to conversation with it (Figure 8(a)). During the conversation, the experimenter blinked the LED in synchronization with her/his nodding. The experimenter did not know which model s/he was operating remotely. The order of presenting the models was changed randomly. After the conversation, the same procedure was followed with the other model.

After that, the subjects read a scenario for a role-playing game, where a customer is complaining through monitor to subjects who are shop clerks. The subjects selected appropriate answers to the customer's questions from options to deal with the difficult customer although all options just increased the customer's anger. This process was expected to increase

---

[1] The time interval was determined based on the fact that the SD model needed 131 seconds to make the subjects to perceive the illusion in the first experiments.

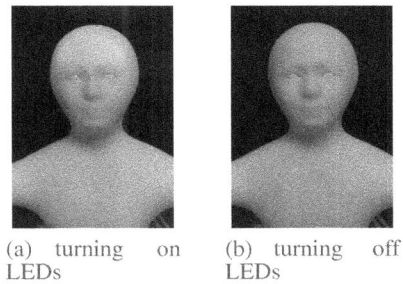

(a) turning on LEDs   (b) turning off LEDs

Figure 7. No-nodding case. LEDs on the left and right side of Elfoid's head (4 and 5 in Figure 3) are blinked.

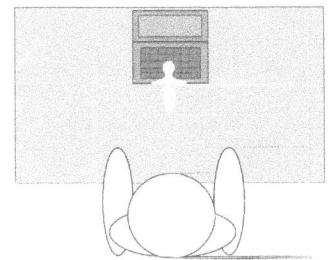

(a) Instruction and Free talk phases

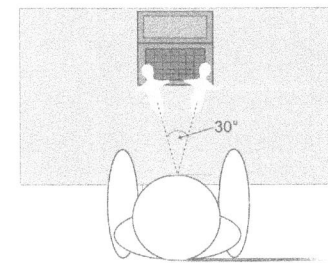

(b) Grumbling task

Figure 8. Experimental setting

the subject frustration. After the role play was finished, they were asked to complain to two Elfoids at the same time, as shown in Figure 8(b): one is the illusion model and the other is the no-illusion one. These Elfoids were randomly placed on the left side or right one for every subject. The subjects were informed that each Elfoid was operated by two different experimenters, though both Elfoids were actually operated by one experimenter, who blinked the LEDs when s/he nodded. The time of onset of blinking is slightly delayed between two models. Note that the operator did not talk to the subjects. The subjects only evaluated the Elfoids from the blinking patterns. After the subjects grumbled to the Elfoids, they completed questionnaires. We also interviewed them about their impression of the Elfoids to collect more detailed information about their feelings.

Evaluation

We evaluated the extent of the ease of frustration with subjective measures based on the one proposed in [11]. Six questions are asked to the subjects: (Q1) Which Elfoid made you feel better?; (Q2) Which Elfoid satisfied your feeling?; (Q3) Which Elfoid was more fun?; (Q4) Which Elfoid was more friendly?; (Q5) To which Elfoid could you say everything you wanted to say?; (Q6) Which Elfoid showed empathy?

The subjects were asked to answer which Elfoid on the left and right sides was appropriate for each question and then rated how strongly they felt on a three-point scale. If they selected the illusion model, the point was used as a score. A negative value was scored if the no-illusion model was selected. For example, when a subject selects the right Elfoid which is no-illusion model and gives it two points, the score was -2. If the subjects failed to find any difference between the two Elfoids, we gave a score of zero.

Result

We removed some subjects from the analysis because they reported that they could not perceive the illusory head nodding. So the data of eleven subjects (six men and five women) were analyzed. The average age of the subjects was 21.7 (SD = 2.7).

Figure 9 shows the average scores for each question. The negative scores indicate that the no-illusion model was selected. The illusion model received a higher average score than the no-illusion one. We tested whether the average score of each question exceeded zero. We used a t-test for Q1 and Q6 whose normality can be assumed by the Shapiro-Wilk test. We found significant difference for Q6 (Which Elfoid showed empathy?) ($t(10) = 3.32, p < 0.01$). There was no significance in the other questions by the Wilcoxon-test.

The extent of the ease of frustration varied in individuals. This is because it is not always true that persons have the same feeling when they complain to others. The average score of all questions will help us evaluate the overall effect of illusory motion on the ease of frustration. Therefore, we also tested whether the sum of all the scores exceeded zero with a t-test since we confirmed normality (Figure 10). We found a significant difference between the sum of the scores and zero (($t(10) = 2.88, p < 0.01$)). These results show

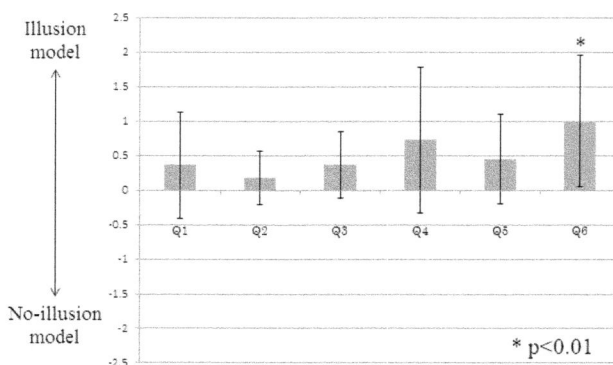

Figure 9. Averages and standard deviations of scores for each question

that the illusion model significantly eased the subject frustration more than the no-illusion model. Especially, the subjects felt greater empathy from the Elfoid with the illusory-head-nodding model.

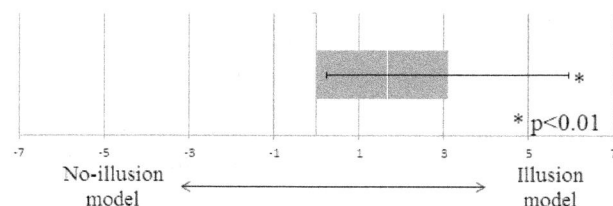

Figure 10. Average and standard deviation of the sum of scores for all questions

DISCUSSION

Before the first and second experiment, we expected that the biological motion-based patterns could create illusory motions since people generally perceive a human-like motion from a biological motion. However, the shadow motion-based pattern with diffused lights is a more natural pattern to recognize nodding motions than the biological motion-based one. One possibility for its low performance is that the point-light motion was not continuous but intermittent while the original biological motion is expressed as a continuous change of lights. However, in preliminary experiments, we confirmed that we can recognize nodding motions when only the light pattern is presented in a dark room. Therefore, the projection of the light pattern to the surface of Elfoid disturb the perception of biological motions.

Although the experiment 2 result shows that the pattern SD can produce a natural nodding motion, it is a concern whether this result really reflects the illusory motions. It still remained the possibility that the participants merely perceived the blinking lights as a sign of nodding. The experiment 1 result indicates that the participants more easily perceived the illusory motion of pattern SD than the other patterns. Additionally, almost all of the participants (22 of 23) announced that they perceived the illusory motion for pattern SD (other patterns: 16 in BD, 12 in SP, and 9 in BP). If they perceived the blinking lights as a sign, we infer that there is no large time difference among the four patterns since before the experiment they knew that the blinking lights expressed nodding motions. Furthermore, almost all of the participants (14 of 15) in experiment 2 admitted in interviews after the experiment that they felt that Elfoid's face actually moved. These results suggest that the participants perceived the illusory motions especially for pattern SD with a mechanism that resembles the illusory motions from shadows [5]. The natural impression of pattern SD might come from the illusory motion rather than the blinking pattern.

The result of the last experiment showed that grumbling to the illusory head-nodding model eased subject frustration more than grumbling to the simply blinking pattern even though a previous study reported that a blinking LED gave positive impressions to people [6]. This implies that robot avatars with human-like appearance should express nonverbal information including facial expressions and gestures as humans do because it is intuitively understandable for other people. This corresponds to the fact that humans anticipate a robot's ability based on its appearance [2, 7]. Our proposed method has the potential to achieve human-like gestures on portable robot avatars without any actuators. However, we have not compared illusory motions with actual motions to investigate whether the illusory motions have the same effect as actual ones. Such comparison should be conducted in future.

It should be pointed out that the subjects needed instruction and about two minutes to perceive head-nodding motions in our experiment. Subjects often failed to perceive the motions if any instruction is presented. One might consider this as a crucial problem for practical use. However, many subjects reported that they can perceive the illusory motion easily once they have perceived the illusory. Therefore, that is not problem for practical use because illusory motion is always recognizable for users after short training.

Nevertheless, a well-designed structure should be explored so that people can strongly perceive illusory motions without any instruction because long instruction time is needed as the number of illusory motions increases. The research on optical illusions might help us build design principle for illusory motion of human gestures. Another solution might be to integrate other sensory information. For example, vibrations synchronized with illusory head-nodding motions might improve the perception of head nodding.

Our proposed method should also be applicable to other gestures such as shaking heads or hands, even though we focused on a head-nodding motion here. Implementation of other gestures is challenging as future work.

CONCLUSION
We proposed a method that enables users to convey nonverbal information, especially their gestures, through portable robot avatar based on illusory motion. We realized the illusion of head nodding with blinking lights for a human-like mobile phone called Elfoid. The comparison between the illusions of head nodding and biological motions presented with LEDs showed that illusions allowed people to perceive head nodding motions more naturally and more quickly. We

also tested whether the illusory motion of head nodding provided more positive effects than just blinking lights. The experiment results where subjects grumbled to Elfoid showed that grumbling with illusory head nodding eased subject frustration. Our approach is noiseless and has low energy requirements while servomotors consume more energy and make noise, which might disturb smooth communication. We hope this approach provides a new idea to realize a portable robot avatar that allows us to feel the presence of a person who is communicating through it.

ACKNOWLEDGMENTS
This work has been supported by JST CREST (Core Research of Evolutional Science and Technology) research promotion program "Creation of Human-Harmonized Information Technology for Convivial Society" Research Area.

REFERENCES
1. Adalgeirsson, S., and Breazeal, C. Mebot: a robotic platform for socially embodied presence. In *Proceeding of the 5th ACM/IEEE international conference on Human-robot interaction*, ACM (2010), 15–22.

2. Goetz, J. Matching robot appearance and behavior to tasks to improve human-robot cooperation. *Proc. of IEEE International Workshop on Robot and Human Interactive Communication, 2003* (2003).

3. Ishiguro, H. Android science–toward a new cross-interdisciplinary framework. *Robotics Research 28* (2007), 118–127.

4. Johansson, G. Visual perception of biological motion and a model for its analysis. *Attention, Perception, & Psychophysics 14*, 2 (1973), 201–211.

5. Kersten, D., Knill, D. C., Mamassian, P., and Bulthoff, I. Illusory motion from shadows. *Nature 379*, 6560 (1996), 31.

6. Kobayashi, K., Funakoshi, K., Yamada, S., Nakano, M., Komatsu, T., and Saito, Y. Blinking light patterns as artificial subtle expressions in human-robot speech interaction. In *In Proceedings of the 20th IEEE International Symposium on Robot and Human Interactive Communication (RO-MAN 2011)* (2011), 182–186.

7. Komatsu, T., and Yamada, S. Adaptation gap hypothesis: How differences between users' expected and perceived agent functions affect their subjective impression. *Journal of Systemics, Cybernetics and Informatics 9*, 1 (2011), 67–74.

8. Komatsu, T., Yamada, S., Kobayashi, K., Funakoshi, K., and Nakano, M. Artificial subtle expressions: Intuitive notification methodology of artifacts. In *Proceedings of the 28th international conference on Human factors in computing systems*, ACM (2010), 1941–1944.

9. Matarazzo, J., Saslow, G., Wiens, A., Weitman, M., and Allen, B. Interviewer head nodding and interviewee speech durations. *Psychotherapy: Theory, Research & Practice 1*, 2 (1964), 54.

10. Matarazzo, J., Wiens, A., Saslow, G., Allen, B., and Weitman, M. Interviewer mm-hmm and interviewee speech durations. *Psychotherapy: Theory, Research & Practice 1*, 3 (1964), 109–114.

11. Matsubara, D., and Ueda, H. A robot listening to user's grumble. *IPSJ SIG Technical Report 2011-EC-20*, 9 (2011), 1–6. (in Japanese).

12. Nakaya, S. Variation of scheffe's paired comparison. In *Proceedings of the 11th Sensory Evaluation Convention* (1970), 1–12. (in Japanese).

13. Nishio, S., Ishiguro, H., and Hagita, N. Geminoid: Teleoperated android of an existing person. *Humanoid robots-new developments. I-Tech* (2007).

14. Okubo, M., and Watanabe, T. Effects of interactor's nodding on a collaboration support system. In *Proc. of IEEE International Workshop on Robot and Human Interactive Communication*, IEEE (2005), 329–334.

15. Paulos, E., and Canny, J. Social tele-embodiment: Understanding presence. *Autonomous Robots 11*, 1 (2001), 87–95.

16. Rutter, D. R., Stephenson, G. M., and Dewey, M. E. Visual communication and the content and style of conversation. *British Journal of Social Psychology 20* (1981), 41–52.

17. Sakamoto, D., Kanda, T., Ono, T., Ishiguro, H., and Hagita, N. Android as a telecommunication medium with a human-like presence. In *Proc. of the ACM/IEEE int. conf. on Human-robot interaction* (2007), 193–200.

18. Sekiguchi, D., Inami, M., and Tachi, S. Robotphone: Rui for interpersonal communication. In *Proceedings on the ACM SIGCHI Conference on Human Factors in Computing Systems*, ACM (2001), 277–278.

19. Shimada, M., and Ishiguro, H. Motion behavior and its influence on human-likeness in an android robot. In *Proc of the annual conf. of the cog. sci. society* (2008), 2468–2473.

20. Sidner, C., Lee, C., Morency, L., and Forlines, C. The effect of head-nod recognition in human-robot conversation. In *Proceedings of the 1st ACM SIGCHI/SIGART conference on human-robot interaction*, ACM (2006), 290–296.

21. Tachi, S., Kawakami, N., Nii, H., Watanabe, K., and Minamizawa, K. Telesarphone: Mutual telexistence master-slave communication system based on retroreflective projection technology. *SICE Journal of Control, Measurement, and System Integration 1*, 5 (2008), 335–344.

22. Tsumaki, Y., Fujita, Y., Kasai, A., Sato, C., Nenchev, D., and Uchiyama, M. Telecommunicator: A novel robot system for human communications. In *Proceedings of 11th IEEE International Workshop on Robot and Human Interactive Communication*, IEEE (2002), 35–40.

23. Watanabe, T., Okubo, M., and Ogawa, H. An embodied interaction robots system based on speech. *Journal of Robotics and Mechatronics 12*, 2 (2000), 126–134.

Empirical Study of a Vision-based Depth-Sensitive Human-Computer Interaction System

Farzin Farhadi-Niaki
School of Electrical Engineering
and Computer Science
University of Ottawa, Ottawa,
Canada
ffarh101@uottawa.ca

Reza GhasemAghaei
School of Computer Science
Carleton University, Ottawa,
Canada
rgaghaee@connect.carleton.ca

Ali Arya
School of Information
Technology
Carleton University, Ottawa,
Canada
arya@carleton.ca

ABSTRACT

This paper proposes the results of a user study on vision-based depth-sensitive input system for performing typical desktop tasks through arm gestures. We have developed a vision-based HCI prototype to be used for our comprehensive usability study. Using the Kinect 3D camera and OpenNI software library we implemented our system with high stability and efficiency by decreasing the ambient disturbing factors such as noise or light condition dependency. In our prototype, we designed a capable algorithm using NITE toolkit to recognize arm gestures. Finally, through a comprehensive user experiment we compared our natural arm gestures to the conventional input devices (mouse/keyboard), for simple and complicated tasks, and in two different situations (small and big-screen displays) for precision, efficiency, ease-of-use, pleasantness, fatigue, naturalness, and overall satisfaction to verify the following hypothesis: on a WIMP user interface, the gesture-based input is superior to mouse/keyboard when using big-screen. Our empirical investigation also proves that gestures are more natural and pleasant to be used than mouse/keyboard. However, arm gestures can cause more fatigue than mouse.

Author Keywords
3D; gesture interaction; HCI; usability; vision.

ACM Classification Keywords
H.5.2 [User Interfaces]: Input Devices and Strategies; I.3.6 [Methodology and Techniques]: Interaction Techniques.

INTRODUCTION
While the field of Human-Computer Interaction (HCI) have always aimed to improve the interaction by making computers more practical and responsive to the user's requests, and minimizing the incompatibility between the human's cognitive model and the computer's ability to understand and respond properly [1], lately the research in HCI is showing a significant focus on creating interfaces that are more user-friendly, by applying natural communication and human skills in the user interface design. The new wave of input systems in video game consoles (such as Nintendo Wii, Xbox Kinect, and PlayStation Move) are examples of the trend toward a more "natural" interfaces, where computers adapt to human behavior rather than the other way around. Input/output techniques, interaction styles, and evaluation methods are the challenging fields of research in such gesture-based improvement [2].

With availability of in-expensive 3D cameras, many researchers have improved the quality of gesture-based systems by incorporating depth information as well as employing robust computer vision methods such as those provided by toolkits like OpenCV. On the other hand, a consolidated and reliable usability analysis has not been fulfilled for gesture-based input systems to see how and where they can be used. This paper is based on a prototype that combines a 3D camera with advanced vision software, and offers a novel study of usability of such system in performing common desktop tasks like accessing files, opening and resizing windows, etc. The study has considered a variety of factors such as complexity of tasks, screen size, and human factors like pleasantness, fatigue, and naturalness.

RELATED WORK

Technical
Recent studies have demonstrated that hand gesture systems are not only technical and theoretical in nature but are also very practical since they can be implemented into numerous types of application systems and environments. For example, Ahn et al. [3] developed a method for virtual environment slide show presentations.

Another example is the study by Jain [4], which describes a way to estimate hand poses for mobile phones that only have one pointing gesture based on a vision-based hand gesture approach. The sign language tutoring tool developed by Aran et al. [5] is also very practical because it is designed to interact with users to teach them the fundamentals of sign language [6].

Several researchers have conducted similar studies in tracking, such as the Viola-Jones-based cascade classifier, which is typically used for face tracking in rapid image processing [7,8] and is regarded as more robust in pattern recognition against noise and lighting conditions [9]. Other researchers have shown that cascade classifiers can also be utilized to recognize hands and various parts of the human body [9,10,11,12,13].

In order to detect gestures, Marcel et al. [14] proposed a method of hand gesture recognition based on Input-Output Hidden Markov Models that track variations in the skin color of the human body. Similarly, Chen et al. [15] applied the hidden Markov model in training method to enable systems to detect hand postures, even though it is more complex than Cascade classifiers in training hand gestures.

A simple Human-Computer Interactive system that could detect predefined hand gestures for the numbers 0 to 6 was proposed by Liu et al. [6]. This system could better implement the Number Input Management in Word documents. The AdaBoost algorithm was revised and used to automatically recognize a user's hand from the video stream, which is based on Haar-like features as a representation of hand gestures. A Multi-class Support Vector Machine was employed to train and detect the hand gesture based on Hu invariant moments features and the Human Computer Conversation was then implemented for hand gesture interaction instead of a traditional mouse and keyboard.

The other research, by Yu et al. [17], proposes a hand gesture feature extraction method (with a dataset of 3500 images) that employs multi-layer perception. By binarizing the image and enhancing the contrast, the silhouette and distinct features of the hand are accurately and efficiently extracted from the image. The Gauss-Laplace edge detection approach has been utilized to get the hand edge. A feature vector that can recognize hand gestures is developed from combinational parameters of Hu invariant moment, hand gesture region and Fourier descriptor.

In above mentioned related works, accuracy and usefulness of gesture recognition software have remained a challenging issue. Noise, inconsistent lighting, items in the background, distinct features, and equipment limitations can also be named as the constraints associated with some of those image-based gesture recognition systems. Technological incompatibility may also cause difficulties in the general usage to match various image-based gesture recognition systems. For instance, a calibrating algorithm for one camera might not work properly for another different camera. Kinect camera uses some more stable methods and very useful techniques such as: background removal, image segmentation, depth and connectivity detection, and hand gesture recognition. Last but not least, Kinect also works well in an extensive variety of lighting conditions which itself helps in reducing the need for a high power of CPU. Having all these features enables Kinect to simulate a number of controllers properly. Using Kinect unit enables us to identify the depth of every single pixel in the frame and ultimately conserve the developing (no need for making samples and efforts in training, and testing sessions) and running time comparing to the learning-based traditional methods that have been used in the above mentioned related works. Moreover, applying a depth thresholding removes the wrist and its unwanted defects from the depth map, based on Z (creates a binary image). Cropping the wrist out of the frame can also help in improving accuracy. On the other hand, OpenNI and NITE secure the system with a high stability and efficiency by decreasing the effect of ambient disturbing factors such as noise and improper light conditions. In addition, programming with NITE provides some gesture detector options, e.g. Velocity or Angle features in a push detector in order to make a desirable setting for the push gesture recognition.

Usability

As for the multimodal interfaces, Cabral et al. [18] discuss numerous usability issues associated to the use of gestures as an input mode. A simplistically strong 2D computer vision based gesture recognition system was introduced by the authors and was successfully used for interaction in VR environments. Three different scenarios were employed to test the interface: as a regular pointing device in a GUI interface, as a navigation tool, and as a visualization tool. Their results illustrated that it is more time consuming, as well as more fatiguing to complete simple pointing tasks than using a mouse. However, several advantages are revealed by the use of gestures as a substitute in multimodal interfaces. These include immediate access to computing resources using a natural and intuitive way, and that balances properly to joint applications, where gestures can be used infrequently.

A proposition by Villaroman et al. [19] suggests that using Kinect to classroom training on natural user interaction creates a prospect and innovative method. Examples are presented to demonstrate how Kinect-assisted instruction can be utilized to accomplish certain learning results in Human Computer Interaction (HCI) courses. Moreover, the authors have confirmed that OpenNI, in addition to its accompanying libraries, are adequate and beneficial in enabling Kinect-assisted learning activities. For students, Kinect and OpenNI offer a hands-on experience with its gesture-based, natural user interaction technology.

In a study on 3D applications using Kinect, Kang et al. [20] introduced a control method that naturally regulates the application with the use of distance information and joints' location information. Furthermore, the recognition rate was more successful, as well as the use of the proposed gestures in the 3D application, which was 27% quicker than a mouse.

Code Space, introduced by Bragdon et al. [21], is a system that combines touch + air gesture hybrid interactions to jointly carry small developer group meetings. This method enables access, control and sharing of information through several different devices such as multi-touch screen, mobile touch devices, and Microsoft Kinect sensors. In a formative study, professional developers were positive about the interaction design, and most felt that pointing with hands or devices and forming hand postures are socially acceptable.

A gesture user interface application, Open Gesture, is available for standard tasks, for instance making telephone calls, operating the television, and executing mathematical calculations. This prototype uses a television interface to carry out various tasks by using simple hand gestures. Based on a usability evaluation, Bhuiyan and Picking [22], recommend that this technology can improve the lives of the elderly and the disabled users by creating more independence while some challenges still remain to be overcome.

During a study, on touch-free navigation through radiological images, analyzed by Ebert et al. [23], ten medical professionals tested the system by rebuilding a dozen images from a CT data. The experiment measured the response period and the practicality of the system compared to the mouse/keyboard control. An average of ten minutes was required for the participants to be at ease with the system. The response time was 120 ms, and the image recreation time using gestures was 1.4 time longer than using mouse/keyboard. However it does remove the potential for infection, for both patients and staff.

In a usability study, in order to have more accurate results, it is suggested to design a simple and minimalistic as possible simulated desktop interface with neutral colors to reduce user error or bias, while focusing on common desktop tasks to be relatively general. Moreover, we believe that studying more features in a usability study than those have been studied in above mentioned related works develops the models and theories of interaction.

METHODOLOGY

Our research aims as verifying the following hypothesis: On a WIMP (Windows, Icons, Menus, Pointers) user interface, the gesture-based input is superior to mouse/keyboard when using with a big-screen, but not on a small screen. In order to verify this hypothesis, we (1) designed a simple yet effective simulated WIMP interface, (2) defined a set of criteria for evaluation, (3) selected natural gestures, (4) implemented a gesture recognition engine, and (5) performed usability studies.

User Interface and Gesture Recognition Modules

This project uses a simulated WIMP interface. The design is kept as simple and minimalistic as possible, with neutral colors to reduce user error or bias (Figure 1). The simulated desktop includes icons with operations such as selecting, opening/closing, moving and resizing.

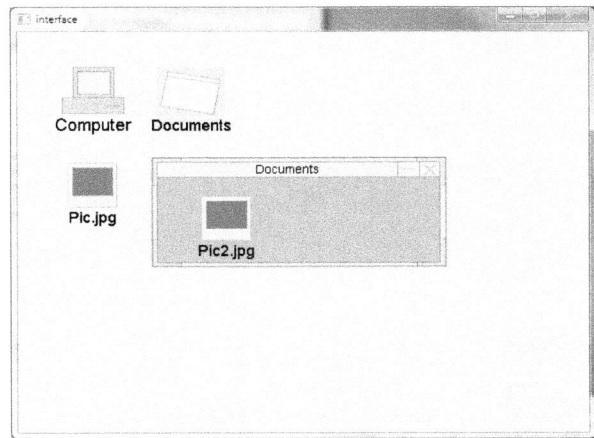

Figure 1. User interface.

Tables 1 and 2 show our chosen gestures and their corresponding mouse/keyboard events. We have used a combination of Kinect sensor, OpenCV, Allegro graphics library, OpenNI, and NITE to create the simulated desktop interface and interact with users.

Processes	Arm
Selecting/Running/Closing	Hand pushing
Moving curser	Hand moving
Grabbing/Resizing	Hand circling

Table 1. Final design for arm/hand set.

Arm Gestures	Mouse	Actions
Push	Dbl-click	Run/close objects
Circle + move + push	Drag & drop	Move/resize

Table 2. Arm gestures' definitions, mouse analogies, and actions.

The details of the gesture recognition engine are not within the scope of this paper that is focused on usability study. Figure 2 illustrates our gesture-based UI algorithm.

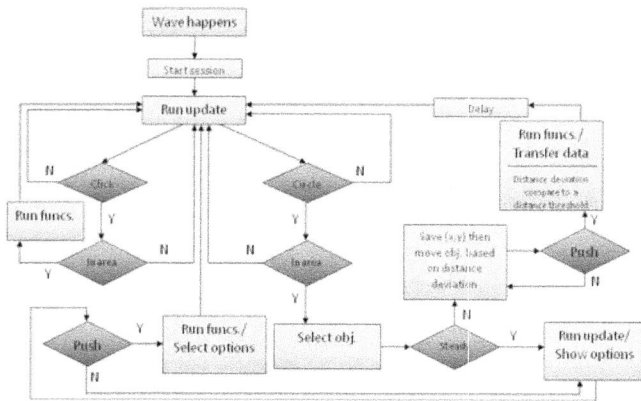

Figure 2. The algorithm controlling UI using arm gestures recognition.

User Experiments

In our usability experiments we have focused on common desktop tasks to be relatively general, and have included ratings by typical university users and also objective measures by observation, such as number of trials, errors, etc.

The experiment process has the following sessions:

Training session

Training consists of thirty minutes of practicing the "simple" tasks, including selecting desktop objects (icons and windows), opening and closing, moving and resizing. Complex tasks are combination of 5 simple ones through a script.

Test session

Test sessions include two tasks (simple and complex), two devices (mouse and gesture), and two types of screen (desktop and big-screen), i.e. eight units.

Questionnaire and observation

During the test sessions the users are requested to rate their satisfaction on a scale of 1 to 5 (1 for absolutely unsatisfied and 5 for extremely satisfied) on eight respective task tables, and to answer some extra questions on the questionnaire while the testing persons measure the observations.

RESULTS AND DISCUSSIONS

This study is conducted using 20 participants (10 males and 10 females) and in the age range of 11 to 40 (average of 29 years old). Nineteen participants were right-handed and one was left-handed.

Hypotheses and Analyses

For the different factors being studied, 3-way repeated analysis of variances (ANOVA) is carried out for three independent variables:

1- Difficulty (simple task vs. complex task)
2- Input device (mouse vs. arm gestures)
3- Output device (desktop vs. big-screen)

All analysis are concluded at p < 0.05 significance level and for 20 participants. Our ANOVA analysis is accompanied by an extra t-test analysis particularly for naturalness and fatigue. This redundancy is carried out in order to confirm our multi-factor analysis with a single-factor analysis. The results of the t-test support the ANOVA analysis.

Notation: In the following analyses, we show the mean and standard deviation for different variables in the forms of $M_{variable}$ (e.g. M_{simple} is the mean for simple task) and $SD_{variable}$ (e.g. $SD_{gesture}$ is the standard deviation for arm gestures). Moreover, F(df,MS) is the test statistic (F-ratio) in which df and MS are the degree of freedom and mean square respectively for the variables (within variables when more than one, and within subjects). The F-ratio is calculated using $MS_{variable(s)}/MS_{error(s)}$ and P is the probability value.

Time (duration of test session):
Hypothesis- using a mouse is faster than using arm gestures as inputs.
The analysis illustrates that for variable 1, F(1,2504.306) = 66.994, P = 0.0000 (M_{simple} = 17.83, SD_{simple} = 7.67 vs. $M_{complex}$ = 25.74, $SD_{complex}$ = 9.80). This illustrates that task complexity has significant effect on time. This effect is as expected since the two tasks were initially designed to illustrate different difficulty levels for using the system.

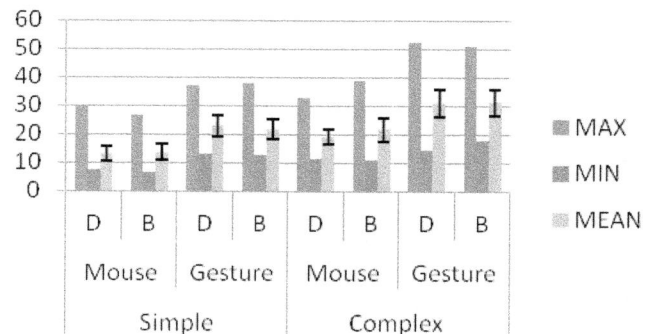

Figure 3. Temporal MAX/MIN/MEAN/ST DEV facts (D≡desktop, B≡big-screen).

For variable 2, F(1,3820.070) = 41.163, P = 0.0000 (M_{mouse} = 16.90, SD_{mouse} = 7.0868 vs. $M_{gesture}$ = 26.67, $SD_{gesture}$ = 9.3749), which implies that using gestures also has significant effect on time. For variable 3, F(1,10.404) = 0.646, P = 0.4316 which illustrates that the screen type does not have a significant effect on time. Moreover, the analysis shows no significant effect on time for variables 1 and 2 combined F(1,29.929) = 1.371, P = 0.2562, variables 1 and 3 combined F(1,28.392) = 1.641, P = 0.2156, and finally variables 2 and 3 combined, F(1,37.056) = 1.131, P = 0.3008. Combination of the three variables (1, 2, and 3) F(1,0.121) = 0.006, P = 0.9370 also do not show any significant effect on time. Based on the above, the initial hypothesis is confirmed meaning gesture inputs are significantly slower than using a mouse (as shown also in Figure 3).

Easiness (how easy to interact with the UI):
Hypothesis- Using arm gestures as inputs is easier than mouse.

Analyzing the feedback from participants regarding easiness of experiments given the 3 variables defined earlier shows that the only significant effect is caused by variable 2, $F(1,19.600) = 23.059$, $P = 0.0001$ ($M_{mouse} = 4.3750$, $SD_{mouse} = 0.8325$ vs. $M_{gesture} = 3.6750$, $SD_{gesture} = 0.9517$). This means that according to participants, the only variable with significant effect on easiness is the input device (mouse vs. gesture). For variable 1, $F(1,0.100) = 0.134$, $P = 0.7181$ and for variable 3, $F(1,1.225) = 2.730$, $P = 0.1149$. For combination of variables 1 and 2, $F(1,0.100) = 0.409$, $P = 0.5303$, variables 1 and 3, $F(1,0.225) = 0.371$, $P = 0.5497$, variables 2 and 3, $F(1,4.225) = 4.219$, $P = 0.0540$, and finally for variables 1, 2, and 3, $F(1,0.225) = 0.609$, $P = 0.4449$ which indicates that there is no significant effect. According to the provided statistics, the initial hypothesis is rejected which indicates that using a mouse is significantly easier than using arm gestures.

Fatigue (how fatiguing to interact with the UI):
Hypothesis- Using arm gestures produces more fatigue compared to mouse.

In this experiment the participants have been asked to rank higher if more fatigue is experienced. The feedback obtained from participants indicates that similar to easiness, variable 2 is the only one with significant effect $F(1,45.156) = 31.813$, $P = 0.0000$ ($M_{mouse} = 1.4000$, $SD_{mouse} = 0.7730$ vs. $M_{gesture} = 2.4625$, $SD_{gesture} = 0.9929$). This indicates that the input device is the only determining parameter in fatigue. For variable 1, $F(1,1.406) = 3.065$, $P = 0.0961$ and for variable 3, $F(1,0.506) = 1.351$, $P = 0.2595$ respectively. For combination of variables 1 and 2, $F(1,0.006) = 0.015$, $P = 0.9050$, variables 1 and 3, $F(1,0.006) = 0.018$, $P = 0.8949$, variables 2 and 3, $F(1,0.756) = 0.657$, $P = 0.4276$, and finally variables 1, 2, and 3, $F(1,0.756) = 1.322$, $P = 0.2645$. Based on the above mentioned figures, the initial hypothesis is approved, meaning arms gestures significantly causes more fatigue compared to using a mouse. Table 3 shows an extra t-test analysis for fatigue which supports the ANOVA analysis.

Phase	Mean		p-value
	Mouse	Arm	
Simple/Desktop	1.10	2.45	3.756e-06
Simple/Big-screen	1.5	2.3	0.002506
Complex/Desktop	1.45	2.50	0.002502
Complex/Big-screen	1.55	2.60	0.002173

Table 3. Fatigue and results of t-test.

Naturalness (how natural/intuitive to interact with the UI):
Hypothesis- Using arm gestures is more natural than using a mouse.

For this factor, none of the variables shows any significant effect.

The calculated statistical values for variable 1, $F(1,0.000) = 0.000$, $P = 1.0000$, for variable 2, $F(1,10.000) = 4.153$, $P = 0.0557$, and for variable 3, $F(1,0.225) = 0.851$, $P = 0.3679$. These results indicate that variables 1, 2, and 3 do not have any significant impact on naturalness of tasks. However, combination of variables 2 and 3 show significant effect $F(1,5.625) = 6.628$, $P = 0.0186$ ($M_{mouse-desktop} = 3.4500$, $SD_{mouse-desktop} = 1.1082$, vs. $M_{mouse-bigscreen} = 3$, $SD_{mouse-bigscreen} = 1.1983$, vs. $M_{gesture-desktop} = 3.5750$, $SD_{gesture-desktop} = 0.9306$, vs. $M_{gesture-bigscreen} = 3.8750$, $SD_{gesture-bigscreen} = 0.8530$). This means that the input device when combined with a particular output device will show significant effect on naturalness. Multiple one-way ANOVAs further indicate that mouse when used on desktop is significantly more natural than mouse used on big-screen. Moreover, gestures used on big-screen are significantly more natural than mouse used on both desktop and big-screen. Combination of variables 1 and 2, $F(1,0.400) = 0.910$, $P = 0.3520$, variables 1 and 3, $F(1,0.225) = 0.533$, $P = 0.4744$, and finally variables 1, 2, and 3 , $F(1,0.625) = 1.067$, $P = 0.3145$, show no significant effect. According to the above mentioned figures, the hypothesis is rejected, meaning arm gestures as inputs do not feel significantly more natural compared to mouse. However, it is shown that using arm gestures on big-screen is significantly more natural than using a mouse on both the desktop and the big-screen. Table 4 shows an extra t-test analysis for naturalness which supports the ANOVA analysis.

Phase	Mean		p-value
	Mouse	Arm	
Simple/Desktop	3.30	3.65	0.2804
Simple/Big-screen	3.05	3.90	0.006697
Complex/Desktop	3.6	3.5	0.7647
Complex/Big-screen	2.95	3.85	0.01963

Table 4. Naturalness and results of t-test.

Pleasantness (how pleasant to interact with the UI):
Hypothesis- Using arm gestures as inputs is more pleasant than using mouse.

When analyzing the participant feedback for pleasantness, a similar trend to that of naturalness is observed. Variable 1, $F(1,0.006) = 0.016$, $P = 0.9020$, variable 2, $F(1,6.806) = 3.824$, $P = 0.0654$, and variable 3, $F(1,0.506) = 1.351$, $P = 0.2595$ show no significant effect. Combination of variables 1 and 2, $F(1,1.056) = 3.055$, $P = 0.0966$, variables 1 and 3, $F(1,0.306) = 1.347$, $P = 0.2601$, and variables 1, 2, and 3, $F(1,0.506) = 1.572$, $P = 0.2251$ show no significant effect as well. Similar to naturalness, the only set of variables which illustrate an effect are combination of factors 2 and 3, $F(1,8.556) = 7.716$, $P = 0.0120$ ($M_{mouse-desktop} = 3.7250$, $SD_{mouse-desktop} = 0.9868$ vs. $M_{mouse-bigscreen} = 3.1500$, SD_{mouse-}

bigscreen $= 1.0266$, vs. $M_{gesture-desktop} = 3.6750$, $SD_{gesture-desktop} = 0.8590$, vs. $M_{gesture-bigscreen} = 4.0250$, $SD_{gesture-bigscreen} = 0.8317$). Therefore there is significant interaction between input and output device when pleasantness is being analyzed. Multiple one-way ANOVAs further indicate that mouse when used on desktop is significantly more pleasant than mouse used on big-screen. Furthermore, arm gestures used on big-screen is significantly more pleasant than mouse used on desktop, mouse used on big-screen, and arm gestures used on desktop.

Based on these results, similar to naturalness, the initial hypothesis is rejected. But again, it is revealed that the hypothesis does hold true on big-screens, meaning using arm gestures is significantly more pleasant than mouse when performed on big-screens. Also it is shown that arm gestures used on big-screen is significantly more pleasant compared to when it is used on desktop.

Overall Satisfaction (how overall satisfactory to interact with the UI):
Hypothesis- Overall, using arm gestures as inputs is a more popular experience compared to mouse.
In the overall ranking obtained from participants, no particular variable shows significant effect. This can be due to the fact that while some parameters such as naturalness are ranked higher for gesture on the big-screen, the fatigue level is increased at the same time. This experience, we believe leads to an overall insignificant ranking. The calculated values are as follows: For variable 1, $F(1,0.006) = 0.019$, $P = 0.8928$, for variable 2, $F(1,0.306) = 0.341$, $P = 0.5662$, and for variable 3, $F(1,0.306) = 0.721$, $P = 0.4063$. Similarly for combination of variables, no effect is observed since for variables 1 and 2, $F(1,0.156) = 0.704$, $P = 0.4120$, variables 1 and 3, $F(1,0.006) = 0.022$, $P = 0.8833$, variables 2 and 3, $F(1,3.906) = 4.249$, $P = 0.0532$, and finally for all three variables 1, 2, and 3, $F(1,0.006) = 0.035$, $P = 0.8531$. Based on this analysis, the hypothesis is rejected, meaning neither input hold a significant popularity over the other.

Hypotheses Verification
According to the provided statistical analyses, we summarize our hypotheses verification as follows:

The time and the fatigue factors analyses support our initial hypotheses, meaning gesture inputs are significantly slower and more fatiguing than using a mouse. The initial hypotheses for the easiness and overall satisfaction factors are rejected which indicate that using a mouse is significantly easier than using arm gestures while neither inputs hold a significant popularity over the other. For the naturalness and the pleasure factors, the hypotheses are rejected as well, meaning arm gestures as inputs do not feel significantly more natural or more fun to use compared to mouse. However, it is revealed that using arm gestures on big-screen is significantly more natural and more pleasant than using a mouse on both the desktop and the big-screen. Also it is shown that arm gestures used on big-screen is

significantly more pleasant compared to when it is used on desktop.

Extra Observations

Timing:
Using mouse on big-screen is slower than on desktop. As expected, due to not being familiar with controlling a UI using gestures, the result with mouse is faster than with gestures. However, we believe that having more practice and getting used to the gesture application, allows the users to perform the tasks almost as fast as using a mouse.

Satisfaction:
Most of the participants preferred "equally use of mouse and gesture" as a combination of gesture and mouse inputs.

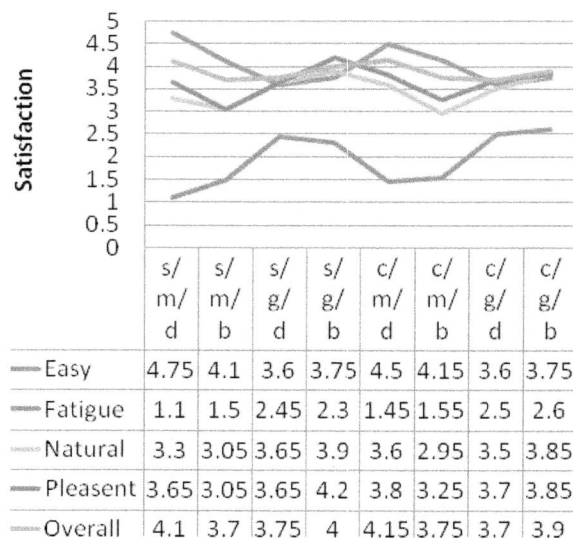

	s/ m/ d	s/ m/ b	s/ g/ d	s/ g/ b	c/ m/ d	c/ m/ b	c/ g/ d	c/ g/ b
Easy	4.75	4.1	3.6	3.75	4.5	4.15	3.6	3.75
Fatigue	1.1	1.5	2.45	2.3	1.45	1.55	2.5	2.6
Natural	3.3	3.05	3.65	3.9	3.6	2.95	3.5	3.85
Pleasent	3.65	3.05	3.65	4.2	3.8	3.25	3.7	3.85
Overall	4.1	3.7	3.75	4	4.15	3.75	3.7	3.9

Figure 4. Satisfaction comparison (s≡simple, c≡complex, m≡mouse, g≡gesture, d≡desktop, b≡big-screen).

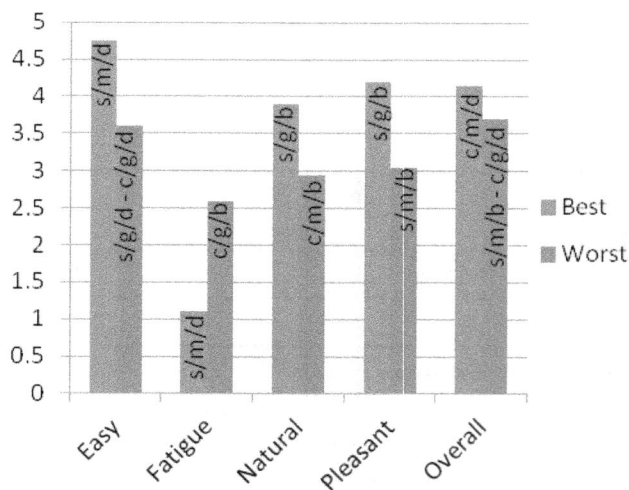

Figure 5. Best/Worst satisfactions (s≡simple, c≡complex, m≡mouse, g≡gesture, d≡desktop, b≡big-screen).

As shown in Figures 4 and 5, doing simple-task with gestures on desktop caused more fatigue than on big-screen, although it is reverse in doing complex-task. Performing simple-task, using mouse on desktop is the easiest and the lightest (least fatigue) and on big-screen is the least pleasant and the least overall satisfactory, while using gestures on big-screen is the most natural, and the most pleasant. In addition, the complex-task using gestures on desktop is the most difficult and the least overall satisfactory. In other words, a short time usage of mouse on big-screen, and a long term usage of gesture on desktop have the least popularity from users' feedback. Doing complex-task, using mouse on desktop is the most overall satisfactory and on big-screen is the least natural, while using gesture on big-screen is the heaviest (most fatigue).

Based on the results, opening a window (Running action) using gesture was the easiest task overall.

This study compared arm gestures with mouse/keyboard in two different settings (desktop and large-scale displays), and two different task difficulties (simple and complex). Based on the participants' feedback, multimodal UI makes more attentive and immersive than the conventional UI. There are still remaining issues to solve such that users feel fatigue while using arms in the air.

CONCLUSION
A new gesture-based interface has been presented and compared with traditional input systems for typical desktop tasks. Through an efficient implementation using Kinect 3D camera and computer vision software libraries, and with comprehensive user experiments, we compared our defined arm gestures to the conventional input devices (mouse/keyboard), in two different settings (desktop and big-screen displays), and during two sets of tasks (simple and complex) for precision, efficiency, easiness, pleasantness, fatigue, naturalness, and overall satisfaction to verify the following hypothesis: the gesture-based input is superior to mouse/keyboard when using big-screen. Our experiment has analytically showed that using gestures on a big-screen display is more natural and pleasant than using a mouse/keyboard in a HCI. On the other hand, arm gestures are more fatiguing than mouse.

There are a few efforts that can be undertaken to improve our prototype system. The current prototype only supports single hand gestures for interaction. Hence, multiple hands gesture interaction can be proposed in order to have more gestures available, reduce the error rate, and ultimately increase the accuracy, speed rate, and user satisfaction, while more hand postures will be selected to support the controlling activities. However, a robust approach in hand gesture recognition is necessary since the multiple hands increase the computational costs and complexity of the system. Using other types of body gestures and studying other types of tasks are among our objectives for further research.

ACKNOWLEDGMENTS
The authors wish to thank S. Ali Etemad for his great contribution in the usability part of this research, and also Colin Killby for his aid in designing our user interface.

REFERENCES
1. Harper, R., Rodden, T., Rogers, Y. and Sellen, A. Being human: Human-computer interaction in the year 2020. *Microsoft Corporation*, (2008).

2. Erol, A., Bebis, G., Nicolescu, M., Boyle, R.D. and Twombly, X. Vision-based hand pose estimation: A review. *Computer Vision and Image Understanding. Special Issue on Vision for Human-Computer Interaction.* vol. 108, (2007), 52-73.

3. Ahn, S.C., Lee, T.S., Kim, I.J., Kwon, Y.M. and Kim, H.G. Computer vision-based interactive presentation system. *Proceedings of Asian Conference for Computer Vision*, (2004).

4. Jain, G. Vision-based hand gesture pose estimation for mobile devices. *University of Toronto*, (2009).

5. Aran, O., Ari, I., Benoit, F., Campr, A., Carrillo, A.H., Fanard, P., Akarun, L., Caplier, A., Rombaut, M. and Sankur, B. Sign language tutoring tool. *eNTERFACE, The Summer Workshop on Multimodal Interfaces*, (2006).

6. Pang, Y.Y., Ismail, N.A. and Gilbert, P.L.S. A real time vision-based hand gesture interaction. *Fourth Asia International Conference on Mathematical/Analytical Modelling and Computer Simulation*, (2010), 237-242.

7. Viola, P. and Jones, M. Robust real-time object detection. *2nd International Workshop on Statistical and Computational Theories of Vision*, (2001).

8. Viola, P. and Jones, M. Rapid object detection using a boosted cascade of simple feature. *IEEE Computer Vision and Pattern Recognition*, vol. 1, (2001), 551-518.

9. Chen, Q., Cordea, M.D., Petriu, E.M., Varkonyi-Koczy, A.R. and Whalen, T.E. Human-computer interaction for smart environment applications using hand-gesture and facial-expressions. *International Journal of Advanced Media and Communication*, vol. 3 n.1/2, (2009), 95-109.

10. Kolsch, M. and Turk, M. Robust hand detection. *International Conference on Automatic Face and Gesture Recognition*, (2004).

11. Kolsch, M. and Turk, M. Analysis of rotational robustness of hand detection with a Viola-Jones detector. *In IAPR International Conference of Pattern Recognition*, (2004).

12. Zhang, Q., Chen, F. and Liu, X. Hand gesture detection and segmentation based on difference background image with complex background. *International Conference on Embedded Software and Systems*, (2008), 338- 343.

13. Anton-Canalis, L., Sanchez-Nielsen, E. and Castrillon-Santana, M. Hand pose detection for vision-based

gesture interfaces. *Conference on Machine Vision Applications*, (2005), 506-509.

14. Marcel, S., Bernier, O., Viallet, J.E. and Collobert D. Hand gesture recognition using input-output hidden Markov models. *Conference on Automatic Face and Gesture Recognition*, (2000).

15. Chen, F., Fu, C. and Huang, C. Hand gesture recognition using a real-time tracking method and hidden Markov models. *Image and Vision Computing*, (2003), 745-758.

16. Liu, Y. and Zhang, P. Vision-based human-computer system using hand gestures. *International Conference on Computational Intelligence and Security*, vol. 2, (2009), 529-532.

17. Yu, C., Wang, X., Huang, H., Shen, J. and Wu, K. Vision-based hand gesture recognition using combinational features. *Sixth International Conference on Intelligent Information Hiding and Multimedia Signal Processing*, (2010), 543-546.

18. Cabral, M.C., Morimoto, C.H. and Zuffo, M.K. On the usability of gesture interfaces in virtual reality environments. *Proceedings of the 2005 Latin American conference on Human-computer interaction*, (2005), 100-108.

19. Villaroman, N., Rowe, D. and Swan, B. Teaching natural user interaction using OpenNI and the Microsoft Kinect sensor. *Proceedings of the 2011 conference on Information technology education*, (2011), 227-232.

20. Kang, J.W., Seo, D.J. and Jung, D.S. A study on the control method of 3-dimensional space application using Kinect system. *International Journal of Computer Science and Network Security*, vol.11, no.9, (2011), 55-59.

21. Bragdon, A., DeLine, R., Hinckley, K. and Morris M.R. Code space: Touch + air gesture hybrid interactions for supporting developer meetings. *Proceedings of the ACM International Conference on Interactive Tabletops and Surfaces*, (2011), 212-221.

22. Bhuiyan, M. and Picking, R. A gesture controlled user interface for inclusive design and evaluative study of its usability. *Journal of Software Engineering and Applications*, (2011), 513-521.

23. Ebert, L.C., Hatch, G., Ampanozi, G., Thali M.J. and Ross, S. You can't touch this: Touch-free navigation through radiological images. *Surg Innov Journal*, (2011).

Brain–Computer Interface (BCI): Is It Strictly Necessary to Use Random Sequences in Visual Spellers?

Manson Cheuk-Man Fong, James William Minett, Thierry Blu, and William Shi-Yuan Wang
The Chinese University of Hong Kong
Hong Kong, China
cmfong@ee.cuhk.edu.hk, jminett@ee.cuhk.edu.hk, tblu@ee.cuhk.edu.hk, wsywang@ee.cuhk.edu.hk

ABSTRACT

The P300 speller is a standard paradigm for brain–computer interfacing (BCI) based on electroencephalography (EEG). It exploits the fact that the user's selective attention to a target stimulus among a random sequence of stimuli enhances the magnitude of the P300 evoked potential. The present study questions the necessity of using random sequences of stimulation. In two types of experimental runs, subjects attended to a target stimulus while the stimuli, four in total, were each intensified twelve times, in either random order or deterministic order. The 32-channel EEG data were analyzed offline using linear discriminant analysis (LDA). Similar classification accuracies of 95.3% and 93.2% were obtained for the random and deterministic runs, respectively, using the data associated with 3 sequences of stimulation. Furthermore, using a montage of 5 posterior electrodes, the two paradigms attained identical accuracy of 92.4%. These results suggest that: (a) the use of random sequences is not necessary for effective BCI performance; and (b) deterministic sequences can be used in some BCI speller applications.

Author Keywords

Brain–computer interface (BCI); P300 speller; ERP-based visual speller; electroencephalography; oddball paradigm; linear discriminant analysis (LDA).

ACM Classification Keywords

H.5.m. [**Information interfaces and presentation (e.g., HCI)**]: Miscellaneous; H.5.2. [**User Interfaces**]: User-centered design.

INTRODUCTION

A brain–computer interface (BCI) [37] is a device which translates brain signals into commands that control applications. Currently, scalp electroencephalography (EEG) is the predominant technology for realizing non-invasive BCI systems, not only because of the portability of EEG systems, but also due to the continual progress being

made in eliciting different types of prominent control signals in a range of EEG-based BCI paradigms (for a review, see [5]).

The P300 speller, the focus of the present study, represents one of the most successful EEG-based BCI paradigms. Primarily, it exploits the fact that selective visual attention to a target stimulus can enhance the average electrical potential elicited, referred to as the event-related potential (ERP [14]), compared to that elicited by other stimuli that are either unattended or deliberately ignored. More precisely, it is known that when subjects respond mentally to rare, target events that are *randomly* interspersed among frequent, non-target events (the so-called *oddball paradigm*), the target events (the *oddballs*) tend to elicit a stronger ERP component, termed P300, than the non-target events [10, 33]. The component is so named as it is a positive deflection in electrical potential that peaks around 300 ms post-stimulus, and is usually more prominent at central-parietal sites. In the original formulation of the P300 speller by Farwell and Donchin in 1988 [11], a 6 × 6 matrix of symbols, analogous to a virtual keyboard, is displayed on-screen to the user as choices—henceforth, we shall refer to this speller as the *matrix speller* to distinguish it from other variants. To select a choice, the user is required to attend to that choice, while the rows and columns of the matrix are intensified successively in random order. Intensification of a row or column that contains the intended choice, by virtue of its rare and random occurrence, constitutes an oddball, so eliciting a stronger P300 than that elicited by intensification of other rows and columns. This difference forms the basis for the intended choice to be identified. Recent works confirmed the validity of the matrix speller as a practical BCI, through online assessment with both able-bodied [8, 13] and pathological groups [24, 30]. Numerous optimization schemes have been explored in order to increase the communication rate [21], from adjusting the various system parameters associated with the speller (e.g., matrix size [2, 29], inter-stimulus interval (ISI) [29], method of intensification [16, 34, 35], stimulus type [15, 22], etc.) to improving the methods of signal processing and classification [6, 15, 20]. This collective effort has allowed the mean input rate for the matrix speller to increase from about 12 bits/min, as estimated offline in Farwell and Donchin's original study, to about 23 bits/min, as determined online in a recent study [35]. In another line of study, other visual paradigms in which different geometric configurations are used to arrange the choices have been tested. These included a four-choice paradigm in which four stimuli ('YES', 'NO', 'PASS', 'END') were successively presented centrally [28]; a 2D cursor control system, wherein four arrows were arranged on the periphery of a square [25]; and a two-level speller, referred to as Hex-o-Spell, in which six discs containing either one or multiple symbols were arranged in the corners of a hexagon [6, 36].

The present study has two primary motives, one theoretical and one practical. On the theoretical side, we examine one of the most important, but often understated, working assumptions of the P300 speller paradigm, namely, that the performance of the BCI is the best when the choices are intensified in a random order. Specifically, we compare the classification accuracies obtained for two paradigms—a random paradigm, in which the choices are successively intensified in random sequence; and a deterministic paradigm, in which the choices are successively intensified in fixed sequence (i.e., in the same order repeatedly). The use of random intensification sequences has two clear advantages: (a) rare targets in a random sequence are known to elicit a larger P300 than non-targets for almost every subject [10], providing a general basis for discriminating between the two types of stimuli; (b) although its amplitude is modulated by attention [26], the P300 can be elicited without active attention by visual oddballs, hence can be considered an automatic response [18, 31]. It is unclear, however, to what extent the utility of the P300 speller hinges on the use of random sequences for choice intensification. More precisely, is selective attention to target choices alone sufficient for the choices to be identified, regardless of whether the sequence of intensification is random or deterministic? Given that the P300 amplitude elicited by targets increases as the subjective expectancy towards the target occurrences decreases [9, 32], it is tempting to conclude that, since the target occurrences in a deterministic sequence are not only predictable, but also entirely known, the degree of subjective expectancy is maximal, which would in turn imply that the P300 amplitude elicited by the targets should be smallest under such circumstances. However, the findings regarding subjective expectancy have been obtained using random sequences, and there is no guarantee that they can be generalized to the case of deterministic sequences. In fact, a recent study reported that targets following a predictive sequence, i.e., one which allowed the subject to precisely learn of the exact times of occurrences of the targets, elicited a P300 component whose magnitude was not significantly different from that elicited by targets following a random, non-predictive sequence [12]. Although that study was not conducted within a BCI context, its findings clearly cast doubts on the assumption that the P300 amplitude elicited by the targets in deterministic sequences will be reduced. Adding to these uncertainties are the recent findings that ERP components

other than P300 can also be used to discriminate targets and non-targets. In particular, for the matrix speller, these components include P2 [1, 19] and N2 [1, 20, 22, 36]. For paradigms in which the choices are arranged differently, these include a range of both earlier and later components, such as P1, N1, P2, N2 and N3, in Hex-o-spell [6, 36], and again, N2, when the stimuli are centrally presented one-by-one [3]. Given that the modulation of such a wide range of components might not all hinge on the use of random sequences, it is clearly a valid question as to whether some of these components will be modulated in the case of the deterministic paradigm.

Apart from the theoretical interests above, there are practical concerns over the use of random sequences, especially from the point of view of user-centered design. Thus far, there have been a number of unresolved weaknesses associated with the matrix speller. To attain high accuracy, it is necessary to visually intensify all symbols for multiple times, and then average the resultant responses to produce a robust signal for classification. The sustained visual stimulation of rows and columns, however, can cause discomfort [16, 17], and discourage long use. Intensifying symbols one at a time can reduce the discomfort, but this results in a reduction in the communication rate [13]. Intuitively, the random stimulation might contribute to such discomfort, since the randomness requires the user to maintain a high-level of concentration throughout the symbol-selection process, which may last up to 10 seconds. In contrast, if the sequence of stimulation is deterministic, users can vary their level of concentration accordingly during a selection, e.g., to relax between target stimulations. Thus, if the deterministic paradigm can achieve a similar accuracy as the random paradigm, it will provide the target users with an alternative system that is potentially more user-friendly.

In the present study, as a starting point for studying the differences between using random and deterministic sequences within a BCI context, a simple four-choice paradigm similar to [25] in terms of geometrical arrangement was used. The results are of direct relevance to the Hex-o-Spell paradigm, whose accuracy has been demonstrated recently to be higher than that of the matrix speller [36].

EXPERIMENTAL METHODS

Participants
Six healthy Chinese subjects (S1–S6; 3 male and 3 female), aged 22–37 (mean 26.3), took part in the experiment as volunteers. Three subjects (S2, S4 and S5) had not previously sat an EEG experiment; the other three subjects (S1, S3 & S6) all had prior experiences with the P300 speller paradigm using random sequences, but not using deterministic sequences. Informed consent was obtained from each subject.

Data Acquisition

Each subject was seated in a quiet room 60 cm in front of a 19' LCD monitor (resolution: 1280 × 1024) that displayed the experimental stimuli as images. Each image was composed of four Chinese characters, arranged geometrically according to their respective meanings (left, up, right and down). Figure 1 exemplifies an intensification of the stimulus "left". Each character is about 80 pixels wide (visual angle: 2.0°), with its center being 140 pixels (visual angle: 3.6°) from the center of the screen.

EEG data were acquired at a sampling rate of 1024 Hz using a 32-channel ActiveTwo EEG system (BioSemi B. V., Amsterdam, The Netherlands). Figure 2 shows the positionings of the 32 pin-type, Ag/AgCl active electrodes. Two flat-type electrodes were attached over the left and right mastoids for offline re-referencing. Two additional electrodes, common mode sense (CMS) and driven right leg (DRL), positioned at C1 and C2 respectively, were used to complete a feedback loop, such that the average electrical potential over all electrodes was driven to as close a voltage as possible to the amplifier reference voltage [4]. Stimulus presentation was controlled using the software E-Prime 2.0 (Psychology Software Tools, Inc.).

Experimental Procedure

Each subject completed two sets of four blocks for each of the two paradigms: *random paradigm* (**RP**) and *deterministic paradigm* (**DP**). Each block consisted of 24 experimental runs. The details of a run are as follows:

1. At the beginning of each run, subjects were shown a prompt ("Please attend to: X") on-screen for 2 seconds, where X represented one of the four possible target choices (left, up, right and down), displayed in Chinese. Each choice was selected as the target choice exactly

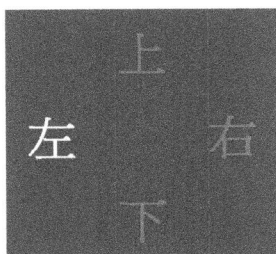

Figure 1. An intensification of the choice "left", printed in Chinese.

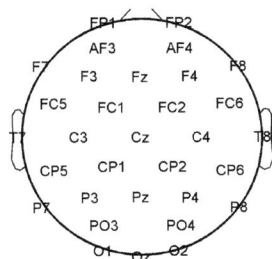

Figure 2. 32-channel ActiveTwo EEG system.

once every 4 runs. Thus, within a block, each choice was selected as target 6 times.

2. An image showing the four choices in fully-lit color (as exemplified for "left" in Figure 1) was then presented for 2 seconds, after which all four choices were displayed in dimly-lit color for a further 2 seconds.

3. The choices were then intensified in succession for 12 sequences, each consisting of 4 intensifications. Each intensification consisted of the display of two images: the first image, in which one of the choices was fully-lit (while the others were dimly-lit), was displayed for 133 ms; the second image, in which all choices were dimly-lit, was displayed for 33 ms. The inter-stimulus interval (ISI) was therefore 166 ms. For convenience, a sequence of intensifications is referred to as a *trial* and a single intensification a *sub-trial*.

4. For the **RP** runs, the choices were intensified in pseudorandom sequences, meaning that the following criteria were satisfied: (a) each choice was intensified exactly once in a trial; and (b) across trials, none of the choices was intensified twice consecutively. For the **DP** runs, the choices were intensified in fixed sequence, i.e., in the same order for all twelve trials. The order was selected to be "left, up, right & down", i.e., clockwise starting from the Chinese character for "left".

5. Following the standard procedure for the matrix speller, subjects were asked to respond to every intensification of the target character by maintaining a mental count of the number of times the target character had been intensified within the run.

6. The duration of each run was approximately 14 seconds, and there was a 3-second rest period between runs.

Each block lasted for approximately 7 minutes, and there was an optional pause after 12 runs. The total time for one recording session was about 1 hour.

The order of the two sets of blocks was counterbalanced across subjects, to control for any potential training effect. That is, for half of the subjects, the 4 **RP** blocks were administered first, while for the other half, the 4 **DP** blocks were administered first.

DATA ANALYSIS

To compare the projected performance attainable by the random and deterministic paradigms, the EEG data acquired for their corresponding runs were analyzed using the same procedure, to be detailed in this section. In brief, for both paradigms, four-fold cross-validation was performed for each subject. Specifically, for a given fold of analysis, the runs from three of the four blocks were used to train a classifier, which was subsequently applied to classify the target choices in the remaining block; the analysis was repeated four times such that each block served once as the testing data.

Preprocessing

Six preprocessing steps, all handled using EEGLAB [7], were carried out in the order stated below.

1. *Filtering.* The cutoff frequencies of the band-pass filter were set to 1.0 Hz and 40 Hz.

2. *Segmentation.* The band-passed data were segmented into sub-trials of duration 833 ms. Each sub-trial started at 333 ms pre-stimulus, and lasted until 500 ms post-stimulus. For each block, a total of 1152 sub-trials were extracted, corresponding to 288 and 864 sub-trials that were time-locked to a target and a non-target stimulus, respectively. These sub-trials are referred to as target sub-trials and non-target sub-trials.

3. *Re-referencing.* Within each sub-trial, the time-series associated with the two mastoid electrodes were averaged, and subtracted from that associated with each of the 32 main electrodes.

4. *Baseline correction.* For every sub-trial, a baseline potential between 333 ms pre-stimulus to 333 ms post-stimulus was estimated for each electrode. Such a baseline period was chosen such that it covered one sequence of intensifications, and contained, on average, one target trial and three non-target trials for both random and deterministic blocks.

5. *Artifact rejection.* EEG data are often contaminated by artifacts whose presence can be attributed to oculomotor activities, such as eye blinks and eye movement, which are reflected as large amplitude signals that are most prominent at anterior frontal sites. To reduce the effects of such outliers, sub-trials in which an absolute potential exceeding 50μV was recorded from either of the two anterior frontal sites (FP1 and FP2; see Figure 2), within a time-window spanning 333 ms pre-stimulus to 500 ms post-stimulus, were rejected. The other sub-trials belonging to the same trial were also rejected. On average, the percentage of trials that remained were 83.0 ± 16.1% and 78.0 ± 17.4% for the random and deterministic paradigms, respectively.

6. *Downsampling.* Each sub-trial was downsampled from 1024 Hz to 128 Hz.

Classification

After preprocessing, machine-learning was applied to recognize the target choice in each run. Since artifact rejection had been applied, the number of trials available for training was different for each subject and each fold of cross-validation. On average, out of a maximum of 864 trials, there were 717 and 674 trials remaining for training, for the random and deterministic paradigms, respectively.

Feature selection

The 2048 time-samples from 0–500 ms post-stimulus, corresponding to the 64 time-samples in the 32 electrodes, were first standardized, and were then used as the candidate features for constructing a feature vector. That is, given a sub-trial, the potential x measured at a particular electrode and time-point was transformed as follows:

$$x' = (x - \mu_x)/\sigma_x \qquad (1)$$

where μ_x and σ_x were the pooled estimates of the mean and standard deviation of x, based on the training data and without taking classes (targets vs. non-targets) into account. The time-window covered most of the ERP components previously reported to be modulated in the random paradigm, including P1, N1, P2, N2 and P300. To optimize the classification performance and to control for effects of over-fitting, the maximum number of spatiotemporal features (K) selected for inclusion was examined at 6 levels: 50, 100, 200, 500, 1000, and 2048. Specifically, based on the training data, the two-sample t-statistics were obtained for every spatiotemporal feature, i.e., the corresponding potentials in target sub-trials and non-target sub-trials were subject to the Student's t-test. The K most-discriminative features whose t-statistics had the largest absolute values were then selected [23] for the given fold of analysis.

Linear discriminant analysis

Fisher's linear discriminant analysis (see [15], for example) was applied to the training data to obtain a binary classifier for discriminating between target and non-target sub-trials. The classifier corresponds to a decision hyperplane defined by:

$$\boldsymbol{w} \cdot \boldsymbol{x} - b = 0 \qquad (2)$$

where $\boldsymbol{x}$ is a vector in the space of feature vectors, $\boldsymbol{w}$ a normalized vector of feature weights, and b a bias term. The sum $\boldsymbol{w} \cdot \boldsymbol{x} - b$ is referred to as the standardized discriminant function [27], which tends to be positive for targets and negative for non-targets. In this paper, the elements of $\boldsymbol{w}$ will be referred to as the standardized discriminant function coefficients.

Calculation of classification performances

To determine the minimum number of intensification sequences necessary to achieve accurate performance, runs were classified using the data associated with N trials, for $N = 1,...,12$. Specifically, the intended choice in each run was determined using the classifier obtained, and compared to the actual choice that was specified to the subject. For a given run, N scores were calculated for each choice c as follows:

$$Score(N,c) = \sum_{k=1}^{N} s_{k,c} = \sum_{k=1}^{N} \boldsymbol{w} \cdot \boldsymbol{x}_{k,c}, N = 1,...,12 \qquad (3)$$

where $s_{k,c}$ represents the sub-score for the sub-trial that was timelocked to the intensification of the choice c in the kth trial within the run, and $\boldsymbol{x}_{k,c}$ the feature vector associated with that sub-trial. The choice with the highest score was determined to be the target for the given run. Note that: (a) the constant, bias term b in (2) was not included in calculation of the sub-scores, since this term would have no effect on the relative scores across choices; (b) the sub-scores associated with a rejected sequence were all replaced by zeros. Overall, the above calculations were performed for both training and testing runs, to evaluate whether or not there was serious problem of over-fitting.

RESULTS

Classification Performances

Figure 3 summarizes the mean classification accuracies obtained with different number of trials (N = 1, ..., 12) for both the random paradigm (**RP**) and the deterministic paradigm (**DP**). Each curve represents the accuracies obtained for a particular number of features (K = 50, 100, 200, 500, 1000 and 2048). Individual accuracies were averaged across the four folds of validations. As expected, the average accuracy generally increased with increasing N for both paradigms. Also, since it was evident that the average accuracy increased with K, only the cases for K = 2048 are reported in detail from this point onward. Most importantly, accurate performance was obtained for both paradigms, with the accuracies for $N = 3$ and $N = 12$ being $95.3 \pm 1.7\%$ and $99.0 \pm 1.3\%$ for **RP**, and the corresponding accuracies were $93.2 \pm 4.9\%$ and $98.3 \pm 1.4\%$ for **DP**. The training accuracies were also obtained for both paradigms. Although the testing accuracy for each N was lower than the corresponding training accuracy for both paradigms, such effects of over-fitting were not serious. Specifically, the differences between training accuracy and testing accuracy (training – testing) at $N = 3$ and $N = 12$ were $2.7 \pm 1.3\%$ and $0.2 \pm 0.6\%$ for **RP**, and $3.1 \pm 2.2\%$ and $0.4 \pm 0.5\%$ for **DP**, respectively.

The Spatiotemporal Features Underlying Classification

In this sub-section, the basis for discriminating target and non-target sub-trials in the present experiment is demonstrated and characterized using three methods: (a) event-related potentials; (b) standardized discriminant function analysis; and (c) supplementary classification

analyses, by montages (i.e., subsets of electrodes) and by time-intervals. For practical considerations, it is essential to determine whether accurate performance is attainable with only a small set of electrodes. Thus, our main focus is on locating the electrodes that are the most informative. The temporal aspects were also inspected systematically to determine which time-interval was the most informative.

(a) Event-related potentials

Figure 4 shows the grand-averaged ERP waveforms (i.e., average ERP waveforms across subjects) elicited by both targets and non-targets for both paradigms, as recorded over various positions on the scalp, taking all 4 experimental blocks into account for all subjects. In both cases, a prominent positivity peaking between 150–300 ms post-stimulus was observed for the waveform elicited by targets but not by non-targets, over a broad range of electrodes, as highlighted in Figure 4 for the electrodes Fz, Cz and Pz. However, the grand-averaged ERP waveforms do not capture the individual differences across subjects. Thus, this positivity between 150–300 ms does not necessarily comprise the most informative features on a per-subject basis. To demonstrate the individual differences, the two-sample t-statistics comparing the potential associated with every spatiotemporal feature in the target and non-target sub-trials were obtained for all six subjects. These t-statistics are shown as feature maps in Figure 5 for both paradigms. A highly positive (or negative) value would imply that the mean potential for target sub-trials was significantly greater (or less) than that for non-target sub-trials. Consistent with the grand-averaged ERP shown in Figure 4, prominent positivities within the 150–300 ms interval post-stimulus were observed for most subjects at many frontal, central and parietal locations, for both paradigms. However, for all subjects except S4, a prominent peak that emerged within the 100–200 ms interval post-stimulus was also observed at some occipital locations. For S1–S3, the peak was positive, while for S5–S6, the peak was negative.

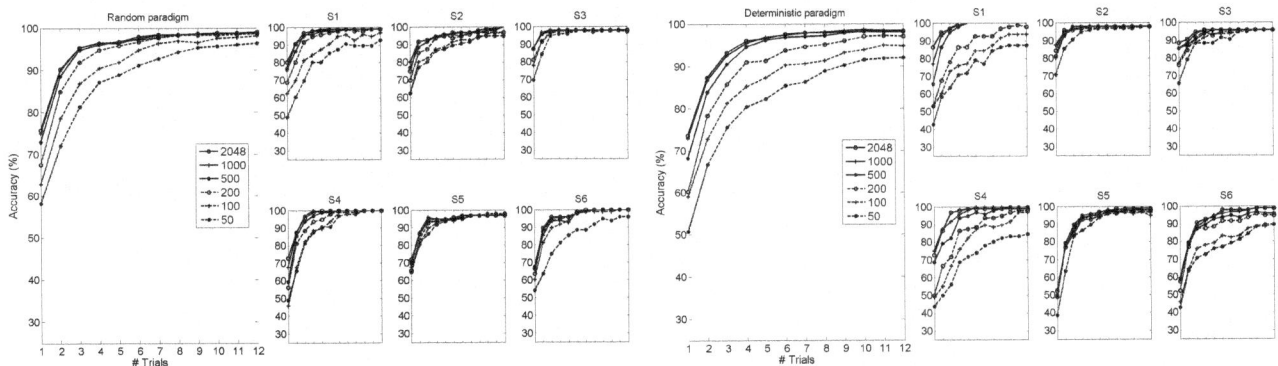

Figure 3. Mean classification accuracies versus the number of trials employed for classification, for the random paradigm (left) and deterministic paradigm (right). Each curve was obtained using a different number of features (K = 50, 100, 200, 500, 1000, and 2048) for classification.

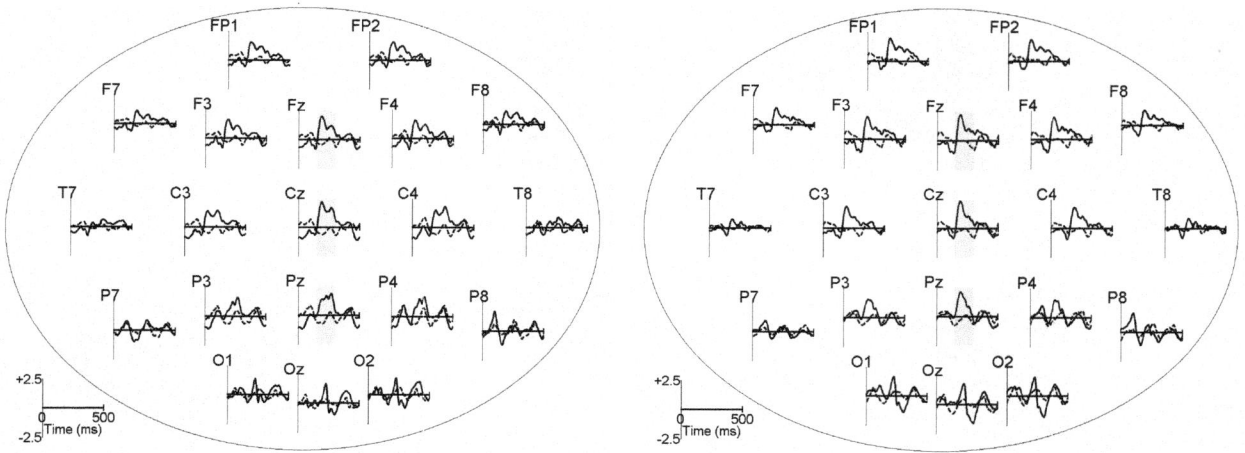

Figure 4. Grand-averaged event-related potential (ERP) obtained at 20 selected electrodes, for both the random (left) and deterministic (right) paradigms. The interval between 150–300 post-stimulus is highlighted in gray for Fz, Cz & Pz, to illustrate the positivity observed.

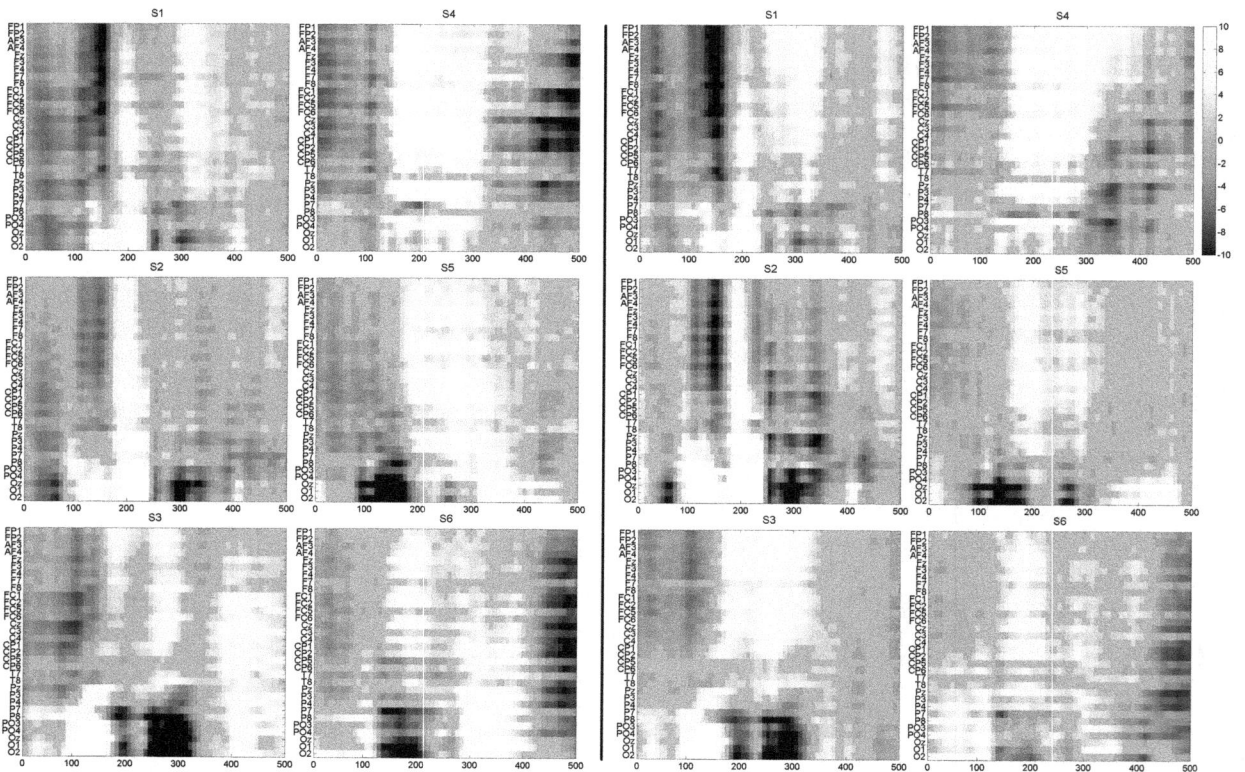

Figure 5. T-value maps obtained for individual subjects, for both the random (left) and deterministic (right) paradigms. The t-statistics associated with the features for which the difference across the target and non-target conditions was non-significant (p>0.05) were displayed as zero-values.

(b) Standardized discriminant function analysis

The contribution made by each spatiotemporal feature for group separation can be ranked according to its associating coefficient in the standardized discriminant function [27]. To shed light on the nature of the primary features, the square of the coefficients were summed over time, to compare the contributions of different electrodes, and over space (i.e., electrodes), to measure the contributions of different time-points. Figure 6 shows, for both **RP** and **DP**, the variation in contributions (by percentage) along the

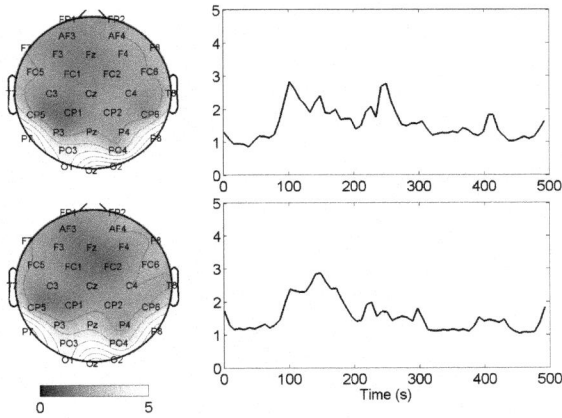

Figure 6. The contributions (by %) made by different electrodes, shown as a topomap (left), and different time-points, shown as a time-series (right), as indicated by the sum of squares of the standardized discriminant function coefficients along the appropriate dimension. Top: random paradigm; bottom: deterministic paradigm.

spatial and temporal dimensions, averaged across the six subjects and for the four folds of analyses. The results of the spatial analysis are shown in detail in Table 1 for the seven most important electrodes in each paradigm. Had the relative contributions been the same for the 32 electrodes, the total contributions made by each electrode would have

been 3.125 %. Consistent with the similarities shown in Figure 6, the first six electrodes were the same across paradigms, namely Oz, O1, O2, P7, P8, and PO3—all posterior electrodes. Also, their order of importance was almost identical, except that O2, by proportion, was consistently found to contribute to the discrimination more for **RP** than for **DP**, for all six subjects.

Table 2 shows the total contributions made by four time-intervals (T1: 0–125 ms, T2: 125–250 ms, T3: 250–375 ms & T4: 375–500 ms), for each subject and for both paradigms. It is apparent that the feature weights tend to be concentrated in time-interval T2 (125–250 ms), exceptions being S3 and S5 for **RP**, wherein the feature weights were more concentrated in T3 and T1, respectively. These temporal characteristics suggest that the time-interval from 125–250 ms was more responsible for the discrimination than the other time-intervals.

(c) Supplementary classification analyses
Two types of classification analyses were performed to characterize the spatiotemporal characteristics present in the two paradigms. In the first analysis (the spatial analysis), the data associated with 8 montages (see Figure 7), each comprising 5 electrodes, were used for classification. In half of the montages, a midline electrode (Fz, Cz, Pz or Oz) was included together with four neighboring electrodes; in the other half, a midline electrode was included together with four laterally arranged electrodes.

Sub.	Random							Deterministic						
	Oz	O2	P7	P8	O1	PO3	T7	Oz	P7	P8	O2	O1	PO3	PO4
S1	10.5	7.9	9.9	4.8	6.1	3.1	4.1	9.9	9.4	7.7	7.1	5.2	3.1	2.7
S2	11.9	7.1	8.1	7.3	5.8	4.7	2.7	7.7	8.4	7.8	5.9	6.0	2.3	4.6
S3	10.5	8.5	5.6	8.7	4.0	3.5	3.3	12.6	7.5	9.8	6.5	5.6	2.1	3.2
S4	2.1	3.9	11.8	9.5	3.0	5.4	4.0	2.0	11.6	8.4	3.2	2.3	11.8	3.0
S5	13.1	9.1	3.5	8.8	4.3	5.7	1.8	12.7	5.3	7.0	7.5	4.3	5.0	3.3
S6	7.6	12.2	8.4	4.0	5.5	3.2	3.4	12.3	6.7	2.8	11.4	5.5	1.8	3.7
Avg.	9.3	8.1	7.9	7.2	4.8	4.3	3.2	9.5	8.2	7.3	6.9	4.8	4.3	3.4

Table 1. The relative contributions made by the 7 most informative channels, for both the random and deterministic paradigms. Note that the two sets of informative electrodes were largely the same.

Sub.	Random				Deterministic			
	T1	T2	T3	T4	T1	T2	T3	T4
S1	19.9	**36.0**	22.8	21.3	26.7	**32.4**	17.8	23.0
S2	25.3	**30.3**	22.8	21.6	24.8	**31.5**	23.5	20.3
S3	18.8	29.6	**30.9**	20.7	21.7	**36.8**	23.2	18.2
S4	20.1	**35.8**	24.7	19.3	19.9	**40.4**	22.1	17.6
S5	**32.9**	23.9	21.9	21.2	27.8	**28.6**	21.1	22.5
S6	23.8	**28.7**	26.7	20.7	25.8	**29.9**	21.2	23.1
Avg.	23.5	**30.7**	25.0	20.8	24.5	**33.3**	21.5	20.8

Table 2. The relative contributions made by different time intervals (T1: 0–125 ms; T2: 125–250 ms; T3: 250–375 ms; T4: 375–500 ms), for both the random and deterministic paradigms. The value corresponding to the most informative interval per-subject was shown in bold. Note that on average, T2 was the most informative for both paradigms.

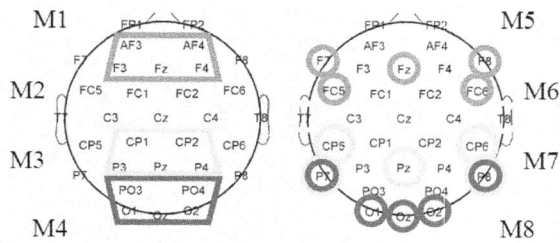

Figure 7. Eight candidate montages (M1–M8), each consisting of 5 electrodes, for which classification accuracy was obtained.

Given that the standardized discriminant function analysis in part (b) indicated an advantage for posterior electrodes, it was expected that the two montages M4 (Oz, O1, O2, PO3 & PO4) and M8 (Oz, O1, O2, P7 & P8) would give rise to the most accurate performances. However, the standardized discriminant function is multivariate in nature, i.e., it indicates the importance of a set of variables in the presence of other variables. Thus, it is not necessary that the set of features carrying the most weights in the analysis in section (b) give rise to the highest classification accuracies when employed separately. In the second analysis (the temporal analysis), consistent with the analyses in part (b), the four time intervals (T1–T4) were examined by using the data from all 32 channels for classification.

Figure 8 shows the results of the two analyses. For the spatial analysis, it is clear that the classification accuracies for both paradigms increased along the anterior-posterior axis, reaching a maximum at M4 and M8 (Figure 8, top panel). In particular, using 3 trials for classification, the accuracies for **RP** and **DP** were respectively 92.4 ± 8.4% and 92.4 ± 6.2% for M4, and 89.4 ± 10.0% and 88.4 ± 14.5% for M8. For the temporal analysis, the classification accuracies peak at T2 (125–250 ms) for both paradigms (Figure 8, bottom panel). Thus, both results are consistent with the conclusions made in part (b).

DISCUSSIONS

In the random and deterministic paradigms, by using the 32-channel data associated with 3 trials, target choices could be recognized at a mean accuracy of 95.3% and 93.2%, respectively. Moreover, for both paradigms, the accuracy reached at least 90% for all six subjects by the end of the fourth trial. In addition, consistent with the indications from the standardized discriminant function analysis, the highest accuracy was achieved by a montage consisting of 5 posterior electrodes (Oz, O1, O2, PO3 & PO4), being 92.4% for both paradigms. Evidently, as far as the classification performance is concerned, neither paradigm has an apparent advantage over the other. Consistent results regarding the temporal aspects were also obtained for the standardized discriminant function analysis and the supplementary classification analyses; in both analyses, the time-interval between 125–250 ms was found to be the most informative for both paradigms. Such

spatiotemporal distributions of primary features are not typically associated with P300 responses, which have a central-parietal distribution that peak around 300 ms post-stimulus. They are, nonetheless, consistent with the growing evidence accumulated that the P300 responses do not necessarily comprise the primary features for classification in this type of visual paradigms. For this reason, some authors have advocated the more generic term of ERP-based visual speller [36]. In the present experiment, the early responses recorded at the posterior sites were found to be the primary features for both the random and deterministic paradigms, suggesting that these responses, unlike the P300 responses, might be qualitatively similar across paradigms, and might not be modulated by randomness in the intensification sequences. These conclusions have to be confirmed with a larger data set.

In terms of classification performance, our results compare favorably with a previous study in which a four-choice paradigm was employed [28]. In that study, the best-performing subject managed an accuracy of 75% at 4 trials, and 92% at 19 trials. A possible explanation for our much higher accuracies is our use of a much shorter ISI (166 ms, vs. 1,400 ms in [28]). In the original matrix speller study

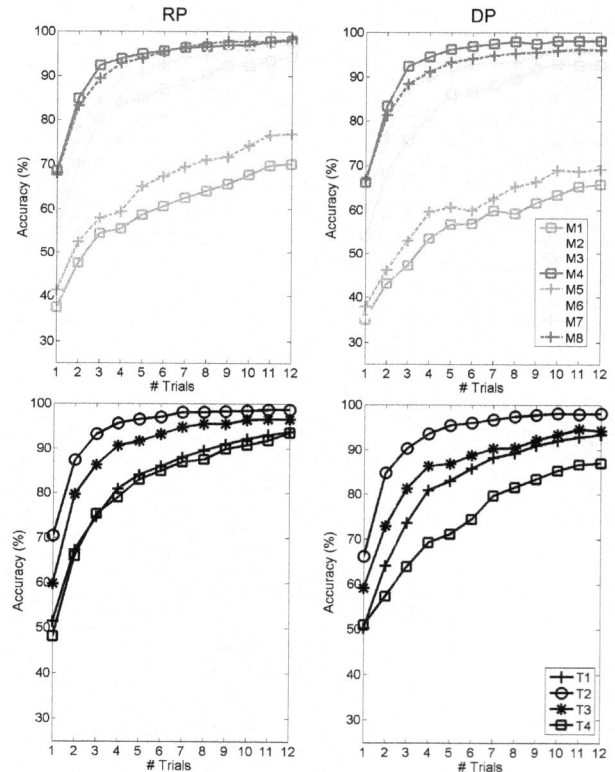

Figure 8. Mean classification accuracies versus the number of trials employed for classification, for the random (left) and deterministic (right) paradigms. Top panel: each curve was obtained using different montages (M1–M8; see Figure 7) for classification. Bottom panel: each curve was obtained using different time-intervals (T1–T4) for classification.

[11], a higher accuracy was observed at an ISI of 500 ms than at 125 ms, suggesting that a longer ISI could be helpful for good performance. On the other hand, as pointed out in [15], this conclusion might hold only within certain limits of ISIs. Our result that the classification performance is higher at an ISI of 166 ms (than at 1,400 ms) is consistent with this view. A systematic investigation of the ISI variable, after controlling for other confounding factors (such as geometrical configuration), is necessary to determine if any general conclusion could be drawn regarding the dependence of accuracy on ISI.

Finally, of the two criteria (randomness and low target probability) necessary for an oddball sequence, the present study has investigated only the former criterion. For practical considerations, it is especially important to determine if the present results, obtained with a four-choice paradigm, can be extended to other paradigms that allow more choices to be selected. If so, the use of deterministic sequences may offer a more user-friendly alternative than random sequences for ERP-based visual spellers. Work is under way to test if the deterministic paradigm works as well as the random paradigm as the number of choices is increased, e.g., from 4 to 8.

CONCLUSION

The primary aim of the present study was to determine whether the use of random sequences for stimulus intensification is crucial for accurate performance in ERP-based visual spellers by comparing the accuracies obtained when the choices were intensified either in random or deterministic sequences. It was found that the intended choices could be recognized at a mean accuracy of 95.3% and 93.2%, respectively, using the 32-channel data associated with 3 intensification sequences. The time-interval from 125–250 ms post-stimulus was found to be the most informative. To assess the projected performance of a BCI system in which the number of electrodes available is expected to be limited, further analyses were performed using the data associated with 8 candidate montages, each comprising 5 electrodes. A comparable mean accuracy of 92.4% was achieved in both paradigms for the best montage, consisting of 5 posterior electrodes: Oz, O1, O2, PO3 & PO4. These results suggest that: (a) the use of random sequences is not necessary for effective BCI performance; and (b) deterministic sequences can be used in some BCI speller applications.

ACKNOWLEDGMENTS

This work is supported in part by grants made to the Chinese University of Hong Kong by the Research Grants Council of the Hong Kong SAR (T. Blu: CUHK410110), the Office of the Government Chief Information Officer (W.S-Y. Wang: af-006), and the Patent Committee of The Chinese University of Hong Kong (TBF/11/ENG/001).

REFERENCES

1. Allison, B.Z. and Pineda, J.A. Effects of SOA and flash pattern manipulations on ERPs, performance, and preference: Implications for a BCI system. *International Journal of Psychophysiology 59*, 2 (2006), 127-140.

2. Allison, B.Z. and Pineda, J.A. ERPs evoked by different matrix sizes: implications for a brain computer interface (BCI) system. *IEEE Transactions on Neural Systems and Rehabilitation Engineering 11*, 2 (2003), 110-113.

3. Bandt, C., Weymar, M., Samaga, D. and Hamm, A.O. A simple classification tool for single-trial analysis of ERP components. *Psychophysiology 46*, 4 (2009), 747-757.

4. BioSemi. *Active Two User Manual (Version 3.2, July 3, 2007)*. Amsterdam.

5. Birbaumer, N. Breaking the silence: Brain–computer interfaces (BCI) for communication and motor control. *Psychophysiology 43*, 6 (2006), 517-532.

6. Blankertz, B., Lemm, S., Treder, M., Haufe, S. and Müller, K.-R. Single-trial analysis and classification of ERP components — A tutorial. *NeuroImage 56*, 2 (2011), 814-825.

7. Delorme, A. and Makeig, S. EEGLAB: an open source toolbox for analysis of single-trial EEG dynamics including independent component analysis. *Journal of Neuroscience Methods 134*, 1 (2004), 9-21.

8. Donchin, E., Spencer, K.M. and Wijesinghe, R. The mental prosthesis: assessing the speed of a P300-based brain–computer interface. *IEEE Transactions on Rehabilitation Engineering 8*, 2 (2000), 174-179.

9. Duncan-Johnson, C.C. and Donchin, E. On Quantifying Surprise: The Variation of Event-Related Potentials With Subjective Probability. *Psychophysiology 14*, 5 (1977), 456-467.

10. Fabiani, M., Gratton, G., Karis, D. and Donchin, E. The definition, identification and reliability of measurement of the P300 component of the event-related brain potential. In Ackles, P., Jennings, J. and Coles, M.G.H. eds. *Advances in psychophysiology*, JAI Press, Greenwich, CT, 1987, 1-78.

11. Farwell, L.A. and Donchin, E. Talking off the top of your head: toward a mental prosthesis utilizing event-related brain potentials. *Electroencephalography and Clinical Neurophysiology 70*, 6 (1988), 510-523.

12. Fogelson, N., Wang, X., Lewis, J.B., Kishiyama, M.M., Ding, M. and Knight, R.T. Multimodal Effects of Local Context on Target Detection: Evidence from P3b. *Journal of Cognitive Neuroscience 21*, 9 (2009), 1680-1692.

13. Guger, C., Daban, S., Sellers, E., Holzner, C., Krausz, G., Carabalona, R., Gramatica, F. and Edlinger, G. How many people are able to control a P300-based brain–computer interface (BCI)? *Neuroscience Letters 462*, 1 (2009), 94-98.

14. Handy, T. *Event-Related Potentials: A Methods Handbook*. The MIT Press, Cambridge, MA, USA, 2004.

15. Hoffmann, U., Vesin, J.-M., Ebrahimi, T. and Diserens, K. An efficient P300-based brain–computer interface for disabled subjects. *Journal of Neuroscience Methods 167*, 1 (2008), 115-125.

16. Hong, B., Guo, F., Liu, T., Gao, X. and Gao, S. N200-speller using motion-onset visual response. *Clinical Neurophysiology 120*, 9 (2009), 1658-1666.

17. Ikegami, S., Takano, K., Saeki, N. and Kansaku, K. Operation of a P300-based brain–computer interface by individuals with cervical spinal cord injury. *Clinical Neurophysiology 122*, 5 (2011), 991-996.

18. Jeon, Y.-W. and Polich, J. P3a from a passive visual stimulus task. *Clinical Neurophysiology 112*, 12 (2001), 2202-2208.

19. Jin, J., Allison, B.Z., Brunner, C., Wang, B., Wang, X., Zhang, J., Neuper, C. and Pfurtscheller, G. P300 Chinese input system based on Bayesian LDA. *Biomedizinische Technik Biomedical engineering 55* (2010), 5-18.

20. Krusienski, D.J., Sellers, E.W., McFarland, D.J., Vaughan, T.M. and Wolpaw, J.R. Toward enhanced P300 speller performance. *Journal of Neuroscience Methods 167*, 1 (2008), 15-21.

21. Mak, J.N., Arbel, Y., Minett, J.W., McCane, L.M., Yuksel, B., Ryan, D., Thompson, D., Bianchi, L. and Erdogmus, D. Optimizing the P300-based brain–computer interface: current status, limitations and future directions. *Journal of Neural Engineering 8*, 2 (2011), 025003.

22. Minett, J.W., Zheng, H.-Y., Fong, M.C.-M., Zhou, L., Peng, G. and Wang, W.S.-Y. A Chinese text input brain–computer interface based on the P300 speller. *International Journal of Human-Computer Interaction 28*, 7 (2012), 472-483.

23. Müller, K.-R., Krauledat, M., Dornhege, G., Curio, G. and Blankertz, B. Machine learning techniques for brain–computer interfaces. *Biomedizinische Technik 49*, Suppl 1 (2004), 11-22.

24. Nijboer, F., Sellers, E.W., Mellinger, J., Jordan, M.A., Matuz, T., Furdea, A., Halder, S., Mochty, U., Krusienski, D.J., Vaughan, T.M., Wolpaw, J.R., Birbaumer, N. and Kübler, A. A P300-based brain–computer interface for people with amyotrophic lateral sclerosis. *Clinical Neurophysiology 119*, 8 (2008), 1909-1916.

25. Piccione, F., Giorgi, F., Tonin, P., Priftis, K., Giove, S., Silvoni, S., Palmas, G. and Beverina, F. P300-based brain computer interface: Reliability and performance in healthy and paralysed participants. *Clinical Neurophysiology 117*, 3 (2006), 531-537.

26. Polich, J. Updating P300: An integrative theory of P3a and P3b. *Clinical Neurophysiology 118*, 10 (2007), 2128-2148.

27. Rencher, A.C. *Methods of Multivariate Analysis*. John Wiley & Sons, NY, USA, 2002.

28. Sellers, E.W. and Donchin, E. A P300-based brain–computer interface: Initial tests by ALS patients. *Clinical Neurophysiology 117*, 3 (2006), 538-548.

29. Sellers, E.W., Krusienski, D.J., McFarland, D.J., Vaughan, T.M. and Wolpaw, J.R. A P300 event-related potential brain–computer interface (BCI): The effects of matrix size and inter stimulus interval on performance. *Biological Psychology 73*, 3 (2006), 242-252.

30. Silvoni, S., Volpato, C., Cavinato, M., Marchetti, M., Priftis, K., Merico, A., Tonin, P., Koutsikos, K., Beverina, F. and Piccione, F. P300-based brain–computer interface communication: evaluation and follow-up in amyotrophic lateral sclerosis. *Frontiers in Neuroscience 3*, 60 (2009).

31. Sommer, W., Leuthold, H. and Matt, J. The expectancies that govern the P300 amplitude are mostly automatic and unconscious. *Behavioral and Brain Sciences 21*, 01 (1998), 149-150.

32. Squires, K., Wickens, C., Squires, N. and Donchin, E. The effect of stimulus sequence on the waveform of the cortical event-related potential. *Science 193*, 4258 (1976), 1142-1146.

33. Sutton, S., Braren, M., Zubin, J. and John, E.R. Evoked-potential correlates of stimulus uncertainty. *Science 150*, 3700 (1965), 1187-1188.

34. Takano, K., Komatsu, T., Hata, N., Nakajima, Y. and Kansaku, K. Visual stimuli for the P300 brain–computer interface: A comparison of white/gray and green/blue flicker matrices. *Clinical Neurophysiology 120*, 8 (2009), 1562-1566.

35. Townsend, G., LaPallo, B.K., Boulay, C.B., Krusienski, D.J., Frye, G.E., Hauser, C.K., Schwartz, N.E., Vaughan, T.M., Wolpaw, J.R. and Sellers, E.W. A novel P300-based brain–computer interface stimulus presentation paradigm: Moving beyond rows and columns. *Clinical Neurophysiology 121*, 7 (2010), 1109-1120.

36. Treder, M. and Blankertz, B. (C)overt attention and visual speller design in an ERP-based brain–computer interface. *Behavioral and Brain Functions 6*, 1 (2010), 28.

37. Vidal, J.J. Toward direct brain–computer communication. *Annual review of biophysics and bioengineering 2* (1973), 157-180.

Area Gestures for a Laptop Computer Enabled by a Hover-Tracking Touchpad

Sangwon Choi, Jiseong Gu, Jaehyun Han and Geehyuk Lee
Human Computer Interaction Lab, KAIST
291 Daehakro, Yuseong, Daejeon, 305-701, South Korea
{sangwonchoi7, gstarcastle, jay.jaehyun, geehyuk}@gmail.com

ABSTRACT

A touchpad has been the most popular pointing device for laptop computers. As large, multi-touch sensing touchpads are now common, we came to think about extending its input vocabulary by adding area gestures. In order to explore this possibility, we constructed a laptop-like mock-up with an optical, proximity sensing touchpad, and implemented a few area gestures that may be useful in such an environment. We conducted a user test and ran a task walkthrough with a realistic scenario in order to verify the feasibility of the area gestures in a laptop environment.

Author Keywords

Area gesture, ThickPad, hover tracking touchpad, laptop computer

ACM Classification Keywords

H.5.m. Information Interfaces and Presentation: User Interfaces. - Input devices and strategies

INTRODUCTION

A touchpad is the de facto standard pointing device for laptop computers. Typically, it has been a small rectangular area below the keyboard area, operated by a single finger. It has been in this typical style for a long time since its introduction, but it recently started to change. One of the most important changes is the support of multi-finger operations. This seems to be influenced by the multi-touch interfaces popularized by smart phones. Many laptop computers in the market these days have a large touchpad that can recognize basic multi-finger gestures, such as a two-finger scrolling gesture and a four-finger swipe gesture.

As large multi-touch-sensing touchpads are now common, we came to think about extending its input vocabulary by adding area gestures. Area gestures in fact have a long history as some early examples [4, 9, 13] show, but have not been considered in the context of a laptop computer. We could think out a few area gestures that would be relevant in a laptop setting, such as covering the left half of a touchpad to activate a widget panel, and attempted to test

the ideas with a multi-touch touchpad. However, we soon realized that detecting a covered area using a multi-touch touchpad is not an easy task because a multi-touch touchpad does not report a touch area but the centroid of a touch area. A more fundamental problem was that we do not usually keep the whole palm area in contact with a touchpad. This means that we needed a touchpad that does not only detect contact points but also takes the whole image of a hand in proximity. Therefore, we constructed a proximity-sensing touchpad before we could start to test the feasibility of area gestures for a laptop computer. The touchpad that we constructed was an optical one that is basically the same as the touchpad of RemoteTouch [3] but has a larger form factor. We call the touchpad a ThickPad in order to emphasize its large sensing range compared with a usual touchpad as illustrated in Figure 1. With a ThickPad, we could implement a working prototype that allowed us to try out some area gestures that we expected to be useful in a laptop environment. We conducted a user test with the prototype to see whether the gestures are easy to perform and whether they are not in conflict with existing common gesture. We also implemented a simple application to test the area gestures in a realistic context, and conducted another user study to see how the area gestures would be accepted by users.

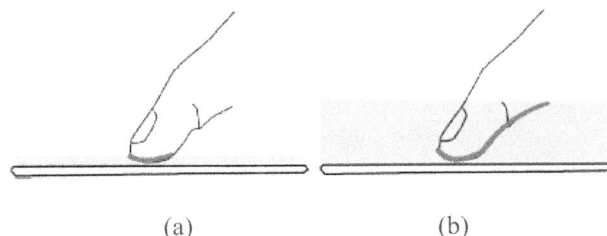

(a)   (b)

Figure 1. The sensing range of (a) a usual touchpad, and (b) a ThickPad, a proximity-sensing touchpad

RELATED WORK

An early example of an interaction technique using an area is found in Videoplace by Krueger et al. [7], where a user interacts with virtual objects using a silhouette of his or her hands. As large multi-touch surfaces became commonly available, many examples of using areas for interaction were introduced. Rekimoto demonstrated interaction techniques on SmartSkin, where a contact area shape was used to form a simulated potential field for manipulating objects [9]. Cao et al. augmented touchscreen interaction by taking into consideration hand shapes and friction between touch areas and object [2]. More recently, Bartindale et al. showed an interaction technique where a user calls a mouse on a tabletop using a hand shape after a mouse grip [1]. Wigdor et al. showed an interaction technique where a user uses a hand shape to select a translation mode [12]. Interaction techniques using area gestures are now common, but the use of area gestures in a laptop environment is still an unexplored possibility.

We needed a hover-tracking touchpad to implement area gestures in a laptop environment. The hover-tracking function of a touch sensing surface has been in focus in many multi-touch interaction studies. SmartSkin by Rekimoto uses a capacitive sensing technology that can detect a hand approach as well as a hand touch. iGesturePad by Westerman [10] is another example of a capacitive sensing technology with a similar capability. There were also optical sensing approaches for hover-tracking. Hodges et al. introduced ThinSight [5], which uses multiple sets of infrared emitters and receivers to detect fingers near the screen. Choi et al. introduced an optical touchpad for RemoteTouch [3] that uses matrices of infrared LEDs and phototransistors to enable hover and touch tracking. There were also camera-based approaches for hover-tracking [6, 11]. Hover-tracking was desired in many applications for different purposes as these examples show. In our case, hover-tracking made it possible to detect a covered area by a hand even when the hand is not in complete contact with the touchpad, which is a good feature for both users and algorithm developers. Our research will be another example supporting the importance of a hover tracking feature of a touchpad.

DESIGN OF AREA GESTURES

We designed a set of area gestures that would be useful and feasible in a laptop environment. The area gestures were not meant to replace but to extend finger gestures that are already popular among laptop users. One of the most important design constraints was to avoid conflict with existing finger gestures. Therefore, the gesture set that we tested in a user study includes existing multi-finger gestures as shown in Figure 5.

Hand Gestures

For a MacBook touchpad, the number of touched fingers is an important gesture modifier. Usually, as the number of the touched fingers increases, the same dragging operation may invoke a heavier or hierarchically upper command. As a heavy version of a finger tap, we added a hand tap gesture. Also, as a heavy version of a finger swipe, we added a hand swipe. These hand gestures may join the continuum of corresponding finger gestures and may be mapped to a command accordingly. Alternatively, they may be mapped to a command based on their own metaphors. For example, a hand swipe may look like a sweeping action and therefore may be mapped to a close command.

Cover Gestures

A cover gesture means putting a hand over the touchpad. We defined 3 cover gestures: left, right, and full cover gesture. We did not consider horizontal cover gestures such as top and bottom cover because they are not easy to perform on a laptop. To avoid conflict between hand gestures and cover gestures, a user has to maintain a static pose for some amount of time, e.g., for 0.5 second.

Non-Dominant-Hand Pointing

In a usual laptop usage, the non-dominant hand is rarely used. However, as a multi-touch sensing touchpad becomes popular, we expect that users will develop a skill to use both hands. In this case, distinguishing touch points by the left hand and the right hand may be useful. For example, one may use a left-hand tapping to open a menu and use a right-hand tapping to select an item in the menu. For another example, one may use a left-hand dragging to scroll a page and use a right-hand dragging to move a picture on the page. A non-dominant-hand pointing in fact is not an area gesture but is included here as a new area gesture because the detection of the handedness of a pointing action is possible by looking at the shadow of the pointing fingers.

Typing-Mode Gesture

This is not really a gesture but is a hand pose that a user makes when he or she uses the keyboard above the touchpad. Detecting the typing pose will be very useful because it will enable automatic deactivation of the touchpad when a user is using the keyboard. Typing pose detection is a lot easier with a hover-tracking touchpad than with a usual touchpad because a user usually covers the upper two corner areas of the touchpad in this pose.

IMPLEMENTATION

Figure 2 shows a mock-up of a laptop environment with a ThickPad, a hover-tracking touchpad of the same size as that of MacBook 13. A ThickPad shares the same operating principle as the touchpad for a TV remote introduced in RemoteTouch [3], but has a larger dimension and a larger number of sensor cells. A ThickPad consists of three layers: a touch-sensing layer, a hover-sensing layer, and a press-sensing layer. The hover-sensing layer is the main layer containing 10x8 LEDs and 11x9 photo-transistors at regular 9mm intervals. The LEDs are turned on and off sequentially, and phototransistors, which are working as a single photo sensor, measure the reflection of the LED lights from the fingers. A ThickPad takes a 10x8 hover image about 30 times a second. Its hover-tracking range is about 10 mm from the surface. A hover-tracking range of 10mm might be somewhat too short to detect the exact pose of hands on the pad. For our current gesture set, however, this was long enough because the gestures were covering, swiping, or sliding right above the surface. The touch-sensing layer is a single transparent electrode just for discriminating a touched state from a hover state, which is difficult with a hover image alone. The press-sensing layer is a single button switch under the touchpad for a 'click' operation.

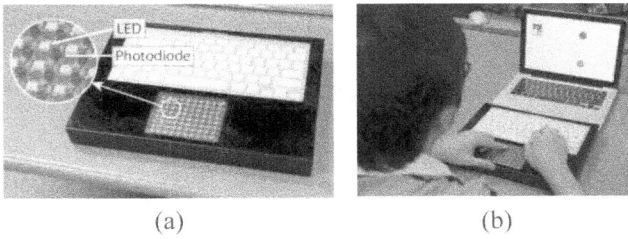

(a)   (b)

Figure 2. (a) A mock-up of a laptop environment with a ThickPad, and (b) a snapshot of a feasibility test

Figure 3 shows a flow chart explaining signal processing steps from preprocessing of a hover image to gesture recognition. The preprocessing step performs normalization of sensor values, a gamma correction, and a bi-cubic interpolation into 30x24 image. The next step is to determine whether it is currently a typing mode by using a typing mode detection mask. If not, the next step is to test whether it is an area gesture mode or a pointing mode by using an area mode detection mask. In the pointing mode, a convolution operation with a 7x7 fingertip mask is used to obtain a fingertip image, and the positions of fingertips are determined by a thresholding operation. In the area gesture mode, detection of cover gestures and hand gestures is performed. The left, right and full cover gestures are determined by the corresponding masks shown in Figure 3. To recognize a left cover gesture, for example, the average pixel values in the white region should be larger than 70 and the average pixel values in the black region should be smaller than 20. The gray region represents "don't-care". For the hand gesture, blobs are obtained by a thresholding operation, and the biggest blob becomes the hand blob. The

centroid of the hand blob is used to recognize a hand swipe and a hand tap. Finally, the touch and area data are combined in a gesture recognizer to declare area gestures such as a swipe and a tap gesture.

EVALUATION

We conducted a user test to verify the feasibility of the proposed area gestures in a laptop environment. More specifically, the main goal of the experiment was to see how well the area gestures can be performed without confusion among each other. Additionally, we hoped to evaluate the relative usability of the area gestures for future refinement of the area gestures.

We recruited 10 university students (average age of 25, 1 female), who have some experience with the laptop touchpad. With each participant, we conducted the following two experiments in succession.

Experiment 1: Testing Gesture Confusions

A test program, as shown in Figure 4, prompted participants to perform the following 13 gestures and gave its recognition result.

- Hand tap (HT)

- Left/Right-hand swipe (LHS/RHS)

- Full/Left/Right cover (FC/LC/RC)

- Left/Right-hand pointing (LHP/RHP)

- Typing mode (TM)

- 2/3 left/right finger swipe (2LS/2RS/3LS/3RS)

The last four gestures are not area gestures but are included

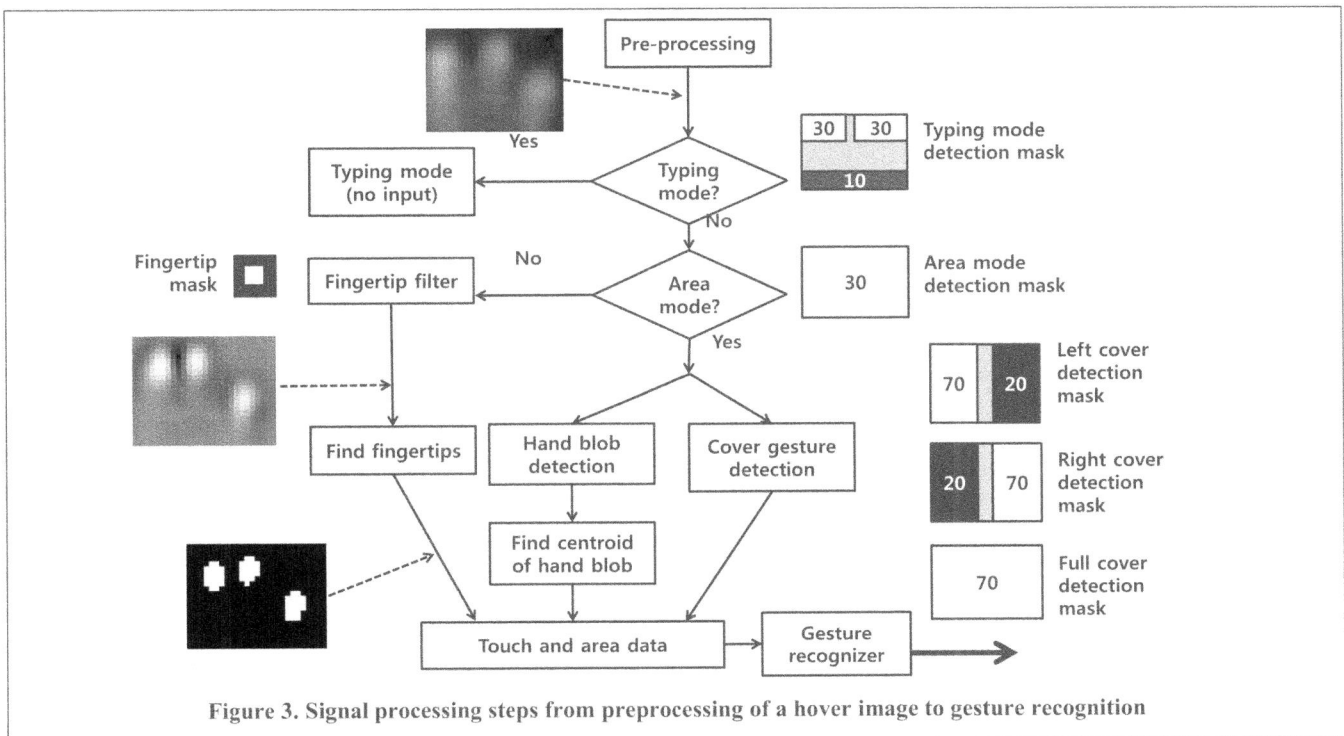

Figure 3. Signal processing steps from preprocessing of a hover image to gesture recognition

in the experiment to verify whether the new area gestures go well without confusion with existing finger gestures.

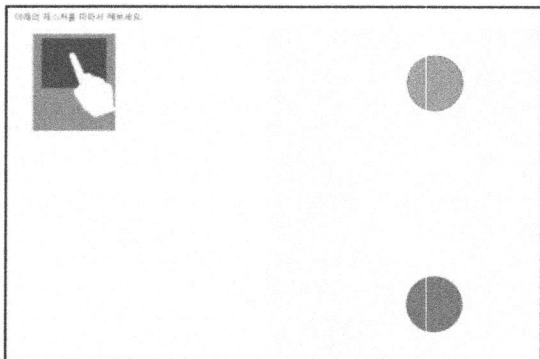

Figure 4. A screen shot of the test program for Experiment 1 (A Fitts' law task for RHP). The instruction above the icon says "Perform the following gesture.")

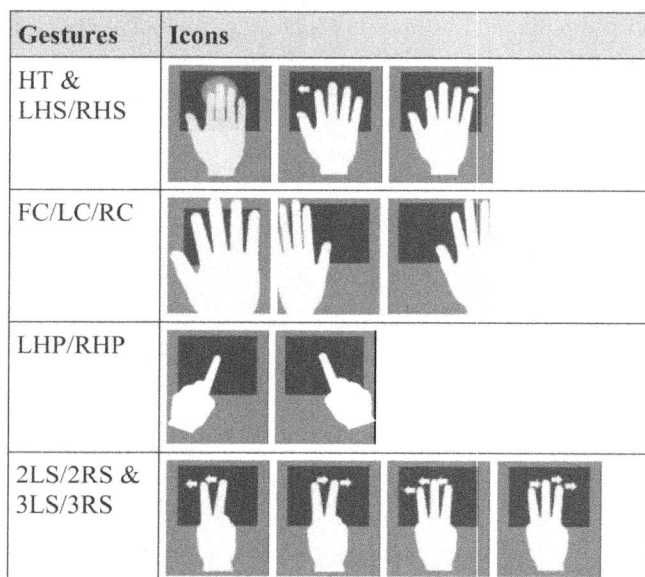

Gestures	Icons
HT & LHS/RHS	
FC/LC/RC	
LHP/RHP	
2LS/2RS & 3LS/3RS	

Figure 5. The icons for the 13 gestures used in Experiment 1. No icon for TM to avoid a bias about a typing pose.

Figure 5 shows the icons for these gestures that we used in the test program. The test program used these icons to prompt the participants to perform designated gestures as shown in Figure 5. An auditory and a visual feedback were provided in response to gestures like a swipe, a tap, and cover gestures, while only an auditory feedback was provided for other gestures. For pointing operations, a Fitts' law test was used, where targets appeared in the four directions in the same distance. For a typing operation, one random sentence was given to the participants. The participants had to repeat a trial if there was an error. The order of trials was randomized. 10 trials were performed for each gesture, and 130 trials in total were performed by each participant. The participants had a short practice session before an experiment, where they had a chance to try all of the gestures twice. We measured the number of errors in

recognizing the gestures. We also recorded all touchpad events for a possible post-analysis.

The result of the experiment is summarized in Table 1, where the row labels show the gestures that we asked the participants to perform and the column labels show the classification of the system. For instance, for the 100 trials of the HT gesture, 89 of them were recognized as a HT gesture, 6 of them as a LHS gesture, and 5 of them as a RHS gesture. We could observe in the system log that the detection of a pointing gesture often occurred before or after the detection of a swipe gesture. Since such pointing events before or after a swipe gesture may be safely filtered out in a real application, we ignored them. Despite insufficient time to practice the new gestures, the participants could perform the 13 gestures without too much confusion and the system could classify the gestures relatively accurately.

	HT	LHS	RRS	FC	LC	RC	LHP	RHP	TM	2LS	2RS	3LS	3RS
HT	89	6	5	0	0	0	0	0	0	0	0	0	0
LHS	6	84	0	0	0	3	1	4	0	0	1	0	1
RHS	4	1	92	0	2	1	0	0	0	0	0	0	0
FC	2	0	0	98	0	0	0	0	0	0	0	0	0
LC	4	0	0	1	95	0	0	0	0	0	0	0	0
RC	5	1	0	0	0	93	0	1	0	0	0	0	0
LHP	0	0	0	0	0	0	98	2	0	0	0	0	0
RHP	0	0	0	0	0	0	11	89	0	0	0	0	0
TM	0	0	0	0	0	0	0	0	100	0	0	0	0
2LS	0	1	0	0	0	0	0	10	0	89	0	0	0
2RS	0	0	0	0	0	0	1	1	0	0	98	0	0
3LS	2	0	0	0	0	0	6	5	0	1	10	76	0
3RS	2	2	0	0	0	0	1	3	0	16	0	0	76

Table 1. The confusion matrix of the 13 gestures: The row labels show the gestures that the participants performed and the column labels show the classification of the system.

By analyzing the system log, we could identify two main causes of the gesture confusions. First, the individual difference in the speed of the hand movement was an important cause, especially for confusion among area gestures, such as hand swipes, a hand tap and cover gestures. The system sometimes misrecognizes a hand swipe as a hand tap or a cover gesture. A hand swipe was misrecognized as a cover gesture when the hand movement was too slow or as a hand tap when the hand movement was too fast. A hand tap was sometimes recognized as a hand swipe. This might be that users lifted up their hand more slowly than the system expected. Cover gestures were sometimes recognized as a hand tap. This might be that the participants lifted up more quickly than the system expected. This observation suggests that the temporal parameters of the classifier should be determined more carefully or should be controlled more adaptively considering the individual difference of users and the context of gesture usages.

The second cause for the gesture confusions were the resolution limitation of the ThickPad. The ThickPad often recognized two close finger blobs as one single blob, thereby making a mistake in counting the number of fingers on it. As shown in Table 1, 2-finger swipes (2LS/2RS) were

122

sometimes recognized as pointing gestures (LHP/RHP), and 3-finger swipes (3LS/3RS) as 2-finger swipes or pointing gestures. We could observe that this type of errors occurred more frequently among novice users. We divide users into two groups according to their experience with a multi-touch touchpad, and counted the number of errors in making finger swipe gestures. The average number of the errors was 5.5/50 for the experienced participants (#) and 10/50 for inexperienced participants (#). This observation suggests that this type of errors may be overcome by practice and experience. Of course, we do understand that a more ultimate cure will be by improving the resolution of the ThickPad in the next iteration.

Experiment 2: Testing the Gestures in Context

Figure 6 shows the screen shot of the test application that we implemented for testing the usability of the area gestures in a realistic context. The application is a simple web browser with the minimal functionality of showing web pages in multiple tabs. Table 2 shows the mapping between the 13 gestures and the application functions. RHP was used for the usual pointing function and therefore is not shown in the table. TM is not shown in the table, either, because its function is not application dependent; it is for disabling the touchpad to avoid accidental inputs while typing.

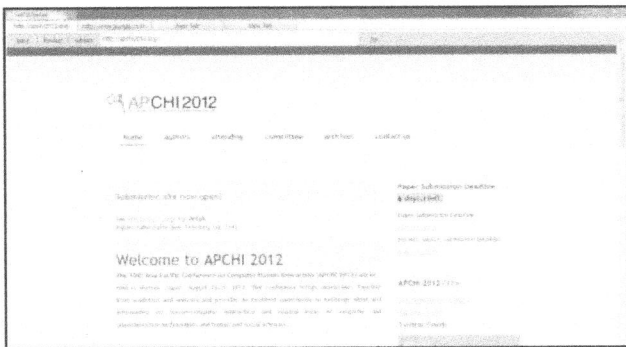

Figure 6. A screen shot of the test application (a simple web browser) for Experiment 2.

Gestures	Mapped commands
HT	Add a bookmark
LHP	Scroll the page
FC	Access the desktop (toggle)
LC (RC)	Show the left (right) menu
2LS (2RS)	Backward (Forward)
3LS (3RS)	To left (right) browser tab
LHS (RHS)	Change the window size

Table 1. Gesture mapping in the web browser application

We explained this gesture mapping to the participants, and gave them 10 minute for practicing them freely with the application. Then, we conducted a task-walkthrough with the participants according to a predetermined scenario. After the walkthrough, we asked the participants to complete a questionnaire. They answered the following six questions about the usability of the gestures and their usage

in the application using a five-point Likert scale (1: strongly disagree, 5: strongly agree): 1) the intuitiveness of the gestures, 2) ease of learning, 3) the level of fatigue, 4) input difficulty, 5) enjoyment, and 6) relative preference over the existing touch gestures. We also interviewed the participants to discover possible usability issues.

Figure 7 shows the result of the questionnaire study. All gestures seemed to receive good scores for ease of learning. Also, all received good scores (low values) for input difficulty and level of fatigue. It was rather disappointing to see that the preference scores for most of the hand gestures were low. It seems that the preference scores do not only reflect the usability of the gestures themselves but also the combined benefits the gestures brought to the participants in the context of the test application. For instance, some participants said "I rarely use a bookmark." The evaluation of a gesture was strongly affected by how the mapped function is important for them. Some gesture mapping was not favored because the participants were already accustomed to an existing gesture mapping. For instance, some participants said "I prefer a two-finger gesture to the left-land pointing for scrolling a page." Familiarity with existing multi-touch operations seemed to affect the evaluation result a lot. For instance, the participants gave positive answers to most of the usability questions for finger swipe gestures. In fact, 5 among the 10 participants were currently using a multi-touch touchpad, and they were already accustomed to using finger swipe gestures. The low preference scores for a hand tap and cover gestures may be explained in part by the 500ms time delay that we added to the gesture recognizer in order to solve the ambiguity between these gestures and hand swipe gestures. The participants said "I have to wait too much after these cover gestures." "I want the system to response faster."

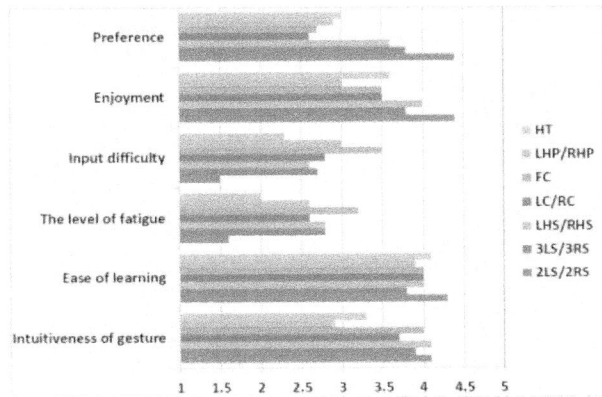

Figure 7. The result of the questionnaire study with 6 usability questions

DISCUSSION

As we look back upon what we did and obtained in this research, we have to say that we are still in a formative evaluation stage than in a summative evaluation stage. The current gesture recognizer and the test applications were not mature enough to enable a proper evaluation of the new gestures. For instance, the participant complained about the 500ms time delay in the recognition of cover gestures as mentioned earlier. If the time delay was unavoidable, we could have provided a continuous visual feedback until a cover gesture was confirmed by the recognizer in order to make the system appear more responsive to the participants. It seems to be still too early to draw a conclusion about the feasibility of the area gestures in a laptop environment. We will have to go through another interaction design cycle with a more refined prototype based on what we learned in the current cycle of interaction design.

This was another chance for us to learn that the design of gestures cannot be done separately from other components or factors of a user interface. The evaluation of a gesture seems to be highly dependent on the usefulness of the associated function in a test application. The evaluation of a gesture seems to be also highly dependent on the responsiveness of an application while a gesture is performed. In this respect, we think that we will have to improve in the next iteration the gesture mapping and the visual feedback of the test applications, as well as the gestures themselves and their recognizer.

We observed that the detection of a typing mode was pretty reliable. We expect that typing mode detection will be more reliable if the ThickPad can see more of the hands, i.e., if we have a larger ThickPad. In fact, we felt the need for a larger ThickPad throughout the current research. For example, the current ThickPad was too small for bimanual operations. Also, when we pose a cover gesture to invoke a menu, the remaining uncovered area was often too small for the other hand to choose a menu item. It is interesting to think that a larger ThickPad will enable a better detection of a typing mode and a reliable detection of a typing mode will enable the use of an even larger ThickPad. We are currently designing a ThickPad that will fill the entire area below the keyboard area.

CONCLUSION

We implemented a ThickPad, a hover-tracking touchpad for a laptop and used it to enable area gestures in a laptop environment. We could show that the new area gestures could be performed easily and recognized well without a lot of confusions with existing multi-touch gestures. The participants' feedback about their usability was not very positive, but enabled us to discover and understand the problems of the current design, which will be addressed in the next interaction design cycle of the area gestures.

ACKNOWLEDGEMENT

This work was supported by the IT R&D program of MKE/KEIT. [10039161, Development of core technologies for high-physicality control interfaces and personalized intelligent user interfaces based on Smart TV user experience]

REFERENCES

1. Bartindale, T., Harrison, C., Olivier, P., and Hudson, S. E. Surfacemouse: supplementing multi-touch interaction with a virtual mouse. In *Proc. TEI 2011*, ACM Press (2011), 293–296.

2. Cao, X., Wilson, A., Balakrishnan, R., Hinckley, K., and Hudson, S. Shapetouch: Leveraging contact shape on interactive surfaces. *TABLETOP 2008*. IEEE (2008), 129–136.

3. Choi, S., Han, J., Lee, G., Lee, N., and Lee, W. Remotetouch: touch-screen-like interaction in the tv viewing environment. In *Proc. CHI 2011*, ACM Press (2011), 393–402.

4. 5. Epps, J., Lichman, S., and Wu, M. A study of hand shape use in tabletop gesture interaction. In *Proc. CHI EA 2006*, ACM Press (2006), 748–753.

5. Hodges, S., Izadi, S., Butler, A., Rrustemi, A., and Buxton, B. Thinsight: versatile multi-touch sensing for thin form-factor displays. In *Proc. UIST 2007*, ACM Press (2007), 259–268.

6. Kane, S. K., Avrahami, D., Wobbrock, J. O., Harrison, B., Rea, A. D., Philipose, M., and LaMarca, A. Bonfire: a nomadic system for hybrid laptop-tabletop interaction. In *Proc. UIST 2009*, ACM Press (2009), 129–138.

7. Krueger, M. W., Gionfriddo, T., and Hinrichsen, K. Videoplace - an artificial reality. In *Proc. CHI 1985*, ACM Press (1985), 35–40.

8. Malik, S., and Laszlo, J. Visual touchpad: a two-handed gestural input device. In *Proc. ICMI 2004*, ACM Press (2004), 289–296.

9. Rekimoto, J. Smartskin: an infrastructure for freehand manipulation on interactive surfaces. In *Proc. CHI 2002*, ACM Press (2002), 113–120.

10. WESTERMAN, W. 1999. Hand Tracking, Finger Identification and Chordic Manipulation on a Multi-Touch Surface. PhD thesis, University of Delaware.

11. Wigdor, D., Forlines, C., Baudisch, P., Barnwell, J., and Shen, C. Lucid touch: a see-through mobile device. In *Proc. UIST 2007*, ACM Press (2007), 269–278.

12. Wigdor, D., Benko, H., Pella, J., Lombardo, J., and Williams, S. Rock & rails: extending multi-touch interactions with shape gestures to enable precise spatial manipulations. In *Proc. CHI 2011*, ACM Press (2011), 1581–1590.

13. Wu, M., and Balakrishnan, R. Multi-finger and whole hand gestural interaction techniques for multi-user tabletop displays. In *Proc. UIST 2003*, ACM Press (2003), 193–202.

An Interaction System Using Mixed Hand Gestures

Zhong Yang, Yi Li, Yang Zheng, Weidong Chen, Xiaoxiang Zheng

Qiushi Acad. for Adv. Studies, Zhejiang University

Zheda Road No.38, Hangzhou, China 310027

{jason.yang1228, liyi9810857, xdzy2426}@gmail.com,

chenwd@zju.edu.cn, zxx@mail.bme.zju.edu.cn

ABSTRACT

This paper presents a mixed hand gesture interaction system in virtual environment, in which "mixed" means static and dynamic hand gestures are combined for both navigation and object manipulation. Firstly, a simple average background model and skin color are used for hand area segmentation. Then a state-based spotting algorithm is employed to automatically identify two types of hand gestures. A voting-based method is used for quick classification of static gestures. And we use the hidden Markov model (HMM) to recognize dynamic gestures. Since the training of HMM requires the consistency of the training data, outputted by the feature extraction, a data aligning algorithm is raised. Through our mixed hand gesture system, users can perform complicated operating commands in a natural way. The experimental results demonstrate that our methods are effective and accurate.

Author Keywords

Hand gesture recognition; mixed hand gesture; spotting algorithm; data aligning; hidden Markov model (HMM).

ACM Classification Keywords

H.1.2 [User/Machine Systems]: Human information processing.

INTRODUCTION

Hand gesture has become a powerful interaction media between human and computers. It is of utmost importance in designing an intelligent and efficient human-computer interface. The applications of hand gesture are manifold, ranging from sign language through medical rehabilitation to virtual reality [10].

Gesture data fetching is a significant procedure in hand gesture recognition. Although many works have been done, the methods can be mainly divided into two categories [8]: glove-based and vision-based. The glove-based method uses data glove and other sensors to gather information of hand movements. Although the extra sensors make it easy and accurate to collect gesture data, the devices are quite expensive and cumbersome for users. In contrast, the vision based method requires only some cameras. Therefore, more and more researches are focused on vision-based methods.

Hand gesture can be static or dynamic. Static hand gesture means a still hand posture, while dynamic hand gesture is made up of continuous hand movements and posture variations. There are many different methods for recognizing static hand gestures. Zhang et al. [16] raise a fast algorithm for hand posture recognition. An adaptive complexion model is used to segment hand area. In the training stage, they calculate a mean vector for each gesture. Then for recognizing an unknown gesture, voting theory is employed. The final result is the category which obtains the highest score. Triesch et al. [14] develop a hand posture recognition system using elastic graph matching. Their system can run under complex backgrounds and need no segmentation stage. Bretzner et al. [3] adapt particle filtering for hand gesture recognition. Multiscale color features are used to compute blob and ridge features from the image. They use the number of opened fingers to define different hand postures. Brik et al. [2] realize a real-time system for hand alphabet gestures recognition. Principal component analysis (PCA) is used to extract features from images. Then a Bayes classifier is employed to classify gestures. They get a high recognition rate of 99% on 1500 samples.

As to dynamic hand gesture recognition, many works are focusing on recognizing hand trajectory. Yoon et al. [8] develop a graphic editor system operated by hand gestures. They use color analysis to locate hand area. In order to split useful gestures from image sequence, they adapt a time-varying-based spotting algorithm. Location, orientation and velocity features are extracted and vector quantization is performed to create discrete symbols for training HMMs. Their system has an overall recognition of 96.10% on 48 different gestures. Chen et al. [4] combine the information of motion, skin color and edge to segment hand area. Then they apply fourier descriptor (FD) to describe spatial features and motion analysis to describe temporal features. These features are used to train different HMMs. They test on 20 different gestures and have a recognition rate over 90%. Alon et al. [1] raise a unified framework for simultaneously performing spatial segmentation, temporal segmentation and recognition. A spatiotemporal matching algorithm is designed to accommodate multiple candidate hand detections. And they use a classifier-based pruning framework for early rejection of meaningless gestures. Meanwhile, a sub-gesture reasoning algorithm is

Gesture	Posture variation	Hand trajectory	Description
Forward	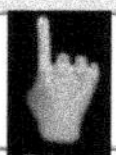	None	Move forward.
Backward	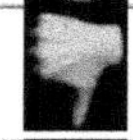	None	Move backward.
Turn left	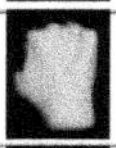		Turn left by 90 angle.
Turn right	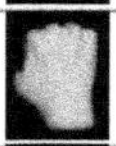		Turn right by 90 angle.
Stop		None	Stop moving.
Grasp		None	Grasp objects.
Release		None	Release objects.
Push		Move hand forward	Push objects away from you.
Pull		Move hand backward	Pull objects to you.
Turn on			Turn on an object if it can be.
Turn off	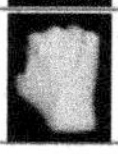		Opposite to "Turn on".

Figure 1. Gestures defined in the system

adapted to detect gestures that falsely match parts of other gestures. There also exist a lot of works concerning posture variations as well as hand trajectories [12].

Although either static gestures or dynamic gestures can be used for interaction, it may be obscure for conveying some certain instructions. For example, consider performing a "shoot" action in a shooting game controlled by static hand gestures. When the player make the designed gesture, the gun shoot a bullet. But if the player wants to shoot again, he may feel uneasy: he needs to change hand posture to others and then change back, or other strategies. Using dynamic gestures alone may run into similar problems. The problem lies in that static gestures are not suitable for expressing one-time actions, while dynamic gestures are not suitable for stating sustained actions. In order to deal with this issue, we propose the conception of mixed hand gestures. The word "mixed" contains two meanings. Firstly, hand gestures are composed of static and dynamic ones. Secondly, the presence orders of static and dynamic hand gestures are unknown, and they may occur alternately. This is consistent with our habit of gesticulating in the daily life.

Some former research works has been done on recognizing both static and dynamic hand gestures. Chen et al. [5] raise a two level approach to solve the problem of hand gesture classification. In the lower level, haar-like features and AdaBoost learning algorithm [7] are used to recognize hand posture. In the higher level, they propose implementing the linguistic

hand gesture recognition by using a context-free grammar-based syntactic analysis. However, the higher level is complicated and they have not realized it. Liu's work [9] utilizes depth images to perform hand gesture recognition. Depth data are employed to detect hand area, then a set of features are extracted. They define a simple but not natural method to split hand gestures, which takes no hand stage as split point. Although their system can recognize static and dynamic hand gestures, but in fact, static hand gestures are completely treated as dynamic ones. In [15], RGB and ToF cameras are combined to set up a system for real-time 3D hand gesture interaction. Hand area can be precisely located by using both RGB and depth images. In the system, 6 key hand postures are defined, and a classifier which relies on a dimensionality reduction is set up for recognizing them. Other 4 dynamic hand gestures as operating commands are defined based on these key postures. Through analyzing the postures of two hands and their moving directions, the operating command can be determined. This method is simple but the command set is limited.

In our research, we adapt the mixed hand gesture system for user interacting with a virtual house system. Users can roam in the house and operate objects in the environment, such as moving a chair or turning on a TV. The system defines 11 different gestures, containing 3 static gestures and 8 dynamic gestures. 5 gestures are used for roaming in the virtual house, including forward, backward, turn left, turn right, and stop. Other gestures are used for operating virtual objects in the virtual house. All gestures are described in Figure 1. We just use a single camera to capture hand gesture images, and gestures in the image sequence are automatically extracted by our state-based spotting algorithm. Considering the recognition speed, different recognition methods are used for static hand gestures and dynamic hand gestures. The threshold-based judgement can automatically reject meaningless gestures. Our system are convenient to set up, easy to use, and can run under complex environments.

GESTURE IMAGE FETCHING
We use a common web camera placed in front of people to gain RGB images. The resolution of images outputted by the camera is 640×480 pixels. And the image fetching speed is 20 frames per second. Considering the camera's field of view and hand size in the image, the best distance between performer and camera is from 50 to 100 centimeters.

Hand Segmentation
Skin color is the most important clue for extracting hand area in an image. However, there will be a lot of potential hand areas when there are many skin-like areas in the background. In order to make our system work well under complex background, we combine background model and skin color to segment hand area. Users should best cover other skin areas with dark clothes except hand. This can make the hand segmentation result pretty good, which benefits following gesture recognition. We segment hand area by following steps. Suppose the image prepared to be divided is I_t.

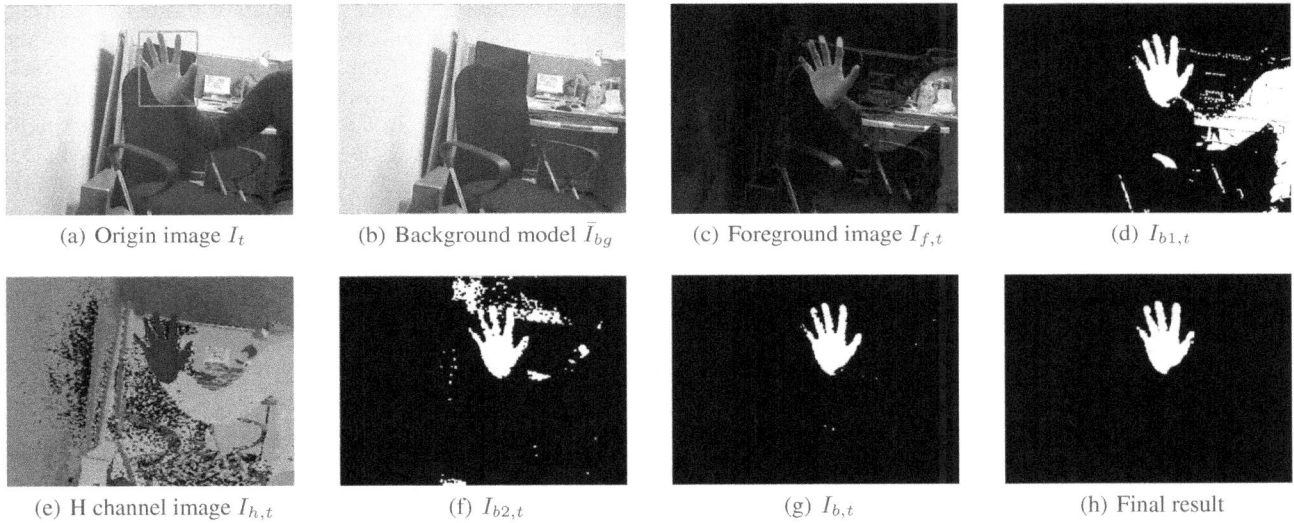

(a) Origin image I_t (b) Background model $\bar{I}_{bg}$ (c) Foreground image $I_{f,t}$ (d) $I_{b1,t}$

(e) H channel image $I_{h,t}$ (f) $I_{b2,t}$ (g) $I_{b,t}$ (h) Final result

Figure 2. The results of hand segmentation

1. Create a simple average background model using 100 continuous images. This process takes about 5 seconds. During the procession, there should be no people and no obvious movement in the camera view. The average model is calculated by the following equation:

$$\bar{I}_{bg} = \frac{1}{n}\sum_{t=1}^{n} I_{g,t}, n = 100 \qquad (1)$$

where $\bar{I}_{bg}$ stands for the background model, $I_{g,t}$ means the gray image of I_t, and $\sum_{t=1}^{n} I_{g,t}$ add values of each corresponding pixel in all gray images. $\bar{I}_{bg}$ is a gray image. This work needs to be done only once.

2. Extract foreground image $I_{f,t}$ from I_t:

$$I_{f,t} = |I_{g,t} - \bar{I}_{bg}| \qquad (2)$$

3. Fragment $I_{f,t}$ to get foreground area by a threshold. In the system, the threshold is selected to be 10. Values bigger than the threshold are set to 1, otherwise are set to 0. Then we can get a binary image $I_{b1,t}$ in which pixels with value 1 stand for foreground. There may be lots of noises in $I_{b1,t}$. So we use image morphology operations to filter noises in the binary image. Exactly, erosion operation is used first to clear small separated areas, and then dilation operation is performed to stuff small holes.

4. Transform the color space of I_t from RGB to HSV and extract the H channel image $I_{h,t}$. The values in $I_{h,t}$ are normalized to locate between 0 and 255.

5. Fragment $I_{h,t}$ to get skin like areas by two thresholds: upper threshold and lower threshold. Values bigger than upper threshold or smaller than lower threshold are set to 0, otherwise are set to 1. Here, pixels with value 1 stand for skin area. Through a few of tests under different lighting conditions, we set the thresholds to be 5 and 35. The result image is denoted as $I_{b2,t}$. Also, we filter noises in $I_{b2,t}$ using the method described in step 3.

Figure 3. Hand location (X_t, Y_t)

6. Calculate the intersection of $I_{b1,t}$ and $I_{b2,t}$:

$$I_{b,t} = I_{b1,t} \cap I_{b2,t} \qquad (3)$$

Areas with value 1 in $I_{b,t}$ stand for skin like areas in the foreground. Hand area will be picked out from these areas.

7. Delete areas which are lying on the image edge and choose the biggest area as the hand area. We do this on the assumption that hand is always in the image and hand area is the biggest skin area. We also set an area threshold here to filter wrong hand areas which may occur when there is no hand in the image.

The results are shown in Figure 2.

Motion State Detection

Motion state of hand is significant in splitting continuous gestures, including static and dynamic gestures. The states of hand can be divided into two classes: still and moving. Here, "moving" includes two situations: the change of hand location, and the variation of hand posture. Therefore, in order to determine whether the hand is moving, we have to evaluate changes in these two aspects. We get hand location by the method shown in Figure 3. The rect with red edges is the minimum external rectangle of the detected hand area. And we choose the centroid of the rect as hand location.

127

The variation of hand location is calculated by the distance between continuous frames. That is:

$$\Delta d = \sqrt{(X_t - X_{t-1})^2 + (Y_t - Y_{t-1})^2} \qquad (4)$$

And we use the variation of the rectangular area to express the alteration of hand posture. The equation is:

$$\Delta s = |Area_t - Area_{t-1}| \qquad (5)$$

where $Area_t$ means the area of the external rectangle at time t.

After these two values are prepared, we can get the result by the following equation:

$$r = \begin{cases} 1, & if(\Delta d \geq T_1) \ or \ (\Delta s \geq T_2) \\ 0, & otherwise \end{cases} \qquad (6)$$

where T_1 and T_2 are thresholds for filtering jitters in hand detection and $r = 1$ means moving state.

Spotting Algorithm

Since gestures exist in continuous image sequences, in order to get useful gestures, we need to divide image sequences by some rule. There are both static and dynamic gestures in our gesture system. Static gestures exist in single images, while dynamic gestures are composed of continuous frames. They may occur randomly. Meanwhile, the image sequences captured by the camera may contain garbage gestures that have to be discarded, such as the move-in and move-out of the hand. The system use a state-based spotting algorithm to resolve these problems.

As to an image I_t, through hand segmentation and motion detection, we can get one of these three results: no hand, still hand, moving hand. We use three states: S_0, S_1, S_2 to stand for them. Exactly, S_0 means no hand, S_1 means still hand and S_2 means moving hand. Using these states, we can label all images in the image sequence. Apparently, continuous sequences of images with state S_2 are dynamic gestures, and images with state S_1 are static gestures. However, the segmentation results may not be perfect if we just rely on states of single frames to split gestures. For example, if the user makes a careless movement when performing a static gesture, the hand state will change from S_1 to S_2 in an instant. Then a bad dynamic gesture will be outputted. Similarly, when a subtle halt occurs during a dynamic gesture, the gesture will be divided to two gestures. We call these frames as singular points. In order to boost the robustness of our method, we set a threshold N to filter these points. Step 6, 12, 25 of Algorithm 1 ensures that. Here N is set to be 5. Therefore, there has to be a pause about $0.3s$ before and after gestures to create a point for separating gestures. The pause is very short and consistent with our custom.

STATIC GESTURE RECOGNITION

We use a simple and fast algorithm raised by Zhang et al. [16] to recognize static gestures. Their method is based on voting theory and relief algorithm.

The training stage is done off line. For each static gesture, segmented hand images have to be prepared. In order to make our static gestures recognition individual-independent and position-independent, hand images need to be normalized to an uniform size. In our system, the size is selected to be 160×120. Then every hand image is represented by a column vector. For each gesture category k, we calculate a mean vector $\vec{D}_k$:

$$\vec{D}_k = \frac{1}{n} \sum_{i=1}^{n} \vec{V}_i \qquad (7)$$

where $\vec{V}_i$ is the ith column vector and n is the count of samples.

Algorithm 1 State-Based Spotting Algorithm

Initialization:
    Define $n_0 = 0$, $n_1 = 0$, $flag_1 = 0$, $flag_2 = 0$; Create an empty list L for storing possible dynamic gestures.

Iteration:
1: **for all** image I_t **do**
2:     $flag_1 = 0$, $flag_2 = 0$;
3:     Run hand segmentation and motion detection to get a result r;
4:     **if** $r = S_0$ **then**
5:         $n_0 + +$;
6:         **if** $n_0 \geq N$ **then**
7:             $flag_1 = 1$, $n_0 = 0$;
8:         **end if**
9:     **else**
10:         **if** $r = S_1$ **then**
11:             $n_1 + +$;
12:             **if** $n_1 \geq N$ **then**
13:                 $flag_1 = 1$, $flag_2 = 1$, $n_1 = 0$;
14:             **end if**
15:         **end if**
16:     **else**
17:         **if** $r = S_2$ **then**
18:         Insert I_t to the back of L;
19:         $n_0 = 0$, $n_1 = 0$;
20:         **end if**
21:     **end if**
22:     $n = length(L)$;
23:     **if** $flag_1 = 1$ **then**
24:         **if** $n \geq N$ **then**
25:         Output L as a dynamic hand gesture;
26:         **end if**
27:         Clear L;
28:     **end if**
29:     **if** $flag_2 = 1$ **then**
30:         Output I_t as a static hand gesture;
31:     **end if**
32: **end for**

To recognize an unknown static gesture denoted as a vector $\vec{G}$, we score for each category by this rule:

$$s_{k,i} = \begin{cases} D_{k,i}, & G_i = 1 \\ 1 - D_{k,i}, & G_i = 0 \end{cases} \qquad (8)$$

where G_i is ith element of $\vec{G}$, $D_{k,i}$ is the ith element of $\vec{D}_k$, and $s_{k,i}$ is the score of ith element in $\vec{G}$ gives to category k.

$G_i = 1$ means this element corresponds to a skin-like pixel. The total score of each category is represented as $s_k = \sum s_{k,i}$. And the recognition result is the category which has the highest score. In order to reject gestures that don't belong to our trained categories, we set a threshold here. If the highest score for an unknown gesture is lower than the threshold, this gesture will be discarded.

DYNAMIC GESTURE RECOGNITION
After we have extracted hand area and divided hand gestures, dynamic gestures are represented by hand image sequences. We use an HMM-based approach to recognize dynamic gestures.

Feature Extraction
Position and velocity are the most common features used in hand gesture recognition. They are both two-dimensional and easy to get, however, they do not include information of hand posture and hand depth. In order to recognize complex gestures we defined, we add other two features: hand size and hand shape. Combine all of these features, we can get a six-dimensional vector.

Hand Position
The position feature used in this research measures the relative difference between the current hand location and the center of gravity of the gesture. The reason we use the difference rather than the origin is that different starting points can generate for the same gesture. The relative difference solves this problem so that gestures are independent of starting position.

We can calculate the position feature by using the following formulas:

$$(C_x, C_y) = (\frac{1}{n}\sum_1^n X_t, \frac{1}{n}\sum_1^n Y_t) \qquad (9)$$

$$(P_{x,t}, P_{y,t}) = (X_t - C_x, Y_t - C_y) \qquad (10)$$

where (C_x, C_y) is the center of gravity of the gesture and (X_t, Y_t) is the hand location in current frame shown in Figure 3.

Hand Velocity
The velocity feature represents the moving speed and direction of hand during the gesture. It measures the difference between the hand location in current frame and that in previous frame. The equation is:

$$(V_{x,t}, V_{y,t}) = (X_t - X_{t-1}, Y_t - Y_{t-1}) \qquad (11)$$

Hand Size
We use the area of bounding rectangle of the hand to describe hand size. The area will change along with the variation of hand depth, which means the distance between hand and camera. The area may also be affected by the hand posture. So, the reason we introduce the size feature is that we want to describe the change of hand depth and hand posture. We calculate it with the following formula:

$$S_t = Area_t - Area_1 \qquad (12)$$

Hand Shape
The shape feature is used to track the changes of hand posture. Although the prior feature contains information of hand posture, it is too harsh. We use the ratio of length and width of hand size to present the shape. This feature can just roughly express the variety of hand posture. Therefore, it works well when the hand posture changes clearly.

These features are all easy to get. Then we can get a six-dimensional vector composed by these features, that is

$$\vec{F}_t = \langle P_{x,t}, P_{y,t}, V_{x,t}, V_{y,t}, S_t, R_t \rangle$$

where R_t is the shape feature. We normalize each element of $\vec{F}_t$ to locate between -1.0 to 1.0 before training.

Hidden Markov Model
A hidden Markov model (HMM) is a statistical Markov model in which the system being modeled is assumed to be a Markov process with unobserved (hidden) states. In an HMM, the state is not directly visible, but output, dependent on the state, is visible. Each state has a probability distribution over the possible output tokens. Therefore the output sequence generated by an HMM gives some information about the sequence of states. Formally, an HMM is defined as follows [13]:

- N, the number of states in the model. The state set is denoted as $S = \{S_1, S_2, \ldots, S_N\}$, and the state at time t is q_t.

- M, the number of distinct observation symbols per state. The observation set is denoted as $V = \{v_1, v_2, \ldots, v_M\}$, and the observation at time t is O_t.

- The state transition probability distribution $A = \{a_{ij}\}$ where
$$a_{ij} = Pr(q_{t+1} = S_j | q_t = S_i), 1 \leq i, j \leq N$$
$a_{ij} = 0$ means the model will never change state from S_i to S_j.

- The observation symbol probability distribution in state j, $B = \{b_j(k)\}$, where
$$b_j(k) = Pr(O_t = V_k | q_t = S_j), 1 \leq j \leq N, 1 \leq k \leq M.$$

- The initial state distribution $\pi = \{\pi_i\}$ where
$$\pi_i = Pr(q_1 = S_i), 1 \leq i \leq N.$$

From the above description, a complete set of parameters of an HMM can be compactly expressed as $\lambda = (A, B, \pi)$. To accurately describe a real-world process such as hand gesture with an HMM, we need to appropriately select the HMM parameters.

Generally, there are three basic problems that must be solved for the model to be useful in real applications: (1) Evaluation problem. Given the observation sequence O and a model $\lambda = (A, B, \pi)$, how do we efficiently evaluate $Pr(O|\lambda)$. The solution is Forward-Backward algorithm [13]. (2) Decoding problem. Given the observation sequence O and the model $\lambda = (A, B, \pi)$, how do we determine an optimal state sequence Q that best explains the observation. The solution is Viterbi algorithm [6]. (3) Training problem. How do we adjust the model parameters $\lambda = (A, B, \pi)$ to maximize $Pr(O|\lambda)$. The solution is Baum-Welch algorithm [13].

Data Aligning Algorithm

There is a problem to be solved before training. The training data input to an HMM must have the same sequence length. However, as to the same kind of dynamic gesture, different people may take different time, even the same people can't guarantee that he performs it many times in the same time. So the length of sample data has different value. We have to align them so that gestures belong to the same category have identical sequence length.

Algorithm 2 Data Aligning Algorithm

Initialization:

Calculate the average length $\bar{L}$ for the training gesture:

$$\bar{L} = \frac{1}{n} \sum_{1}^{n} |F_i|$$

where n is the sample count, F_i stands for one sample, $|F_i|$ means the length of F_i.

Iteration:

1: **for all** F_i **do**
2:    Define F_i as

$$F = \{\vec{F}_1, \vec{F}_2, \ldots, \vec{F}_n\};$$

3:    Define an array D to record the distance between adjacent vectors in F, where

$$D[i] = \|\vec{F}_{i+1} - \vec{F}_i\|, 1 \leq i \leq n - 1;$$

4:    **while** $length(F) > \bar{L}$ **do**
5:       Select the minimum value $D[k]$ from D;
6:       Define $\vec{F}'$ where

$$\vec{F}' = \frac{(\vec{F}_k + \vec{F}_{k+1})}{2};$$

7:       Delete $\vec{F}_k$ and $\vec{F}_{k+1}$;
8:       Insert $\vec{F}'$ to the position k of F;
9:       Update array D;
10:    **end while**
11:    **while** $length(F) < \bar{L}$ **do**
12:       Select the maximum value $D[k]$ from D;
13:       Define $\vec{F}'$ as Step 6;
14:       Insert $\vec{F}'$ to the position $k + 1$ of F;
15:       Update array D;
16:    **end while**
17: **end for**

Algorithm 2 describes our data aligning algorithm. First we calculate the average length of samples in the gesture. Then we check each sample whether the length is equal to the average length. If it is shorter, we expand it until the length of it reaches the average length. Else we compress the sample to get the same length. The method we used to expand or

Gesture	$\bar{L}$	M	Q
Turn Left	11	4	4
Turn right	13	2	3
Grasp	5	3	4
Release	4	2	2
Push	12	6	5
Pull	9	4	4
Turn On	18	3	2
Turn Off	19	6	4

$\bar{L}$: Average length of gestures.
M : The state number.
Q : The mixture number of Gaussians.

Table 1. $\bar{L}$, M and Q for dynamic gestures

compress data is based on interpolation algorithm. By using this algorithm, users are not limited to finish gestures in certain times. This method can work well as long as the time differences between different individuals are not too large.

Training and Recognition

We use an HMM toolbox written by Murphy [11] to do the training and recognition work. This toolbox supports learning for HMMs with mixtures of Gaussians output. Therefore we can train HMMs with the six-dimensional vector sequences directly, without vector quantization. Every dynamic gesture has an HMM to be trained by according training data. After we have prepared aligned training data for each gesture, we run the training procedure using these data as input. In order to get a good HMM for each gesture, we have to appropriately set a state number M and a mixture number Q for each HMM. Each HMM may need to be trained many times along with the adjustment of M and Q until it has a good likelihood on the training data.

After training, we call the recognition procedure to recognize coming gestures. The new gesture will be evaluated by each trained HMM to output a likelihood. The recognition result is the category which gives the highest likelihood. Similar to static gesture recognition, a threshold is set here to reject unknown gestures.

EXPERIMENTAL RESULTS

In our experiment, each gesture has 70 samples. Then the total gesture database contains 770 gestures. For each static gesture, 20 samples are used to create the mean vector. The remained 50 samples are employed to set up the test data set. As to dynamic gestures, an HMM is trained for each category by using 20 samples. Other samples are also put into the test data set. The average length of each dynamic gesture in our system is shown in Table 1. Through a lot of experiments, we get reliable HMMs that have high likelihood using values of M and Q in Table 1.

The recognition results are presented in Table 2, in which first three lines are about static gestures and others are results of dynamic gestures. The total recognition rate on test data set is 95.45%. From the recognition results, we can see that our

Gesture	Test Data	Correct	Error	Recognition (%)
Forward	50	49	1	98.00
Backward	50	48	2	96.00
Stop	50	48	2	96.00
Turn Left	50	50	0	100.00
Turn right	50	50	0	100.00
Grasp	50	44	6	88.00
Release	50	48	2	96.00
Push	50	43	7	86.00
Pull	50	45	5	90.00
Turn On	50	50	0	100.00
Turn Off	50	50	0	100.00

The total recognition rate is 95.45%.

Table 2. Recognition results

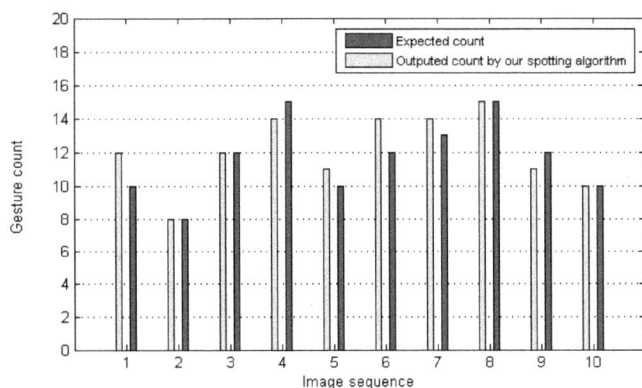

Figure 4. Tests on spotting algorithm

methods have pretty good performance on recognizing static gestures. And some dynamic gestures which contain obvious hand trajectory also get perfect recognition rates. However, the recognition rates are apparently lower on other dynamic gestures. This is due to our approach of feature extraction. During the extracted features, hand position and hand velocity can well express the hand trajectory, while hand shape and hand size can just describe big variations on hand posture and depth. We should make great efforts to optimize our feature extraction method later.

Meanwhile, we test our spotting algorithm on 10 different image sequences. Thought our spotting algorithm, each dynamic gesture is followed by a static gesture. There static gestures can be fast recognized for acceptance or rejection. Therefore, we don't count them in the experiment. We just consider meaningful dynamic gestures in the sequence. The results are presented in Figure 4. Some sequences are divided to more gestures than we expect. It is because there are meaningless gestures in the sequence, such as the action during the alteration from "forward" to "backward". While fewer gestures are outputted from some sequences because

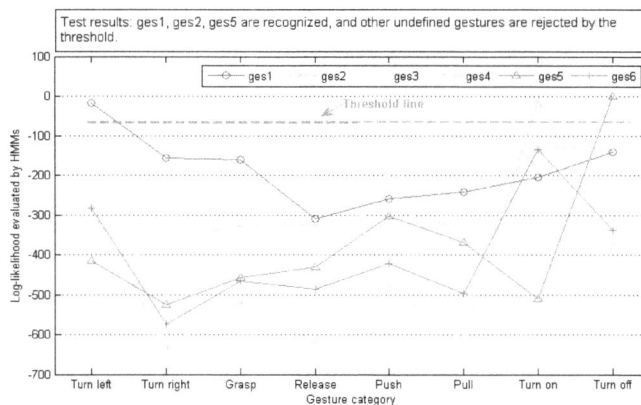

Figure 5. The recognition results on some defined or undefined dynamic gestures

that the pause between some gestures is so short that they are combined by the algorithm.

Luckily, these meaningless gestures can be rejected by our threshold-based method. Some recognition results are demonstrated in Figure 5. There are 6 dynamic hand gestures to be recognized, in which 3 gestures belongs to defined categories and others are undefined. Through the evaluation of trained HMMs, each unknown gesture gets eight values of log-likelihood. The bigger value stands for better similarity on corresponding gesture. From the curves shown in the figure, we can see that defined gestures have an excellent similarity on a certain category, while values of undefined gestures are much smaller. Therefore, we can set a threshold to cut them. In our system, the threshold is set to be -80.0. Then we get the right results. Figure 6 shows some scenes in the virtual house during the manipulation.

CONCLUSION

In this paper, we describe a novel mode for natural interaction in virtual environment. Static and dynamic hand gestures are both used for manipulation according to their characteristics. Users can make their gestures continually. Our gesture spotting algorithm will precisely segment gestures contained in the image sequence. Static gestures are recognized by a simple approach based on voting theory, while dynamic gestures are recognized by HMMs. The experimental results prove the effectiveness of our methods.

Future works may focus on the recognition of meticulous hand gestures. If meticulous hand gestures can be recognized, such as the movement of fingers or hand joints, the application field of gesture recognition will be greatly expanded. Recently, our feature extraction method can only describe hand trajectory and big variation of hand posture. We would look for other features to deal with this issue. Meanwhile, we can try other recognition methods except HMM-based.

ACKNOWLEDGMENTS
This work is supported by National Natural Science Foundation of China (No.61031002), Zhejiang provincial key science and technology program for international cooperation

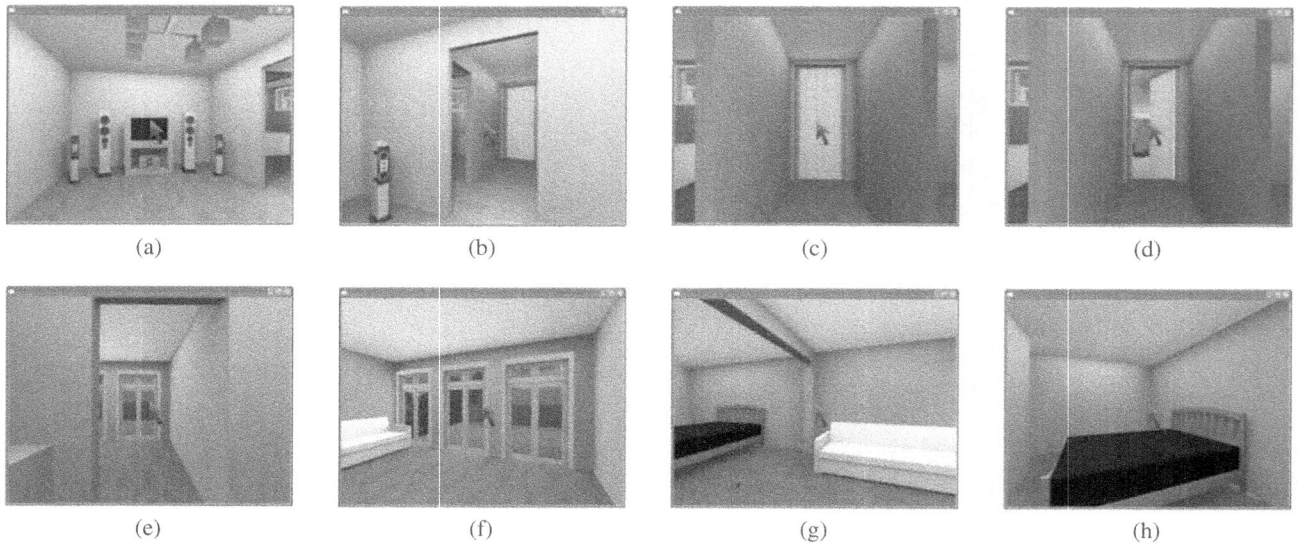

(a) (b) (c) (d)

(e) (f) (g) (h)

Figure 6. Some scenes during the manipulation

(No.2011C1405) and National High Technology Research and Development Program of China (No.2012AA011602).

REFERENCES

1. Alon, J., Athitsos, V., Yuan, Q., and Sclaroff, S. A unified framework for gesture recognition and spatiotemporal gesture segmentation. *Pattern Analysis and Machine Intelligence, IEEE Transactions on 31*, 9 (sept. 2009), 1685–1699.

2. Birk, H., Moeslund, T., and Madsen, C. Real-time recognition of hand alphabet gestures using principal component analysis. In *In Proc., SCIA* (1997).

3. Bretzner, L., Laptev, I., and Lindeberg, T. Hand gesture recognition using multi-scale colour features, hierarchical models and particle filtering. In *Automatic Face and Gesture Recognition, 2002. Proceedings. Fifth IEEE International Conference on* (may 2002), 423–428.

4. Chen, F.-S., Fu, C.-M., and Huang, C.-L. Hand gesture recognition using a real-time tracking method and hidden markov models. *Image and Vision Computing 21*, 8 (2003), 745–758.

5. Chen, Q., Georganas, N., and Petriu, E. Real-time vision-based hand gesture recognition using haar-like features. In *Instrumentation and Measurement Technology Conference Proceedings, 2007. IMTC 2007. IEEE* (may 2007), 1–6.

6. Forney, G. D. The viterbi algorithm. In *Proc. of the IEEE*, vol. 48 (1973), 268–278.

7. Freund, Y., and Schapire, R. E. A short introduction to boosting. *Journal of Japanese Society for Artificial Intelligence 14*, 5 (1999), 771–780.

8. Garg, P., Aggarwal, N., and Sofat, S. Vision Based Hand Gesture Recognition. *Engineering and Technology 49*, 3 (2009), 972–977.

9. Liu, X., and Fujimura, K. Hand gesture recognition using depth data. In *In Proc., FGR2004* (2004), 529–534.

10. Mitra, S., and Acharya, T. Gesture Recognition: A Survey. *IEEE TRANSACTIONS ON SYSTEMS, MAN, AND CYBERNETICSIPART C: APPLICATIONS AND REVIEWS 37*, 3 (2007), 311–324.

11. Murphy, K. Hidden Markov Model (HMM) Toolbox for Matlab. http://www.cs.ubc.ca/~murphyk/Software/HMM/hmm.html.

12. Patwardhan, K. S., and Roy, S. D. Hand gesture modelling and recognition involving changing shapes and trajectories, using a predictive eigentracker. *Pattern Recognition Letters 28*, 3 (2007), 329 – 334.

13. Rabiner, L. R. A tutorial on hidden markov models and selected applications in speech recognition. In *Proc. of the IEEE*, vol. 77 (1989), 257–286.

14. Triesch, J., and von der Malsburg, C. Classification of hand postures against complex backgrounds using elastic graph matching. *Image and Vision Computing 20*, 13-14 (2002), 937–943.

15. Van den Bergh, M., Zurich, E., Zurich, Switzerland, and Van Gool, L. Combining rgb and tof cameras for real-time 3d hand gesture interaction. In *Applications of Computer Vision (WACV), 2011 IEEE Workshop on* (2011), 66–72.

16. Zhang, J., Lin, H., and Zhao, M. A fast algorithm for hand gesture recognition using relief. In *Sixth Int. Conf. on Fuzzy Systems and Knowledge Discovery* (2009), 8–12.

Robots in My Contact List: Using Social Media Platforms for Human-Robot Interaction in Domestic Environment

Xiaoning Ma[1], Xin Yang[1], Shengdong Zhao[1], Chi-Wing Fu[2], Ziquan Lan[1], Yiming Pu[1]

[1] NUS-HCI Lab
Department of Computer Science
National University of Singapore

[2] School of Computer Engineering
Nanyang Technological University
Singapore

{xiaoning84, yangxinnus, ziquan111, yiming3478}@gmail.com; zhaosd@comp.nus.edu.sg; cwfu@ntu.edu.sg

ABSTRACT

This paper proposes to put domestic robots as buddies on our contact lists, thereby extending the use of social media in interpersonal interaction further to human-robot interaction (HRI). In detail, we present a robot management system that employs complementary social media platforms for human to interact with the vacuuming robot Roomba, and a surveillance robot which is developed in this paper on top of an iRobot Create. The social media platforms adopted include short message services (*SMS*), instant messenger (*MSN*), online shared calendar (*Google Calendar*), and social networking site (*Facebook*). Hence, our system can provide a rich set of user-familiar, intuitive and highly-accessible interfaces, allowing users to flexibly choose their preferred tools in different situations. An in-lab experiment and a multi-day field study are also conducted to study the characteristics and strengths of each interface, and to investigate the users' perception to the robots and behaviors in choosing the interfaces during the course of HRI.

Categories and Subject Descriptors

H.5.2. User Interfaces – [Interaction styles]; I.2.9 Robotics - [Commercial robots and applications]

General Terms

Human Factors, Experimentation.

Keywords

Human-robot interaction, domestic robots, social media platforms, intuitive interaction.

1. INTRODUCTION

Robots are starting to enter our homes, evidenced by the increasing proliferation of domestic helpers like the vacuuming robot Roomba (by iRobot Corp.), lawn mowing robot Robomower (by Friendly Robotics Ltd.), etc. In the future, homes are likely to be equipped with one or more robots to serve the need of users, especially those who may not stay at home all the time and thus have to rely on domestic robots to take care of the household and family. Therefore, it is crucial to provide a management system to enable people to efficiently, ubiquitously

and intuitively interact with domestic robots, and hence bridge the gap between domestic robots and the general public.

To serve this purpose, the system between robots and users must provide intuitive interfaces for the users to learn and use since domestic robots target ordinary home users who often have limited computing knowledge. Moreover, it must be able to handle the varying contexts and scenarios of interaction in order to ubiquitously connect human with their robots. It will be desirable if the system could provide complementary HRI interfaces which fit in different interaction contexts, such as working in stationary office environment, standing on a bus, walking, etc.

To the best of our knowledge, we are unaware of any such systems that allow users to ubiquitously interact with multiple robots through a set of complementary and non-exclusive interfaces. Thus, in this paper, we present a highly-accessible and extensible robot management system which employed social media platforms to provide intuitive and easy-to-learn user interfaces. Specifically, four types of social media platforms are adopted in the system, including short text message services (*SMS*), instant messenger (i.e., MSN), shared online calendar (i.e., Google Calendar) and social networking sites (i.e., Facebook), to interact with domestic robots. Our two robots include a vacuuming robot Roomba, and a surveillance robot developed by us on top of an iRobot Create in the purpose of making our system more capable of doing household chores. The proposed approach, including the four social media platforms adopted, the picture of our robots and the user scenarios, is shown in Figure 1.

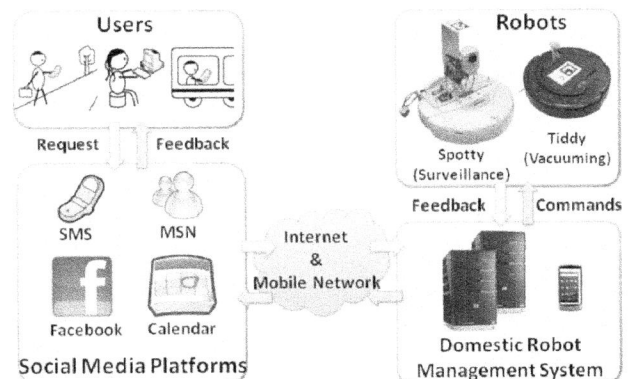

Figure 1. Using social media to interact with domestic robots.

We choose existing social media platforms to provide the user interfaces because social media platforms are highly popular with a large population of skilled users; therefore, reusing these platforms as the interaction media to domestic robots can minimize users' efforts for learning. Besides, since different social media platforms are designed to serve different kinds of needs in different scenarios, supporting multiple complementary platforms as in our system can thus cater to user's needs emerged from different scenarios, such as on the road or in the office.

The followings highlight the contributions of this paper:

First, this is the first paper we are aware of that harness complementary social media platforms to achieve better user experiences in HRI.

Second, we implemented a working system as described in this paper, deployed it into a multi-room apartment, and recruited users to try out the system in a real home environment for three days. To the best of our knowledge, we are unaware of any other work that attempted to deploy such a system into a real home to study its effect on HRI for a period of multiple days.

2. RELATED WORK

A growing number of researchers have begun to explore the field of domestic robots. While some researchers focused on the implementation and algorithmic aspects of domestic robots, such as [10, 17], others studied the application of domestic robots (a majority of them focused on the vacuuming robot, *Roomba*), e.g., on how design can influence HRI in home setting, e.g., [2, 4, 12]. Many researchers are also interested in designing novel interaction methods to enable natural and intuitive HRI, which includes the design of paper tag interfaces to facilitate implicit robot control [22], the use of tangible objects such as toys [8], accelerometer-based Wii-mote [7], laser pointers [9], sketching on a tablet computer [18], using gaze and blink (BlinkBot [15]), and using enhanced projector-camera (LuminAR [13]) to control robots. Moreover, researchers also worked on extending robots to other housework tasks beyond simple vacuum cleaning, such as [16] and [20].

So far, studies on social media platforms mostly concerned with human-to-human interaction [5] instead of human-robot interaction, except [3, 6, 11, 14], where intelligent virtual agents were used to communicate with humans via instant messengers [6], and to help humans plan their calendars [3]. In addition to virtual agents, an *SMS* interface has also been proposed to control home appliances [11]. Cellbots, an open source library available at http://www.cellbots.com/, also allows users to control different robots (iRobot, LEGO Mindstorm, etc.) using SMS. Moreover, Mavridis, *et al.* [14] proposed a social robot is used to wander in the lab, attempting to talk to people it encountered. This robot obtained people's information via Facebook to enhance conversation and face recognition performance. In a separate effort, a Facebook-connected desktop pet robot called "Pingo" (by Arimaz Inc.) was brought to the market, which can read Facebook updates, news, sing songs, and give weather forecasts. While all these work leverages social media platforms, our work differs from them because our system involves autonomous robots instead of virtual agents [6] or stationary machines [11]. Being "robots" sets them apart from other types of electronic devices such as "desktop computers" or "home appliances." More than these stationary devices, robots can share physical space with people and can take the initiative to display a variety of autonomy and intelligence over the information world as well as the physical world [21]. Moreover, unlike entertainment and social robots, domestic robots play a dual role of doing housework and act like human companions or even family members. These

distinguish our work from [14] and "Pingo," which employed Facebook only for socializing or entertainment.

3. USAGE SCENARIOS

We designed the following scenarios to illustrate how our approach can employ complementary social media platforms to facilitate HRI. All the tasks and interfaces in these scenarios have been developed in our system and were used to conduct the lab experiment and multi-day field study.

3.1 Profile

Jason and Maggie are a professional working couple who works from 9am to 6pm on working days. Their son Mike is studying abroad. They have two domestic robots, Tiddy (vacuuming) and Spotty (surveillance), to take care of household chores which include preparation work for the upcoming Christmas Eve party.

3.2 Party Scheduling through Calendar

On Dec. 20, Jason uses the Google Calendar to schedule a Christmas Eve party starting at 6pm on Dec. 24th. The calendar shows that Tiddy has been scheduled to vacuum the living room during that time. Hence, Jason reschedules Tiddy's cleaning task to another time slot via the calendar interface. Due to the rescheduling, Tiddy sends an automatic SMS to Maggie (the owner of the previous cleaning task) to inform her about the change. The calendar interface is shown in Figure 2.

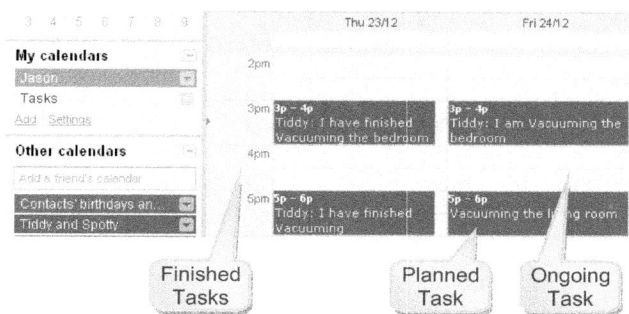

Figure 2. Using Google Calendar to interact with the robots.

3.3 Progress Update through Facebook

Since Jason has confirmed the schedule of the Christmas Eve party, Spotty and Tiddy start to post the tasks they have done for the party on Facebook. On Dec.22, Spotty receives a message from one of Jason's Facebook friends asking about the Christmas tree in the living room. Hence, Spotty moves to the living room, takes a picture using its wireless camera and shares the picture on its Facebook wall. This scenario is shown in Figure 3.

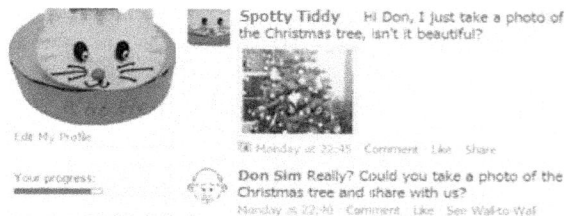

Figure 3. Using Facebook to interact with domestic robots.

3.4 Video Chatting through IM

Mike could not join the party since he is aboard, but he still hopes to take a look at the Christmas tree. Hence, he starts an MSN video chat with Spotty, as shown in Figure 4:

Mike: Could you show me the Christmas tree in living room?
Spotty: I am moving to living room ...
Spotty: I am in the living room now.
Spotty: I am looking at the Christmas tree now.
Mike: Can you turn left a bit?
Spotty: I am turning left.
Mike: Thanks Spotty. It's fantastic!

Figure 4. Using MSN to interact with domestic robots.

3.5 Arranging a Urgent Task by SMS

Early in the morning of the Christmas Eve party, Jason is on a bus heading to work, and suddenly remembers of the bits of paper he left in the bedroom. Realizing that he may not have time to clean them up before the guests arrives, Jason immediately sends an SMS to Tiddy, as shown in Figure 5. Soon after that, Tiddy acknowledges Jason with an SMS; ten minutes later, Tiddy sends another SMS to inform him of the task completion.

Figure 5. Using SMS interface to interact with the robots.

4. SYSTEM IMPLEMENTATION

We envision a flexible and extensible domestic robot management system which could accommodate both single and multiple users, with each user free to choose the desirable client to interact with each robot at home. Based on the above vision, we designed and implemented a working system based on the client-server architecture. Figure 6 depicts both the hardware setup and the software components in the client and server side.

4.1 Client Side

The client side requires no development or maintenance efforts from users, the only step required is to install (if needed) the standard version of the social media platforms in their computer/tablet/smartphone, then add the robot's account to their contact list (just like adding a friend). For example, adding a robot to the user's MSN simply means installing the standard version of MSN and then adding the robot to one's contact list.

While there are a variety of social media available, we choose the following four platforms (*SMS*, *MSN*, *Google Calendar* and *Facebook*) due to their popularity and complementary abilities to serve a range of users' needs.

4.1.1 Short Message Service (SMS)

We choose to support SMS because it is arguably the most widely used data application in the world, with 4.16 billion active users by the end of 2010 [1]. SMS is commonly used in mobile scenarios as it takes relatively short setup time and can be used almost anywhere covered by mobile phone network, hence supporting SMS in our system helps increase the system ubiquity. However, most phone models support only short text-based messages in chunks without graphics and video feeds, which may limit the type of feedback that the robots might send to the users.

4.1.2 Instant Messenger (IM)

Similar to SMS, Instant Messenger (*IM*) clients are also widely adopted. Some popular clients have over hundreds of millions of active users (i.e., Windows Live Messenger: 330 million active users by June 2009; Yahoo Messenger: 248 million active users by Jan 17, 2008). IM offers well-designed notification functionality so that it can easily get user's attention while he is working with other computer applications. The video chat capability of IM also enables additional services to be used with domestic robots. On the other hand, video chatting in IM typically need fast internet connection, which may make it less ubiquitously available for HRI as compared to SMS. In our system, we currently support the Windows Live Messenger client (*MSN*) as it is one of the mostly commonly used IM clients. To interact with a robot using MSN, users only need to add the robot's MSN account to their contact lists, and then communicate with the robot just like chatting with anyone else.

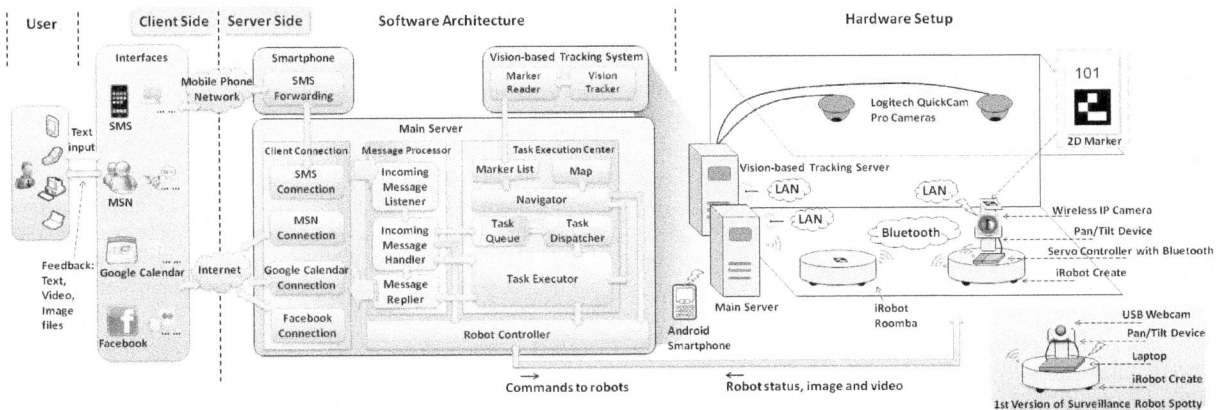

Figure 6. Overview of system implementation: users, social media interfaces, software architecture, and home-robot system.

4.1.3 Shared Online Calendar

Shared calendars are designed for both individual and group to manage, plan, and overview schedules. Hence, interacting with robots via shared calendar not only allows users to manage robot tasks together with their own workflow, but also allows robots to check each family member's schedule and suggest reschedule existing tasks if there is any overlap of activities. Our system adopted Google Calendar to interact with robots. Unlike our SMS and MSN clients, Google Calendar does not support real-time communication because excessively frequent data retrieval is prohibited by the Google server. According to our experience, the minimum time between successive accesses is around 40 seconds. Thus, Google Calendar functions more as a shared task-planning interface than a real-time communication interface in our system.

4.1.4 Social Networking Site

Facebook is included in our system as a representative social networking site due to a number of reasons. As of January 2011, it has more than 600 million active users. Besides, Facebook is a community-based website designed for interaction amongst a large group of people for social networking purposes. It has also been largely explored for many research purposes, such as [14, 19]. Facebook mixes robots' activities with those of human's, and the viral and snowballing effect of Facebook could possibly help promote robot adoption to more users.

In order to talk to robots in Facebook, users can just add the robots' Facebook account as a friend, then talk to them by leaving messages on robots' walls. Feedbacks from robots are sent back via posts on users' wall. However, to prevent spamming, Facebook does not allow frequent data retrieval, which makes it unsuitable for performing real-time interaction with robots.

4.2 Server Side Design

The bulk of the implementation is done on the server side, as illustrated in Figure 6. In the following sections, we first briefly introduce the hardware setup, and then describe the software components in detail.

4.2.1 Hardware Setup

Main Server. There is a dedicated desktop computer (referred to as the main server in later sections) used to host the entire server side software components. The model number is Dell OptiPlex 780, which runs Windows 7 Professional. A smartphone, a wireless IP camera, and a vision-based tracking server (all described in later sections) communicate with the main server via Wi-Fi network, and the robots communicate with it via Bluetooth.

Smartphone. There is also an Nexus One smartphone with Android 2.3.3 which runs an in-house developed Java application that exchanges messages between the main server and the phone.

Vision-based Tracking System. Aside from the dedicated main server mentioned previously, there is also a dedicated vision-based tracking server which connects two Logitech QuickCam® Pro cameras that installed in the ceiling 2.5 meters above the floor and covered an area of 2m×4m. This server tracks the robots' coordinates in real-time by using a vision tracking method [22] to recognize the markers on top of the robots, and send the coordinates to the main server via Wi-Fi network.

Robots. We built our robots according to the hardware design shown in Figure 6. Both the *Roomba* and *Create* are connected with Bluetooth-to-serial converters called RooTooth so that they can communicate with main server over Bluetooth connection. Figure 7 shows a photo of the two robots.

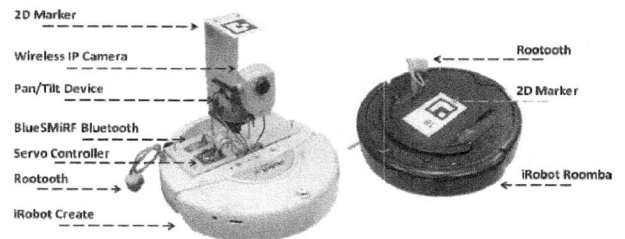

Figure 7. Spotty the surveillance robot (left) and Tiddy the vacuuming robot (right).

The *iRobot Create* is augmented with additional hardware components to enable it to work as a surveillance robot, which include a BlueSMiRF Bluetooth module, a servo controller, a two degree of freedom (2-DOF) CrustCrawler S3 Pan/Tilt device, and an Axis 207MW wireless IP camera mounted on the Pan/Tilt device. The BlueSMiRF Bluetooth module enables the servo controller to receive commands from main server. The servo controller, upon receiving the commands, will control the Pan/Tilt device to make the corresponding movement, which will alter the viewing angle of the wireless camera. Images from the wireless camera are then sent to the main server via Wi-Fi.

4.2.2 Software Components

A simplified work flow of the system is described as follows (illustrated in the middle part of Figure 6). Once a message is sent from the client-side, it will be received by its corresponding receiver within the client connection component on the server side. The client connection component will then pass the message along with the information of the sender and client type to the message processor, which further analyzes and converts such input into executable tasks. After a message is processed, the message processor will send feedback to the user via the client connection component. Depending on the urgency of the task, it will either be buffered in the task queue or executed immediately by the task executor. The real-time location information of the robots and objects in the environment are supplied by the vision-based tracking component. To control the robot, the task execution center needs to communicate with the robot controller, which handles specific commands to each robot.

4.2.2.1 Client Connection

This component serves as the bridge connecting all clients, hence it is the only component needed to be changed when new social media platforms are introduced into the system. This component allows the server to receive and extract the necessary information from different types of clients, and it is also responsible for sending server-generated messages back to the clients. Currently, this component includes four client connection modules to communicate with the four social media platforms we mentioned. All the messages come from different clients or users are converted into the unified format [user-client-message], and then passed to the message processor.

SMS connection module. Sending and receiving SMS from the server is done by an in-house-developed Java application on an Nexus One smartphone which is connected to standard mobile phone network and co-located with the main server via local wireless network, so that the application can exchange text messages effectively with the main server.

MSN connection module. An open source application MSNPSharp (MSNP18 Release: 3.1.2 Beta by Xih Solutions) is used to develop an MSN client program running on the main server to communicate with the user's MSN. Currently, only the surveillance robot is equipped with a wireless camera, so the video conferencing capability is only enabled with this robot.

Google Calendar connection module. This module is implemented using the Google calendar data API 2.0. It runs on the main server to communicate with the Google calendar client website. Since the Google calendar website will not inform our server upon users' update, data are pulled from the client website every 40 seconds.

Facebook connection module. Using the official Facebook Client Library (facebook-0.1.0), we built the Facebook connection module as a Facebook application running on our main server. This module queries message updates on robots' Facebook wall every 90 seconds, and responds to users' requests by posting text and photos on users' wall.

4.2.2.2 Message Processor

The message processor is responsible for translating the incoming messages from the client connection component into executable tasks. It analyzes the incoming messages using a simple natural language processing (NLP) method: Each input sentence is first broken into words, and matches against the keywords from the following three categories in descending priorities: tasks (e.g., "vacuum the bedroom now"), general contextual inquiry (e.g., what's your schedule?), and socialization (e.g., hello). If a sentence contains keywords in more than one category, keywords of the highest-priority category are used.

Task sentences are identified by a few action keywords (e.g., vacuum). Once a sentence is identified as tasks, we will further look for other details of the tasks such as time (e.g., "now", "5 pm"), location (e.g., "bedroom"), item (e.g., "trash can"), and convert the message into a task object. The currently supported tasks and their corresponding keywords are listed in Table 1.

Table 1. Tasks supported by the two robots.

Robots	Tiddy (vacuuming robot)	Spotty (surveillance robot)
Specific Tasks	vacuum/clean	take photo/picture look forward look up/down/left/right
Common tasks	move/go forward/backward turn/spin left/right/around stop; go home, dock, charge/charging	
Target Locations	bedroom, bed, window, door, flower/flowers, dog/pet	
Time	now/10am/5pm/etc.	

4.2.2.3 Task Executor Center

The task executor center consists of several parts: a task queue, a task dispatcher, a task executor, and a navigator. Each task in the task queue will be assigned to a task executor by the task dispatcher in a first-in-first-out (FIFO) order.

The navigator is responsible for navigating the robots to some specific locations. Robot and object locations are updated in real-time by a vision-based tracking system (which will be introduced

in more detail in subsection 4.2.3). Certain fixed locations are pre-stored in the system map. Based on the robots' and locations' coordinates, the navigator computes the routes, and directs the robot controller to move the robots to the required location.

4.2.2.4 Robot Controller

The robot controller is responsible for communicating with the robots through wireless connection. Since multiple household tasks can be received simultaneously, a queue is built for buffering the tasks. The robot controller retrieves each task from the queue, translates it (such as "take a photo of the window") into a series of basic movement commands for each robot (such as "move forward", "stop", "turn right"), and sends the commands to the robots via Bluetooth connection. The robot controller currently supports *iRobot Roomba* and *iRobot Create* by using the roombacomm Java library provided by hackingroomba.com.

4.2.3 Vision-based Tracking System

As described in former subsections, we set up a vision-based tracking system to support robot navigation. The vision tracking component uses proprietary 2-D planar ID-markers as shown in Figure 6 (upper right), which were similar to those in earlier work such as CyberCode [16] and ARTag [4]. A marker consists of a 3×3 black-and-white matrix pattern within a black border surrounded by white margin. Each marker is about 5×5 cm^2, in which we managed to recognize stably using two 960×720 resolution ceiling cameras (2.5m high) covering a 2m×4m region on the floor.

5. USER STUDY

We conducted our user studies in order to seek answers for the following questions: (i) Will the users feel comfortable, natural and intuitive to "chat" with robots using the interfaces which are originally designed for interpersonal communication? (ii) What are the factors that affected users' feeling and decisions in choosing different interfaces? (iii) Do these interfaces complement each other when interacting with domestic robots in varying contexts/scenarios? We first conducted usability experiments in our lab to seek answers for questions (i) and (ii). Then we conducted a multi-day field study, attempting to seek answers for questions (i), (ii) and (iii) in real setting.

5.1 Usability Experiment

5.1.1 Participants

Twelve participants (6 females and 6 males, aged 19 to 30; mean 24.4, median 24.5) are involved in this experiment. Among them, 9 are from the university and 3 are from the community (working professional). Each received ~10 US dollars for the experiment. Table 2 summarizes their prior experience with the four employed social media platforms.

Table 2. Participants' prior experience on the four platforms.

		Participant ID											
		p1	p2	p3	p4	p5	p6	p7	p8	p9	p10	p11	p12	Average
Frequency	SMS	3	3	1	3	3	1	2	2	3	2	3	3	2.42
	MSN	3	3	3	2	3	3	3	3	3	2	3	1	2.67
	Calendar	1	3	2	2	0	0	1	1	0	0	1	0	0.92
	Facebook	2	2	2	3	3	3	2	2	2	2	3	2	2.33

0: never, 1: at least once a month, 2: at least once a week, 3: everyday

5.1.2 Environment

We decorated a 4m×2m space in our lab to turn it into a simulated living room and a simulated bedroom, as shown in Figure 8. In Figure 8, the two robots were decorated with colorful paper to make the participants feel familiar with the whole environment. The experimental setup is described in the "System Implementation" section.

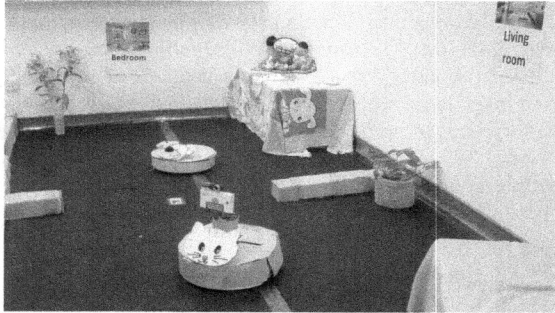

Figure 8. Experiment setup for the usability experiment in the lab.

5.1.3 Procedure

Upon arrival, each participant was asked to first complete the pre-study questionnaires. During the experiment, each participant performed a task for each of the four interfaces in a random order without any prior training, see Table 3. For each task, the participant was given a 2-minute time limit. If he/she failed to complete the task within this limit, the experimenter will demonstrate the procedure to him/her and ask him/her to complete it again. Upon finishing the experiment, the experimenter will do a post-study questionnaire and interview on each participant. The entire study, including questionnaires and interviews, is performed at one sitting within about 30 minutes.

Table 3. Task List for the Usability Experiment.

Interfaces	Tasks
SMS	Ask Tiddy to vacuum the floor
MSN	Ask Spotty to check if the bedroom window is closed
Google Calendar	Ask Tiddy to start vacuuming the floor on 3pm
Facebook	Ask Spotty to take a photo of the flowers in your bedroom and upload it to your Facebook album

5.1.4 Results

In summary, all participants completed the assigned tasks using the specified interface within 2 minutes without help from the experimenter, except one who failed in a Facebook task.

We recorded the *learning time* and *response time* taken by each of the twelve participants in each of the four tasks as listed in Table 3. The *learning time* is defined as the time taken from when the participant was given the task until he/she started typing on the interface; the *response time* is defined as the time taken from when the participant was given the task until he/she received the first response from the robot. The average *learning time* and *response time* for each interface are shown in Figure 9.

Both our observation during the experiments and the data presented in Figure 9 showed that Google Calendar and Facebook took longer learning time than SMS and MSN, which is mainly because SMS and MSN are one-to-one conversation interfaces while the Google Calendar and Facebook interfaces provide a variety of functionalities; hence the participant needed more time to figure out

how to start the interaction. As for response time, SMS takes the longest time because it is slower and more troublesome to type on a phone than a computer. The Google Calendar and Facebook also take about one minute to respond as they are not designed for instant communication, so the users need to manually refresh the page to see the feedback. MSN is obviously the most instant and responsive interface among the four since it is a specialized tool for instant communication.

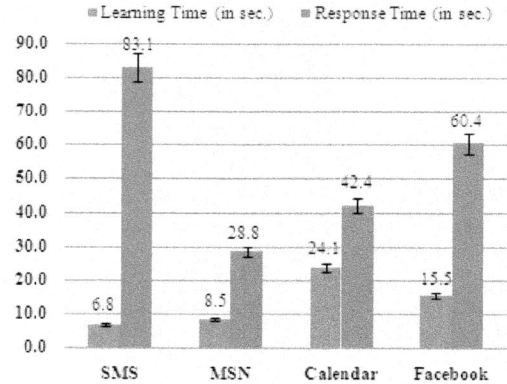

Figure 9. Task preparation time and completion time taken on the four interfaces in usability experiment.

In the post-study questionnaire, we asked the participants to rank their perception towards the robots across the four interfaces, from a Likert scale of 1 (machine-like) to 7 (lifelike). Results are summarized in Figure 10.

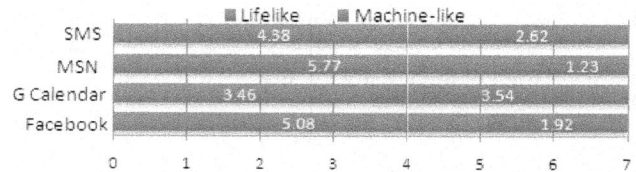

Figure 10. Average scale of lifelikeness for each interface.

Figure 10 shows that among the four social media platform interfaces, MSN (5.77) makes the participants feel that the robots appear to be the most lifelike. Facebook (5.08) also made the robots appear to be quite lifelike compared with the Google Calendar interface (3.46) and SMS interface (4.38), whereas the Google Calendar interface made the robots appear the least lifelike. Based on the data shown in Figures 9 and 10, and the comments obtained from the post-study interviews, we identified the following factors that contribute to such variation in users' perception towards the robots.

Interface Design. Participants commented that both MSN and Facebook made them feel robots to be more lifelike because they contain more "human" elements, such as icons and images representing people on their contact lists with profile pages. They also found both interfaces richer and more entertaining.

Prior Experiences. For most participants, interacting with robots using the MSN and SMS interfaces feels more sociable because they usually use these two interfaces to interact with other people.

Responsive-ness. The feedback speed is also a key factor that influences the participants' perception to robots. Most users rank MSN higher than Facebook because they feel that robots in MSN respond much faster than in Facebook.

5.2 Field Study

5.2.1 Participants

Two participants were recruited. Their background information is listed below. Each participant spent 3 days for this study and received an amount of ~64 US dollars.

Table 4. Participants' background in the field study.

		Participant 1	Participant 2
Gender		Female	Female
Age		30	27
Occupation		Computer Engineer	Assessment Officer
Prior Experience	**SMS**	Everyday	Everyday
	MSN	At least once a week	Everyday
	Google calendar	Once over a month	Once over a month
	Facebook	At least once a week	Once over a month

5.2.2 Environment and Apparatus

We rent a multi-room apartment for this field study and deployed the entire system in one of the bedrooms. The bedroom is about 3 meters × 5 meters, while the available space for robots to roam is only about 1.5 meters × 3 meters; therefore two ceiling cameras are enough to cover the entire space for robot navigation.

To hide the supporting equipment from participants' normal lives, we installed the vision tracking server and main server in an empty wardrobe. The only equipments exposed to the participants are the two robots and their charging docks, and two ceiling cameras, as shown in Figure 11. Please refer to our supplementary video for a visual description of the settings.

5.2.3 Procedure

The 3-day field study consists of two sessions. The first session was conducted in the first day of the 3 days. During the first day, participants needed to remotely carry out the tasks in Table 3 while working in the office. This session served as a tutorial of the four HRI interfaces. In the evening of the first day, the experimenter interviewed the participants for feedback.

The second session was conducted in the next two days, where the participants were free to use the robots as they like. In addition, the experimenter also sent some requests to the participants through SMS to trigger certain interactions. We carefully picked the time to send these messages so that we can cover more diverse set of scenarios that the participants may encounter (such as on the way to work, walking, sitting next to a computer, having meal with others, talking, etc.). The participants were so busying working that they ignored some of our notifications, therefore the numbers of tasks both participants actually completed are not equal.

After the second session, the experimenter interviewed the participant again to collect their overall feedback.

5.2.4 Results and Discussion

In summary, both participants enjoyed using existing social media platforms to interact with domestic robots. Although the robots' capability is limited, both participants are convinced about the potential of domestic robot systems.

(a) The two robots in the bedroom.

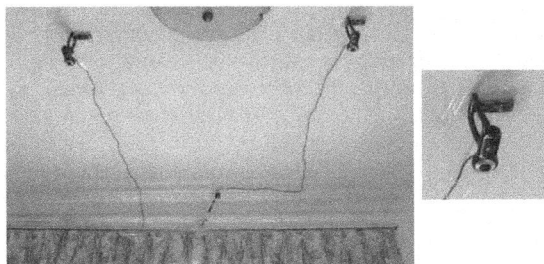
(b) Ceiling cameras for the vision-based tracking system.

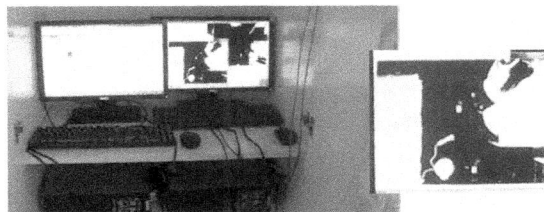
(c) Main server and vision-based tracking server in the wardrobe.

Figure 11. System setup in the experimental apartment.

During the second session, Participant 1 chose to use SMS for 50% of the tasks (4 out of 8 tasks) and Facebook for the other 50%, whereas Participant 2 chose to use MSN for 100% of the tasks (7 out of 7). This is coherent with their prior experiences summarized in Table 4, which indicated that Participant 1 uses Facebook much more often than participant 2 (at least once in a week vs. once over a month), while she uses MSN much less often than participant 2 (at least once in a week vs. everyday). This demonstrated that prior experience in using the social media for interpersonal communication have strong influence on the participants' choice to interact with the robots.

It is also obvious that both participants were trying to keep using the same social media platforms for various types of tasks, no matter whether they were using a phone or a computer, working in the office or walking down the street. Both of them never used Google Calendar at all throughout the second session even when they received request to schedule a repetitive routine task. In the post-study interview, both participants expressed that they do not have the habit of using Google Calendar and it makes them feel that the robots are less interactive.

The above observations seem to be contrary to our design purpose that different interfaces would be used in different contexts/scenarios. However, we argue that this is because the prior experience has greater effect on interface selection than the complementary ability of different platforms, and the Google Calendar interface could be more useful for overviewing scheduled tasks, in particular when the same robot is being deployed to more than one family members (which is not covered in our field study as it is hard to find a whole family to try out the system). More specifically, the users would only switch between those interfaces that they prefer to use. This is supported by Participant 1's behavior in the second session because she chose Facebook whenever there is available Internet connection and SMS whenever there is no Internet. Participant 2 also explained in the interview that she would probably switch from MSN to SMS if she is driving or when the Internet is not available.

When asked about suggestions, both participants suggested to include more popular clients such as Skype, Google Talk, etc. in our system. More interestingly, participants hope to see more human-like features attached to robots by the interfaces. For instance, Participant 2 said she expects to see the notification "Tiddy is typing…" in MSN chat window while talking with the robot, although she is aware that the robots are wirelessly communicating with the MSN client rather than physically tapping on keyboard. These suggestions made us believe that using social media platforms to interact with robots is a promising approach to bridge the gap between robots and ordinary users.

6. CONCLUSION

This paper explores the application of multiple popular social media platforms to support interaction between human and domestic robots. A working system integrating four complementary social media platforms (SMS, MSN, Google Calendar and Facebook) and two domestic robots (a vacuuming robot and a surveillance robot) was developed to extend our interpersonal communications further to domestic robots. We have conducted lab experiments and multi-day field studies which showed that the approach can contribute to delivering a more user-familiar, flexible, and intuitive interface for common users to interact with robots.

Our approach of leveraging complementary social media platforms for HRI could open up new prospective research directions. Researchers are encouraged to study the longer term effects, e.g., the security and privacy issues, of using the proposed (and other forms of) social media platforms when interacting with robots. With advancement in robot technologies, we envision the potentials of our approach as a practical and natural interaction style with robots, more easily to be adopted by the public.

7. ACKNOWLEDGEMENT

This research is supported by National University of Singapore Academic Research Fund R-252-000-375-133 and by the Singapore National Research Foundation under its International Research Centre @ Singapore Funding Initiative and administered by the IDM Programme Office.

8. REFERENCES

[1] T. T. Ahonen, *Time to Confirm some Mobile User Numbers: SMS, MMS, Mobile Internet, M-News*. 2011.

[2] C. Breazeal. Affective Interaction between Humans and Robots. *Advances in Artificial Life, Lect. Notes in Comp. Sci.* 2001; 2159: 582-591.

[3] A. Faulring and B. A. Myers. Enabling Rich Human-Agent Interaction for a Calendar Scheduling Agent. *ACM CHI EA* 2005, ACM (2005), 1367-1370.

[4] J. Forlizzi. How Robotic Products Become Social Products: An Ethnographic Study of Cleaning in the Home. *ACM/IEEE HRI* 2007, ACM (2007), 129-136.

[5] E. Gilbert and K. Karahalios. Predicting Tie Strength With Social Media. *ACM CHI* 2009, ACM (2009), 211-220.

[6] O. S. Goh, C. C. Fung, A. Depickere, and K. W. Wong. An Analysis of Man-Machine Interaction in Instant Messenger. *Advances in Comm. Sys. and Electrical Engr.* 2008. 197-210.

[7] C. Guo and E. Sharlin. Exploring the Use of Tangible User Interfaces for Human-Robot Interaction: a Comparative Study. *ACM CHI* 2008, ACM (2008), 121-130.

[8] C. Guo, J. E. Young, and E. Sharlin. Touch and Toys: New Techniques for Interaction with a Remote Group of Robots. *ACM CHI* 2009, ACM (2009), 491-500.

[9] K. Ishii, S. Zhao, M. Inami, T. Igarashi, and M. Imai. Designing Laser Gesture Interface for Robot Control. *INTERACTION, Lect. Notes in Comp. Sci.* 2009; **5727**: 479-492.

[10] K. Kawamura, R. T. Packa, M. Bishaya, and M. Iskarous. Design Philosophy for Service Robots. *Rob. and Aut. Sys.* 1996; **18**(1-2): 109-116.

[11] M. S. H. Khiyal, A. Khan, and E. Shehzadi. SMS Based Wireless Home Appliance Control System (HACS) for Automating Appliances and Security. *J. Issues in Informing Sci. & Info. Tech.* 2009; **6**: 887-894.

[12] H. Kim, H. Lee, S. Chung, and C. Kim. User-centered Approach to Path Planning of Cleaning Robots: Analyzing User's Cleaning Behavior. *ACM/IEEE HRI* 2007, ACM (2007), 373-380.

[13] N. Linder and P. Maes. LuminAR: Portable Robotic Augmented Reality Interface Design and Prototype. *ACM Symposium on User Interface Software and Technology* 2010, ACM (2010), 395-396.

[14] N. Mavridis, C. Datta, S. Emami, A. Tanoto, C. BenAbdelkader, and T. Rabie. FaceBots: Robots Utilizing and Publishing Social Information in Facebook. *ACM/IEEE HRI* 2009, ACM (2009), 273-274.

[15] P. Mistry, K. Ishii, M. Inami, and T. Igarashi. BlinkBot - Look at, Blink and Move. *ACM Symposium on User Interface Software and Technology* 2010, ACM (2010), 397-398.

[16] K. Okada, T. Ogura, A. Haneda, J. Fujimoto, F. Gravot, and M. Inaba. Humanoid Motion Generation System on HRP2-JSK for Daily Life Environment. *IEEE Intl. Conf. on Mechatronics & Automation* 2005, IEEE Press (2005), 1772-1777.

[17] P. Roßler and U. D. Hanebeck. Telepresence Techniques for Exception Handling in Household Robots. *IEEE Intl. Conf. on Systems, Man, and Cybernetics* 2004, IEEE Press (2004), 53-58.

[18] D. Sakamoto, K. Honda, M. Inami, and T. Igarashi. Sketch and Run: A Stroke-based Interface for Home Robots. *ACM CHI* 2009, ACM (2009), 197-200.

[19] D. J. Sim, X. Ma, S Zhao, J. T. Khoo, S. L. Bay, Z. Jiang Farmer's Tale: A Facebook Game to Promote Volunteerism.. *ACM CHI* 2011, ACM (2011), 581-584.

[20] Y. Sugiura, D. Sakamoto, A. Withana, M. Inami, and T. Igarashi. Cooking with Robots: Designing a Household System Working in Open Environments. *ACM CHI* 2010, ACM (2010), 2427-2430.

[21] J.-Y. Sung, L. Guo, R. E. Grinter, and H. I. Christensen. "My Roomba is Rambo": Intimate Home Appliances. *UbiComp* 2007, Springer-Verlag (2007), 145-162.

[22] S. Zhao, K. Nakamura, K. Ishii, and T. Igarashi. Magic Cards: A Paper Tag Interface for Implicit Robot Control. *ACM CHI* 2009, ACM (2009), 173-182.

Facial Design for Humanoid Robot

Ichiroh Kanaya
Graduate School of
Engineering, Osaka
University
2-1 Yamadaoka, Suita,
Osaka, Japan
kanaya@pineappledesign.org

Shoichi Doi
Graduate School of
Engineering, Osaka
University
2-1 Yamadoka, Suita,
Osaka, Japan
doi@design.frc.eng.osaka-u.ac.jp

Shohei Nakamura
Graduate School of
Engineering, Osaka
University
2-1 Yamadoka, Suita,
Osaka, Japan
nakamura@design.frc.eng.osaka-u.ac.jp

Kazuo Kawasaki
Graduate School of
Engineering, Osaka
University
2-1 Yamadoka, Suita,
Osaka, Japan
info@design.frc.eng.osaka-u.ac.jp

ABSTRACT

In this research, the authors succeeded in creating facial expressions made with the minimum necessary elements for recognizing a face. The elements are two eyes and a mouth made using precise circles, which are transformed to make facial expressions geometrically, through rotation and vertically scaling transformation. The facial expression patterns made by the geometric elements and transformations were composed employing three dimensions of visual information that had been suggested by many previous researches, slantedness of the mouth, openness of the face, and slantedness of the eyes. In addition, the relationships between the affective meanings of the visual information also corresponded to the results of the previous researches.

The authors found that facial expressions can be classified into 10 emotions: happy, angry, sad, disgust, fear, surprised, angry*, fear*, neutral (pleasant) indicating positive emotion, and neutral (unpleasant) indicating negative emotion. These emotions were portrayed by different geometric transformations. Furthermore, the authors discovered the "Tetrahedral model," which can express most clearly the geometric relationships between facial expressions. In this model, each side connecting the face is an axis that controlled the rotational and vertically scaling transformations of the eyes and mouth.

Author Keywords

Facial expression; Emotion; Design; Human factors

ACM Classification Keywords

H.5.2; H.1.2

INTRODUCTION

When human beings communicate with each other, their faces convey the most important and richest information, and their facial expressions are by far the most essential element for understanding the other's emotion. Various elements such as the eyes, mouth, and nose are contained in the face, and these are transformed to form facial expressions. Transformation is the method we use to make expressions. For many primates including human beings, the eyes are one of the most important factor used to recognize a face as a face [1-3]. In addition, visual preference for face figures (patterns in which three figures are arranged at the top of an upside-down triangle) [4,5] and research on perceptions of upside-down faces [6,7] are well known regarding facial recognition. These research results have suggested that primates recognize faces as sets of configural information comprised of facial elements, and in particular, the eyes and the mouth are the most important elements of all.

Meanwhile, these days there are two theories regarding the recognition of facial expressions: the "category perception theory" and the "dimension theory" [8-10].

The category perception theory states that human beings judge the meaning of facial expressions through 7+/-2 universal categories common to all human beings. This theory is based on a basic theory of cognition and emotion [12] stemming from evolutionary theory [4]. Those who advocate this theory insist that facial expression is not a continuous variate but a discrete variate, and deny the presence of the psychological dimension described later in the cognitive process of expression [10]. In terms of emotional categories, the six basic emotions (happy, angry, sad, disgust, fear, and surprise) advocated by Ekman and many other researchers are the most typical. Basic emotions synchronize with physiological responses and signals to the body such as facial expressions [14], and it is proposed that facial expressions can be classified under one of the six basic emotions without exception irrespective of culture [15-21].

The dimension theory proposes that affective category judgment is conducted following previous judgment that the facial expression is located as one point in two or three dimensional space [8,10], and that facial expression is a continuous variate. In addition, those who advocate this theory insist that the universal factor for human beings is not category but dimension [13]. Dimension theory begins with Schlosberg's theory of the dimension of emotion, for example the circular ring model [22] comprising two dimensions, namely pleasant vs. unpleasant and attention vs. rejection, and the circular cone model [23] comprising the previous two dimensions plus tension vs. sleep [8, 10, 24]. Since this research, many researchers have discussed such affective meaning dimensions and have repeatedly encountered three dimensions: the pleasantness dimension (pleasant vs. unpleasant), the attention vs. rejection dimension, and the activeness (awareness) dimension (aware vs. asleep) [8-10, 24]. Especially in recent times, the circumplex model comprising a pleasantness dimension and an awareness dimension suggested by Russell [13] has been validated in terms of its universality and robustness by many previous researches [24, 25].

Thus, since Schlosberg's research [22, 23], many researches have been conducted attempting to find an affective meaning dimension (psychological variable) relating to the recognition of facial expressions. However the visual information related to the recognition of facial expressions has been little researched. This means that the relationship between the psychological variable and the physical variable has not yet been identified regarding human cognizance of emotion by facial expression.

Yamada [26] conducted a study to clarify visual information (the physical variable) related to the cognition of facial expressions using a line-drawing figure in which eight points of the eyebrows, eyes and mouth are manipulated. From the results, two physical variables have been found: slantedness, meaning the curve and indication of face elements; and openness and curvedness, meaning the level of curve and openness of facial elements. In addition, they have suggested that there are strong relationships between slantedness and the pleasantness dimension, and between openness and activeness [27, 28]. Based on this knowledge, they proposed that there are three processes used to cognize facial expressions: (1) acknowledgement of visual information (the physical variable) of the face, (2) evaluation of affective meaning based on the physical variable, and (3) judgment of the emotional category based on affective meaning [10].

Moreover, from similar research using actual human faces, it has been suggested that there are three physical variables of visual information—openness, slantedness of mouth, slantedness of eyebrows and eyes [29] — and that the same results as those from in a three-dimensional structure would be produced in the case of using a line-drawing face [30]. Furthermore, it has been determined that there is a strong relationship between the slantedness of the mouth and the pleasantness dimension, and between the slantedness of the eyebrows/eyes and activeness, as well as a moderate relationship between openness and both forms of slantedness [31]. Through competing research using line-drawing faces and actual human faces, a strong relationship was also found between the openness of the eyes and mouth and pleasantness [32]. In this respect, there is a close relationship between visual information (the physical variable) and emotional information (the affective variable).

The objective of this thesis is to validate the relationship between the physical variable and the affective variable discovered by previous researches using geometrical faces, and to apply the existing knowledge to robot facial design. Clarification of this relationship is one of the most important aspects for research on cognition of facial expression. The geometrical face used for this thesis is comprised of the minimum necessary elements for recognizing the face, and the elements are transformed geometrically to form the various facial expression patterns. The author introduces the physical variables, slantedness and openness, to the geometrical transformation. These facial patterns are classified by basic emotions, and evaluation of the relationship between the physical and affective variables is conducted by applying principal component analysis to the facial expression space centered on physical variables. Based on the results of the research, the author finally developed a model to create facial expressions.

In addition, in this thesis the author researched the neutral face, a concept that has rarely been mentioned by previous researches. In recent research, it has been suggested that the neutral face does not strictly speaking show a neutral emotion, but rather conveys some meaning concerning an actual circumstance of life.

By not using a realistic-looking human face, but rather a face made with limited elements and employing geometrical transformation, the relationship between the elements and factors used in making facial expression is shown more clearly. In addition, the result of this relationship expands in application to not only robot facial design, but also to medical fields such as curing cognitive impairment of facial expression. Thus, it is aimed to apply the results of this research to other fields.

EXPERIMENT CONCERNING COGNITION AND STRUCTURE OF FACIAL EXPRESSIONS

In this chapter, an expression pattern is generated using the geometrical transformation of a face made with the minimum necessary elements, the eyes and the mouth. Elements are transformed by the parameters of slantedness and openness.

The category of basic emotions is used to classify the facial patterns. The classified facial expression patterns are evaluated by analyzing the spatial distribution of the facial expression patterns generated based on the values of the transformation parameters.

These processes are aimed at discovering the geometrical, spatial and quantitative relations between the elements and the factors used to make facial expressions.

Making Expression Patterns

The elements composing the face are limited to just three: the two eyes and the mouth, composed of precise circles and placed on the top of the upside-down triangle, the face figure (Fig. 1). Facial expression patterns are made by adding transformations to the three elements within the two parameters of slantedness and openness, comprising the physical variable for cognition of facial expressions. Slantedness of the eyes is a parameter that expresses the curve according to the opening of the eyes by their rotational deformation, while slantedness of the mouth expresses the rise or fall of the corners of the mouth. Openness is a parameter that expresses the change in the opening state of the eyes and mouth by the change in the vertically scaling transformation of the precise circle. Fig. 2 and Fig. 3 show the changes to the eyes and mouth according to the value of the parameters. The eyes make 19 patterns and mouth makes 7 patterns as shown in Fig. 2,3, making a total of 133 expression patterns. The facial expression is assumed to be completely facing the observer, and all faces are symmetrical.

Thus, each facial expression is defined by four values: two parameters of the eyes and two of the mouth, namely slantedness and openness respectively. So, the coordinates of one face can be shown as in the following mathematical expression.

$$\vec{f_i} = \begin{pmatrix} Es_i \\ Eo_i \\ Ms_i \\ Mo_i \end{pmatrix}, \quad i \in \{1, 2, \cdots, n\}$$

The above mathematical expression shows the coordinates of the ith facial expression, where Es and Eo represent the eyes' slantedness and openness respectively, and Ms and Mo represent the mouth's slantedness and openness respectively.

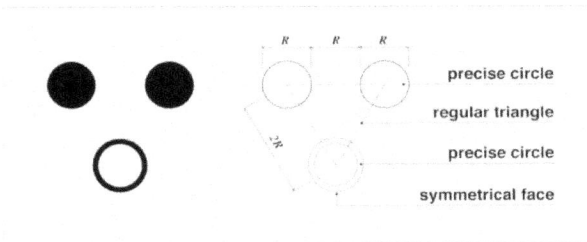

Fig. 1 Basic face before transformation

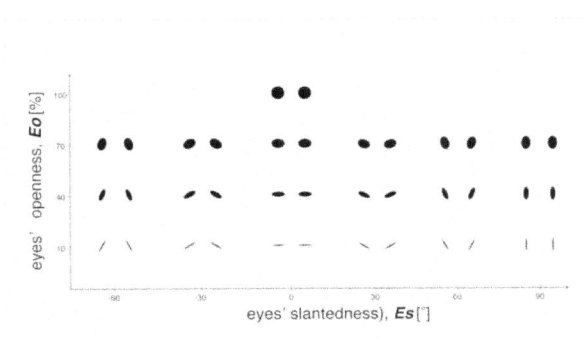

Fig. 2 Transformation of eyes by each parameter

Classification of Facial Expression Patterns

The obtained expression patterns are classified by emotional category. For the emotional categories, the author uses the six basic emotions (happy, angry, sad, disgust, fear, and surprised) advocated by Ekman and many other researchers. In this thesis, the author additionally utilizes a neutral (pleasant) emotion, displaying no emotion but showing a pleasant expression, and a neutral (unpleasant) emotion, showing no emotion but displaying an unpleasant expression, in order to research the facial expressions of neutral emotions. Clarification of the neutral face is important for robot faces, especially for humanoid robots without the function of forming facial expressions. In total, the eight emotional categories are defined.

Classification of facial expression patterns is conducted through an identification task. There are three rules for this task as follows: (1) the answerer must choose one emotion category for one face; (2) the answerer may adopt the same emotion category for more than one face; (3) the answerer does not need to select an emotion category if no category fits the face.

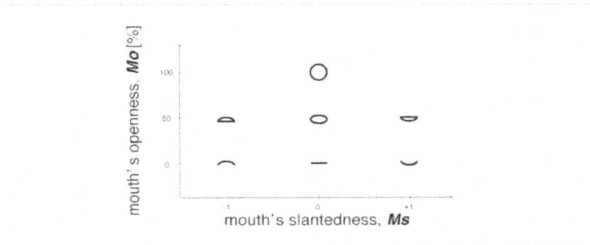

Fig. 3 Transformation of mouth by each parameter

Distributing Facial Expression Patterns in Mathematical Space

As described in 2.1, each expression is defined by four-dimensional coordinates. Based on these coordinates, the author distributes the classified facial expression patterns in four-dimensional space. The facial patterns distributed in space are the faces selected by more than $p/2$ answerers (p is the maximum number of answerers selecting the face as the emotion category).

After creating the facial expression space, analysis is applied to the space and the dimensions of the space are reduced to render it perceptible to the human eye. Through this analysis and visualization, the author can observe the difference in spatial distribution and parametric values of each facial pattern.

RESULT OF CLASSIFICATION AND SPATIAL DISTRIBUTION OF FACIAL EXPRESSIONS

From the results of the principal component analysis, the face distribution space is composed of three variables: openness of the mouth, slantedness of the eyes, and openness of the face. Moreover, this result almost completely concurs with expression distributions in the space composed of the emotional meaning dimension in previous research, and shows similarity to the results of expression cognition research using faces of actual human beings.

In addition, the research of the past is consolidated, and 10 basic facial expressions—happy, angry, angry*, sad, disgust, fear, fear*, surprised, neutral (pleasant), and neutral (unpleasant)—are advocated.

Three-Dimensional Space for Distribution of Face

The identification task was undertaken by 140 men and women ranging in age from their teens to their 60s. (average age in their 20s). The results of the principal component analysis of four-dimensional space are shown in Table 1. Four-dimensional space can be reduced to three-dimensional space from the result of the cumulative proportion from principal component-1 to principal component-2, shown to be 0.807. In addition, the value of each principal component is shown in Table 2. Principal component-1 was be judged to mean the slantedness of the mouth; principal component-2 shows the slantedness of mouth; and principal component-3 shows the openness of the face, meaning openness of both eyes and mouth, according to this value. This result corresponded to the three types of visual information (the visual variable) that had been obtained by previous researches [12-16].

To assess the relationship between the emotional meaning dimension obtained by this research and the visual information dimension obtained by previous researches, the author compared two planes, a projection plane of three-dimensional space obtained by this research comprising slantedness of mouth and openness of face, and a plane comprising the pleasantness dimension and the activeness dimension [10], which have strong relationships with the slantedness of the mouth and the openness of the face [17,18]. The former plane is shown in Fig. 4, and the latter in Fig. 5. Each facial expression is assigned a weight according to the number of selections. An important point in Fig. 5 and Fig. 6 is that the average coordinates of each emotion category took these weights into consideration.

Comparing Fig. 4 and Fig. 5, the distribution of *happy*, *surprised*, and *fear* can be seen to almost correspond, and in addition, *angry*, *sad*, and *disgust* were also seen to correspond in terms of closeness of distribution. Moreover, *fear* could be seen to separate into two clusters in terms of distribution, which could be read in Fig. 4. As mentioned above, the author determined that the distribution of the facial expressions in three-dimensional space obtained through this thesis was valid.

In addition, *angry*, *sad* and *disgust* were separately observed by constructing and observing a projection plane of three-dimensional space comprising slantedness of the eyes and openness of the face (Fig. 6). From this result, by considering the third dimension, the slantedness of the eyes, the distribution of each facial expression was easy to separate and read. Thus the author discovered that the

Table 1 Result of principal component analysis

Principal Component (PC)	PC1	PC2	PC3	PC4
Standard Deviation	1.119	1.034	0.951	0.873
Cumulative Proportion	0.313	0.581	0.807	1.00

Table 2 Meaning of each principal component

Principal Component (PC)		PC1	PC2	PC3
Eyes	Slantedness	0.280	-0.773	-0.298
	Openness	0.557	0.125	0.749
Mouth	Slantedness	0.674	-0.137	-0.160
	Openness	-0.396	-0.606	0.570
Meaning of Principal Component		Mouth's slanbtedness	Eyes' slantedness	Face's Openness

visual information dimension (physical variable) comprises three variables for cognizance of facial expressions.

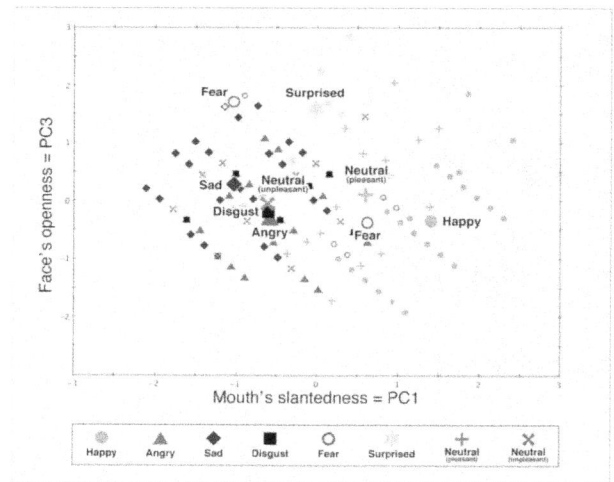

Fig. 4 Projection plane of three-dimensional space for facial expression composed of slantedness of the mouth and openness of the face

Eight Facial Expressions and Two Neutral Facial Expressions

In addition to the observation of face distributions in space, the author found 10 basic facial expressions, eight basic facial expressions: happy, angry, angry*, sad, disgust, fear,

fear*, and surprised; and two neutral facial expressions: neutral (pleasant) and neutral (unpleasant), according to the parametric values and actual facial patterns. Fig. 7 shows each typical facial expression. The difference between angry and angry* is especially apparent in terms of the openness of the eyes and mouth, so angry can be separated in terms of the facial expression showing the anger emotion. Moreover, it can be seen that fear and fear* can be separated because the slantedness of the eyes and the mouth indicate an opposite value.

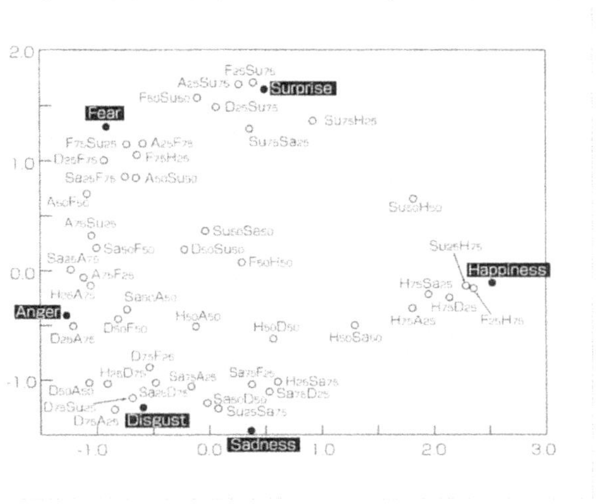

Fig. 5 Circumplex mode constructed by Takehara & Suzuki (2001)

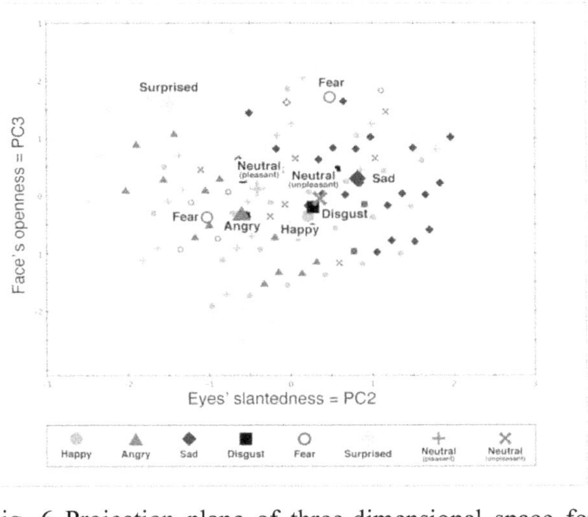

Fig. 6 Projection plane of three-dimensional space for facial expressions composed of the slantedness of the eyes and the openness of the face

Furthermore these facial expressions are distributed in three-dimensional space based on continuous geometrical transformation of the eyes and mouth, and it is understood that each facial expression generates a network comprising a visual and a physical variable (geometrical transformation).

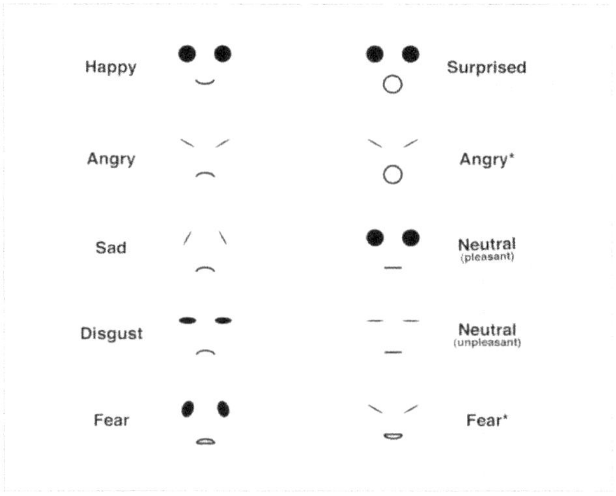

Fig. 7 Typical facial patterns of 10 basic facial expressions

DISCUSSION

In this chapter, a tetrahedral model for making facial expressions is advocated. This model comprises the geometrical and spatial relationships between the 10 facial expressions, and the actual facial patterns and the parametric values of each element.

Relationship Between The Visual Variable Dimension and The Affective Meaning Dimension

Through the facial expression pattern presented in this thesis, the visual variable dimension was obtained, namely, the slantedness of the eyes, the slantedness of the mouth, and the openness of eyes and mouth. Moreover, by observation and comparing with three-dimensional space and the results of previous research, it was found that there is a strong relationship between the slantedness of the mouth and the pleasantness dimension, and the openness of the eyes and mouth and activeness, as indicated in previous research.

In addition, based on observation of the distribution in three-dimensional space, the slantedness of the eyes is an effective means of discerning the distribution areas of the facial expressions, especially *angry*, *sad* and *disgust*. Thus the third effective variable's dimension serves to aid cognition of facial expression, and bears a strong relationship with the judgment of *angry*, *sad* and *disgust*.

Limitation of Facial Elements and Cognition of Facial Expressions

In many previous researches, various experiments on recognition of facial expressions was conducted using actual human faces and pictures or line-drawing faces closely resembling the human face. On the other hand, in this thesis, the minimum elements needed to recognize the face as a face were selected, and the face used for the experiment consisted of only two eyes and a mouth. The eyes and the mouth were used to make facial patterns through geometrical transformations based on precise circles.

From the results, it was found that human beings could recognize faces and judge facial expressions and emotions even when observing a face composed of limited elements subjected to geometrical transformations, as well as being able to recognize the expressions of actual human beings.

Thus, it is possible to read emotion sufficiently, not only from the facial expression of an actual human being, but also from the expression made by a geometrical transformation (rotation and vertically scaling transformation) of the minimum geometrical elements (two eyes and a mouth) needed to recognize a face.

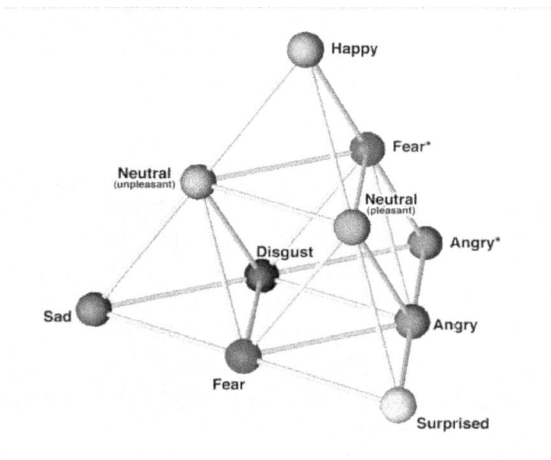

Fig. 8 Tetrahedral-model on structure of facial expressions

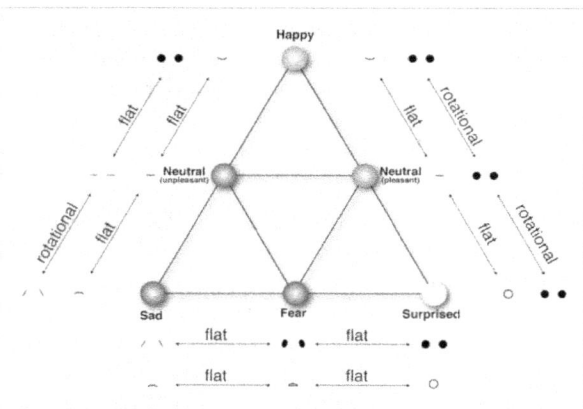

Fig.9 Happy-Sad-Surprised surface of tetrahedral model

Tetrahedral Model to Make Facial Expressions

According to the results and discussion, a tetrahedral model used to make facial expressions is advocated using the 10 basic facial expressions. The model's structure is shown in Fig. 8. This facial model's target is a face made with two eyes and a mouth, and facial patterns made by rotation and vertically scaling transformation of the elements. The 10 emotions are placed in four locations, on top of the body and at a middle point on each side. The position in which each expression is produced is expressed with the ball. The sides between the balls are the axes of transformation of the eyes and the mouth in a constant direction. The actual transformation of the elements is shown in Figs. 9, 10, and 11.

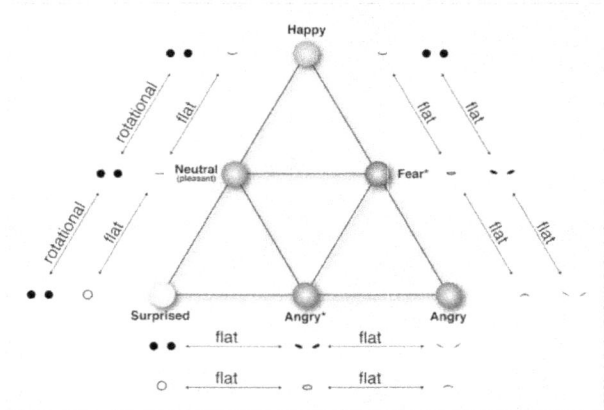

Fig.10 Happy-Surprised-Angry surface of tetrahedral model

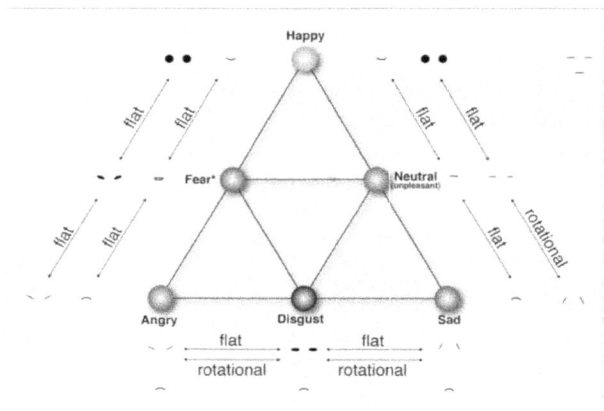

Fig.11 Happy-Angry-Sad surface of tetrahedral model

These figure show the equilateral triangle plane made from each of the three tops of the tetrahedral model. Rotation and vertically scaling transformation adds the eyes, while vertically scaling transformation alone adds the mouth, along the axis (side) connecting each expression. By these transformations and the relationships between each parametric value, the facial expressions can be made to change.

To take the triangle in Fig. 9 as an example, on the side connecting *happy* and *sad*, first of all the eye flatness rate is changed to 10% (this forms the eye for *neutral (unpleasant)*), and secondly, rotation is added and the angle of the eye is changed to -60 degrees, creating the eye for *sad*. Meanwhile, the mouth's form is changed to flat, (*neutral (unpleasant)*), after that it is changed to form the *sad* face. The *happy* face's mouth and the *sad* face's mouth indicate fully opposite values. As shown in Figs. 9, 10, and 11, the topological distance between each emotion is equal, and each facial expression changes to the adjacent facial expression along the side connecting the emotions.

The tetrahedral model can be applied to all face making facial expressions by using geometrical elements and their transformation. For instance, facial expression is assumed to become very important in future communications between humanoid robots, as well as for communication with human beings. In such situations, making facial expressions of humanoid robots is easier using the tetrahedral model, because this model has succeeded in creating facial expressions by geometrical elements and transformation. As well as in the robot field, the application range of the tetrahedral model in the future is thought to be vast, encompassing the realm of healing, curing cognitive impairment, and so on.

Facial Expression of Neutral Facial Expression

In this thesis, the *neutral (pleasant)* and *neutral (unpleasant)* expressions were added to the classification of facial expressions. These expressions were found to exist even though they do not show a specific emotion, and these neutral facial expressions can be generated through transformation of facial elements. Moreover, according to the facial pattern, the *neutral* face can be divided into two facial expressions, showing pleasant and unpleasant emotions respectively. From the results of observing the spatial and geometrical differences between faces, and the tetrahedral model, the author defined the *neutral (pleasant)* facial expression as between *happy* and *surprised*, and the *neutral (unpleasant)* expression as between *happy* and *sad*.

CONCLUSION

In this research, the authors succeeded in creating facial expressions made with the minimum necessary elements for recognizing a face, and enabling human recognition of the expressions created. The elements used for the minimal face were two eyes and a mouth made by precise circles and transformed to make facial expressions geometrically, through rotation and vertically scaling transformation. The facial expression patterns made by the geometric elements and transformations comprised three dimensions of visual information (visual variables) that had been suggested by many previous researches: slantedness of the mouth, openness of face, and slantedness of the eyes. Thus the results of this research indicate that human beings can classify expression patterns of minimal faces to particular emotional categories just as they would with an actual human face. In addition, the relationships between visual affection dimension and the affective meaning dimension also corresponded to the results of the previous researches. These relationships were strong between the slantedness of the mouth and pleasantness; and between the openness of the face and activeness; and the existence of a third

affective variable strongly related to the slantedness of the eyes was also suggested.

The authors found that facial expressions could be classified into 10 different facial expressions: happy, angry, sad, disgust, fear, surprised, and angry*, fear*, neutral (pleasant) showing a positive emotion, and neutral (unpleasant) showing a negative emotion. These facial expressions are composed by different geometric transformations and combinations of the eyes and the mouth. Furthermore, the authors discovered a tetrahedral model that could express most clearly the geometric relationships between the facial expressions. This model is structured in the form of a tetrahedron, with each facial expression located on the top or the middle of the sides of the tetrahedron. Each side connecting faces is an axis determining the rotation and vertically scaling transformation of the eyes and the mouth.

In future, it hoped to research the affective dimension for recognition of facial expressions and to clarify the relationship between the visual variable dimension and the emotional information dimension, and to actually apply the tetrahedral model to humanoid robots and to other wide-ranging fields.

REFERENCES

1. Ellis. H. D, Shepherd. J. W, Davis. G. M., "Identification of familiar and unfamiliar face from internal and external features: Some implications for theories of face recognition," *Perception*, Vol.8, pp.431-439, 1979.

2. Shepherd. J. W, Davis. G. M, Ellis H. D, "Studies of cue saliency," *Perceiving and Remembering Faces*, Academic Press, pp.105-131. 1981.

3. Young. A. W., Hay. D. C., McWeeny. K.H., Fluid. B. M., Ellis. A. W., "Matching familiar and unfamiliar faces on internal and external features," *Perception*, Vol.14, pp.737-746, 1985.

4. Yin. R. K., "Looking at upside-down faces," *Journal of Experimental Psychology*, Vol.81, pp.141-145, 1969.

5. Diamond R., Carey. S., "Why faces are and are not special: An effect of expertise," *Journal of Experimental Psychology*, Vol.115, pp.107-117, 1986.

6. Goren, C., Sartty, M., & Wu, P., "Visual scan patterns of rhesus monkeys viewing faces," *Perception*, Vol.11, pp.133-140, 1975.

7. Johnson, M. H., & Morton, J., "Biology and cognitive development:The case of face recognition," Cambridge, UK: Blackwell, 1991.

8. Ekman P., Friesen W. V., Ellsworth P., "What emotion categories or dimensions can observers judge from facial behaviour?", *Emotion in the human face*, Cambridge University Press, pp. 39-55, 1982.

9. Smith C. A., Ellsworth P. C., "Patterns of cognitive appraisal in emotion," *Journal of Personality and Social Psychology*, Vol.48, No.4, pp.813-838, 1985.

10. Yamada H., "Expression model for process of perceptive estimation of facial expression" [in Japanese], *Japanese Psychological Review*, Vol.43, No.2, pp.245-225, 2000.

11. Darwin C., "The expression of the emotions in man and animals," Oxford University Press, 1998.(original work published 1872)

12. Ekman P., "Basic emotions, Handbook of cognition and emotion," pp.45-60, 1999.

13. Russell J. A., "Reading emotions from and into faces: Resurrecting a dimensional-contextual perspective," *The psychology of facial expression*, Cambridge University Press, pp.295-320. 1997

14. Ekman, P., Basic Emotions. In Daglesh T. & Power M. (Eds.), *Handbook of cognition and emotion*, New York: Wiley, pp.45-60, 1999.

15. Ekman P., "Universals and cultural differences in facial expressions of emotion," Nebraska Symposium on Motivation, Vol.19, pp.207-283, 1972.

16. Ekman P., "Cross-cultural studies of facial expression," *Darwin and facial expression: A century of research in review*, Academic Press, pp.169-222, 1973.

17. Ekman P., "An argument for basic emotions," *Cognition and Emotion*, Vol.6, no.3, pp.169-200, 1992.

18. Ekman P., "Constants across cultures in the face and emotion," *Joumal of Personality and Social Psychology*, Vol.17, No.2, pp.124-129, 1971.

19. Ekman P., "Pan-cultural elements in facial displays of emotions," *Science*, Vol.169, pp.86-88, 1969.

20. Ekman P., "Conceptual ambiguities," *Emotion in the human face*, Cambridge University Press, 1982.

21. Ekman P., "Universals and cultural differences in the judgments of facial expressions of emotion," *Journal of Personality and Social Psychology*, Vol.53, No.4, pp.712-717, 1987.

22. Schlosberg H., "The description of facial expressions in terms of two dimensions," *Journal of Experimental Psychology*, Vol.44, No.4, pp.229-237.1952.

23. Schlosberg H., "Three dimensions of emotion," *Psychological Review*, Vol.10, No.5, pp.81-88, 1954.

24. Shah R., and Lewis M. B., "Locating the neutral expression in the facial-emotion space," *Visual Cognition*, Vol.1-, No.5, pp.549-566, 2003.

25. Takehara T., Suzuki N., "Robustness of the two-dimensional structure of recognition of emotionality," *Perceptual and Motor Skills*, Vol.93, No.3, pp.739-753, 2001.

26. Yamada H., "Visual information for categorizing facial expression of emotions," *Applied Cognitive Psychology*, Vol.3, No.7, pp.252-270, 1993.

27. Yamada H., Shibui S., "The relationship between visual information and affective meanings from facial expressions of emotion," *Perception*, Vol.27, pp.133, 1998.

28. Watanabe N., "Research of distribution of facial expressions in emotional space by using affect grid method" [in Japanese], *Japanese Psychological Research*, Vol.65, pp.274, 2001.

29. Yamada H., Matsuda T., Watari C., Suenaga T., "Dimenson of visual information for categorizing facial expressions of emotion," *Japanese Psychological Research*, Vol.35, No.4, pp.172-181, 1993.

30. Watanabe N., Suzuki R., Yamada H., "Visual information related to facial expression recognition - Research of 3 dimensional structure," The Technical Report of The Proceeding of The Institute of Electronics, Information and communication Engineers, Vol.102, No.598, HCS2002-35, pp.43-48, 2003.

31. Watanabe N., Suzuki R., Yamada H., "Re-consideration about relationship between mental and physical information for facial expression recognition" [in Japanese], The Japanese Society for Cognitive Psychology, 2003.

32. Russell J. A., Weiss A., Medelsohn G. A., "Affect grid: A single-item scale of pleasure and arousal," *Journal of Personality and Social Psychology*, Vol.57, No.3, pp.493-502, 1989.

33. Kawahara H., Matsumoto N., "A cognitive analysis to the variety in facial features of prehistoric figurines: An approach from cognitive and esthetic archaeology" [in Japanese], Technical report of IEICE. HIP, Vol.107, No.369, pp.79-84, 2007.

34. Carrera P., Fernandez-Dos J. M., "Neutral faces in context, Their emotional and their function," *Journal of Nonverbal Behavior*, Vol.18, pp.281-299, 1994.

35. Okamoto T., Numerical experiment for assessment of reproducibility of each method of multiple classification analysis [in Japanese], Behaviormetric Society of Japan, Vol.18, No.2, pp.47-56, 1991.

Empirical Evaluation of Mapping Functions for Navigation in Virtual Reality using Phones with Integrated Sensors

Amal Benzina
Fachgebiet Augmented Reality
Technische Universität
München Fakultät für
Informatik Boltzmannstraße 3,
85748 Garching b. München,
Germany
benzina@in.tum.de

Arindam Dey
University of South Australia
Adelaide, Australia
arindam.dey@unisa.edu.au

Marcus Tönnis
Gudrun Klinker
Fachgebiet Augmented Reality
Technische Universität
München Fakultät für
Informatik Boltzmannstraße 3,
85748 Garching b. München,
Germany
toennis, klinker@in.tum.de

ABSTRACT

Mobile phones provide an interesting all-in-one alternative for 3D input devices in virtual environments. Mobile phones are becoming touch sensitive and spatially aware, and they are now part of our daily activities. We present *Phone-Based Motion Control*, a novel one-handed travel technique for a virtual environment. The technique benefits from the touch capability offered by growing number of mobile phones to change viewpoint translation in virtual environments, while the orientation of the viewpoint is controlled by built-in sensors in the mobile phone. The travel interaction separates translation (touch based translation control) and rotation (steer based rotation control), putting each set of degrees of freedom (DOF) to a separate interaction technique (separability).

This paper examines, how many DOF are needed to perform the travel task as easy and comfortable as possible. It also investigates different mapping functions between the user's actions on the mobile phone and the viewpoint change in the virtual environment. Therefore, four techniques are implemented: rotate by heading, rotate by roll, rotate by roll with fixed horizon and a merged rotation. Each technique has either 4 or 5 DOF and different mappings between phone and viewpoint coordinates in the virtual environment. We perform an extensive user study to explore different aspects related to the travel techniques in terms of DOF and mapping functions. Results of the user evaluation show that 4 DOF techniques seem to perform better the travel task. Even though, the results were not statistically decisive in favor of the usage of the mobile roll to control the viewpoint heading in the virtual environment despite the good results, there is a clear tendency from the users to prefer the mobile roll as the desired mapping.

Author Keywords

Interaction; Navigation; degree of freedom; User study; Mobile devices.

ACM Classification Keywords

H.5.2 [Information interfaces and presentation]: User Interfaces - Input devices and strategies.

General Terms

Design; Human Factors; Experimentation.

INTRODUCTION

Nowadays, we are emerged in a rich and heterogeneous ubiquitous computing world, where we need to interact with different resources like large displays. Mobile devices have shown to be an excellent candidate as 3D input devices. Mobile phones provide a rich set of features enabling us to interact with virtual environments.

To explore geographical features of large virtual worlds, user interfaces that adopt flying metaphors are usually well accepted because many people are used to games and 3D game controllers imitating airplanes flighting like the Wii. Our visualization system [4] renders high resolution 3D geographical data and in the near future will incorporate further spatial simulations that will require explorations in all possible DOF. Another pseudo requirement is that only one hand of the user should be able to use the system so that fatigue of very long use can be distributed over both hands and the second hand can execute additional activities, such as manipulation of simulation parameters or selection.

The increasing availability of mobile phones and the integration of various sensors and touch sensitive displays make such devices candidates for investigation. Although sensors of various kinds with higher accuracy are available, mobile phones however offer an all-in-one integrated and compact solution. Having both, built in sensors and a touch screen available, creates a large and diverse design space.

Our approach is to investigate navigation techniques by employing such mobile phones to enable the user to travel and explore virtual environments (VE). Following the recommendations of Hinckley et al. [11] to constrain the dimensions (i.e. degrees of freedom) of an input device to a certain meaningful value, we developed a one-handed system that has been outlined in an earlier work [2]. The travel task distinguishes between translation and rotation, putting each set of DOF to a separate interaction technique. For translation i.e. for controlling the direction of the viewpoint, we use the touch capability of the display of the phone. For rotation we employ the motion sensors to make it spatially aware.

With the separation between translation and the rotation, four travel techniques with different DOF and mappings have been developed and tested in an initial study [2]. The study aimed on collecting information about the general quality of the techniques and brought insights about drawbacks in technical matters, that were improved in the new implementation. Even if the test had been run in terms of dimensionality and mapping functions, no empirical user study had been conducted. Nevertheless, the initial study showed some observations. 4 DOF seem to be sufficient to control 5 DOF in the VE. Moreover, it also revealed that techniques incorporating a device roll seem to be the desired mappings to control the heading in the VE. This paper presents the extensions incorporated to the different travel techniques and now provides an extensive user study with statistical analysis of calculated quality measures.

This paper contributes in two ways. First, a few novel interaction techniques are proposed to use a mobile phone as a 3D input device to travel in VEs. Second, results of a rigorous user evaluation of a traveling task in VE providing valuable insights about the effectiveness of different DOF possibly be mapped between the input device and VE and their mapping functions.

The next sections first cover related work and then develop our concept. Then, the four travel techniques with the respective DOF and the mapping functions are presented. In the following section, the outcome of the formative shaping process is illustrated. Then we present the user study we conducted. Results of the statistical analysis are then presented and discussed. Finally, we conclude the paper by directing towards the future work.

RELATED WORK

Handheld and multi-touch capable devices, and mobile phones have been used recently for various interaction techniques, often for travel tasks. The sensors embedded in mobile phones and built-in cameras have been used for sensing the users' gestures or what was called in several publications sensing-based interaction or travel [12].

Sensing-based Interaction within Handheld Devices

Hinckely et al. [9, 10] investigated different sensing techniques for mobile interaction with spatially aware mobile devices and demonstrated several new functionalities. They used touch sensors, accelerometers or what they call tilt sensors and proximity sensors to introduce functionalities such as recording memos when the device is held vertically, switching between portrait and landscape display modes by

changing the device orientation, power management of the device when the user picks the device up and start using it, and scrolling the display using tilt. Their usability study showed that a careful usage of the phone integrated sensors is necessary to deliver a mobile interaction that is as simple and pleasant to use as possible. In a earlier work, Hinckley et al. [11] presented a survey of previous research on spatial input techniques. They gathered some interaction techniques involving 3D input devices and presented a design framework for the development of interaction techniques using spatial input devices. Accelerometers have also been used to control mobile 3D games, [13] describe how accelerometers provide the feature of a no-button control for mobile game. they discuss that tilt motion is suitable for mobile phones for a 3-D graphics first-person driving game 'Tunnel Run'. They compare the game user experience with a traditional phone joypad interface and with a tilt interface in two phases. The results show that the tilt interface was more attractive and fun to players. Rohs et al. [12] presented three sensor technologies in small-scale handheld devices for spatial tracking: camera-based tracking, optical motion estimation, and accelerometer and magnetometer readings for tilt and rotation detection. They performed a comparison of user performance using the three sensor technologies to navigate in a map. The evaluation procedure consisted of the users searching 10 individual targets in sequence using each time one of the three navigation techniques and hence each time a sensing technique. Accelerometer and magnetometer sensing showed good performance just below optical marker grid tracking. Others explored different physical operations, such as contact, pressure, tilt and motion, that can be applied to handheld devices for navigation tasks in mobile phones [14, 5]. Zhai [7] introduced the TinyMotion prototype that tracks the users hand movements by analyzing image sequences captured by the phone built-in camera. They found out that their Tiny-Motion method could be quite reliably used for text-input and gaming. They also made an analytical comparison between their camera phone based motion sensing TinyMotion and accelerometers. They mentioned that even though the accelerometers, to the contrary of the TinyMotion, will not have any influence from illumination conditions and require a fairly low processing power on the mobile side, they might suffer from a higher accumulative drift error.

Sensing-Based Travel in VE using Handheld Devices with External Resources

Boring et al. [17] introduced and compared three different interaction techniques for continuous control of a pointer located on a remote display using a mobile phone: scroll, tilt, and move. The interaction in their work is more about selection on a large display, but the results can be related to our approach for traveling in VEs, because especially the tilt technique uses acceleration sensors. The evaluation showed that users applying the move and tilt techniques perform the selection task faster, but they also suffer from higher error rates. The paper by Jeon [18] presents user interaction especially for object selection and manipulation using camera built-in mobile phones in large display environments. They proposed three approaches: motion flow based, marker-object based and marker-cursor based. Bednarz [19] introduced an interaction technique in immersive virtual environment. They used the iPhone to get the orientation data pertaining to accelerational and rotational attributes, such as, pitch, roll and yaw as well as the touch screen for navigation and manipulation of virtual objects in an immersive VR mining environment. Zhai investigated the relation between the sensed property and and the transfer function [15]. He also shows that isotonic sensors work better for position control techniques, while elastic sensors and isometric sensors should be used with rate control. According to Zhai's work, travel task use mostly rate control. Kulik et al. [1] introduced a one-handed input device for 3D interaction called two - 4 - six. They analyzed the specific interaction task to choose a specific spatial arrangement of the sensors in the input device, and discussed the required DOF in appropriate combinations. They provided 6 DOF for the travel task with a separation between orientation and translation. Also Hinckley et al. [11] pointed out that it is important to look at the number of available DOF for the interaction task, and to relate this to the ability of the users to control the DOF simultaneously.

PHONE BASED MOTION CONTROL

We introduce a novel one-handed travel technique in a VE. We call the travel technique *Phone-Based Motion Control* technique, since the travel in the VE is completely performed using a mobile phone with integrated sensors as a 3D input device.

As our travel technique aims for the exploration of large scale data sets, for long distance movements it is better to use rate control instead of position control during the travel to avoid unnecessary clutching that decreases performance. This has been discussed in the work of Casiez et al. [3] where they presented a prototype RubberEdge position-rate hybrid control device for selection task. They also discuss in their work the fact that position control provide better precision performance, but since in our work we are dealing with travel task where clutching would have a dramatic influence and fine precision is not that crucial. With a spatially aware mobile device, we can provide up to 6 DOF, however, we want to answer the question of whether or not more DOF contribute to a better execution of the travel task. The control of the VE viewpoint is divided into two parts. We use the *touch screen* of the mobile phone to control the *translation* of the viewpoint, and the *built-in sensors* to control the *orientation* of the viewpoint. For translation, a *touch based translation control* technique is conceptualized. For rotation, the orientation of the device is mapped to the orientation of the viewpoint in the VE, defining the *steer based rotation control* technique.

In addition to the separability, we aim to make the mappings between the user actions on the mobile phone and the effect or reactions onto the viewpoint in the VE smooth and meaningful. The main underlying principle here is that a translation maps to a translation and a rotation, or more specifically, a tilt, maps to a turn or a rotation in the VE.

Beforehand, conventions on the coordinate systems used in later concepts are illustrated and the general activation model of the interaction techniques is introduced.

Conventions of Coordinate Systems

To ease understanding in the following paper sections, we define the coordinate systems both of the mobile phone and the VE.

1. **Coordinate system of the mobile phone touch screen:** The coordinate system is relative to the phone screen. The origin of the coordinate system is the lower left corner of the screen. The X-Axis extends horizontally and to the right, the Y-Axis extends vertically and to the upper direction, and the Z-Axis extends outside the front of the screen (see Figure 1(b) and (c)).

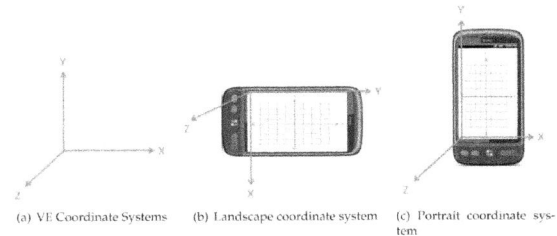

(a) VE Coordinate Systems   (b) Landscape coordinate system   (c) Portrait coordinate system

Figure 1. Coordinate System

2. **Coordinate system of the mobile phone (sensors):** Many programming interfaces of mobile phone functionality internally fuse the readings from built-in sensors, in most cases a 3-axis accelerometer sensor and a magnetic field sensor. Accelerometers cannot be used for motion in all axes. The gravitational field of the earth can provide an absolute reference and rotation relative to the gravitational field can be measured reliably. Other rotations are only measurable if more than one sensor is built into the phone. At the moment, most mobile phones only provide one sensor for acceleration. This is the reason behind combining both the readings from the 3-axis accelerometer and the magnetometer to get the orientation around the three axes. The three angles representing the orientation of a mobile phone are usually heading, pitch, and roll, as described below:

   (a) *Heading* or *Azimuth* represents the orientation around the Z-Axis. It represents the angle between the magnetic north direction and the Y-Axis. The angle ranges from 0 to 359 where 0 indicates north, 90 east, 180 south, and 270 west directions. Figure 2(a)

   (b) *Pitch* to represent the orientation around the X-Axis. The angle ranges from -180 to 180, positive angle when the Z-Axis moves toward the Y-Axis. Figure 2(b).

   (c) *Roll* is defined as the representation of the orientation around the Y-Axis. The angle ranges from -90 to 90; positive angle when X-Axis moves toward the Z-Axis. Figure 2(c).

3. **Coordinate system of the virtual world:** The coordinate systems of the VE are depicted in Figure 1(a). The X-axis extends into positive space to the right, the Y-axis increases upwards and the Z-axis extends into positive space from the center of the screen towards the viewer.

151

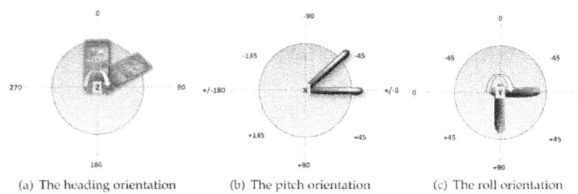

(a) The heading orientation   (b) The pitch orientation   (c) The roll orientation

Figure 2. Orientation Sensor Readings

Since the coordinate systems of the mobile phone and the VE are not the same, we transform the coordinates accordingly and also depending on whether the user is holding the mobile phone in the portrait or landscape side. For simplicity, in this paper all examples are considering the phone in the portrait mode.

Activation State of Travel Mode

The user needs to trigger a dedicated action on the mobile phone to activate the start or to end the motion in the VE; otherwise, the viewpoint would change continuously, every time the user moves the hand holding the mobile phone whether intentionally or not. As the system uses accelerometer and magnetometer readings, we need to calculate the relative rotation of the mobile phone. For this reason, we need an initial rotation angle of the mobile phone. Therefore, we use the touch capabilities of the mobile phone as a start indication to maintain the system control task for activation and deactivation of the traveling action. To stop steering and translating, users have two options: either to remove the thumb from the screen to enter a smooth deceleration phase, or to set the mobile phone back to its start orientation and in parallel to move the finger to the start position on the screen. We also implemented a short tap on the screen to allow the user stop instantly if needed to avoid overshooting a target position in VE.

Touch Based Translational Control

As the thumb moves over the display, the relative displacement of the finger to the initial touch-down position is calculated. The mobile direction vector is hence calculated indicating the viewpoint motion direction. The finger displacement on the mobile screen is mapped to a translation in the virtual environment. The users can press any initial point on the screen and move the finger in any direction. Not having a conceptual start-stop button for motion control benefits us in terms of avoiding accidental clicking on the button. The users can perform the translation without looking at the mobile screen and can keep their eyes on the VE as desired. As long as the thumb is still pressing the touch screen the translation continues in the indicated direction.

The mobile displacement vector is then sent asynchronously to the VE server application where the displacement of the viewpoint in the VE is calculated. The VE vector is calculated by multiplying the mobile displacement vector received from the mobile with the elapsed time between each two frames to obtain a smooth motion.

Steer Based Rotation Control

The orientation is controlled by tilting the mobile phone. The sensors in general provide angles for heading, pitch and roll. Those angles are calculated from the difference between the initial orientation value (once the thumb presses the mobile screen) and the current orientation at each point in time. The delta orientation of the mobile is then mapped to the viewpoint orientation speed in the VE. The delta angles are first "filtered" and then sent to the VE, where the angles are multiplied by the elapsed time between each two frames and added to the previous VE orientation values (heading, pitch and roll). As a result we obtain a smooth transition from one orientation state to another.

The orientation sensor is a virtual sensor, provided by the phone programming interface, combining the readings from both the 3-axis accelerometer sensor and the magnetic field sensor.

Three techniques are implemented for the steer based rotation control with different number of degrees of freedom and different mapping functions. A fourth technique is a combination of the rotate by heading and the rotate by roll technique, having the maximum number of DOF used.

1. **Rotate By Heading Technique**: This technique simulates a bicycle or walking metaphor. In this technique heading and the pitch of the mobile are mapped to the heading and pitch of the VE application. The roll is not used, the horizon is kept horizontal in that case. The user has to rotate or tilt the mobile around the Z axis (up vector). Since the coordinate system is relative to the mobile phone, as shown in Figure 1, rotating the mobile using the hand wrist or the hand elbow will not make a difference in sensor readings for the heading; see Figure 3(a).

2. **Rotate By Roll Technique**: The rotate by roll technique is simulating an airplane metaphor. The change in the mobile roll is mapped to both the heading and the roll in the VE. The change in the roll values in the VE provides an animation to make the user feel like flying. Here, the mobile pitch is mapped to the pitch of the viewpoint in the VE; see Figure 3(b).

3. **Rotate By Roll With Fixed Horizon Technique**: The rotate by roll with fixed horizon technique is similar to the rotate by roll technique; the only difference is that the horizon remains aligned horizontally. Hence the mobile roll is mapped only to the heading of the VE and the mobile pitch is mapped to the pitch of the viewpoint in the VE. This technique simulates a car steering behavior; see Figure 3(c).

4. **Merged Rotation Technique**: This technique is a combination between the Rotate by Heading and the Rotate by Roll techniques. We are merging both techniques, rotate by roll and rotate by heading. Both the heading and the roll values from the mobile phone are mapped to the heading in the VE. The delta heading will be calculated based on the change in both the roll and the heading values of the mobile, the delta heading is the average of both the delta heading and the delta roll. The mapping of the

mobile phone roll to the roll in the VE is done to provide the flying effect. The mobile orientation on the three axes (heading, roll and pitch) is mapped to the VE orientation of the viewpoint (heading, roll and pitch); see Figure 3(d).

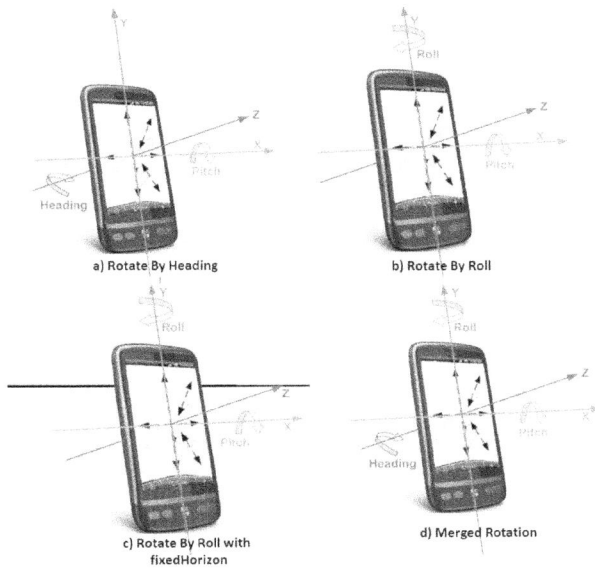

Figure 3. Steer Based Rotation Control Techniques

Travel in a Virtual Environment

With the translation and rotation mechanisms at hand, users can travel through the VE freely. The touch translation combined with the four rotation techniques gives the four techniques of concern of investigation in a user experiment. With these techniques at hand we either can investigate the suitability of different DOF for maintaining exploratory travel tasks and also can inspect different coordinates' mapping between the phone tilt and the VE rotation.

1. **Touch translation and rotate By Heading Technique**: In this technique four DOF in the mobile device (translation (X, Y) and rotation (heading, pitch)) are mapped to four DOF in VE (translation (X, -Z) and rotation (heading, pitch)); see Figure 4(a).

2. **Touch translation and rotate By Roll Technique**: In this technique four DOF in the mobile device (translation (X, Y) and rotation (roll, pitch)) are mapped to five DOF in VE (translation (X, -Z) and rotation (heading, roll, pitch)); see Figure 4(b).

3. **Touch translation and rotate By Roll With Fixed Horizon Technique**: In this technique four DOF in the mobile device (translation (X, Y) and rotation (roll, pitch)) are mapped to four DOF in VE (translation (X, -Z) and rotation (heading, pitch)); see Figure 4(c).

4. **Touch translation and merged Rotation Technique**: In this technique five DOF in the mobile device (translation (X, Y) and rotation (heading/roll, roll, pitch)) are mapped to five DOF in VE (translation (X, -Z) and rotation (heading, roll, pitch)); see Figure 4(d).

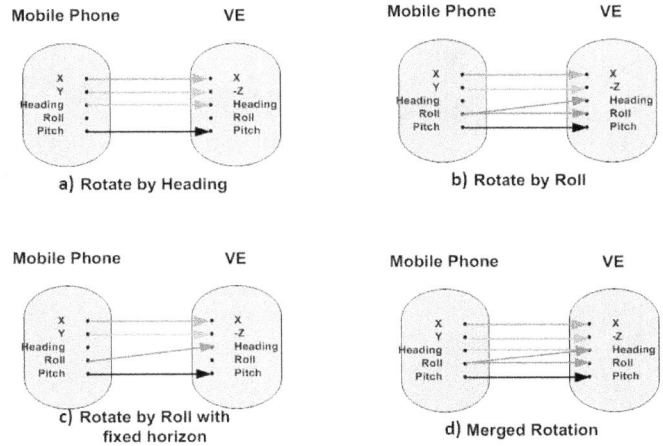

Figure 4. (a) Rotate by Heading. (b) Rotate by Roll. (c) Rotate by Roll with fixed Horizon. (d) Merged Rotation

FORMATIVE SHAPING OF TRAVEL USER INTERFACE

Evaluating user interfaces during development facilitates stability and usability. Following [16], we integrated discussion partners and test subjects at early stages to discuss drawbacks and to identify further issues. This formative shaping during system development helped us learn about behaviors of test users in terms of used dimensionality while performing the travel task.

Intermediate Implementation

An intermediate implementation of the touch based translation control technique, was a small modification of the finger walking in place (FWIP) [8] to have one handed interaction. The users had to keep "rolling" their thumb to control the viewpoint translation. In other words, we simulate the behavior of a mouse scrolling wheel on the screen such that the user will have to "roll" the virtual wheel on the screen to control the translation in the (X,Y) plane (2 DOF) depending on the movement of the scrolling. Early observations of the users however showed that the majority never used the scrolling method. The users, for example, moved the thumb forward on the screen while keeping their thumb pressed on the screen and expected the translation to continue, like a virtual joystick. Moreover, when this "virtual scrolling wheel" was used at the same time with the steer based rotation control, users had trouble controlling translation and rotation of the device simultaneously. To move forward and to steer at the same time in a sharp turn, most users first had to roll their thumbs for the virtual mouse wheel on the screen to translate, then stopped, and steered the mobile device. Users translated and steered sequentially. Also, due to the continuous finger rolling to simulate the "virtual scrolling wheel", we noticed a clear cross influence between the touch and orientation sensors. While rolling the finger, the users were unintentionally also changing the accelerometers roll readings as they could keep their hand stable. Therefore, we modified the touch based translation control technique to support a "joystick" metaphor, as described in Section . This modification was instantly accepted by the users, as it removed the undesired sensor cross influence and it relieved the users' hand fatigue.

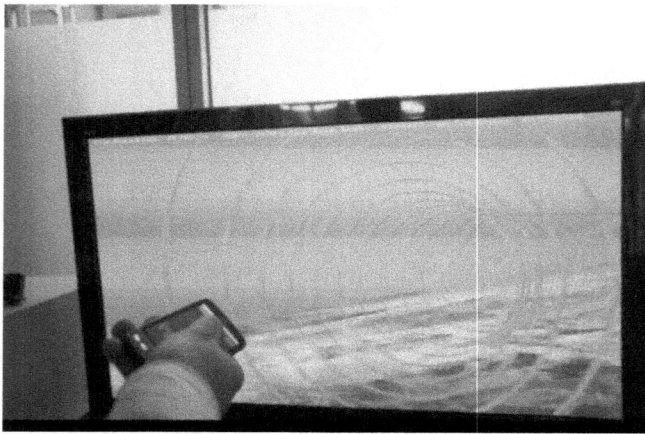

Figure 6. Evaluation Tunnel

With the new implementation, they did not have to move their thumbs extensively. Small displacements on the screen were enough to perform the translation.

USER STUDY ON STEERING METAPHORS

In this user study, we performed a *mixed − factorial* evaluation to compare the performance of the different steering techniques (rotate by roll, rotate by roll with fixed horizon, rotate by heading, and merged rotation) with their different DOF and mapping functions in terms of Accuracy, Errors, Time, and Steering Quality. The overall design goal of this experiment is to evaluate whether users could complete a given travel task better with less or more DOF as presented through our steering techniques. We have also collected data to analyze whether the mapping functions had an influence on the performance. Twenty participants (18 male), ages ranging from 22 to 36 years (M=27, SD=3.8), were recruited from the student population of the university. All of the participants had normal vision.

Experimental Environment

The mobile device used for the evaluation is a HTC Desire phone. The mobile phone provides a multi-touch display, a 3-axis accelerometer, and a digital compass. The mobile phone run the Android operating system [6]. The work is evaluated on 3D terrain visualization environment [4]. We used a 3D TV (50") during the evaluation, the participants had to wear shutter glasses for the 3D effect and semi-immersivity in the VE. The lighting condition of the environment was controlled and remained identical throughout the entire experiment. To be able to carry out the evaluation we drew three different tunnels, we call them *paths*, with different steering complexities in the VE application as shown in Figure 5. However, all of the paths had an equal length of 98 km. The coordinates of the paths are taken from a prerecorded flight. The recording was done using a keyboard for the translation and a mouse for the orientation in the VE. This way the four techniques have the same fairness of travel. Each of the tunnels were composed of rings having a diameter of 2000 meters at 250 meters interval.

Experimental Task

Participants were placed in front of the 3D TV at a distance of 1 meter during the evaluation. The display was placed at a convenient height and fixed throughout the experiment. However, participants were allowed to move their body freely during the experiment. There were two repetitions for each participant, and in each repetition participants had to travel through nine tunnels (randomly presented one at a time) (see Figure 6) using the assigned steering technique. We have randomly distributed participants in four groups. They were instructed to be within the tunnel as much as they can and reach the end of the tunnel as quickly as possible. Participants were allowed to take a rest between each repetition. Participants were provided with a training session to try out the experimental technique before the experiment. Data collection for each trial started when a participant entered the tunnel from the start point, and ended when she reached the end of the tunnel.

Variables

There were four independent and five dependent variables in this experiment. The entire experiment was based on 4 (techniques) × 3 (paths) × 3 (speeds) × 2 (repetitions) × 5 (participants per technique) = 360 data points.

Independent Variable

- **Steering Technique** ∈ {Rotate by Roll, Rotate by Roll with fixed horizon, Rotate by Heading, Merged Rotation} *between subjects*
  Please see Section *Steer Based Rotation Control* for detailed description of the four steering techniques used in this experiment. Each group of participant performed their experimental task using only one technique.

- **Path Complexity** ∈ {Simple, Moderate, Complex} *within subjects*
  We have designed three different paths with varying complexity namely Simple, Moderate, and Complex. The paths were verified by a panel of researchers in our group to ensure the quality of the paths are appropriate for their respective levels. All of the experimental paths had an equal length of 98 km. We have carefully designed the paths and verified them with a pilot study to avoid any unrealistic turns that could force participants to cause errors.
  Simple: In this type of path we have carefully manipulated the curves to have moderate complexity at the turns (large turns). Along the entire path there were just two turns, straight paths and minimal change in the height along the path. See Figure 5(a).
  Moderate: Moderate path had a mixture of sharp and moderate turns along with a straight path. We also varied the height along the path more than that of Simple path. See Figure 5(b).
  Complex: This type of path had all sharp turns and frequent change in the pitch. See Figure 5(c).

- **Speed** ∈ {Slow, Medium, Fast}   *within subjects*
  Increasing speed decreases the accuracy of traveling in

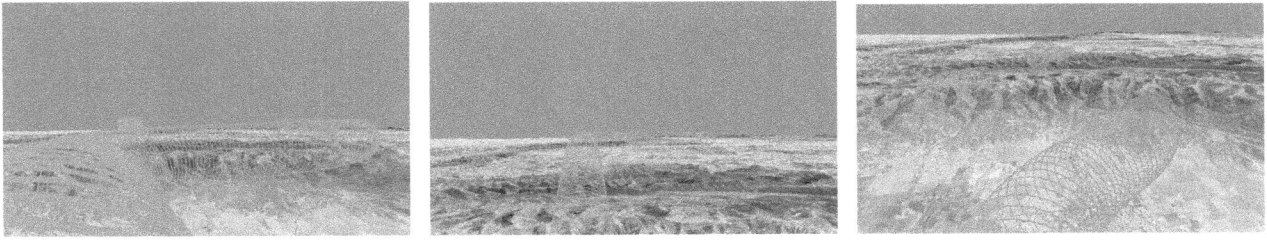

(a) Straight paths and two large turns and no change in the pitch   (b) Mixture of sharp and moderate turns along with a straight path   (c) Sharp turns and frequent change in the pitch

Figure 5. Path Complexities: (a) Simple Path, (b) Moderate Path, and (c) Complex Path.

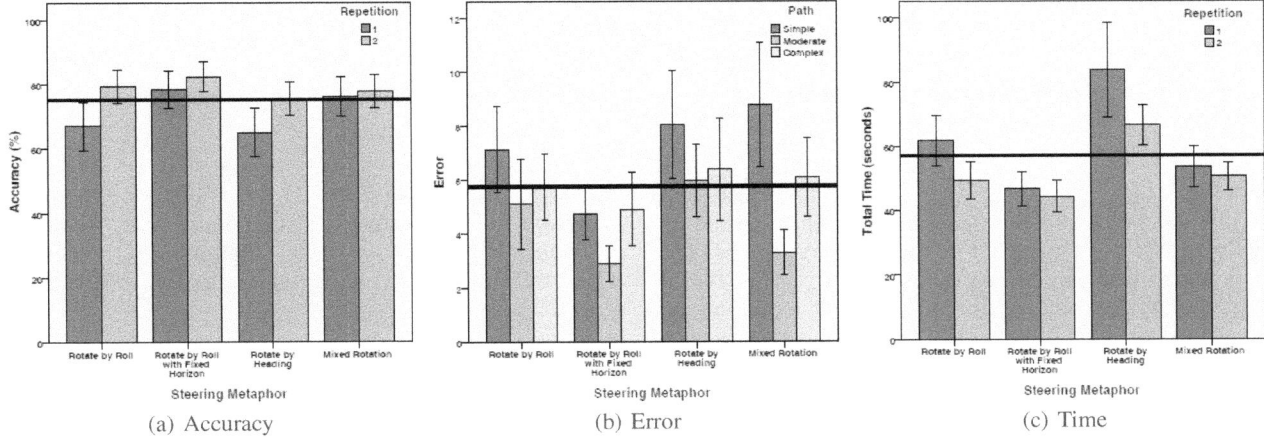

(a) Accuracy   (b) Error   (c) Time

Figure 7. Rotate by Roll with fixed horizon appeared to be the best alternative among all of the techniques experimented in terms of Accuracy (a), Error (b), and Time (c). Moderate path had significantly less Error. Thick Black lines represent the overall mean and whiskers represent ±95% confidence interval.

VE. We were interested to know how the increasing speed affects our four novel techniques. We have systematically varied the speed: Slow (20km./sec), Medium (35km./sec), and Fast (50km./sec).

- **Repetition** $\in \{1$ to $2\}$ *within subjects*
  We have crossed the variables Path and Speed to achieve nine unique stimuli and then randomly presented these nine conditions to each participant in one set of trials. A same set of nine trials were repeated two times for each participant resulting them to perform eighteen different trials, where they traveled through one path in each of them. Participants were allowed to take a break between two trials and also a longer break after each repetition.

Dependent Variable

As dependent variables we measured Accuracy, Error, Time and Steering Quality.

Accuracy: We measured the accuracy of traveling using these steering techniques with the Equation 1.

$$Accuracy = \frac{Time_{in}}{Time_{total}} \times 100\% \qquad (1)$$

Hence, an accuracy of 100% is perfect.

Error: The number of times participants went outside the tunnel's rings during each travel was measured as an Error.

Time: In each trial the time to reach the end of the tunnel was measured in Seconds. The stopwatch started when the participant entered through the first ring of the tunnel.

Steering Quality: We decided to measure a composite measure that takes all aspects of the travel into account and call it *Steering Quality*. It was measured using the following Equation 2.

$$Steering\ Quality = Error \times Time_{out} \times Deviation \qquad (2)$$

Where, Deviation is the *area* covered outside the tunnel during each travel. Hence, 0 is the veridical steering quality and lower values indicate higher quality.

Hypotheses

Initially we have hypothesized the following.
[H1] Overall, performance will increase with the increase of DOF in the techniques as participants will have more flexibility in the traveling task. Hence, Merged rotation will be the best among all of the techniques.
[H2] The higher the speed is and the more complex the tunnel is, the worst is the accuracy for the travel task.

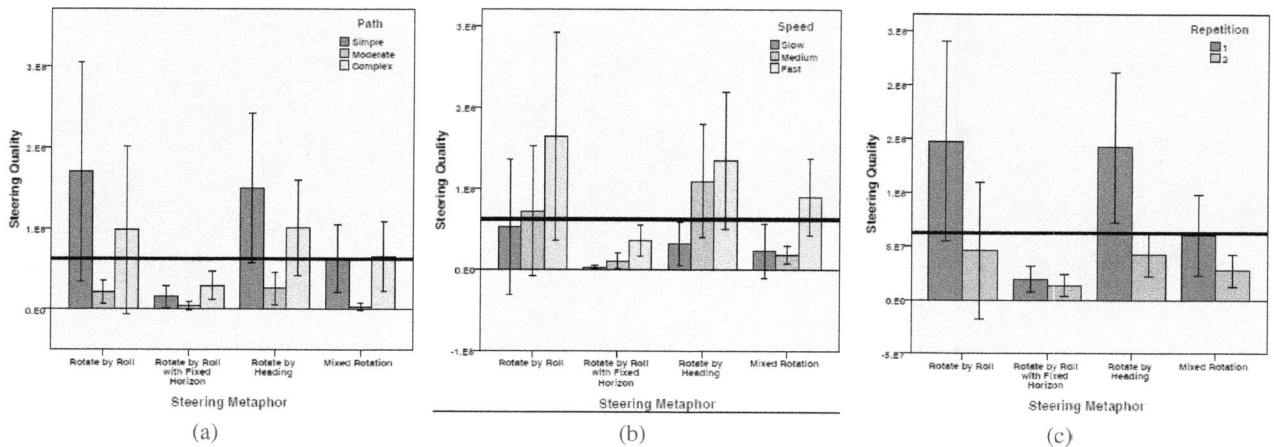

Figure 8. Rotate by Roll with Fixed Horizon had the highest steering quality among all of the steering techniques. The thick Black line represents the overall mean and whiskers represent ±95% confidence interval.

Results

To analyze the effect of four steering techniques on the dependent variables we ran a set of mixed factorial ANOVAs, one for each of the dependent variables using the statistical package SPSS. Once getting a significant main effect through the ANOVA, we used Tukey's HSD post-hoc test to analyze between-subject effects (Techniques) and pair-wise comparisons with Bonferroni adjustments for within-subject effects (Path, Speed, and Repetition).

Accuracy: The analysis did not show a significant main effect of Technique $F(3, 16) = 1.071; p = .389; \eta_p^2 = .167$ (see Figure 7(a)). However, among all of the techniques Rotate by Roll with fixed horizon was the best (M=80.44, SD=17.61) and Rotate by Heading was the worst (M=70.28, SD=22.21).

Error: There was a significant main effect of Technique on Error $F(3, 16) = 3.51; p = .04; \eta_p^2 = .397$ (See Figure 7(b)). In this case also, Rotate by Roll with Fixed Horizon (M=4.17, SD=2.9) was significantly ($p = .03$) better than Rotate by Heading (M=6.79, SD=4.77). Expectedly, there was main effect of Speed ($p < .001$) as Slow speed being significantly better than both Medium and High speeds. We have found a main effect of Path on Error ($p < .05$). Interestingly, Moderate path (M=4.3, SD=3.41) had significantly ($p = .02$) better performance than both Simple (M=7.17, SD=4.96) and Complex (M=5.77, SD=4.04) paths. Surprisingly, the Simple path had most errors.

Time: Steering techniques had a significant main effect on the total time $F(3, 16) = 5.244; p = .01; \eta_p^2 = .496$ (See Figure 7(c)). Rotate by Roll with Fixed Horizon (M=45.48, SD=16.92) was significantly ($p = .008$) faster than Rotate by Heading (M=75.15, SD=38.52).

Steering Quality: Though Rotate by Roll with fixed horizon was the best technique in term of steering quality, but ANOVA did not report any main effect of steering techniques on steering quality ($p = .13$). Expectedly, Path had a significant main effect on Steering Quality $F(1.42, 22.74) = 9.13; p = .003; \eta_p^2 = .363$ (Greenhouse-Geisser adjustment),

and so had Speed $F(2, 32) = 9.396; p = .001; \eta_p^2 = .37$. While the Moderate path had significantly better steering quality than other paths (see Figure 8(a)), High speed had significantly worst quality than both of the other speed levels (see Figure 8(b)).

Discussion

We needed to consider all of the quality measures: Accuracy, Time, and Error at the same time, because it is not enough to draw any conclusions without looking at all those aspects together. Accuracy gives an indication of the percentage of the time users spend steering inside the tunnel with respect to the the total time. However, we need to know how many times users exited the tunnel, and what is the area of the path they covered outside the tunnel until they steered back inside the tunnel. Therefore, we calculated the steering quality as a product of the deviation, time, and error. From the results presented in the previous section, we can draw the following conclusions: The *rotate by roll with fixed horizon*, seems to have the best performance in general, it is also the most consistent technique. This is due to the fact that the performance of this technique shows consistent results through both repetitions, in other words even though the learning effect is the smallest among all the techniques, the first repetition is already better than the second repetitions of all the other techniques. Moreover, rotate by roll with fixed horizon, has more stable results even in different speeds and path complexities. Interestingly, despite the fact that rotate by roll technique and rotate by roll with fixed horizon have the same DOF, the only difference is the fact that in rotate by roll with fixed horizon the roll is mapped to both the heading and the roll in the VE, the later performed better than the earlier. In other words, the roll dimension in the VE provides a nice animation to simulate flying, but does not improve steering quality. This is due to the fact that participants in rotate by roll with fixed horizon had a fixed frame (i.e. the horizon) during their traveling task and it was easier for them to constantly relate their current orientation with that fixed frame. Hence this worked as a visual cue and helped them to maintain orientation. Also, some test users mentioned that they felt some kind of dizziness due

156

the fact that roll was changing in the VE. Another interesting observation is the fact that all techniques performed worst in all quality measures (time, error, steering quality) in the simple path. A simple path had the characteristics of containing straight paths and only two wide turns. It is worth mentioning that we identify the path to be *simple*, since it has mostly straight paths elements. However, it appeared to be difficult to steer in a straight path, meaning it was challenging for the participants to hold the hand still, and not to change the rotation of the mobile phone, even if we introduced thresholds and separated the translation and rotation on different sensors. When the speed is fast, the Accuracy of the four techniques is almost the same and around 50 percent, in other words, the users were almost half of the time outside the tunnel. This is expected, because when the speed is too high, the performance of steering experiences a negative impact.

On a more subjective level, we observed the following. Even though, we expected the use of the mobile phone heading to steer left and right in the VE to be more natural and intuitive than the use of roll, because this is actually how humans turn left and right in the real world. However, the opposite showed to be true. When using the rotate by heading technique and rotating the mobile phone over the Z axis, the users complained about wrist fatigue. We think that the reason behind that could be the fact that rotating the hand over the wrist joint is not a too common hand movement. Other participants used the rotate by heading technique and used their elbow to change the heading, they expected a larger change in the heading value compared to using their wrist. This is not the case as the delta change in the heading value is the same (the sensor coordinate system of the mobile phone). On the other hand, while using the roll to control the heading, participants felt that the rotation over the Y axis is easier, e.g., a *screw driver* movement, and they could take better control of the roll change. In addition to that, in the merged rotation technique, participants disliked the fact that they could not separate the heading control from the roll control in the VE. As a result, participants were not able to turn left using only heading. With this technique, a heading change was inseparable from a roll change with the mobile phone and vice versa.

Analyzing the sensors readings for the merged rotation, users actually used mostly the roll to control the heading. When the heading value was below a certain threshold, only the mobile roll was used to control the heading in the VE. We could also notice that during the user study and the observation of the users' hand gestures.

CONCLUSION AND FUTURE WORK
Incorporating mobile phones as self-contained input devices for travel control tasks in VEs is a challenging task. Especially the built in sensors are not yet perfectly suitable for sensing in all DOF.

To investigate the usability of phones, we developed a concept for a one-handed travel technique. We use the touch capability of the mobile phone for translation, and the built-in sensors in the mobile phone for VE viewpoint rotation control. To gain experience about the self-referring combination of the number of DOF that can be handled by a user and the

variety of mapping functions, we developed four differing interaction techniques for traveling and shaped them in formative studies. The four travel techniques are: rotate by roll, rotate by roll with fixed horizon, rotate by heading, and merged rotation. Each technique has either 5 or 4 DOF and different mappings of the phone coordinates to the VE viewpoint coordinates.

We performed an empirical user study to investigate the number of DOF that are necessary to travel in a VE as easy as possible and to study the different coordinates mappings. The results of the user study show that the rotate by roll with fixed horizon with 4 DOF have decent performance and showed a strong acceptance and favoritism among the users. Also the usage of the roll in the mobile phone to control the heading in the VE, seems to be the desired mapping. Finally, we find that an extra not needed dimension in the VE could also make a significant difference in terms of performance, in our case the VE roll.

In the future, we are planning to compare both the rotate by roll techniques with classical existing systems, like joysticks. Also, we will enhance the technique by adding some more visual cues showing for example what gestures users actually execute on the mobile phone. Visual guidance when the users leave the tunnel will also be investigated. Some participants also mentioned the fact that haptic feedback on the mobile phone when they hit the tunnel borders would be beneficial. Finally, we are planning to perform also a subjective evaluation and to also estimate to fatigue factor.

ACKNOWLEDGMENTS
Authors would like to thank the participants for their voluntary participation in the user studies.
This publication is based on work supported by Award No. UK-c0020, made by King Abdullah University of Science and Technology (KAUST).

REFERENCES
1. Alexander Kulik, Bernd Frohlich and Roland Blach. two - 4 - six - A Handheld Device for 3D-Presentations. In *VR '06 Proceedings of the IEEE conference on Virtual Reality* (2006), 139.

2. Benzina, A., Tönnis, M., Klinker, G., and Ashry, M. Phone-based motion control in vr: analysis of degrees of freedom. In *Proceedings of the 2011 annual conference extended abstracts on Human factors in computing systems*, CHI EA '11, ACM (New York, NY, USA, 2011), 1519–1524.

3. Casiez, G., Vogel, D., Qing, P., and Chaillou, C. RubberEdge: reducing clutching by combining position and rate control with elastic feedback. In *UIST '07: Proceedings of the 20th annual ACM symposium on User interface software and technology* (2007), 129–138.

4. Dick, C., Schneider, J., and Westermann, R. Efficient Geometry Compression for GPU-based Decoding in Realtime Terrain Rendering. *Computer Graphics Forum* 28, 1 (2009), 67–83.

5. Harrison, B. L., Fishkin, K., A. Squeeze me, hold me, tilt me! An exploration of manipulative user interfaces. In *CHI'98* (1998), 17–24.

6. HTC. HTC Desire, http://www.htc.com/www/product/desire/specificati on.html. Accessed Nov 2010.

7. J. Wang, S. Zhai and J. Canny. Camera Phone Based Motion Sensing: Interaction Techniques, Applications and Performance Study. In *UIST'06* (2006), 101–110.

8. Ji-Sun Kim, Denis Gracanin, Kresimir Matkovic, and Francis Quek. iphone/ipod touch as input devices for navigation in immersive virtual environments. In *IEEE Virtual Reality 2009* (2009), 261–262.

9. Ken Hinckley, Jeff Pierce, Mike Sinclair and Eric Horvitz. Sensing techniques for mobile interaction. In *Proceedings of the 13th annual ACM symposium on User interface software and technology* (2000), 91–100.

10. K.Hinckley, J. Pierce, E.Horvitz and M. Sinclair. Foreground and background interaction with sensor-enhanced mobile devices. In *ACM Transactions on Computer-Human Interaction*, vol. 12 (2005), 31–52.

11. K.Hinckley, R.Pausch, J.C.Goble, and N.F.Kassell. A survey of design issues in spatial input. In *Proceedings of the 7th annual ACM symposium on User interface software and technology* (1994), 213–222.

12. Michael Rohs and Georg Essl. Sensing-based interaction for information navigation on handheld displays. In *Proceedings of the 9th international conference on Human computer interaction with mobile devices and services* (2007), 387–394.

13. P. Gilbertson, P. Coulton, F. Chehimi and T. Vajk. Using Tilt as an Interface to Control No-Button 3-D Mobile Games. In *Computers in Entertainment (CIE) - SPECIAL ISSUE: Media Arts*, vol. 6 (2008).

14. Rekimoto, J. Tilting Operations for Small Screen Interfaces. In *UIST'96* (1996), 167–168.

15. S. Zhai. Human Performance in Six Degree of Freedom Input Control. In *PhD-Thesis, University of Toronto* (1995).

16. Schwerdtfeger, B. *Pick-by-Vision: Bringing HMD-based Augmented Reality into the Warehouse*. PhD thesis, Technische Universität München, 2010.

17. Sebastian Boring, Marko Jurmu and Andreas Butz. Scroll, tilt or move it: using mobile phones to continuously control pointers on large public displays. In *Proceedings of the 21st Annual Conference of the Australian Computer-Human Interaction Special Interest Group: Design: Open 24/7* (2009), 161–168.

18. Seokhee Jeon, Jane Hwang, Gerard J. Kim and Mark Billinghurst. Interaction Techniques in Large Display Environments using Hand-held Devices. In *VRST '06 Virtual Reality Software and Technology* (2006), 100–103.

19. Tomasz P Bednarz, Con Caris, Jeremy Thompson, Chris Wesner, Mark Dunn. Human-Computer Interaction Experiments - Immersive Virtual Reality Applications for the Mining Industry. In *AINA'10 Proceedings of the 2010 24th IEEE International Conference on Advanced Information Networking and Applications* (2010), 1323–1327.

Building Interactive Prototypes of Mobile User Interfaces with a Digital Pen

Clemens Holzmann
University of Applied Sciences Upper Austria
Softwarepark 11, 4232 Hagenberg, Austria
clemens.holzmann@fh-hagenberg.at

Manuela Vogler
University of Applied Sciences Upper Austria
Softwarepark 11, 4232 Hagenberg, Austria
manuela.vogler@students.fh-hagenberg.at

ABSTRACT

Paper prototyping is commonly used to identify usability problems in the early stages of user interface design, but it is not very well suited for the evaluation of mobile interfaces. The reason is that mobile applications are used in a rich real-world context, which is hard to emulate with a paper prototype. A more powerful technique is to test the design on a mobile device, but building a functional design prototype requires much more effort. In this paper, we try to get the best of both worlds by building interactive prototypes with a digital pen. We developed a system which allows for sketching a user interface on paper and manually associating the interface elements with functionality. This enables designers to bring their design ideas to paper without any restrictions, define the meaning of selected interface elements, and test them on a mobile device instantaneously. We conducted a user study in which the participants had to design and test a small application with our system. The results provide evidence for the feasibility and positive aspects of our approach, but also showed some limitations and missing functionalities of its current implementation.

Author Keywords

Mobile interfaces; paper prototyping; pen-based computing

ACM Classification Keywords

H.5.2. Information Interfaces and Presentation: User Interfaces—*Prototyping*

INTRODUCTION

Paper prototyping is a technique for designing, testing and refining user interfaces, which is commonly used in the early stages of user interface design [12, 18]. A prototype consisting of hand-drawn sketches is presented to the user, who is asked to perform certain tasks with the prototype.

According to Snyder [18], the most important benefits of paper prototyping are that it enables collecting user feedback before the actual implementation is started, that it facilitates rapid iterative development, and that it does not require any technical skills. Paper prototyping can be easily integrated

into the design process, because most designers prefer sketching in early design stages [10, 12, 14]. The main reasons for the widespread creation of sketches are that they are quick to produce, that the use of paper and pencil is natural, and that the sketches avoid focusing on unimportant details [10].

In the domain of desktop system design, paper prototyping provides solid user feedback and allows to uncover many possible problems. When comparing the results of a usability evaluation with a paper prototype and a high-fidelity prototype, Virzi et al. [19] found little difference regarding the number of problems discovered with these prototypes.

However, paper prototypes are not that adequate for the evaluation of a mobile application design. Many usability problems of mobile applications can be best discovered when evaluating a prototype in realistic settings, making it necessary to take the prototype out of the lab [7]. This can be difficult with a paper prototype due to its fragility, for example a prototype can be destroyed when put into the user's pocket [6]. Additionally, paper prototypes are often not realistic regarding the size of controls and the amount of information presented on a sketched screen, which can confuse and mislead users during the evaluation [7].

The best way to enable a realistic testing experience is to create a high-fidelity prototype that looks like a final product and that can be tested on the actual mobile device. Lumdsen and MacLean observed that using interactive prototypes on mobile devices enables users to identify more usability problems [16]. Additionally, users are more satisfied when using mobile devices, because of the fact that they get real feedback [9].

Summing up, paper prototypes have the advantages of low development costs and short production time [5], but they are not well suited for the evaluation of mobile applications because of the unrealistic testing experience they provide [7]. In contrast, high-fidelity prototypes improve the testing experience and the quality of the evaluation results [8, 16], but increase the costs and the time needed for creating them [5].

In this paper, we introduce a system which combines the advantages of both low- and high-fidelity prototyping for the evaluation of mobile application designs, with the goal to improve the evaluation results without creating additional costs or effort. First, we present the system's initial version that generated high-fidelity prototypes from hand-drawn sketches, and present our lessons learnt from this approach. We then discuss how the adaption of the system's concept towards the building of interactive low-fidelity prototypes helped us to solve these problems, and describe the pen-based generation of these prototypes in detail. We proceed with discussing the results of a user study performed at our university to test the general concept and the system's current implementation. Finally, we survey and compare related work about sketch-based generation of interactive prototypes, and describe future research goals.

TOWARDS THE AUTOMATED GENERATION OF MOBILE APPLICATION PROTOTYPES

As explained in the previous section, there is a dilemma in the early stages of mobile application design. On the one hand, paper prototypes, which are fast and simple to create, do not provide a sufficiently realistic testing experience. However, this is an important factor for identifying many usability problems. On the other hand, high-fidelity prototypes are much more complex to create, and thus and slow down the design process.

Our first attempt to solve this dilemma, namely to enable both short iteration cycles and more realistic testing at the same time, was to combine the advantages of low- and high-fidelity prototyping by developing a system that automatically generates high-fidelity prototypes based on paper sketches of the user interface. The goal was to end up with a tool which allows fast and natural designing like in traditional paper prototyping, but also offers the possibility to use high-fidelity prototypes for testing without additional effort. We expected that the use of this system would increase the quality and usability of the resulting mobile applications, and that it would help to reduce the time-to-market and development costs.

In order to enable the automated generation of high-fidelity prototypes, the hand-drawn sketches have to be captured digitally before they can be processed by the system. For this purpose, we decided to use the Anoto digital pen and paper technology [2]. The pen, which is equipped with an embedded infrared camera, takes snapshots of a special pattern printed on the paper, and uses this information to calculate its current position. By recording the position information, it is possible to reconstruct the sketches.

To evaluate our idea, we implemented a first version of the system enabling the automated generation of high-fidelity prototypes based on sketches drawn with an Anoto pen. Figure 1 shows the sketches which define the content of a single screen as well as its resulting representation in the high-fidelity prototype. As can be seen, a special template showing the front side of a mobile phone was printed on the Anoto paper. The template had the same size as the mobile device, with the goal to make both sketching and data processing easier.

During the sketching of a prototype, the system tried to recognize the sketches as soon as they were drawn. For this purpose, an application running on a mobile phone was responsible for receiving the data captured by the Anoto pen via a Bluetooth connection and for forwarding the data to a server that executed the sketch recognition. As the only supported widgets in the first prototype were buttons, every stroke forming a rectangle was recognized as a button. Handwriting within a button was transformed into text and was

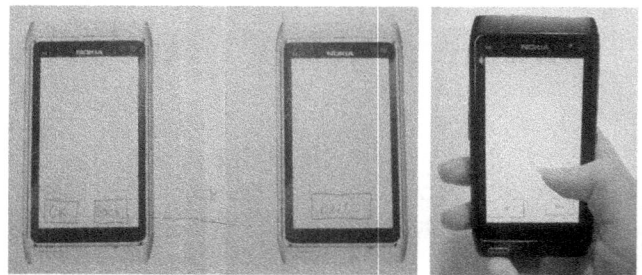

Figure 1. Two templates containing sketched user interface elements with a defined screen change triggered by the "Back" button (left) and the high-fidelity representation of the sketched screen on the left hand side (right).

stored as the button's caption. A line connecting a button and another screen template was interpreted as a definition of screen changing behavior, meaning that a click on the button should lead to the displaying of the other screen.

As soon as the sketching was finished, the designer could trigger the generation of the according high-fidelity prototype. The system then used the stored sketch data to generate a set of HTML pages, where each page contained the content drawn into one of the sketching templates. During the generation, the sketched button elements were converted into HTML buttons considering the positions and dimensions defined by the sketches. Additionally, the HTML pages were linked to implement the screen changing behavior. The generated prototype could then be tested using the mobile phone's browser.

During the implementation and testing of the system, which was still in a quite premature stage, we came across several problems and shortcomings of our approach:

- There was no feedback for the designer during the sketching process, so that the designer had to rely upon the correct recognition of all sketches.

- The system was highly dependent on the correct recognition of sketch types and handwritten texts, because there was no mechanism for correcting wrong recognition results.

- The system supported the definition of buttons, but we were not sure how to sketch and process more complex and dynamic user interface elements like scrollbars or combo boxes.

These problems encouraged us to revise the system's basic concept in order to develop a tool that is easy and comfortable to use for designers, works reliably and supports the definition of a wide range of commonly used user interface elements. The following section describes our new prototyping approach, which has been developed based on the lessons learnt from the first attempt.

PEN-BASED GENERATION OF INTERACTIVE LOW-FIDELITY PROTOTYPES

Most of the problems listed in the previous section are related to the need for shape and handwriting recognition, which was essential for transforming the sketches into interactive user interfaces. Therefore, we assumed that a change in concept reducing the need for sketch recognition would help to solve most of these problems.

Adapted Concept

There are several other projects generating digital prototypes from sketches which do not require sketch recognition (e.g. Paper-in-Screen [3] and ActiveStory [20]). The resulting prototypes look like the original sketches, but allow at least simple interaction during the prototype evaluation. The sketchy look of these prototypes makes them well-suited for the early design stages, because low-fidelity prototypes force users to concentrate on general concepts like layout, terminology and navigation [17]. In contrast, test participants often focus on details like fonts or colors when evaluating a high-fidelity prototype, but this kind of feedback is not that relevant in early design stages. Because the generated prototypes are interactive and can be tested on the targeted devices, they enable a more realistic usage experience than simple paper prototypes, which is important for the evaluation of a mobile application design [7].

The concept of interactive low-fidelity prototypes seems to be applicable to the system described in this paper, which is mainly targeted at the early phases of mobile application design. Besides combining the gathering of more valuable feedback due to the sketchy look of the prototypes and the enabling of interactive prototype testing on the target devices, this new approach also reduces the need for shape and handwriting recognition, which was one of our most important goals.

In the system's previous version, all the sketch data had to be sent to a server for recognition, as the mobile platform did not provide appropriate recognition libraries. The reduced need for sketch recognition makes it possible to process the sketches directly on the mobile device as soon as they are drawn. As a result, the displaying of immediate feedback for the designer during the sketching becomes possible without having to cope with potentially slow data transmission and latency.

Another major conceptual change affected the technology used for building the interactive prototypes. In the system's first version, the prototypes consisted of a set of HTML pages that could be accessed using the mobile phone's browser. However, this approach did not provide the most realistic testing experience, because the look and feel of websites is not the same as that of a real application. Additionally, the browser's behavior (e.g. appearing browser controls like the URL input field or the screen rotation behavior) could confuse the user. In order to make the handling of the prototype more realistic, for example to allow for its start from the phone's menu, the system was adapted to generate installable and executable applications representing the sketched user interfaces.

Supported Widgets

For the implementation of our adapted concept for generating low-fidelity prototypes, we decided to use the Android platform. The main reasons for this decision were its huge market share on the one hand, and the simple Bluetooth connection with the Anoto pen on the other hand. We analyzed the widgets provided by Android (see [1] for a list of all widgets) in order to define which ones can be supported by our new system. However, please note that our approach is not limited to a certain platform, as other mobile operating systems provide similar sets of user interface elements. In the following list, a classification of widgets is given, which provides the basis for the implementation of interaction in our system:

- **Buttons**: Clickable elements that trigger screen changes (e.g. *Button*, *ImageButton*).

- **Two-states buttons**: Buttons that can either be checked or unchecked and use an icon to visualize their current state (e.g. *CheckBox*, *RadioButton*).

- **Popup elements**: Elements that trigger the displaying of a content popup after being clicked (e.g. *Spinner*, which is the Android equivalent to a combo box).

- **Elements with simple predefined behavior**: Elements with simple type-dependent behavior that do not support the definition of further behavior (e.g. *EditText*, *RadioButtonGroup*, *ScrollView*).

- **Elements with complex predefined behavior**: Elements with more complex appearance and predefined behavior (e.g. *AnalogClock*, *DigitalClock*, *DatePicker*, *TimePicker*).

- **Non-interactive elements**: Elements that just display information, but do no enable interaction (e.g. *TextView*, *ImageView*).

- **Elements without user-controlled behavior**: Widgets with behavior that can only be controlled by the application logic, but not by direct user interaction (e.g. *Toast*, *ProgressBar*).

Defining Prototype Behavior

The low-fidelity prototypes generated by the system introduced in this paper enable basic interaction like screen changes, the use of combo boxes and the selection of options using radio buttons or checkboxes. In order to make a sketched widget interactive, the designer has to manually define its type and the associated behavior. Several interaction concepts, which have been developed for this purpose, are shown in table 1. Elements without user-controlled behavior are not supported in the current version of our system, and remain an open issue for future work.

For widgets that should not be interactive, none of the listed interaction concepts has to be used during the sketching of a prototype. The designer just has to write or draw the non-interactive content into a screen template, and the sketches are later displayed in the generated prototype without allowing for any kind of interaction.

All interactive widgets require at least one additional step after sketching what they look like. For most of them, it is necessary to assign type information using a concept similar to that of ActiveStory [20], namely to tag areas of a prototype screen with type information. The left picture in figure 2

	Type		Behavior			
	Toolbox assignment	Snippet use	Screen linking	Popup sketching	Snippet embedding	Icon definition
Button	X		X			
Two-states button	X					X
Popup elements	X			X	X	
Elements with simple predefined behavior	X					
Elements with complex predefined behavior		X				
Non-interactive widgets						

Table 1. Overview of used interaction concepts

shows the two steps that are necessary for defining a widget type using the toolbox. First, the type has to be selected by touching one of the toolbox elements printed on the paper with the Anoto pen. The user can then define the area to tag with this type information by drawing its bounding box with a single stroke. After the stroke has been finished, the mobile phone, which is responsible for processing the sketches, immediate displays feedback by changing the color of all included parts of the sketch (there are different colors for different widget types). In the resulting prototype, the widget looks exactly like the sketched element.

Figure 2. Defining a widget's type with the Anoto pen (left) results in immediate feedback (middle). In the generated prototype, the widget keeps its original look (right).

Similar approaches for adding metadata to content written or drawn with an Anoto pen have been used in several other projects. NiCEBook [4] for example, a paper notebook enabling the digital capturing and organization of notes written with an Anoto pen, allows to assign a category to a note by first ticking the according checkbox and then defining the note's area by selecting two corners of the region. Papier-Craft [13] uses special gestures to tag content with keywords and select areas that should be sent via e-mail.

For most of the widget types, the designer can define specific behavior after having assigned the type information. For example, it is possible to define a screen change triggered by a button click using the screen linking concept shown in figure 3. After touching the triggering button area with the Anoto pen, the user has to touch the template containing the target screen. Again, the mobile client application provides immediate feedback: the left screen contains the triggering button, and the right one is the resulting screen. If the designer wants to edit the screen change definition, this can be done by first touching the triggering button element again and by touching another screen template afterwards. Additionally, it is also possible to delete a screen change by repeating the original definition steps.

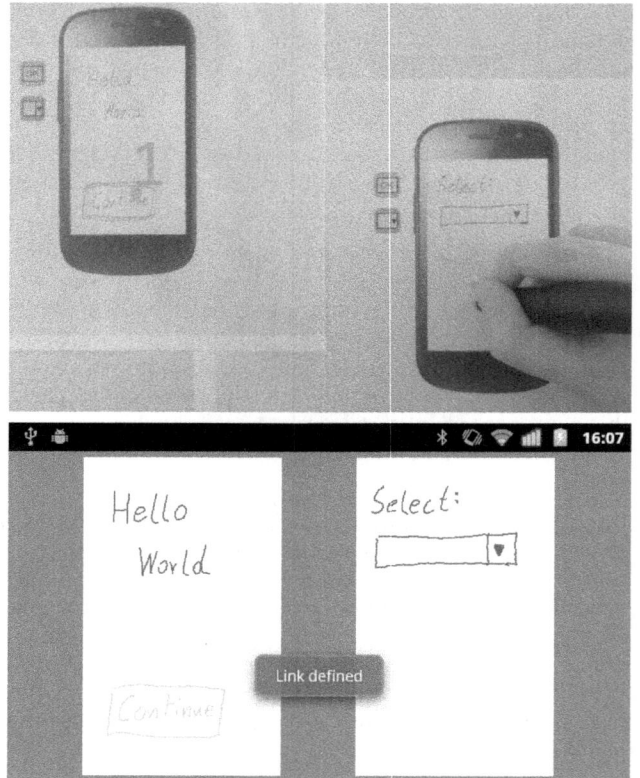

Figure 3. The definition of a screen change triggered by a button click (top) is also visualized by the mobile client application (bottom).

Popup elements like combo boxes require sketching the content of the popup on a special template that is also printed on Anoto paper. The size of this snippet can be adapted by cutting off unneeded space or by folding it, which enables to make the popup just as big as necessary. To link the spinner element with its content popup, the designer first has to touch the element with the Anoto pen, followed by the steps of the snippet embedding concept described below. In the generated prototype, a popup overlay shows the content after the spinner element is clicked.

To embed a snippet (i.e. a separate piece of paper) into a screen template, the snippet has to be put onto the screen template first. As shown in figure 4, the designer has to draw two lines afterwards, which connect the corners of the snippet with the screen template. These two lines enable the determination of both the snippet's position and its size. Again, it is possible to remove an embedded snippet by repeating these steps. This interaction concept is similar to that used in NiCEBook [4] for the tagging of an entire page of the notebook with a specific topic through a dog-ear, which has to be registered by stroking over the folded corner.

Figure 4. After embedding the popup snippet into the screen by drawing two lines (left), it is also visible in the mobile client application (middle). In the generated prototype, the popup is only displayed after clicking the spinner element (right).

The snippet embedding concept is not only used for popup elements, but also for the integration of widgets with complex type-dependent behavior and appearance like clocks or date and time pickers. In this case, the snippet consists of a sketchy-looking print of the according widget on Anoto paper, which allows the designer to integrate complex interactive widgets without having to sketch them. The type of the widget is implicitly given by choosing the right snippet and does not have to be assigned using the toolbar. In figure 5, a date-picker snippet and its representation in the generated prototype is shown.

Figure 5. A date picker snippet (left) and its representation in the generated prototype (right).

The last concept for defining behavior, the icon definition, is only used for two-states buttons (radio buttons and checkboxes) which consist of an icon indicating their current state. In the generated prototypes, the icons are supposed to change in order to visualize the current state (e.g. an x marks a checked checkbox). This makes it necessary for the system to know which part of the sketched element represents the icon.

For this purpose, the stroke that was first drawn within the widget area is assumed to be the icon after defining a two-states button using the toolbox, because most people might start to sketch a two-states button by drawing its icon. The stroke recognized as the icon is highlighted by the mobile client application using a thicker stroke. If the designer is not satisfied with this selection, it is possible to change it by first touching the two-states button area and by then drawing the icon with a single stroke afterwards.

EVALUATION AND DISCUSSION

Although the prototyping system introduced in this paper is still in an early implementation stage, we performed a first user study using a version of the system that only supported a limited set of the previously listed interactive widgets and interaction concepts. The study focused on the general feasibility as well as the usability of our adapted concept. However, the intention was not to provide information about the usefulness of the system compared to traditional paper prototyping, which will be investigated in a later development stage. The objectives of the study were

1. to check if the participants like the system's general concept and feel comfortable when using the system,

2. to observe how the participants use the system for designing simple prototypes (e.g. design flow, use of interactive widgets, . . .),

3. to verify that the used interaction concepts are intuitive and easy to learn,

4. to identify problems arising when using the system for a real design task, and

5. to find out which user interface elements besides the already implemented ones are considered to be important when designing a prototype.

Procedure

As it was more important at this stage to eliminate simple usability issues before we evaluated a fuller system version with professional designers, we recruited 12 volunteers, 9 males and 3 females, at the university campus. All of them were computer science students (10 undergraduate and 2 graduate students), and they were between the age of 20 and 26 years (M=22.5, SD=2.0). While all of them had developed mobile applications before, only 6 of them had experience in user interface design and 4 participants in prototyping (one of them in paper prototyping). Only 4 of the participants used the Anoto technology before.

For each of the participants, the evaluation session took approximately 30 minutes. After welcoming the participants, they were informed about the purpose of the study as well as the basic idea of our prototyping system. They were then given a brief demonstration of how to use the system. This demonstration included the handling of the mobile client application and the Anoto pen, the sketching of user interfaces, the definition of widgets types and associated behavior, as well as the editing of previously defined information. In every evaluation session, the prototype which was created for demonstration purpose was basically the same, and it contained the two interactive widget types supported by the system's version used for the evaluation: buttons and spinner elements. At the end of the demonstration, the generated prototype was shown to the participants to complete the overview of the system's features.

After the demonstration, each participant received a sheet of paper listing several requirements of a mobile task management application that should be designed using our system. The requirements only specified a very simple application and were kept rough in order to allow for a creative design process. Basically, there were only two features the prototype had to contain: (i) the displaying of an overview of all tasks and (ii) the possibility to add a new task. It was also defined that it should be possible to specify at least a description, priority, due date and category for every task entry. Additionally, participants were told that the prototype should consist of 2 to 4 screens.

Afterwards, the participants started to design the user interface of the specified task management application. They were told to talk about their thoughts during the sketching as well as to ask questions. One researcher took notes about how the participants performed the tasks, the questions they asked and the problems that occurred.

After finishing the task, users were asked to give feedback about the system and to name ideas for its extension and improvement, with a focus on other interactive user interface elements which should be supported in the future. Finally, they were asked to complete the Post-Study System Usability Questionnaire (PSSUQ) [11].

Results and Timing

All but one participants were able to create a prototype meeting the specified requirements. This participant created just an overview screen containing a single task entry which leads to a detail page when clicked, but he did not design a possibility to add new tasks.

Figure 6 shows how much time it took the participants to complete the designs. It was between 143 seconds for the fastest and 1016 seconds for the slowest participant, with a median value of 650 seconds. The fastest participant was also the one who did not meet the requirements.

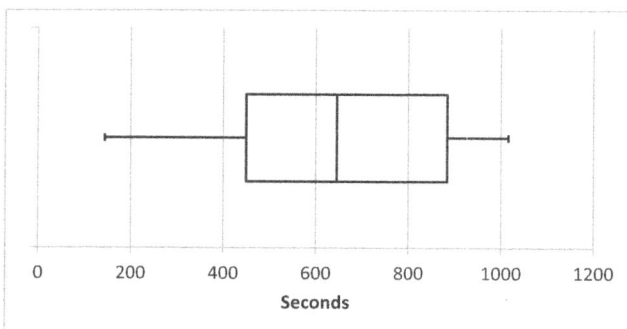

Figure 6. The distribution of time needed for creating the prototype.

7 participants used 2 screens for their prototype, the required time was between 143 and 927 seconds with a median value of 450 seconds, while 5 participants used 3 screens and needed a time between 519 and 1016 seconds and with a median value of 679 seconds. None of the participants used four screens.

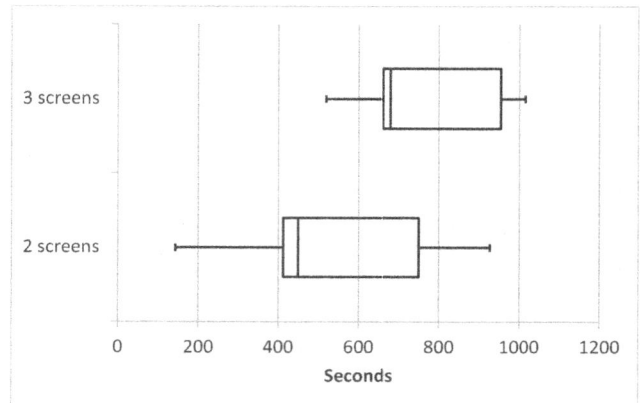

Figure 7. The time needed for creating the prototype depending on the number of used screens.

User Feedback

After finishing the creation of their prototype, the participants were asked to give feedback in an interview, focusing on ideas for improving and extending the system. Generally, the participants recommended that the system should support all the common user interface elements that are also supported by typical UI builders. Other ideas were to enable the selection of different colors for the presentation of the sketches in the generated prototypes and to allow the definition of properties for some widget types (e.g. the font size for a text field). One participant suggested to support different screen types like screens containing a list or a gallery, and to let the designer define the type of the screen by using according sketching templates.

As mentioned previously, it was one of the objectives of the user study to find out which other interactive user interface elements are considered to be important by the test participants and therefore should be supported by our system. The following widget types were named:

- Text fields (for text input)
- Checkboxes, radio buttons
- Images
- Date picker, calendar
- Lists with click-able elements
- Tab views
- Scroll areas

After the interview, the participants were asked to complete the Post-Study System Usability Questionnaire (PSSUQ) [11]. For the questionnaire, a 7 point Likert scale from strongly disagree (1) to strongly agree (7) was used. Figure 8 shows a summary of the given answers.

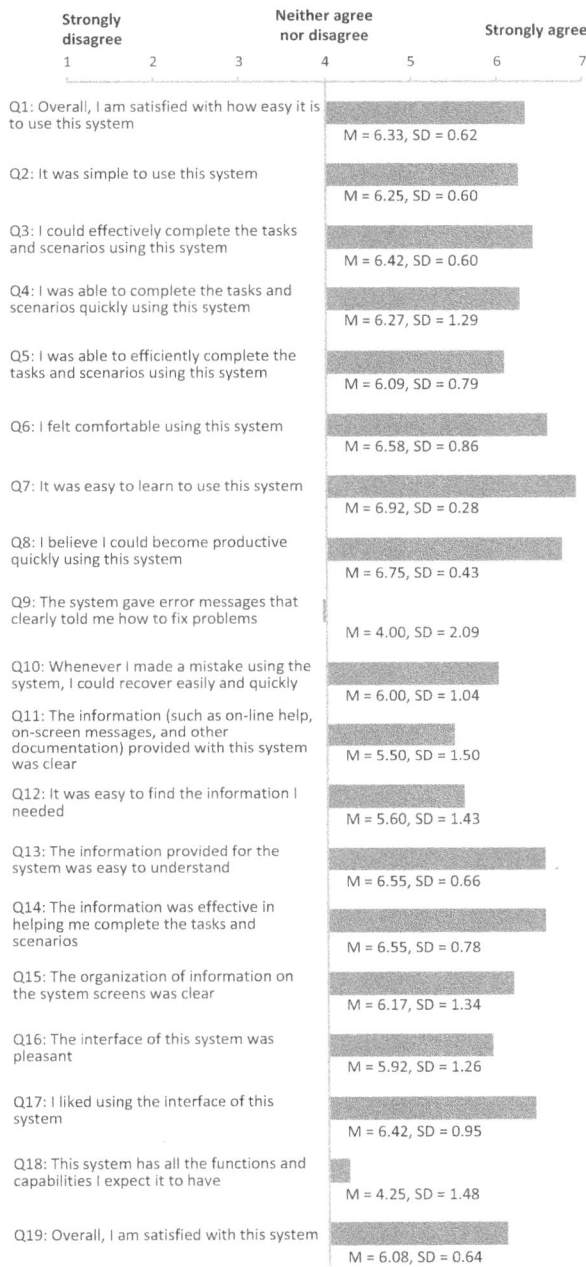

Figure 8. Average user answers to the questions of the PSSUQ questionnaire.

The questionnaire helped us to get the information and feedback we wanted to gather from the study. First of all, it showed that the participants liked to use the system and felt comfortable while using it. In general, the participants were satisfied with the system and also with how easy it was to use. Therefore, they felt able to effectively and quickly complete their task using the prototyping system. Most participants agreed to Q6 ("I felt comfortable using this system"), just one neither agreed nor disagreed. 10 participants found the interface of the system pleasant (Q16), and 11 participants – except one, who neither agreed nor disagreed – liked using it (Q17).

The questionnaire also verified that the use of the system is easy to learn and that the supported interaction concepts are intuitive. All participants agreed that it was easy to learn to use the system (Q7) and that it was simple to use (Q2). The participants also strongly agreed that they believe to be able to become productive quickly using our system (Q8).

Some aspects of the system, especially the handling of errors, were not rated that well. On average, the participants neither agreed nor disagreed to Q9 ("The system gave error messages that clearly told me how to fix problems") and some of them also stated not to feel able to recover easily and quickly after a mistake (Q10). We also noticed that during the sketching of the prototypes, as we often had to intervene and tell the participants how to proceed in cases of problems and mistakes. Of course, it is essential to improve the error handling capabilities in following system versions.

Another aspect which has been criticized by the participants was the range of provided functions and capabilities. The answers to Q18 ("This system has all the functions and capabilities I expect it to have") emphasize the need for supporting more interactive user interface elements than those listed before on the one hand, and for extending the system's feature set on the other hand. Only 5 users agreed to this question, while 3 neither agreed nor disagreed and 4 disagreed.

Problems Encountered

One of the objectives of our study was to identify problems occurring when performing a realistic task with the prototype system. Some of the observed problems were related to the inaccurate printing of the sketching templates. Unfortunately, we did not notice that the printer used for printing the Anoto pattern worked not accurately enough due to its paper feed, so that the Anoto pattern was positioned lopsidedly on several pages. When printing the sketching templates on these pages, this resulted in differences between the template's position on the Anoto pattern and the position defined in the system. As the positioning offset was not the same for all templates, it was not possible to correct it by simply redefining the position in the system. In the future, it will be necessary to pay more attention to the exact printing of the templates to avoid the offset and the subsequently listed resulting problems:

- There was a distracting offset between the representation of the sketches on the paper and in the feedback displayed by the mobile client application, which confused some of the test participants.

- Participants were not able to define the content popups for spinner elements, because the system was not able to correctly handle the snippet embedding interaction concept. Because of the positioning offset, the system could not recognize when the Anoto pen was moved into the screen template during the drawing of the two lines connecting the snippet and the underlying screen, and therefore cancelled the processing of the captured data.

Other problems that occurred during the sketching were caused by the system's sketch processing capabilities:

- The tested version of the system regularly crashed when users sketched fast. Although we asked the study participants to sketch slowly, 5 of them were not able to reduce their sketching speed and therefore caused system crashes. As users should not have to change their drawing style and speed in order to use our system, we definitely have to improve the implementation of our system to make it also robust during faster sketching.

- Due to the strictly defined position and size of the sketching template, there were problems when participants sketched close to the borders of the template. Althought the tip of the Anoto pen was still inside the defined drawing area, the camera already captured positions outside the area due to a little offset between tip and camera. To solve this, the system's flexibility regarding sketches outside the drawing area has to be increased by e.g. making the defined area a little bit bigger than it is.

Some of the test participants were interrupted while sketching their prototype because of technical problems, for example:

- Crashes of the wireless network that made it impossible to transmit the captured sketches to the server

- Crashes of the Bluetooth connection between Anoto pen and mobile client application

- Communication problems between Anoto pen and mobile client application which made it impossible for the system to capture the sketches

For the further implementation of the system, it will be important to improve the monitoring of the connections to the server and the pen, so that users can be better informed about occurring communication problems and can be told how to proceed.

Discussion

The early user study described in this section gave us a lot of information and feedback that will be of value for the further improvement of our system. During the sketching sessions, we could observe that users really enjoyed using the tool and that they were impressed when testing the generated interactive prototypes. This observation is also confirmed by the results of the post-study questionnaire, where the participants stated that they were satisfied with the system and liked using its interface.

The participants quickly learned how to use the tool and were able to create sophisticated interactive prototypes despite the limited range of supported widget types. Some of the participants got really creative regarding the usage of the supported user interface elements for the building of more complex elements, for example they created task lists containing clickable elements by defining the list entries as buttons. By assigning screen change information to these elements, they were able to implement a detail-screen for selected tasks. One of the participants also tried to create a date picker control using a spinner element and a linked popup.

When observing how the participants used the prototyping tool for their design task, we identified several problems regarding the currently used interaction concepts:

- The drawing of a bounding box for defining the area of an interactive widget might not be optimal, because it requires the adding of a stroke that does not belong to the actual design. This makes the resulting screen sketches messy, especially in cases where the type definition fails and has to be repeated. Therefore, it might be necessary to find another concept for defining the area to tag with type information, for example by just drawing the top left and the bottom right corner of the bounding box as proposed in [4] for assigning categories to notes. One of the participants also suggested using the plastic pen tip instead of the ink cartridge for defining widget types.

- The interaction concept for embedding a snippet into a screen used for defining the popup of a spinner element appeared to be not as intuitive as the screen linking concept. We observed that several participants tried to apply the screen linking approach to the popup definition, so that they simply clicked the popup and the containing screen instead of drawing the necessary connection lines. One participant had the idea to make the embedding of snippets easier by letting the user set the position and size of the popup within the screen template by defining its bounding box (e.g. by drawing two corners of the bounding box), and then to link the area and the popup by clicking the popup and the defined area, which is similar to the concept for defining screen changes.

The study revealed two main aspects of the system that have to be improved to make the users more satisfied: (i) the set of supported widget types and (ii) the error handling. Although some participants were able to use the supported widgets for the building of more complex elements, they still stated that other common user interface elements like checkboxes and text fields are also important for their designs. The second point, the currently inappropriate error handling, seemed to affect the user satisfaction more negatively than the limited set of features.

RELATED WORK

Various research projects deal with the usage of sketches as a basis for the generation of interactive prototypes. Table 2 provides an overview of the projects that are subsequently explained in more detail.

Some of these tools create sketchy-looking interactive prototypes like our system. A simple way for achieving this is to digitize paper prototypes, e.g. by taking photos. Paper-in-Screen [3] uses this concept to display application prototypes on mobile devices, but has the disadvantage that the user is just able to flip through the images. The *pseudo*-paper prototypes proposed by Lumsden and MacLean [16] use a similar approach, but support the definition of clickable areas enabling basic interaction like button clicks.

	Fidelity	Interactivity
Paper-in-Screen [3]	Low	Flip through images
Pseudo-paper [16]	Low	Clickable areas
ActiveStory [20]	Low	Clickable areas
De Sá et al. [9]	Low, mid and high	Fully interactive
SILK [10]	High	Fully interactive
DENIM [15]	Low	Fully interactive

Table 2. Overview of sketch-based prototyping tools

ActiveStory's [20] concept is similar to that of our system. It does not only support input in form of images, but also allows for the pen-based generation of interactive low-fidelity prototypes as well as the definition of clickable areas. In contrast to our system, these clickable areas cannot be tagged with type information, but can only be used to trigger screen changes. ActiveStory also differs from our system because it collects data during the evaluation of a prototype, for example mouse trails, page durations and comments entered by the participants.

De Sá et al. [9] developed a software framework allowing the creation of low-, mid- and high-fidelity prototypes that can be evaluated on mobile devices. Scanned images can be used for the low-fidelity prototypes and high-fidelity prototypes can be built by selecting pre-configured user interface elements, but the system does not allow for pen-based input. Another difference to the concept of our system is that the framework encourages test users to actively participate in the design process, because they can edit the prototype during the evaluation. For example, it is possible to change the location and size of elements, to delete screens and components, and to rearrange the screen sequence.

In contrast to our system, SILK [10] uses shape recognition to convert a sketched prototype into a functional interface that can be reused in later stages of the design cycle. To avoid the problems caused by sketch recognition our system had to cope with, SILK uses a trainable recognizer, provides feedback about the recognition results and allows the correcting of recognition errors.

DENIM, a tool for the sketch-based design of web sites using digitizing tablets, enables to test designs in their original sketchy look [15]. The implemented visual language allows the definition and usage of components for reusable user interface elements. In contrast to our system's widget type concept, DENIM distinguishes between intrinsic components built into the visual language like text fields and buttons and custom components that can be freely designed. The prototype behavior that can be defined with the visual language goes beyond that of our system, because it supports different events for triggering screen transitions (e.g. left mouse clicks, double clicks and timeouts) and the definition of conditional behavior.

CONCLUSIONS AND FUTURE WORK

Realistic prototypes, which can be tested on the targeted device, are considered to improve the quality of prototyping re-

sults in the domain of mobile application development and should thus be preferred over simple paper prototypes. The problem about using interactive prototypes is that the effort to create them is much higher than the effort for creating low-fidelity prototypes, which can quickly be sketched on paper. This makes interactive prototyping inadequate for the early phases of the design process, where short iteration cycles are crucial.

This paper presents our research aiming for combining the advantages of paper prototypes and interactive prototypes by using an Anoto pen for sketching a user interface and by automatically generating interactive prototypes based on these sketches. It describes the first version of the system responsible for the processing of the sketched prototypes, which generated HTML-based high-fidelity prototypes. Due to several problems and limitations mainly caused by the need for reliable shape and handwriting recognition, it was necessary to change the system's concept towards the generation of interactive low-fidelity prototypes.

Our adapted concept of generating interactive low-fidelity prototypes instead of high-fidelity ones is supported by the work of other researchers, who found out that sketchy looking prototypes are better suited for the evaluation of a user interface in the early design stages. The reason is that they enable test participants to focus on the general concepts like content and navigation instead of details like colors. Although the prototypes look rough, they can be tested on mobile devices to provide a realistic testing experience.

A first user study showed that novice users are able to quickly learn how to use our prototyping system, and that they like the system's approach. Most participants were able to complete a given design task and successfully created interactive prototypes, even though an early version of the system providing only a limited set of features was used. The study also revealed several system aspects that have to be improved to increase user satisfaction. The most important ones are error handling and the provision of clear error messages as well as the support of more interactive user interface elements.

Besides improving the system according to the feedback collected during the user study, it is also planned to implement support for collaborative design, because user interface design is usually done by a team of designers. This support could include several features like the maintenance of different prototype versions or the possibility to give feedback to a colleague's draft. Multimodal input and output could be useful to facilitate collaborative design, like for example audio recordings which could be used to collect feedback. Another interesting feature would be to generate an overview picture showing the prototype's navigation structure (e.g. which button leads to the displaying of which screen). This could help designers to review the navigation in design meetings and to explain the application's basic concept to customers.

Summing up, there are various possible improvements and extensions for the prototyping system presented in this paper. What has to be kept in mind during the further implementation is that the system has to remain simple to use and should not distract designers from sketching, as it is of utmost importance not to hinder their creativity. For a later development stage, it is planned to perform another user study with designers, in order to evaluate the system's usefulness for professionals and for comparing its efficiency with traditional prototyping approaches.

Acknowledgements

The research presented is conducted within the Austrian project "AIR – Advanced Interface Research" funded by the Austrian Research Promotion Agency (FFG), the ZIT Center for Innovation and Technology and the province of Salzburg under contract number 825345.

REFERENCES

1. android.widget — Android Developers, 2011. http://developer.android.com/reference/android/widget/package-summary.html (Last retrieved October 20, 2011).

2. Anoto Group, 2011. http://www.anoto.com/ (Last retrieved September 29, 2011).

3. Bolchini, D., Pulido, D., and Faiola, A. FEATURE: "Paper in screen" prototyping: an agile technique to anticipate the mobile experience. *interactions 16* (July 2009), 29–33.

4. Brandl, P., Richter, C., and Haller, M. NiCEBook: supporting natural note taking. In *Proceedings of the 28th international conference on Human factors in computing systems*, ACM (2010), 599–608.

5. Coyette, A., and Vanderdonckt, J. A sketching tool for designing anyuser, anyplatform, anywhere user interfaces. *Human-Computer Interaction-INTERACT 2005* (2005), 550–564.

6. de Sá, M., and Carriço, L. Low-fi prototyping for mobile devices. In *CHI'06 extended abstracts on Human factors in computing systems*, ACM (2006), 694–699.

7. de Sá, M., and Carriço, L. Lessons from early stages design of mobile applications. In *Proceedings of the 10th international conference on Human computer interaction with mobile devices and services*, ACM (2008), 127–136.

8. de Sá, M., and Carriço, L. A mobile tool for in-situ prototyping. In *Proceedings of the 11th International Conference on Human-Computer Interaction with Mobile Devices and Services*, ACM (2009), 1–4.

9. de Sá, M., Carriço, L., Duarte, L., and Reis, T. A mixed-fidelity prototyping tool for mobile devices. In *Proceedings of the working conference on Advanced visual interfaces*, ACM (2008), 225–232.

10. Landay, J. *Interactive Sketching for the Early Stages of User Interface Design*. PhD thesis, Carnegie Mellon University, 1996.

11. Lewis, J. IBM computer usability satisfaction questionnaires: psychometric evaluation and instructions for use. *International Journal of Human-Computer Interaction 7*, 1 (1995), 57–78.

12. Li, Y., Cao, X., Everitt, K., Dixon, M., and Landay, J. FrameWire: a tool for automatically extracting interaction logic from paper prototyping tests. In *Proceedings of the 28th international conference on Human factors in computing systems*, ACM (2010), 503–512.

13. Liao, C., Guimbretière, F., Hinckley, K., and Hollan, J. Papiercraft: A gesture-based command system for interactive paper. *ACM Transactions on Computer-Human Interaction (TOCHI) 14*, 4 (2008), 1–27.

14. Lin, J., Newman, M., Hong, J., and Landay, J. DENIM: finding a tighter fit between tools and practice for Web site design. In *Proceedings of the SIGCHI conference on Human factors in computing systems*, ACM (2000), 510–517.

15. Lin, J., Thomsen, M., and Landay, J. A visual language for sketching large and complex interactive designs. In *Proceedings of the SIGCHI conference on Human factors in computing systems: Changing our world, changing ourselves*, ACM (2002), 307–314.

16. Lumsden, J., and MacLean, R. A Comparison of Pseudo-Paper and Paper Prototyping Methods for Mobile Evaluations. In *The International Workshop on MObile and NEtworking Technologies for social applications (MONET'2008), part of the LNCS OnTheMove (OTM) Federated Conferences and Workshops* (2010).

17. Rettig, M. Prototyping for tiny fingers. *Communications of the ACM 37*, 4 (1994), 21–27.

18. Snyder, C. *Paper prototyping: The fast and easy way to design and refine user interfaces*. Morgan Kaufmann Pub, 2003.

19. Virzi, R., Sokolov, J., and Karis, D. Usability problem identification using both low-and high-fidelity prototypes. In *Proceedings of the SIGCHI conference on Human factors in computing systems: common ground*, ACM (1996), 236–243.

20. Wilson, P. Active Story: A Low Fidelity Prototyping and Distributed Usability Testing Tool for Agile Teams. *Univerity of Calgary, MSc Thesis August* (2008).

Mode Switching Techniques through Pen and Device Profiles

Huawei Tu
Kochi University of
Technology, Kochi, Japan
ren.xiangshi@kochi-
tech.ac.jp

Xing-Dong Yang
University of Alberta
Alberta, Canada
xingdong@cs.ualberta.ca

Feng Wang
Kunming University of
Science and Technology
Yunan, China
wf@cnlab.net

Feng Tian
Institute of Software
Chinese Academy of
Sciences, Beijing, China
tf@iel.iscas.ac.cn

Xiangshi Ren
Kochi University of
Technology, Kochi, Japan
ren.xiangshi@kochi-
tech.ac.jp

ABSTRACT

In pen-based interfaces, inking and gesturing are two central tasks, and switching from inking to gesturing is an important issue. Previous studies have focused on mode switching in pen-based desktop devices. However, because pen-based mobile devices are smaller and more mobile than pen-based desktop devices, the principles in mode switching techniques for pen-based desktop devices may not apply to pen-based mobile devices. In this paper, we investigated five techniques for switching between ink and gesture modes in two form factors of pen-based mobile devices respectively: P-DA and Tablet PC. Two quantitative experiments were conducted to evaluate these mode switching techniques. Results showed that in Tablet PC, *pressure* performed the fastest but resulted in the most errors. In PDA, *back tapping* offered the fastest performance. Although *pressing and holding* was significantly slower than the other techniques, it resulted in the fewest errors in Tablet PC and PDA. *Pressing button on handheld device* offered overall fast and accurate performance in Tablet PC and PDA.

Author Keywords

Pen interface, mobile devices, mode switching, ink, gesture.

ACM Classification Keywords

H.5.2 Information Interfaces and Presentation: User Interfaces—*Interaction techniques*

INTRODUCTION

As a familiar tool and a precise input device, the pen has been widely used in Tablet PCs and mobile phones. One of the most common tasks in pen-based handheld devices is to record information by inking [12], which is the prominent feature of this handheld product. Considering the situation where the user quickly records information and wants to change font style or font color to highlight the content, it is beneficial to use an efficient switching technique to switch between the ink task and the gesture task.

Previous studies mainly focused on mode switching in pen-based desktop devices. Li et al. [5] systemically analyzed five mode switching techniques in a Tablet PC fixed on a desktop. Lank et al. [4] investigated the non-preferred hand mode manipulation in a Tablet PC which was fully opened and placed on a desk. Liu and Ren [6] applied pen tilt and azimuth to mode switching in a pen-based desktop device. Unlike desktop devices, handheld devices are mobile and miniature, so the conclusions drawn by previous studies may not apply to pen-based handheld devices.

Mode switching is more urgent issue in pen-based handheld devices than in pen-based desktop devices. As mentioned in [5], the usual methods to alleviate modes in pen-based interfaces are designed by using system defined gestures and appropriate interface layout. However, because of hardware limitations in handheld devices, the ability to discern gestures from other ink strokes in freeform sketches is not as strong as in that of desktop devices. In addition, the small input area also restricts icon size in pen-based devices, which makes mode switching more difficult in pen-based handheld devices. Simple and effective explicit mode switching techniques are needed to provide users advanced mode switching mechanisms in pen-based handheld devices.

Six mode switching techniques were examined in this study. Four of these techniques, *pressing the barrel button on the pen*, *pressing and holding*, *pressing the button on the handheld device* and *using pressure* were previously proposed and examined as they applied to pen-based desktop devices by Li et al. [5]. The other two techniques, *jerking movement* and *back tapping* are proposed in this study based on the features of pen-based handheld devices. The aim of this study is to compare these mode switching techniques and to find the most suitable mode switching technique in two typical sizes of pen-based handheld devices: PDAs and Tablet PCs.

The paper is structured as follows. In the following section, the six mode switching techniques are described. Next, two empirical experiments are reported and the experimental results are analyzed. Finally, several design principles for mode switching techniques and directions for future research are discussed.

RELATED WORK

We reviewed previous studies related to the six techniques used in our study, with consideration of how to better employ these techniques in mobile devices for mode switching. In addition, we reviewed some other mode switching techniques which would be beneficial to the technique design in our study.

Using Pressure

The availability of pressure in pen-based devices has been explored by a number of researchers. Ramos et al. [10] carried out the first systematic investigation of the human ability to select a discrete target by varying stylus pressure under full and partial visual feedback. Ramos et al. [11] designed pressure marks, which employed pressure as a feature for selection and action simultaneously.

Employing pressure is an effective input method for mobile devices. Varying levels of pressure can be used, for example, to convert the case of letters [2]. Miyaki and Rekimoto [7] proposed a single-handed UI scheme to realize multi-state input using pressure sensing.

Stylus pressure can be used to switch input mode from inking to gesturing [5],[6]. Inking is a more common task than gesturing in stylus input, so the normal pressure space can be employed in inking mode and the heavier pressure space can be employed in gesturing mode.

A preliminary experiment was conducted to set a suitable pressure spectrum for gesturing mode and inking mode. Four participants, two males and two females, were asked to do the pie crossing task (described in the section "Experimental Design") which included four blocks for each orientation (one block included four red pie slices and four black pie slices). Participants were asked to draw with their normal pressure to cross the black pie and with their heavier pressure to cross the red pie. No visual feedback other than pressure sensitive ink thickness was given. The stylus pressure in one pie crossing task was recorded per 10 milliseconds.

The formula proposed in [5] was used to calculate the maximum average pressure which is defined as the maximum of the average pressure of one pie crossing task. The average pressure at the time t_i is measured as:

$$\mathrm{AP}_{t_i} = \frac{1}{i+1} \sum_{j=0}^{i} P_j, \; P_j \text{ is the pressure at the time } t_j$$

We set a pressure threshold which was higher than most av-erage pressures in normal input conditions and lower than most average pressures in heavy input conditions. The pressure threshold for Tablet PC and PDA will be given in the section "Experiment One" and "Experiment Two" respectively.

Pressing and Holding

Pressing and holding is a widely used technique in pen-based devices such as PDA and Tablet PC. *Pressing and holding* requires the user to hold the pen tip on the screen for a predefined time, then mode switching feedback is given. The user can lift the pen tip to choose a menu item or move the pen tip to draw a gesture on the screen.

According to the method proposed by Li et al. [5], we designed a *pressing and holding* technique for this study. For a drawing trajectory, the first point was set as the base point. The holding time was defined as the duration from the moment the base point was produced to the moment the pen was moved out of the scope of a circle whose center was the base point and radius was 7 pixels. If the holding time was longer than 1 second, a red circle with a radius of 7 pixels appeared around the pen tip. If the holding time was shorter than 1 second, the subsequent point of the base point would be chosen as the new base point and the holding time would be recalculated. In the case when a red circle appeared, to perform mode switching the participant had to move the pen out of the circle within 800 ms. Otherwise, the red circle would disappear; meanwhile the current pen point would be set as the base point and the holding time would be recalculated.

Pressing the Barrel Button

Pressing the barrel button of the stylus is a commonly used technique, in which the barrel button serves the function of a mouse. Mode switching can be achieved by pressing the barrel button.

Pressing the Button on Handheld Devices

Physical buttons on handheld devices can be used to switch interfaces or functions. Pressing and then releasing the button can be used to affect mode switching.

Back Tapping on the Device

Back operation is an effective way to enhance input capability in handheld devices. Users can input information by fully utilizing the back of the device. Sugimoto and Hiroki [15] mounted a touchpad to the rear surface of a PDA and proposed a new technique called HybridTouch. Yang et al. [20] designed a Dual-Surface technique by means of mounting a touchpad at the back of a PDA, and systematically investigated the ability of backside operation via two experiments. Tapping input was an embedded interaction method for mobile devices [13]. Back tapping was used to trigger a continuous mode in mobile devices [14]. Wobbrock et al. [18] analyzed the performance of pointing tasks with respect to the interaction with one and two hands, thumbs and index fingers, horizontal and vertical movements, and front- and back-of-device manipulation in a mobile device respectively. The results showed that the index finger offered good performance on both the front and the back of the device, and that the thumb performed worse on the front of the device.

In this study, we used a prototype similar to that in [20] where we attached an Ergonomic USB touchpad [?] on the back of the experimental device. Participants were asked to tap on the touchpad to perform mode switching using the index finger of the non-dominant hand.

Jerking Movement

In a noteworthy study, Roudaut [14] used a jerking movement to activate a mode that helped to reach the last opened window. In this study, we used vibration acceleration to detect jerking movements.

Considering the vibration difference is usually small while inking input, we set the normal vibration difference space for inking and large vibration difference space for gesturing.

To determine the jerking direction for *jerking* technique, a pilot study was conducted with four participants, two males and two females. Participants were requested to jerk two handheld devices, PDA and Tablet PC over x, y and z axis respectively (ten times for each exis) by their non-preferred hand. They were asked over which axis the jerking task was easier and fastest to accomplish. For the Tablet PC, all participants reported that the jerking task was easy to accomplish over the z axis. Regarding the PDA, three participants reported that the jerking task was easy to accomplish over the z axis, and a female participant said it was easier to accomplish over the y axis but she admitted that it was faster over the z axis. According to their reports, jerking a handheld device over the z-axis (forward or backward) was the preferred method to perform the mode switching task.

A Phidget Accelerometer 3-Axis [9] which can detect vibration with $\pm$ 29.4 m/s^2 change per axis, was used to measure the vibration over the z-axis. Jerking movement was detected by calculating the difference between the smallest acceleration value and the largest acceleration value in an experimental trial. The acceleration difference is defined as:

$$AD = Max(A_i) - Min(A_j), 0 \le i, j \le t,\ A_i \text{ and } A_j \text{ are}$$

the acceleration values in time i and j, t is the total task time of an experimental trial.

A preliminary experiment was conducted to set a suitable acceleration difference spectrum for gesturing mode and inking mode. Four people, two males and two females, were required to do the pie crossing task (described in section "Experimental Design") which had four blocks for each orientation (one block included four red pie slices and four black pie slices). If a red pie appeared, participants were asked to jerk the device with comfortable jerking movement over the z-axis (forward or backward) and then perform the pie crossing task. If a black pie appeared, participants only needed to do the pie crossing task. The value of device acceleration in one pie crossing task was recorded per 10 milliseconds.

We set an acceleration difference threshold which was higher than most acceleration difference values in the non-jerking condition and lower than most acceleration difference values in the jerking condition. The acceleration difference thresholds for Tablet PC and PDA will be given in "Experiment One" and "Experiment Two" respectively.

Other Mode Switching Techniques

Bi et al. [1] explored how to use pen rolling in pen-based interactions, including the task of mode switching. Pen tilt can also be employed to perform mode switching [19]. We did not use pen rolling or pen tilt in this study as these two input techniques are not available in current mobile devices. The combination of finger gesture on the pen barrel plus device tilt can produce a sense of natural and seamless operation for mode switching [16]. Motion gesture on mobile devices can produce better mode switching for word input [17]. Inspired by the above two techniques proposed in [16] and [17], we designed and tested a technique named *Jerking Movement* in our study.

EXPERIMENTAL DESIGN

Experimental Task

Our experimental design was based on the experimental paradigm proposed in [5]. As shown in Figure 1a, a pie slice was shown with its symmetry axis corresponding to one of the eight major geographical directions. Pie crossing task was the process of crossing a pie slice from its inner edge to its outer edge with the requirement of high speed.

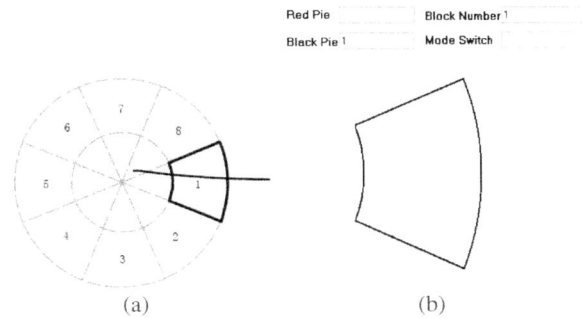

Figure 1. The experimental interface. (a)A ring is equally divided into 8 slices. Supposing the center point of the ring is the origin of the coordinate, the first slice is axial symmetry with x-axis. (b) The numbers and the dashed lines were not shown in the experiment, and only one pie slice appeared each trial.

The experiment consisted of two kinds of tasks: mode switching task and non mode switching task. In the non mode switching task, a black pie was shown in the screen and participants only needed to perform the pie crossing task (see Figure 1b). In the mode switching task, a red pie was shown on the screen. Participants were required to complete the mode switching task before the drawing exceeded the inner edge of the pie target. In both mode switching and non mode switching tasks, the pie color would turn green if mode switching was performed and the mode could not be canceled until pie crossing task was finished. In order to avoid the predictable mode switching [4], the presentation order of black pies and red pies was randomized in each block. Task time in a trial was defined as the time from when the pie slice appeared until the moment the pen was lifted from the screen.

Error Classification

Similar to [5], errors in the experiment were divided into three categories: mode errors, crossing errors, and out-of-target errors. Mode errors included mode-in errors and mode-out errors; mode-in error was crossing a red pie without mode switching and mode-out error was crossing a black pie with mode switching. Crossing errors happened when the trajectory crossed a target slice from a side, or from outer to inner. Out-of-target error means trajectory did not cross the target.

If a participant finished a pie crossing task with an error, a beep sound and a new pie slice with bold edge would be given to remind the participant to redo this task.

EXPERIMENT ONE - MODE SWITCHING IN TABLET PC

Five mode switching techniques, *using pressure, pressing the barrel button, pressing and holding, pressing the button on the Tablet PC* and *jerking movement* were tested in a medium-sized pen-based handheld Tablet PC. *Back tapping* technique was not examined because it was difficult to tap the Tablet PC's back with the non-dominant hand when the participant was holding the device.

Apparatus

The experiment was conducted with a Fujitsu FMV-STYLISTIC Tablet PC running Windows XP Tablet PC Edition. The weight of the device was approximately 1.48 kg. The tablet PC has a Pentium III 933MHz processor and 256MB RAM. The resolution of the screen is 1024x768 pixels with each pixel approximately 0.2055mm. The stylus recognizes 256 levels of pressure and is equipped with a barrel button.

A Phidget Accelerometer 3-Axis [9] was mounted on the top of the Tablet PC's back and connected to the Tablet PC for the detection of jerking movements.

The Tablet PC ran custom software written in C# using Microsoft's Tablet SDK and Visual Studio .NET.

Set Pressure and Acceleration Threshold for Mode Switching

The pressure threshold for mode switching was set as the value of 185 which was higher than 89% maximum average pressure in the normal condition and lower than 89% maximum average pressure in the heavy condition.

We set the acceleration difference threshold for mode switching as 0.3 m/s^2 which was higher than 97% acceleration difference in the non-jerking condition and lower than 99% acceleration difference in the jerk condition.

Participants

Ten right handed volunteers (5 females, 5 males) ranging in age from 25 to 30, participated in this experiment. Two

participants reported that they had experience with *using the barrel button*. Two participants had experienced *pressing and holding*. Four participants had experienced *using pressure*. However, none of them had used *jerking movement* before. Participants were asked to sit in a chair and hold the device by the non preferred hand when performing the experimental task with a stylus which was held in the preferred hand.

Procedure

The experiment consisted of a training phase and an experimental phase. Two mode switching trials and two non mode switching trials in each orientation were performed in the training phase. In the experimental phase, each participant performed the pie crossing task for 8 orientations. Each orientation trial included 6 blocks; for each block, the participant performed 4 pie crossing tasks with mode switching and 4 pie crossing tasks without mode switching. The participant could take a break after finishing a block. A Latin-square design was used to balance the order of the five techniques between the participants. The whole experimental session lasted about 1 hour. In summary, the experiment consisted of:

10 subjects $\times$
5 mode switching techniques $\times$
8 orientations $\times$
6 blocks of trials $\times$
8 pie-crossing tasks
$=19200$ pie-crossing tasks

9600 mode switches were performed in total. The dependent variables measured were task time for mode switching trials and for non mode switching trials, mode-in error, mode-out error, crossing error, and out-of-target error.

RESULTS

Performance Stability over Experimental Blocks

Mode switching time was measured by subtracting the mean non mode switching task time from the mean mode switching task time. Repeated measures analysis of variance showed that there was no significant learning effect on mode switching time for block ($F_{5,45} = 2.15$, $p = 0.08$). Chi-square analysis revealed that no significant learning effect was found on error rate for block ($\chi_5^2 = 2.27$, $p = 0.81$). Therefore, we believed that after the training phase, participants were able to stably perform the five mode switching techniques in the following experimental blocks.

Mode Switching Time

A significant main effect was found on mode switching time for the five techniques ($F_{4,36} = 209.20$, $p < 0.001$) (see Figure 2a).

Post Hoc Tests with the Bonferroni adjustment were applied to multiple comparisons. The smallest mode switching time was the time of *using pressure* with a mean 228ms. Post hoc comparisons showed there was no significant difference ($p = 0.14$) between *using pressure* and *pressing button on Tablet PC* (Mean = 304ms), and no significant difference ($p = 0.18$)

between *using pressure* and *barrel button* (Mean = 374ms). However, there was a significant difference ($p < 0.01$) between *using pressure* and *jerking*. It was found that *jerking* (Mean = 435ms) had no significant difference from *barrel button* (p = 1.00), but a significant difference from *button on Tablet PC* ($p < 0.01$). Post hoc comparisons also showed there was no significant difference ($p = 1.00$) between *button on Tablet PC* and *barrel button*. *Pressing and holding* was the slowest technique with a mean of 1414ms ($p < 0.001$).

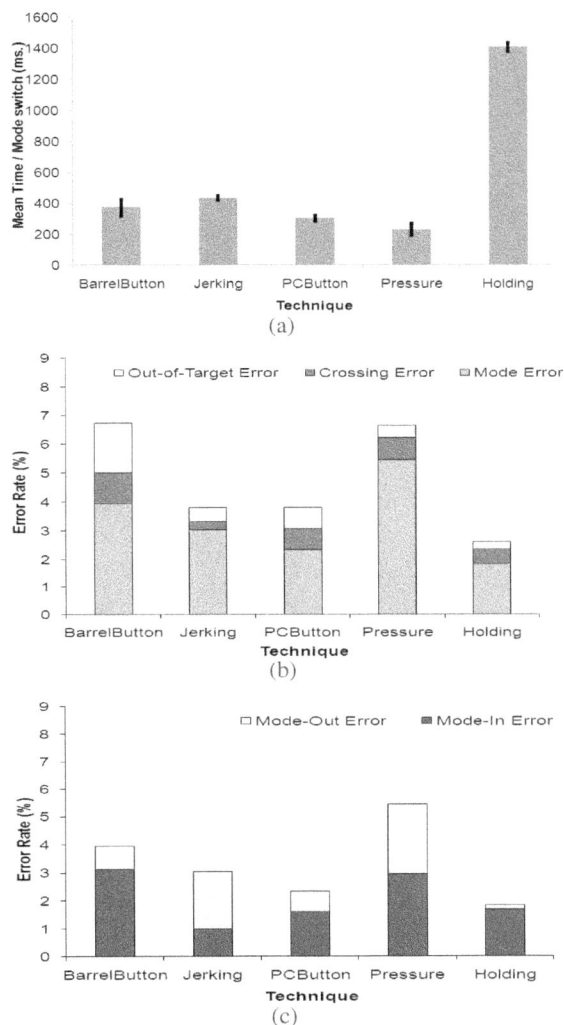

Figure 2. (a) The mean mode switching time of five techniques. Error bars represent 0.95 confidence interval. (b) The error rate on each pie-crossing. (c) The error rate of mode-in and mode-out errors on each pie-crossing.

Error Analysis

Chi-square test revealed that there was a statistically significant relationship between the number of errors and techniques ($\chi_4^2 = 113.53$, $p < 0.001$). *Pressing and holding* resulted in few errors with a standardized residual at -6.0. *Jerking* (z = -2.6) and *pressing PC Button* (z = -2.6) led to the same errors. *Using pressure* resulted in more errors than these three techniques (z = 5.5). *Barrel button* committed the most errors (z = 5.8).

Frequencies of each type of error when using the five different techniques were further analyzed. Chi-square test showed that there was a significant relationship between the five techniques and four types of errors ($\chi_{12}^2 = 161.00$, $p < 0.001$).

The results showed that mode errors, including mode-in and mode-out errors, were the main errors for the five techniques. As shown in Figure 2c, *using pressure* led to the most mode errors, and *pressing and holding* resulted in the least mode errors. *Barrel button* committed more mode-in errors (z = 0.6), and *jerking* resulted in fewer mode-in errors (z = -3.3). *Using pressure* led to more mode-out errors (z = 3.3), and *pressing and holding* resulted in fewer mode-out errors (z = -4.0).

It should be noted that some crossing errors and out-of-target errors occurred along with mode errors. This is because while engaging in a crossing task, subjects accidentally lifted the pen tip to cancel the drawing if they found a mode error happened, even though they were required to continue the pie crossing task. Regarding crossing error, *barrel button* led to more crossing errors (z = 0.5), and *jerking* resulted in fewer crossing errors (z = -2.1). For out-of-target error, *barrel button* resulted in more out-of-target errors (z = 4.4), and *pressing and holding* committed fewer out-of-target errors (z = -1.6) (see Figure 2b).

EXPERIMENT TWO - MODE SWITCHING IN PDA

The aim of this experiment was to compare five mode switching techniques in a small scale pen-based handheld device, PDA. Five mode switching techniques, *using pressure*, *pressing and holding*, *pressing the button on PDA*, *back tapping* and *jerking movement*, were investigated in this experiment. We did not test *Pressing the barrel button* in this experiment, because most styluses for PDA did not have a barrel button.

Apparatus

PDA and Host Computer

We conducted the experiment with an HP iPAQ PDA running Windows Mobile 2003. The weight of the device is 164.4g. The PDA has a PXA270 520MHz processor, 65MB RAM and Wi-Fi card. The resolution of the screen is 240 × 320 pixels with each pixel measuring approximately 0.24mm.

A Tablet PC which has a wireless network card was used as the host computer to receive data from sensors and to send data to the PDA through the wireless network. The sensors were used to detect back taping, pressure and jerking.

Back Tapping Detection Device

A prototype similar to that in [20] was built. In the prototype, an Ergonomic USB touchpad was attached on the back of the PDA and connected to the host computer. A tapping action was detected as a pressing down action on a mouse.

Pressure Detection Device

A device for pressure detection was constructed based on [7] and [8]. Four Force Sensitive Resistor (FSR) sensors

[3], which can detect 1024 levels of pressure, were attached on the bottom of an acrylic cover. The FSR was connected to the host computer via a single-board microcontroller Arduino. The PDA was put on the sensors and the average pressure value of the four pressure sensors was calculated to approximately represent the stylus pressure.

Jerking Detection Device

To detect jerking movement, we mounted a Phidget Accelerometer 3-Axis [9] on the PDA's back and connected it to the host computer.

Experiment software was designed in C# and Visual Studio .NET.

Set Pressure and Acceleration Threshold for Mode Switching

The pressure threshold for mode switching was set to the value of 80 which was higher than 96% maximum average pressure in the normal condition and lower than 89% maximum average pressure in the heavy condition.

We set the acceleration difference threshold for mode switching as 0.7 m/s^2 which was higher than 97% acceleration difference in the non-jerk condition and lower than 98% acceleration difference in the jerk condition.

Participants

Ten right handed volunteers (4 females, 6 males) ranging in age from 25 to 32, participated in the experiment. Six of them had participated experiment one. The other four participants reported that they had no experience using the stylus before. In the experiment, participants were asked to sit in a chair and hold the device in the non preferred hand, while performing the experimental task with a stylus held by the preferred hand.

Procedure

The experiment procedure was similar to that in experiment one. We recorded the task time in mode switching trials and non mode switching trials, mode-out error, mode-in error, crossing error and out-of-target error.

RESULTS

Performance Stability over Experimental Blocks

Mode switching time was measured by subtracting the mean of non mode switching task time from the mean of mode switching task time. Repeated measures analysis of variance showed that there was no significant learning effect on the mode switching time between six blocks ($F_{5,45} = 2.04$, $p = 0.09$). Chi-square analysis also revealed that no significant learning effect was found on error rate between six blocks ($\chi_5^2 = 2.40$, $p = 0.79$). The overall results showed that the learning effect was minor and participants had already reached a steady performance from block one.

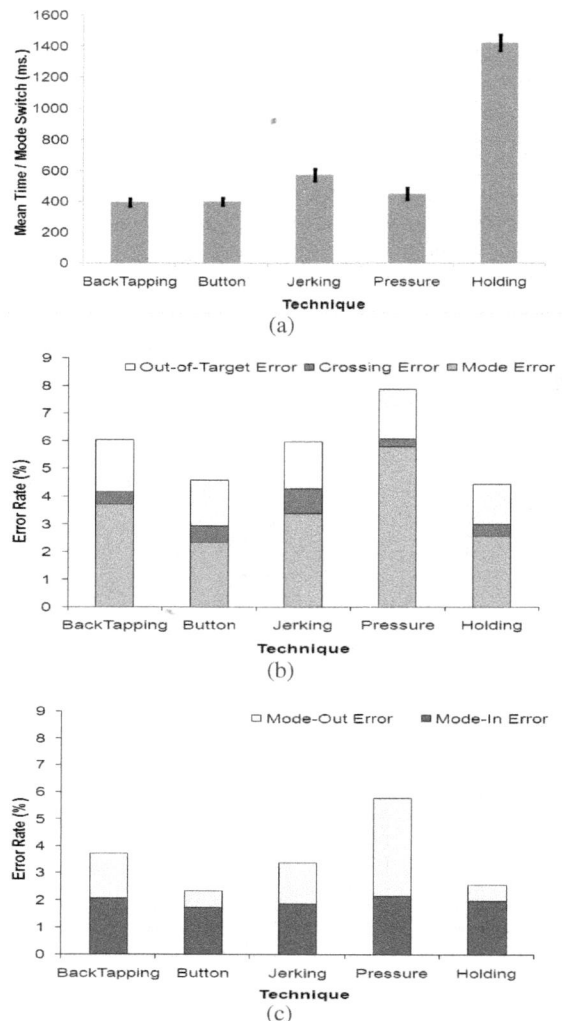

(a)

(b)

(c)

Figure 3. (a) The mean mode switching time of five techniques. Error bars represent 0.95 confidence interval. (b) The error rate on each pie-crossing. (c) The error rate of mode-out and mode-out errors on each pie-crossing.

Mode Switching Time

Repeated measures analysis of variance was performed on mode switching time for five techniques. Mauchly's test indicated that the assumption of sphericity had been violated (chi-square = 17.98, p < 0.05), therefore degrees of freedom were corrected using Huynh-Feldt estimates of sphericity (epsilon = 0.86). A significant main effect was found on mode switching time for the five techniques ($F_{3.458,31.118} = 288.61$, $p < 0.001$) (see Figure 3a).

Post Hoc Tests were performed using the Bonferroni adjustment for multiple comparisons. *Back tapping* produced the smallest mode switching time with a mean 393ms. Although *back tapping* had no significant difference with *pressing button on PDA* (Mean = 399ms, $p = 1.00$), it had a significant difference with the three other techniques(*jerking* (Mean = 572ms, $p < 0.05$), *using pressure* (Mean = 450ms, $p < 0.05$) and *pressing and holding* (Mean = 1424ms, $p < 0.001$)). *Pressing button on PDA* also had a significant difference with *jerking* ($p < 0.05$), *using Pressure* ($p < 0.05$) and *press-*

ing and holding ($p < 0.001$), which means that *pressing button on PDA* and *back tapping* resulted in the similar mode switching times. Post hoc comparisons showed there was no significant difference ($p = 0.85$) between *jerking* and *pressure*, indicating that these two techniques can be grouped on their efficiency in switching modes. *Pressing and holding* produced the largest mode switching time than the other four techniques.

Error Analysis

A Chi-square test revealed that there was a statistically significant relationship between the number of errors and the technique ($\chi_4^2 = 51.26$, $p < 0.001$) (see Figure 3b). *Pressing and holding* resulted in few errors with a standardized residual at -3.5. And *Pressing the button on PDA* led to few errors ($z = -3.1$). *Jerking* resulted in many more errors than these two techniques ($z = 0.5$). *Back tapping* made almost the same error as *jerking* ($z = 0.68$). *Using pressure* resulted in more errors ($z = 5.4$) than the other techniques.

Frequencies of each type of error were further analyzed. The Chi-square test showed that there was a significant effect between five techniques and four types of errors ($\chi_{12}^2 = 103.20$, $p < 0.001$).

Mode errors, including mode-in and mode-out errors, were the main errors for the five techniques. *Using pressure* led to the most mode errors, and *pressing button on PDA* resulted in the least mode errors. *Using pressure* resulted in more mode-out errors ($z = 5.8$), and *pressing the button on PDA* resulted in fewer mode-out errors ($z = -3.6$). *Using pressure* resulted in more mode-in errors ($z = 1.0$). *Pressing button* ($z = -1.9$) resulted in fewer mode-in errors (see Figure 3c).

In this experiment, some crossing errors and out-of-target errors occurred along with mode errors. This is because while engaging in a crossing task, participants accidentally lifted the pen tip to stop the drawing if they found a mode error happened. In addition, the slippery screen and small stylus made it difficult for participants to control the trajectory. As shown in Figure 3b, *jerking* led to more crossing errors ($z = 2.9$), and *using pressure* resulted in fewer crossing errors ($z = -3.1$). *Back tapping* resulted in more out-of-target errors ($z = 2.2$), and *pressing and holding* resulted in fewer out-of-target errors ($z = -0.8$).

DISCUSSION

Regarding Tablet PC, *using pressure* allowed users to smoothly switch between gesturing and inking, so it offered the fastst performance. However, this technique resulted in more errors. We set the pressure threshold according to the pressure data from four participants, so personalized pressure profiles may reduce the error rate for *using pressure*. Some participants felt it uncomfortable to press the button on Tablet PC for mode switching while holding the experimental device, and this may lead to a longer mode switching time. *Using Barrel button* resulted in the most crossing errors and out-of-target errors, suggesting that this technique may be difficult to use in handheld devices. Some participants complained that the Tablet PC was too heavy to jerk, so *jerking*

technique may perform slower than other techniques except *pressing and holding*. However, *jerking* resulted in fewer errors than other techniques except *pressing and holding*, indicating that it can serve as a promising mode switching technique.

With respect to PDA, *back tapping* performed faster than *pressing button on PDA*, which is consistent with the results in [18]. However, *back tapping* resulted in more errors than *pressing button on PDA*. In the experiment, we found that many errors were caused by inadvertently touching the touchpad. An optimal input area for *back tapping* technique may reduce errors and keep high efficiency for mode switching. In further study, we will investigate the performance of *back tapping* technique in different input areas for mode switch. *Using pressure in PDA* did not perform as well as in Tablet PC, which may be due to the fact that it is difficult to use the small stylus on the smooth PDA screen. *Jerking technique in PDA* led to larger mode switch time than *jerking technique in Tablet PC*. Jerking the PDA was performed by using the wrist as a fulcrum, while jerking the Tablet PC required the use of the elbow as a fulcrum; jerking the Tablet PC may be easier to perform for participants.

Overall, *pressing button on handheld device* performed faster and more accurately on the Tablet PC and the PDA, which was consistent with the results in [5]. Although *pressing and holding* technique resulted in longer mode switching time than the other techniques, it led to fewer errors. Furthermore, this technique requires the least hardware support, so it has been widely used in handheld devices.

Jerking technique and *back tapping* are two techniques proposed in this paper with a view to better meeting the requirement of efficient mode switching for mobile devices. Although these two techniques did not perform as well as we expected, the results still shed some light on the use of these two techniques in mode switching technique design. First, regarding *jerking technique*, we found that the mode switching time for the tablet PC was shorter than that for the PDA. This is an interesting result: although the tablet PC is heavier than the PDA, it seems that users feel more control over the tablet PC. This indicates that *jerking technique* is more suitable in large scale mobile devices for mode switching tasks. Second, although the area of the touchpad used in *back tapping* is larger than that of the button in *pressing button on handheld device*, *back tapping* did not produce significant shorter mode switching times than *pressing button on handheld device*. This may be due to the differences between one handed and two handed input; *back tapping* is a two-handed input technique but *pressing button on handheld device* is a one-handed input technique. Mode switching technique design should pay attention to the use of one-handed and two-handed input. Last, *pressing the barrel button on the pen*, *pressing and holding*, *pressing the button on the handheld device*, *using pressure* and *back tapping* were performed on a 2D surface, such as the touch screen and the button surface. Unlike the above techniques, *jerking technique* is a motion-based technique. This technique did not perform well in the sitting posture, but due to its distinct property, it may be useful in other postures, such as walking. Future study will explore the impact of user posture (sitting, standing and walking) on the performance of mode switching.

CONCLUSION

In this paper, we investigated five mode switching techniques in two typical pen-based handheld devices respectively: a PDA and a Tablet PC. Two experiments were conducted to evaluate the performance of these techniques. Some interesting results were found here. For the PDA, *back tapping* offered the fastest performance. *Pressing the button on PDA* technique was slower than *back tapping* technique, but there was no significant difference between them. Regarding Tablet PC, *pressure* led to shorter time but more errors than the other four techniques. *Pressing button on Tablet PC* technique was slower than *pressure* technique, but there was no significant difference between them. *Jerking* resulted in fewer errors than the other techniques except *pressing and holding*. In both devices, *pressing and holding* was significantly slower but less prone to error. *Pressing button on handheld device* offered overall fast and accurate performance in both the Tablet PC and the PDA. Two methods proposed here, *back tapping* and *jerking* are two promising mode switching techniques, which should be deeply explored in future study. The experimental results can be beneficial to the design of mode switching techniques in pen-based handheld devices.

ACKNOWLEDGMENTS

This study has been partially supported by Grant-in-Aid for Scientific Research (No. 23300048) in Japan and NSFC of China (No. 61063027). We thank the members of Ren Lab in Kochi University of Technology for their assistance.

REFERENCES

1. Bi, X., Moscovich, T., Ramos, G., Balakrishnan, R. and Hinckley, K. An exploration of pen rolling for pen-based interaction. In *Proc. UIST 2008*, ACM Press (2008), 191-200.

2. Brewster, S. A. and Hughes, M. Pressure-based text entry for mobile devices. In *Proc. MobileHCI 2009*, ACM Press (2009), 1-4.

3. Interlink electronics: Force Sensing Resistors, http://www.interlinkelectronics.com/force_sensors.

4. Lank, E., Ruiz J. and Cowan, W. Concurrent bimanual stylus interaction: a study of non-preferred hand mode manipulation. In *Proc. GI 2006*, ACM Press (2006), 17-24.

5. Li, Y., Hinckley, K., Guan, Z. and Landay,J.A. Experimental analysis of mode switching techniques in pen-based user interfaces. In *Proc. CHI 2005*, ACM Press (2005), 461-470.

6. Liu C. and Ren, X. Experimental analysis of mode switching techniques in pen-based user interfaces. *International Journal of Innovative Computing, Information and Control*, 6, 4(2010), 1983-1990.

7. Miyaki T. and Rekimoto J. GraspZoom: zooming and scrolling control model for single-handed mobile interaction. In *Proc. MobileHCI 2009*, ACM Press (2009), 1-4.

8. Mizobuchi, S., Terasaki, S., Keski-Jaskari, T., Nousiainen, J., Ryynanen M. and Silfverberg, M. Making an impression: force-controlled pen input for handheld devices. *Ext. Abstracts CHI 2005*, ACM Press (2005), 1661-1664.

9. Phidget: PhidgetAccelerometer 3-Axis, http://www.phidgets.com/.

10. Ramos, G. A., Boulos, M. and Balakrishnan, R. Pressure widgets. In *Proc. CHI 2004*, ACM Press (2004), 487-494.

11. Ramos, G. A. and Balakrishnan, R. Pressure marks, In *Proc. CHI 2007*, ACM Press (2007), 1375-1384.

12. Ren, X. and Moriya, S. Improving selection performance on pen-based systems: a study of pen-based interaction for selection tasks. *TOCHI, 7*, 3(2000), 384-416.

13. Ronkainen,S., Häkkilä,J., Kaleva, S., Colley A. and Linjama, J. Tap input as an embedded interaction method for mobile devicess. In *Proc. TEI 2007*, ACM Press (2007), 263-270.

14. Roudaut, A., Baglioni M. and Lecolinet, E. TimeTilt: Using Sensor-Based Gestures to Travel through Multiple Applications on a Mobile Device. In *Proc. INTERACT 2009*, Springer Press (2009), 830-834.

15. Sugimoto M. and Hiroki K. HybridTouch: an intuitive manipulation technique for PDAs using their front and rear surfaces. In *Proc. MobileHCI 2007*, ACM Press (2007), 137-140.

16. Sun, M., Cao, X., Song, H., Izadi, S., Benko, H., Guimbretiere, F., Ren, X. and Hinckley, K. Enhancing naturalness of pen-and-tablet drawing through context sensing. In *Proc. ITS 2011*, ACM Press (2011), 83-86.

17. Wang, J. Zhai, S. and Canny, J. SHRIMP - solving collision and out of vocabulary problems in mobile predictive input with motion gesture. In *Proc. CHI 2010*, ACM Press (2010), 15-24.

18. Wobbrock, J.O., Myers B.A. and Aung, H.H. The performance of hand postures in front- and back-of-device interaction for mobile computing. *Int. J. Hum.-Comput. Stud, 66*, 12(2008), 857-875.

19. Xin, Y., Bi, X. and Ren, X. Acquiring and pointing: an empirical study of pen-tilt-based interaction. In *Proc. CHI 2011*, ACM Press (2011), 849-858.

20. Yang, X.D., Mak, E., Irani P. and Bischof, W.F. Dual-Surface input: augmenting one-handed interaction with coordinated front and behind-the-screen input. In *Proc. MobileHCI 2009*, ACM Press (2009), 1-10.

HomeOrgel: Interactive Music Box for the Aural Representation of Home Activities

Maho Oki
Ochanomizu University
okimaho@acm.org

Koji Tsukada
JST PRESTO
tsuka@acm.org

Kazutaka Kurihara
AIST
qurihara@unryu.org

Itiro Siio
Ochanomizu University
siio@acm.org

ABSTRACT

We propose a music-box-type interface, "HomeOrgel", that can express various activities in the home using sound. Users can also control the volume and content using common methods for controlling a music box: opening the cover and winding the spring. Users can hear the sounds of past home activities, such as cooking and the opening/closing of doors with the background music (BGM) mechanism of the music box. We developed the HomeOrgel device and installed it in an actual house. We also verify the effectiveness of our system through evaluation and discussion.

Author Keywords

Auditory display; music box; ubiquitous computing; smart home.

ACM Classification Keywords

H.5.2 [Information Interfaces and Presentation]: User Interfaces – input devices and strategies, user-centered design, Prototyping.

INTRODUCTION

In the near future, it will be common for a large number of computers and sensors to be installed in the home. There have been many research projects on the design of smart homes as test-beds for new technologies in a future environment [2,9,17]. While most projects focused on activity recognition [10,13], representation methods of these activities have also attracted attention in recent years [3,14,16]. To design such representation systems, we need to consider emotional factors: for example, when a user wants to know the status of his/her family member, the presentation method using a picture of the family member [12] is more comforting than a text presentation such as email.

We focused on a music box to present home activities because the music box is familiar to most people, particularly when they look back on their memories. We

propose an auditory interface modeled on a music box, "HomeOrgel", which helps users look back on past activities in the home using sounds, imitating the recall of memories using a music box [11].

First, we introduce the concept and implementation of the HomeOrgel. Next, we explain the installation of our system in an actual home. Then, we report the evaluation method used to verify the effectiveness of our system using actual data. Finally, we provide discussion and present future works.

HOMEORGEL

The HomeOrgel presents various activities in the home using sounds. Users can control the HomeOrgel using common methods for controlling a music box: when a user winds the spring and opens the cover, he/she can hear the sounds of home activities (e.g., conversations and the opening/closing of doors) with the background music (BGM) mechanism of the music box. The user can easily perceive the home activities by listening to these sounds in the same manner as listening to music from a common music box (Figure. 1).

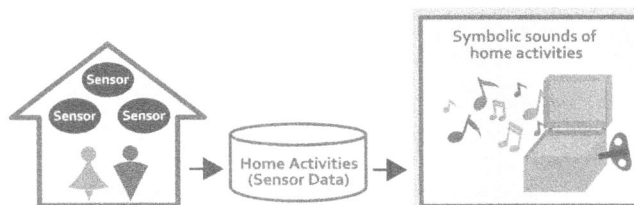

Figure 1. Concept of the HomeOrgel.

Usage

The basic usage of the HomeOrgel is shown in Figure 2. The HomeOrgel provides three main interactions similar to general music boxes by simply using the cover and spring. The procedures are as follows:

1. The user winds the spring on the back of the HomeOrgel by a half-turn.

2. When the user opens the cover, the HomeOrgel starts to play BGM and sounds of past activities (e.g., from 1 hour ago).

3. Sounds of past activities are compressed into a certain length (e.g., 20 sec).

4. The user can change the volume by adjusting the angle of the cover: the volume is increased (decreased) according to the degree to which the cover is opened (closed).

5. When the user closes the cover, the music stops.

When the user winds the spring through more cycles, the HomeOrgel will play the sounds of activities further back in the past. For example, when the user winds the spring three times, he/she can hear sounds of home activities for the past 3 hours. These sounds are compressed into short length to help users look back on past activities more effectively.

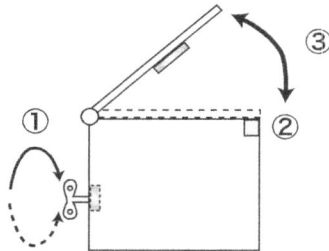

Figure 2. Usage of the HomeOrgel:
(1) winding a spring to rewind to past activities, (2) opening/closing the cover to play/stop music, and (3) adjusting the tilt of the cover to control volume.

Design of sounds

There are several research projects that express activities in the real world using sounds [6, 15]. In such systems, users' activities are expressed by changing the rhythm and pitch of music; however, users often have difficulties in finding meaning in these changes since they must learn the mapping between musical changes and activities in advance. To avoid these difficulties, the HomeOrgel adopts "symbolic sounds" to express home activities

Symbolic sounds of home activities

The HomeOrgel adopts "symbolic sounds" to present home activities for the following reasons:

- Clear mapping between sounds and activities

- Protecting privacy of users

The "symbolic sound" is similar to Blattner's concept of "representational sound" [1] and that of "iconic sound" reported by Gaver [5]. These approaches help listeners understand the meaning of sounds without learning them in advance by mapping sounds directly to events in the real world. Similarly, the HomeOrgel helps users recognize the meaning of sounds using pre-recorded symbolic sounds corresponding to home activities. For example, when someone opens/closes an entrance door in the home, the HomeOrgel plays the sound of a door opening/closing (e.g., "bang"). Although we could also record sounds each time using a microphone attached near the entrance, such "raw" sounds may become difficult for users to hear due to surrounding noises. In particular, users may have difficulty

in understanding multiple raw sounds at once. Moreover, raw sounds may cause privacy problems since they may include unintentionally captured sounds (e.g., conversations around the entrance). For these reasons, we basically applied pre-recorded symbolic sounds. The HomeOrgel generates various symbolic sounds based on home activities detected by sensors at various locations inside the home: entrance, living room, kitchen and so on. When multiple events occur within a short period, the HomeOrgel generates symbolic sounds corresponding to these events simultaneously.

Music length

We discuss here the total length of music generated by the HomeOrgel. We decided to limit the length of the music to several minutes in consideration of the basic usage of the HomeOrgel: casually looking back over daily activities. Since the system needs to present many activities within a limited time, we compress activities into shorter sounds. The details of this are shown in the Implementation section.

BGM

The HomeOrgel play symbolic sounds in combination with the BGM of music boxes for following reasons: (1) enhancing the attraction of the music and (2) informing the user of the state of the music. When the system plays symbolic sounds without BGM, the music becomes quite boring for listeners after several minutes. Moreover, it is difficult for listeners to distinguish the end from the rest of the music.[1]

Usage scenarios

We introduce several scenarios using the HomeOrgel.

- Scenario 1: A father living away from his family comes home at midnight every day since he is quite busy at his business, meaning he cannot call his family as often he wants. One midnight, he thinks about his family and uses the HomeOrgel. He opens the cover after winding the spring. He can catch up with the activities of his family by hearing the music on the HomeOrgel: his children left home in the morning; his wife cooked before children came home. This allows the father to feel at ease.

- Scenario 2: Grandparents live in the country apart from other family members. They always want to see their grandchildren who just started primary school. On Sunday afternoon, they think about their grandchildren: "are they are at home or out?" The grandparents winded the spring and open the cover of the HomeOrgel. First, the HomeOrgel plays the chimes of the intercom, then plays many more sounds than they had expected. They guess that their

---

[1] The rest of the music here indicates the absence of any home activities for a period.

grandchildren's friends have come for a small party. Thus, they call their grandchildren later to ask about the event.

- Scenario 3: A daughter studying in her room happens to open the HomeOrgel after winding the spring a little. She hears several sounds: cutting vegetables on the board and sautéing in a pan. She can recognize that her mother just started cooking and leaves for the kitchen to help her mother.

IMPLEMENTATION

We developed a HomeOrgel prototype with the above features. The HomeOrgel device consists of several sensors and a speaker in a ready-made music box (Figure 3).

We attached a rotation sensor on the spring to measure its rotation angle, a magnetic sensor on the edge of the box to detect the opening/closing of the cover, and an acceleration sensor inside the cover to detect its tilt angle. These sensors are connected to a host PC (Windows XP) via a Phidgets Interface Kit. [2]

The HomeOrgel software can control the above sensors using the PhidgetServer[3] via the Phidget Interface Kit. The software controls the playing of the music based on the magnetic sensor, and adjusts the volume of music based on the value of the acceleration sensor; the system increases the volume when the cover is opened more widely. The software can extract past events in chronological order. The recall period is determined by number of time the spring is wound.

As mentioned in the previous section, the software compresses home activities into a shorter period as shown in Figure 4. First, we prepared symbolic sounds of home activities lasting no more than 5 seconds in consideration of the balance between simplicity and expressiveness.

There are three variables for the compression process: "rewind interval", "music interval" and "compression threshold of each event" (Table 1). Next, we explain these variables.

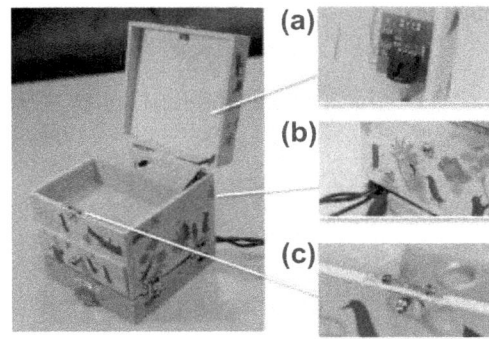

Figure 3. The HomeOrgel prototype: (a) acceleration sensor, (b) knob with a rotation sensor, (c) magnetic sensor.

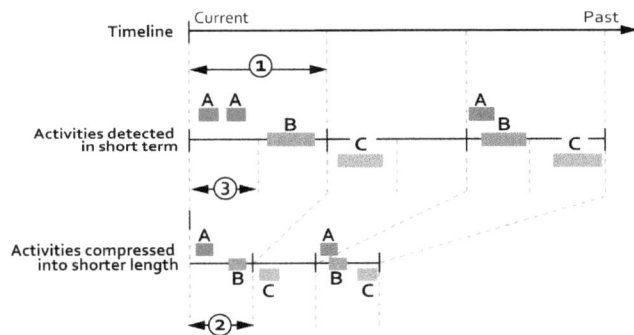

Figure 4. Activity compression procedure: (1) rewind interval of past activities (e.g., 1 h), (2) Music interval (e.g., 10 sec), (3) Compression threshold of each activity (e.g., 30 min).

Variable name	Range of value	Setting value
Rewind interval	1 minute —24 hours	1 hour
Music interval	1 seconds—1minutes	10 seconds
Compression threshold of each activity	1 minute —24 hours	30 minutes

Table 1. Variables of the HomeOrgel software.

Rewind interval

When a user winds the spring by a half-turn, the target activities presented by the HomeOrgel are recalled for a certain time interval, the "rewind interval" (Figure 4-1). We set the rewind interval at 1 hour in the prototype in consideration of its use to recall activities for approximately one day.

---

[2] http://www.phidgets.com/

[3] PhidgetServer: middleware for easy control of Phidget devices.

Music interval

When the HomeOrgel generates music, activities in the rewind interval are compressed into a shorter length, the "music interval". We calculated the music interval using the following formula: "music_interval = music_length/ (waking_hours/rewind_interval)".

We assumed the music length to be no more than several minutes (e.g., 2.5 minutes) and the waking hours per day as 16 hours. To present the home activities for a day within 2.5 minutes, we set the music interval at 10 seconds in the prototype. [4]

Compression threshold of each activity

When many activities are detected in a short term, the system needs to summarize them to avoid complicated aural presentations. The HomeOrgel functions to pack the multiple activities occurring within the "compression threshold" and generate the corresponding sounds simultaneously. We set the compression threshold at 30 min based on the following formula: "compression_threshold = rewind_interval/(music_interval / sound_length)". The length of the symbolic sounds is up to 5 seconds. [5]

SYSTEM INSTALLATION

We installed a simple activity recognition system in an actual house "Ocha House"[6] to verify the effectiveness of the HomeOrgel using actual data. We report the installation details in this section.

Sensor modules

First, we explain the installation of wireless sensor modules in Ocha House. Each module consists of a wireless communication module (Digi International XBee[7]) and a human detection sensor (Panasonic Electric Works NaPiOn) to detect user movements (Figure 5). We installed the sensor modules in various locations in Ocha House, including the entrance, passage, kitchen, dining room, living room, bedroom and bathroom (Figure 6 and Figure 7).

Ocha House has frames and catwalks suited to the installation of sensor modules and computers (Figure 5, left). Therefore, we attached sensor modules on the frame and catwalk to keep people's attention from the sensors. Figure 6 shows the sensor positions on the frames and their detection area: A (bedroom), B, C (living room) and D, E (dining room). Sensors on the catwalks detect users in J

(entrance), K (passage), L (changing room) and M (bathroom). We also installed four sensor modules under the cooking table in the kitchen. These sensors can detect users in F (in front of the stove), G, H (in front of the cutting board) and I (in front of the sink) as shown in Figure 7.

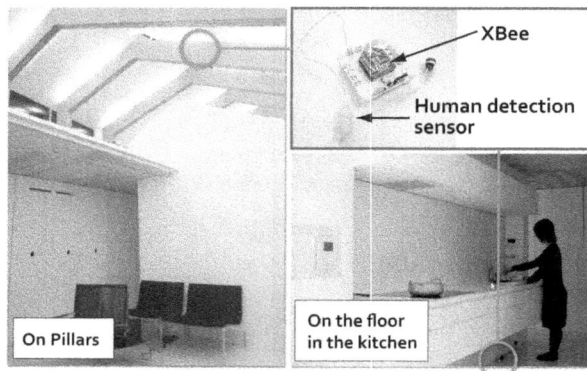

Figure 5. Installation of wireless sensor modules in Ocha House.

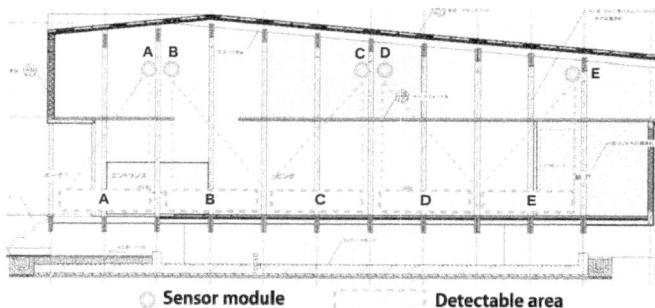

Figure 6. Sensor modules on frames and their detection areas.

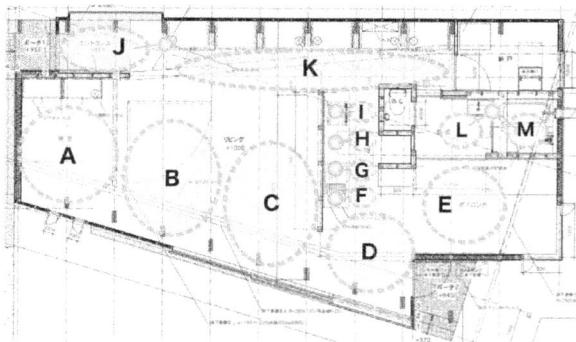

Figure 7. All sensor module detection areas.

---

[4] $150/ (16/1) = 9.375$ (sec)

[5] $60/ (10/5) = 30$ (min)

[6] Ocha House: an experimental smart house for evaluating ubiquitous computing applications in Ochanomizu University.

[7] XBee: a wireless communication module based on the 802.15.4/ZigBee standard.

Middleware

We developed two types of middleware, "XBeeServer"[8] and "OchaHouseManager", to control the above sensor modules. Figure 8 shows our system architecture. The XBeeServer collects sensor data from XBee modules (XBeeEndPoints) and translates them into simple messages. The OchaHouseManager receives these messages from the XBeeServer via TCP Sockets and converts them into location/status parameters (e.g., living room/motion, entrance/open) and saves them to the database (Microsoft SQL Server).

The HomeOrgel software determines the recall period by the number of times the spring is wound and extracts the relevant past data from the database. The HomeOrgel estimates the activity (or "event") from the detection areas of sensors. The mapping of detection areas and events is as follows: "working" (in the living room: B~C shown in Figure 7), "eating" (in the dining room: D~E), "cooking" (in the kitchen, in front of the stove: F), "cutting vegetables" (in the kitchen, in front of the cutting table: G~H), "washing dishes" (in the kitchen, in front of the sink: I), "coming home/going out/receiving a guest" (in the entrance: J).

Since the motion sensors continuously react for a while after detecting human motion, our system distinguishes activity from noise using the "activity threshold"; that is, activities are recorded only when they continue beyond the threshold. We set the activity threshold at 15 seconds because a user tended to perform activities at the same location for more than 15 seconds in our preliminary observations.

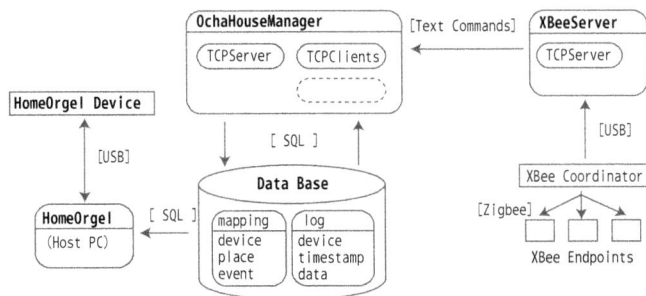

Figure 8. Sensor modules on frames and their detection areas.

EVALUATION

To verify the performance of aural representations by the HomeOrgel, we undertook an evaluation from two perspectives: (1) performance in informing users about home activities by sounds alone" and (2) attractiveness of the HomeOrgel music.

That is, the goal of the evaluation was to explore the two following questions: (A) "Can the subject understand the content of activities by hearing sounds from the HomeOrgel?" and (B) "Did the subject receive a favorable impression from the HomeOrgel music?"

Method

First, an experimenter spent seven hours in Ocha House as shown in Table 3 and used the system to create activity data. Next, the experimenter had each test subject listen to the HomeOrgel music generated from these activities. We selected 7 test subjects (1 male and 6 females, age 22-27). None of them had ever heard the HomeOrgel. Before starting the experiment, we explained the basic functions of the HomeOrgel to the subjects as follows:

- The HomeOrgel represents past home activities using sound.

- The recall period is about 7 hours a day.

- The home activities occurring in 1 hour are compressed into 10 seconds of music.

Next, we obtained feedback from the subjects both by questionnaires and oral discussion. First, the experimenter asked the subjects to answer the two following questions while listening to the HomeOrgel music:

- Q1: "Please write all sounds you hear?"

- Q2: "Please write all events you imagine occurring from the sounds?"

After hearing the HomeOrgel music, the subjects were asked to answer the three following questions:

- Q3: "Please write the time period in which activities most frequently occurred?"

- Q4: "Please write all sounds that you cannot understand?"

- Q5:"Do you experience a pleasant feeling while listening to the HomeOrgel music? (1: not at all - 5: very pleasant)"

Table 2 shows the mapping of activities, symbolic sounds and locations. Table 3 shows actual data for home activities and generated symbolic sounds in chronological order. Figure 9 shows the detailed transitions between activities and the generated sounds.

---

[8] XBeeServer: middleware for easy control of XBee devices.

Location	Activity	Symbolic Sound
Living room	Reading a book	Flipping through a book
Dining room	Eating	Dish clatter, munching food
Kitchen (stove)	Cooking using a stove	Igniting a stove, shaking a pan
Kitchen (cooking table)	Cooking using a cutting table	Cutting veggies slowly/quickly
Kitchen (sink)	Cooking using water, washing dishes	Running water, washing dishes
Entrance	Coming/leaving home, Welcoming a guest	Intercom

Table 2. The mapping of activities, symbolic sounds, and locations.

Time	Actual activity	Symbolic sound
14:30~15:30	Coming home, working in living room	Intercom, flipping a book
15:30~16:30	Working in living room, opening refrigerator door	Flipping through a book, cutting veggies slowly, shaking a pan
16:30~17:30	Working in living room	None
17:30~18:30	Working in living room	Flipping through a book
18:30~19:30	Working in living room, opening refrigerator door	Igniting a stove
19:30~20:30	Going to shopping, coming home, cooking	intercom, cutting veggies quickly, igniting a stove
20:30~21:30	Having guests, cooking, eating	Igniting a stove, running water, cutting veggies slowly, dish clatter, munching food

Table 3. The actual data for home activities and generated symbolic sounds in the experiment.

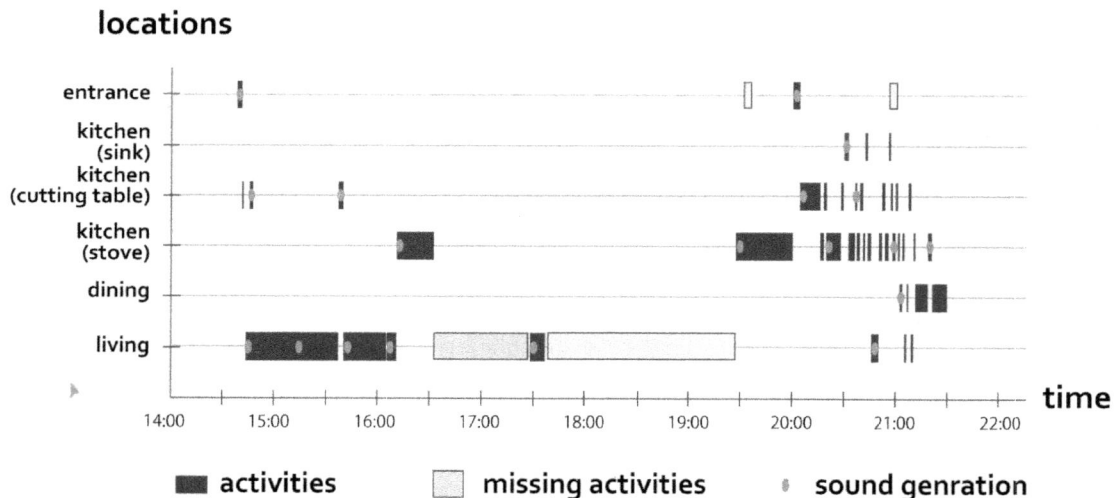

Figure 9. Detailed transitions between activities and generated sounds in the experiment.

Result and Consideration

The results of Q1 - "Please write all sounds you hear?" - are shown in Table 4. All subjects wrote symbolic sounds related to entrance and water, and six subjects wrote the sounds related to cutting/cooking.

Next, the results of Q2 - "Please write events you imagine occurring from the sounds" - are shown in Table 5. All subjects wrote "cooking", six subjects wrote "coming home/receiving guests". Since these answers include expressions such as "cutting vegetables using a kitchen knife" and "washing dishes", some subjects seemed to imagine the details of the cooking events. Although the experimenter did not indicate subjects to write activities in chronological order, one subject answered with almost the exact order: "First, someone comes home, next he/she starts cooking, and finally he/she eats something". As shown in Table 3, this answer corresponds with actual data of home activities. These results suggest that subjects could understand the activities just by hearing the sounds from the HomeOrgel. In contrast, some subjects could not understand the precise activities from the sounds in several cases. For example, although all subjects could recognize "water sounds" in Q1, they imagined different activities, such as "washing dishes" or "running a bath," in Q2. In addition, three subjects answered in Q4 that the water sounds were difficult to understand as they imagined many candidate events (Table 6). Considering this feedback, we saw the need to provide more concrete aural presentations for activities related to water.

Similarly, the intercom sounds were interpreted as multiple activities: "Someone came home" and "Having guests" in Q2. However, since both activities are related to entering the house, the current mapping may be sufficient to represent an "entrance event".

Next, in Q3 - "Please write the time period in which the activities most frequently occurred "- six subjects answered "the last three hours". This result corresponds with the experimenter's behavior as shown in Table 3.

In Q 5 - "Do you experience a pleasant feeling while listening to the HomeOrgel music? (1: not at all - 5: very pleasant)"- five subjects answered "5: very pleasant" or "4: rather pleasant" (M: 3.71, SD: 0.88). Additional comments were as follow: "I had fun imagining the behavior of the person" and "the representation of home activities using sounds like a music box is comforting". These results suggest that most subjects had a favorable impression of the HomeOrgel music.

Evaluation summary

In this evaluation, subjects could understand the correct activities and their frequency of occurrence. Moreover, most subjects had a favorable impression of the HomeOrgel music. These results indicate that the HomeOrgel performs sufficiently well for users to look back on home activities casually.

Category	Raw Answers (number)
Sound of entrance	"Ding Dong"(3), "sound of intercom"(1), "chime"(3)
Water sound	"water sound"(3), "sound of flowing water"(1), "splash"(1), "sound of bathroom"(1),
Sound of cutting	"cutting using knife"(4),"cutting something on cutting board"(1), "thock-thock-thock (cooking)"(1)
Sound of using fire in the kitchen	"sound of frying"(4), "sizzling"(1), "sound of burning"(1)
No sound	

Table 4. The categorized answers to question (1): Please write all sounds you hear?

Category	Raw Answers (number)
Cooking	"cooking"(7), "cutting veggies with knife"(1), "pan frying something"(2), "washing dishes"(1)
Coming home or receiving a guest	"someone came home"(3), "having guests"(1), "someone visited"(1), "someone visited or the resident came home"(1)
Eating	"eating something"(1), "having food"(1)
Others	"turning on taps"(2), "running a bath"(2)

Table 5. The categorized answers to question (2): "Please write all events you imagine occurring from the sounds? "

Sound	Answer number	Reason
Water sound	3	I don't know the difference between bathroom sounds and cooking sounds.
Rest of sounds	2	I don't know the difference between absence and sleeping.
Intercom sound	1	I don't know the difference between the sound of receiving guests and coming home.
Others	1	The volume was not loud enough to hear clearly.

Table 6. The categorized answers to question (4): "Please write symbolic sounds that you cannot understand?"

183

DISCUSSION

We discuss the HomeOrgel based on the results of the evaluation in following aspects: " Extension of sound expression", "Extension of sensors" and "Controlling variables".

Extension of sound expression

As mentioned above, our system used symbolic sounds in consideration of sound quality and privacy issues. However, some subjects wanted more realistic, sounds such as conversation, laughter, footsteps and the sound of typing on a PC keyboard. Here, we discuss the possibility of applying such sounds to the HomeOrgel.

First, we discuss the possible improvement of the HomeOrgel in terms of the "improvement of symbolic sounds" and "expression based on the frequency of activities." Next, we discuss the advantage of using "family voices" and its potential problems. We also discuss the possibility of designing additional sounds to capture the "characteristic sounds of each family".

Improvement of symbolic sounds

In the evaluation, subjects could generally understand the activities taking place and their frequency of occurrence. This indicates that the symbolic sounds are effective in representing home activities.

However the results of the evaluation also reveal limitations to the symbolic sounds with the subjects having difficulty in understand the activities based solely on water sounds. To avoid these limitations, we need to provide more concrete aural presentations for activities related to water. To this end, we plan to use a combination of symbolic sounds. For example, we would express the activity of "washing dishes" by combining several sounds sequentially: "water flowing", "dish clatter" and "dish cleaning". Similarly, we would express the activity of "taking shower" by combining the sounds of "turning on the faucet" and "water droplets falling like rain".

Expression based on activity frequency

Our current system applied fixed parameters (e.g., volume and pan) for each activity. We plan to vary these parameters based on the frequency of activities for further expressiveness. For example, the system would increase the volume of sounds when (1) the same activity occurs more than once in a short period or (2) a "rare" activity occurs after a long interval (e.g., someone comes into an area which is seldom frequented).

Since excessive changes to the sound parameters may cause difficulties for users to actually hear the music and recognize the activities, we should consider the balance between simplicity and expressiveness.

Using "family" voices.

Since some subjects wanted family voices (e.g., conversation and laughter) in the evaluation, we also considered the possibility of using family voices. By hearing the voices of their family members, listeners can feel the presence of their families and become familiar with the system. Additionally, listeners may recognize the family status more accurately from voice tones. However, the system requires the attachment of many microphones in the home to record the voices.

Moreover, these raw voices may cause privacy issues. To avoid these problems, we consider limiting the recording locations (e.g., only at the entrance and living room).and modifying the recorded voices (e.g., playing voices backwards).

Characteristic sounds of each family.

Each home has its own characteristic sound depending on each family's habits (e.g., child's hobby). These sounds may help listeners recall their family members more directly. For example, when a user has a piano at home, he/she can imagine that his/her daughter is practicing the piano from piano sounds. Moreover, when a user has a cat at home, he/she may imagine the cat's status (e.g., eating and playing) by hearing the cat's voice based on its status. However, these extensions need additional sensors to detect each event (e.g., installing a magnetic sensor on the cover of a piano). We will discuss this point in greater detail in the following section.

Extension of sensors

In this evaluation, the activities the system detected were occasionally incorrect because we applied a simple detection method based on location. For example, when the experimenter went to the refrigerator to get a drink, the HomeOrgel generated the sound of "cutting vegetables" because the refrigerator was located in front of the cooking table. This problem can be solved by attaching additional sensors at various locations (e.g., installing a magnetic sensor on the refrigerator).

Moreover the system occasionally failed to detect activities. For example, the system failed to detect the activity for "16:30-17:30" when the experimenter was working in the living room (Table 3). This problem is caused by the characteristic of motion sensors in only detecting human "movement". Therefore, the sensor could not detect the experimenter because she hardly moved while working on the PC at "16:30-17:30" (Figure 9). Similarly, the current system cannot distinguish staying at home without movement (e.g., sleeping) from going out from home. To solve these limitations, we plan to apply a recognition method based on historical data of user's movements between locations For example; the system may estimate the user's status using the "final location" before movement ceased: when the final location is an entrance, the user probably left home, since he/she hardly stays at entrance for long periods. Similarly, when the final location is a bedroom, the user is probably sleeping. As mentioned above, the system needs additional sensors to extend sound expression. For example, we need to attach a magnetic sensor into the cover of the piano to detect the activity of "playing a piano". However, we should take into consideration the difficulties associated with installation in an everyday household environment. The results of this evaluation verified that the current system is effective to some degree because the subjects could understand the correct chronological order of the experimenter's activities. We should improve the system further through consideration of the trade-off between the accuracy of event detection and the number of sensors.

Controlling variables

We discuss here some variables of the HomeOrgel: "rewind interval" and "music interval". In the current system, the home activities for a 1-hour period (=rewind interval) are compressed into 10 seconds (=music interval) of music to help users recall activities from approximately one day. However, we may need to change these settings based on situations. For example, a shorter rewind interval (e.g., 10 minutes) is appropriate in the case of scenario 3 because the user here wants to check current home activities. Although these variables can be changed by software settings, we plan to provide more intuitive methods to control them. For example, when we attach a RFID reader inside the device and RFID tags onto small objects, the user can select settings simply by placing the object[9] into the device.

RELATED WORKS

Bottles[7] is an interface to access digital information using glass bottles as "containers" and "controls". Although this system focuses on different applications from our system, the basic approach of using familiar objects for representing sound information is similar.

Several research projects have adopted visual content to represent home activities. For example, Video Window System [4] records the users' rooms using video cameras, and shares the data among users via a permanent connection. Although this system allows users to provide and receive complete information, it may cause privacy problems. Additionally, users need to focus on the display to obtain the information.

There have been several research projects that represent home activities using ambient information. Digital family portrait [12] provides qualitative visualizations of a family member's daily life. Leveraging a familiar household object, the picture frame, this system populates the frame with iconic imagery summarizing for several weeks. The ambientROOM [8] is an interface to information for processing in the background of awareness. This

information is displayed through various subtle displays of light and sound. Although these ambient displays can solve problems of privacy and user disturbance, users may have difficulty in understanding multiple simultaneous activities as they need to learn the mapping between activities and representations in advance. In contrast, our system can provide clear mappings between sounds and activities using symbolic sounds.

There have also been several research projects that represent home activities using sounds. Music Monitor [15] illustrated how music can be used to balance attention between two active rooms in a home, with an initial focus between the kitchen and living room. InPhase [16] proposed a new method of communicating the "happy coincidences" between a pair of remote locations using sounds. While these systems represent rather limited activities, HomeOrgel represents a wide range of activities in the home using symbolic sounds. Moreover, a user can understand most activities simply by listening to the corresponding sounds without any advance study of the mapping. Additionally, our system can help users look back on past activities easily using techniques common to the control of a music box.

CONCLUSION

This paper proposed a music-box type interface, "HomeOrgel", which can express various activities in the home using sound. We developed the HomeOrgel prototype, which consisted of several sensors and a speaker in a ready-made music box, and installed a simple activity recognition system in an actual house, "Ocha House". Based on the actual data collected in Ocha House, we performed an evaluation study to verify the performance of the aural representations of the HomeOrgel. Results showed that subjects could understand most activities correctly as well as their frequency of occurrence just by listening to the HomeOrgel music. Moreover, most subjects had a favorable impression of the music. These results indicate that the performance of the HomeOrgel was adequate for the users to review and recall home activities on a casual level. Our current aim is to further improve the HomeOrgel system in terms of sounds, sensors, and interaction.

ACKNOWLEDGMENTS

This project is partly supported by JST PRESTO program.

REFERENCES

1. Blattner, M.M., D.A.Sumikawa and R.M.Greenberg: Earcons and Icons:Their Structure and Common Design Principles, Human-Computer Interaction,Vol.4, No.1, 11-44 (1989).

2. Cook,D., Schmitter-Edgecombe,M., Crandall,M., Sanders,C., Thomas,B.: Collecting and disseminating smart home sensor data in the CASAS project, Proceedings of the CHI Workshop on Developing Shared Home Behavior Datasets to Advance HCI and Ubiquitous Computing Research(2009).

---

[9] Many music boxes have a space for holding small objects

3. Dodge,C., The bed: a medium for intimate communication, CHI '97 Extended Abstracts on Human factors in computing systems: looking to the future, 22-27 (1997).

4. Fish, R.S., Kraut, R.E. and Chalfonte, B.L.: The VideoWindow system in informal communication, Proceedings of the 1990 ACM conference on Computer-supported cooperative work, 1 -11 (1990).

5. Gaver, W.W.: The SonicFinder: An Interface That Uses Auditory Icons, Human-Computer Interaction, Vol.4, No.1, 67-94 (1989).

6. Hirai S., Keyaki F. and Fujii G.:Toward for Realization of an Entertainment Bathroom in Daily Life, IPSJ SIG Technical Report, vol.2006 No.24(EC-3), 1-8(in Japanese).

7. Ishii, H., Mazalek, A. and Lee, J.: Bottles as a minimal interface to access digital information, Extended Abstracts of CHI 2001 , 187-188 (2001).

8. Ishii, H., Wisneski, C., Brave, S., Dahley, A., Gorbet, M., Ullmer, B. and Yarin, P.: ambientROOM: integrating Ambient Media with Architectural Space, Summary on CHI 1998, 173-174 (1998).

9. Kidd, C.D., Orr, R., Abowd, G.D., Atkeson, C.G., Essa, I.A., MacIntyre, B., Mynatt, E., Information, T. E. S.C. and Newstetter1, W.: The Aware Home: A Living Laboratory for Ubiquitous Computing Research, Adjunct Proceedings of the Second International Workshop on Cooperative Buildings, Integrating Information, Organization, and Architecture, 191-198 (1999).

10. Kuznetsov, S. and Paulos, E.: UpStream: motivating water conservation with low-cost water flow sensing and persuasive displays, Proceedings of CHI 2010, 1851-1860 (2010).

11. Oki.M, Tsukada.K, Kurihara.K, and Siio.I, HomeOrgel: Interactive music box for aural representation, Adjunct Proceedings of Ubicomp 2008, 45-46 (2008).

12. Rowan, J. and Mynatt, E.D.: Digital Family Portrait Field Trial: Support for Aging in Place, Proceedings of CHI2005, 521-530 (2005).

13. Sposaro,F. and Tyson,G., iFall: An android application for fall monitoring and response, Proceedings of IEEE Eng Med Biol Soc, 6119-6122 （2009）.

14. Strong,R. and Gaver, W.Feather: Scent, and Shaker: Supporting simple intimacy, Proceedings of CSCW 1996, 29-30(1996).

15. Tran, Q.T. and Mynatt, E.D.: Music Monitor: Ambient Musical Data for the Home, Extended Proceedings of the HOIT 2000, 85-92 (2000).

16. Tsujita, H., Tsukada, K. and Itiro, S.: InPhase: Evaluation of a Communication System Focused on"Happy Coincidences"of Daily Behaviors, Proceedings of CHI 2010, 2481-2490 (2010).

17. Yamazaki.T: Ubiquitous Home: Real-life Testbed for Home Context-Aware Service, Proceedings of Tridentcom2005 (First International Conference on Testbeds and Reserch Infrastructures for the DEvelopment of NeTworks and COMmunities), 54-59(2005).

Cooking Support with Information Projection onto Ingredient

Yu Suzuki
Kyoto Sangyo University
Motoyama, Kamigamo,
Kita-ku, Kyoto 603-8555
JAPAN
suzu@cse.kyoto-su.ac.jp

Shunsuke Morioka
Kyoto Sangyo University
Motoyama, Kamigamo,
Kita-ku, Kyoto 603-8555
JAPAN

Hirotada Ueda
Kyoto Sangyo University
Motoyama, Kamigamo,
Kita-ku, Kyoto 603-8555
JAPAN
ueda@cc.kyoto-su.ac.jp

ABSTRACT

Recipes once only appearing in cookbooks are being digitalized, now accessible through PCs and on mobile devices, including smart phones. Researchers endeavor to provide details of the cooking processes in these computerized recipes, however, cooking support systems tailored to novice cooks remain a matter of research. This paper details a cooking support system for novices that specifically takes into consideration the needs of inexperienced cooks. This system provides concrete instructions for cooking by superimposing a cutting line and a knife CG over ingredients. In addition, a conversational Robot "Phyno" provides additional verbal and gestural support. This system not only provides detailed visual support for cooking novices, but also contributes to enhancement of the safety of those novice cooks. This paper explores the advantages and drawbacks of this system and reflects on its adequacy based on trial evidence.

Author Keywords

Human robot interaction; recipe presentation; visual and acoustic instructions.

ACM Classification Keywords

H.5.m. Information Interfaces and Presentation (e.g. HCI): Miscellaneous

General Terms

Human Factors; Design.

INTRODUCTION

Numerous researchers in the Human Computer Interaction (HCI) field are actively working to create future living environments. Similar to the work at other universities and institutes, our research group has created a an experimental house named "Ξ Home" (Figure 1) in one of its research buildings and is conducting comprehensive research on the living environment within this house. We aim to create an experimental house where livelihood support can be provided from any location in the house, whether it be the living room, bathroom, or even the restroom. Especially, we have used a kitchen and conducted a research for cooking support [8].

Recipes once only appearing in cookbooks are being digitalized, now made accessible through PCs and on mobile devices, including smart phones. Websites, such as Cookpad[1], allows viewers to browse through these recipes online. Moving beyond simply providing a recipe online, some researchers [9, 11] have endeavored to provide explicit details of the cooking processes on LCDs. With the passage of time, digital cooking systems continue to evolve, however, systems tailored to novice cooks remain a matter of research.

We have attempted to address this issue by developing a novice-friendly cooking support system that takes into consideration some of the difficulties that inexperience cooks face. One large stumbling block for those just learning to cook is the unintelligibility of cooking methods provided in recipes. For instance, novices would find it difficult to fillet a fish without being shown how to do it, even if the steps for filleting a fish were written within the recipe. We hypothesize that visual presentation of cooking instructions would prove more effective for novices because text-based instructions are difficult to understand. We have developed a cooking system that superimposes images over cooking ingredients to help guide food preparation and cooking. In this paper, we describe our cooking support system and a concrete example of the instructions.

RELATED WORK

There is an abundant amount of research being conducted on how to support cooking activities [5, 11]. Hamada et al., [3] developed a task model from a cookbook as a challenge for modeling cook's activities in the kitchen. Based on the task model, a cooking support system using LCDs [9] was developed.

Other researchers aim to improve cooking efficiency through systems that recognize the position or type of foods [4], and systems that records the users cooking and also play video of the cooking processes [9]. In addition, researchers aim to improve the interaction in the kitchen. For instance, the augmented reality kitchen [2] provides visual information around

[1] Cookpad http://cookpad.com/

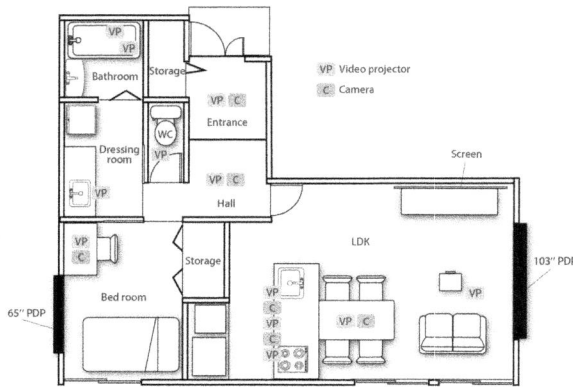

Figure 1. Layout of our experimental home "Ξ Home"

the kitchen and Ju et al. [6] has introduced an interactive cookbook.

The majority of the systems described above utilize LCDs or projection on to a tables to provide visual representations of recipes. We suppose that these systems do not provide cooking novices with adequate support. We aim to present a cooking instruction easily understandable for the novices. Through the system described below, we have aimed to provide a cooking environment where inexperienced cooks can receive easy-to-understand instructions so that they can complete successfully complete a recipe.

DESIGN OF COOKING SUPPORT SYSTEM

We aim to develop a novice-friendly cooking support system. One major issue particular to novices is unfamiliarity of techniques often found in recipes. For instance, often times when the preparation of an ingredient in recipes is described in a recipe, the name of the technique may be noted, but how to perform this technique is not described. Therefore, a person new to cooking who is not proficient in techniques such as icho-giri (cutting into quarters), tanzaku-giri (cutting into rectangles) or fish filleting may know what the technique is, but cannot perform the technique to satisfaction without being shown how to do it. In addition, cooking support systems include a problem of input interfaces as many researcher mentioned. When cooking, it is difficult to use a mouse or keyboard because the cook's hands are tied up with the cooking process.

Therefore, our cooking support system attempts to address these two issues with the following approaches:

- Overlaying the cooking instruction over ingredients to guide cooks in performing cooking techniques

- Equipping the system with an conversational robot

Overlaying the Cooking Instruction over an Ingredient

In order to help cooks understand how to prepare an ingredient for a recipe, our system superimposes an image over cooking ingredients as a guide. The types of guiding images can be broken down into three categories: process instruction images, procedural images, and progression images. Process instruction images include those that show how to cut an item,

such as computer graphics (CG) cutting line, accompanied with an image of a moving knife that demonstrates how to maneuver the knife. Procedural images provide text or graphics, such as arrows, that show the steps in preparing an item, such as turning an ingredient over. Progression images link steps in a recipe. If it is necessary for an item to be transferred to a dish for instance, text will appear instructing the cook to do so.

With such detailed instruction as provided by this system, even a novice cooks can successfully complete a recipe from start to finish with ease. Furthermore, the system optimizes the safety of the cook in two ways. First, by providing superimposed images in the cooking area, the cook can keep their attention on the cooking process. When vertically-placed LCD interfaces are utilized in cooking support systems, the cook must divert their gaze between the cooking table and the LCD to receive directions. Unlike these systems, our system allows the cook to stay focused and concentrate the task at hand. When using a vertically-placed LCD like previous researches, the cook has to move his/her gaze between the cooking table and the LCD many times. On the other hand, the system improves the safety because it decreases the gaze movement and lets the cook concentrate his/her works. Secondly, our system encourages the cook to properly use cutting tools without injury. With interfaces that use video to demonstrate how to cut ingredients, we have found that novices tend to focus more on the object they are cutting rather than proper and safe use of the cooking implements, potentially leading to injury. By using a CG movie of a knife, for instance, novices can acquire the skills to use knives safely, thereby enhancing the safety of the cook and preventing injury.

Equipping the System with an Conversational Robot

We used a robot to interact with a computer because current interfaces are not suitable for use with the kitchen. There are other two reasons why we adopted the robot for interaction.

One of the authors of this paper previously conducted research in installing a cooking support system in an experimental home using a conventional robot [10, 11] in what was referred to as "ubiquitous home" at the National Institute for Computer Technology (NICT). In the NICT project, it was found that the robot successfully allowed users to proceed through the cooking process without the necessity of a mouse or keyboard. The robot also significantly decreased the amount of mistakes that users made while cooking process as well. Finally, when a user made a mistake while cooking, the robot could pinpoint the mistake by having a conversation with the user. In addition, it displayed a recording of the user cooking to compare against a pre-installed video showing how to cook so that the user could discover where they made a mistake during the process. Due to the successes of this project, we decided to adopt a robot in our cooking system.

Another reason we decided to utilize an interactive robot in the cooking system is because the potential for a robot to serve as a cooperative partner. While spoken interaction between a user and cooking support system can be achieved through the use of a speaker and microphone, this leaves the

188

Figure 2. Photograph of entire kitchen facility

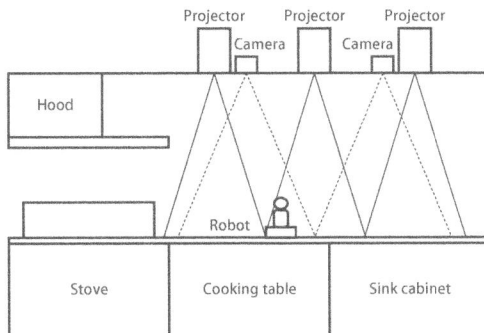

Figure 3. Diagram of kitchen from an elevated view

Figure 4. Appearance of a conversational robot Phyno

user feeling detached. Recently, new role of the robot has been proposed; the role of the robot shifts from "human-like interaction partner" to a social entity which stimulates constructive, cooperative activities between people and improves the quality of their interpersonal interactions [1]. We believe that introducing the conversational robot into a cooking support system enables to achieve conversation without empty feeling and to stimulate the cooking activity.

THE KITCHEN ENVIRONMENT AND THE ROBOT

Kitchen Environment
The kitchen environment (Figure 2 and 3) is equipped with a sink cabinet (user's left), cooking table (center), and stove with a hood (user's right). Two cameras and three projectors have been installed in the ceiling in addition to lighting equipment. The camera and projector have been strategically placed so that footage of the entire kitchen, except for the hooded-stove, can be captured. We used high-speed cameras in order to record the quick movements of the kitchen users. For safety purposes, the kitchen is always kept highly illuminated. We use high-power projectors so that fine picture detail can be provided in the bright kitchen environment.

Conversational Robot "Phyno"
We installed a Phyno robot, a small conversational robot in the kitchen (Figure 4). Measuring 260mm × 210mm × 340 mm and weighing 3 kg, it is placed on a control box containing computer. Phyno does not move but has a degree of freedom (DOF) totaling to five - 3 DOF in its head and 1 DOF in the arms and torso respectively. Phyno can record images

with the movement of its eyes, as well as sounds, because its head is equipped with a camera and microphone. Phyno is controlled by a computer via RS-232C on the control box.

With the purpose of capturing the cook's speech, even in the noisy kitchen environment, we installed a separate speaker and microphone. With the speaker and microphone, the cook and Phyno can hear each other. We placed Phyno at the back of the cooking table so as not to interfere with the cooking work. We used an open-source large vocabulary CSR engine Julius [7] to recognize the cook's speech.

COOKING SUPPORT FOR FILLETING A FISH
From the viewpoint of a novice, cooking a fish requires some complicated techniques. Therefore, we developed a support system to guide a novice through filleting a fish.

Cooking Process
The cooking support system instructs cooks through projected CG, speech, and the Phyno. CG is projected on the cooking table and speech is outputted by the external speaker. The following details the steps for filleting a fish provided by the cooking system.

Step 1: Starting cooking
The system instructs the cook to put a fish on the cutting board through speech commands of Phyno and CG projections. After detecting the fish on the cutting board, the system displays a CG and announces in speech "Let's start cooking. Good luck!" to encourage the cook. At this point, a bounding box appears around the fish to demonstrate to the cook that the system has properly detected the fish.

Step 2: Removing scales
The system instructs the cook on how to remove the scales utilizing CGs.

Step 3: Flipping the fish
The system instructs the cook to flip the fish in order to remove scales on both sides of the fish. In addition to speech, a CG of an arrow is shown on the fish as illustrated in Figure 5. This allows the cook to easily understand the process. After the fish is flipped, the instructions from step 2 are repeated so that both sides of the fish are scaled.

189

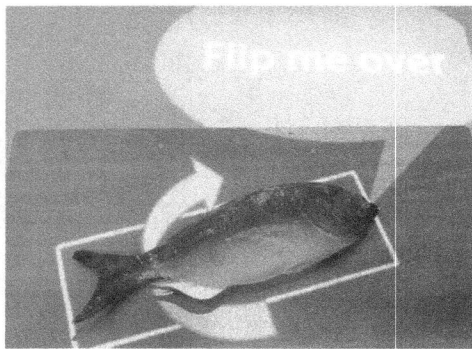

Figure 5. Projection of an arrow over the fish instructing to flip it

Step 4: Removing the offal

The system instructs the cook to remove the internal organs. The system projects a CG of a cutting line and demonstrates how to move the knife, providing detailed instruction on how to remove the entrails from the fish, as illustrated in Figure 6, to facilitate a novice in this potentially complicated task.

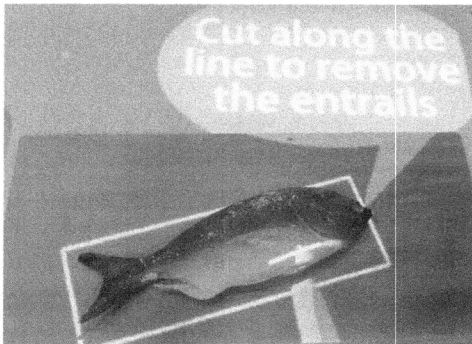

Figure 6. Projection of a cutting line and movement of the knife over the fish

Step 5: Removing remaining offal

The system instructs the cook to wash the fish in the sink to remove the remaining offal. In this case, speech is used instead of a CG projection because it is difficult to maintain a CG on the fish when it is being moved to the sink.

Step 6: Cutting off the head of the fish

The system instructs the cook to cut off the head of the fish. The system projects CG of a cutting line and knife onto the fish for cutting off the head of the fish.

Step 7: Inserting the knife into the abdomen

We adopted a cooking technique for effectively removing the flesh from the fish that requires a knife to be inserted into both the abdomen and back of the fish. First, the system instructs the cook to insert the knife into the abdomen of the fish by projecting onto the fish a CG of a cutting line and image showing how to maneuver the knife.

Step 8: Rotating the fish horizontally

To maintain the safety of the cook, the system instructs the cook to rotate the fish 180 degrees in the horizontal direction. Then, the system projects a CG of an arrow around the fish (Figure 7) so that the cook can easily understand this step.

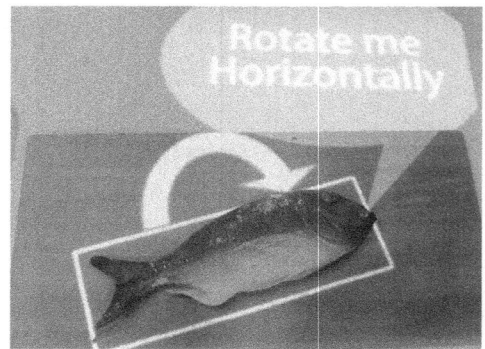

Figure 7. Arrow projected over the fish instructing to rotate it

Step 9: Inserting the knife into the back of the fish

In order to cut off all of the flesh from the fish properly, the system instructs the cook to insert the knife into the back of the fish by projecting a CG cutting line and showing how to move the knife.

Step 10: Finishing cooking

After all of the steps are complete, the system announced through both speech and a CG, "Completed. Well done."

Implementation

In order to determine whether a step in the cooking process has been completed or not, we have installed functions into the system to both recognize the fish and judge whether or not a step has been completed or not. Detecting the fish is also important so that the CG projections, such as cutting lines, can be properly calibrated. The system can use a cue from the cook as the judgment because it can recognize the cook's speech. However, cooking novices have worry whether they have proceeded the cooking process well or not if putting the judgment in the cook's hand. Therefore, the system eliminates the concern by asking the cook whether s/he finished the process or not. The judgment has to be implemented to achieve this. While cooking processes may vary with fish of different sizes or species, currently the system is only equipped to handle certain fish.

Fish recognition

The system utilizes two computer-vision techniques: a background-differencing technique and a pattern-matching method.

First, the system detects objects on the cooking table using a background-differencing technique. Prior to cooking, it captures an image of the cooking table to use as a background image (Figure 8(a)). The system then takes another photo when something is put on the table at the start of cooking to use as an input image (Figure 8(b)). With background-differencing, it extracts a foreground image (Figure 8(c)) from the background image to isolate the input image. Then, labeling (Figure 8(d)) is done to detect multiple objects included in the foreground image. The system extracts object images after detecting the contour definition of each detective object by analyzing their rotation on the smallest rectangle. The rotational angle is used to determine the direction of the fish.

(a) Background image captured in advance

(b) Input image

(c) Extracted foreground image

(d) Labeling and contour definition

(e) Extracted object image (1)

(f) Extracted object image (2)

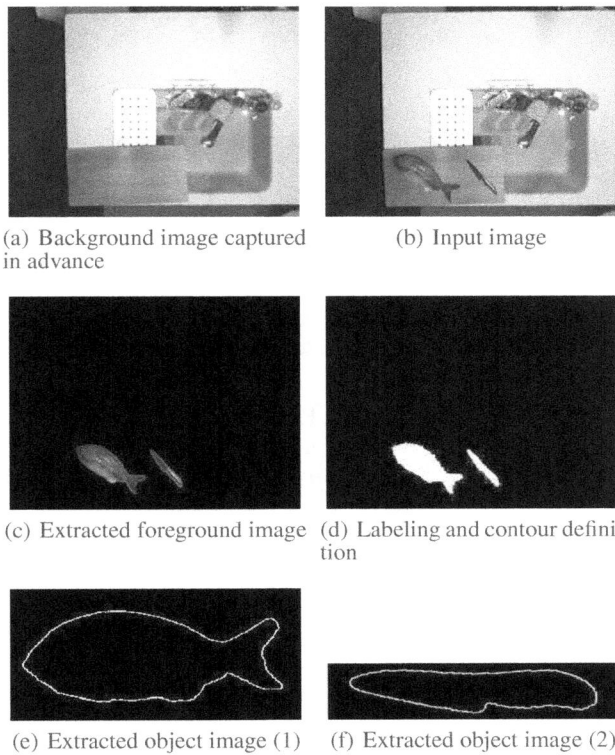

Figure 8. How to detect objects put on the cooking table

(a) Template image of a fish

(b) Hand image caused false identification

(c) Object (fish) image divided into right and left

Figure 9. Images using in template matching

Next, to identify whether previously extracted objects (Figure 8(e) and 8(f)) are fish or not, the system utilizes a template matching technique. The system tries to match the extracted image to a template image of a fish stored in the system in advance (Figure 9(a)). While the system is successful in distinguishing between a knife and a fish, it has difficulties discriminating between the cooks' hands (Figure 9(b)) and fish because the shape of the hands is similar to the shape of fish. We have developed a technique that divides captured images into right and left parts (i.e., head and tail of fish) and then respectively matches them with images stored in the system (Figure 9(c)). Consequently, we succeeded to decrease the incidence of misidentification of items and increase the recognition rate of the system higher than simpler methods employed in the past.

The system temporarily halts the CG projection when the camera is capturing images as projected images can complicate the recognition result. Since the detection process is relatively quick, the cook can continue cooking without difficulties.

Determining the completion of cooking processes
Some judgment techniques [4] have been explored. However, it is difficult to automatically judge all steps. Therefore, we have developed a hybrid technique that combines image processing and speech recognition.

This technique is completed in two steps. First, the system implements image processing to determine if a cook is touching an ingredient or not. The system detects the ingredient

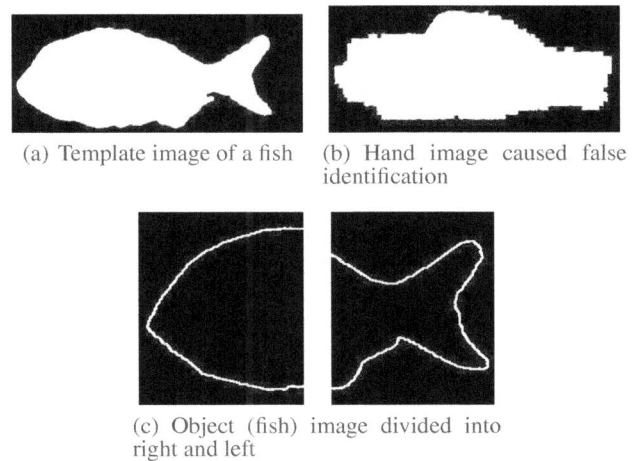

and its state by the background differencing technique in the same way as the fish recognition. The system judges as during cooking when the cook is touching on the ingredient (Figure 10(a)). On the other hand, it judges as finished when finishing touching on the ingredient (Figure 10(b)).

The second step utilizes speech interaction. Phyno prompts the cook for a response by asking, "Have you finished this step?" once it has judged through image processing that the cook is no longer touching the ingredient. If the cook answers "Yes.", the system will judge as the process is finished. If s/he answers "Not yet.", the system will start again from the first judgment.

This two-step judging technique improves the efficiency of the cooking system in determining the completion of cooking steps. Furthermore, cook anxiety can be relieved through communication with the Phyno.

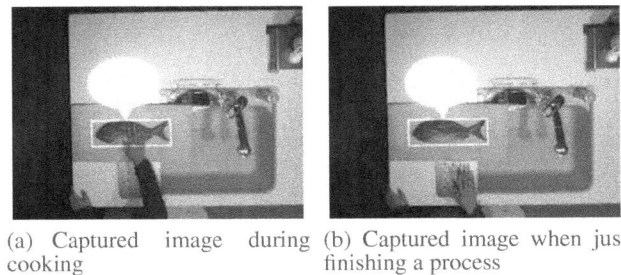

(a) Captured image during cooking

(b) Captured image when just finishing a process

Figure 10. The judgment whether a cooking process is done or not by image processing

DISCUSSION

After taking the cooking support system on a trial run, we found that a user was able to successfully complete all of the steps of the cooking process. The user easily comprehended the CG projections and took interest in the system as a whole.

In contrast, we discovered three stumbling blocks. First, the system still lacked the detailed support needed for novices at certain points in the cooking process. Specifically, the user was uncertain of how to proceed with the removal of the offal because there were no CG but only speech. Second, the system is not yet equipped to provide advanced cooking instructions that cannot be conveyed by the visual and acoustic senses. For instance, when removing the flesh from the fish, the cook has to cut it by relying on a haptic sense generated by a knife and the bones of the fish. However, our system does not have the ability to provide this kind of detail instruction. Finally, while cutting and knife CG were provided, our system does not instruct users on how to hold ingredients when performing different techniques. The user found difficulty in moving the knife in the same manner as the CG because they were holding the knife incorrectly.

While some of these concerns can be easily addressed by making adjustments to the system, more research needs to be conducted on how to convey instructions that require the sense of touch. We hope to tackle these issues in trials of future cooking support system.

CONCLUSIONS

We aimed to ease the difficulties that novices face when confronting the cooking process by making cutting instructions, and other instructions, as clear as possible. CG projected onto ingredients, and speech interaction with a conversational robot Phyno, were two techniques we adopted to achieve this. The system detects the ingredient by image processing to calibrate a position of the CG projection. This enables to automatically project CG of a cutting line and a knife movement onto the ingredient. In addition, to judging whether steps in the cooking process have reached completion, we developed a unique hybrid process that utilizes image processing and speech interaction. This effectively tackles the concerns faced with systems that automatically determine step completion that cause novices to feel the system is unreliable or that their cooking is inadequate. It also allows novices to feel confident that they have completed a step properly by prompting the cook to indicate if they are ready to proceed to the next step. The cook is encouraged because the system recognizes that a step may be near completion.

While, at this point, our system does not provide instructions that related to the tactile senses, the instructions given that employ visual and acoustic senses, have proved to be a great improvement, especially for novice cooks. We will conduct further investigation to tackle these issues.

REFERENCES

1. *Journal of the Robotics Society of Japan [special issue] "Human Robot Symbiosis" 29*, 10 (2011).

2. Bonanni, L., Lee, C.-H., and Selker, T. Attention-based design of augmented reality interfaces. In *Proceedings of the SIGCHI Conference on Human Factors in Computing Systems (CHI'05)* (2005), 1228–1231.

3. Hamada, R., Ide, I., Sakai, S., and Tanaka, H. Structural analysis of cooking preparation steps in japanese. In *Proceedings of the fifth international workshop on on Information retrieval with Asian languages (IRAL'00)* (2000), 157–164.

4. Hashimoto, A., Mori, N., Funatomi, T., Yamakata, Y., Kakusho, K., and Minoh, M. Smart kitchen: A user centric cooking support system. In *Proceedings of Information Processing and Management of Uncertainty in Knowledge-Based Systems (IPMU'08)* (2008), 848–854.

5. Ide, I., Ueda, M., Mase, K., Ueda, H., Tsuchiya, S., and Kobayashi, A. Planning a menu(<special section> media processing for daily life: The science of cooking activities). *The Journal of The Institute of Electronics, Information and Communication Engineers 93*, 1 (2010), 33–38.

6. Ju, W., Hurwitz, R., Judd, T., and Lee, B. Counteractive: An interactive cookbook for the kitchen counter. In *Proceedings of the SIGCHI Conference on Human Factors in Computing Systems (CHI'01)* (2001), 269–270.

7. Lee, A., Kawahara, T., and Shikano, K. Julius—an open source real-time large vocabulary recognition engine. In *Proceedings of 7th European Conference on Speech Communication and Technology* (2001), 1691–1694.

8. Morioka, S., and Ueda, H. Cooking support system utilizing built-in cameras and projectors. In *Proceedings of The 12th IAPR Conference on Machine Vision Applications (MVA'11)* (2011), 271–274.

9. Siio, I., Hamada, R., and Mima, N. Kitchen of the future and applications. In *Proceedings of the 12th International Conference on Human-Computer Interaction (HCI International 2007)* (2007), 946–955.

10. Ueda, H., Minoh, M., Chikama, M., Satake, J., Kobayashi, A., Miyawaki, K., and Kidode, M. Human-robot interaction in the home ubiquitous network environment. In *Proceedings of the 12th International Conference on Human-Computer Interaction (HCI International 2007)* (2007), 990–997.

11. Yamakata, Y., Funatomi, T., Ueda, H., Tsuji, H., Minoh, M., Nakauchi, Y., Miyawaki, K., Nakamura, Y., and Siio, I. Cooking(<special section> media processing for daily life: The science of cooking activities). *The Journal of The Institute of Electronics, Information and Communication Engineers 93*, 1 (2010), 39–47.

Elderly User Mental Model of Reminder System

Fariza Hanis Abdul Razak
Universiti Teknologi MARA
40450 Shah Alam, Selangor,
MALAYSIA
fariza@tmsk.uitm.edu.my

Rafidah Sulo
Universiti Teknologi MARA
40450 Shah Alam, Selangor,
MALAYSIA
rafidahsulo@yahoo.com

Wan Adilah Wan Adnan
Universiti Teknologi MARA
40450 Shah Alam, Selangor,
MALAYSIA
adilah@tmsk.uitm.edu.my

ABSTRACT

The growing numbers of elderly is inevitable. As we get older, we will experience some memory declines, thus an assistive technology such as reminder system is recommended. However, the uptake of reminder system is still low. Many researchers from the western countries are interested in exploring the use of reminder system as part of assistive technology for the elderly. Nevertheless, no research is solely focused on what actually elderly users expect from a reminder system. Hence, this paper attempts to assess and propose elderly mental model on reminder system. We conducted a series of studies: interview, usability evaluation and drawing activity with eight (8) participants. Our results revealed that elderly users expected that a reminder system should be simple, familiar, flexible and recognizable to them. We also learned that drawing and user study can be effective methods for assessing a mental model depending on type of user groups involved in the study.

Author Keywords

Mental model; elderly; older adults; reminder; usability; drawing

ACM Classification Keywords

H.5.2 [Information Interfaces and Presentation]: User Interfaces - Interaction styles.

INTRODUCTION

Elderly population keeps on increasing year by year. Ageing population has become a major concern globally. As reported in the World Population Ageing: 1950-2050, *"The older population is growing faster than the total population in practically all regions of the world – and the difference in growth rates is increasing* [23]. As stated by Arch [1], in few decades time, there will be a supreme escalation in the number of older people compared with any other period in human history.

As for Malaysia's context, the increase in ageing population cannot be denied [12]. The number of elderly population (60 and above) in Malaysia are projected to grow to 2.2 million by the year 2020 [8]. Recently, *thestaronline* has published an article entitled "Malaysia likely to reach ageing nation by 2035". In the article, Halijah Yahaya, Welfare Department deputy director-general (Operations) said that, *"The government should therefore view seriously the ageing rate among the population especially because old people have their own requirements"* [13].

With the significant size of elderly in the near future, it is important to see them as large-scale group user for technology. For the past few years numerous researchers have investigated how Information and communication Technologies (ICT) can be used by older people. In HCI communities, the last few years had shown an increasing interest in generating scientific and methodological knowledge about how to design interactive system for elderly.

An emerging trend related to elderly is the assistive technology. Assistive technology is defined as a product or service that enables independence for older or disabled people [5]. Example of assistive technology is a reminder.

Reminder is generally used to prompt or aid the memory. Regardless of the age, we use reminders everyday; be it calendars, diaries, sticky notes or visual reminders around the home or workplace. However, as we age, we are more likely to have cognitive ageing problems such as being more forgetful thus reminder becomes important for us to structure the day or managing our lives.

According to Lennon et al. [10], research done on presentation design of reminders is still comparatively low even though it is important. Indeed, good design is crucial to success and uptake of reminder systems. Currently, research on reminder systems mainly focuses on when to deliver reminders and how reminders should be delivered. Reminders are effective when users can understand what they are supposed to be doing if they attend appropriately to the reminder. Acceptable reminders quickly become part of life. The acceptance key of any technological product is that the design matches with the user's mental model.

However, Lennon [10] highlights that there is little effort to assess older adult user mental model on reminder system. Without assessing user's mental model on reminder system, the designer cannot predict what the user expects from the reminder system. When the design does not match with the user mental model, then it will lead to user's frustration on the end product.

According to Lorenz et al. [11], it is always a challenge to develop applications that specifically meet the requirements of the user group of 50+. Interestingly, some studies have proven that systems designed for older and disabled people can offer much more usable systems for everyone.

The aim of this paper is therefore to propose a mental model of elderly users to help the designers to better understand the needs, expectation and requirements of the older adult users in using reminder systems.

METHODOLOGY

To assess mental model of the older adult users, we incorporated three techniques: interview, usability evaluation and drawing.

Participants

There is a debate on the age that defines 'old' or 'elderly'. O'Neill and his colleagues [15] define 60 as the new 55 in terms of retirement from full-time work as life expectancy, health, and economic expectations increase. The American Association of Retired Persons' (AARP) 2004 study found that previous studies (undertaken during 2000 - 2004) of the elderly and their use of the ICT and the Web used a variety of definitions, from 50+ years through to 65+ years [2].

The AARP itself considers 'older adults' to be those over 50 years, while many western countries (including the USA) consider the retirement age to be 65 years. Hanson [6] argues that the age of 50 is often used to define an older adult and there is clinical evidence to suggest that some age related declines begin at this age. However, most studies agree to use the retirement age to indicate old or elderly.

In Malaysia, people retire as early as at the age of 58. However, 50s are often regarded as 'young old' for Malaysians [7]. Thus, in this study, eight (8) working professionals aged 52-68 years old were identified and agreed to take part.

Location

It is important to consider the location of the study to ensure that the participants were comfortable with the environment and surrounding of the location. This study took place at two different locations: for lecturer participants, our lab known as UseLab (User Science and Engineering Laboratory) was used. Meanwhile, for teacher participants, the study was done at their school.

At the study location, the participants were first briefed on the purpose and a series of study. The participants were also given a declaration form before the session started to avoid any ethical issues. The declaration informed that the participants would be observed and their answers would be recorded, and the outcome from this research was only for research purposes. If they had agreed with the terms and conditions, then only could we conduct the study.

Methods for Assessing Mental Model

This study basically consisted of three parts. The first part was Interview session. Here, the participants were asked about their experience with a reminder system. The interview lasted about 10 minutes for each participant.

After the interview, we asked them to evaluate two identified reminder systems. The purpose of this study was to elicit user experience with reminder systems. In this user study, they were asked to perform two simple tasks with AIV Reminder (see Figure 1) and Lucky Reminder (see Figure 2). The tasks were (1) set alarm for a meeting in INTEKMA that starts at 3pm today and (2) set alarm for a daily discussion at 10am. After they had completed the tasks, they were later asked about their experiences with these reminders.

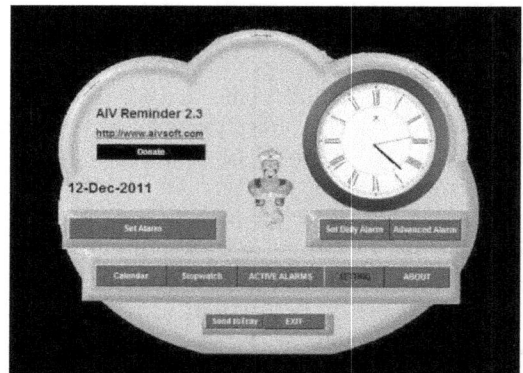

Figure 1. AV Reminder

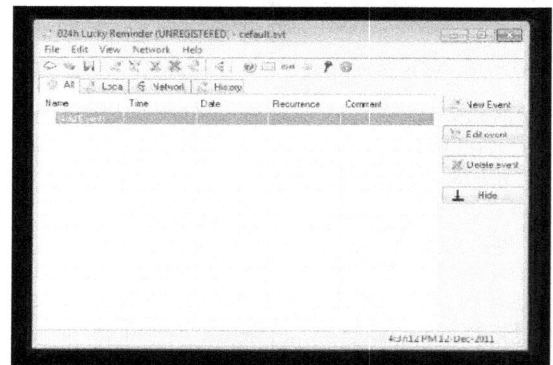

Figure 2. Lucky Reminder

Both AIV and Lucky reminders can be downloaded from the Internet. The reason we chose AIV was because in our opinion it was different: it's got genie to 'entertain' you. Meanwhile, Lucky was chosen due to its 'familiar', typical office interfaces.

The last part of the study was drawing. This drawing activity was meant to assess participant's thought and expectation on a reminder system. This technique has been applied by many researchers and drawing is actually an effective tool in assessing people's mental model [22]. [17], [18], and [24] have recently applied drawing techniques in assesing mental models.

For the drawing activity, the participants were given some blank papers and a pencil. Their task was to draw interfaces for a reminder system. To help them deliver what we wanted, we asked our participants to imagine themselves as a designer. We, too, encouraged them to talk about their ideas and opinions while drawing.

RESULTS

We report our findings individually according to phases of the study: interviews, user study and drawing.

Interview Session

Our participants were all young elderly professionals aged between 52-68 years old. Table 1 summarises the participants' background information.

From the interviews, as predicted, we found that our participants used reminders for two reasons: *work* (i.e., meetings, appointments and deadlines) and *personal* purposes (i.e., birthdays, event invitations, wakeup calls, to-do (or buy) list & time for medication).

Table 2 highlights the type of reminder technology used by

Age	Gender	Type of IT User	Career
58	Male	Frequent	Senior Lecturer
68	Male	Frequent	Professor
55	Female	Frequent	Professor
55	Female	Frequent	Associate Prof
55	Female	Frequent	Teacher
52	Male	Frequent	Teacher
57	Female	Intermittent	Teacher
53	Female	Frequent	Teacher

Table 1. Participants' Background Information

our participants:

From the table, we found that:

- three (3) participants (P1, P2 & P6) used more than one type of reminder

- six (6) participants used mobile phone as their reminder tools

- two participants (P4 and P7) used manual reminders only

- only one participant (P1) used desktop reminder

- two (2) participants (P2 and P6) used mobile phone and manual as their reminders   and

- four (4) participants still rely on manual reminders such as physical alarm clock, calendar and planner

Participant	Reminder Technology		
	Desktop	**Mobile Phone**	**Manual**
P1	√	√	
P2		√	√
P3		√	
P4			√
P5		√	
P6		√	√
P7			√
P8		√	
Total	1	6	4

Table 2. Type of Reminder Technology

From this study, we found that mobile phone was the most commonly used technology for reminders. The participants used some of mobile phone features such as calendar, notes and alarm clock as their reminder tools. There is evidence that mobile calendar and alarm clock are used to help people coordinate their everyday life activities ([18] and [19]).

It was interesting, nevertheless, to note that there were some participants who did not know that they were actually using a reminder. When we told them that the tools they were using were actually reminders, they were very surprised because they often thought that the *reminder system* should be on a computer (computer-based reminder).

We also learned some interesting behaviours from our participants. For example, there were some of our participants did not set the reminders by themselves. Instead, they 'passed' this responsibility to others. For example, P5 and P8 would ask their children to set alarm (reminder) for them. This similar behaviour was also highlighted in an earlier study on the use of mobile phone alarm clock by Razak and Dix [18].

However, in this study, the reason why these participants relied on others was because they believed that the children 'knew better' in using technology. Therefore, it was common to have someone else do it for us instead.

Another interesting behaviour was also noted when using mobile phone as a reminder tool. For example, P2 would ask someone (i.e., his student) to send him a text message to remind him about his appointment or meeting. This is a special type of message that we send to ourselves or others, to notify us about some activity that we need to engage in near future [5]. P2 further highlighted that this method was even more effective than using the technology alone as a reminder.

Partic -ipant	AIV Reminder	Lucky Reminder		Partic -ipant	AIV Reminder	Lucky Reminder
P1	• "Like the calendar but expect more function on the calendar part."	• "Better than AIV." • "Much easier to set the date and time." • "More flexible in term of reminding duration." • "Quite similar to the previous system that has been used."		P5	• "More interesting." • "Easier to understand the interface."	• "Do not know where to start." • "Much easier to give input because the calendar is provided to set the date, no need to key-in."
P2	• "Don't know where to click." • "Easier steps to follow than Lucky reminder." • "Simpler than Lucky."	• "Don't know where to click."		P6	• "Many sections and inflexible, different places to set one-time event and daily alarm."	• "Better compared to AIV reminder in term of setting the date." • "All in one place: to set daily, monthly, yearly and one-time event."
P3	• "The size consumes so much space and the location is distracted." • "Messy" • "The other function is not relevant such as stopwatch." • "The organization of menu is not suitable." • "The watch is not significant." • "Troublesome." • "The genie is distracting."	• "Simpler since the interface design is similar to other system." • "Used to boxes."		P7	• "Clearer that I can see as a whole."	• "Do not like table because I have to analyze."
P4	• "More user friendly and interesting than Lucky reminder but have to understand first." • "Lots of redundancy." • "Troublesome to set the date." • "Can navigate around without assistant." • "The genie is irritating."	• "Better use in terms of set time and date." • "Require a lot of input." • "Have familiarity with other system." • "Less information on what needs to be done." • "A lot of texts (main interface)." • "Need to understand the text and button." • "Look like for administrative."		P8	• "Hard to use since there are many fields" • "It requires typing to set the date and time."	• "Easier to set the date and time." • "The symbols and buttons in main interface are confusing."

Table 3. Participants' Feedbacks on AIV and Lucky Reminders

Usability Evaluation

Participants were required to evaluate AIV and Lucky reminders. The evaluation study provide them with ideas on how a reminder should work. The following table highlights their feedbacks after evaluating AIV and Lucky reminders.

Drawing

The last part of the study was drawing. Although the participants had to draw the interfaces of their 'ideal' reminders, there were some participants who just could not draw. They said that they had no idea at all on how to draw the interfaces. However, they suggested that they could describe or at least give some ideas about a reminder system. Due to this limitation, we asked them to write instead. The following are the drawings and the descriptions or perceptions that our participants had on their reminders.

Figure 3. Drawing by P1

P1 explained that reminder must have categories of events and/or activities. Then for every activity, there should be an extra information. For example, if the user had an appointment on 24/12/11 at 3.50pm, then the reminder should allow the user to add extra information such as the appointment venue, meeting person, the person contact number and others. He highlighted that synchronization should be made between computer and mobile phone as it was illustrated in the drawing. He also suggested an extra feature in the reminder: reminder can be viewed from two perspectives - personal or employer use. In this design, if you are a superior, you can send a reminder to your subordinates.

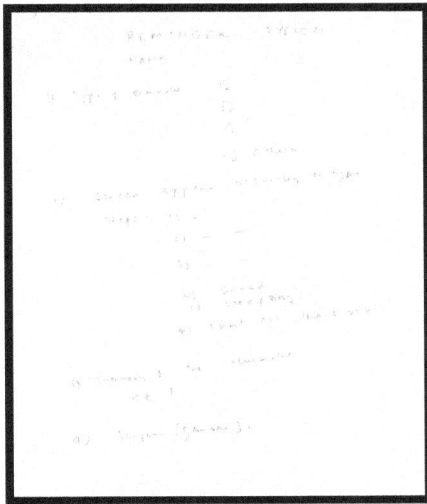

Figure 4. Drawing by P2

In this drawing, P2 stressed on a step-by-step procedure in setting up a reminder. To get started, we must first select a type of reminder. A screen would then appear according to the selected type. Afterwards, we must key-in all the required information according to the steps. After all information needed has been keyed in, the system would summarise our reminder information. After we have confirmed the information, only then the reminder will be set. Once the reminder has successfully been set, a smiley icon will appear to show an accomplishment.

Figure 5. Drawing by P3

P3 emphasised that a reminder should prioritise the events. In other word, the reminder should be able to detect the most urgent or important event, thus that event will be in the highest ranking of priority. She also emphasized on simple design and the design should be able to differentiate between alert and alarm.

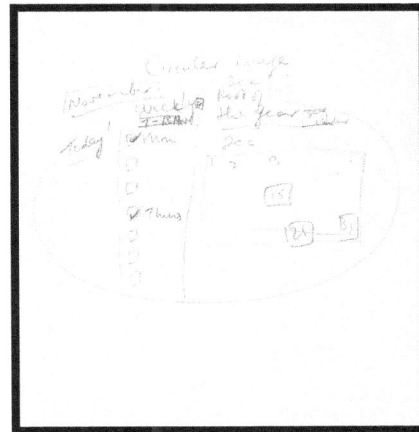

Figure 6. Drawing by P4

For P4, the reminder should also be simple and easy to use. In her drawing, she stressed on a 'bird-eye' view design in which a user can see what activities he/she has on that day, in that week and in that month from the main page.

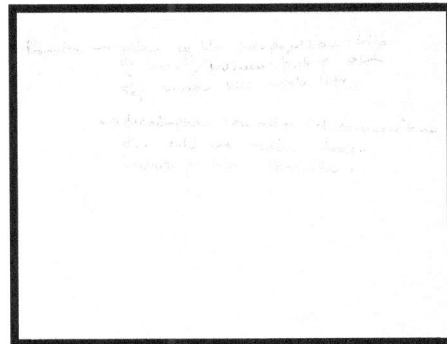

Figure 7. Description by P5

In this activity, P5 often reminded us of the importance of a reminder. For her, a reminder should be an independent tool – not a computer nor a mobile phone. She said, "We do not always turn our PC on, as for mobile phone, we may use it for other purposes. If possible, the reminder can be brought anywhere and we can put it on the table (at workplace) where we can directly see it".

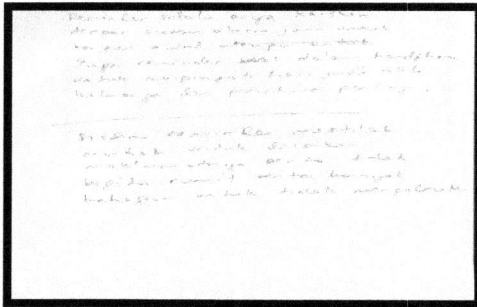

Figure 8. Description by P6

P6 defined reminders based on his own understanding. For him, reminder was related to wakeup calls and important events. He expected that a reminder should be simple and easy to use.

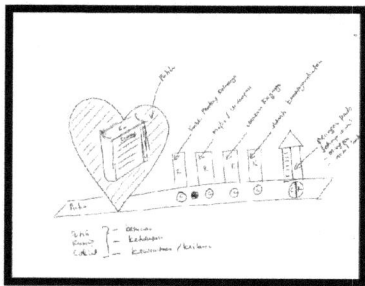

Figure 9. Drawing by P7

Like P5, P7 also expected a reminder as a one independent tool as shown above. She focused on categories of activities/events (similar to P1). She also emphasized on a 'bird-eye' view on what needed to be done for a particular week (similar to P4). In her drawing, interestingly, she added three colour codes according to her interpretation: white (clean), yellow (purity) and brown (woman).

Figure 10. Description by P8

At first, she thought that reminder was only used to remind us of birthdays. Then later, she realized that reminders could also be used for other things, not only restricted to events/ activities/tasks; but also for important numbers and facts, for example, using a note to save account numbers.

Partici-pant	Feedbacks
P1	• "It is good if the reminder application start with **calendar** first. Only then, the user can add their activities or set alarm on the particular date." • "Reminder application should be flexible in terms of reminding duration." • "It is better if the application can check the availability of time in the case of there is same time for different meeting." • "**Flexible**: can be synchronized in mobile phone and computer."
P2	"There must be a procedure or checklist to ensure that user has done all tasks in order to set a reminder." "Make the reminder flexible in which we **can bring it anywhere**. We are not all the time in front of our desktop/laptop, thus there is no use of reminder."
P3	• "**Simple** design." • "Flexible: we **can bring anywhere** such as mobile phone."
P4	• "It is better if the reminder is flexible whereby we can bring it anywhere."
P5	• "It is better if the reminder is **a tool without depending on computer or mobile phone.** We can bring it and put it anywhere."
P6	• "The design should be **simple** and not complicated." • "Font size must be large."
P7	• "The reminder should be **one tool like alarm clock** without depending neither to computer nor mobile phone."
P8	• "The font size should be larger." • "Do not put icons that the user does not understand." • "Synchronization between mobile phone and computer."

Table 4. Participants' Perceptions on Reminder System

DISCUSSION

The term 'mental model' was first introduced in 1943 by Scottish Psychologist named Kenneth Craik. The book titled "The Nature of Exploration" written by Craik, states that *"the mind constructs "small-scale-models" of reality that it uses to reason, to anticipate and to underlie explanation"* as cited by [21].

In HCI, Norman defines mental model as *"a set of beliefs how a system works"*. Norman has introduced three models of a system which is (1) system model, (2) user's mental model and (3) Design Model (as cited by [3]).

According to McDaniel [9], mental model can be presented in using several key parts including an image, a script, a set of related mental models, a controlled vocabulary, and a set of assumptions. Based on the results, we proposed two types of mental models: definition and design of a reminder according to older adult users.

Elderly User Mental Model

Based on design principles, for these older adults, reminders should be simple, familiar, recognizable and flexible.

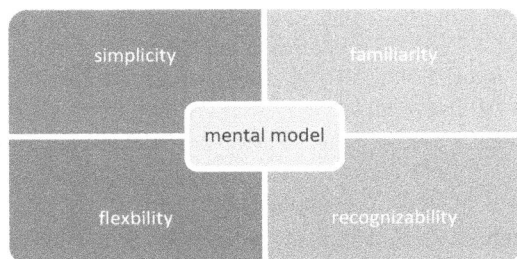

Figure 11. User Mental Model

Simplicity

As highlighted in the literature of interface guidelines for elderly people, simplicity is the most important element in designing for elderly people. Therefore, functions should be made easy and quick to access for these people.

Familiarity

We suggest that simple design can be presented based on the concept of **familiarity**. In this study, P1 suggested to apply the 'calendar' concept or P2 suggested 'to-do list' in the design. Both calendar and to-do list provide features such as simple and easy to use and an overall view of the tasks or activities.

From our study, we discovered that the participants expected that they could see their activities/ events on the main page. The main page should provide a quick view on what they need to do for a particular day, week or month. It might be as simple as list of activities that the users need to do for that particular date. As for interaction design, it is important to ensure that the reminder system requires less effort from the users in order to set the reminder message. For instance, instead of required the user to type the date, the system should provide a calendar in which the user just needs to click on the desired date.

Since manual reminders such as diaries and calendar are still widely used, thus it might be good if the interface of the reminder is easy and similar to this kind of presentation.

Flexibility

Reminders should be similar to another **everyday technology**, not anything like computers. The essential characteristic of this ubiquitous reminder is **mobility**.

Recognizability

For elderly users, reminders should be a technology that can be brought and put everywhere that is easily visible and **recognizable** to them. This ubiquitous technology can be a mobile phone, however, from our study we found that some of the participants did not want reminders to be associated with computer or mobile technologies. This is perhaps due to anxiety with ICT technologies [16]. Participants who often work on computers and with mobile phone, on the other hand, prefer if the reminder can be synchronized between these two technologies.

LESSONS LEARNED

We learnt some important lessons from our studies:

- From our study, we found that both usability evaluation and drawing methods yielded similar results. Therefore, we suggest that if these methods are used together, they can be very effective in assessing mental models.

- Drawing technique appears to be more effective to some of our participants (P1, P2, P3, P4 and P7). Some possible reasons are (1) they are IT professionals (P1, P3 & P4) and/or (2) they knew what they expected from a reminder (P1, P2, P3, P4 & P7). If they understood their own requirements, they could design the usable interfaces.

- Usability evaluation can be a helpful technique for some people (P5, P6 and P8) who may not know what to expect from a technology, but, by evaluating interface design, it indirectly helps elicit their requirements and expectations. Talking method used in this study works better for these participants because talking helps them to be more expressive in their feedbacks.

CONCLUSION

The mental model that we proposed here may or may not be applicable for 'old' non-working elderly. Thus, the study with this user group needs to be replicated to improve the user mental model.

REFERENCES

1. Arch, A. Web Accessibility for Older Users - Successes and Oppurtunities. In *18th International World Wide Web Conference (W4A2009)*, ACM Press (2009), 1-6.

2. Chisnell, A., Lee, A. and Redish, J. *Recruiting and Working With Older Participants.* AARP article (2004). http://www.aarp.org/olderwiserwired/oww-features/Articles/a2004-03-03-recruiting-participants.html

3. Davidson, M. J., Dove, L., & Weltz, J. Mental Models and Usability, 1999.

4. Dewsbury, G. What do elderly people want from Assistive Technology. Manchester, UK, 2004.

5. Dey, A. K., & Abowd, G. D. CybreMinder: A context - Aware System for supporting reminders. *Symp. Handheld and Ubiquitous Computing*, 172-186, 2002.

6. Hanson, V. L. Age and Web Access: The Next Generation. In *Proceedings of the 2009 International Cross-Disciplinary Conference on Web Accessibililty (W4A)*, ACM (2009), 7-15.

7. Hassan, H and Nasir, M. H. N. M. The Use of Mobile Phones by Older Adults: A Malaysian Study. SIGACCESS Newsletter, 92, 2008, 11-16.

8. Khadijah Alavi, Rahim M. Sail, Khairuddin Idris, Asnarulkhadi Abu Samah & Christine Chan. Emotional Support Needs in Caring For the Elderly Parents by the Adult Children. *Journal of Social Science and Humanity*, 6 (1), 102-114.

9. McDaniel, S. *What's Your Idea of a Mental Model?* (2003) Retrieved October 23, 2011, from boxesandarrows: http://www.boxesandarrows.com/view/whats_your_idea_of_a_mental_model_

10. Lennon, M. M., Wolters, M. K., & Brewster, S. User-Centred Multimodal Reminders for Assistive Living. *CHI 2011*, Vancouver: ACM (2011), 2105-2114.

11. Lorenz, A., Mielke, D., Oppermann, R., & Zahl, L. (2007). Personalized Mobile Health Monitoring for Elderly. *Mobile HCI'07*, Singapore: ACM (2007), 297-304.

12. Mohamed, M. The Problems And Challenges Of The Aging Population Of Malaysia. *Malaysian Journal of Medical Sciences* , 1-3, 2000.

13. *Nation - Malaysia likely to reach ageing nation status by 2035.* (2011, April 27). Retrieved December 1, 2011, from thestaronline. http://thestar.com.my/news/story.asp?file=/2010/4/27/nation/20100427160245&sec=nation

14. Newell, A. F., & Dickinson, A. Designing a Portal for Older Users: A Case Study of an Industrial/Academic Collaboration. *Computer- Human Interaction,* 13(3), 347–375, 2006.

15. O'Neill, J., Lawson, S. and Purushothaman, R. *60 Is the New 55: How the G6 Can Mitigate the Burden of Aging.* (September 2005). http://www2.goldmansachs.com/ideas/demographic-change/60-is-the-new-55-pdf.pdf

16. Otjacques, B., Krier, M., Feltz, F., Ferring, D. & Hoffmann, M. Designing for Older People: A Case Study in a Retirement Home. In *HCI in Work and Learning, Life and Leisure*, LNCS (2010), 6389, 177-194.

17. Qian, X., Yang, Y., & Gong, Y. The Art of Metaphor: A Method for Interface Design Based on Mental Models. *VRCAI 2011,* Hong Kong: ACM, 171-178, 2011.

18. Razak, F. H. A. and Dix, A. Mobile phone: A tool for expressing co-actualisation. Proceedings of the 13th ECCE: Trust and control in complex socio-technical systems. Vol. (250), pp. 100-104. Zurich, Switzerland: ACM Press. September 20 - 22, 2006.

19. Razak, F. H. A. Single Person Study: Methodological Issues. PhD Thesis, Lancaster University, 2008. www.hcibook.net/people/Fariza/

20. Roth, S. P., Schmutz, P., & Pauwels, S. L. Mental models for web objects: Where do users expect to find the most frequent objects in online shops, news portals, and company web pages? *Interacting with computers* , (2010), 140-152.

21. Soegaard, M. *Mental Models.* Retrieved 12 1, 2011, from Interaction-Design.org: http://www.interaction-design.org/encyclopedia/mental_models_glossary.html

22. Thatcher, A., & Greyling, M. Mental Model of the Internet. *International Journal of Industrial Ergonomics 22* , 299-305, 1998.

23. *World Population Ageing 1950-2050.* New York: Department of Economic and Social Affairs (Population Division), 2001.

24. Zhang, Y. The influence of mental models on undergraduate students' searching behavior on the Web. *Information Processing and Management 44* , 1330-1345, 2008

Restrain from Pervasive Logging Employing Geo-Temporal Policies

Mohsin Ali Memon
University of Tsukuba
1-1-1, Tenno-dai, Tsukuba,
Ibaraki, 305-8573 Japan
mohsin@iplab.cs.tsukuba.ac.jp

Jiro Tanaka
University of Tsukuba
1-1-1, Tenno-dai, Tsukuba,
Ibaraki, 305-8573 Japan
jiro@cs.tsukuba.ac.jp

Tomonari Kamba
NEC BIGLOBE, Ltd.
1-11-1, Osaki, Shinagawa,
Tokyo, 141-0032 Japan
kamba@biglobe.co.jp

ABSTRACT

Life logging has been a prominent research concern in recent years with the invention of wearable life capture gadgets and it has played a significant role in some situations such as helping Alzheimer disease patients. However, at the same time, it has raised privacy concerns among ordinary people. At present, life log devices are pervasively capturing information, including people in the vicinity without their consent. This will produce a great concern in the future if the majority of people come to have life log devices that record continuously what is happening around. In this paper, we propose a mechanism to restrict people from capturing a person in their personal digital diaries in real time by introducing Geo-temporal privacy framework. Furthermore, the system ensures that the unwilling party is not revealed to the life logging system users and privacy is sustained when the Geo-temporal framework discontinues the log activity after an encounter with the reluctant party. The prototype is developed on an Android-based smart phone that works as a life log device with a policy controller. The phone is connected to an Infrared Transmitter/Receiver with an interface board, for identifying human proximity.

Author Keywords

Life log; geographical; temporal; pervasive; neighbor; privacy.

ACM Classification Keywords

H.5 INFORMATION INTERFACES AND
PRESENTATION: H.5.1 Multimedia Information Systems--
-*Evaluation/methodology*.

General Terms

Human Factors; Security; Privacy.

INTRODUCTION

Life logging is a strenuous activity where our day to day activities such as dining, travelling, congregating, etc. are

recorded. The invention of compact and portable capture devices have driven people towards saving and maintaining their personal life experiences. Several attempts have been made by various researchers to digitize day to day activities, thus, increasing the social acceptance of personal life logging. Among them, "My life bits" [1] project by Gemmell et al. used Microsoft SenseCam to capture everything beyond legacy content, like papers, photos, and videos, into a second level that included real time capture of conversations, meetings, sensor readings, health monitors and computer activity, collecting around 1-2 thousand photos every day. In [2], Kim et al. used body worn sensors including audiovisual device, GPS, 3D-accelerometer and processed logged information to create metadata to be retrieved easily afterwards.

Without denying the benefits of the above mentioned research, we naturally pose the following question: what if people do not want to be captured by someone's life log device? This is where the Geo-temporal privacy framework comes into play. The proposed idea redefines the meaning of privacy in terms of life logging, because while detaining these personal experiences and activities, we inadvertently capture numerous people without their consent, thus negating the idea that life logging is a solipsistic activity, since the captured crowd may include friends, family members or strangers. Because these life log devices are consistently retaining everything in our life from watching TV to waiting for the train and so on, the problems arise when our personal life log device is obtaining pictorial and auditory information of our neighbors in the course of maintaining the record of our life. Such situations may be unsettling for those who love their privacy and do not like to be captured or recorded by someone they are unaware of, at a particular location and time.

In order to avoid circumstances where users are always concerned that their movements are captured by someone, the proposed system permits them to employ privacy policies on various life log sensors and hence decide by themselves whether anonymous people can capture them at a certain place and time. These policies facilitate the people to select specific locations and time slots when their neighbors will not be able to confine their activities. The exploitation of such systems can be practical in various situations. For example, a person might restrain anonymous people from taking pictures of them in informal company gatherings or they may feel uncomfortable when their colleagues try to capture them when they fail in an assessment.·

In general, the purpose of life log is to recall previous events including the people we came across or what others said when we were in a gathering in a natural setting. At the same time, it may compel us to be vigilant when we come to know that our daily lives are being captured, resulting in unnatural behavior. Furthermore, the use of such logs in lawsuits is also a matter of concern, which still needs to be addressed.

VARIOUS CONCERNS IN NEIGHBOR'S LOGGING

Let us assume we are using a messenger service on the internet, where we have various status options to choose from, such as, *away*, *busy* or *offline* mode, and we select one depending on our mood or availability of time to interact with others. The activity of capturing neighbors via life log devices is not much different because the neighbor's consent to be a part of one's life log is indispensable. Life log devices are capturing the events and objects without any intervention. When it comes to taking a picture or recording a person's voice, many people dislike to be recorded by an anonymous person and like to have the control of their privacy, depending on the place and people they are surrounded by. A survey conducted by Karkkainen et al. in [3] supported the idea that people were content with life logging when they had the authority to share the photos and videos taken by the life log device, but showed utmost care in case of neighbor's pictures as no proper privacy mechanism was available to deal with such situations. Allen et al. in [4] also showed concerns over legal and ethical problems of life logging and named the work of [1] as an act of sousveillance or surveillance when the SenseCam takes snapshots of people around the owner of life log device. They also wondered whether this data can be used in lawsuits to prove criminal acts. The purpose of research by Cheng et al. in [5] was to emphasize legal and social questions while pervasively logging everything in life. They proposed an authenticity mechanism ensuring the originality of the data being logged. According to them, the life logging systems will be commonly used by people in future just like cell phones and credit cards, exposing where we were and when. The survey conducted in [6] to gain feedback about the use of SenseCam revealed that most of the people preferred to be informed and asked before any recorded data was to be shared.

Hence, there are various privacy concerns pertaining to what a person does with our pictures, videos or recorded conversations and poses a clear threat if shared on social networking sites without our knowledge, thus placing us in an uneasy situation. Therefore, the need to cope with such situations is clearly arising in the course of logging neighboring information. The next section explains our approach to halt logging others unless given permission to do so.

OUR APPROACH

Life log sensors can be categorized as Personal log generator and Neighbor log generator. Personal log generators are obligated to log user's daily activities and trace visited locations, where as neighbor log generators are capable of capturing the people around. The research presented in [7,8,9] shows the most suitable examples of personal logs generation, because the sensors used by the authors help to recall events related to a particular location and assist in diagnosing a disease through previous health records.

Here, we have no concern over personal logging, but we are interested in developing a Neighbor log generator which may capture the neighbors only with their agreement. This happens because if we make our neighbors aware that we are observing them with our life log device, it may induce spuriousness in their conduct. Therefore, we present Geo-temporal privacy framework which empowers people to defend themselves from unauthorized logging. The following subsection illustrates this framework in detail.

Geo-Temporal Privacy Framework

Geo-temporal privacy framework helps a user to inscribe privacy in the context of location, time, or both, over the explicit sensors worn by neighbors posing a threat to his day to day dealings. The constraints or privacy policies are classified as geographical (location based) and temporal (time based), which are to be applied on the neighbor log generator as shown in Figure 1. We call these constraints "geo-temporal."

Neighbor log generator is capable of observing people around, by recording their conversations and capturing videos and pictures. The competence of such sensors is best explained in [1,2,10,11] and these sensors work without the owner's intervention, as they are fairly sensitive. Although, the neighbor log may contain geo tags adhering to the captured data; in this case, audio and pictorial information of people around is of immense privacy concern.

The users of the proposed system are allowed to apply either geo, temporal or both constraints on each neighbor log

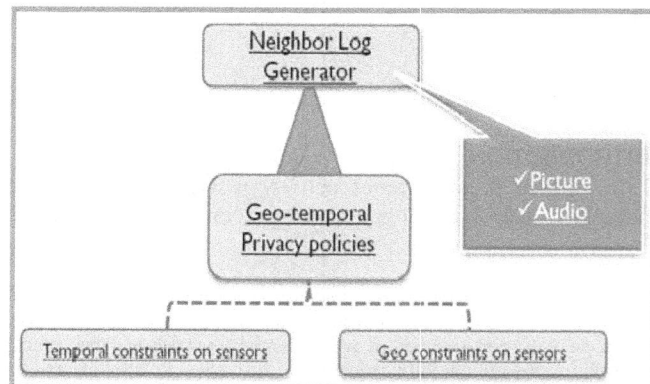

Figure 1. Geo-Temporal Privacy Framework

generator carried by the people in their vicinity. These privacy constraints or policies facilitate a user to hide from unidentified people, depending on specified location and time, thus imposing a selection criterion over anonymously produced content by life log devices of the people in a close proximity.

The above mentioned framework, when applied in a life log device, grants the authority to hide from unnecessary sensing. This framework is effective even if extended to more than two neighboring log generators. In the broad perspective, it encourages people to continue their routine activities as they please, without being secretive or restrained in any way.

Privacy Policies

Every privacy policy resides in the owner's life log device. The policy is a tuple of:

<sensor, accessibility, validity, provision>,

determining how the restriction should behave on the neighbor's life log sensors when triggered. These policies are inscribed by the life log device possessor and values for the type of sensor, accessibility level, validity period and provision of policy are to be selected. Figure 2 depicts the way each privacy policy is infixed in the life log device so as to keep a user from being recorded by pervasive logging devices in his/her neighborhood.

The Sensor can be a camera, microphone or any other device capable of logging passerby's information. Accessibility determines the restriction level of the policy, where, *strictly restricted* means no one is allowed to capture, *moderate restricted* means family members are allowed, whereas, *standard restricted* means family, friends as well as neighbors are allowed to log the person. In figure 2, neighbor refers to the person who lives in the neighborhood. The user may select certain levels of reservation from people in his/her vicinity depending upon his/her frame of mind. Validity specifies the lifetime of a policy after which the policy dies and this parameter is frequently monitored to keep checks on policies that have expired and to delete them as well. Here, *present day* policy expires after the day comes to an end but *everyday* policy never expires. Provision is allowed either by restricting a particular location, a certain time span or both. It depends upon circumstances where preferring the location is more significant because of indefinite time duration, or selecting a time slot regardless of location.

The attributes of each policy such as sensor type, accessibility level, validity period and provision are to be decided by the user for appropriate situations. For example, people may inscribe an everyday policy for restricting a stranger to picture them at a fitness center/dance club. In this example, the restriction is applied on the camera of people around who are unknown. The validity of that policy is every day because visits to that place are frequent with no time restrictions. The privacy policies are activated automatically

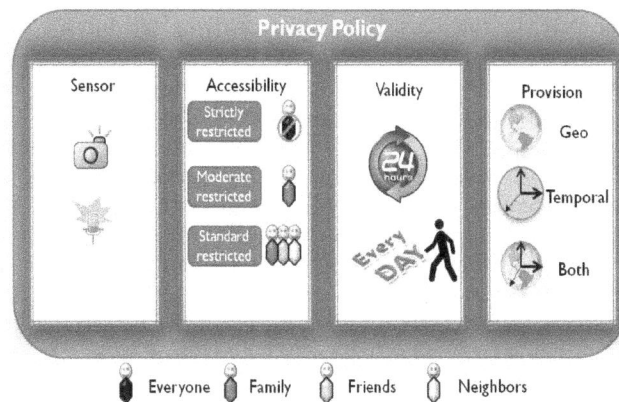

Figure 2. Privacy Policy attributes

when a person enters the location inscribed on their devices or when the time specified for a particular policy commences, thus, enabling the restrictions to be applied on the passerby's life log devices.

Policy overlapping

A policy is assumed to be weak and may be triumphed over by a strong policy only if changes occur in policy accessibility and temporal values but the rest of the parameters remain the same. This phenomenon is named as 'Policy overlapping'. The overlapped policy is always a one day policy, which means that the lifetime of overlapped policy is for the current day, after which that policy is no longer effective.

Policy overlapping may be suitable in situations where an everyday policy may be overlapped by an occasional one day policy due to some changes in the schedule. For example, a person who wishes to spend more time at work simply changes the temporal value of his/her privacy policy, leaving the other parameters untouched, hence s/he achieves policy overlapping. Similarly, a standard restricted policy is overlapped by strictly restricted policy in situations such as when a person is at a party and s/he is revealing hard facts about something/someone which s/he does not want logged by anybody.

SYSTEM DESIGN

The proposed system presumes that everyone wears identical life log devices which are capable of communicating with each other. A life log device in this approach is composed of a GPS enabled smart phone connected to an infrared Transmitter/Receiver pair. The smart phones have built in Bluetooth, thus making them compatible to communicate or share information within a certain range. Each user wears the smart phone with the help of a 15 inch long neck strap and plants an infrared LED on it with a receiver facing others. Here, infrared Transmitter/Receiver is used to detect and identify people in sight or face to face interaction. Choudhury et al. first used this technique to measure face to face interaction between people in [12].

Policy Implementation

The privacy concerns of a user employing the life logging device are advocated in the form of privacy policies, which are stored on the user's life log device. Once these policies are set, the user's location and time is being monitored for the privacy policy to be activated. To apply privacy restrictions, users share their privacy concerns relating to current location and time, along with contact and infrared ID to the people nearby via Bluetooth. The infrared LED worn by the users emits distinctive signals within regular intervals, while the infrared receiver detects the beam of infrared light. Once the human proximity is perceived, the passerby's life log device is directed to act according to the privacy concerns of the person in sight. Figure 3. shows the steps being followed in the course of logging bystander's activities, in this case, taking pictures, while considering the individual's privacy policies delineated by him/her for that location/time or both.

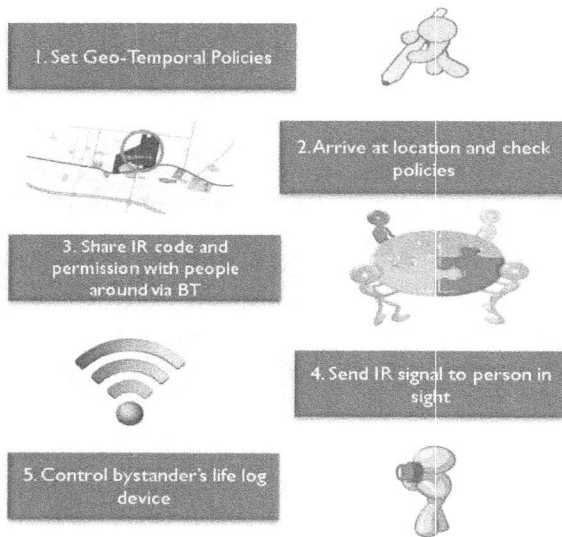

Figure 3. Steps followed to prevent oneself from pervasive logging

Potential Scenario

The system mentioned above fits best in situations where we are visiting a crowded place such as a social gathering with our family members, but it also saves us from scrutiny of others in the confines of our own home. Let us envision that we have invited our relatives, friends and neighbors to a gathering at our home. Here, we may not mind our family members to log us, but hesitate to permit friends or neighbors capturing us or other family members in their pervasive life log devices. Therefore, we make a moderate restricted privacy policy to discontinue the camera operation being performed by life log devices on our friends and neighbors. We broadcast our infrared ID and logging permissions to the people in our home. Figure 4 explains a situation where the privacy concerns are being shared among four users of the system within Bluetooth range and the Access control list (ACL) is maintained by all four users. Here, user A

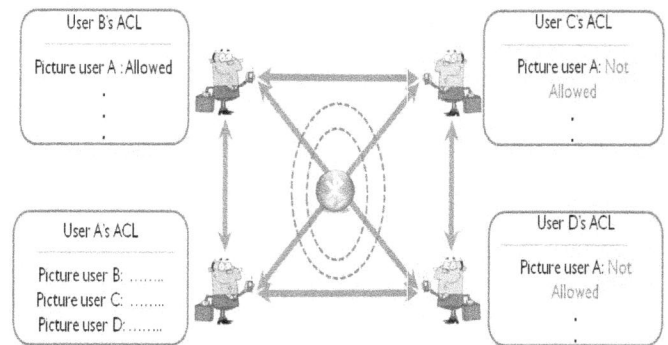

Figure 4. Policy sharing among Bluetooth enabled devices

represents the host, user B is a family member, whereas user C and user D represent a friend and a neighbor respectively. The ACL contains information of who can capture user A with their life log devices. Thus, in this example, user B is permitted to take user A's picture but when there is a face to face contact with user C or user D, their life log device is unable to capture User A. The privacy policy inscribed by the host, who is represented as user A, and its influence on people arrived at a gathering is shown in Figure 5.

The proposed approach protects an individual from being logged by others' life capture devices, depending on the policies prescribed by him/her for a particular place, time or both. It also ensures that the unwilling participants in life logging are not disclosed to the person monitoring the life log device content at that time, but instead, it only records the identification and contextual details to help maintain the owner's life log.

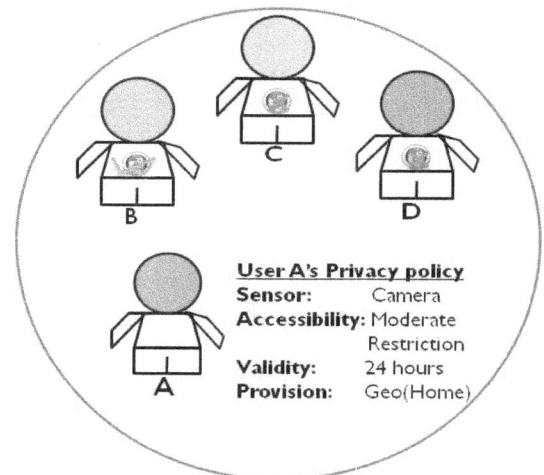

Figure 5. Scenario explaining the proposed approach

SYSTEM FUNCTIONALITY

Device prototype

Our life log device used as a prototype for the proposed approach consists of a Nexus S smart phone employing Android 2.3.6. The infrared Transmitter/Receiver communicates with the smart phone through an Arduino Mega ADK board [13]. The transmitter used for the prototype is a 5mm round infrared LED and the infrared remote control receiver module helps in detecting the signals arriving from a distance of 9 meters at an angle of ± 30°.

The current prototype is wearable, as shown in Figure 6, but it is limited to only control the built-in smart phone camera of the life log device wearer. The camera captures the surroundings with a regular interval of 60 seconds unless interrupted by the reluctant party. Figure 7 shows some pictures stored in the gallery of the smart phone and taken while wearing the proposed life log device on a certain day. The pictures stored on the life log device can be viewed date wise as well as location wise. Being a smart phone, the capabilities of the prototype life logging device are quite restricted since it is not meant to be literally used in logging everything. Thus, a discussion about the efficiency of the life log device and the way it helps to remember the past events is outside the scope of this paper.

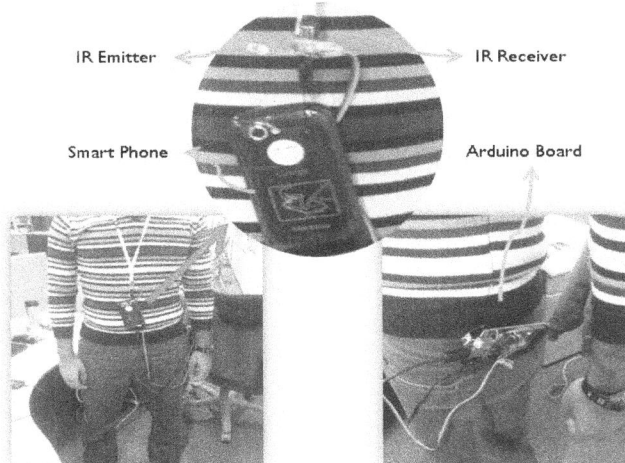

Figure 6. Life log device prototype

Policy Inscription

The privacy policies are inscribed using an android application and stored in the SQLite database. These policies are continuously being monitored so as to apply specified restrictions on passerby's life log devices. Each user is entailed to explicitly determine the privacy policy by picking the sensor type, accessibility, validity and provision values as shown in Figure 8(a). By default, a policy is 'standard restricted', which means that the family, friends and neighbors, determined by the contact list on the user's cell phone or social network, are allowed to capture. A policy is being checked for an overlap if the validity of newly created policy is set for *present day*. If a user selects 'Geo' provision, then a map is shown to mark locations to activate the privacy, as shown in Figure 8(b). Here, the user's current location is marked by a green pin and the restricted location is marked by a blue circle. The restricted location is where the privacy policy is activated. The user can select multiple locations for a single policy, but can only deselect the last selected location by pressing the 'Remove' button. Each selected

Figure 7. Proposed Life log device capturing neighborhood

location on the map means that the policy applies around a 100 meter radius of that location. If the user selects 'Temporal' provision, then a timer box appears to determine the time slot for maintaining the user's privacy during the prescribed timing. By selecting 'Both' provision, the user is requested to determine both location and time parameters to restrict bystanders from logging when s/he is in their vicinity. This is decided by the user or owner of life log device to either guard his/her privacy at a particular location for a specific time duration or for the whole day.

The provision of selecting either location or time may be useful in various circumstances. For example, if we are doubtful about the duration of staying at a particular location and desire no unidentified person to capture our activities, then we may choose geo provision for that privacy policy. On the other hand, when we are uncertain about our prospected location, but we do not want anyone to bother us during a particular period of time, then we make a temporal constraint. The owner of the privacy policies is given the liberty to edit everything, including accessibility, sensor type, validity, etc, except for the main values of location and time. This is because doing so would result in an entirely new

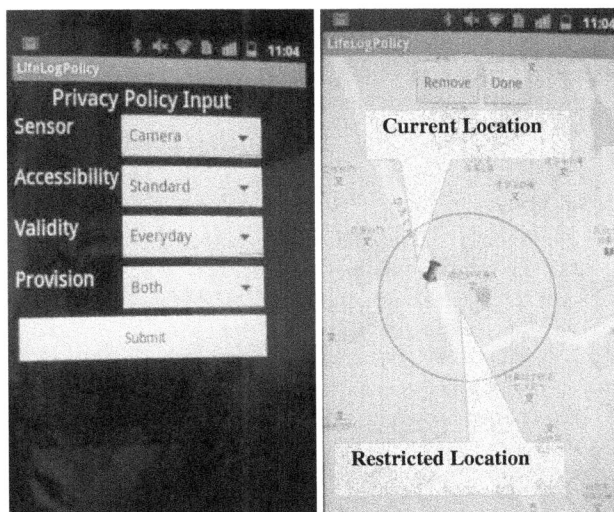

(a)   (b)

Figure 8. Life Log Privacy Policy Android App

policy. Hence the best option would be of constructing a new policy instead of editing the old one.

System Execution

On arrival at a particular location, user's privacy policies are examined for a possible policy overlap for that location or time and then the user's consent about that location and time along with infrared ID is shared among other life log devices within the Bluetooth range in order to maintain an individual's ACL for that location. The infrared LED worn by the user is emitting signals at an interval of every 5 seconds. Whenever there is a person in sight, the receiver detects the infrared ID and transmits it to the smart phone, where the ACL is referred and the sensor is signaled, whether to sense the information around or not. As the infrared light is not viewable by human eye, thus, it substantiates the invisibility of unwilling person. The life log system keeps the identification of the passerby who has restricted others to capture him/her; hence, in this unique way the spirit of the life logging is still preserved, even while the privacy policies are in operation.

The system ensures that the privacy constraints defined by the user of the system are strictly followed during the course of maintaining personal life log. These constraints desist anonymous capturing by the life log devices of the people in the vicinity of the person wearing the proposed life log device.

EVALUATION

At first, we identify the key research challenges of this study which are being listed in the next subsection. Subsequently, the results of experiments being performed on the prototype application are presented. The motivation behind the first and second research challenges is to emphasize the need of a restriction mechanism which may help the users feel more contented while wearing the life log device. The third and fourth research challenges are related to the efficiency and effectiveness of the proposed mechanism.

Research Challenges

The research tries to answer the following questions.

1. Does the user wearing life log device literally amend the neighbor's behavior if the restriction policies are not in function?
2. How does the user feel when s/he has the trigger to the life log sensor of the person in sight?
3. Are the contextual parameters, in this case geographic location and time allocation for privacy constraints, enough or is there is a need to add another parameter?
4. Is the proposed mechanism influential in eradicating the threat of anonymous logging and what is the success rate of the system?

Experiments and Results

The first question was answered by asking 16 users (12 male and 4 female) to allow a stranger to take a picture of them during their routine work. All the users denied being captured

by a stranger and most of them agreed that they would intentionally change their behavior in case they knew they were being photographed.

In the next step, the users were asked if they had the authority over the remote control of the camera shutter directed towards them. In response to the second question, 87.5% users replied that, in this case, the decision would depend upon their mood and situation. The rest of the users declined of allowing unfamiliar person to capture them even when they were given the command over their camera shutter. This conclusion strengthens the idea of creating a mechanism which may protect from anonymous logging.

The next two questions were asked by allowing the users to utilize the prototype application and select the restricted locations and timings of where and when they would not tolerate someone else to record them. The system was assessed by users in pairs to verify the prototype working and the results are shown in Figure 9.

In answer to question 3, 75% of the users warranted that the geo and temporal constraints are enough to ensure privacy and that the system is very easy to operate. Four users claimed that there can be some other contextual parameters apart from geo and temporal constraints, two of them had no other option in mind at that time. One user asserted that an option of broadening and curtailing of the restricted area should be supplemented in the prototype, which positively allots more authority in the hands of the user. The other user replied that while performing a certain activity we may switch off being logged by neighbors.

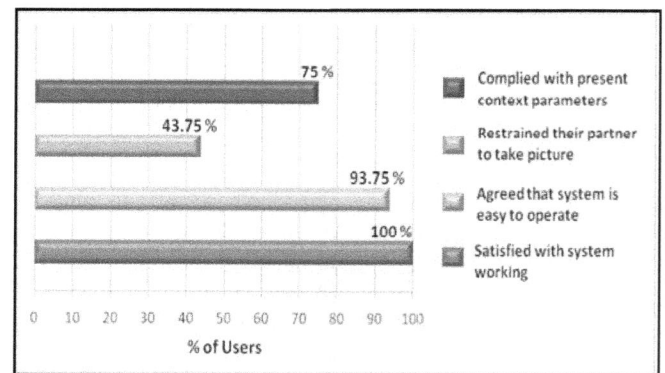

Figure 9. Evaluation of the prototype application

Question 4 was answered with 43.75% users inhibiting their partner from capturing them, while the remaining users allowed their partner to log them at their current location. The users who refrained from being captured were satisfied with the working of the system, because they were cloaked from the sensors of the partner, and the only information being logged was their name, time and location. According to them, it was easy to inscribe a privacy policy and apply restrictions over the passerby's life logging device. The system worked successfully all the time due to the fine range of the infrared LED and receiver that helped in instant detection of human proximity.

The users were also asked to specify which of the constraints suited them the most. Among them, 43.75% voted for geo constraints, 6.25% voted for temporal constraints and 50% voted for both. The reasons behind their preferences were very definite. One of the geo constraint preferring users presented the argument that he would not want his lab mates to capture him while in the lab, because at times he is found slumbering in his chair. A temporal constraint preferring user on the other hand did not want to be captured the whole day when he was wearing lousy clothes. Table 1 shows the users' preference towards geo-temporal constraints.

A weak spot of the prototype appeared when four users complained that the pictures taken with the smart phones were either blurry or the people in sight were sliced. The reason is that, even though the length of the neck strap on all users was the same, the people wearing it differed in their respective heights. Moreover, the smart phone camera did not produce very good results when the users were in motion.

RELATED WORK

There are two ways to impose privacy over the life log data. One method addresses privacy during live capture while the other deals with post capture distortion to maintain privacy. Most of these approaches employ computer vision techniques which has some serious flaws such as missed detection and false alarm, as discussed in [14].

Various privacy issues while capturing video or recording voice were discussed in [15]. The wearable life log system attempted to protect the privacy of life log video recordings in real time. The system used face detection, tracking and blocking algorithm to obfuscate the faces of the subjects with solid-color block, but this approach is vulnerable to missed detection in bad light conditions. Furthermore, the system depends upon skin color detection algorithm, which fails even with a tiny movement of the shoulder where the camera is mounted. The audio identity of the subject is distorted using a time-based pitch shifting algorithm.

In [3], the users were allowed to decide whether to log and share photos or videos taken by the life log device and concerns were shown for neighbors' pictures and videos; however, no mechanism was proposed to avoid such circumstances.

In [15], Makino et al. developed a tactile sound based life logging system employing a piezoelectric device on finger nail and recording the touch sound propagating through a fingertip. The mechanism enhanced privacy by avoiding camera, microphone and GPS sensors, however, the essence of life logging cannot be achieved as the captured information of touched objects is not rich enough to assist in the course of reminiscence.

In contrast to these techniques, we have developed a runtime mechanism to stop neighbors' logging unless acknowledged

	Geo context	Temporal context	Both
Users	7	1	8
%	43.75%	6.25%	50%

Table 1. User's preference towards geo-temporal constraints

by the owner, hence inducing a sense of consent before being captured by the life log device of others.

CONCLUSIONS AND FUTURE WORK

In the near future, wearable life log devices will be widespread and dominant. The act of logging everything and everyone is cumbersome, but easy to achieve at the same time. The threat of being monitored might drive people to behave in an unnatural way. The proposed framework attempts to prevent anonymous logging by specifying the privacy policies on the user's life logging devices, thus, ensuring their privacy pertaining to a specific location or during certain time slots of the day, or both. Furthermore, the system conceals the reluctant individuals who insist on their privacy and disagree to expose themselves to other users of the system.

The prototype system has gained a positive feedback from the experimenters and strengthened the idea of applying geo-temporal policies to restrict others to capture people in their daily life. In the next step, we are planning to extend the framework which can recognize hand gestures at runtime and discontinue the operation of life logging devices worn by people in the vicinity, since we might forget to inscribe a privacy policy for a place or time span where we are not willing to be recorded by others.

ACKNOWLEDGMENTS
Many thanks to Simona Vasilache for her valuable suggestions and comments.

REFERENCES
1. Gemmell, J., Bell, G., Lueder, R., Drucker, S., Wong, C. MyLifeBits: fulfilling the Memex vision . In *Proc.* Multimedia (2002). ACM; 2002 . p. 235–238.

2. Kim, I.J., Ahn, S.C., Kim, H.G. Personalized life log media system in ubiquitous environment. In *Proc.* Ubiquitous convergence technology 2007. Springer-Verlag; 2007. p. 20–29.

3. Kärkkäinen, T., Vaittinen, T., Väänänen-Vainio-Mattila, K. I don't mind being logged, but want to remain in control: a field study of mobile activity and context logging. In *Proc.* Human factors in computing systems 2010. ACM; 2010. p. 163–172.

4. Allen, A.L., Gemmell, J. Dredging up the past: Lifelogging, memory, and surveillance. The University of Chicago Law Review. 2008;75(1):47–74.

5. Cheng, W.C., Golubchik, L., Kay, D.G. Total recall: are privacy changes inevitable? In: *Proc.* Continuous archival and retrieval of personal experiences 2004. ACM; 2004. p. 86–92.

6. Nguyen, D.H., Marcu, G., Hayes, G.R., Truong, K.N., Scott, J., Langheinrich, M., et al. Encountering SenseCam: personal recording technologies in everyday life. In *Proc.* Ubiquitous computing 2009. ACM; 2009. p. 165–174.

7. Intille, S. S., Tapia, E.M., Rondoni, J., Beaudin, J., Kukla, C., Agarwal, S., Bao, L., Larson, K. Tools for studying behavior and technology in natural settings. In *Proc.* UBICOMP 2003; Springer; 2003: 157–174.

8. Kern, N., Schiele, B., Schmidt, A. Recognizing context for annotating a live life recording. Personal Ubiquitous Comput. 2007 Apr;11(4):251–263.

9. Li, Y., Landay, J.A. Activity-based prototyping of ubicomp applications for long-lived, everyday human activities. In *Proc.* SIGCHI Human factors in computing systems 2008. ACM; 2008. p. 1303–1312.

10. Blum, M., Pentland, A., Troster, G. InSense: Interest-Based Life Logging. IEEE Multimedia. 2006 Dec;13(4):40–48.

11. Aizawa, K., Tancharoen, D., Kawasaki, S., Yamasaki, T. Efficient retrieval of life log based on context and content. In: *Proc.* Continuous archival and retrieval of personal experiences 2004. ACM; 2004. p. 22–31.

12. Choudhury T., Pentland A. The Sociometer: A Wearable Device for Understanding Human Networks. In Workshop on Ad hoc Communications and Collaboration in Ubiquitous Computing Environments. 2002.

13. Arduino Mega ADK Board http://www.arduino.cc/en/Main/ArduinoBoardADK

14. Senior, A., Pankanti, S., Hampapur, A., Brown, L., Tian, Y.L., Ekin, A., et al. Enabling video privacy through computer vision. IEEE Security & Privacy. 2005 Jun;3(3):50– 57.

15. Chaudhari, J., Cheung, S. S., Venkatesh, M.V. Privacy Protection for Life-log Video. In: IEEE Workshop on Signal Processing Applications for Public Security and Forensics, 2007. SAFE '07. IET; 2007. p. 1–5.

16. Makino, Y., Murao, M., Maeno, T. Life log system based on tactile sound. In *Proc.* Haptics 2010. Springer-Verlag; 2010. p. 292–297.

Multi-Tapping Shortcut: A Technique for Augmenting Linear Menus on Multi-Touch Surface

Kentaro Go
Interdisciplinary Graduate School
of Medicine and Engineering
University of Yamanashi
4-3-11 Takeda, Kofu 400-8511 Japan
go@yamanashi.ac.jp

Hiroki Kasuga
Department of Computer Science
and Media Engineering
University of Yamanashi
4-3-11 Takeda, Kofu 400-8511 Japan
kasuga@golab.org

ABSTRACT

In this paper, we propose the Multi-Tapping Shortcut (MTS), a technique aimed at augmenting linear menus on multi-touch surfaces. We designed this multi-finger two-handed interaction technique in an attempt to overcome limitations of direct pointing on interactive surfaces while maintaining compatibility with traditional interaction techniques. Multi-tapping Shortcuts exploit multi-tapping by simply tapping a finger on the surface several times. This report describes the results of an experimental evaluation of our technique, with comparison to the Radial Stroke Shortcut (RSS) technique. Results show that the mean task completion time with MTS is 21.7% faster than that with RSS. MTS also outperformed RSS in terms of error and some users' assessments of comfort.

Author Keywords

Menu selection techniques; menu shortcuts; multi-touch; multi-finger interaction; two-handed interaction

ACM Classification Keywords

H.5.2 [Information Interfaces and Presentation]: User Interfaces - Interaction styles.

INTRODUCTION

A menu is a set of command options consisting of visually similar words and/or icons on a computer screen that are available to a user for selection. Menus are ubiquitous computer schemes in current human–computer interaction because they are easy to learn and use. Most menu techniques have been designed for the windows, icons, menus, and pointers (WIMP) interface used on personal computers. In recent years, however, development of interactive surface technologies such as touchscreens has proceeded rapidly, necessitating research and development of menu techniques.

Bailly, Lecolinet, and Guiard (2010) recently summarized

five major challenges for menu operation on interactive surfaces [1].

D1: Occlusion. The hand and the fingers might hide parts of the menu display.

D2: Accuracy. The large surface area of finger–screen contact might induce item selection errors.

D3: Lack of shortcuts. In the absence of a keyboard, the expert mode of Linear menus based on keyboard shortcuts are unavailable.

D4: Reachability. The length of the human arm being what it is, the menubar might be difficult to reach.

D5: Groupware. Collaborative work often requires the user identity to be known. So long as a menu technique relies on pointing in the absence of specific technology, this information is missing [8].

D1, D2 and D3 are applicable to all interactive surfaces of any size. D4 and D5 are specifically applicable to large interactive surfaces such as tabletops and interactive walls.

As described in this paper, we propose the Multi-Tapping Shortcut (MTS), a technique aimed at augmenting traditional linear menus on multi-touch surfaces. This technique is designed to overcome the five drawbacks above. We designed this multi-finger, two-handed interaction technique to overcome important limitations of direct pointing on interactive surfaces while maintaining compatibility with traditional interaction techniques. Multi-tapping Shortcuts exploit multi-tapping by simply tapping a finger on the surface several times.

In subsequent sections, we begin by discussing selection techniques aimed at alleviating the shortcomings described above. Specifically, we introduce the Finger Count Shortcut (FCS) and Radial Stroke Shortcut (RSS) proposed in [1]. Then we introduce our MTS. We discuss its evaluation with implementations on a single-touch device and a multi-touch device following a discussion of evaluation results. The paper concludes with a summary of the current project and a description of future work.

RELATED WORK

Recent development of interactive techniques for multi-touch surfaces has fundamentally improved traditional graphical user interface elements. Menu selection is no exception. Several works describe improvements of menu usage [2, 3, 4, 5], yet important shortcomings remain.

Two-handed approaches [12, 13] on interactive surfaces can improve interaction by providing natural operations and commands [6, 7, 8]. However, they present weaknesses such as the absence of expert mode. Marking menus and stroke-based shortcuts [3, 5, 9] specifically apply to expert modes of use. They are applicable to interactive surfaces and provide efficient menu selection from multilayered menus when a user becomes proficient at recalling the assigned strokes. Nevertheless, such approaches provide no specific means for efficient menu activation.

To deal with the five challenges for menu operation on interactive surfaces, Bailly, Lecolinet, and Guiard [1] proposed the Finger Count Shortcut (FCS) and Radial Stroke Shortcut (RSS), which respectively use coding systems and strokes to augment traditional menu systems.

Finger Count Shortcut
The Finger Count Shortcut is a coding technique based on touching several points simultaneously. Each hand can produce five fingerprints at most. Consequently, *"with two hands a user can specify 5×5=25 favorite items in a classical two-level hierarchical menu bar"* [1].

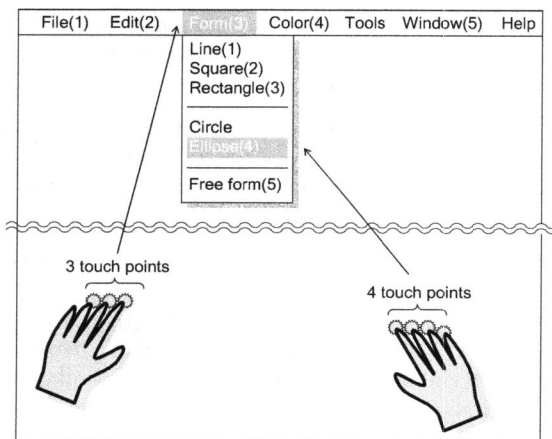

Figure 1. Finger Count Shortcuts [1].

Figure 1 depicts an example of a Finger Count Shortcut. Each menu item has a digit, so the user puts the appropriate number of fingers on the interactive surface with the non-dominant hand to select the corresponding menu item. Each menu item on the selected menu has a digit, so the user puts the appropriate number of fingers on the interactive surface with the dominant hand to select the corresponding menu item. As an example shown in Figure 1, the user makes three finger touches on the interactive surface to select the Form menu item from the menu bar. Then the user makes four finger touches on the interactive surface to select the Ellipse menu item from the displayed menu.

The number of selection items is limited to five items in each menu, but the Finger Count Shortcut presumably provides maximum selection speed because each item can be selected with a single coding action.

Radial Stroke Shortcut
The Radial Stroke Shortcut, which shares the basic concept with [9] and [14], employs a sequence of short strokes to select a desired menu item. Strokes are designed to choose eight directions: the four cardinal directions and the four diagonal directions. Consequently, *"two short strokes executed successively suffice to specify one from a set of 8×8=64 favorite commands."* [1].

Figure 2 portrays an example of a Radial Stroke Shortcut. To activate the menu bar, the user presses at least two fingers with the non-dominant hand on the interactive surface. Each menu item on the menu bar has an arrow sign, so the user expresses the appropriate short radial stroke on the interactive surface with the dominant hand to select the corresponding menu item. Similarly, each menu item on the selected menu has an arrow, so the user performs the appropriate short radial stroke on the interactive surface with the dominant hand to select the corresponding menu item. In the example shown in Figure 2, the user makes two finger touches on the interactive surface to activate the menu bar. Subsequently, the user makes a short stroke to the right with the right index finger to specify the Form menu item from the menu bar. Finally, the user performs a short stroke to the bottom right with the right index finger to specify the Ellipse menu item from the Form menu.

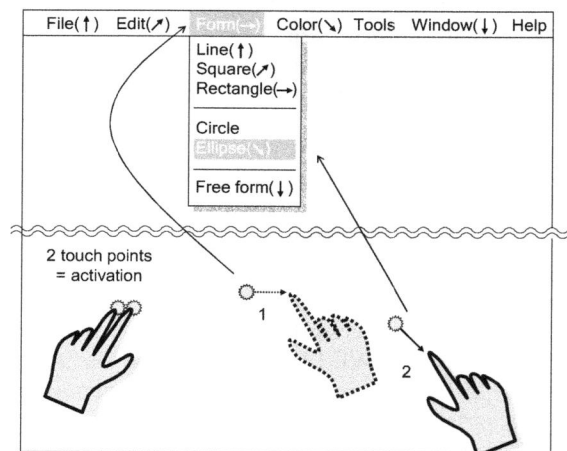

Figure 2. Radial Stroke Shortcuts [1].

In summary, although FCS and RSS are designed to address the five challenges described in the Introduction, their design solution is limited to a two-level hierarchical menu system and five or eight menu items for selection. To remove these restrictions, we propose MTS.

MULTI-TAPPING SHORTCUT

Motivation

Multi-tapping operation is employed by standard mobile phone keypads for text entry. Touchscreen mobile phones also have onscreen software keypads, giving users opportunities to tap certain areas multiple times on the interactive surface to create text messages for SMS and micro-blogging.

Multi-tapping is a basic skill cultivated from daily mobile phone experience. Therefore, users can naturally and easily transfer this skill to other command input techniques such as menu selection. Most users are already proficient at multi-tapping. Therefore, we expect that multi-tapping command input can achieve higher performance than other command input techniques.

Interaction Design

Multi-Tapping shortcuts augment traditional menu systems using taps. Users express their choices within the menu bar and the selected menu by tapping at some convenient location on the interactive surface.

State Transition Models

Figure 3 depicts state transition models of the Multi-Tapping shortcut, which is a similar schematic notation to [6]. Figure 3(a) depicts the state transition model for single-layer menus such as icons and ribbons currently displayed on screen or context menus. The model includes two states: State 0 and State 1. State 0 is that in which the menu is inactivated. When the menu is activated, it moves to State 1, where the menu cursor (or pointer) is displayed on screen. In this state, the user taps some convenient location on the interactive surface and makes a corresponding move of the cursor position. The user repeats tapping until the cursor points at a desired menu item. When the cursor points at the desired menu item, the user sends a selection command by single tapping of a certain area on the interactive surface. It makes the state change from State 1 to State 0. A user who wishes to cancel the operation in State 1 then just issues the cancel command and returns to State 0.

Figure 3(b) extends the single-layer menu model in (a) to a two-layer model. Standard dropdown menus for OS X (Apple Inc.) and Windows (Microsoft Corp.) can be represented as a two-layer model. They consist of three states: State 0, State 1, and State 2. Basic behaviors and events for State 0 and 1 are the same as those of the single-layer menu model, except for selection events. A tap for selection in State 1 goes to State 2, which enables a new menu such as a dropdown menu and its cursor (or pointer) to display on screen. Four choices exist for a user in State 2: Tap for pointing, Tap for selection, return from the menu mode (Inactivate), and go back to the previous menu (Tap for Return). Although the first three choices have the same behavior and events as State 1 of the single-layer menu model shown in Figure 3(a), the last choice is novel. If the user wishes to return to the previous menu in State 2 of

Figure 3(b), then the user sends a cancel command by single tapping of a certain area on the interactive surface. Then the current menu reverts to the previous menu with its cursor for selection (State 1). Now, we can extend the menu model to more than three states (e.g., Three-Layer Menu as in Figure 3(c)).

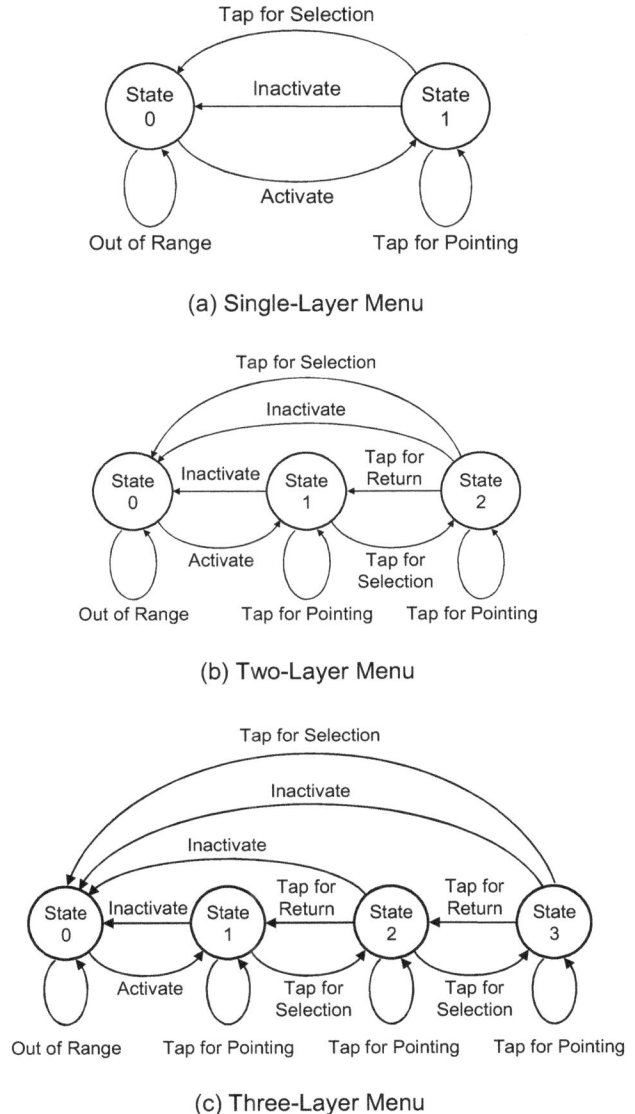

(a) Single-Layer Menu

(b) Two-Layer Menu

(c) Three-Layer Menu

Figure 3. State Transision Models of MTS.

Design Example

Figure 4 presents a design example of an MTS system for a two-layer menu used in the experiment to be described later in the paper. We assigned two-point simultaneous touches for the non-dominant hand as the activation command of the menu mode. It can be done naturally by right-handed users with the left index and middle fingers. The touches should be kept during the menu mode and released if the user wishes to cancel the operations and inactivate the menu mode. We assigned one finger tap for the dominant hand as a Tap for Pointing, which can be done with the right index finger for right-handed users. Additionally, we assigned one finger tap for the non-dominant hand as Tap for Selection, which can be done with the left thumb for right-handed users.

A normal operation sequence of MTS is the following (note that in the following, State corresponds to the State in Figure 3(b)).

Step 1: In State 0, the user touches on the left side area on the touchscreen by the left index and middle fingers, which sends the menu activation command to the computer. Then, it moves to State 1.

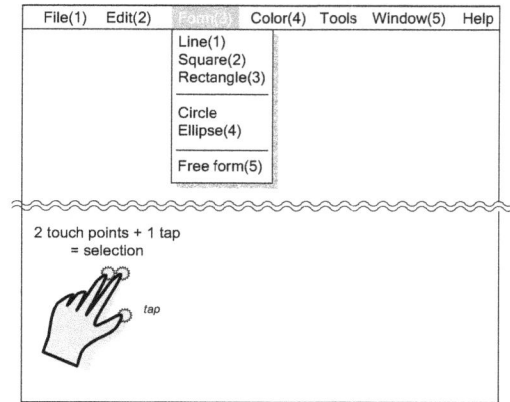

Step 3: Tapping as selection.

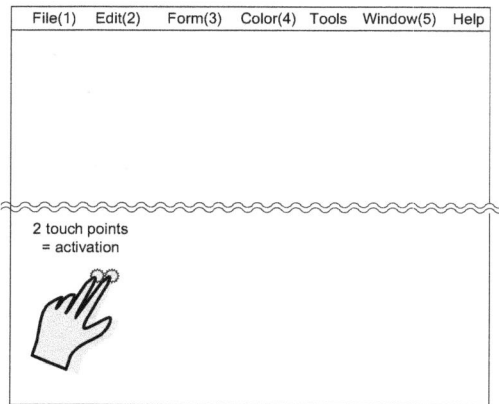

Step 1: Activation.

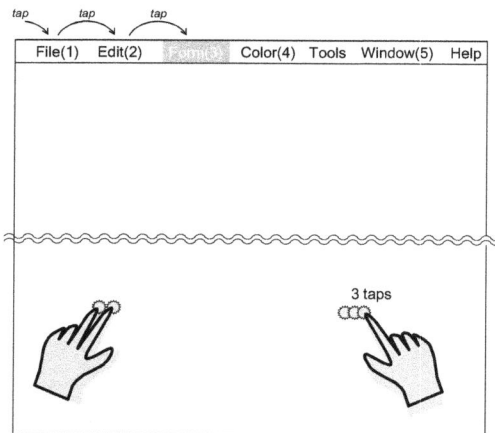

Step 4: Multi-tapping as pointing.

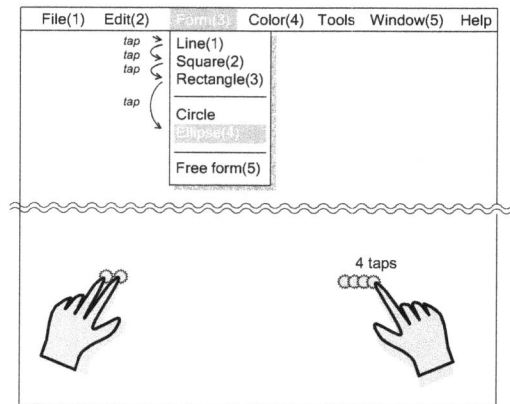

Step 2: Multi-tapping as pointing.

Figure 4. Multi-Tapping Shortcuts (Continue to the next column).

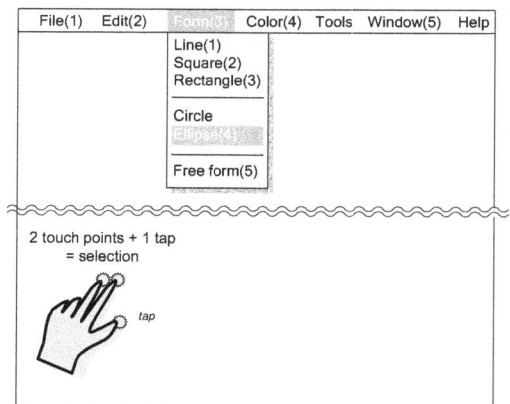

Step 5: Tapping as selection.

Figure 4 (Cont'd). Multi-Tapping Shortcuts.

Step 2: In State 1, the user keeps touching with the left two fingers. The user taps the right side area on the touchscreen with the right index finger. The selection cursor appears on the first selection item and shifts its position as the user taps. In the example, the user taps three times to find the Form item highlighted.

Step 3: The user taps with the left thumb when finding a desired menu item highlighted. The thumb tap sends the command as Tap for Selection. Then it displays the corresponding menu on screen and moves to State 2. In the example, the Form menu shows up on screen.

Step 4: In State 2, the user keeps touching with the left two fingers. The user taps the right side area on the touchscreen with the right index finger. The selection cursor appears on the first selection item and shifts its position as the user taps. In the example, the user taps four times to find the Ellipse item highlighted.

Step 5: The user taps by the left thumb when finding a desired menu item highlighted. The thumb tap sends the command as Tap for Selection. Then it executes the corresponding command and moves to State 0. In the example, the Ellipse format is applied to a pre-selected object.

Another possible design is that the left thumb is used for Tap for Return and the right thumb for Selection. Thereby, the left hand consolidates the mode operations for menu: Activation, Inactivation, and Tap for Return. The right hand does the item operations for menu: Tap for Pointing and Tap for Selection.

Multi-layered Menus and Other Issues
Menu layers can be extended to more than two layers by cascading State 2 of the two-layer model in Figure 3(b). For a three-layer model, State 3 is added as portrayed in Figure 3(c).

A menu structure might be designed to have uneven depths. For example in the two-layer menu, the top menu might contain a selection item that shows no next menu but issues a command. Thereby, State 1 of the two-layer model in Figure 3(b) should have the edge to State 0 labeled as Tap for Selection. A similar discussion is applicable to States 1 and 2 of the three-layer model in Figure 3(c).

In MTS, selection items consist of a ring structure at the same selection level, as inferred from the fact that any number of the Tap for pointing event can be done in the state transition models in Figure 3. In the menu bar in Figure 4, for example, the next tap to Window(5) means File(1). In general, the File item is selected when the number of taps **mod** 5 is 1. Similarly, the Edit item is selected when the number of taps **mod** 5 is 2. Another example is one of dropdown menus. In the Form menu depicted in Step 4 of Figure 3, the next tap to Free form(5) means Line(1). In general, the Line item is selected when

the number of taps **mod** 5 is 1. Similarly, the Square item is selected when the number of taps **mod** 5 is 2.

Characteristics and Hypothesis
Along the same lines described in an [1], MTS can deal with the shortcomings of direct finger contact on interactive surfaces. The occlusion (D1), accuracy (D2) and reachability (D4) are not issues because the user can perform MTS away from the menu display area. It also provides an expert mode (D3) by tapping a rhythm [10] corresponding to a sequence of taps to reach a selection item. Furthermore, it can be used with eye-free tapping actions, and it can be done by more than one user (D5).

Table 1 presents Finger Count, Radial Stroke, and Multi-Tapping shortcut characteristics: FCS employs the number of fingerprints for detection; RSS employs short strokes on interactive surface; and MTS employs the number of taps.

Shortcut method	Detection	# of shortcuts	# layers in hierarchy	Selection speed
Finger Count	Fingerprints	25	Two	Fastest
Radial Stroke	Strokes	64	Two	TBD
Multi-Tapping	Taps	Any	Any	TBD

Table 1. Shortcut Method Comparison Table.

FCS can specify 5×5=25 selection items in a classical two-level hierarchical menu. RSS can specify more items with the upper limitation at the resolution of gestures on screen: 8×8=64 selection items in a classical two-level hierarchical menu. MTS can specify virtually any number of items on any number of layers without limitation.

However, FCS can achieve the fastest selection speed among the three shortcut methods because a user can specify any item merely with a touch action. RSS and MTS are theoretically slower than FCS, but no empirical evidence shows which is the faster.

In summary, although it is the fastest approach to select a menu item, we exclude FCS from our discussion because its number of shortcuts is limited to 25 and the hierarchy is limited to two layers. For the rest of the paper, we compare RSS and MTS empirically. Our hypothesis is the following.

Hypothesis: Multi-Tapping Shortcut is faster in menu selection tasks than Radial Stroke Shortcut.

We set the hypothesis based on our prior experience on text entry methods on an interactive surface [11]. It proved that multi-tapping is a prominent method with practical advantages for finger motor skills and learning.

PILOT STUDY: SINGLE-TOUCH DEVICE

To test our hypothesis—the tap-based shortcut (Multi-Tapping Shortcut) is faster for menu selection than the gesture-based shortcut (Radial Stroke Shortcut)—we first developed a touch-screen-based menu system for a single-touch device. We tested the hypothesis in a minimalist setting.

Simulated Single-touch Shortcuts

We developed a prototype menu system that simulates RSS and MTS on a single-touch device.

Single-touch RSS is a version of RSS with no activation. It is useful with the dominant hand only. Therefore in Figure 2, the left hand is not necessary. Since it is implemented for testing purposes, no other action than pointing and selecting a menu item is allowed.

Similarly, Single-touch MTS is a version of MTS with no activation. In Figure 3, Step 1 is not necessary. In Step 2 of Figure 3, the left hand is not necessary. In Step 3, the selection command is sent to the computer by tapping an area, which has a certain distance from the last tap point with the right hand. Most users usually tap the bottom left corner of the screen with the left hand while others shift the right hand, maintain a certain distance, and tap the screen as a selection. Similar discussions are applied to Step 4 and Step 5 of Figure 3 for pointing and selecting a menu item with Single-touch MTS. It is implemented for testing purpose. Therefore, no other action than pointing and selecting a menu item is allowed.

Equipment and Menu Configuration

The experiment was conducted on a 21.5-inch Multi-Touch monitor (SX2210Tb; Dell Inc.) connected to a PC (Endeavor Pro7000; Hewlett-Packard Co.) running Windows 7 (Microsoft Corp.). We developed a prototype of menu system in C# (Visual Studio 2010; Microsoft Corp.). A sub-monitor (SyncMaster 712N; Samsung Electronics) was provided for the participant to consult the experimental task to be completed at any time during the test session. Figure 5 shows an experimental session during the pilot study.

The menu bar has five selection items, whereas each pull down menu has 2–5 selection items. It partially emulates standard menu systems on the Windows (Microsoft Corp.) operating system. Figure 6 presents an example of the menu system used for the pilot study. In this example, the View menu has five menu items; the third item, Icons, is selected.

Task and Procedure

Four undergraduate students participated in this pilot study. They were asked to activate a target menu item as quickly and accurately as possible. The experimenter observed the participant's tasks, evaluated the task effectiveness, and measured the task completion time.

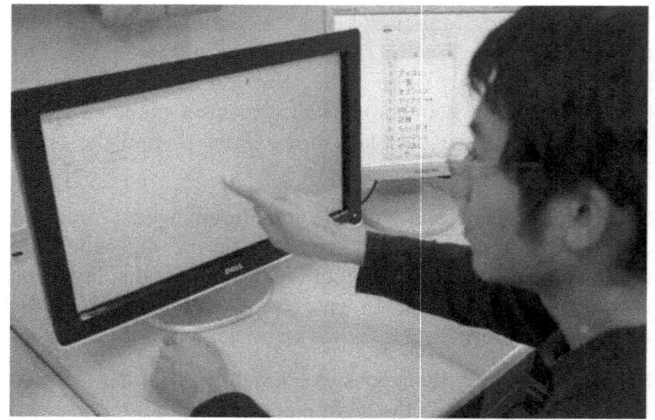

Figure 5. Experimental session of the pilot study.

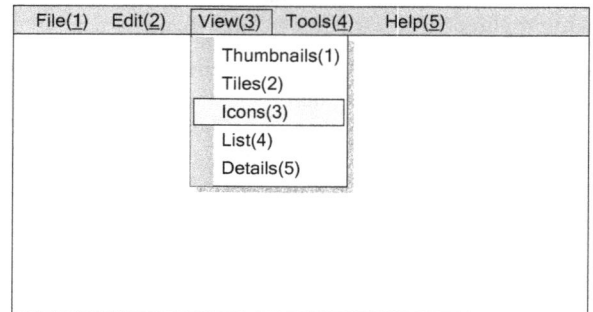

Figure 6. Overview image of the menu system used in the pilot study. The figure is an English version, but the experiment was conducted using a corresponding Japanese version.

Experimental sessions are conducted with the following procedure:

1. The experimenter gives instructions to the participant about the menu selection method to be tested: Single-touch RSS or Single-touch MTS.

2. The participant is given five minutes to practice similar tasks several times in the test environment.

3. The participant performs four experimental sessions.

4. The participant is provided a short break and repeats Steps 1–3 using another shortcut method.

The presentation order of Single-touch RSS and Single-touch MTS is counterbalanced.

Results

Figure 7 presents each participant's average task completion time with single-touch Radial Stroke and single-touch Multi-Tapping shortcuts.

Figure 7 shows that single-touch MTS took 42.4 s (SD = 5.90) on average to complete the task whereas single-touch RSS required 49.1 s (SD = 7.35).

Based on this preliminary result with the pilot study, we expected that further formal experiment with multi-touch device supports our hypothesis. On the multi-touch versions, we implement the menu system activation process also.

EXPERIMENT: MULTI-TOUCH DEVICE

Our goal was to test our hypothesis: a multi-tapping shortcut is faster in menu selection than a slide-based shortcut in a multi-touch tabletop environment. To this end, we developed a touchscreen-based menu system for a multi-touch device.

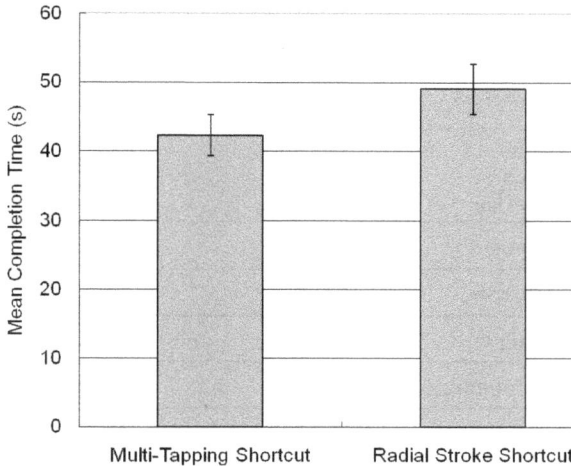

Figure 7. Mean task completion time for single-touch version shortcuts.

Equipment and Menu Configuration

We made a tabletop multi-touch screen using the Frustrated Total Internal Reflection (FTIR) sensing technique [4].

We used the TUIO tracker of Community Core Vision [7] software to detect touch points on screen with a Web camera. The detected touch-point positions are transmitted to our original software using TUIO protocol. The original software, written in C# (Visual Studio 2010; Microsoft Corp.), acts as a TUIO client and implements the menu systems, shortcut methods and testing environment. It creates the look-and-feel of the touchscreen. Visual feedback is displayed on the tabletop screen from the bottom of the table with a projector. Figure 8 portrays the overall architecture of our tabletop system. Figure 9 depicts an overview.

The main PC had the following specifications: Touch Smart PC tx2 (Hewlett-Packard Co.) with a Turion X2 Ultra Dual-Core Mobile ZM-84 2.30 GHz processor (AMD Inc.) running on Windows Vista Home Premium (Microsoft Corp.). In the Web camera (V-UJ16; Logitec Corp.), we replaced the internal infrared filter with an infrared transmitting one. We used a projector (EMP-760; Seiko Epson Corp.).

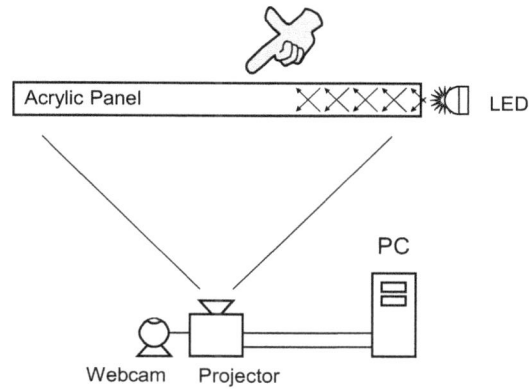

Figure 8. Basic components of FTIR-based interactive surface.

Figure 9. Overview of the experimental setting.

The table height was 920 mm, which is assumed to be operated when standing (see Figure 10). The tabletop, which is made from 10 mm thick acrylic, is 1,030 mm wide × 730 mm depth. A sheet of tracing paper is placed on the table-top as a projector screen. It provides users a smoother feeling of touch also.

As Community Core Vision parameters, the calculation time is set to 5 ms, camera resolution to 320 × 240, and camera frame rate to 30 fps.

Figure 11 presents a sample touchscreen menu used for the Multi-Tapping shortcut condition in the experiment. The menu bar has five selection items. Each pull down menu has five selection items. The items of the menu bar are labeled with alphabetical letters from A to E. The items of each menu are labeled randomly created four letters. It requires user visual search in the menu items and emulates a situation in which a non-expert user uses the environment.

The target menu item to be selected is displayed on the bottom left area on screen so that the participant can easily confirm it during the experimental session.

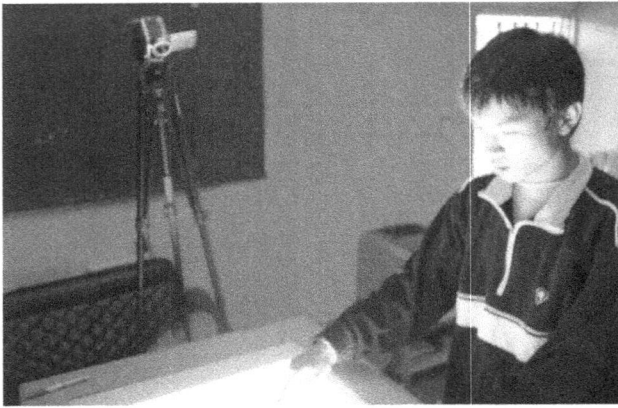

Figure 10. Scene from the experiment. The user operates objects on the tabletop standing up.

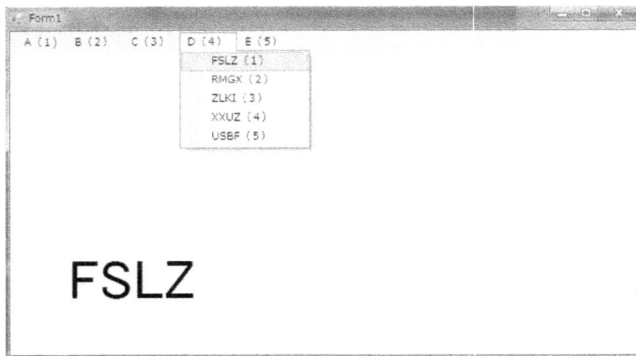

Figure 11. Overview of the experimental setting.

Evaluation Item	Rating Scale		
	1	...	7
Force required for actuation	Very uncomfortable	...	Very comfortable
Smoothness during operation	Very rough	...	Very smooth
Effort required for operation	Very high	...	Very low
Accuracy	Very inaccurate	...	Very accurate
Operation speed	Unacceptable	...	Acceptable
General comfort	Very uncomfortable	...	Very comfortable
Overall operation of input device	Very difficult (to use)	...	Very easy (to use)
Finger fatigue	Very high	...	None
Wrist fatigue	Very high	...	None
Arm fatigue	Very high	...	None
Shoulder fatigue	Very high	...	None
Neck fatigue	Very high	...	None

Table 2. Independent 7 point rating scale used in the study (Assessment of comfort in ISO9241-9).

Task and Procedure

The purpose of the experiment is to test our hypothesis that Multi-Tapping Shortcut is faster than a Radial Stroke Shortcut in a multi-touch environment. Consequently, the principal independent variable for the experiment is the shortcut method.

Nine undergraduate students (males in their twenties; right-handed) participated in this experiment. Five students were proficient at operating touchscreens, although four students were not. They were asked to activate a target menu item as quickly and accurately as possible.

Design

The experiment used within subjects design to evaluate performance across the two conditions: Radial Stroke Shortcut and Multi-Tapping Shortcut. The principal dependent variables for the experiment were selection time and accuracy, which were recorded within the menu system software. In addition, each participant's subjective assessment on the shortcut and task was recorded. Table 2 presents the independent 7 point rating scale used in the study, which is referred from the assessment of comfort in ISO9241-9.

Results

Figures 12 and 13 present mean selection times and mean errors, respectively. Mean task completion time for Multi-Tapping Shortcut was 183.3 s (SD = 24.7); that for Radial Stroke Shortcut is 234.0 s (SD = 44.8). Results show that MTS significantly outperforms RSS in mean task completion time ($p = 0.0081$, paired t-test). Mean error for MTS is 0.67 (SD = 0.70); that for RSS is 5.11 (SD = 3.33). Results show that MTS significantly outperforms RSS in mean error ($p = 0.0039$, paired t-test). In summary, the mean task completion with MTS is approximately 21.7% faster than that of RSS.

Figure 14 presents the participants' subjective values for the assessment of comfort. A Wilcoxon signed-rank test was performed, revealing significant differences in three items: smoothness during operation ($p = 0.028$), general comfort ($p = 0.036$), and overall operation of the input device ($p = 0.025$). Although no other significant difference exists in the evaluation items, participants' subjective values for MTS were generally higher than for RSS.

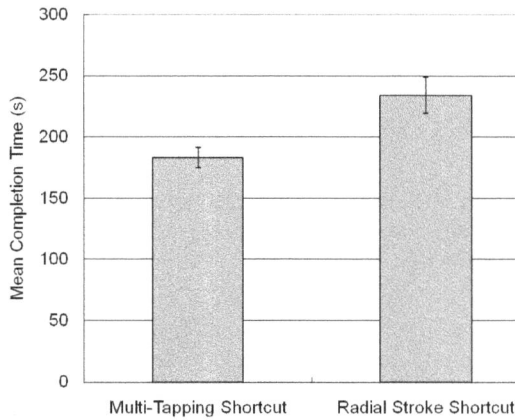

Figure 12. Mean task completion time

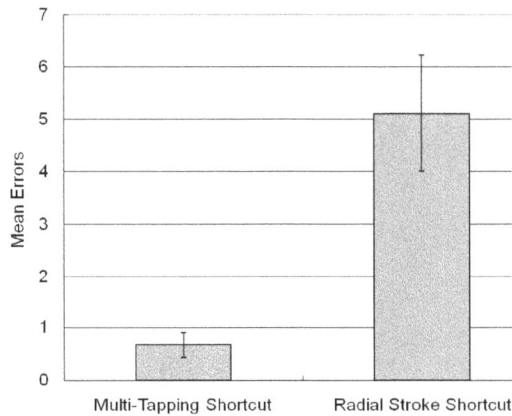

Figure 13. Mean errors

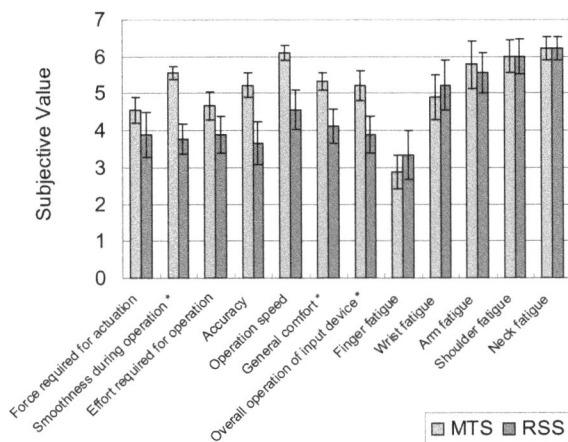

Figure 14. Assessment of comfort for the experiment.

DISCUSSION

Results support our hypothesis that the Multi-Tapping Shortcut is faster in the menu selection task than the Radial Stroke Shortcut. The former also surpasses RSS in mean error. MTS is 21.7% faster than RSS with less operation error.

Participants' subjective values for MTS are generally higher than for RSS except, with respect to the finger fatigue item. Although no significant difference was found, MTS apparently requires more finger actions than RSS does.

Overall, the results indicate MTS as a better approach than RSS from a performance viewpoint. Finally, we revise the shortcut method comparison table as Table 3.

Shortcut method	Detection	# of shortcuts	# layers in hierarchy	Selection speed
Finger Count	Fingerprints	25	Two	Fastest
Radial Stroke	Strokes	64	Two	Fast
Multi-Tapping	Taps	Any	Any	Faster

Table 3. Shortcut Method Comparison Table (revised on Table 1)

CONCLUSION

We conclude from our comparative experiments that Multi-Tapping Shortcut for augmenting traditional layered menu is an effective, efficient, and robust shortcut technique for multi-touch interactive surfaces. Results show that MTS is superior Radial Stroke Shortcut in mean task completion time and mean error. MTS also outperforms Finger Count Shortcut because it can accommodate menus with more than two layers. Furthermore, MTS provides ease of learning: users can readily transfer their prior skill and experience in multi-tapping text entry for mobile phones to the menu shortcut method.

In future work, we plan to investigate which finger is best to assign commands such as activate, inactivate, pointing, selection, and return. We also plan to investigate combination techniques such as coding plus tapping to incorporate more commands into a single tap action.

ACKNOWLEDGMENTS

This research was partially supported by the Ministry of Education, Science, Sports and Culture, Grant-in-Aid for Scientific Research (C) 24500144 and 23500160.

REFERENCES

1. Bailly, G., Lecolinet, E., and Guiard, Y. Finger Count and Radial Stroke Shortcuts: Two Techniques for Augmenting Linear Menus. In *Proc. CHI 2010*, ACM Press (2010), 591-594.

2. Bier, E. A., Stone, M. C., Pier, K., Buxton, W., and DeRose, T. D. 1993. Toolglass and magic lenses: The see-through interface. In *Proc. SIGGRAPH '93*. ACM Press (1993), 73-80.

3. Fitts, P. M., and Seeger, C. MS-R Compatibility: Spatial Characteristics of Stimulus and Response Codes. JEP, 1953, 46, 199-210.

4. Han, J. Y. Low-Cost Multi-Touch Sensing through Frustrated Total Internal Reflection. In *Proc. UIST '05*, ACM Press (2005), 115-118.

5. Nacenta, M. A., Baudisch, P., Benko, H., and Wilson, A. 2009. Separability of spatial manipulations in multi-touch interfaces. In *Proc. GI '09*, ACM Press (2009), 175-182.

6. Buxton, W. (1990). A Three-State Model of Graphical Input. In *D. Diaper et al. (Eds), Human–Computer Interaction - INTERACT '90*. Amsterdam: Elsevier Science Publishers B.V. (North-Holland), 449-456.

7. Community Core Vision. http://ccv.nuigroup.com/.

8. Dietz, P. and Leigh, D. DiamondTouch: a multi-user touch technology. In *Proc. UIST '01*, ACM Press (2001), 219-226.

9. Appert, C. and Zhai, S. Using strokes as command shortcuts: cognitive benefits and toolkit support. In *Proc. CHI '09*. ACM Press (2009), 2289-2298.

10. Wobbrock, J. TapSongs: tapping rhythm-based passwords on a single binary sensor. In *Proc. UIST '09*. ACM Press (2009), 93-96.

11. Go, K. and Tsurumi, L. Arranging touch screen software keyboard split-keys based on contact surface. In *Proc. CHI EA '10*, ACM Press (2010), 3805-3810.

12. Fitzmaurice, G., Baudel, T., Kurtenbach, G., and Buxton, B. A GUI paradigm using tablets, two-hands and transparency. In *Proc. CHI '97*, ACM Press (1997), 212-213.

13. Guiard, Y. 1987. Asymmetric division of labor in human skilled bimanual action: The kinematic chain as a model. *Journal of Motor Behavior*, 19(4), 486-517.

14. Zhao, S. Balakrishnan, R. Simple vs. compound mark hierarchical marking menus. In *Proc UIST '04*, ACM Press (2004), 33-42.

Designing a User Interface for a Painting Application Supporting Real Watercolor Painting Processes

Jiho Yeom
Graduate School of Culture Technology, KAIST
335 Gwahangno, Yuseong-gu,
Daejeon 305-701, Korea
Jiho6493@kaist.ac.kr

Geehyuk Lee
HCI Lab, KAIST
335 Gwahangno, Yuseong-gu,
Daejeon 305-701, Korea
geehyuk@gmail.com

ABSTRACT

While research on non-photorealistic rendering is providing simulation-based realistic watercolor painting effects, the current digital painting interfaces are yet to be improved for providing realistic watercolor painting experience. This study proposes a digital watercolor painting interface to support real watercolor painting processes. We evaluated the new interface in comparison with a conventional digital watercolor painting interface with respect to effectiveness, efficiency, and satisfaction. The new interface was not different in terms of efficiency, but was shown to be more effective in that it enabled the users produce more satisfactory paintings than the conventional interface. It was also favored in terms of satisfaction. This result suggests that a user interface supporting real watercolor painting processes is important for the usability of a simulation-based digital watercolor painting system.

Author Keywords

Digital Painting; Interface Design.

ACM Classification Keywords

H.5.2 [Information interfaces and presentation]: User Interfaces. – Interaction styles; I.1.34 [Computer Graphics]: Graphics Utilities.–Paint systems.

General Terms

Human Factors; Experimentation; Design.

INTRODUCTION

Digital painting systems have evolved greatly over the past few decades. In particular, research on non-photorealistic rendering is providing simulation-based realistic watercolor painting effects [8, 21]. However, existing digital painting interfaces are not suitable for providing realistic watercolor painting experience. Some studies pointed out that the conventional digital painting systems are so sterile that they only took a shallow view of the processes of real painting [4, 5]. For example, painters iteratively change the

properties of the painting brush with watercolor painting tools, but the conventional digital painting interfaces do not support this kind of real watercolor painting processes.

The following three requirements are essential for a digital painting system to support realistic watercolor painting experience. First, it should provide a direct manipulation environment. Some digital painting systems use a graphics tablet, thereby providing an indirect manipulation environment. This can cause an eye-hand coordination problem. A direct manipulation environment will be essential for users to have realistic painting experience. Second, the basic properties of real painting tools should be respected. For example, a brush is flexible, dynamic, and area-based tool. A graphics tablet pen, on the other hand, is a hard-pointed and point-based input device. The use of a brush-like input device will enable users experience more realistic digital watercolor painting. Finally, real painting processes has to be respected. Existing digital painting systems usually provide slide bars and select boxes for controlling painting parameters such as color and brightness. Users in this case adjust painting parameters individually with the slide bars and the select boxes. However, in real watercolor painting, the adjustment of the painting parameters is done using painting tools, such as a brush and water, and more than one painting parameters are usually controlled together. For example, a user controls the wetness and the intensity of a brush at the same time by adding water.

Among these three requirements, the first two have been considered often in early studies pursuing realistic digital painting experience. For example, there are studies proposing a direct-manipulation, digital painting environment with a real brush or a brush-like device [12, 14, 17, 22, 23]. On the other hand, the third requirement has rarely been considered, i.e., no studies so far paid a serious attention to the requirement of a digital painting environment supporting the processes of real watercolor painting. In fact, there are some studies paying attention to the processes of real oil painting, but oil painting processes are different from watercolor painting processes.

In the study presented in this paper, we investigated real watercolor painting processes, and designed a digital watercolor painting interface with real watercolor painting tools to support real watercolor painting processes. We evaluated the usability of the new interface in comparison with a conventional digital watercolor interface.

RELATED WORK

There have been a number of studies suggesting solutions for the usability problem of using a tablet stylus and for bridging the real painting and the digital painting. CoolPaint, IntuPaint, and MAI Paint Brush proposed digital painting systems that use a brush-like device in a direct manipulation environment like a tabletop environment or a mixed-reality environment [12, 14, 22]. Digital Canvas and FluidPaint suggested digital painting systems that use a real painting brush [17, 23].

There are also studies proposing a user interface with painting tools [3, 4, 19]. HabilisDraw proposed a tool-based drawing interface, and showed that a tool-based approach has some advantages in terms of intuitiveness and ease of use [19]. Baxter's works suggested an immersive painting environment mimicking a real painting environment [3, 4]. By the way, the proposed interfaces by these studies cannot be applied to our case because their target domains were different from watercolor painting. However, these studies support our expectation that bringing the tools of real watercolor painting into a digital painting interface may have possible advantages.

In our study, we adopted a tabletop interface using a real brush from early works to handle the problems of an indirect manipulation environment and a graphics tablet. On top of the existing platform, we propose a user interface with real watercolor painting tools to support real watercolor painting processes.

WATER-COLOR PAINTING

Watercolor Painting Processes

Watercolor painting consists of two steps as shown in Figure 1: sketching and painting. Sketching is a process independent of watercolor painting, which is done before watercolor painting. Painting consists of two steps: adjustment of brush properties and stroke. To adjust brush properties, a user adjusts the color, its intensity, and wetness of the brush. Stroke is a step that makes a footprint of the brush on the canvas. These two steps are iteratively done during the watercolor painting process.

Adjustment of brush properties

This step is adjusting brush properties for intended watercolor effects. It consists of adjusting the color, intensity of the color, and wetness of the brush. Adjusting the color can be either by selecting an existing color on a palette or by mixing more than two colors. Adjustment of brush properties may or may not be required depending on the situation. Adjusting brush properties is done iteratively with watercolor painting tools.

Stroke

Stroke is a major activity in watercolor painting, making a footprint of the brush on the canvas. Various watercolor effects may be possible depending on the brush properties.

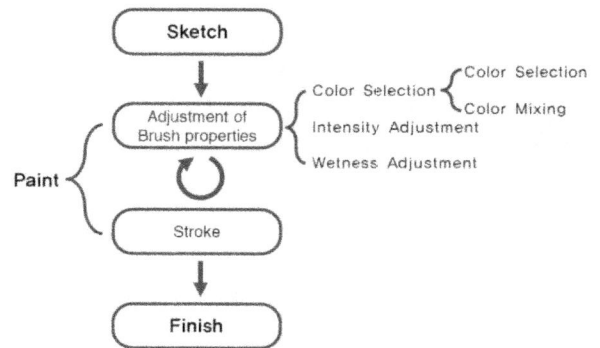

Figure 1. Watercolor painting processes

Watercolor Painting Tools

Brush

In real watercolor painting, brush footprints are created on the touched area of the canvas. The brush is used for adjusting brush properties with water, a towel, and a palette. Various kinds of watercolor effects like dry-brush, edge darkening, back-runs, granulation, and flow patterns are created by adjusting the wetness and the color intensity of the brush. In addition, a brush tip shows the current value of brush properties. As the tip of the brush shows the brush shape and color, a painter can predict the thickness and the color of a stroke. Also, a painter can guess the approximate value of the intensity and the wetness of the brush through the tip of the brush.

Watercolor paints and palette

Watercolor paint determines color, and the amount of the watercolor paint on the brush determines the intensity of the color. A palette is used to keep watercolor paints, and to mix them to create a new color.

Water and towel

Water is one of the most important materials in watercolor painting. A user rinses the brush with the water, increasing the wetness of the brush. At the same time, this decreases the intensity of the color. Various watercolor effects are possible depending on the wetness of the brush. A towel is used to dry the brush after rinsing. The function of a towel is to decrease the wetness of the brush.

Basic Skills of Watercolor Painting

There are various watercolor painting techniques in watercolor painting. In the following, we define six basic skills of watercolor painting: Flat Wash, Graded Wash, Glazed Wash, Wet-In-Wet. Dry Brush, and Lifting.

Flat Wash is the most basic skill, which is painting the area with a consistent intensity of the color and wetness. It does not need any adjustment of the brush properties in digital painting. **Graded Wash** is painting the area gradually by changing the brush properties. This skill is often used to express the background such as the sky. **Glazed Wash** is creating a glazed effect, adding thin watercolor layers on a dried layer. **Wet-In-Wet** adding layers of wet paint on a wet canvas. Accidental effect of watercolor is shown by the flow of water. **Dry Brush** is painting with little wetness. It is mostly used to express rough textures, applying paint only to the raised areas of the paper [8]. **Lifting** is removing the layers of watercolor with a clean brush. It can be easily done when the layer is wet, and the lifted area will be lightened. This skill is used not only to remove the painted area but also to express light and pale effects like clouds.

Figure 2. 6 basic skills of watercolor painting

PAINTING APPLICATION PROTOTYPE

We made a prototype supporting real watercolor painting process. The prototype has tools that resemble the look, use and function of real watercolor painting tools.

System

The prototype is developed for a tabletop environment. The tabletop detects a blob of a touched area of the brush, and creates the footprint of the brush based on the information of the position and the size of the blob. The tabletop is of Rear-DI (diffused illumination) type [20], and has the dimension of 102cm x 79cm x 80cm. The camera in the tabletop had the resolution of 640 x 480 pixels and the frame rate of 22 FPS and was equipped with an infrared passing filter. The tabletop uses a projector of 2,200 ANSI lumens.

To detect the touched area of the brush, the prototype used Community Core Vision (CCV) which was customized to send TUIO 2D blob messages [7]. CCV detects and sends the position, the orientation, and the width and height of the touched area of the brush. In addition, WetDream was used to simulate realistic watercolor effect. WetDream is an open source semi-realistic watercolor simulation tool made by Raph Levien [13]. It produces watercolor effects by a flow simulation with watercolor brush properties in real-time, and can be used for an interactive digital watercolor painting system. The prototype ran on a desktop PC with a 3.2 GHz dual-core CPU and 2GB RAM.

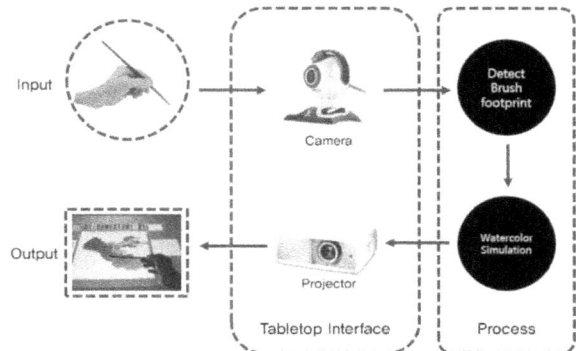

Figure 3. The structure of the painting application prototype

User Interface

We made a user interface for digital watercolor painting as shown in Figure 4. It consists of a canvas, a palette, water, a towel, a dashboard, and a test board.

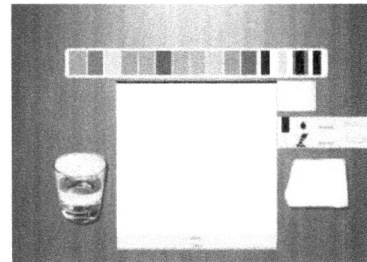

Figure 4. The user interface of the painting application prototype

Canvas

The 500 x 500 pixels canvas is in the center of the screen, and generates the footprints of the brush as an ellipse according to the information of the touched area. Footprints generated on the canvas are different depending on the brush properties as shown in Figure 5. When the brush is wet, the brush stroke has white diagonal lines on it. These lines gradually disappear as the stroke dries. The stroke with a low wetness displays a Dry Brush effect, applying paint only on the raised areas of the paper.

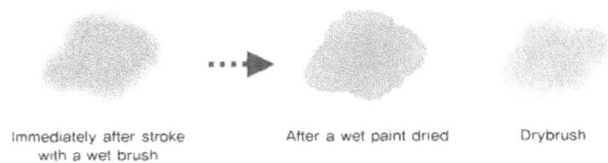

Figure 5. The stroke on the canvas

Palette

A palette is placed above the canvas. It has three gray scale colors, pure water, and eleven colors introduced in Curits' work: Quinacridone Rose, Indian Red, Cadmium Yellow, Hookers Green, Cerulean Blue, Burnt Umber, Cadmium Red, Brilliant Orange, Hansa Yellow, Phthalo Green, and French Ultramarine [8]. Since every watercolor paint is transparent except opaque white, a blended color appears when the user dubs multiple colors on the canvas except opaque white. Opaque white is used for erasing or highlighting. As one of the three grayscale colors is opaque, the three grayscale colors are shown with black background and white background together so that the user can distinguish an opaque color. The palette has pure water on the rightmost cell to reset the brush to a transparent state immediately without using water for convenience. The palette is used to load watercolor paint, increasing intensity of the color. As a user rubs paint on the palette, the intensity of the selected color increases as shown in Figure 6.

Figure 6. The function of the palette

The palette is also for mixing colors like in real watercolor painting. When a user rubs on paint on the palette, the color of the brush will be mixed with the paint color gradually. For example, when the current color is yellow and a user rubs on blue paint, the color of the brush becomes green. When the user rubs on blue paint again, the color turns blue. As all colors except opaque white are transparent, mixing with the opaque white and pure water is not allowed. When a user rubs on opaque white or on pure water, the color of the brush immediately changes to the selected color.

Water

The water is an image of water contained in a transparent glass, placed on the left side of the canvas. The function of the water is to decrease the intensity of the color and increase the wetness of the brush at the same time as shown in Figure 7. A user can dilute the paint by varying the rubbing speed on the glass of water on the screen as in real watercolor painting. When the user continuously rubs the water on the screen, the intensity of the color becomes zero, and then the color of the brush becomes transparent just like pure water. This act can be compared to rinsing the brush in real watercolor painting.

Figure 7. The function of the water

Towel

A towel is located on the right side of the canvas. The function of the towel is to decrease the wetness of the brush. When the user rubs on the towel on the screen, wetness of the brush decreases depending on the number of rubbing as shown in Figure 8.

Figure 8. The function of the towel

Dashboard

A dashboard is on the right side of the canvas, presenting the current status of the brush properties which cannot be shown on the brush tip in digital painting. As shown in Figure 9, the color of the brush is shown with black background. Also, the wetness and the intensity of the color are shown by the slide bars without numeric value. The slide bars are only for a display purpose and cannot be adjusted. As in real watercolor painting, the wetness and the intensity of the color are not presented precisely, letting the user guess the approximate levels of the wetness and the intensity from the slide bars.

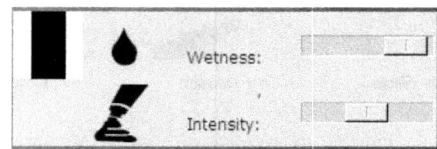

Figure 9. The dashboard showing the brush state

Test board

A test board is on the right side of the canvas. A user can test his or her brush strokes on the test board before making strokes on the canvas. The stroke on the test board disappears as time goes. The test board may not be needed when an undo function is implemented later.

EVALUATION OF THE USER INTERFACE

We did an experiment to compare the usability and the advantages of the interface that we designed with that of a conventional digital watercolor painting interface.

Apparatus

The experiment was conducted with the two painting interfaces shown in Figure 10 on the same tabletop. Interface A is the digital watercolor painting interface introduced in the prototype section, and Interface B imitates a conventional digital painting interfaces. It has slide bars for controlling the wetness and the intensity of the color independently. Also, the values of the brush properties are presented with numeric values on the slide bars. The palette of the interface B is not for adjusting the intensity of the color, but is only for selecting a color. Also, it does not support mixing colors, and therefore a color picker was offered. The color picker enabled the user select an exact color that a user wants. The size of the canvas, color representation, and watercolor simulation are the same as Interface A. Also, both interfaces were run on the same hardware environment described in the prototype section. Two round brushes were used in the experiment: number 15 round and number 20 round. Participants could change between the two brushes freely while they were painting.

Participants

Twelve volunteers (9 females, between 21 and 32 years old) participated. All participants were familiar with watercolor painting and had knowledge about watercolor painting tool usage, but not all participants were familiar with digital painting. Six participants were familiar with digital painting. One of the participants was an active physical painter, and another majored in pure painting. Two other participants majored in industrial design.

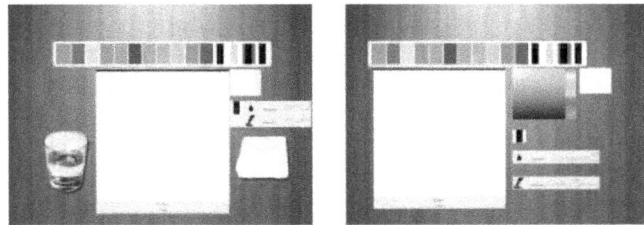

Interface A.
Proposed Digital Watercolor
Painting Interface

Interface B.
Existing Digital Watercolor
Painting Interface

Figure 10. Experimental setup

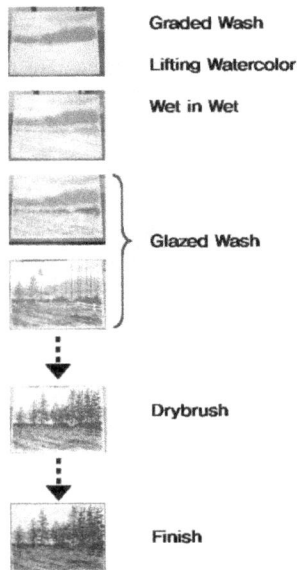

Graded Wash

Lifting Watercolor

Wet in Wet

Glazed Wash

Drybrush

Finish

Figure 11. Tutorial painting task and the basic skill of watercolor painting corresponding to each step

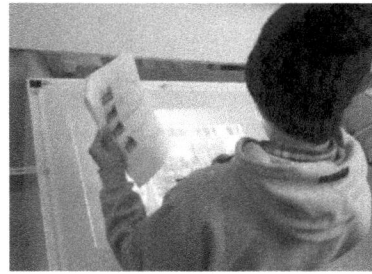

Figure 12. Task performing participant

Tasks

The experiment consisted of two tasks: tutorial painting and free painting. Tutorial painting included an instruction to complete each painting. We used a tutorial from Watercolorpainting.com, about the six basic skills of watercolor painting [24]. In the tutorial painting task, the pictures for each step were given, and the description of the step was given in natural language without the name of the skills. The skill required for each step is illustrated in Figure 11. A picture of a participant performing a tutorial task is shown in Figure 12. In free painting tasks, participants were asked to paint an apple freely. The photograph of an apple was given. The participants could paint in however they wanted. Samples paintings from the experiment are shown in Figure 13.

From Interface A   From Interface B

Figure 13. Samples from the experiment

Procedure

The subjects participated in the experiment after a brief introduction of the two interfaces. Before the experiment, they were asked to go over the six basic skills on both interfaces. The test session lasted about an hour and a half per each participant. It included a brief introduction session of the two interfaces and exercise of the six basic watercolor skills. Participants were divided into two groups, and each group started with a different interface. Every participant did a free painting task after the tutorial painting task. Participants were asked to paint naturally as usual. After each task, we asked the participants to fill out a user questionnaire with 7-step in Likert scale and had a short debrief session.

Measures

To evaluate the usability of the two interfaces, we measured the effectiveness, efficiency, and participants' satisfaction level of the interfaces. Effectiveness of the digital watercolor painting system is closely related to how much the user can make an aesthetically satisfactory work. To measure the effectiveness, we asked the users to rate the aesthetic satisfaction of his or her work done with each interface. To measure the efficiency, total time spent of painting and the time spent for 6 watercolor painting skills were measured. To measure the participants' satisfaction level, questionnaire for the interfaces was used. It included the questionnaire of the perceived usefulness, perceived ease of use, and preference of the system.

Besides measuring these aspects, the user's overall feelings about the experiment were measured by using a self-report questionnaire with the scale developed by Jeong. [11] It consists of 6 categories: Aesthetics, Satisfaction in Usability, Novelty, Uncomfortableness, Pleasure, and Excellence. Aesthetic is a positive emotion expressed due to various visual information of the system. Satisfaction in Usability is the positive emotion due to usability or practical aspect of the system. Novelty is the positive emotion expressed due to originality of the system. Uncomfortableness is uncomfortable or unpleasant feeling while using the system. Excellence is a positive emotion expressed due to outstanding aspects of the system. Each question is presented with related adjectives extracted by Jeong for convenience.

RESULTS AND DISCUSSION

Effectiveness

Satisfaction of the work
An average score of the satisfaction of the work done by each interface is shown in Figure 14A. The average score of participants' satisfaction about their work with the interface A was higher than that of the interface B significantly (paired samples t-Test, p = 0.001). The participants could make aesthetically more satisfactory work with proposed interface. More than half of the participants indicated that they felt like they painted with real painting tools and used watercolor painting skills more naturally. They also indicated that the watercolor effects were well expressed in

the paintings from the interface A rather than the interface B. It seems that the participants could make use of their experience of real watercolor painting process with the interface A, and it helped them make more satisfactory work.

In addition, a blind evaluation was performed on aesthetic satisfaction of work with people who did not participate in the experiment. We recruited 38 participants (16 males, 22 females), 20-30 years old, from online community related to painting. We showed paintings from two interfaces from same person without telling anything, and asked to choose more aesthetically satisfying one. The result of the blind evaluation is shown in Figure 14B. The paintings from the interface A were preferred by viewers with significant difference (paired samples t-Test, p = 0.0). The paintings from the proposed interface were aesthetically more satisfactory.

Efficiency

We measured the total time spent and time spent for 6 basic watercolor painting skills during the tutorial painting task. In the tutorial, each step represented a different watercolor skill. We did not measure the time spent for the flat wash because it is a simple skill without adjusting the brush properties so there was no difference between the two interfaces.

The total time spent in the interface B was shorter than that of the interface A. From this we know that the participants did painting quickly with existing interface, but it has no significant difference (paired samples T-test, p=0.174). In addition, the participants took less time in using Lifting Watercolor under the interface A than the interface B with a significant difference (paired samples T-test, p=0.017). Other skills had no significant differences between the two interfaces. Compared to the interface B, the user could not easily get the precise brush property values with the interface A, so the participants might need more activities to get the brush property values they want with the interface A. However, it was not that significant difference. Consequently, we can say that there was no significant difference in efficiency between the two interfaces.

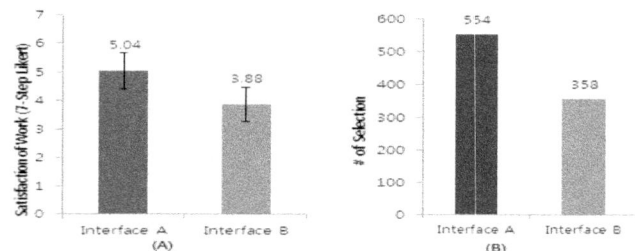

Figure 14. Mean of aesthetic Satisfaction of the Work (A) from participants (B) from blind evaluation

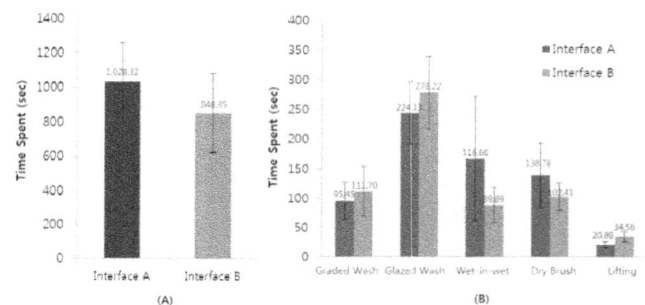

Figure 15. Mean time spent on tutorial painting: (A) total time (B) time for each of the basic skills of watercolor painting

Satisfaction

Perceived Usefulness and Perceived Ease of Use

Perceived usefulness shows how a user thinks the interface is useful, and perceived ease of use can show the easiness of the interface user thinks.

Perceived usefulness and perceived ease of use of the two interfaces are shown in Figure 16. The result of the perceived usefulness was higher in the interface A than in the interface B, but it had no significant difference (paired samples T-test, p=0.067). However, the perceived ease of use of the interface A was higher than that of the interface B with significant difference (paired samples T-test, p=0.0). The usefulness perceived by the participants was different by individual participants. Some participants accustomed with conventional digital painting interface indicated that the interface B was effective, but the opposite case indicated that the interface A was effective. However, every participant agreed that the interface A was easy. We can say that the proposed interface is easier to use than the existing digital watercolor painting interface.

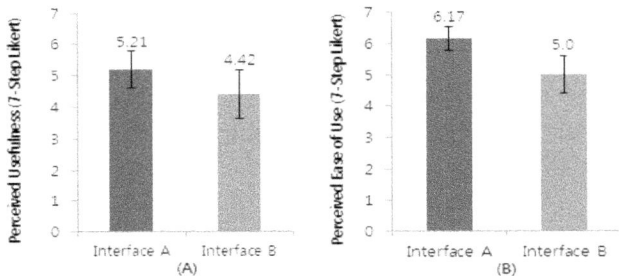

Figure 16. Mean of (A) perceived usefulness (B) perceived ease of use

User's overall emotions while painting

We asked the participants to rate 6 types of emotions during the painting tasks, and the results are shown in Figure 17. The interface A had higher scores than the interface B in Aesthetic, Satisfaction in Usability, Novelty, Uncomftableness, Pleasure, and Excellence, and all of them had significant differences (paired samples T-test, p=0.0, p=0.014, p=0.0, p=0.06, p=0.0, and p=0.09 each).

The interface A had better score than the interface B in Aesthetics. Placement of water and towel and the real watercolor painting tools might have invoked aesthetically positive emotion from the users. Four participants liked the placement of the real watercolor painting tools because it was natural.

A higher score in Satisfaction in Usability of the proposed interface could have been influenced by the function of the watercolor tools. More than half of the participants indicated that the function of the watercolor painting tools resembled the real watercolor painting tools and they could adjust the brush properties easily and intuitively with them.

All of the participants were impressed by the interface and indicated that they had never seen this kind of digital painting interface. While painting, ten participants said they enjoyed painting on the screen and felt it was like a real watercolor painting. It might have influenced Novelty and Pleasure of the interface.

Participants felt that the interface B was more uncomfortable. There were some complaints from the existing digital watercolor painting interface. Three participants were confused the interface B when adjusting the brush properties, and the other three participants felt uncomfortable adjusting the brush properties independently. One participant indicated that the interface B required great skill and it was hard to use.

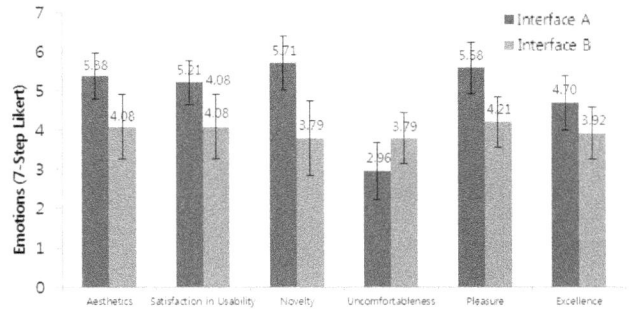

Figure 17. Mean of overall emotions while painting

User Preference

The preference scores of the two interfaces were 5.92 and 4.33 for Interface A and B, respectively, and their difference was statistically significant (paired samples T-test, p=0.032). Participants preferred the proposed interface because the interface was fun, easy, and intuitive. In addition, more than half of them indicated that they could paint more satisfactorily with the proposed interface. Also, over a half of the participants indicated that they could concentrate better on painting in the proposed interface because of the easiness and intuitiveness than existing digital watercolor painting interface. All participants said that the proposed interface would be good for kids and people who are not familiar with digital painting.

There were some limitations of proposed interface. About one third of the participants wanted to keep the mixed color on the palette, which was not supported. Also six participants wanted the visual feedback when the brush properties changing. There was no visual feedback of brush properties changing except a dashboard. Visual feedback like showing the rinsed paint while rinsing the brush would give user more natural feeling of painting.

In addition, there were some feedbacks related to the function of digital painting system. Eight participants wanted the function like zooming the canvas or undoing, supported other typical digital painting systems. Supporting these kinds of function would help the user paint effectively.

CONCLUSION

In this paper, we proposed the digital watercolor painting interface suitable for simulation-based watercolor painting by supporting real watercolor painting processes. We explored the real watercolor painting processes and tools, and drew a design requirement for painting the interface with real watercolor painting tools. Then we made the prototype of the painting interface with the real watercolor painting tools, and compared the usability of the proposed interface with existing digital watercolor painting interface.

The results of the experiment show the interface with real watercolor painting tools did not have much difference in efficiency. However, the proposed interface was more effective in a sense that participants could produce more satisfactory paintings with the proposed interface, and it was easier and more intuitive which made the users more satisfied with the proposed interface. In conclusion, the digital watercolor painting interface with the real watercolor painting tools to support the real watercolor painting process is effective and satisfactory for painting.

ACKNOWLEDGEMENT

This work was supported by the IT R&D program of MKE/KEIT.[KI10041244, SmartTV 2.0 Software Platform]

REFERENCES

1. Adobe. http://www.adobe.com

2. Alwym Crawshaw, Sharon Finmakr and Trevor Waugh. Watercolour for the Absolute Beginner: Great Value with More Than 70 Step-by-Step Excercises, HarperCollins UK, 2007.

3. Baxter, W., Chu, N. S., Govindaraju, N. Project Gustav: Immersive Digital Painting. in SIGGRAPH 2010, Talks.

4. Baxter, W. Physically-Based Modeling Techniques for Interactive Digital Painting. University of North Carolina at Chapel Hill, North Carolina, USA, 2004.

5. Cockshott, T. Wet and Sticky: A novel model for computer based painting, University of Glasgow, Glasgow, Scotland, 1991.

6. Corel. http://www.corel.com

7. Nui group community, Community Core Vision(CCV). http://nuicode.com/projects/tbeta

8. Curtis, C., Anderson, S., Seims, J., Fleischer, K., and Salesin D. Computer-generated Watercolor. in SIGGRAPH 1997.

9. ISO. Ergonomic requirements for office work with visual display terminals (VDTs) Part 11: Guidance on usability (ISO9241-11:1998(E)). Geneva, Switzerland, 1998.

10. Jeong, S. and Lee, K. Development of Tools for Measuring the User's Emotions expressed while Using a Product. Journal of Korean Society of Design Science, Vol.19 (2). 69-80.

11. Jeong, S. Development a self-report questionnaire-type scale for measuring user's emotions while using a product. The Korean Society for Emotion & Sensibility, Vol. 10 (3). 403-410.

12. Lang, D., Findlater, L., and Shaver, M. CoolPaint: Direct Interaction Painting. in UIST 2003, Poster.

13. Leiven, R., Wet Dream. http://www.levien.com/gimp/wetdream.html

14. Mai Otsuki, Kenji Sugihara, Asako Kimura, Fumihisa Shibata, and Hideyuki Tamura. MAI Painting Brush: An Interactive Device That Realizes the Feeling of Real Painting. in UIST 2010.

15. Mayer, R. The Aritsit's Handbook of Materials and Tehcniques. Viking Books, New York, 1991.

16. Merilyn Scott. The Watercolor Artist's bible. Chartwell Books, Inc., Edison, NJ, USA, 2009.

17. Park, J. Digital Canvas: A Projection-Space Interaction Tool. in Edutainment 2006, Lecture Notes in Computer Science(LNCS), Vol. 3942, 1171-1179.

18. Schning, J., Brandl, P., Daiber, F., Echtler, F., Hilliges, O., Hook, J., Lchtefeld, M., Motamedi, N., Muller, L., Olivier, P., Roth, T., and Zadow, U.V. Multi-touchsurfaces: A technical guide. Technical Report TUMI0833, University of Munster. 2008.

19. St. Amant R. and E. Horton, Thomas. Characterizing tool use in an interactive drawing environment. in 2nd International Symposium on SmartGraphics (2002).

20. Teiche, A., Rai, A. K., Yanc, C., Moore, C., Solms, D., Cetin, G., Riggio, J., Ramseyer, N., Intino, P. D., Muller, L., Khoshabeh, R., Bedi, R., Bintahir, M.T., Hansen, T., Roth, T., and Sandler, S. Multi-touch Technologies. http://nuigroup.com/, 2009.

21. Van Laerhoven, T., and Van Reeth, F. Real-time Simulation of Watery Paint: Natural Phenomena and Special Effects. Computer Animation and Virtual Worlds, Vol. 16 (3-4), 429-439.

22. Vandoren, P., Van Laerhoven, T Claesen, L., Raymaekers, C., and Reeth, F. IntuPaint: Bridging the Gap between Physical and Digital Painting. in TABLETOP 2008.

23. Vandoren, P., Claesen, L., Van Laerhoven, T., Taelman, J., Raymaekers, C., Flearackers, E., Reethm F., FluidPaint: an interactive digital painting system using real wet brushes. in ITS 2009.

24. Watercolorpainting.com, http://www.watercolorpainting.com

25. Watercolorpaintingandprojects, http://www.watercolorpaintingandprojects.com

Docking Window Framework:
Supporting Multitasking by Docking Windows

Hirohito Shibata

Research and Technology Group,

Fuji Xerox Co. Ltd.

430 Sakai, Nakai-machi, Ashigarakami-gun,

Kanagawa, 259-0157, Japan

hirohito.shibata@fujixerox.co.jp

Kengo Omura

Research and Technology Group,

Fuji Xerox Co. Ltd.

6-1 Minatomirai, Nishi-ku, Yokohama,

Kanagawa, 220-8668, Japan

kengo.omura@fujixerox.co.jp

ABSTRACT

When performing tasks using computers, multiple documents are used with multiple applications. During working with computers, multiple tasks, perhaps involving multiple documents, are switched. This paper presents the *Docking Window Framework*: an extended multi-window system supporting such multitasking situations. It enables construction of workspaces comprising multiple windows with simple switching of workspaces. Although previous systems emphasized the support of task-switching after workspace construction, the proposed system characteristically supports construction of workspaces through a docking user interface. It also supports operation of multiple windows simultaneously, provides a tile layout of windows to reduce the overhead of window operations, and supports saving and restoration of workspaces. We conducted two experiments to evaluate the system. In window arrangement tasks, participants performed tasks faster using the proposed system than when using a popular window system (Windows XP). Moreover, in task-switching tasks, participants using our system performed multiple tasks in parallel more efficiently.

Author Keywords

Window systems; workspaces; multitasking

ACM Classification Keywords

H.5.2 [Information interfaces and presentation]: User Interfaces – Windowing systems

INTRODUCTION

When performing a task using computers, one cannot necessarily complete the task using a single document or a single application. Users often refer to multiple documents of various applications to perform a single task. For example, when writing an academic paper, people usually make use of their own papers, papers written by other people, dictionaries,

Before

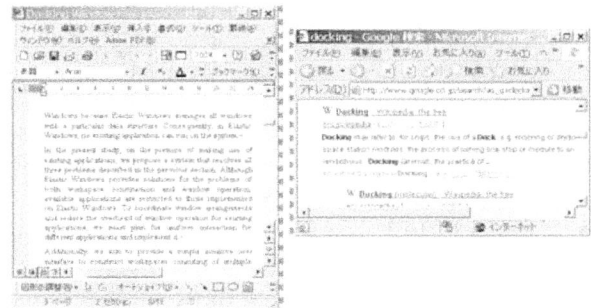

After

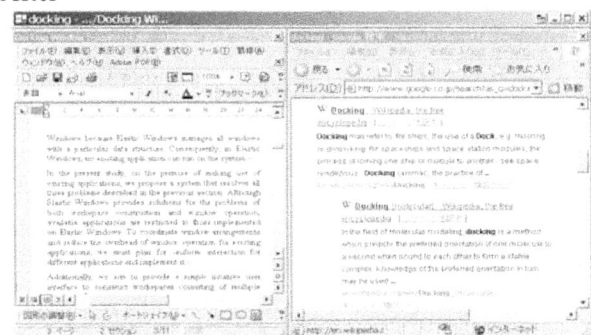

Figure 1. Before and after the docking operation. The right window was docked to the left window.

drawing tools to create figures, and spreadsheets to calculate data, as well as a word processor to compose the paper. When programming, people usually use an editor to edit source code, a developing environment to compile and debug the code, manuals of libraries, and a web browser to search quickly as necessary. To perform such tasks, people implicitly construct their own working spaces by arranging multiple windows [3,7,13].

In addition, people usually perform several tasks in parallel such as writing reports, exploring information, and reading news or mail. They conduct their work while switching their attention among these tasks. Furthermore, tasks are sometimes interrupted unintentionally by external events such as scheduled meetings or urgent requests from colleagues. Such phenomena are known collectively as *multitasking*, which is frequently observed in office work [8,12,14,19,20,22,34]. For example, Gonzalez and Mark [12] observed that workers of an investment company switched tasks every three minutes. O'Conaill and Frohlich [22] reported that tasks of knowledge workers were interrupted four times per hour for extraneous reasons. Although those analyses do not specifically examine PC work, we can consider that similar phenomena are observable in PC work because most knowledge work these days is performed using PCs.

When performing such multitasking work with traditional window systems, users must activate multiple windows by clicking all of them one by one whenever task-switching is necessary. This procedure is operationally demanding. Furthermore, in such a situation, it is difficult to grasp the kind and number of workspaces they are using. It is cognitively demanding because users must manage multiple workspaces in their head. Therefore, it is desirable to support construction of workspaces consisting of multiple windows and to allow easy switching of workspaces.

This paper presents a proposal of a framework called the *Docking Window Framework* (*DWF*) to manage multiple windows and support multitasking in PC work. The most characteristic point of the system is in the user interface to construct workspaces. In the rest of this paper, we present our approach to support multitasking in PC work, the design and implementation of our prototype system, and the evaluation of it.

APPROACH

Constructing workspaces
The importance of supporting the construction and switching of workspaces has been noted since the late 1980s. Rooms [7,13] is a pioneer in this research area. It supports management of windows using a room metaphor. Each room corresponds to a workspace; users switch workspaces by moving virtual rooms. Solutions of various types have been proposed for problems of this kind [16,17,18,21,24,25,33]. All are aimed at supporting switching workspaces after the construction of workspaces. They provide original visualization of workspaces so that users can readily grasp multiple workspaces and readily select a desired one.

Nevertheless, previous systems have emphasized the support of task switching after workspace construction. In contrast, our system was designed to support the creation of workspaces through a simple intuitive user interface. To construct workspaces in previously proposed systems, users needed to determine what kind of workspace to create, to specify which windows should be included in the workspace, and to organize the layout of windows in each workspace. Therefore, users were required to formalize group structures of windows in advance for performing tasks in workspaces; such formality apparently impedes the task performance [32]. Furthermore, workspaces are often restructured while performing tasks. For example, while performing tasks, users

might realize that they must refer to other documents to perform tasks, or they might find that some documents are not necessary yet. In other words, workspace construction is not a one-time procedure that occurs only at the initial setup of tasks. It occurs dynamically during task performance. Therefore, we consider that improvement of the user interface to construct workspaces can improve work efficiency meaningfully during computer use.

In our framework, as a simple intuitive user interface to construct workspaces, we provide an interaction technique called *docking* that enables connecting windows as if users were to plug in a piece of a jigsaw puzzle. Toolbars in some applications of Windows OS can be detached from a window and can be attached again to the window. We adopt a similar feature between windows and use this interaction to construct workspaces. In this framework, users need not specify any group relation or hierarchical relation between windows. Users merely need to lay out windows. Therefore, we expect that users can construct workspaces easily and thereafter concentrate on their primary work.

We also provide a feature to save and restore workspaces. When constructing a workspace, users must execute multiple applications, arrange the window layout, and open all necessary documents. They must perform this procedure to set up a task environment every time they start up a PC. Furthermore, users might want to return to a previous state of a workspace so that they can recall the situation of the work or they can redo their work again. In our system, we provide features to save the status of workspaces such as applications, the position of windows, and documents opened in each window, and to restore the status of workspaces merely using a single action.

Reducing window operation costs
Reducing the cost of window operations is an important challenge. According to an analysis of window operation logs of workers at an intellectual property management department [31], they spent 7.4–9.1% of time in window operations such as activating, moving, and resizing of windows. Users spend no small amount of time performing operations that have nothing to do with jobs that users must perform with PCs.

Demonstrably, there is room to improve the operability of window operation. According to our previous experiments, the performance of reading with PCs is markedly inferior to the performance of paper-based reading in cross-reference reading among multiple documents and multiple pages [29,30]. Such a style of reading is frequently observable in actual work situations [1,23,27]. Moreover, screen space has become larger and larger recently, thereby encouraging users to open many windows having large size [15,26,31]. The greater the number of windows in a workspace, the more that overlapping of the windows increases. Consequently, users frequently need to switch, move, and resize windows to refer to multiple sources simultaneously, thereby increasing the cost of window operations.

Many systems and techniques have been proposed to improve the operability of window operations. They facilitate selection and switching of windows [4,11,35,36], coordinate the window layout [2], and support the exchange of data between windows [6,10]. They are all apparently effective proposals to reduce the window operation cost.

However, those systems and techniques do not consider multitasking-related circumstances. To reduce window operation costs in multitasking of PC work, we provide a feature to operate multiple windows of the same workspace simultaneously. Using this feature, users can operate windows using fewer operations. Furthermore, to avoid the overlapping of windows, we take a tiled window approach with regard to the layout of windows within a workspace.

According to an experiment conducted by Bly and Rosenberg [5], in information extraction tasks, users were able to complete the task faster using a tiled window system than when using an overlapping window system. Overlapping window systems were developed originally to display many documents in a small display area. As we described above, displays have become larger and cheaper recently. On the assumption that many people use large monitors or multiple monitors, it is important to provide environments that make use of large display space [9,26].

DOCKING WINDOW FRAMEWORK

The Docking Window Framework (DWF) has four main features: a docking user interface to construct workspaces, multiple window operations, tile layout to avoid overlapping, and saving and restoring workspaces. It runs on .NET Framework 2.0; it is implemented with C#.

Docking user interface

Figure 1 presents the docking appearance. The top of the figure shows the situation before docking. When a user drags a window, if another window is near the dragged one, jagged hooks appear on edges of both windows, as shown in the top of the figure. These hooks show that the two windows can be mutually docked. At that time, the edges with the hooks would be connected if the windows were docked. When the user drops the window in this state, docking of windows starts. The bottom of Figure 1 portrays the docking result. After docking, the position and size of the dropped window are changed so that the two connected windows constitute a single rectangle. The process of changing the dropped window layout is visualized as an animation so that the user can follow the change of the window layout.

Two windows connected by the docking operation are activated and moved simultaneously; they behave as if they were a single window. Therefore, we call the connected windows a *docking window*.

After docking, in addition to connected two windows, a new title bar, called a *docking bar*, appears at the top of the two windows. It provides commands to operate all windows of the workspace such as closing the workspace, minimizing and maximizing the workspace, releasing the connected windows of the workspace, saving the workspace, and changing the title and icon of the workspace.

Users can connect windows without limitations in the number of windows. They can also connect two docking windows. Figure 2 presents two examples of a window layout consisting of four windows. To construct the left layout of the figure, users might dock window 2 beneath window 1, dock window 3 beneath window 2, and finally dock window 4 at the right of the created docking window. To construct the right layout, users might dock window 2 beneath window 1 (or window 1 on window 2), dock window 4 beneath window 3 (or window 3 on window 4), and finally connect the two docking windows horizontally.

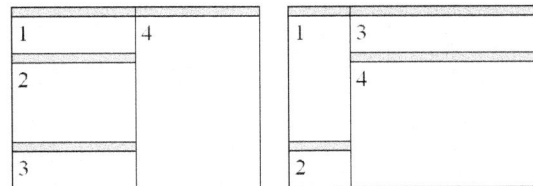

Figure 2. Examples of window layout in workspaces

Detaching of docking windows is also possible. All docked windows can be released using the release command of the docking bar. Detaching only a single window from a docking window is possible (we describe the usage later). At that time the size of other remaining windows is coordinated so that they all constitute a single rectangle again. For example, when window 1 is detached in the left of Figure 2, window 2 expands vertically so that it covers the area of window 1. When window 4 is detached in the left of Figure 2, window 1, 2, and 3 all expand horizontally so that they cover the area of window 4.

Additionally, when docking is performed, two separate icons in the Windows task bar are integrated into a single one. This can prevent an overflow of icons in the task bar. The name of the icon, and therefore the title of the docking window, is created automatically by connecting each window title, but it can be modified later to facilitate discrimination among windows.

Users might want to put windows side by side sometimes without connecting windows, i.e., without creating a workspace. In such a case, if users drag windows with pressing the Shift key, then the jagged hooks do not appear and windows are not connected each other.

A docking window consisting of multiple windows visually resembles a single window. In addition, users can activate all windows of a docking window simultaneously. It works as a feature to support task switching. Users can use a docking window as a workspace to support multitasking. In all

229

previous systems, before performing tasks, users must determine what kind of workspace they create. They must specify which windows should be included in the workspace. In our framework, when multiple windows are docked, they function as a single window. The connected windows can be used as a workspace. When docking windows, users can construct a workspace through the action of juxtaposing windows without declaring a group structure of windows. In other words, in DWF, when a user allocates windows side by side, then these windows are mutually connected and the workspace is created automatically without selecting any command to create a workspace and without arranging a window layout.

As a user interface to connect windows, a window-snapping technique is well known. Its third party tools have been developed (MagnetWindow, Virtual Desktop for Win32, etc.). In these systems, when two windows are placed closer together, the two windows are *magnetized* and connected to contact each other. However, the connected windows do not constitute a rectangle as a whole and are not arranged in a tile layout. Furthermore, window icons in a taskbar are not integrated and users cannot assign a title for the windows. In this situation, users would not become conscious of constructing workspaces. Additionally, users cannot move the connected windows to the foreground and change their positions simultaneously. Although window snapping is an effective technique to arrange the window layout, it does not improve multitasking efficiency.

Multiple window operation

People often organize paper documents as piles and move them simultaneously. Similarly, users might want to operate on multiple documents within a workspace simultaneously. Not only do such operations reduce the window operation load; they also help users to realize a workspace consisting of multiple documents as a single window. DWF supports the following simultaneous operations for connected multiple windows.

Activating When users click any area of a workspace or the icon of the workspace in the task bar of Windows OS, all windows of the workspace are activated simultaneously. Using this feature, users can switch tasks easily with one click.

Moving When users drag any window or a docking bar of a workspace, all windows within the workspace are moved simultaneously. Using this feature, users can arrange and organize workspaces easily.

Resizing DWF always maintains the workspace shape as a rectangle, which helps users to realize a workspace as a single window. It also enables the effective use of the display area. When users change the size of any window, the size of other windows is changed to maintain the rectangular shape. Figure 3 shows a situation where the resizing of window B engenders resizing of window A.

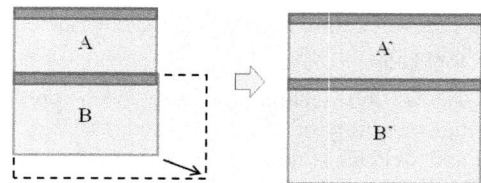

Figure 3. Resizing windows.

Enlarging/Narrowing DWF provides a feature to display a specified window as large (or small) as possible with all remaining window contents visible. This feature is called *enlarging* (or *narrowing*). It differs from maximizing (or minimizing) of traditional window systems in that maximized windows cover the entire display area such that users cannot view any contents of other windows (or users cannot view any content of minimized windows). Maximizing and minimizing are features that were invented to use a small display space efficiently. In contrast, enlarging and narrowing are features to make use of large display space, enabling users to work more productively. When users enlarge a window, other windows change size, as shown in Figure 4. The process of layout change resulting from enlarging and narrowing can be visualized as an animation so that the user can follow the change of the window layout.

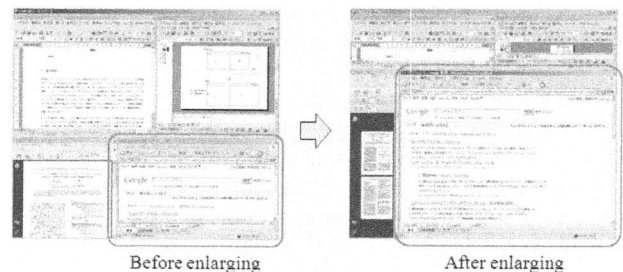

Before enlarging   After enlarging

Figure 4. Before and after the enlarging operation.

Opening/Closing When users open a workspace, all windows and documents of the workspace are opened simultaneously. The layout and documents of these windows are restored. Furthermore, when users close a workspace, all windows of the workspace are closed simultaneously. Using these features, users can establish and finish workspaces easily.

To provide uniform interaction for windows of different applications, the Task Gallery [24] provides a solution that pops up original command buttons. Our system uses this solution. When a mouse cursor is on a title bar of any window, the system pops up a *floating bar*, as shown in Figure 5. It provides commands for the individual window positioned below the floating bar. The system currently provides the following commands: detaching the window from the workspace, enlarging and narrowing the window, and closing the window.

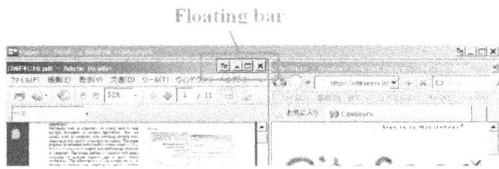

Figure 5. Floating bar.

Using this interaction technique, the system can provide its own commands, such as detaching and enlarging, for various applications through a uniform user interface. Moreover, although all applications have a "close" command, the command execution differs slightly among applications in terms of confirming modified documents. Using this feature, the system can replace application-dependent behavior of such commands to uniform behavior in our framework.

Tile layout

Most currently available window systems use an overlapping window approach. However, that approach is not necessarily superior to a tiling window approach [5]. The tiled window approach is apparently more effective to perform each task in a large screen space.

In our system, we use a tiling window approach that does not cause window overlapping. This approach sustains a tiling layout at all times. Even if users change the size of a certain window, the window layout remains tiled, which is to say that the change of the window size propagates to other windows so that the total window layout is coordinated, thereby avoiding overlapping. This basic behavior is the same as that of Elastic Windows [16]. Below, we explain the behavior of the window size propagation with restriction to the point that it differs from that of Elastic Windows.

Figure 6 presents how to propagate the change of window size within a workspace. At the top of this figure, two cases are possible: window A is made larger or window B is made smaller. The behavior of Elastic Windows differs depending on the two cases. When window A is made larger, both window A and B are made smaller with conserving the proportion of size of both windows. On the other hand, when window B is made smaller, only window B is made smaller. Window C size does not change.

However, in this situation, users cannot discern which window has been resized because window A and window B are mutually connected. Nonetheless the window C size is changed or not changed according to time and circumstances. This difference of changes creates confusion among users. We observed such scenes many times during preliminary experiments. Therefore, in DWF, the window size change is propagated only to windows adjoining the original one. That is, the behavior of the lower bottom of Figure 6 is always performed independently of whether window A is made larger or window B is made smaller.

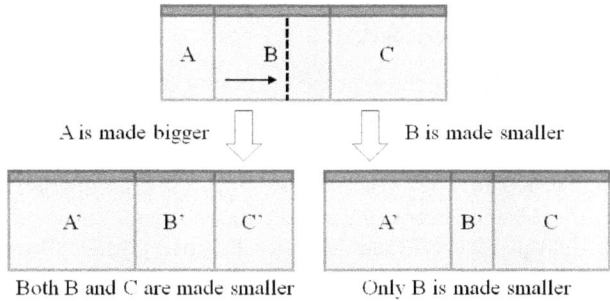

Figure 6. Propagation of the change of window size.

Saving and restoring workspaces

DWF provides a feature to save the state of workspaces (title, icon, applications, position and size of windows, and documents) to a file and to restore the previous state of workspaces later. Using this feature, users need not reconstruct workspaces from scratch whenever a PC is started up. We describe implementation of this feature later.

EVALUATION

Using DWF, we expect the following effects: users can (1) arrange windows and construct workspaces easily using a docking user interface, (2) switch tasks easily by switching workspaces, and (3) perform tasks efficiently using the tile layout of windows. To confirm effect (1), we conducted an experiment using a window arrangement task (Experiment 1). To confirm effects (2) and (3), we conducted an experiment for a task-switching task (Experiment 2).

Experiment 1: Window arrangement

To construct workspaces in DWF, users must connect windows and adjust the window layout. Our hypothesis is that DWF yields faster performance than traditional window systems for window arrangement because it provides an easy docking user interface and multiple window operations after docking. We also hypothesize that the performance difference between two systems is remarkable when using many windows.

Method

Design and participants The experimental design was a 2×3 within-participant design. The first factor was the system condition (a traditional window system and DWF). The second factor was the number of windows (2, 4, and 6 windows). Each participant performed all conditions of tasks and performed two trials in each condition. The order of the system conditions and the number of windows in the series of participants' trials were counterbalanced to cancel the overall effect of the trial order.

Participants were 12 people (6 men, 6 women). Their ages were 21–38 years (avg. 28.0). Each had three or more years' experience using a PC. The vision of each, after correction, was better than 0.7.

Apparatus The PC used in the experiment (Dimension C512; Dell Inc.) was connected to a 23-inch TFT display (FlexScan; Eizo Nanao Corp.). The OS was Windows XP.

Procedure Before the experiment, participants learned about and trained with DWF for 20 min.

The experiment task was to arrange windows. The initial window layout was a cascade layout, as shown at the left of Figure 7. We presented the target window layout as shown in the right of Figure 7, and requested that participants allocate windows to match the target layout. We drew a four-by-four lattice in pink on the desktop and required allocation of the specified number of windows to the specified position.

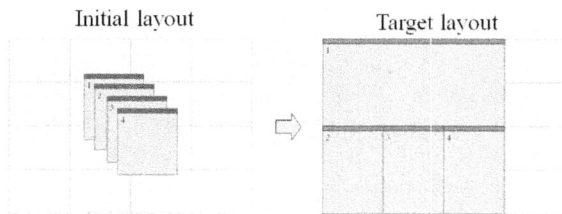

Figure 7. Initial layout and target layout in the window arrangement task.

In each trial, participants pushed a start button, arranged windows, and pushed an end button. We required them to do this procedure as quickly and as accurately as possible. We measured the time from the push of the start button to the push of the end button as the task completion time.

After the experiment, we conducted interviews and solicited impressions related to each system condition.

Results and discussion
Figure 8 presents the task completion times. The error bar shows plus or minus one standard error from the average. Two-way repeated measures analysis of variance was conducted to assess the task completion time. Results show that the main effects of the system condition [$F(1, 11)=26.3$, $p<.001$] and the number of windows [$F(2, 22)=144.5$, $p<.001$] were significant. Interaction of the two factors was significant [$F(2, 22)=3.4$, $p<.05$]. Then we tested the simple main effects for each number of windows. They were all significant [for 2, 4, an 6 windows, $F(1, 11)=17.2$, $p<.01$; $F(1, 11)=21.4$, $p<.001$; $F(1,11)=12.4$, $p<.01$, respectively]. In DWF, participants arranged windows 22.9%, 23.4%, and 23.4% more quickly than when using the traditional system for 2, 4, and 6 windows, respectively.

We compared the accuracy of window layouts among the system conditions. The distance between two windows was defined as the sum of the four Euclidean distances between corresponding vertices of the windows. Furthermore, we defined the window layout accuracy as the distance between the target layout and the actually allocated layout. Two-way repeated measures analysis of variance was conducted to assess the accuracy of the window layout. Although the main effect of the number of windows was significant [$F(2,$

$22)=59.8$, $p<.001$], the main effect of the system condition was not significant [$F(1, 11)=0.4$, $p>.1$].

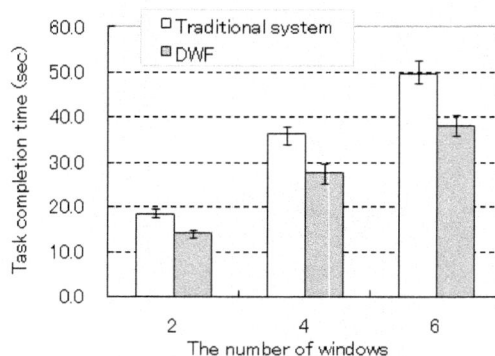

Figure 8. Task completion time in window arrangement tasks.

According to the results, participants arranged windows with DWF 20.9–23.4% faster than when using the traditional window system. No difference in the accuracy of the window layout was found between DWF and the traditional window system. Results show that users of DWF can arrange windows rapidly without sacrificing accuracy.

A noteworthy point in this experimental task is that DWF users not only arranged windows but also created workspaces by connecting windows. In DWF, users adjust the window layout after creating a workspace, but they can still arrange windows more than 20% faster than when using the traditional window system. We consider the following two reasons for this point.

First, the operation of window allocation doubles as the operation of workspace construction. Therefore, no cost accrues to construct workspace, where we can consider that the cost to construct a workspace is included in the cost to allocate windows.

Second, in DWF, users can operate multiple windows simultaneously after the construction of workspaces, which engenders rapid window organization. Furthermore, because DWF create a tile layout automatically, users need not devote attention to trivial layout adjustment of windows if they merely set up a rough window layout.

In this experiment, the target layouts were all tiled. For arranging windows in layouts of other types such as cascading layouts, DWF requires users to continue to press the Shift key to avoid docking windows unintentionally. Although that requirement might bother users, our framework is designed on the basis that the tiling approach is superior to an overlapping approach when used for a large display space.

We are also interested in the comprehensibility of systems because DWF provides an unusual user interface in terms of the docking and the tile layout. In the post-task interview, one participant described that he "became accustomed to DWF right away after actual use of it." Some participants reported that it "felt fun to use DWF" and that they "felt a pleasurable sensation when docking windows." These comments suggest that the framework of window docking is easy to learn; it also provides a pleasurable experience for users sometimes.

Experiment 2: Task switching and performing tasks

Although the most characteristic point of DWF is in the mode of workspace construction, the aim of constructing workspaces is to support task switching. The second experiment takes up a multitasking situation and compares the user performance between DWF and a traditional window system.

Multitasking requires multiple documents. Therefore, the initial layout of windows is apparently an important factor affecting the user performance. In the traditional window system, we set two initial layouts: the tile layout and the cascade layout. Furthermore, observations revealed that physical paper effectively supported the reading of multiple documents [23,27]. We are interested in whether or not DWF is superior to physical paper when performing multitasking. Our hypothesis is that DWF yields faster performance than the conditions of the traditional window systems, but it does not reach the level of physical paper.

Method

Design and participants The experimental design was a one-way within-participant design. We set the following four conditions as factors: using paper documents (Paper), using our system (DWF), and using a traditional window system in which the initial window layout was a tile layout, as shown at the left of Figure 9 (Tile), and using a traditional window system in which the initial window layout was a cascade layout, as shown at the right of Figure 9 (Cascade).

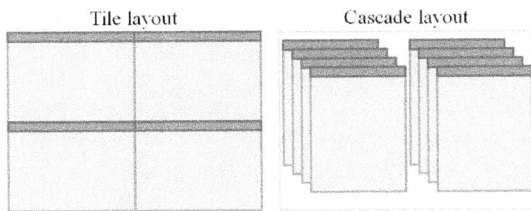

Figure 9. Initial window layout in task-switching tasks.

Participants were 18 people (9 men, 9 women). Their ages were 21–39 years (avg. 29.5). Each had three or more years' experience of using a PC. The vision of each, after correction, was better than 0.7.

Each participant performed two trials in each condition. The order of conditions and document sets in the series of participants' task trials was counterbalanced to cancel the overall effect of the order.

Apparatus The display and the PC used in this experiment were the same as those described for Experiment 1.

Materials In this experiment, participants performed two independent tasks in parallel, where each task is to count products that match the specified conditions.

We created documents used in the experiment related to products specifications such as digital cameras, printers, and TFT displays. For each task, four one-page documents were used. Three of the four were product lists. The remaining one was a question list for which participants were asked to count products matching the condition in the product lists. We created eight document sets consisting of these four documents for the experiment and two document sets for exercises.

In the product list, each item was created using product names, manufacturers, weights, prices, sales rankings and other attributes of products. Each page of a product list consisted of 16 products; all products in each counting task included 48 items in total. Each document set included six questions. Samples of questions are shown for TFT displays in the following.

- How many displays for which the manufacturer is ACER are there?

- How many displays for which the power consumption is less than 20 W are there?

Procedure Before the experiment, participants learned about and trained with DWF for 20 min.

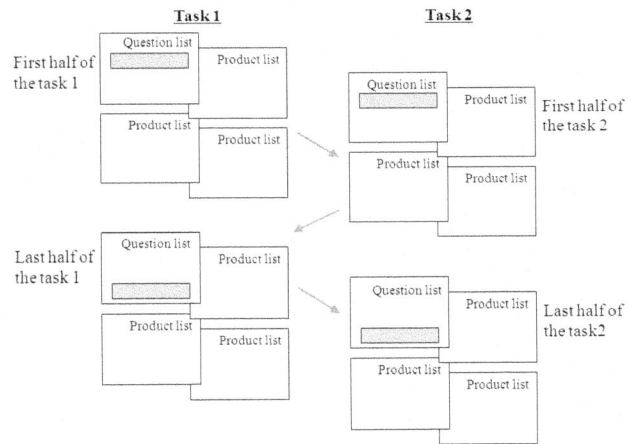

Figure 10. Order of performing task-switching tasks.

The experimental task was to perform two counting tasks in parallel while switching them. Figure 10 shows that participants answered the initial three questions of the first task and then answered the initial three questions of the second task. Next, they answered the last three questions of the first task and then answered the last three questions of the second task. This procedure was written in question lists to prevent mistakes in the order of answering questions.

In each task, participants switched between the two counting tasks three times. They were asked to perform this procedure as quickly and as accurately as possible.

In the paper condition, electronic documents were printed on one side of A5 paper in black and white. Electronic documents were all given in PDF and displayed with Adobe Reader 9. We adjusted the character size of electronic documents to be the same size as those of paper documents. We prohibited changing of the display character size.

In all conditions, we delivered answer sheets of question lists printed in paper and requested that participants write down the answers on the sheets. We required that they refer to the answer sheets only when they wrote down the answers and they refer to electronic and paper documents for performing tasks. Participants wrote down answers on additional answer sheets to unify the mode of writing between paper and electronic conditions, thereby excluding the effect of the mode of writing. In electronic conditions, participants need to change the device from a mouse to a pen to write answers. Therefore, we prohibited participants from performing tasks while holding a pen when counting products in the paper condition.

In each task, participants used eight documents (eight sheets of paper in the paper environment and eight windows in electronic environments). In the paper condition, the initial documents were provided as two piles corresponding to two counting tasks. The initial layout of the DWF condition was two workspaces, where each consisted of four tiled windows, as shown on the left of Figure 9. The initial layout of the tile condition was the same as that in the DWF condition, except that all windows were independent and unconnected. The initial layout of the cascade condition was two stacks of cascading windows, as shown in the right of Figure 9. Regarding window size, in the DWF and the tile conditions, participants were requested to use both horizontal and vertical scrolls to overview contents of documents. On the other hand, they were requested to use only horizontal scrolling in the cascade condition.

After the experiment, we conducted interviews to elicit participants' impressions of respective conditions.

Results and discussion
Figure 11 presents the task completion times in each condition. The error bar shows plus or minus one standard error from the average. Repeated measures analysis of variance was conducted to assess the task completion time. Results show that the main effect of conditions was significant [$F(3, 51)=20.35$, $p<.001$]. According to multiple comparison using the LSD method, the task completion time in the paper condition was significantly shorter than in the DWF condition [$p<.01$]. The task completion time in the DWF was also significantly shorter than in the tile condition [$p<.01$]. A tendency was also apparent by which the task completion time in the tile condition was shorter than that in the cascade condition [$p<.1$]. In the paper condition, the tasks were performed 14.9% faster than in the DWF condition, 26.8% faster than in the tile condition, and 33.6% faster than in the cascade condition. Additionally, regarding DWF, the

tasks were performed 13.9% faster than in the tile condition and 21.9% faster than in the cascade condition.

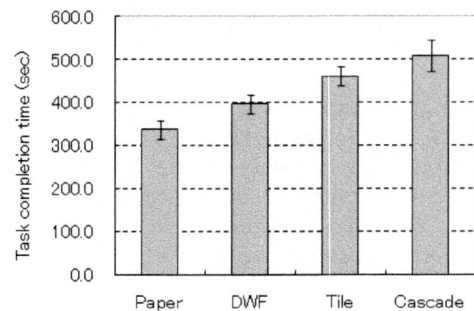

Figure 11. Task completion time in task-switching tasks.

We compared the accuracy of product counting. The percentage of the correct answers was highest in the cascade condition (79.9%) and lowest in the tile condition (71.5%). However, the difference was not significant [$p>.1$].

We provide the following three suggestions based on the results. First, using DWF, the participants were able to perform multitasking more efficiently than with traditional window systems. According to the participants' report, they felt that, using DWF, they were able to switch tasks quickly, understand what tasks they engage in, and grasp an overview of all tasks. With DWF, users can switch workspaces with one click and can view whole contents of the document by enlarging and narrowing them. The use of these features was frequently observed while performing tasks. We consider that these features engender efficient task performance.

Second, even if users used the same window system, the task completion time differed depending on the initial window layout. Users were able to perform multitasking more efficiently when using the tile layout than when using the cascade layout, which demonstrates that the tile layout is superior to the cascade layout in multitasking when opening many windows. This result underscores the validity of the DWF approach, which avoids window overlapping.

Third, the use of paper enables performance of multitasking far more efficiently than electronic environments, which demonstrates that physical paper is an excellent tool to support multitasking. DWF is an extended window system that provides many features that physical paper cannot provide, such as tile layout, multi-window activation, and enlarging. However, paper remains superior to DWF, which indicates that we can learn a methodology to support multitasking by analyzing human interaction with paper.

IMPLEMENTATION
In the implementation of DWF, a resident application called a *DWF manager* monitors the behavior of all windows and controls the positions and sizes of windows.

To save and restore the states of workspaces, including files opened in each window, and to make the task state persistent, the DWF manager must ascertain which file is opened in each window. However, in the current Microsoft Windows architecture, no general solution for this issue works for any application [24]. Therefore, DWF takes an approach that each application running on DWF sends messages of opening files and closing files to the DWF manager. Existing applications can be run on DWF by being added as plug-ins to send messages.

We briefly describe the development cost of applications running on DWF, which we call *DWF clients*. When we implement a new DWF client, programmers merely add one line of source code to specify the use of a DWF library. To make an existing application run on DWF, they must implement a plug-in for the application. However, the logic of plug-ins is simple and we can easily implement plug-ins with a small quantity of source code (about 50 lines). To date, we have implemented plug-ins for MS Office and Internet Explorer, and have confirmed their operations.

However, this architecture is one example implemented within the restriction of Windows OS. We do not regard it as ideal. We believe that our framework should be implemented as one module of an OS from the perspectives of reliability and processing speed.

CONCLUSION

We proposed a framework to support multitasking as an extension of traditional window systems. The framework, called the Docking Window Framework (DWF), enables workspace construction and load reduction of window operations. The most characteristic point is the way to construct workspaces by connecting windows through a simple intuitive user interface called docking.

We verified the effectiveness of our system using two experiments. The first experiment of window arrangement tasks revealed that DWF enabled setting up of a window layout more than 20% more quickly than when using a traditional window system. The task completion time of window arrangement in DWF includes the time to construct workspaces. Previous systems supporting task-switching necessitate the selection of additional commands to create workspaces, which indicates that DWF enables more rapid workspace construction than when using previous systems.

The second experiment of multitasking revealed that users were able to perform multiple tasks in parallel rapidly in the order of using paper documents, DWF, a traditional window system with a tile layout, and a traditional window system with a cascade layout. These results suggest the following points. First, DWF enables users to perform multitasking 13.9–21.9% more quickly than when using a traditional window system, which demonstrates the superiority of DWF for traditional systems. Second, users can perform multitasking in the tile layout faster than in the cascade layout, indicating the validity of our approach, which adopts a tile layout of windows within workspaces. Third, paper documents are excellent tools to support multitasking. We

can learn how to improve window systems through examining human interaction with paper.

After the experiments, not a few participants expressed their strong desire to use our system in their daily activities. We are currently preparing the use of DWF in real-world settings. Additionally, our system can be extended so that connected windows exchange data and change behavior according to the status change of other windows. We would like to examine the methodology of such coordination among windows.

TRADEMARKS

- Microsoft®, Windows®, and Internet Explorer® are trademarks or registered trademarks of Microsoft Corp.

- Adobe® Reader is a trademark or registered trademark of Adobe Systems Inc.

- All brand names and product names are trademarks or registered trademarks of their respective companies.

REFERENCES

1. Adler, A., Gujar, A., Harrison, B., O'Hara, K., and Sellen, A.J. A diary study of work-related reading: Design implications for digital reading devices. In *Proc. CHI '98*, ACM Press (1998), 241-248.

2. Badros, G.J, Nichols, J, and Borning, A. SCWM: An intelligent constraint-enabled window manager. In *Proc. AAAI Spring Symposium on Smart Graphics*, (2000).

3. Bannon, L., Cypher, A., Greenspan, S., and Monty, M.L. Evaluation and analysis of users' activity organization. In *Proc. CHI '83*, ACM Press (1983), 54-57.

4. Beaudouin-Lafon, M. Novel interaction techniques for overlapping windows. In *Proc. UIST '01*, ACM Press (2001), 153-154.

5. Bly, B. and Rosenberg J. A comparison of tiled and overlapping windows. In *Proc. CHI '86*, ACM Press (1986), 101-106.

6. Chapuis, O. and Roussel, N. Copy-and-paste between overlapping windows. In *Proc. CHI '07*, ACM Press (2007), 201-210.

7. Card, S.K. and Henderson, J.A. A multiple, virtual-workspace interface to support user task switching. In *Proc. CHI '87*, ACM Press (1987), 53-59.

8. Czerwinski, M., Horvitz, E., and Wilhite, S. A diary study of task switching and interruptions. In *Proc. CHI '04*, ACM Press (2004), 175-182.

9. Czerwinski, M., Robertson, G., Meyers, B., Smith, G., Robbins, D., and Tan, D. Large display research overview. In *Proc. CHI '06*, ACM Press (2006), 69-74.

10. Dragicevic, P. and Sabatier, U.P. Combining crossing-based and paper-based interaction paradigms for dragging and dropping between overlapping windows. In *Proc. UIST '04*, ACM Press (2004), 193-196.

11. Faure, G., Chapuis, O., and Roussel, N. Power tools for copying and moving: Useful stuff for your desktop. In *Proc. CHI '09*, ACM Press (2009), 1675-1678.

12. Gonzalez, V. and Mark, G. "Constant, constant, multi-tasking craziness": Managing multiple working spheres. In *Proc. CHI '04*, ACM Press (2004), 26-29.

13. Henderson, J.D.A. and Card, S.K. Rooms: The use of multiple virtual workspaces to reduce space contention in a window-based graphical user interface. *ACM Transactions on Graphics, 5*, 3 (1986), 211-241.

14. Hudson, J.M., Christensen, J., Kellogg, W.A., and Erickson, T. "I'd be overwhelmed, but it's just one more thing to do:" Availability and interruption in research management. In *Proc. CHI '02*, ACM Press (2002), 97-104.

15. Hutchings, D.R., Smith, G., Meyers, B., Czerwinski, M., and Robertson, G. Display space usage and window management operation comparisons between single monitor and multiple monitor users. In *Proc. AVI, '04*, ACM Press (2004), 32-39.

16. Kandogan, E. and Shneiderman, B. Elastic Windows: Improved spatial layout and rapid multiple window operations. In *Proc. AVI '96*, ACM Press (1986), 29-38.

17. Kandogan, E. and Shneiderman, B. Elastic Windows: Evaluation of multi-window operations. In *Proc. CHI '97*, ACM Press (1997), 250-257.

18. MacIntyre, B., Mynatt, E., Voida, S., Hansen, K., Tullio, J., and Corso, G. Support for multitasking and background awareness using interactive peripheral displays. In *Proc. UIST '01*, ACM Press (2001), 41-50.

19. Mark, G., Gonzalez, V. and Harris, J. No task left behind? Examining the nature of fragmented work. In *Proc. CHI '05*, (2005), 321-330.

20. Mark, G., Hausstein, D., and Kloecke, U. The cost of interrupted work: More speed and stress. In *Proc. CHI '08*, ACM Press (2008), 107-110.

21. Matthews, T., Czerwinski, M., Robertson, G., and Tan, D. Clipping lists and change borders: Improving multitasking efficiency with peripheral information design. In *Proc. CHI '06*, ACM Press (2006), 989-998.

22. O'Conaill, B. and Frohlich, D. Timespace in the workplace: Dealing with interruptions. In *Proc. CHI '95*, ACM Press (1995), 262-263.

23. O'Hara, K.P., Taylor, A., Newman, W., and Sellen, A.J. Understanding the materiality of writing from multiple sources. *International Journal of Human-Computer Studies, 56*, 4 (2002), 269-305.

24. Robertson, G., Dantzich, M., Robbins, D., Czerwinski, M., Hinckley, K., Risden, K., Thiel, D., and Gorokhovsky, V. The Task Gallery: A 3D window manager. In *Proc. CHI '00*, ACM Press (2000), 494-501.

25. Robertson, G., Horvitz, E., Czerwinski, M., Baudisch, P., Hutchings, D., Meyers, B., Robins, D., and Smith, G. Scalable Fabric: Flexible task management. In *Proc. AVI '04*, ACM Press (2004), 85-89.

26. Robertson, G., Czerwinski, M., Baudisch, P., Meyers, B., Robbins, D., Smith, G., and Tan, D. The large-display user experience. *IEEE Computer Graphics and Applications, 25*, 4 (2005), 44-51.

27. Sellen, A.J. and Harper, R.H. *The myth of the paperless office*. The MIT Press (2001).

28. Shibata, H. and Omura, K. Proposal and evaluation of a window system that enables constructing workspaces. *Transactions of the Japanese Society for Artificial Intelligence, 26*, 1 (2011), 237-247. (in Japanese)

29. Shibata, H. and Omura, K. Effects of paper in moving and arranging documents: A comparison between paper and electronic media in cross-reference reading for multiple documents. *Journal of the Human Interface Society, 12*, 3 (2010), 301-311. (in Japanese)

30. Shibata, H. and Omura, K.: Effects of paper on page turning: Comparison of paper and electronic media in reading documents with endnotes. In *Proc. HCI International '11, LNCS, 6781*, Springer (2011), 92-101.

31. Shibata, H. Operational efficiency of single and multiple display systems in an actual work environment. In *Proc. IDW '11*, SID (2011).

32. Shipman, F.M. and Marshall, C.C. Formality considered harmful: Experiences, emerging themes, and directions on the use of formal representations in interactive systems. In *Proc. CSCW '99*, ACM Press (1999), 333-352.

33. Smith, G., Baudisch, P., Robertson, G., Czerwinski, M., Meyers, B., Robbins, D., Horvitz, E., and Andrews, D. GroupBar: The TaskBar evolved. In *Proc. OZCHI '03*, ACM Press (2003), 34-43.

34. Sproull, L.S. The nature of managerial attention. *Advances in Information Processing in Organizations, 1* (1984), 9-27.

35. Tashman, C. WindowScape: A task oriented window manager. In *Proc. UIST '06*, ACM Press (2006), 77-80.

36. Xu, Q. and Casiez, G. Push-and-pull switching: window switching based on window overlapping. In *Proc. CHI '10*, ACM Press (2010), 1335-1338.

RIM: Risk Interaction Model for Vehicle Navigation

Linmi Tao
Tsinghua University
Beijing 100084 P.R.China
linmi@tsinghua.edu.cn

Lixia Meng
Tsinghua University
Army Aviation College
mlx08@mails.tsinghua.edu.cn

Fuchun Sun
Tsinghua University
Beijing 100084 P.R.China
fcsun@tsinghua.edu.cn

ABSTRACT

Interactive auto-driving systems are used for disabled and elderly persons. In such systems, human errors during operation or interaction could lead to serious consequences during motion. A novel human-robot interaction model, termed risk interaction model (RIM), is proposed for quantitative evaluation of the risk for complex interactive systems in terms of human safety. The risk elements for system-human interaction are defined, and quantitative relations among the elements are formalized based on experimental analysis. Extensive experiments are used to validate RIM.

Author Keywords

Human Robot Interaction; Risk Interaction model;
Auto-driving System.

ACM Classification Keywords

H.5.2 User Interfaces: Theory and method:
H.1.2User/Machine System

INTRODUCTION

Human errors can occur during actions and decision-making and in human robot interactions. Many studies have investigated human error in the field of cognitive science [4, 7, 8]. According to James Reason, user operation errors (mistakes, lapses and slips) can lead to risks, but he did not quantitatively model the consequences of human errors. To the best of our knowledge, there have been no studies on interaction risk for human robot interaction (HRI) and human computer interaction (HCI), since computer systems are designed to reduce losses due to human interactive errors via reversible operations. Unfortunately, reversal is not applicable for many interactive systems, such as vehicle driving, aircraft control, and management of large factories. In these systems, operation errors can lead to serious consequences. Therefore, the interaction risk for these systems has to be modeled and carefully calculated.

In current HCI theories, models such as GOMS [5], PIE [2], Fitts Law [3, 9] and keystroke-level models [1, 6] focus on the operation efficiency for interaction and do not consider the consequences of interaction. For interactive auto-driving systems, experimental methods cannot be used to assess system safety because operational errors can lead to serious consequences. Therefore, a theoretical model is needed to evaluate risk for such systems, independent of the interactive mode. A risk interaction model (RIM) for quantitative assessment of system risk is proposed. RIM is defined and formalized in Section 2. Risks for an interactive auto-driving system are analyzed in terms of usability tests in Sections 3 and 4. Conclusions are presented in Section 5.

RISK INTERACTION MODEL

RIM is a task-oriented interaction model. Operation risk is calculated after task decomposition into a series of operations, and the system risk can be theoretically assessed through the analysis of task risks.

Risk analysis

The main factors in generating and influencing risks are:

- **System state s**: Each system state has an inherent risk, and each operation may produce state transformation. Transformations between different states will lead to additional risks.

- **Risk probability p**: This is the probability of risk generated by one operation, in other words, the probability of operation error. Its value is decided in the system design or interface design.

- **Operation urgency u**: This is the time between an operation request and its performance. The shorter the time, the more difficult is successful completion of the operation and the more prone it is to risk. Operations requiring a higher response speed (such as brake operation) are urgent.

- **Cognitive load c**: This is the number of continuous operations executed before a new operation. The greater this number is, the more fatigued the user is, and the greater is the risk.

The risk structure of RIM is shown in Figure 1.

The various risks are as follows:

- **Original risk R_0**: inherent risk for a correct operation in normal system operation. It is usually defined by an expert according to the system state and the actual situation.

- **Basic risk R_1**: risk value for an operation due to operation error or system error. The risk is decided by R_0 and the corresponding risk probability p.

- **Operation risk R_2**: final risk value for an operation. It is affected by operation urgency u and the user's cognitive load c based on R_1.

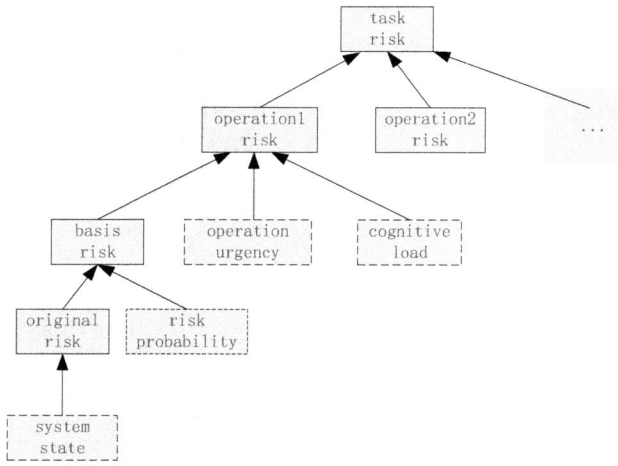

Figure 1. Risk structure of RIM

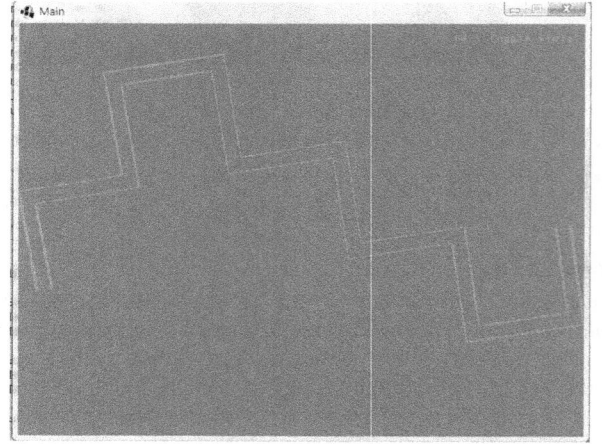

Figure 2. Road platform for $K_1(u)$ analysis.

- **Task risk** R_T: risk value for the entire task, determined by all operations arising from task decomposition.

Formalization of RIM

Definition. RIM is a tuple $M = (S, O, R_T, T)$ where S is a set of states of the system, T is the whole task that needs to be completed by the interaction system, R_T is the task risk and O is a set of atomic operations arising from task decomposition, defined as:

$$O = \{(O_l, O_p, O_r)^i | i = 1, 2, ...\} \tag{1}$$

where O_l is the operation label, $O_p = \{p, u, c\}$ is a set of properties of the operation, $O_r = \{R_0, R_1, R_2\}$ is a set of risk values of the operation.

For instance, an interactive auto-driving car is runing on a small road straightly, the current state S is "running straightly". At a time, the user wants to stop the car, and sends a command to the auto-driving system. When the system received and confirmed this "stop" command, the system current task T is "to stop the car at some place". Unfortunately, the car cannot be stopped immediately on the center of a small road. The nearest parking lots is on the left, only a hundred meters away which is estimated based on the current location and in-car map. Therefore, the task T is decomposed into a set of atomic operations O, which includes "go straight", "turn left", "slow down", etc. Finally, the car is stopped, and the state S is "still" now.

Risk values are calculated as follows:

$$R_1^i = \sum_j (R_0^j \times p_i^j) \quad (\sum_j p_i^j = 1) \tag{2}$$

where p_i^j is the probability that the wrong operation j will be carried out instead of the intentional operation i.

$$R_2 = R_1 \times K_1(u) \times K_2(c) \tag{3}$$

where $K_1(u)$ is a penalty function for operation urgency u and $K_2(c)$ is a penalty function for cognitive load c.

$$R_T = \frac{\sum R_2^i}{n} \tag{4}$$

where n is the number of operations arising from task decomposition.

Function parameter analysis in RIM

The characteristics of the two penalty functions $K_1(u)$ and $K_2(c)$ were further analyzed experimentally.

We implemented a Java 3D vehicle driving simulation program. The user controls the vehicle via driving operations on a road displayed on a screen. A road map can be drawn, including inflexions, as read from a text file. The road bends are 90 and can be used to preserve as much familiarity with the turning angle as possible.

Driving operation involves clicking the up-arrow button to control vehicle movement or to stop. The left-arrow button is clicked to turn left, and clicked again to complete a vehicle turn and to continue in a straight line. Turning right is similar to turning left.

Function $K_1(u)$ analysis: As shown in Figure 2, the road for $K_1(u)$ analysis had 10 turns. The straight parts are long enough to ensure that users have enough time to rest after turning each corner to avoid a cognitive burden. The turning speed is variable, the same as for the straight part, to ensure a perfect driving experience. In experiments, 10 subjects simulated driving at different turning speeds (i.e. different u). A score of 10 was assigned for successful completion of the road network and a score of $n - 1$ for failure at the nth turn. The car is reset if an error occurs. Each subject performed five tests and the mean results are shown.

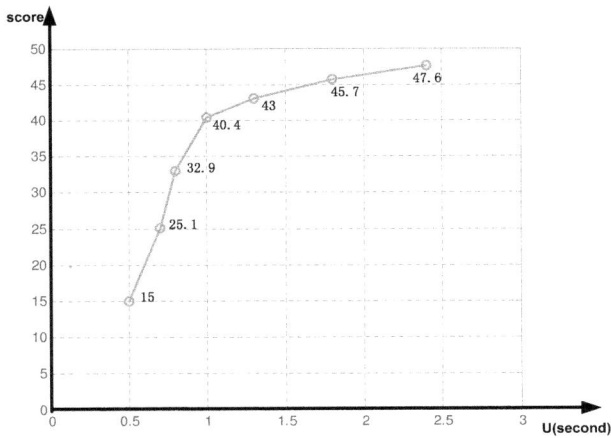

Figure 3. Experimental results for $K_1(u)$ analysis.

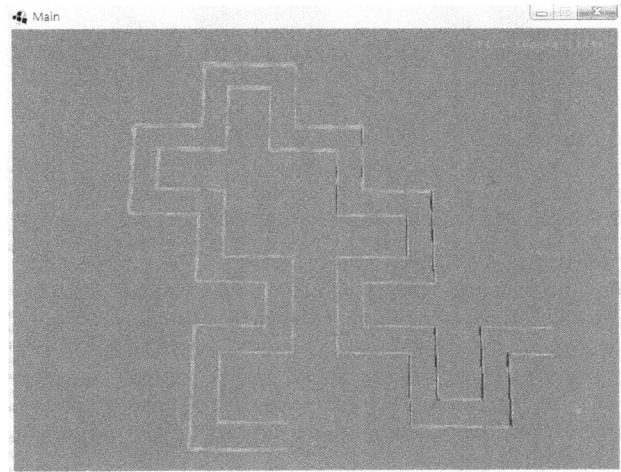

Figure 4. Road platform for $K_2(c)$ analysis.

The experimental results are shown in Figure 3. The rate of decrease in the score is relatively small as the turning speed increases (decerasing u), so the risk is less. As the turning speed continues to increase, the score then rapidly decreases at an inflexion point corresponding to $u = 1.0s$, corresponding to a significant increase in risk. When u is greater than a threshold, the operation time is sufficient, the operation error rate is low and the operation risk is small. For times less than the threshold, the operation time is insufficient, the operation error rate greatly increases, and the operation risk is greatly affected by u.

Function $K_2(c)$ analysis: As shown in Figure 4, the road for $K_2(c)$ analysis had 22 corners. The length of the straight parts is short enough to ensure that users have to turn immediately after the previous turn to increase the cognitive load. The turning speed is fixed (i.e. u fixed) at a moderate level for continuous operation and a good driving experience. In experiments, 10 subjects simulated driving and the number of successes were recorded at the fifth, 10th, 15th, 20th, and 25th corners. The car is reset if an error occurs. Each subject performed five tests and the mean results are shown.

In Figure 5, the horizontal axis represents the number of corners successfully turned and the vertical axis represents the success rate. It is evident that because of the continuous operation required, the user's cognitive load and the operation error rate both increase; consequently, the risk also increases. In addition, as can be seen from the graph, a curve is fitting the points very well. This proves that the increase in cognitive load is not linear, but is similar to a power law function. Thus, further risk is created as the cognitive load increases.

RISK ANALYSIS FOR THE INTERACTIVE AUTO-DRIVING SYSTEM

An interactive auto-driving system is an outdoor vehicle system for disabled and elderly individuals. Users can interactively control the system by defining the destinations and indicating the paths along which to travel. The vehicle will automatically drive itself to the destination via the path planned by the system. Users can also operate the automatic driving

system via the interactive interface at any time. For instance, the users can change their destination, or want to stop at some place.

Interaction operation and interface

The interaction interface of the system is shown in Figure 6. The driver inputs their intention by BCI (brain-computer interface) system. Only five buttons are designed on screen to complete the whole operation for the limited input of BCI. The buttons are "mode switch", "forward/stop", "left", "right", "destination" and "display switch".

To reduce operation risks caused by human error, we designed two driving modes, auto mode (automatic driving by the system based on global path planning) and free mode (the driver may intervene during travel). The user can switch between them by choosing "mode switch". Only "forward/stop" operation is allowed in auto-mode driving. The vehicle will automatically turn at the next junction when the user chooses "left" or "right".

If "destination" is chosen, the intelligent vehicle system maps out a minimum-risk path instead of the normal shortest path based on the vehicle's current location and the electronic map, as shown in Figure 6a. The vehicle will reach the destination along this path in auto-mode driving. To change the path, the driver must choose "stop" first and then "destination", or else choose "mode switch" to select free driving mode, in which turning operation is allowed. Meanwhile, the video from the camera mounted on the vehicle is shown in the interaction interface (Figure 6b).

System Risk Analysis

System risk comprises two components: risk in global path planning and operation risk in local navigation. For the latter, task risk is calculated for system assessment. The specific analysis carried out involved the following steps.

- Analyze risk in global path planning.

239

- Define the original risk R_0 for all operations in the system, which takes an integer value from 0 to 5, and calculate the other risks.

- Choose representative interaction tasks.

- Draw an interaction flow chart.

- Calculate the task risk for selected tasks.

Risk analysis in global path planning

For the path identified by global path planning, road conditions will affect the inherent safety of driving, including road width (w), the number of corners (n_1), the number of continuous turns (n_2), and the turning angle for each intersection (a). These parameters are potential factors in operational risk. Therefore, we use the following formula to evaluate global planning risk:

$$R_G = F(w, n_1, n_2, a) \qquad (5)$$

The minimum-risk path can be obtained by optimization of Eq. 5. In our system, roads are categorized into four classes according to road information. The first plan uses roads in the best class; if this does not provide a solution, second-class roads are included, and so on.

Calculation of various risks

Risk does not arise when the vehicle is immobile in this system. Thus, risks are only generated by system commands via the main interface. Therefore, we only discuss risks for the five buttons on the main menu.

- **Original risk R_0:** A transition in the system state occurs when "forward/stop", "left" or "right" is clicked. We define $R_0 = 1$ for "forward/stop" because the system transition is between immobile and mobile, $R_0 = 2$ for "left" and "right" because the system transition is between mobile and mobile, and $R_0 = 0$ for other commands.

- **Basic risk R_1:** The input accuracy is approximately 90% for the brain-computer interface, and the remaining 10% is recognized as an error, randomly assigned to the other four commands. Basic risks arising from the command operation via the interface buttons can be calculated according to Eq. 2, which are shown in Table 1.

- **Operation risk R_2:** In the system design there are no time limits for any operations. The BCI is assigned a long response time (2-4s seconds) and urgent operations are handed over to the sensors (radar, cameras and other intelligent devices) on the vehicle. Thus, $K_1(u) = 1$ and $K_2(c) = a^c$ in Eq. 3 for any operation in the system, where $a = 1.1$ in our experiments.

- **Task risk R_T:** The task risk depends on the specific task and is calculated according to Eq. 4.

Interaction tasks in experiments

Task 1: Starting from the east gate of Tsinghua University, proceed to the west gate and stop at ERXIAOMEN intersection once using auto-mode driving;

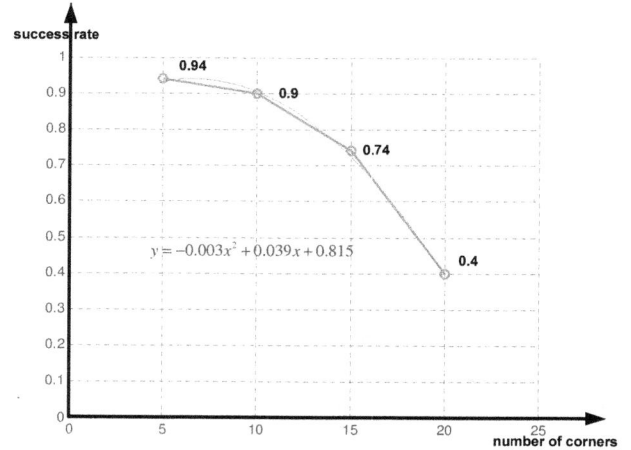

Figure 5. Experimental results for $K_2(c)$ analysis.

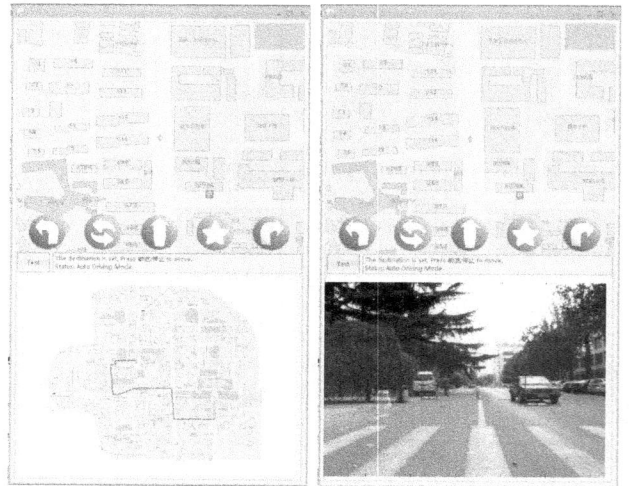

Figure 6. Interaction interface

R_1	immobile	mobile(auto-mode)	mobile(free-mode)
forward/stop	0.9	0.9	1.0
left	0.025	0.025	1.875
right	0.025	0.025	1.875
mode switch	0.025	0.025	0.125
destination	0.025	0.025	0.125

Table 1. Basis risk of five commands.

Task	Risk
1	0.5687
2	0.4361
3	1.2313

Table 2. Task risk

Task 2: Starting from the west gate of Tsinghua University, proceed to the north gate of the library using auto-mode driving.

Task 3: Starting from the north gate of the library, switch to free-mode driving at the EASTMAINBULDING intersection (the driver may choose his own route, but if the time taken for the task is too long, this results in task failure).

The three tasks are representative since they include all possible operations in the system using both auto-mode and free-mode driving with minimal cost.

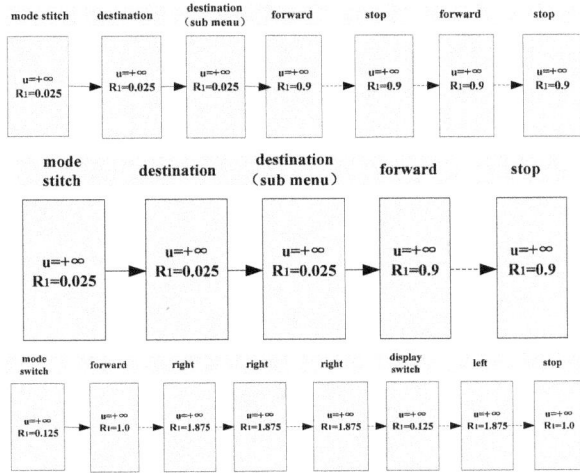

Figure 7. Interaction flow chart of Task 1, Task 2, and Task 3

Interaction flow chart
The interaction flow chart is shown in Figure 7. Solid arrows indicate a short time interval between two operations, which can be regarded as a continuous operation for which the cognitive load will gradually increase. Dotted arrows indicate discontinuous operations for which there is no increase in cognitive load.

Task risks and model analysis
The risk for the three tasks described above (R_{T1}, R_{T2}, R_{T3}) was calculated. The results are shown in Table 2.

The results show that R_{T1} and R_{T2} are small and of similar magnitude. This is because the main operations are static operations with low risk and forward/stop operations with medium risk in tasks 1 and 2. Furthermore, continuous static-state operations occur with less risk. R_{T1} is slightly greater than R_{T2} because task 1 has more forward/stop operations with relatively high risk than task 2, which reflects the high sensitivity of the proposed model.

R_{T3} is much greater than R_{T2} and R_{T1} and is close to three times R_{T2}. The reasons are (i) the main operations in task 3

	Task 1	Task 2	Task 3
Number of error operation Per capita	0.6	0.4	1.1
Number of error operation Per capita with risk	0	0	0.9
probability of Error operation	0.086	0.08	0.138
probability of Error operation with risk	0	0	0.113

Table 3. Operation errors and its probability.

are high risk, such as turn right and turn left and (ii) task 3 involves free-mode driving. The basic risk in free-mode driving is much greater than that in auto-mode driving, as shown in Table 1. The quantitative results reflect the qualitative analysis of the actual situation.

In practice, free-mode driving will occasionally be used when somewhere is not reachable by auto-mode driving. Thus, auto-mode driving (similar to tasks 1 and 2) is the predominant driving mode. Therefore, our interactive system has lower risk and better interactive safety according to model comparisons.

USABILITY TEST
To assess the usability of the model, we carried out a user test and compared the results with model calculations. For the risks in real automatic driving system, we designed a simulation system by collecting the real situation of the environment in the test driving tasks.

User study
Ten users performed simulated driving to complete the three tasks mentioned above. The goal was to identify possible operation errors leading to risk by observing user operations, especially errors. During the tests, the number and position of user operation errors were recorded, together with whether the errors involved risk. For example, in the three tasks, when an operation occurs during a static operation, it does not lead to risk. On the contrary, when an operation error occurs during a dynamic operation, this leads to risk. Test results for the 10 users are shown in Table 3.

As shown in Table 3, the number of operation errors per capita and the probability of operation errors are relatively low for all three tasks. Operation errors with risk are basically avoided during auto-mode driving (tasks 1 and 2), while a few operation errors occur during free-mode driving (task 3). However, since the probability of free-mode use is low in practice, this risk has little effect on system safety. In addition, the number of incorrect operations increases with road unfamiliarity.

In addition, a user survey of subjective feelings (safety, convenience, fatigue) provided important information. The score results (range 0-5) are shown in Table 4. The users assigned high scores to all three parameters.

According to our test results, the interactive auto-driving system is safe and has a user-friendly interaction interface.

Factor	Score
Safety	4.25
Convenience	4.07
Fatigue	4.85

Table 4. User survey

Comprehensive evaluation

Model analysis and users test proved that the interactive auto-driving system has relatively low risk and high safety according to risk calculations and statistical error probability. Model analysis revealed that risk is lower in auto-mode than in free-mode driving, which echoes the probability distribution of operation errors with risk from the user tests. This confirms that RIM is a valuable application.

CONCLUSION AND FUTURE WORK

Safety cannot be evaluated experimentally in complex systems in which operation or interaction errors could lead to serious consequences. To overcome this problem, RIM is proposed for quantitative evaluation of system risk for operation or interaction. Operation and task risks can be easily calculated according to the characteristics of RIM. The influence of two important properties of the model, operating urgency and cognitive load, on errors was analyzed experimentally. Trends for the penalty functions were obtained; these will be important for application of RIM. A safety evaluation of a BCI-based interactive auto-driving system was used as an example for quantitative calculation of system risks based on the model. Overall system safety was evaluated in comparisons between theoretical calculations and user tests, which also demonstrated the use of RIM. RIM and its formalization were only tested on one real system. The system has many imperfections. Accurate expressions for the two penalty functions in RIM have yet to be determined even though influence trends were observed in experiments. In addition, an interaction style that can reduce free-driving risk as part of the driving system design was not considered. These issues will be addressed in future work.

ACKNOWLEDGMENTS

This research was jointly supported by the National Natural Science Foundation of China (Grant Nos. 90820304 and 61075027) and the Tsinghua National Laboratory for Information Science and Technology (TNList) Cross-discipline Foundation (042003023). We are grateful to Mu Yu for the experimental work he carried out.

REFERENCES

1. Card, S. K., Moran, T. P., and Newell, A. *The psychology of human-computer interaction*. Lawrence Erlbaum Associates, 1983.

2. Dix, A., and Abowd, G. Modelling status and event behavior of interactive systems. *Software Engineering Journal 11*, 6 (1996), 334–346.

3. Fitts, P. M. The information capacity of the human motor system in controlling the amplitude of movement. *Journal of Experimental Psychology 47* (1954), 381–391.

4. Jain, S., and Bhattacharya, S. Predictive error behavior model of on-screen keyboard users. In *Proc. CHI 2011*, ACM Press (2011), 1435–1440.

5. John, B. E., and Kieras, D. E. The GOMS family of user interface analysis techniques: Comparison and contrast. *ACM Transactions on Computer-Human Interaction 3*, 4 (1996), 320–351.

6. Rabdulin, E. Using the keystroke-level model for designing user interface on middle-sized touch screens. In *Proc. CHI 2011*, ACM Press (2011), 673–686.

7. Reason, J. Generic error-modeling system (gems): a cognitive framework for locating common human error forms. In *Rasmussen J., Duncan K. and Leplat J. eds. New Technology and Human Error*, John Wiley & Sons Ltd. London, UK (1987), 63–83.

8. Reason, J. Human error: models and management. *British Medical Journal 320*, 7237 (2000), 768–770.

9. Wobbrock, J. O., Jansen, A., and Shinohara, K. Modeling and predicting pointing errors in two dimensions. In *Proc. CHI 2011*, ACM Press (2011), 1653–1656.

Scan Modeling: 3D Modeling Techniques using Cross Section of a Shape

Tatsuhito Oe, Buntarou Shizuki, and Jiro Tanaka

University of Tsukuba

Tennoudai 1-1-1, Tsukuba, Ibaraki, Japan 305-8571

{tatsuhito,shizuki,jiro}@iplab.cs.tsukuba.ac.jp

ABSTRACT

In clay modeling, a creator makes a model by using the shapes of objects, including hands. In contrast, in traditional 3D modeling environments, shapes are assigned by the systems a priori, i.e., no real world object's shape is used. In this paper, we present *Scan Modeling*, in which the creator performs 3D modeling by scanning any real object. To realize Scan Modeling, we developed an input device called "*Wakucon*". Wakucon is square-shaped with 245 millimeters per side. The creator uses it to scan a cross section of a shape by placing it inside of the device. By moving the Wakucon or the objects inserted into the device spatially while scanning these objects, the creator can perform 3D modeling. In this paper, we show interaction techniques and implementation of Scan Modeling. Additionally, we present an evaluation of the accuracy of reconstructed 3D models when using the Wakucon.

Author Keywords

3D modeling; 3D user interface; input device; cross section; shape reconstruction; virtual reality; rapid prototyping; interaction techniques.

ACM Classification Keywords

H.5.2. User Interfaces: Input Devices and Strategies; H.5.1. Multimedia Information Systems: Artificial, Augmented, and Virtual Realities

General Terms

Design; Human Factors.

INTRODUCTION

In clay modeling, which is used as a method for rapid prototyping, a creator makes a model by using the shapes of objects, including hands. Examples of such objects are tools such as spatulas, knives, and prick punches and materials such as wood, leaves, and metals. By using these objects, which include hands, the creator shaves, marks, and smoothes the model. Note that these modifications are performed by direct contact of an object's or hand's shape to the model, i.e.,

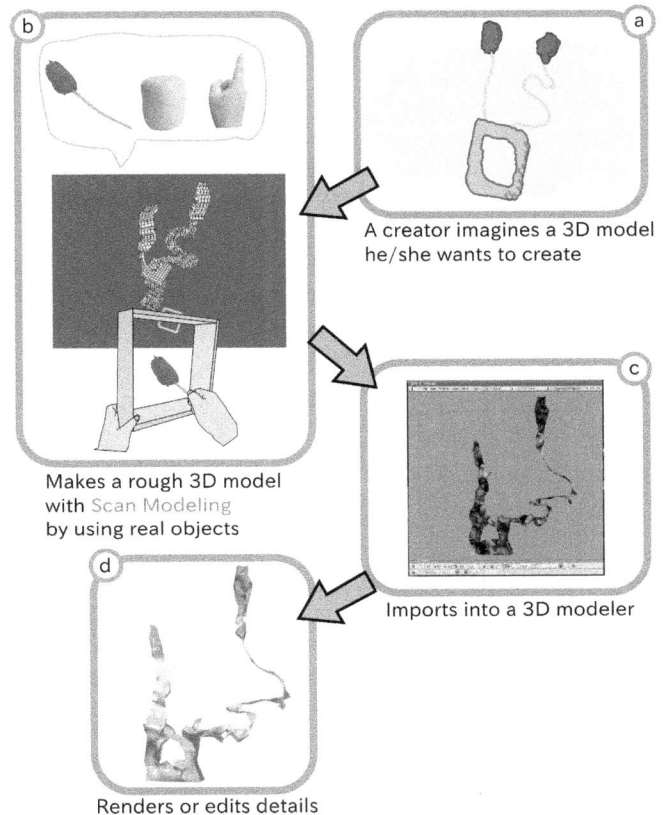

Figure 1. A typical 3D modeling process using Scan Modeling. a: The creator imagines a 3D model that he/she wants to create. b: The creator makes a rough 3D model using Scan Modeling. c: The creator imports the model into a popular 3D modeler from Scan Modeling. d: The creator renders or edits details by using the 3D modeler.

the shape becomes the interface that affects the target. This interface has a rich power of expression in rapid prototyping for three reasons: changing the object's or hand's contact point can be performed quickly since the creator is used to using these tools in the real world, changing the object's shape (i.e., changing the object itself) or the hand's shape can be performed rapidly, and the shape can be freely chosen.

In contrast, in traditional digital 3D modeling, a mouse or a stylus is used. In such modeling, the interface affecting a target is a single point whose position is controlled by using a mouse or a stylus. Moreover, a creator performs 3D modeling by selecting one of multiple modification modes given by the system a priori. Due to these limitations, the amount of freedom for expression is limited.

To address this problem, 3D modeling environments that use real objects have been researched. This research includes 3D modeling environments in which the shape of a hand is used and ones in which real tools are used. In these 3D modeling environments, the interface to a 3D model becomes a surface represented by a hand's or device's shape. Therefore, the amount of freedom for expression increases compared to traditional 3D modeling. Nevertheless, the shapes used in these 3D modeling environments are assigned by the systems a priori, i.e. no real world object's shape is used.

Our goal is to realize a 3D modeling environment in which a creator can make rough 3D models rapidly by using the shape of any real world object. To achieve this goal, we introduce Scan Modeling, in which the creator performs 3D modeling by scanning real objects readily available. As shown in Figure 1, an example of a typical 3D modeling process with Scan Modeling is:

a: The creator imagines a 3D model that he/she wants to create. In Figure 1a, he/she wanted to make a 3D model of a holed vase with two flowers.

b: The creator makes a rough 3D model by using Scan Modeling. In this case, the creator scans the clay, the flower, and his/her finger in the real world.

c: The creator imports the 3D model into a popular 3D modeler from Scan Modeling to edit its details. In Figure 1c, he/she imports it into Blender[1].

d: After editing, he/she renders the 3D model.

We developed an input device called *"Wakucon"* to realize Scan Modeling. The Wakucon is square-shaped with 245 millimeters per side. A creator uses it by inserting an object inside of it to scan a cross section of the shape of the object. To scan a cross section, the Wakucon has four cameras attached on each inner side of the it that face inward. Additionally, our 3D modeling environment recognizes the Wakucon's 3D position and rotation. To recognize these, we use a depth camera and a degrees-of-freedom (9DOF) sensor, respectively. The creator can perform 3D modeling by moving either the Wakucon or objects inserted into the device while scanning these objects.

RELATED WORK

Scan Modeling consists of 3D modeling techniques performed by moving the Wakucon or objects inserted into the device while scanning these objects. Therefore, related works relate Scan Modeling to interaction techniques for 3D modeling or an implementation of our system. These works include research on 3D modeling environments in which hands' or devices' spatial movement, position, posture, and shape are used and research on scanning an object's shape.

---

[1] http://www.blender.org/

Spatial 3D Modeling

There is research on 3D modeling environments in which various devices are used. Saso et al. presented the Beyond-Me Site, in which 3D modeling is performed by using a camera held in one hand and a marker held in the other [12]. Keefe et al. presented CavePainting, in which 3D models are created by using a real brush in the CAVE environment [5]. Sachs et al. presented 3-Draw, in which a creator holds a stylus and a palette in the hands and draws 3D curves by moving the stylus [11]. A common feature among this research is that the shape of a vertex or a surface to be added into VR space is given by each 3D modeling environment a priori; that is, a creator makes a 3D model by selecting modes that define how to modify the 3D model. In contrast to this research, in Scan Modeling, 3D modeling is performed by scanning a cross section of a real object dynamically. The creator makes a rough 3D model by changing the position of an object for scanning or its posture or by changing the Wakucon's position or rotating it.

Some research has tried to use the shapes of hands in 3D modeling. Gloss et al. presented Gesture Modeling, in which a creator makes a 3D model by using hand postures recognized with computer vision [4]. Moritz et al. presented a 3D modeling environment in which a creator wears Data Gloves on both hands and performs boolean operation on 3D models by using a model of a plane, a sphere, a cube, or a cone [8]. Schkolne et al. presented Surface Drawing, in which a creator wears a glove interface and draws 3D models by shaping with his/her hands [13]. By contrast, in Scan Modeling, not only are hand shapes used but also any object's shape is used. Therefore, Scan Modeling extends this research in which 3D modeling is performed by shaping with the hands.

Malleable device shaping also has been tried. A 3D modeling environment was presented in which a creator holds a malleable device in his/her hands and deforms a 3D model by deforming the device [9, 15]. In an environment created by Sheng et al., a creator edits a 3D model not only by deforming a malleable device with his/her hands but also by pressing a knife against the device [14]. All of this research focused on deforming a 3D model by using press manipulation. In contrast to this research, in Scan Modeling, the press like manipulation is supported by subtracting a 3D model spatially by using a scanned cross section. In addition, we support reconstructing a part or the whole of a real object.

There are pieces of research that use real objects' shapes in 3D modeling environments. Anabuki et al. presented AR-Jig, in which a creator makes a 3D model by using a pin array called a "jig" [1]. With AR-Jig, the creator can copy a real object's contour by pushing the jig against the object and paste the contour to a 3D model. Anderson et al. presented a 3D modeling environment in which a creator builds a model by using physical blocks, and these blocks are reconstructed in VR space [2]. Also, in Scan Modeling, the real object is reconstructed in VR space by using scanning. In addition to reconstruction, complex interaction techniques including holing, shaving, and cutting with a real object as a tool are uniformly supported in Scan Modeling.

Scanning an Object's Shape

Methods for scanning a real object are classified into two classes:

- scanning by pressing an object against a deformable device.
- scanning an object with sensors, which observe the object from different positions in an environment.

Our method belongs in the second class, in which an object's cross section is scanned by using cameras.

The first class is used to reconstruct an object's surface. Pieces of research using this method were shown in the previous section, such as research with deformable devices [9, 15, 14] or the AR-Jig presented by Anabuki et al. [1]. In addition, Sean et al. presented a malleable surface that reconstructs the surface of an object pressed against it [3].

In the second class, light sensors, magnetic sensors, cameras, etc. are used. Moeller et al. presented a multi-touch interface that scans the cross section of an object inserted into a device by using an IR sensors array [7]. Reed presented a method to scan the entire shape of a clay object [10]. In this research, wireless magnetic transceivers were embedded into the clay, and to track these transceivers' positions and postures with a magnetic receiver, the clay's shape was scanned. In contrast to the first class, these pieces of research reconstruct a cross section or the whole of an object.

The first is suitable for texturing a 3D model because an object's surface can be scanned. In contrast, the second suits the prototyping because it can reconstruct a whole object rapidly in VR space by scanning. Therefore, we adopt the second, in which an object's cross section is scanned by using cameras.

OVERVIEW OF SCAN MODELING

Scan Modeling's interaction is performed by spatially moving the Wakucon or a real object inserted into the device. Figure 2 shows an overview of Scan Modeling. The bottom of Figure 2 illustrates both the Wakucon and a real object scanned in our system. The top shows our 3D modeler's display. In the 3D modeler, the created 3D model, the cross section of the shape inserted into the device, and the cursor, which represents the Wakucon's position and rotation, are displayed. 3D modeling is performed by drawing or subtracting 3D voxels by using a real object's cross section.

INTERACTION TECHNIQUES OF SCAN MODELING

There are three manipulations with Scan Modeling: *Scan Subtraction*, *Scan Draw*, and *View Change*. The first is a manipulation that holes, shaves, or cuts a 3D model by using a cross section of a shape. The second is a manipulation that generates a 3D model by drawing voxels spatially by using a cross section. The third is a manipulation that changes the view toward a 3D model in VR space.

Scan Subtraction

Scan Subtraction is a manipulation that holes, shaves, or cuts by subtracting existing voxels by using a cross section. This is similar to modification by using a tool's surface in real clay modeling. In Scan Subtraction, a creator determines how to

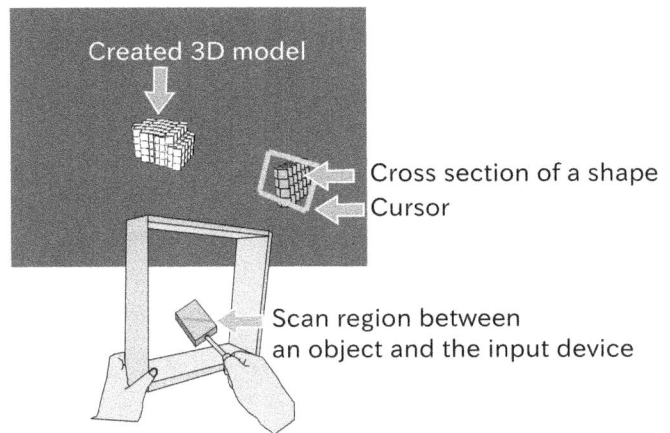

Figure 2. Overview of Scan Modeling.

modify a 3D model by changing a scanned shape or the way to push against the target, like in real clay modeling.

Figure 3 shows a technique of Scan Subtraction, holing. Using this technique, it is possible to hole an arbitrarily shaped hole. A case involving the holing process is described below and is shown in Figure 3.

a: The creator holds the Wakucon in one hand and the object in the other.

b: The creator pushes both hands on the 3D model while scanning the object.

c: The 3D model is holed.

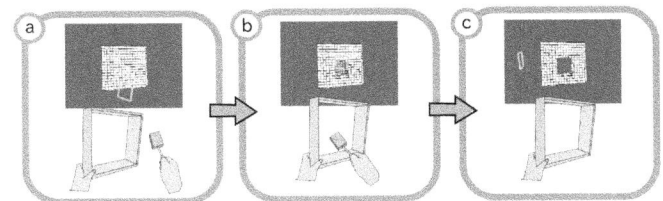

Figure 3. A technique for holing by using Scan Subtraction.

Figure 4 shows a shaving technique. A case involving the shaving process is described below and is shown in Figure 4.

a: The creator holds the Wakucon in one hand and clenches the other.

b: The creator shifts both hands around the right side of the 3D model while scanning.

c: The 3D model is shaved.

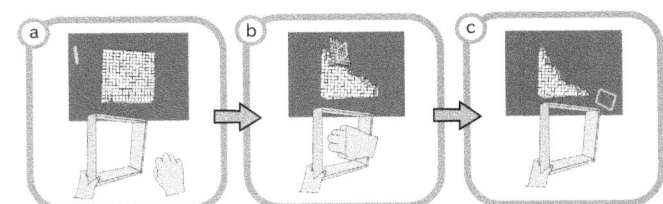

Figure 4. A technique for shaving by using Scan Subtraction.

Figure 5 shows a cutting technique. A case involving the cutting process is described below and is shown in Figure 5.

a: The creator holds the Wakucon and the object.
b: The creator shifts both hands in a longitudinal direction while scanning.
c: The 3D model is cut.

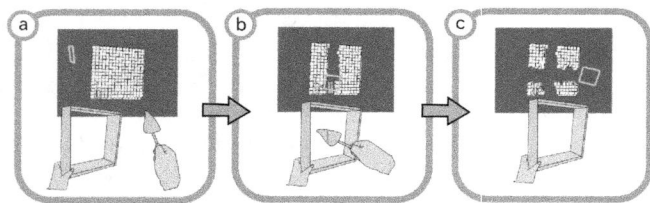

Figure 5. A technique for cutting by using Scan Subtraction.

Scan Draw

Scan Draw is a manipulation that generates one or more 3D models by drawing voxels spatially by using a cross section. A technique with Scan Draw is shown in Figure 6. In Figure 6, the creator is scanning cross sections of two of his/her fingers and shifting both hands while maintaining a relative position between the Wakucon and fingers. This results in two parallel lines in VR space.

Another technique with Scan Draw is shown in Figure 7. This technique copies an entire real object into VR space by scanning a stationary target object. In Figure 7, the creator scans his/her entire hand by making his/her one hand into a specific shape and moving the Wakucon through this hand by using the other hand.

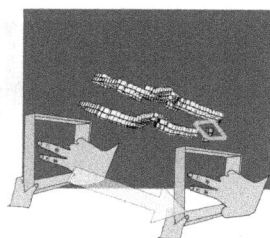

Figure 6. A technique with Scan Draw. The creator draws two 3D lines with two fingers.

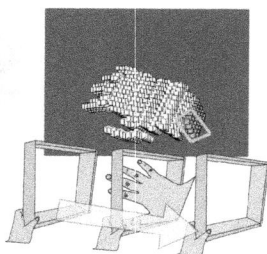

Figure 7. Another technique with Scan Draw. The creator scans his/her entire hand.

View Change

View Change is a manipulation that changes the view to a 3D model in VR space by using Wakucon's pose. By using View Change, a creator can view a 3D model from any direction by rotating the camera in VR space along the x, y, z axes. For example, in the top of Figure 8, the creator is rotating the camera along the x axis, rotating along the y axis on the left, and rotating along the z axis on the right.

IMPLEMENTATION

In this section, we describe an implementation of Scan Modeling. First, we present the system configuration. Second, we present the Wakucon and 3D reconstruction method that uses the device. Finally, we show a method for rotation and position detection.

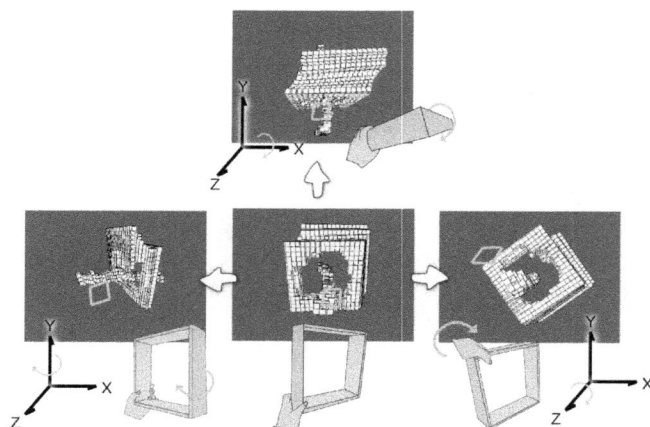

Figure 8. An example of View Change. At the top, the creator is rotating the camera along the x axis, rotating along the y axis on the left, and rotating along the z axis on the right.

System Configuration

As shown in Figure 9, the system consists of the Wakucon, a depth camera, and a display. The Wakucon is used to scan a cross section of a real object. The depth camera is used to detect the 3D position of the Wakucon. At current implementation, we used Microsoft's Kinect[2] as the depth camera. Finally, the display is used to show the 3D modeler.

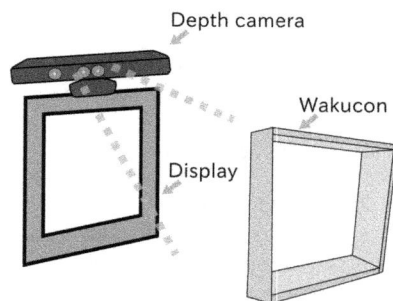

Figure 9. System configuration of Scan Modeling. Our system consists of the Wakucon, a depth camera, and a display.

Wakucon

As shown in Figure 10, the Wakucon consists of four cameras, infrared (IR) LEDs, a microcontroller, a degrees-of-freedom (9DOF) sensor, and buttons. Each element's arrangement and purpose is described below.

Four cameras A camera is attached on each inner side of the Wakucon and faces inward. The camera views the objects inserted into the Wakucon from each position. The frames captured by the cameras are used to reconstruct the cross section of an object. In the current implementation, the FPS of each camera was set to 30.

IR LEDs As shown in Figure 10, the Wakucon has two types of IR LEDs:

IR LEDs for lighting an object In our 3D reconstruction method, an object's silhouette, which is grabbed from

---

[2]http://www.xbox.com/kinect

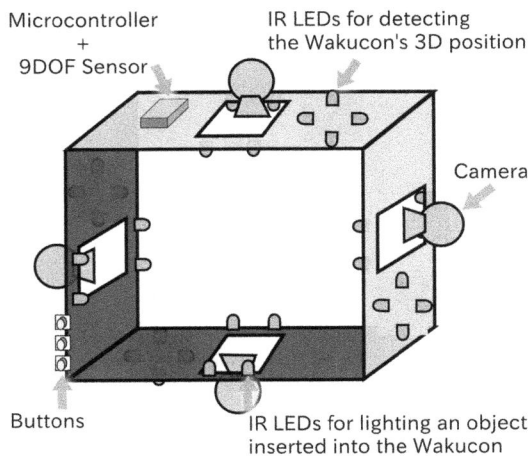

Figure 10. Wakucon configuration. The Wakucon consists of four cameras, IR LEDs, a microcontroller, a 9DOF sensor, and buttons.

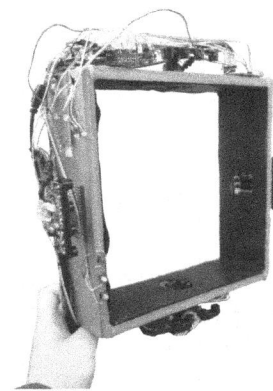

Figure 11. Prototype Wakucon.

a camera frame, is used as an input source. Since detecting the silhouette sometimes fails when the object's color is dark or due to the lighting environment, we use the reflected light of the IR LEDs that are attached around on each camera's lens as the camera's input.

IR LEDs for detecting the Wakucon's 3D position
Wakucon 3D position is detected by tracking with the IR LEDs attached on the outside of the device by using the depth camera.

Microcontroller We use the microcontroller to turn on/off the IR LEDs used for lighting an object inserted into the Wakucon. Because turning on all the IR LEDs is too bright, we only turn on the IR LEDs around the camera used for capturing a frame while turning off all the other IR LEDs. At current implementation, we used an Arduino Pro Mini[3] as the microcontroller.

9DOF sensor The 9DOF sensor attached on the Wakucon consists of a triple-axis accelerometer sensor, a triple-axis magnetometer sensor, and a triple-axis gyroscope. By using the sensor, Wakucon's pitch, roll, and yaw are computed. At current implementation, we used Sparkfun's SEN-10736[4] as the 9DOF sensor.

Buttons Three buttons are attached around the grip of the device. These buttons are triggers of Scan Subtraction, Scan Draw, and View Change.

Our prototype Wakucon is shown in Figure 11. The prototype weighs about 400 grams without cables and about 700 grams with cables connecting the device to a PC. Each side of the device is 245 millimeters.

Reconstruction of a Cross Section
Scan Modeling is a 3D modeling technique that uses a scanned cross section. The Scan Modeling system repeats the following steps: 1) reconstruct a cross section and 2) represent the cross section as voxels in VR space. In this section, first, we describe Shape-From-Silhouette [6] which is an algorithm we use for the first step. Second, we describe how to reconstruct a cross section by using the algorithm as well as how to calculate the rotation and position of the input device for the second step.

Shape-From-Silhouette
Shape-From-Silhouette [6] is a reconstruction method that uses a target object's silhouettes, which are extracted from camera frames captured from different angles. Figure 12 shows the concept of Shape-From-Silhouette. In Figure 12, a camera is attached on each of the sides of the Wakucon and detects the silhouette of an object inserted into the center of the device. Shape-From-Silhouette first defines a volume by extending each silhouette toward the depth direction. The cross region of all the volumes will be the reconstructed model. In our implementation, we use Figure 12's scan region as the cross region, enabling the creator to widen/narrow the width of scanning.

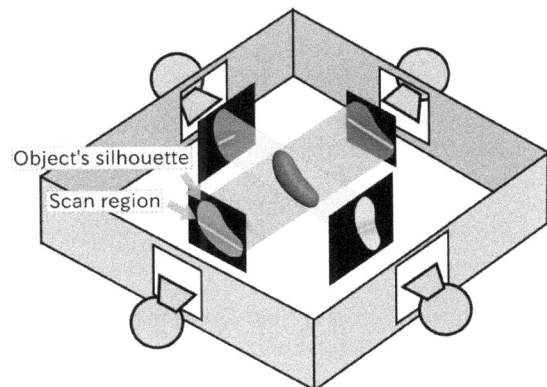

Figure 12. Reconstructing a cross section by using Shape-From-Silhouette. A white line within each object's silhouette is used to represent a scan region in this figure.

---

[3]http://arduino.cc/it/Main/ArduinoBoardProMini
[4]http://www.sparkfun.com/products/10736

Reconstruction of a cross section by using Shape-From-Silhouette

In our implementation, a silhouette is detected in four steps. Figure 13 shows the result of each step. Cam_0~3 represent frames grabbed from each camera. The frames, shown in Figure 13, are raw, synchronized, moving averaged, and binarized frames from left to right. A detailed description of each step is given below.

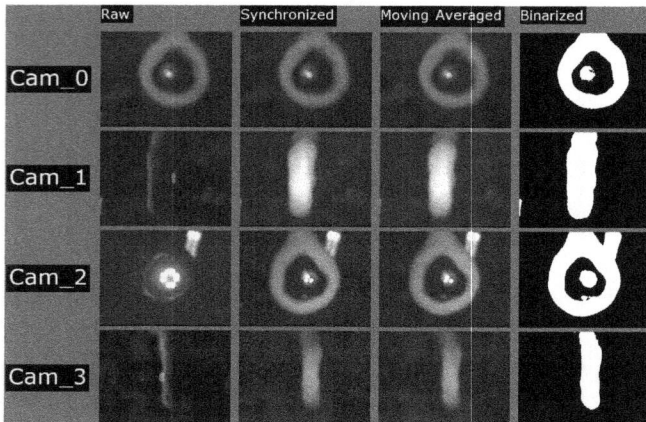

Figure 13. Frames captured from cameras attached on the Wakucon. In this picture, Cam_0~3 represent each camera's frame. Moreover, shown from the upper left are raw, synchronized, moving averaged, and binarized frames.

Raw A raw frame is captured with a camera. At this step, the capture is not synchronized with LEDs. Therefore, as is shown under "Raw" in Figure 13, the object is lit by LEDs' from various directions.

Synchronized Synchronized frames are frames captured under synchronized lighting. That is, the system turns on the LEDs attached around the camera and then captures a frame with the camera.

Moving averaged Moving averaged frames are frames that are taken as a moving average by using some synchronized frames. This is computed to stabilize brightness variations that occur from the blinking of the LEDs.

Binarized Binarized frames are generated by binarizing moving averaged frames.

Since the binarized frames show silhouettes, we use them as the input to the Shape-From-Silhouette algorithm.

An example of reconstruction is shown in Figure 14. In Figure 14, a torus's cross section is reconstructed. Another example is shown in Figure 15. In Figure 15, the creator widens the scan region to the maximum size; that is, the whole of the camera frame. In this case, the torus shaped object and the hand grasping it are reconstructed instantly.

Calculating Rotation and Position of the Input Device

The Wakucon's rotation is computed from the attached 9DOF sensor. The device's position is computed by attached tracking IR LEDs for position detection. Figure 16 shows the process that utilizes the Kinect's RGB depth camera, making the tracking simple but robust. First, an RGB frame is captured with the RGB camera (Figure 16a). To track only the IR

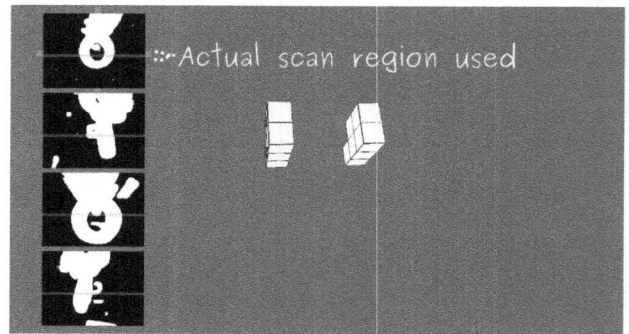

Figure 14. Reconstruction result by using our system. In this result, the torus's cross section is reconstructed.

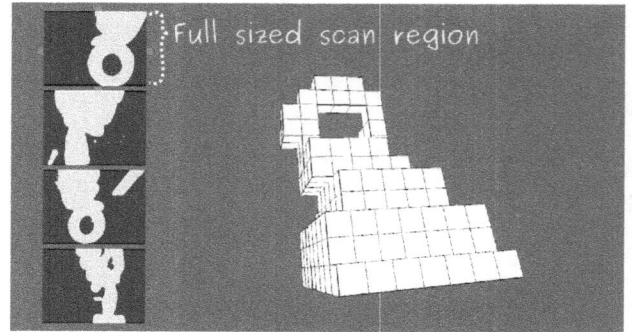

Figure 15. Reconstruction result by using our system. In this result, the torus shaped object and the hand grasping it are reconstructed instantly with a full sized scan region.

LEDs, an IR pass filter is attached to the RGB camera. At the same time, an depth frame is captured with the depth camera (Figure 16b). Second, binarization and dilation are applied to the RGB frame (Figure 16c) to make a mask frame for later use. In the mask frame, white pixels correspond to the Wakucon's IR LEDs. Next, by masking the depth frame with the mask frame shown in Figure 16c as a mask, we can obtain each IR LED's (x, y, z) position (Figure 16d). Finally, from these positions, the Wakucon's (x, y, z) position is computed. In this position, drawing or subtracting voxels is performed in Scan Modeling.

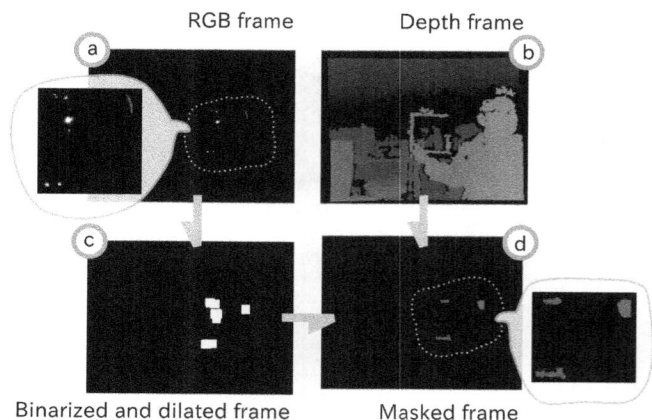

Figure 16. Image processing to obtain a device's 3D position.

EVALUATION OF RECONSTRUCTED 3D MODELS

Our research goal is to realize a 3D modeling environment in which a creator can make rough 3D models rapidly by using any real world object's shape. Because reconstructed 3D models are main tools in Scan Modeling, the accuracy of the reconstructed 3D models is important. Therefore, we examined this accuracy.

Method

We scanned four primitive objects by using Scan Draw. These four objects are shown in Figure 17. From the left, a sphere, a triangle, a rectangle, and a torus are shown. Each object was made of clay beforehand, and a stick was inserted as a grip.

Figure 17. The four objects used in this evaluation. From the left, a sphere, a triangle, a rectangle, and a torus are shown.

We scanned these objects by using Scan Draw multiple times, and the 3D model which was thought to be closest to the source object was used as an experimental result. Additionally, the range for object scanning was from the top of each object to a point attached on the stick.

The experiment was conducted by one of the authors. We used a computer with an Intel Core2 Quad Q9550 CPU, 4GB of RAM, and an ATI Radeon HD 3600 GPU that runs Ubuntu Linux.

Results and Discussion

The experimental result is shown in Figure 18. Figure 18a, b, c, d represent the scanned sphere, triangle, rectangle, and torus, respectively. Each figure shows the source object in the upper left for comparison. Moreover, each figure is the 3D modeling's result created from the following steps.

1. Create 3D voxels by using Scan Modeling with a source object.
2. Import into meshlab[5] to build meshes by using Delaunay triangulation from 3D voxels.
3. Import into Blender to render meshes.

In addition, the time taken to reconstruct the 3D models was 2.6 seconds for the sphere, 1.5 seconds for the triangle, 2.0 seconds for the rectangle, and 3.3 seconds for the torus. Note that each time represents the time taken to create 3D voxels by using Scan Modeling.

As shown in Figure 18, all the reconstructed 3D models roughly reflected the corresponding source objects' shapes. For example, in Figure 18b, the model represents the triangle

---

[5]http://meshlab.sourceforge.net/

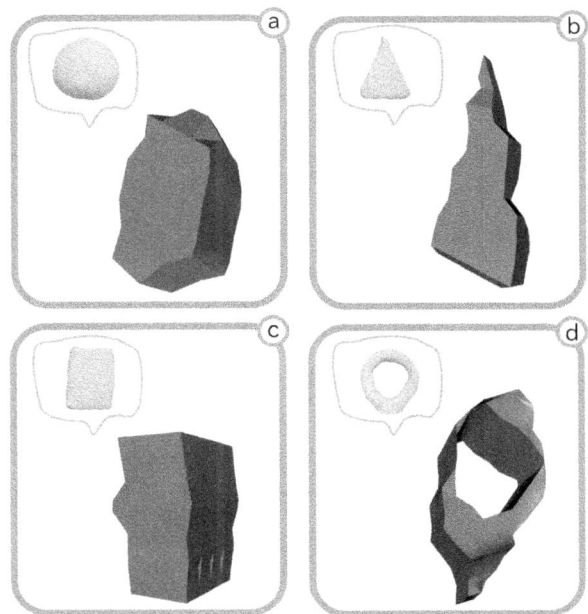

Figure 18. Reconstructed 3D models of real objects by using Scan Draw; a: the sphere, b: the triangle, c: the rectangle, and d: the torus.

shape. In Figure 18d, the model represents the torus, which has a hole in the center. However, problems were found and are described below.

- In current implementation, a sphere was difficult to reconstruct, as shown in Figure 18a.
- A distortion along the scanned direction occurred in the reconstructed 3D models. For example, the rectangle shown in Figure 18c curves loosely in a longitudinal direction. Moreover, the noises of vertices are shown around the center of the model.
- There is variance in the density of the vertices in the reconstructed 3D models. For example, in the torus shown in Figure 18d, the density of the vertices of the tube's left side are low compared to those of the right side.

The first problem was caused by how the cross section scanning was implemented. In current implementation, we use silhouette frames with lower resolution as input sources to reduce the calculation cost of Shape-From-Silhouette. Specifically, we reduced the resolution of raw frames 320×240 into 16×12 to detect the silhouette. This problem can be addressed by using higher resolution; reconstructed 3D models become closer to the source objects. However, real time reconstruction becomes difficult because it takes more time to detect the intersection of the silhouettes' volumes. Therefore, we plan to modify the algorithm to detect an intersection by using parallel computation of CPUs or by using a GPU based Shape-From-Silhouette [16].

The second and third problems were caused by a variance of the Wakucon's position and move speed, respectively. To solve these problems, a creator can scan the whole object instantaneously with a full sized scan region, as shown in Figure 15, in case of reconstructing a whole object. To scan instantaneously, the effect of the variance of the Wakucon's position or speed must be reduced. Moreover, we plan to apply filters, such as the Kalman filter, to smooth the variance.

CONCLUSION AND FUTURE WORK

In this paper, we presented 3D modeling techniques that use Scan Modeling to realize a 3D modeling environment in which a creator can make rough 3D models rapidly by using any real world object's shape. Scan Modeling's manipulations consist of Scan Subtraction, Scan Draw, and View Change. By using these manipulations, a creator can make a 3D model rapidly. We presented an implementation of a square shaped input device called "Wakucon", a method to reconstruct a cross section of a shape, and a method to calculate the rotation and position of the device.

Our future work is to make the precision of the cross section's reconstruction and the Wakucon's position tracking higher, as shown in the "Evaluation of Reconstructed 3D Models" section. By making precision higher, a creator can prototype a 3D model closer to what he/she wants to create with only one interaction. For this reason, we believe that a creator can make a 3D model more rapidly. We also plan to conduct two evaluations in order to validate Scan Modeling's effectiveness and possibility of expression. In the first evaluation, we will employ creators, including 3D modeling novices, as subjects and let them create specific 3D models in a given amount of time by using a typical 3D modeler or Scan Modeling. As a result of the first evaluation, we will confirm that creators can make 3D models rapidly by using Scan Modeling. In the second evaluation, we will employ as subjects professional creators who are used to creating 3D models and let them create 3D models freely by using Scan Modeling. As a result of the second, we will confirm the possibility of expression by using Scan Modeling and analyze various points to make improvements for practical realization.

REFERENCES

1. Anabuki, M., and Ishii, H. AR-Jig: A Handheld Tangible User Interface for Modification of 3D Digital Form via 2D Physical Curve. In *Proc. ISMAR 2007*, IEEE (2007), 1–10.

2. Anderson, D., Frankel, J. L., Marks, J., Agarwala, A., Beardsley, P., Hodgins, J., Leigh, D., Ryall, K., Sullivan, E., and Yedidia, J. S. Tangible Interaction + Graphical Interpretation: A New Approach to 3D Modeling. In *Proc. SIGGRAPH 2000*, ACM (2000), 393–402.

3. Follmer, S., Johnson, M., Adelson, E., and Ishii, H. deForm: an Interactive Malleable Surface for Capturing 2.5D Arbitrary Objects, Tools and Touch. In *Proc. UIST 2011*, ACM (2011), 527–536.

4. Gross, M., and Kemp, A. Gesture Modelling: Using Video to Capture Freehand Modeling Commands. In *Proc. CAAD Futures 2001*, Kluwer Academic Publishers (2001), 271–284.

5. Keefe, D. F., Feliz, D. A., Moscovich, T., Laidlaw, D. H., and LaViola, Jr., J. J. CavePainting: A Fully Immersive 3D Artistic Medium and Interactive Experience. In *Proc. I3D 2001*, ACM (2001), 85–93.

6. Martin, W. N., and Aggarwal, J. K. Volumetric Descriptions of Objects from Multiple Views. *IEEE Transactions on Pattern Analysis and Machine Intelligence* (1983), 150–158.

7. Moeller, J., Kerne, A., and Damaraju, S. ZeroTouch: a Zero-Thickness Optical Multi-Touch Force Field. In *Ext. Abtracts CHI 2011*, ACM (2011), 1165–1170.

8. Moritz, E., Kuester, F., Hamann, B., Kenneth, I. J., and Hagen, H. Towards Immersive Clay Modeling: Interactive Modeling with Octrees. *Proc. SPIE 3957* (2000), 414–422.

9. Murakami, T., and Nakajima, N. Direct and Intuitive Input Device for 3-D Shape Deformation. In *Proc. CHI 1994*, ACM (1994), 465–470.

10. Reed, M. Prototyping Digital Clay as an Active Material. In *Proc. TEI 2009*, ACM (2009), 339–342.

11. Sachs, E., Roberts, A., and Stoops, D. 3-Draw: A Tool for Designing 3D Shapes. *IEEE Computer Graphics and Applications 11* (1991), 18–26.

12. Saso, T., Tamayama, T., and Inakage, M. Beyond-Me Site: Two-Handed Interface for 3D Drawing in MR. In *Proc. GRAPHITE 2003*, ACM (2003), 275–276.

13. Schkolne, S., Pruett, M., and Schröder, P. Surface Drawing: Creating Organic 3D Shapes with the Hand and Tangible Tools. In *Proc. CHI 2001*, ACM (2001), 261–268.

14. Sheng, J., Balakrishnan, R., and Singh, K. An Interface for Virtual 3D Sculpting via Physical Proxy. In *Proc. GRAPHITE 2006*, ACM (2006), 213–220.

15. Smith, R. T., Thomas, B. H., and Piekarski, W. Digital Foam Interaction Techniques for 3D Modeling. In *Proc. VRST 2008*, ACM (2008), 61–68.

16. Yous, S., Laga, H., Kidode, M., and Chihara, K. GPU-Based Shape from Silhouettes. In *Proc. GRAPHITE 2007*, ACM (2007), 71–77.

Spring: A Solution for Managing the Third DOF with Tactile Interface

Robin Vivian
Université de Lorraine
InterPsy-ETIC, EA 4432
User Experience Lab
robin.vivian@univ-lorraine.fr

Jérôme Dinet
Université de Lorraine
InterPsy-ETIC, EA 4432
User Experience Lab
jerome.dinet@univ-lorraine.fr

David Bertolo
Université de Lorraine
LITA EA 3097
Computer Lab
david.bertolo@univ-lorraine.fr

ABSTRACT

Tablets with touch-screens are one of the most widely used interfaces for three main reasons: the effectiveness and efficiency and fun side interactions. Associated with significant increases in power, the multi-touch touchscreen terminals are able to manipulate real-time application of virtual worlds for entertainment or learning. This raises a question that was already current with conventional interfaces (mouse for example) how to define, with 2D input interface, designation, orientation and move actions (simply and intuitively) on objects in 3D space that require at least 6 degrees of freedom (6 DOF for the object and sometimes six other for the camera)? Our study provides a way of managing the depth dimension with the principle of universal interaction: to screw / unscrew. The first part of this paper presents the theoretical framework based on prior studies and the second part describes the formalization of a grammar of gesture allowing the intuitive interaction management of depth component.

ACM Classification Keywords H.5.2 [Information Interfaces and Presentation]: User Interfaces – Interaction : input devices and strategies

Keywords: Interactions, tablets touch-screen, 3DOF, grammar of gesture, Graphical user interfaces, tactile device, gestural grammar.

INTRODUCTION

Interacting with digital objects in two dimensions does not require specific abilities. For instance, an individual can easily understand that an object can be moved from the right to the left of the touch-screen by pointing this object and dragging his/her finger in the correct direction. But to manage the six degrees of freedom (3 DOF for the placement and 3 DOF for rotation or even 6 additional for an observer) imposes to design less conventional actions. As new applications for 3D mobile Touch are built every days, it is important to define a methodology for interaction, certainly not with universal consensus but just

to be able to rotate, forward, backward, scale shapes in space.

How to move and/or rotate an objet along X, Y and/or Z axes? There are many works both in the development of specific interfaces (trackball, 3D mouse, etc.) and in the definition of an interaction with conventional devices such as mouse and keyboard [23, 24, 25, 26, 27].

Unlike the 2D devices, tablets with touch-screen for multi-fingers interfaces allow, with multipoint interactions, to expand possibilities of manipulations.

Gestural and verbal grammars follow the same rules (construction, analyse, syntax). This similitude allows a unification of definition. One of the main goals of gestural grammar related to tablets for multi-fingers interfaces is to define gestures understandable by everyone. For example, there is a consensus to say that to realize a zoom in or a zoom out, you have just to pull up or separate two points of contact on the screen. Microsoft designs this gesture for the first time for the tablet with touch-screen and is used by Apple with the Ipad®. To manipulate an object in 3D digital world is more complex than in a plan space. The main difficulty is to control the third dimension. One finger, n fingers, one hand, two hands? Today nobody has really the solution but we now that multi-touch screens provide lots of possibilities that traditional device never possess.

I have in my office a lithograph of Alexander Calder (see Figure 1: unluckily a reproduction!) that probably sparks off this idea.

Figure 1: My Lithograph of Alexander Calder

These spirals have something haunting (like a endless screw) but reminds me of a gesture that any handyman knows: screw or unscrew. These gestures move a screw along of Z-axis (or –Z). Have we got the possibility to duplicate this gesture to handle an objet in a virtual space? I think that the novel idea comes from this lithograph.

The study presented in this paper aims at improving the understanding of continuous high degree-of-freedom input using tablets for multi-fingers interfaces. Our formalization is based on a rationale rooted in semiotics. After presenting the related work on degrees of freedom integration and separation, as well as 3D manipulation techniques with multi-touch displays, we will introduce the concept of spring (an extension of Calder's spiral) for a specific area: learning 3D geometry.

CATEGORIES AND FORMALISATION
Gestures' classification

Studying the meaning of gestures run up several problems. The first one is probably a lack of formal standardization. The second is the lack of segmentation of linear or combinatorial to built elementary units. That's the reason why a large part of researcher has proposed functional classifications based on the relation between action and pragmatic value that results. In 1941 Efron [1] thought that the human gesture (not only fingers or hand like in our works) must be group in only five categories. These categories were physiographics, kinetographics, ideographics, deictics, and batons. Ekman and Freisen [2] studied classification and will add eleven subdivisions.

In 1991 Tang [3] observed a task group who worked to a collaborative way around a drawing table. Interactions watching and gesture analyse provided important indications about subdivision of space work, the mains areas of exchange and modalities of exchange of information.

These concepts are dependent of context. Weller [4]. Morris et al. [5] presented multi-user gestural interactions for co-located groupware for collaborative work tasks. These are all very useful contributions to the touch/gesture interaction field but a more generalized understanding of touch interaction focused beyond the specific realization of a device, is required. Recently, researchers in human-computer interaction have been exploring interactive laptops for fun use and entertainment [6].

The main goal of our work is to prove that to use tactile devices is more efficient than traditional devices like mouse or/and keyboard.

Most of the time, the designer of digital environment defines interactions with a typical and personal logic. Sometime it's not easy to understand all mechanisms used to define gesture because designers draw ideas from their experiences, culture or life.

But what kinds of gesture can a standard user perform? Do you know his/her mental representation? How many fingers to use to describe a specific action? In 2003 Nielsen proposes a procedure for developing computer interfaces with intuitive and ergonomic gesture [7]. In 2009 Wobbrock [8] preformed an experiment with 20 people to build a grammar of gestures. These authors present the twenty participants a series of twenty-seven commands and ask them to combine and invent the corresponding interactions. Authors show at twenty participants a series of twenty-seven commands and participants were asked to describe the corresponding interactions on a tactile tablet. Different commands more and more difficult to describe are used. On the basis of one thousand different interactions proposed by participants, four groups of gestures have been distinguished (see Figure 2):

Taxonomy of Surface Gesture		
Form	Static pose	Hand pose is held in one location
	Dynamic pose	Hand pose change in one location
	Static pose and path	Hand pose is held as hand moves
	Dynamic pose and path	Hand pose change as hand moves
	One point touch	Static pose with one finger
	One point path	Static pose & path with one finger
Nature	Symbolic	Gesture visually depicts a symbol
	Physical	Gesture acts physically on objects
	Metaphorical	Gesture indicates a metaphor
	Abstract	Gesture referent mapping is arbitrary
Binding	Object centric	Location defined respect object features
	World dependent	Location defined respect world features
	World independent	Location can ignore world feature
	Mixed dependencies	World independent plus another
Flow	Discrete	Response occurs after the user acts
	Continuous	Response occurs while the user acts

Figure 2: Taxonomy of surface gestures based on 1080 gestures.

The authors show a problem with the principle of the approach, namely bias and behaviour change related to feedback. Users were not able to back on the choice of interaction with a consequence that the solutions did not represent the optimum interaction to perform the action. At the opposite of this approach to categorization from the behavioral observation, is an approach called low-level which is to rebuild a library of gestures from a basis grammar and formalizing actions of the user.

Formalization of a grammar for multi-touch gestures

The main goal of the formalization is to unify different definitions, different grammars, different moves and built a library of common gestures. Designing a universal grammar, a gestural language, which can be used by different tactile applications, is the objective research of Lao et al [9]. In 2010, Görg [10] suggested a framewwork for restricted recognition and representation of interactions with tactile devices. Defining a grammar is normally a concept of formalized logic (like a linguistic grammar). Kaindl showed in [11] all the difficulties to develop a specific framework for tactile devices.

A set of standard gesture can be defined if your interactions are limited to a group of objects with only two dimensions. For example, zoom in/out, rotation, translation will be the same if your task is just visualizing pictures, playing chess or reading an electronic book. It's less easy when you need to manipulate some entities in virtual world. For example how can I turn an objet around a point that is not his barycentre? It's necessary to be able to interact with low-level information and define specific gesture. In 2010 Kammer & al. [12] contributed, with GEFORMT (GEsture FOrmalization for Multi-Touch) to discussion of strategies towards a formalization of gestural interaction on multi-touch surfaces. According to the works of Nespoulos [13] Kammer, as a rationale for the formalization of multi-touch gestures, chose semiotics, a technique utilized in linguistics. Like a language, a grammar of gesture has semantic, syntactic and pragmatic rules. Syntax will describe the basic used symbols and their combinations. The semantic will give senses and pragmatic will control the mental representation of users. GEFORM includes all dimensions (see Figure 3).

```
1F(HOLD(o)) + 1F(SEMICIRCLE(o))
```

Figure 3: Rotate gesture described by GeForMT (left) and resulting gesture (right)

MANIPULATING THIRD DIMENSION

The Z technic: a particular and complex case

It's relatively easy to built interactions to manipulate an objet in 2D-space. Everybody can imagine a gesture to swivel a picture on a table (it is a rotation around Y axis). Then it's easy to turn around X, Z axes or the centre of rotation. But how do I do if the centre of rotation is different from centre of object? To developing a library of specific gestures imposes additional constraints. Interacting with objects in 3D world from a 2D interface is a characteristic problem since the first virtual world. In 1986 Nielson [22] defined a series of manipulations from a concept called "Triad Mouse". The main idea was to open the possibility to manipulate (position, orientation) with a 2D device only. In 1988 Chen [19] was interested in methods of rotation in 3D. He demonstrated that the use of a specific device such as a trackball is easier than a simple 2D mouse to perform all manipulations.

Since 2008 and use of multi-touch screens (GPS, Phones, laptop, etc) interacting with our hands has becoming natural and the question was "how can we modify position and orientation of geometric forms with our fingers only?"

The paradigm of the action is essential in the composition and appropriation of the gesture. In 2004 [20] Grossman proposed a model of grammar gestures using two hands (bi-manual interactions) developed for a volumic tactile device. To control a real world is a holistic process. Splitting and allocate 6 Degrees O Freedom only fingers and hands is an unnatural concept, certainly complicate to assimilating for common user. For example, everyone thinks we have just to identify an object by pointing it before moving it with our index (ie., drag-and-drop process). But in reality, this is not the finger that moves: it's the arm. This bio-mecanic characteristic shows limitations of interactions and performing an action with several fingers and/or hands can be very difficult. In 2009 Nacita [21] proved that it's difficult to preform a gesture without motion noise. For instance, he demonstrated that it is impossible for a user to zoom and move an object without rotation or his/her arm.

We must split in two methodologies to interact with objet in virtual space. The first one comes from technical drawing. Space is subdivided in three or four views (Front, top, left, etc). To move an object, user had to turn the work in different windows. In every case user works in two dimensions [14]. The second one is to work in scene space with two hands (right hand to control X,Y axes and left hand to control Z axe). This approach requires that user is able to locate in space, sometime it's very difficult for current user [15][16] (except for pianist).

Martinet [17] showed that both methods are equivalent if you compare efficiency irrespective of precision of placement.

You have the possibility to use two hands or to subdivide screen if you have a surface table by Microsoft [18], it's less easy if your device is a touch pad like iPad® or a Samsung galaxy tab®. It's necessary to create a library of gesture suitable to the circumstances.

DRAW ME A SPRING

In this section, we propose a third solution, a simple alternative to manage the third dimension. We think everyone has seen a screw (cruciform, Allen is not important). You have probably noted a constant that is the screwing direction (with some exceptions). Normally to screw you turn to clockwise way and to unscrew to counter-clockwise way. When you screw, the direction is the same that –Z Axe (see Figure 4).

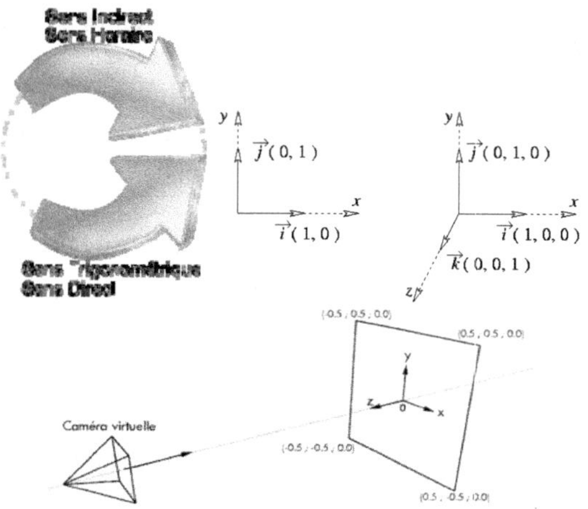

Figure 4 : Clockwise and Viewpoint orientation

We wanted to use this feature to manage the displacements along the depth axis in a virtual space.

Our main idea is possible, with a spring gesture, to control at least two or even three DOF.

Formalization

Formalizing multi-touch interactions requires an exhaustive knowledge that a user will be able to realise. Kammer [12] defines a simple grammar to use when you design some tactile applications. He describes an atypical gesture named Spiral like a combination of two semi circles (see Figure 5).

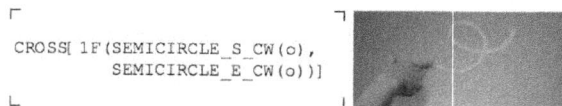

```
CROSS[ 1F(SEMICIRCLE_S_CW(o),
          SEMICIRCLE_E_CW(o))]
```

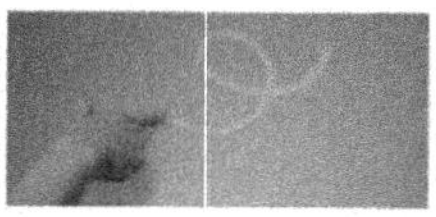

Figure 5 : Curlicue gesture described by GeForMT (left) and resulting gesture (right)

We use this definition of spiral to create a specific gesture name Spring. According to the definition of Kammer, we suggest a new specific grammar. The main idea is to use a spring gesture, like a spiral and a translation, to control depth move with only one and.

```
* = inter1 * inter2= sequence of continuous gesture, with
same fingers, with a continuous contact
+ = inter1 + inter2 = sequence of discontinuous gesture ,
fingers for inter1 and inter2 are different

interaction = gesture
        | interaction <-relation-> interaction

geste = move(type)

type = number* finger

mouve = ponctuel
        | hold
        | line
        | semicircle(sens, direction)
        | spiral (gyre)
        | random

sens = clockwise | anticlockwise

direction= (deltaX, deltaY)

gyre = + (inside) | (outside)

number = 1|...|5

relation= crossed
        | convergence
        | divergence
        | parallel
```

With this grammar we have the possibility to distinguish between direct convergence and indirect convergence, and build four representations of spirals (see Figure 6).

How can we distinguish this ambiguity? If X and Y coordinates are the same in both, you have possibility to differentiate the number of touch points. Of course it's natural to use only one finger to move an objet in plane. That's the reason why we propose to draw a spiral with two fingers.

From Spiral to spring

From Spiral it's easy to imagine designing a spring. It's only necessary to associate a translation along X or Y axis or both, according to Kammer definition (see Figure 8).

- Indirect and Direct Convergences

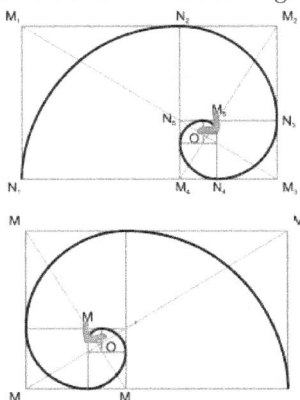

- Indirect and Direct Divergences

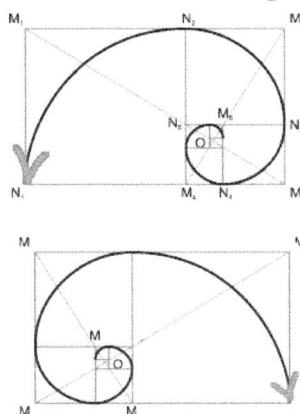

Figure 6: Different forms of spirals

To use

Problem: Drawing of a spiral reveals an ambiguity when you need to understand user's intentions. If you decide to draw a spiral or a set of movements to X and Y directions (see Figure 7), you obtain same results if you look X, Y variations only.

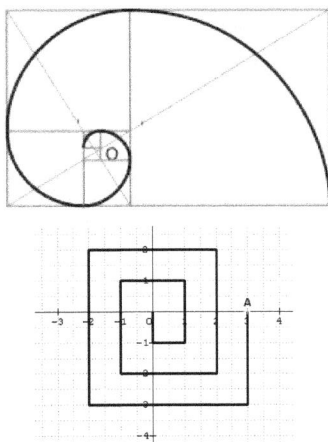

Figure 7: Different interpretations of user's intention

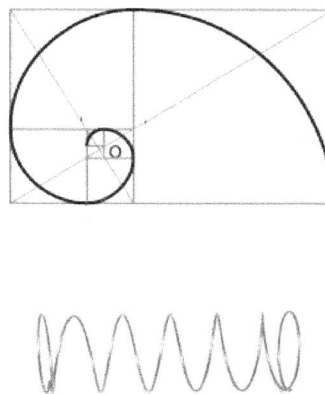

Figure 8: Extrapolation from spiral.

Like any sinusoidal motion, drawing a spring on a touch pad will be characterized by an amplitude and frequency (see Figure 9). The originality of our approach is to combine one of these parameters with translation along Z axis. With only one simple gesture we are able to control two dimensions (We hope three dimensions in a second time).

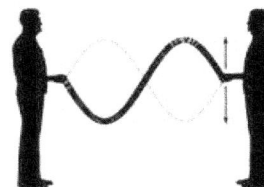

Figure 9: Amplitude and frequency

Drawing a spring on tactile device needs to be defined: a frequency, an amplitude, an orientation (direct, indirect) a direction (X,-X,Y or –Y) and a speed. When you want to move an object in a virtual world, you must just manage five parameters:

- Three parameters for direction (X,Y,Z)
- One parameter for direction (clockwise or counter-clockwise)
- Speed (or Amplitude)

The parameters of a spring control more than five parameters. The notion of frequency is most often associated with the concept of energy (more than I turn fast, more power I store) and as the setting speed of drawing is probably the least simple to control, we don't integrate them. We control moves along X, Y,-X,-Y, we associate these moves to object designated by two contacts (two fingers). The direction to draw spring gives the

255

direction of move along Z axis and amplitude define the speed.

The combinatorial of the parameters permits the creation of a simple gesture to manage all directions (See Table 1).

Move along X with great speed along -Z	
Move along –X with small speed along Z	
Move along –X, -Y with great speed along -Z	
Move along Y with small speed along Z	

Table 1 : Association : Gesture / Actions.

RECOGNIZING A SPRING

We detect direction and orientation of spring with a method of inscribed angles. A spiral can be considered like a sequence of segments (see Figure 10).

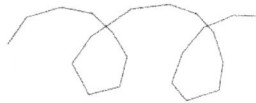

Figure 10: A spring as a list of segments.

The first two segments define the first angle (see Figure 11). This angle gives us the rolling of spring (direction, clockwise, etc). For each new segment, we add the angles (sum of angles included). As long as the sum grows the direction of the spring is constant and when it decreases (negative angle) the direction of the spring can change (see Figure 12).

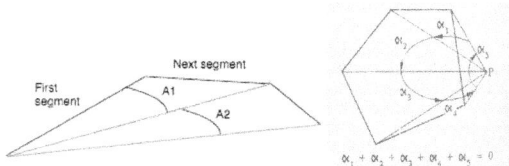

Figure 11: Sum of inscribed angles

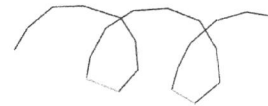

Figure 12: End of half circle

To define the direction of the final sketch we can calculate the gap between the beginning of spring and coordinates of the first red segment (when we change of semicircle). This gap gives the displacement along X or Y axes (see Figure 13).

Figure 13: To ascertain orientation of spring.

Figure 14 shows different recognized situations (number of points used to find first pattern, time to determine first evaluation) on an IPad®. The beginning of sketch is at "left" for screenshots 14a and at "right" for screenshots 14b! This example shows detections for specific directions along X and Z axes. With the same approach, we have possibilities to control a variation along Y and Z axes and we hope using both to manipulate an objet in space with only one hand interaction.

X and Y coordinate values would change while in spring manipulation. Smoothing these interferences we must calculate a linear regression line. A first development proofs that gap, along X and Y directions, is the same during first or second loop and become negligible after four or five rotations.

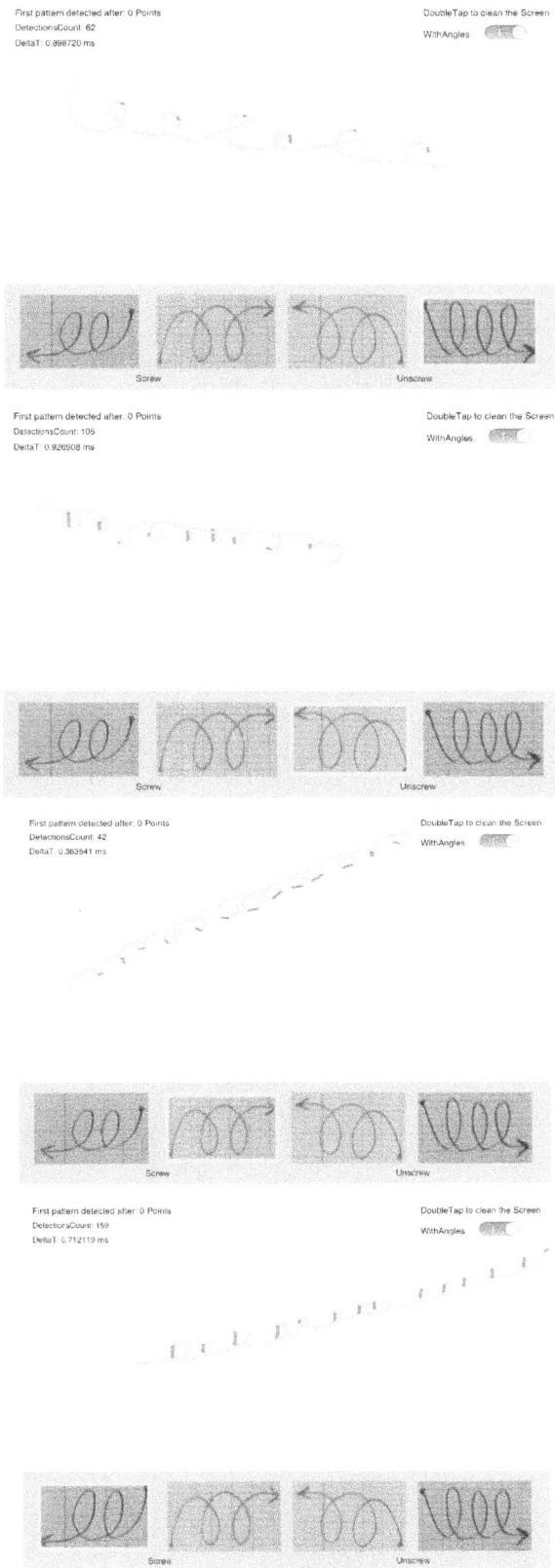

Figure 14a, Figure 14b

Screenshots of spring detection in X and Z directions

CONCLUSION AND FUTURE WORKS

In this paper, we have introduced a new concept for using a simple and intuitive gestural grammar for positioning an object in a virtual space. The main idea is that the three degrees of freedom can be managed by a multi-touch interaction using only one hand. The concept of spiral expanded to spring allows not only the management of the depth but also the combination of two or three directions simultaneously in a single form of interaction. A formal grammar has been proposed for the identification, integration and use of tactile interaction in gestural dialogue. In future experiments conducted with pupils recruited in secondary grade, we would like to compare our approach with 3D interaction in specific context of 3D geometry learning. And finally, if we're thinking about the possibility of extending the method to the management of an observer in a virtual space, the problem is more complex because it requires to control two independent parameters: the position of the observer and his/her point of view.

REFERENCES

1   Efron D., Gesture and Environment. Morningside Heights, New York : King's Crown Press. 1941

2   Paul Ekman and Wallance Friesen, (1969) The Reportorie of Nonverbal Behavior: Categories, Origins, Usage, and Coding, Semiotica, I, 1969. pp 49-98

3   Tang J.C. Findings from observational studies of collaborative work int'l Man-machine studies 43(2) pp 143-160 1991.

4   Wellner P. Interacting with paper on the digitaldesk Communication of ACM 36(7) pp 87-96 1993

5   Morris M.R. Huang A., Paepcke A. Winograd T. Cooperative gesture : multi-user gestual interaction for co-located groupware proc CHI '06 New York ACM Press pp 1201-1210 2006

6   Wilson A.D. Play Anywhere: A compact interactive laptop projection-vision system Proc UIST '05 New York ACM press pp 83-92 2005.

7   Nielsen M., Störring M., Moeslund T.B., Granum E. : A Procedure for developing intuitive and ergonomic gesture interfaces for HCI Int'l gesture workshop 2003 LNCS vol 2915 Heidelberg springer-Verlag pp409-420.

8   Wobbrock J., Morris M., Wilson A. User-defined gestures for surface computing ACM CHI 2009 April 4-9 Boston Massachusetts.

9   Lao S., Zhang G., Ling Y., Wang P.A. Gestural interaction design models for multi-touch displays. Proceeding of British computer society conférence on human-computer interaction Cambridge september 01-05 2009 pp 440-446.

10 Görg, M. T., Cebulla, M., Garzon, S. R., A Framework for Abstract Representation and Recognition of Gestures in Multi-touch Applications, International Conference on Advances in Computer-Human Interaction, pp. 143-147, 2010 Third International Conference on Advances in Computer-Human Interactions, 2010.

11 Kaindl, G. Towards a flexible software framework for multi-touch application design. Engineering Patterns for Multi-Touch Interfaces 2010. A workshop of the ACM SIGCHI Symposium on Engineering Interactive Computing Systems. June 20, 2010.

12 Kammer D., Wojdziak J., Keck M., Taranko S. Towords a formalization of multi-touch gesture ITS'10 novembre 7-10 2010 Saarbrücken

13 Nespoulous, J.-L., Perron, P., Lecours, A. R. Biological Foundations of Gestures: Motor and Semiotic Aspects. Lawrence Erlbaum Associates, Hillsdale, MJ, 1986.

14 Hancock M., Carpendale S., Vernier F. Wigdor D, Shen C. Rotation and translation in Proceedings of the SIGGHI conference on human-computers system pp 79-88 206

15 Reiman J., Davidson P., Han J., A screen-space formulation for 2D and 3D direct manipulation UIST'09 October 4-7 Victoria, British Columbia Canada 2009

16 Hancock M. , Carpendale S., Cockburn A. Shallow-Depth 3D interaction : design and evaluation of one, two, three touch techniques.

17 Martinet A., Casiez G., Grisoni L. The design and evaluation of 3D positioning techniques for mulitouch displays Porceeding of 3DUI'10 IEEE computer society 5the symposium on 3D User Interface 2010.

18 Martinet A., Casiez G., Grisoni L., The effect of DOF separation in 3D manipulation task with multi-touch displays VRST'10 the 17the ACM symposium on virtual reality software and technologies 2010

19 Chen, M., Mountford, S. J., and Sellen, A. 1988. A study in interactive 3-D rotation using 2-D control devices. In *Proceedings of the 15th Annual Conference on Computer Graphics and interactive Techniques* R. J. Beach, Ed. SIGGRAPH '88. ACM, New York, NY, 121-129. 1988

20 Grossman, T., Wigdor, D., and Balakrishnan, R. 2004. Multi- finger gestural interaction with 3d volumetric displays. In *Proceedings of the 17th Annual ACM Symposium on User interface Software and Technology* (Santa Fe, NM, USA, October 24 - 27, 2004). UIST '04. ACM, New York, NY, 61- 70. DOI= http://doi.acm.org/10.1145/1029632.1029644

21 Nacenta, M. A. , Baudisch, P. , Benko, H. , and Wilson, A. 2009. Separability of spatial manipulations in multi-touch interfaces. In Proceedings of Graphics Interface 2009, 175–182.

22 Nielson, G. M. and D. R. Olsen (October 1986,). Direct Manipulation Techniques for Objects Using 2D Locator Devices. Proc. 1986 ACM Workshop on Interactive 3D Graphics, Chapel Hill, NC.

23 Eric A. Bier. Snap-dragging in three dimensions. In Proceedings of the 1990 sym- posium on Interactive 3D graphics, pages 193–204, Snowbird, Utah, United States, 1990. ACM.

24 Richard W. Bukowski and Carlo H. S´equin. Object associations : a simple and practical approach to virtual 3D manipulation. In Proceedings of the 1995 symposium on Interactive 3D graphics, pages 131–ff., Monterey, California, United States, 1995. ACM.

25 Eric Allan Bier. Skitters and jacks : interactive 3D positioning tools. In Proceedings of the 1986 workshop on Interactive 3D graphics, pages 183–196, Chapel Hill, North Carolina, United States, 1987. ACM.

26 Gregory M. Nielson and Jr Dan R. Olsen. Direct manipulation techniques for 3D objects using 2D locator devices. In Proceedings of the 1986 workshop on Interactive 3D graphics, pages 175–182, Chapel Hill, North Carolina, United States, 1987. ACM.

27 Paul S. Strauss and Rikk Carey. An object-oriented 3D graphics toolkit. SIGGRAPH Comput. Graph., 26(2) :341–349, 1992.

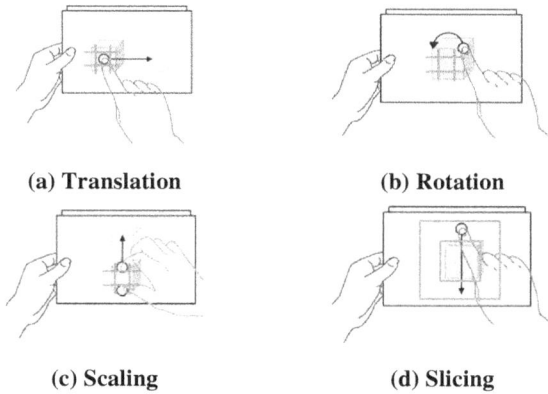

How to Motivate People to Use Internet at Home: Understanding the Psychology of Non-active Users

Momoko Nakatani[1], Takehiko Ohno[1], Ai Nakane[1], Akinori Komatsubara[2], Shuji Hashimoto[2]

[1]Nippon Telegraph and Telephone Corporation
1-1, Hikarino-oka, Yokosuka-shi,
Kanagawa, Japan
{nakatani.momoko, ohno.takehiko,
nakane.ai}@lab.ntt.co.jp

[2]Waseda University
3-4-1, Okubo, Shinjuku-ku,
Tokyo, Japan
{komatsubara.ak, shuji}@waseda.jp

ABSTRACT

Although many Internet services exist that can raise our quality of life, there are still many non-active users who cannot fully enjoy the convenience of the Internet and its potential even when they have computers in the home. To deeply understand this failure to use the Internet, we conducted a field study, and arrived at an integrated model depicting the psychology of active/non-active computer users. Our model enables us to understand the psychology of the users and the external factors affecting them and sheds light on how non-active users are stuck in a negative loop. Users that received a support service designed on our model dramatically changed their attitude and started to use the service actively.

Author Keywords

Technology acceptance; qualitative methods; novices; user support.

ACM Classification Keywords

H1.0. [Models and principles]: General; H.5.2 [Information Interfaces and Presentation]: User-centered design, Training, help, and documentation.

INTRODUCTION

With the rapid spread of the Internet, we have more incentive to extensively use it in everyday life. Many convenient services are available, such as reserving hotels, checking train transfer details, and getting discount coupons for many stores. However, there are still many non-active users who cannot fully enjoy the convenience of the Internet and its potentiality, although the number of the people who possess computers continues to increase [3]. As ubiquitous computing grows more popular in the home environment, it is becoming critical to ensure that non-active users will not be left behind. Thus, our challenge is to activate the non-active users.

Here we acknowledge that each user has a different definition of what constitutes "sufficient" activity that depends on his/her environment or life style. Therefore, activeness in terms of Internet usage is, in this paper, defined as "the degree of how fully each person utilizes Internet from the viewpoint of his/her own life style". This definition avoids the simple metric of frequency of use.

The reasons why some users fail to fully exploit Internet although they possess computers and networks remain unclear. Many studies have indicated the difficulty of using computers [10,12,16,23,24], or the lack of specific user skills [4]. The user's lifestyle, background, and environment may affect her/his usage [2,17,25]. Usage may be determined by not only the interaction between human and the Internet, but also the interaction between human and human, and the surrounding physical/social environment.

While a unified understanding of those factors is essential to identify likely approaches to strengthening the degree of Internet usage, our approach starts by understanding the psychology of non-active/active users and their surrounding environment. We assume that without understanding their intentions or psychological states, our goal may not be achieved.

Although non-active users have limited Internet literacy and low motivation, a seemingly small trigger can yield significant changes. For example, one woman in our survey, had always relied on her husband to access their computer, but just a single opportunity made her change: she began to perform the task by herself once she had noticed that she could do it by herself easily.

In this paper, we propose a new integrated model for user activation, which clearly explains why it's not easy for non-active users to overcome the barrier to active Internet usage and which also indicates how the service provider could assist such users. Understanding of the non-active user will lead to insights on how we can support user activation. As more devices such as smart-phones and other home appliances are being connected to the Internet, activating the usage of the Internet is crucial both for home appliance suppliers and service providers and for the non-active users.

We provide a deep understanding of the differences between non-active and active users by qualitative field studies. Analysis of the results allowed us to identify the inner experience of the interviewees, and so to determine how attitudes are formed; we discover variables rather than assess them [27]. Our field study of households with broadband access was mainly intended to answer two research questions; "Why do non-active users don't use the Internet?", "Under what circumstances do they use the Internet?". The proposed integrated user model derived from our field study allows significant design implications. Our findings will provide conceptual resources for the research community at large that will help guide the design of services that will encourage Internet usage by a wide range of users. It will bring insights to the service planners/providers, call-center managers and operators, whose work covers user-related service design.

In the remainder of the paper, we first discuss related works in activating the Internet usage. We then detail the study plan, and present our new model which elucidates the differences between active/non-active Internet users. We then describe the implications of our research for the service design. One of the solutions, called "concierge support," was tested in the field as a case study.

BACKGROUND AND RELATED WORK

Computers and other interactive devices that allow access to the Internet can be difficult to use [10,12,16,23,24] and extensive studies have been conducted to shed light on the reasons from many different perspectives [4,6,11,13 et al.]. Representative example is the study by Norman [19] whose concern is about the design. Not only the design of the interface, but also other factors involving human properties and environments affect the ease of use. In this section, we overview those studies conducted in the past.

To begin with, it is well known that even experienced users don't necessarily use optimal strategies, which is called "paradox of the active user" [7,14]. They persist in using inefficient procedures in interactive tasks when demonstrably more efficient procedures exist [10,14,18,26]. The reason for this behavior has also been explored in many studies. Fua and Gray [14], for example, indicated that two major characteristics underlie the user's behavior of persisting in suboptimal methods (e.g., using spaces to center a word on a page): (1) the preferred suboptimal procedure is a well-practiced, generic procedure that is applicable either within the same task environment in different contexts or across different task environments, and (2) the preferred suboptimal procedure is composed of interactive components that bring fast, incremental feedback under the external problem states. Carroll [7] indicated that "a production bias" which results in users focusing on the task at hand rather than on learning to use the system more efficiently, was the main reason for the paradox of the active user. Bhavnani [4] describes many of the factors that may influence the paradox of the active

user, such as few opportunities for acquiring effective strategies, and lack of explicit statements of the strategies in instructional material or in help systems.

All of these studies imply that the assistances from others and the opportunities to learn are crucial to acquire an appropriate strategy, thus, lead to be an expert.

Although these studies focus on active users, we assume that the phenomena could also arise in the non-active users. Thus, the way to provide assistance and the opportunities to learn may play a central role in enhancing Internet usage for the non-active users as well.

The determinant of the intention to use the technology devices has been studied in the workplace. According to "Technology Acceptance Model (TAM)" developed by Venkatesh and Davis [29], an individual's behavioral intention to use a system is determined by two beliefs: "the perceived usefulness" which represents the extent to which a person believes that using the system will enhance his or her job performance and "the perceived ease of use" which is referred to as the extent to which a person believes that using the system will be relatively effortless. Learning to use interactive systems requires significant effort, thus, it is important to understand those factors that form the intention to use.

While the workplace has been the focus of attention, interest in ubiquitous computing is stimulating research into the adoption of technology in the home [5,10,15,21,28]. Computer usage in the home is different from that at work, as the goals are different [28]. Venkatesh and Brown found that social influences such as information from TV or newspapers and the barriers, such as rapid change in technology or lack of knowledge influenced the intention of users to adopt computers at home [5,28]; "adopter" and "non-adopter" indicated whether they "purchased" computers at home or not.

Even if a computer is purchased, it is known that its usage is generally restricted to just a few "favorite" applications. According to Beauvisage [3], who had collected extensive computer usage data of 661 households with 1,434 users at home over 19 months, the five most used applications by an individual represented 83% of his PC usage time on average, and the "favorite" one occupied 45% of the time. They also indicated that when there are two computer users in a household, the most active one consumes 83% of the computer usage time on average; with three individuals in the household, the main user grabs three quarters of PC usage time [3]. These results show that having a computer at home does not necessarily imply that everyone uses it equally.

Our study focuses on the reasons for these differences. Some of the determinants can be extracted from previous studies, but no integrated explanation has been given yet. For example, previous studies of technology usage in domestic environments often examined device location as an important factor characterizing its usage [6,13,15]. Usage is also influenced by how the computer is managed and shared among family members [6,11,20,21]. Frohlich [13] suggested that the simple choice of where to locate a computer in the home has a large impact on family life, both in terms of the way individuals use the computer and also in terms of the way they share their time on it. Another study showed that the usage of technology is intertwined with domestic "routines" [8,9,15], which involve communication and collaboration between inhabitants. Crabtree [8] visualized where such communication occurred by examining the "routine communication acts" in residential settings.

Although the factors indicated by previous studies give us many fruitful insights into the problem of enhancing the Internet usage, none of the studies provide an overall framework or an integrated background to understand the obstacles to everyday computer usage from the viewpoint of the situation/circumstances of the user, the history of experiences of the user and the psychology of the user.

This paper, therefore, attempts to provide the integrated framework needed to understand the major factors that influence the Internet usage; it provides a new integrated model depicting the psychology of active/non-active Internet users. Every action or behavior is based on user psychology, so a deep understanding of user psychology is essential to understand user behavior and then provide solutions. Looking at the Internet usage from the perspective of user psychology brings not only a deep understanding of the user, but important implications for designing the services to be provided. We conducted a field study to collect rich data containing information on user psychology: what they think about computers, and how their image changes, with the environment and experience.

METHODS

We conducted semi-structured interviews, which lasted from 1.5 to 2.8 hours, and home tours during which pictures of the domestic setting were taken. The questions targeted the following three topics.

- What applications were they using at the moment? When and why did they start to use computers? What kind of problem had they have and how did they solve them (present/past use of computers)?

- How did they use TV, video recorder, and digital camera (home appliances)?

- What time did they wake up and go to sleep? What kind of work and hobbies did they have (life style)?

The home tours provided us with additional details about the environments of computer usage in the home. Participants consisted of 32 occupants of 17 households in Japan. We interviewed both husband (M01~M15) and wife (F01~F15) in 15 households and only the husbands in 2 households (M16, M17). They all had broadband Internet access, were in their 30's to 50's, and none worked at information technology or telecommunication companies. 4 households were recruited via mailing list of the provider service and the remaining 13 households were recruited via the web site of a survey company that holds 330 million Japanese registrants. Each family was paid to participate in the study.

DATA ANALYSIS

We adopted a method based on the Grounded Theory Approach [27] for the analysis, which allowed us to draw bottom-up conclusions.

In the first step, all interviews, totaling 39 hours and 19 minutes, were transcribed yielding 764172 Japanese characters. In the second step, we conducted open coding, with aim of identifying key themes in the data without imposing pre-conceived categories. This process resulted in about 50 codes. In the third step, the initial set of the phenomena described by the open codes were compared against each other to group them into categories. This process made explicit the connections between categories and sub-categories. The next step, called selective coding, is the process of refining the categories, identifying the core category and then systematically relating it to the other categories. All the causations between the factors were examined in this process. The connections were identified when the users themselves gave their reasons, or when the factor changed when the causal factor was changed. For example, connection from factor 'A' to 'B' (A->B) was identified when the user stated that "A is the reason for B", or when B changed after A was changed. Some of the causations identified in the text (e.g. [C]->[A] in Fig.1) were not adopted in the model, because of the paucity of the data supporting them. Those shortened connections could be consistently explained with the other connections (e.g. [C]->[D]->[A]). This resulted in two psychological loops of the active/non-active users composed of 4 factors. External factors affect either positively or negatively the psychological factors. Our proposed model was finally completed by connecting two psychological loops to describe the transition between the negative and positive factors. The connections do not represent causation but instead the change in status. Thus the connections were represented as cylinders, not single lines.

Although the numbers of the transcriptions classified is shown in the figure (Fig.1, 2) to provide context, our model is derived from a qualitative method, and so is not intended to imply statistical or quantitative significance. Note that we constructed the category by classifying the transcript rather than the users. Thus, some user's transcript was classified into both positive and negative categories (17 out of 31 participants fell into this case). This is because our interviews tackled past episodes as well as the present one.

RESULTS

Although our proposed user model is an integrated model of non-active and active users, we first describe its separate components. We then describe our integrated model.

Non Active Users

Fig.1 presents our model of non-active users; it consists of a negative psychological loop (factors [A] to [D]) and external factors ([I] to [L]). The label represented inside the "< >" are the subcategories of the factor. Numbers in brackets next to the name of the factors indicate the number of people whose transcript was classified as exhibiting that factor. The numbers between the factors (on the arrows) are the numbers of people whose transcript was classified as exhibiting both factors (backward and forward).

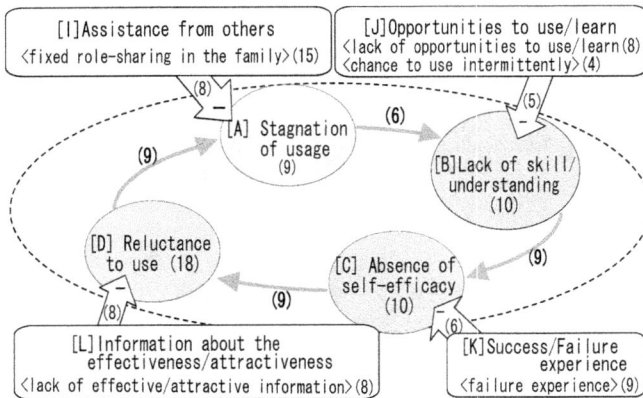

Figure 1. Model of non-active user. It consists of 4 negative psychological factors and 4 external factors.

[A] Stagnation of usage and [I] Assistance from others

Factor "[A] Stagnation of usage" indicates that the non-active user restricted him/herself to a very limited range of tasks. <Fixed role-sharing in the family> is the subcategory of "[I] Assistance from others", which reinforce the negative effect on [A]. For the non-active users, resolving troubles or trying new operations are the job of other members of the family (<fixed role-sharing in the family>), and even when others give support, the non-active users fail to take advantage of the help. An example found in the transcript is shown below.

F01: Use it for... Oh, I can't only use for very very basic things. Shopping.. I suppose, just once or twice a week. Mmn.. Let's see ...Ah, like searching gift bags with Web.. looking at sights like that.
Interviewer: Oh, you're doing net-surfing?
F01: Oh, yeah, right. Only doing net-surfing.
Interviewer: How about putting your pictures from your digital cameras into your computer?
F01: My husband does it, putting them in my computer..I mean, I make him do it.
M01: You make me do it... She just looks at the pictures shown on the display. You don't even know how to do it, do you?
F01: Hmm.. I guess it's kind of enough to have one

person in a family who can take care of it.
M01: Hands-off stance!

Relying on others may not be any problem in the workplace as the user can often turn to in-house professional technical staff or expert coworkers. At home, however, experts and professionals are not readily available, as the live-in expert might be absent, and customer support lines psychological costs that can discourage people from using them [16].

[B] Lack of skill/understanding and [J] Opportunities to use/learn

Not trying to do new things by oneself leads to "[B] Lack of skill/understanding" of how to use functions, applications, and the existence of them. "[J] Opportunities to use/learn" have negative effect on the "[B] Lack of skill/understanding"; they have few and intermittent chances to use/learn computers (<lack of opportunities to use/learn>, <chance to use intermittently>).

"[J] <Lack of opportunities to use/learn>" is mainly because of their lifestyle; they are too busy with other works at home and have no time to spend on the computer, as is shown by the following example.

F01: I have too many things to do, I don't have time to go there (the place where the computer is settled) . I do want to use it, but my husband occupies it all the time, so I can't
Interviewer: Don't you use it when your husband is away?
F01: No, I'm not at home in the daytime, because I work outside. I don't see it and I don't go there unless I have specific need. I'm not there everyday, only once or twice a week.

From her statement, it would appear that the computer was located in a very far place. However, the computer is in the room next to the living room, just few steps from the dining table. This example implies that unless the computer is located with the user's immediate area of movement, the user may feel that it is too far away, which leads to less opportunity to use it. Computer use in the home, especially the use of the Internet, tends to be for hedonistic purposes [28] rather than work, thus computer location and access rights, which might seem to be relatively minor factors, greatly influence the opportunities for computer use in the home.

Even if the opportunities exist, they only tend to have chances to use them intermittently ([J] <chance to use intermittently>). It is hard to acquire sufficient understanding or structured knowledge with this usage pattern.

[C] Absence of self-efficacy and [K] Success/Failure experience

"[B] Lack of skill/understanding" reinforces "[C] Absence of self-efficacy". Self-efficacy refers to one's perceived performance capabilities for a specific activity as defined by Bandura [1]. "[C] Absence of self-efficacy", in our definition, includes also the fear of breaking something, or a negative estimation of the costs incurred to fix the troubles encountered, as shown in the example below.

F04: Oh, I don't like it(the computer). I'm not good at it. (snip) It's the same (for other devices). When something goes wrong, I say Oh, No!!..It's over! (snip) It's kind of my character to break things. (snip) I don't know why, but I always break something, and then, can't fix it. But, computers are too expensive to break. It's far more expensive than other things.

As the transcript shows, "[K] <failure experience>" is another reason for the "[C] Absence of self-efficacy".

[D] Reluctance to use and [L] Information about the effectiveness/ attractiveness

"[C] Absence of self-efficacy" then reduces the user's interest in computers, which is described as "[D] Reluctance to use". When the non-active users have a strong negative feeling that they cannot use computers by themselves ([C]), they tend to state that they are not interested in using them ([D]) as the following description shows.

Interviewer: Do you wish to improve your computer skill?
F04: Ahh.. I'm afraid not. It might be better if I had, but I don't, at all. Yes. I don't have any motivations like, " I wanna do more", or "I'm gonna do something". Well, it's just a collection of information for me.

"[L] <Lack of effective/attractive information>" is another factor underlying "[D] Reluctance to use" computers. The above interviewee F04, for example, didn't have any friends who were active in computers, and thus, couldn't get attractive information from them, which strengthened computer alienation.

"[D] Reluctance to use" again negatively impacts the "[A] Stagnation in usage". When the user enters this negative loop, it is hard to escape, because of these chained factors.

Active users

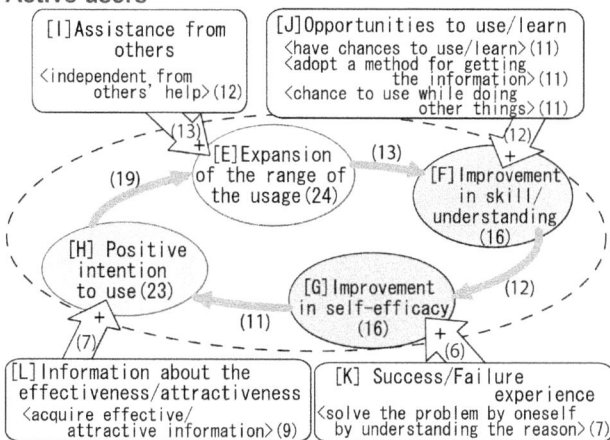

Figure 2. Positive loop of the active user. It consists of 4 positive psychological factors, and 4 external factors.

Fig.2 shows the psychological model of the active user. Factors [E], [F], [G] and [H] represent the positive loop of the active user; they are the inverse of the negative factors mentioned above. External factors ([I] to [L]) are the same factors as shown in Fig.1 although the sub-categories differ, but here they reinforce the positive psychological factors.

[E] Expansion of the range of usage and [I] Assistance from others

The active users had a broad scope ([E]) which was to try to tackle the problems by themselves when faced with something new. Trial-and-error allowed users to expand the range of usage.

M05: When I wish to use something or some new functions, I try to find out how to do it by myself without any hesitation. Unless doing it, my skill doesn't expand. And then, few years later, the person who had more question have more skill, in any case, such as TVs or the computers.

Further, active users didn't excessively rely on others, but rather the "[I] Assistance from others" tended to broaden their range of usage patterns. In detail, active users scarcely relied on others ([I] <independent from others' help>). In this way, active users expand their usage by taking advantage of "[I] Assistance from others" resulting in a positive reinforcement.

[F] Improvement in skill/understanding and [J] Opportunities to use/learn

Through many trial-and-error experiences with new services or functions ([E]), they acquired new knowledge and improved skill ([F]). Not only did they have many more opportunities to use/learn computers ([J] <have chances to use/learn>) but they also tended to adopt learning approaches that suited them ([J] <adopt a method for getting the information>) as is shown below.

M05: (The way to get information about how to use new systems are) Mainly from newspapers, you know. In newspapers, they say like "it's gonna be like this", and so we can get those information. (snip) First, I notice those information from them (newspaper), and then, search for further information on the Web. I always follow that sequence.

Active users knew how to make use of the information around them, which led to improve their skill/understanding ([J]). Another factor that comprises " [J]", is the <chance to use while doing other things>. The episodes included in the sub-category are "starting to use computers on the way to the bath-room" (F08), or operating computers while listening to the television (M05, F09).

[G] Improvement in self-efficacy and [K] Success/Failure experience

Consequently, they gradually improved their self-efficacy ([G]). "[K] <Solve the problem by oneself by understanding the reason" also improves self-efficacy ([G]). The transcript below represents an example of the

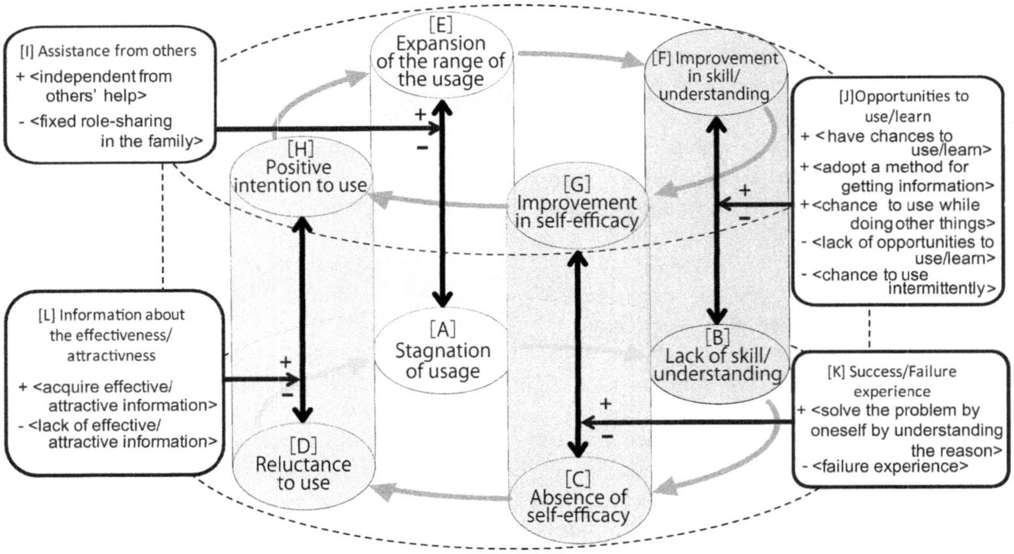

Figure 3. The Integrated Model Based on the Psychology of Active/Non-active Computer Users

user who gained self-efficacy after a successful experience.

> *F07: I've always asked my husband to make greeting cards every year. But once, he was busy for work, and he didn't do it for a while. (snip) He told me like "Well, do it yourself". And so I somehow I did.. well, the sequence was written in the manual, but I thought that I couldn't do it, but, when I tried, I managed to do it against my expectations. So, from that time, I do it myself every year.*

As the description shows, understanding the reason for the trouble is as important after the problem is solved, as it is before the problem is solved.

[H] Positive intention to use computers and [L] Information about effectiveness/attractiveness

Any improvement in self-efficacy ([G]) strengthened their intention to use computers ([H]). "[L] <acquire effective/attractive information>" also enhanced their intention to use computers. The transcript below is from a user who gained a more positive intention to use computers after going to a computer lesson.

> *F05: Well, I became interested in the more effective usage, some function.. I wanna master functions.*
> *Interviewer: The functions you use at your work?*
> *F05: Oh, yes. That's right.*
> *Interviewer:: Does it mean you want to use it more effectively?*
> *F05: Yeah, not only that I wanna use it effectively, but actually, I'm also feeling that I want to study a bit more. (snip) I'd like to increase my abilities.*

She noticed the usefulness of learning new things (spreadsheet, in this case) after going to a computer lesson. In this way, active users gain skill and motivation while traversing the positive loop.

The Integrated Model

We now explain the integrated model, see Fig.3. The model was constructed by connecting the loop of the non-active user (Fig.1) to that of the active user (Fig.2) with the cylinders. Non-active users and active users are not discrete entities, thus the degree of activity is represented by the vertical axis of the cylinder. Each external factor consists of subcategories that have either positive or negative effects as described in Fig.1 and Fig.2.

In some case, there are distinct differences in their lifestyle or the environment depending on their activity level, and thus, the external factors themselves differ. However, even if they were presented with the similar situation, the impact of the external factors differs depending on the activity level because their perception and utilization of the external factors differ; the lower the level is, the more the negative effect is reinforced while the positive effect is weakened.

In the case of "[K] Success/Failure experience", for example, even though they faced a problem that they could not solved by themselves, active users tend to state that the problem was "successfully" solved by asking others (e.g. call-center). Non-active users, on the other hand, tend to perceive that they "failed" to solve the problem because they *had to* ask others, which created the strong impression that they *couldn't* do it by themselves ("[C] Absence of self-efficacy").

The situation is the same for the other external factors, where the non-active users didn't pay attention to them even if they could receive them; non-active users tend to pass on such chances. In this way, the external factors negatively impacted the non-active users, but positively impacted the active users. Therefore, providing assistance ([I]), opportunities ([J]), experience ([K]), and information

([L]) to non-active/active users in a similar manner can worsen the situation for the non-active users. Therefore, the crucial factor to activate computer usage is to carefully design the external factors so as to better suit the activity level.

DESIGN IMPLICATIONS

As mentioned above, the external factors have different effect depending on the activity level, thus the way of designing each external factor is the key to allowing the non-active user to escape from the negative loop. That is, the external factors should be carefully designed to move the psychological factors from the bottom of the cylinder to the top. In addition, it is essential to take into consideration the chained psychological factors (negative loop) when providing the external factors. Our resulting guidelines are described below.

Moving from "[A] Stagnation in usage" to "[E] Expansion in range of usage"

To escape from the stagnation of usage ([A]), the assistance ([I]) must be carefully structured to expand the scope of usage. "[A] stagnation in usage" is also heavily impacted by "[D] reluctance to use", so it is very important that the assistance ([I]) take "[D]" into consideration.

Moving from "[B] Lack of skill/understanding" to "[F] Improvement in skill/knowledge"

To activate non-active users, providing "[J] Opportunities to use/learn" as much as possible is not enough, because a user who is stuck in "[A] stagnation in usage" won't give any attention to those opportunities and will make no use of them. Thus, easing the user's burden is crucial. We have 3 design implications based on the sub-categories of "[J]". First, while intermittent use ([J]<chance to use intermittently>) may not be enough to bring deep understanding and structured knowledge, providing consecutive opportunities (making enough time) may be useful enough to allow the user to concentrate on using it. Second, providing "[J] < chance to use while doing other things>" may reduce the barrier of time concerns. In order to do that, considering the user's lifestyle may be useful. Finally, providing chances to "[J] < adopt a method for getting information>" with a clear emphasis of the value of the information to the user is another solution. Giving opportunities to use/learn in this way may draw the user closer to the services, and escape the negative effect of "[A] stagnation of usage".

Moving from "[C] Absence of self-efficacy" to "[G] Improvement in self-efficacy"

Improvement in self-efficacy", Successful experience ([K]) plays a key role. One simple solution is providing a series of easy to accomplish tasks that reinforce self-efficacy. Another solution is to carefully design instructions so that they do not discourage users even if they fail (e.g. warning messages should not explicitly use the term "error").

Considering that non-active users lack knowledge/skill ([B]), showing the required knowledge and skill in advance may make them better at accepting the failure, and prevent them from losing even more confidence afterwards.

Moving from "[D] Reluctance to use" to "[H] Positive intention to use"

To escape from "[D] Reluctance to use computers", an appropriate way of providing information on effectiveness/attractiveness is the key. We note that the solution is to break the negative pressure of "[C] Absence of self-efficacy". For example, the information should emphasize that anyone can use the attractive new service because it is so simple. The non-active user will perceive that her/his capabilities may actually be sufficient to use the service, which weakens [C].

CASE STUDY

We show an example of a design solution derived from our model, for the purpose of validating the effectiveness of our model. We recruited users with the lowest level of computer literacy. The "concierge support" was carefully designed considering the 4 key factors in our model, and tested in the field study described below.

Concierge support derived from the model.

"Usage Suggestion Support" to provide "[L] Information on effectiveness / attractiveness"
We designed "Usage Suggestion Support", a paper-leaflet that showed a use-case (over 15 possible usages) that matched the user's needs, by providing "[L] information on effectiveness/ attractiveness". Each use-case was drawn as a picture of old woman/man using the service to satisfy their interest, showing that even old people can easily use the service; this should break the negative loop by eliminating "[C] Lack of self-efficacy". The interested shown was selected to match the users' interest as elucidated from the interviews.

"Taking Order Support" to provide "[I] Assistance from others"
Non-active users including those "[D] reluctance to use" the service cannot effectively use the "[I] Assistance from others"; they won't often call support-centers even when they have a problem. We therefore designed "Taking Order Support", which that the call-center operator uses when calling the users to ask whether they have any problem. By asking and giving advices to users, the assistance is expected to eliminate the negative factor of "[D] reluctance to use" and expand the use ([E]) of the service.

"Skill Improvement Support" to provide "[J] Opportunities to use/learn"
The back sides of the paper-leaflets were designed to realize improving the users' knowledge/skill ([F]) by providing the "[J] Opportunities to use/learn", which we call "Skill Improvement Support". So that the opportunities

won't be neglected by the users who had limited scope of usage ([A]), the information given to the user must be recognized as relevant to their daily life. We therefore provided detail procedural information of the use-case on the front side of the paper-leaflets. The point here is that the opportunity for improving their skill/knowledge is designed to suit the user's interest.

"Successful Experience Support" to provide "[K] Successful experience"

Non-active users often experience a failure because they tend to "[B] Lack skill/understanding". We therefore designed "Successful Experience Support" in that the operator asked users to operate the remote controller and assist them to experience new functions, which is intended to "[G] Improve self-efficacy". It should be easier to avoid the [K] <Failure Experience> with the assistance of the call than by trying by oneself.

Method

7-week field study was conducted to validate the effectiveness of our purposed support. We selected different devices and participants from the first study detailed in the previous chapter, for the purpose of verifying the flexibility of our model. An Internet system, "Net-Kun", was provided to the participants, and we observed how the support impacted their usage. Net-Kun can be used as a communication tool and a personal tool. As a communication tool, the image of the computer screen at the remote location can be sent to the TV screen through the Internet and can be printed out. Mothers or fathers, for example, can show their children's pictures or web-sites to their grand-parents who are living apart. As a personal tool, the users can enjoy Internet (web-browsing) on the TV screen through the use of a remote controller.

Via a web-monitoring site, women whose ages ranged from 30-40 and who lived with more than one child under 13 were asked to recruit their parents to participate in the trial. Participants were selected on the condition that they had no prior experience with computers and lived apart from their children-family. Their age ranged from 57 to 75. The reason why we recruited the participants via their children was to find the participants who were computer illiterate. The reason why we asked the women who had children was because "Net-Kun" is a service that can be used as a communication tool between the parents and their grand children. During the trial, participants were free to use Net-Kun. The concierge support (concierge-call and the support leaflet) was provided 3 times. To elucidate the effect of the timing of support provision, we provided support at different times.

They were asked to keep a diary every day, and to record when they used Net-Kun. We visited the participants' house before and after the trial and conducted semi-structured interviews. In the first visit, participants were asked to enter "attitude score" on a 7 point scale for 26 questions. These questions were developed on the 4 key factors of our model and were intended to confirm that the participants were non-active users. Phone interviews were also held after 4 weeks passed. All the interviews and the voices during the concierge-call were recorded and transcribed.

Result

Concierge support was provided through leaflets and call-center support following the 4 external factors of our model. The impact of each was analyzed.

Initial Attitude and the number of usages

Participants used the services 11.4 times on average ranging from 4 to 49. All initial attitude scores were lower than "3", which means that they were all negative about using the service at first. The numbers of service usages, especially the personal usage of Net-Kun, varied widely. There was no significant relationship between the initial attitude scores and the number of service usages. This implies that experience gained during the trial impacted the number of the usages, not the initial attitude.

Reactions to the support leaflets

Reactions to the support leaflets were positive when the timing of sending was suitable and the contents touched on the user's interest. Few users didn't utilize the leaflet, and the common reason was that the timing of sending was not suitable(ID01,05,08). For example, ID05 mentioned that the leaflet was useless because he had already experienced what was written in the leaflet. Another reason was that the content didn't touch on their interest in the first place(ID06, 10). For example, ID10 who received a leaflet with a recipe stated that it was useless, because she doesn't look at the cook books she already has.

The users who reacted positively to the leaflets (ID02, 03, 04, 07, 09) seemed to find the service attractive which means that the factor "[L] Information about the effectiveness/ attractiveness" yielded a positive effect. The following transcription shows that the user broke the negative chain at the negative factor, "[C] Lack of self efficacy", because of the picture shown in the leaflets.

"I felt relieved with it (the leaflet), of course, when I see this beautiful picture. (snip) It's because that there was a picture of grand-pa and grand-ma. I thought that "Oh! Even an old-aged person can do it". (snip) I saw the picture and thought 'Ahh.., pictures like this would appear'. Oh yes, it was easy to understand. (ID03)"

Net-kun, the Internet service, has too many usages for novices, so prior to receiving the leaflet many participants had a hard time finding contents that attracted them and perceived the service to be useless and ineffective. The leaflet, therefore, played the role of informing them of the existence of interesting services. The participants who perceived the leaflet positively also showed improvements in their skill ([F]) after looking at the back side of the leaflet to discover Skill Improvement Support. An example is shown below.

"I saw this, this.. 'Search the TV program' (on the leaflet), and recognized that if I push this, this will come up. I understood this through this paper."

The front and back side of the leaflet, the Usage Suggestion Support and Skill Improvement Support, had a synergistic effect; their motivation of using improved ([H]) looking at the front side which led to expand the scope of the usage ([E]), and the back side provided knowledge of how they could actually do it ([K]).

Reactions to concierge-support-calls

Reactions to the support-call were mostly positive (ID01-05, 07, 09) except for the cases where the users were not available (ID08, 10) or the initial activeness was extremely low (ID06). Even though the participants could call by themselves (the number of the call-center had been given to the participants), most participants asked the operator questions about troubles when the external call was conducted. An example of the first utterance of the participant during a support-call is shown below.

"Oh, it's great to have a call. I've already sent my diary. I can't understand the content (of the service)... I'm low-tech person. (snip) When I tried to do it myself, I couldn't do it at all. (ID02, 1st call)

Many participants stated that the call lead to an expansion in the use of the service ([E]), which is the goal of Taking Order Support. For example, ID07 stated that she didn't know how to delete letters written inside the search-window, but after hearing how to do it from the operator, she started to search many words and expand her usage. She stated as follows.

"I appreciated it (the call), you know. I don't take time to call myself, so if you give me a call, then, I can ask about the troubles I'm facing.(ID07)

During the call, Successful Experience Support played the role of improving users' self-efficacy. One participant, for example, noted that until she experienced the outside support, she didn't feel that she had improved her skill; even when she solved the trouble by herself, she failed to recognize that she had acquired general knowledge.

In this way, the concierge support calls proved to be positive in "[E] Expansion of the range of usage" and "[G] Improvement in the self-efficacy". The support calls also enabled us to understand what service would realize their desire (this information was reflected in the subsequent leaflet).

DISCUSSIONS

Many of the previous studies can be positioned in our model which provides a better understanding of their results. For example, "routines" [8,9,15] and the location of the computer [6,13,15] can be placed under "[J] Opportunities to use/learn", which indicates the importance of considering the user's lifestyle. The way in which

computers are managed and shared by family members [6,11,20,21], or the tendency to create "gurus" that can deal with the computers in the house [16,22,23] can be treated as "[I] Assistance from others" in our model. These external factors in our model are positioned as critical factors that affect the psychological factors either positively or negatively. Based on our model, we showed how to design the external factors so as to suppress the negative effects. Our study is aligned with MATH and TAM [28,29]; the causation that "perceived ease of use" and the "perceived usefulness" strengthen the "Intention to Use". In our model, those are included in the circular loop([C]->[D],[G]->[H]) and the external factors ([L]->[D],[H]). Our model explains why the loop is hard to break free from because the "effect" becomes, in turn, the "cause".

The model is schematic and we make no claim that connections not expressed in our model don't exist. Our intention is not to identify the "complete mechanisms" of the complicated human psychology, but to understand them in a practical manner that will lead to greater assistance to non-active users. The implication derived from our model was proved to be effective in the case study; the leaflet and the concierge support call had the effect of strengthening their intention to use, expanding their usage, and improving their skills/knowledge and self-efficacy. Note that the two support modes (the leaflet and the call) interacted synergistically. The expansion of the usage with the support-call led to improved skills, and the leaflet further enhanced the improvements in their skill and led to improvements in the self-efficacy and so on. All of the external factors affect the psychological loop, and thus are crucial. One of the participants, for example, dramatically changed her attitude during the trial; her motivation decreased because of a repeated failure experience and wrote in the diary that she don't want to use the service in the first half of the trial, but after receiving the leaflet and the support-call the day after, she started to use the service every day and told us that she decided to purchase a computer after the trial. As shown in this example, although non-active users may say initially they are not interested in the Internet, we have shown that providing appropriate support can break the negative loop and make them change their attitude in a positive manner.

CONCLUSIONS

We have developed an integrated model of computer usage and showed its effectiveness. Our model, which is based on empirical data, covers the key factors and leads to a deep understanding of non-active users. To activate non-active users, solutions based on the external factors that help overcome the negative loop are effective. In other words, very careful design is needed to enhance the Internet usage of non-active users. Our model allows practical design solutions to be developed in an entirely manner, rather than an ad-hoc manner, as was confirmed by the field trial. We believe that our findings will provide effective insights for service providers, home appliance suppliers, and related researchers.

REFERENCES

1. Bandura, A. *Self-efficacy: The exercise of control.* Freeman, 1997.

2. Bass, W. and Esselink, A.K. *PC time and money.* Forrester Research Inc., 1996.

3. Beauvisage, T. Computer Usage in Daily Life. *In Proc. CHI 2009*, ACM Press (2009), 575-584.

4. Bhavnani, S.K., Peck, F.A. and Reif, F. Strategy-based instruction: Lessons learned in teaching the effective and efficient use of computer applications. *ACM Transactions on Computer-Human Interaction*, 15, 1 (2008), 1-43.

5. Brown, S.A. and Venkatesh, V. Model of adoption of technology in households: A baseline model test and extension incorporating household life cycle. *MIS Quarterly*, 29, 3 (2005), 399-426.

6. Brush, A.J.B. and Inkpen, K.M. Yours, Mine and Ours? Sharing and Use of Technology in Domestic Environments. *In Proc. UbiComp 2007*, Springer (2007), 109-126.

7. Carroll, J. M., and Rosson, M. B. Paradox of the active user. *Interfacing thought: cognitive aspects of human-computer interaction.* MIT Press (1987), 80-111.

8. Crabtree, A., Rodden, T., Hemmings, T. and Benford, S. Finding a place for UbiComp in the home. In *Proc. UbiComp 2003*, Springer (2003), 208-226.

9. Crabtree, A. and Rodden, T. Domestic routines and design for the home. *Computer Supported Cooperative Work*, 13, 2 (2004), 191-220.

10. Cragg, P.B. and King, M. Spreadsheet modeling abuse: an opportunity for OR? *Journal of the Operational Research Society*, 44 (1993), 743-752.

11. Egelman, S., Brush, A.J.B. and Inkpen, K.M. Family accounts: a new paradigm for user accounts within the home environment. *In Proc. CHI 2008*, ACM Press (2008), 669-678.

12. Franzke, M. and McClard, A. Winona gets wired: technical difficulties in the home. *Communications of the ACM*, 39, 12 (1996), 64-66.

13. Frohlich, D. and Kraut, R. The social context of home computing. *HP Laboratories, 2003.* http://www.hpl.hp.com/techreports/2003/HPL-2003-70.pdf

14. Fua, W., and Gray, W. D. Resolving the paradox of the active user: stable suboptimal performance in interactive tasks. *Cognitive Science.* 28(2004),901-935.

15. Hughes, J., O'Brien, J. and Rodden, T. Understanding Technology in Domestic Environments: lessons for cooperative buildings. In First Int. Workshop, CoBuild'98, Springer (1998), 248-262.

16. Kiesler, S. Zdaniuk, B. Lundmark, V. and Kraut, R. Troubles with the Internet: The dynamics of help at home. *Human-Computer Interaction*, 15, 4 (2000), 323-351.

17. Nie, N., H. and Ebring L. Internet and society: A preliminary report. *IT & Society*, 1, 1 (2000), 275-283.

18. Nilsen, E., Jong. H., Olson, J., Biolsi, I. and Mutter, S. The growth of software skill: A longitudinal look at learning and performance. *In Proc.CHI '93*, ACM Press. (1993), 149–156.

19. Norman, D.A. *The Psychology of Everyday Things*, Basic Books, 1988.

20. O'Brien, J. and Rodden, T. Interactive systems in domestic environments. *In Proc.CHI '97*, ACM Press (1997), 247-259.

21. O'Brien, J., and Rodden, T., Rouncefield, M. and Hughes, J. At home with the technology: an ethnographic study of a set-top-box trial. *ACM Transactions on Computer-Human Interaction*, 6, 3 (1999), 282-308.

22. Poole, E.S., Chetty, M., Grinter, R.E. and Edwards, W.K. More than meets the eye: transforming the user experience of home network management. *In Proc. CHI 2008*, ACM Press (2008), 455-464.

23. Poole, E.S., Chetty, M., Morgan, T., Grinter, R.E. and Edwards, W.K. Computer help at home: methods and motivations for informal technical support. *In Proc. CHI 2009*, ACM Press (2009), 739-748.

24. Poole, E.S., Edwards, W.K. and Jarvis, L. The Home Network as a Socio-Technical System: Understanding the Challenges of Remote Home Network Problem Diagnosis. *Computer. Supported Cooperative Work.* 18, 2-3 (2009), 277-299.

25. Robinson, J. P. and Godbey, G. *Time for Life: The surprising ways Americans use their time.* Pennsylvania State University Press. 1997.

26. Rosson, M. Patterns of experience in text editing. *In Proc. CHI '83*, ACM Press (1983), 171–175.

27. Strauss, A.L. and Corbin, J. *Basics of qualitative research: Grounded theory procedures and techniques.* SAGE Publications. 1990.

28. Venkatesh, V. and Brown, S.A. A longitudinal investigation of personal computers in homes: adoption determinants and emerging challenges. *MIS Quarterly*, (2001), 71-102.

29. Venkatesh, V. and Davis, F.D. Perceived usefulness, perceived ease of use, and user acceptance of information technology. *MIS quarterly*, 13, 3 (1989), 319-340.

Drawing and Acting as User Experience Research Tools

Alexandre Fleury
Aalborg University
Niels Jernes vej 12, 9220 Aalborg Ø, Denmark
amf@es.aau.dk

ABSTRACT

This paper discusses the use of participant-generated drawings and drama workshops as user experience research methods. In spite of the lack of background literature on how drawings can generate useful insights on HCI issues, drawings have been successfully used in other research fields. On the contrary, drama workshops seem to be increasingly popular in recent participatory design research. After briefly introducing such previous work, three case studies are presented, illustrating the use of drawing and drama workshops when investigating the relationship between media technology users and two specific devices, namely televisions and mobile phones. The paper focuses on the methods and discusses their benefits and the challenges associated with their application. In particular, the findings are compared to those collected through a quantitative cross-cultural survey. The experience gathered during the three case studies is very encouraging and calls for additional reports of UX evaluations involving drawing- and theatre-based exercises.

Author Keywords

Acting; drawing; user experience; television; mobile phone.

ACM Classification Keywords

H.5.2 [**Information Interfaces and Presentation (e.g. HCI)**]: User Interfaces – evaluation/methodology.

INTRODUCTION

Exploring detailed aspects of people's life can be done in many ways: Standard ethnographic methods include interviews, activity logging, or remote prompting. These methods help researchers immerse into people's life more or less deeply and over various time periods, from a specific point in time to several weeks, months or even years. However efficient these methods are, they suffer nonetheless from a number of shortcomings, such as being time consuming in planning, conducting and analysing. Sometimes one might need a snapshot of a specific part of people's life from a sample of participant bigger than what can be afforded using the abovementioned methods. Another criticism that these methods can face are the little creativity they rely on. They are indeed not suitable for

developing possible scenarios in which technology meets prior personal experiences.

Two motivations for revisiting the UX researcher's toolbox are at play in the abovementioned scenarios: Firstly, decreasing the resources necessary to measure personal user experiences; and secondly to develop possible future use cases for technological products or services based on prior experiences and personal emotions. Tackling the former issue, rapid UX evaluation strategies have been developed and applied. Beebe for instance introduced and defined "Rapid Assessment Process" [3], and Millen further proposed to focus on three key aspects of evaluation design [13]: Focus and key informants (to limit the amount of data collected), Interactive observations (to improve the quality of the data collected), and Collaborative data analysis (to help analysing the data collected).

Concerning the second issue, participatory design workshops are a common way to investigate how people perceive technology and what is expected from it. Additionally, investigating technology use through the lenses of performative art has been recently called for by researchers interested in practice-led research [7] and ubiquitous media [9]. Theatre-based methods are perceived as a promising way of supporting the design process of mobile IT [17] and for gathering requirements, especially with non-tech savvy populations [15].

This paper examines how drawings and acting can support the two abovementioned challenges in evaluating Human-Computer Interaction with technology, specifically with novel television and mobile technologies. On the one hand, drawing tackles the methodological challenge of providing deep insight on test participants' personal matters in an easy way, in a timely fashion, and using a relatively large sample size. The type of personal stories collected and the level of intimacy user experience (UX) researchers can access through drawings will be exemplified through the application of the method to a specific research agenda, namely investigating the relationship between users of televisions and mobile phones and these devices. On the other hand, acting is used here as part of a workshop mixing reflection upon personal experiences with TV and mobile phones, and generation of creative scenarios involving such technology. Prior to acting mini-plays created in groups, workshop participants reflected on their personal relationship with the technology via simple individual exercises, including story creation and drawing. The results from these exercises are briefly presented, in order to illustrate the approach and discuss the benefits and challenges of including a theatre-based exercise in a technology oriented workshop.

The studies documented in this paper took place in two distinct cultural environments, namely Danish and Japanese universities. The study conducted in Japan happened during a six month visit to the institution as part of the author's doctoral study. The socio-historical approach to media studies taught at the Japanese institution encouraged the author to investigate technology-free user study tools. Moreover the cultural and linguistic gap experienced during the stay provided an excellent opportunity to try non-verbal UX investigation methods. Denmark and Japan are two ICT societies within which media technology is ubiquitous, thus comparing the findings collected in both countries is expected not only to put forward converging trends and differences in how televisions and mobile phones are perceived and used, but also to reveal culture-related issues in the application of drawing and acting as user research methods.

DRAWING AS A RESEARCH METHOD

Drawings and sketches have been part of humans' communication tools palette since their early evolutionary stage. Whether it is for visualizing specific ideas, expressing artistic inspiration, supporting learning process, or ensuring durable memory, drawings are used almost everywhere. In fact when learning how to express themselves, humans rely on drawings very early, prior to writing. In their first years of life, children learn to use drawings as a communication mediator. At the same time, the child gradually includes writing in the drawings, enhancing clarity in the ideas expressed [1]. The important role drawings play in human development explains the vast academic literature available related to children's drawings and their interpretation.

Simple drawings can help convey complex ideas, especially in the business world [16]. Drawings help clarifying ideas, expressing them rapidly without the need for complex technology, and sharing them openly encouraging discussions. It is further argued that "*the value of visual information lies [...] during the action of drawing*", that is during the creation process of the image rather than in the image itself [14]. Mills considers drawing as a visual conversation, for which the performance itself is crucial to make sense of the message conveyed. In design, drawings are widely used in order to illustrate and explore scenarios and ideas through storytelling, and storyboards are considered an efficient and powerful tool for illustrating a succession of events [18]. Exploring people's life, opinions and thoughts through drawing are however less popular.

Recently, ethnographers have used drawings to discuss medical conditions with patients. While using drawings for exploring how people understand illness, Guillemin demonstrated that drawings can indeed generate a broad and in-depth perspective on the study at hand. The author

agrees with Mills in saying that studying the drawing produced alone is not enough, but should be complemented by the analysis of the knowledge built by the drawer while creating the drawing [6]. Additionally, Guillemin notes that a drawing is a snapshot of how the drawer understands a subject at the specific time of the drawing. She reckons the limitations of this visual expression tool and argues that drawings should be used as a complement of additional research methods. Guillemin's findings are corroborated by Kearney and Hyle who identified the following benefits and drawbacks of using drawings as a research method for investigating the emotional effects of change in an educational institution [10].

1. Drawings reveal emotional aspects that would not be covered in word based communication
2. Participant focus on the key aspect of their story
3. Drawings needs to be complemented by participant explanation
4. Response to the drawing task varies according to personal and situational characteristic that may be hard to control
5. The lack of boundaries associated with drawing alleviates participants freedom of expression
6. Likewise, researcher-imposed structure determines interpretation of drawings
7. Drawings is suitable for data triangulation when used in complement to other research tools

Furthermore, considering drawings as a support for focus groups involving children, Yuen presented evidence that drawings had the following positive effects on the study outcome [24].

8. It helped create a relaxed and comfortable atmosphere, and released the pressure to answer immediately
9. It enhanced the communication between the researcher and the children by providing further insight on the children's perspective on the topic discussed, as well as offering children the possibility to express more personal experiences
10. It allowed better identification of groupthink and gave each idea expressed an equal chance for consideration

It should also be reminded that drawings can be culturally reflective. In a study comparing children drawings in Japan and the United States, La Voy et al discovered that when drawing people, Japanese children tend to include more details and represent humans larger but with fewer smiles than their American counterpart. These differences are explained by cultural clues of how children are raised in both societies. [22]

PERFORMING USER EXPERIENCES

Similarly to drawing, acting is deeply integrated into people's life, regardless of the nature of acting (as an artistic performance or as part of everyday routine). Until 2000 acting was primarily used as a research method in social and health science [23]. More recently, designers started including role playing in participatory design workshops occurring at early stages of the design process. In particular a group of Finnish researchers have generated a large body of work regarding the use of drama and dramaturgy in user-centred design processes. For instance Metho et al. introduces state-of-the-art theories, methods, as well as case studies in [12]. In their work, they have identified seven types of drama-based workshops, among which the Drama workshop inspired the activities further described in this paper. Drama workshops consist of a set of collaborative activities (discussions, improvisations, physical exercises, etc.) used to explore a specific issue through the participants' experiences and emotions. Examples of such workshops are reported in [20]. Titta et al. explored the issues associated with retirement using a mixture of user-centred product concept design (UCPCD) and drama-based methods. The methodological lessons learned during the experiment encourage the use of drama-based techniques in complement to more traditional approaches for several reasons. Firstly, the emotional and social dimensions of interaction are more thoroughly investigated. Secondly they provide users a way to explore their experience from a different viewpoint, which can be beneficial especially in early design phases. Last but not least, the ease of conducting drama-based workshops was put forward.

Performance-based user activities are also part of the future technology workshop described in [21]. This collaborative, participatory design technique aims at providing direct input for the design of disruptive technology by relating users to the technology in a pragmatic, open-ended, cost-effective way that requires minimal participant training. It involves participants in a sequence of seven activities, including among others, brainstorming, prototype design, scenario building and role play. The purpose of this latter activity is to contextualize the futuristic and contemporary technology models previously identified during other sessions. The present paper adapted this approach from focusing on a far future to introduce instead an altered, challenging version of current reality.

Even though the Japanese literature available in English concerning performative user experience research is scarce, it seems that theatre-based techniques have been employed in a number of UX research projects. For instance in [8], the authors relate how test subjects first identified typical scenarios of their work and acted out a selection of them in situ. This enabled the research team to thoroughly understand how people relate to these mundane tasks and better inform future design of supportive technology.

Finally, as Metho et al. argue, "the different dramaturgical and performative forms bring up elements that would otherwise go unnoticed" [12]. As a concluding remark, most studies agree on judging the role of facilitator crucial and impacting results. As developed in the next section, this impact is minimized during both drawing and acting activities, letting participants take ownership of the expression medium and use it as they feel.

CASE STUDIES

This section presents three case studies of using drawing or a combination of drawing and acting as a mean of understanding the relationship between media technology users and two media devices: televisions and mobile phones. The first case served as a pilot study in order to test and improve the drawing only approach. Nevertheless, it also generated valuable data which can be analysed. The second iteration builds from the pilot study and was conducted in a different cultural environment for potential comparison. The final case study makes use of both drawing and acting in a drama workshop involving individual and group exercises.

Pilot Study: Project Seminar in Japan

Setup and participants

The pilot study (CS1) took place as a social event during a three-day project seminar. All participants knew each other, for the project had been running for several years. After the second day's dinner, everyone gathered in the meeting room where further discussions about the project were to take place after the drawing experiment. Participants were handed a set of paper sheets. On the first sheet, a description of the author's project and the purpose of the study reminded the participants about the experiment. The four remaining sheets contained a few lines of instructions and a large empty square on the rest of the page for drawing. Pens of various types and colours were available to all participants, who could use any combination of them. Participants were sitting on the floor either in small groups or individually. Interaction between participants during the experiment was possible but not mandatory. Thirty minutes was allocated to the entire test, including introductory speech. The sets of paper sheets were collected after each participant completed his/her drawings, in order to limit potential alterations. Twenty-one participants took part in the pilot study. At thirty-six years old in average, they were mainly males (17 against 4 females), and their occupation was closely related to the academic world.

Tasks

The study investigated participants' relationship with TV and mobile phone separately: The two first sheets focused on television and the two last on mobile phone. On the first sheet participants were asked to draw the layout of their house, indicating the media devices regularly in use. Additionally, participants were instructed to illustrate media devices used simultaneously. For the second drawing, participants were asked to illustrate an impressive memory related to television. It could be a memory about anything that marked them somehow deeply. The drawings concerning the mobile phone followed the same approach: First participants had to picture themselves, depicting the mobile devices they carry around with them. Then they should recall and illustrate an impressive memory associated with their personal mobile phone.

Results

Analysing the data collected solely based on the drawings can be a difficult exercise and has been argued to be insufficient [6]. Nevertheless, as a first step into the analysis it leaves the opportunity to interpret participant answers and identify trends and categories. Later this can be used for selecting a few participants for further examining representative contributions.

Focusing on home media usage, the analysis should filter out the excess of information that appears in most drawings. Sketching the layout of the home is only the support task for studying where and how media devices are used in the home. This comment is actually valid for all drawings regardless of the topic at hand. As illustrated in Figure 1-(a), Japanese home drawings are usually complemented by text clarifying a device, piece of furniture or specific use situation. As the figure also illustrates, sometimes the drawing integrates information that does not relate directly to the topic (such as the location of windows or various rooms in this example). In such cases the researcher needs to separate primary information, directly relevant and to be immediately analyzed from secondary information, which may still be useful to complement the primary findings at a later phase of the analysis.

When asked to depict a memory related to television, the majority of Japanese participants portrayed memories related to the TV content, and little about the device itself or the social interaction around it. Half of the memories involved the participant alone, and one third involved family members (Figure 1-(b)).

Self-depicting oneself leads to reflecting on one's behaviour, which some Japanese participants expressed through there drawings. Additionally, four participants specifically represented several situations in which they carry mobile devices. In general, participants depicted themselves carrying 2.5 mobile devices (such as mobile phones, computers, or music players). A few considered more exotic devices (e.g. watch, transportation cards). Concerning mobile phones, they were mostly located in a pants pocket, often in a bag and sometimes in a jacket pocket. Figure 1-(c) is an example of typical self-depiction.

Finally, memories about mobile phones mostly related to experiences where the device had been broken, forgotten, lost, or otherwise misused (as depicted in Figure 1-(d)), as well as specific use situations. Those memories were mostly associated with negative feelings, rather than positive or neutral ones. Even more than with memories involving TV, mobile phone related memories concerned the participant alone.

Study 2: Graduate Course in Denmark

The second experiment (CS2) repeated the pilot study in a different cultural context, and included a few minor modifications in the setup. The participants also differed in the second study as all were graduate students attending a User Experience Design course. The tasks however remained strictly identical to CS1.

Setup and participants

This study took place during a two-hour lecture introducing students to qualitative methods for user experience research. The exercise was conducted after a short break at the beginning of the second hour of the lecture. The lecturer gave a brief and general introduction to the method before starting the exercise, which lasted about 20 minutes. The task sheets differed from the pilot study by the size allocated to each drawing. In order to avoid potential blank page syndrome, two drawings were expected per page, instead of one per page during the pilot. Participants were sitting at their desk as during the lecture and could interact between each other. Pens were distributed to participants who didn't have one. Thirty-seven graduate students took part in the second study. They were again mostly males (26 against 11 females) and 24 years old in average.

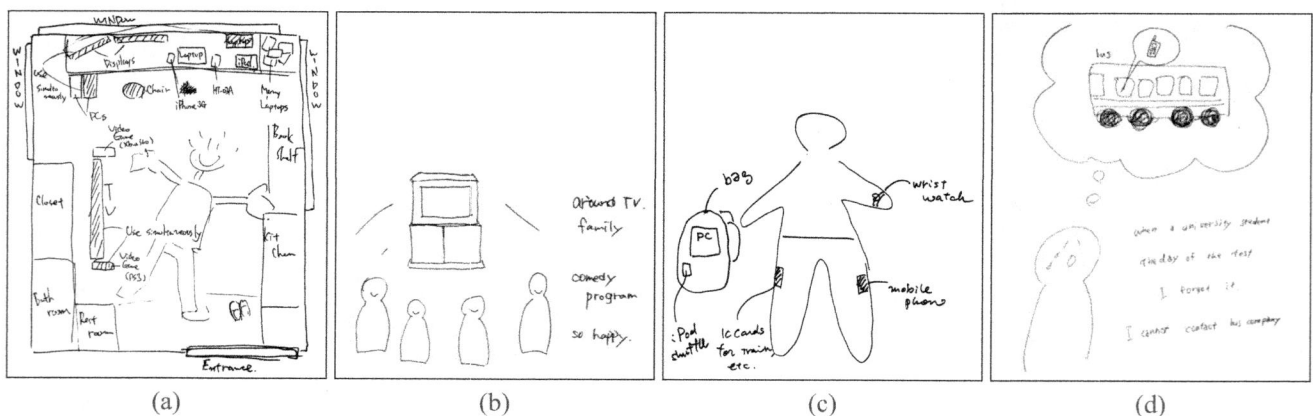

Figure 1. Drawings collected during the Japanese project seminar illustrating a home and media devices in use (a), an impressive memory involving TV (b), a self-depiction including mobile devices (c), and an impressive memory involving mobile phone (d).

Figure 2. Drawings collected during the Danish graduate course illustrating a home and media devices in use (a), an impressive memory involving TV (b), a self-depiction including mobile devices (c) and an impressive memory involving mobile phone (d).

Results

Drawings from the Danish students could be categorized in a similar way than the Japanese ones. The home drawings can be classified in two categories according to the amount of details included. The range of complexity between drawings varied considerably from minimalistic (illustrated in Figure 2-(a)) to very detailed, a short majority belonging to the former category.

When it came to remembering a remarkable event related to television, Danish students mentioned the device itself in majority, mostly illustrating scenes of use or acquisition (illustrated in Figure 2-(b)). Memories related to the TV content as well as the surrounding social environment were also mentioned. The people involved in most of these memories as well as the associated feelings were unclear and were matter of interpretation. This would call for further discussion with the author.

Danish students represented themselves carrying 1.8 mobile devices in average, mostly focusing on the cell phone, sometimes complemented by a laptop or music player. Most participants represented themselves using their mobile phone, hence carrying it in their hand (as illustrated in Figure 2-(c)). The second most popular location for carrying mobile phones was the pants pocket. A surprisingly representative number of drawings pictured the user and devices separately.

Finally, memories related to mobile phones referred equally to situations in which the device was broken, lost, or misused, than to specific use situations (as illustrated in Figure 2-(d)). Those memories involved mostly the participant alone. As with TV-related memories, the feelings associated with mobile phone memories were very

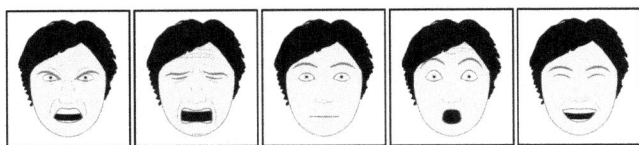

Figure 3. The scale of emotions used to described feelings: anger – sadness – neutral – surprise – joy

hard to identify without making assumptions based on the content depicted.

Study 3: Drama Workshop in Japan

The third study (CS3) reported in this paper illustrates the use of drawing as scenario building and acting as research methods to generate creative use of television and mobile technology based on prior personal experiences with those devices. The workshop took place during the author's stay at the foreign institution mentioned in introduction.

Setup and participants

In this study, 12 undergraduate and graduate university students (aged 26 in average) engaged in a series of individual and group exercises, during a four hour drama workshop. Most of the participants knew each other beforehand, even though they were not necessarily studying together. The workshop took place in a meeting room, in which tables and chairs were arranged to suit groups of 3-4 people working together. In general the workshop followed the approach described earlier as a drama workshop, but the chosen exercises were inspired by McCarty's work on enacting participatory development [11] and Theodor's creative method workshops [19].

Exercises

In order to get the participants in a creative and playful mood, they first took part in an icebreaking group exercise. All participants wrote down a simple sentence about television or mobile phone following the structure "*I <do something with the device>, to <purpose of doing it>*". Half of the participants were asked to create such sentence related to TV, and the other half to mobile phones. The paper sheets on which participants wrote their sentence was then cut at the coma, and the second parts redistributed so each participant would get the ending of a sentence corresponding to the device they did not write about. Each participant then read out loud the newly created sentence, and very briefly tried to argue for its possible meaning. The following is an example of such sentence: "*I change channel to 8, to separate a little bit from business mail*".

Then, the first individual exercise inquired participants about their personal attachment to television and mobile phone, respectively. For each device, participants were asked to (1) indicate on a scale of emotions (anger, fear, neutral, surprise, and joy, as depicted in Figure 3) which ones would likely apply to them in case they didn't have the device anymore, (2) write down on cards up to three functions of the device they consider essential, and (3) select among a list of 36 adjectives those which best describe the device according to them. The emotion scale is derived from cross-culturally validated Ekman's list of six basic emotions [4][5], from which disgust and fear were discarded as deemed irrelevant in a technological context. The list of adjectives consisted of 18 pairs of bi-polar descriptors of objects, such as public and private, hot and cold or polite and rude.

In the second individual exercise, participants integrated the functions they previously identified for both devices into illustrated mini-stories. They were provided with a set of cards representing a problem (lost, fire, late, etc.), a location (workplace, plane, restaurant, etc.), a mood (anger, fear, joy, etc.), and a social setup (family, best friend, colleagues, etc.), which they should integrate in their stories. The purpose of randomly setting up the scene for participants was to provoke them into imagining using familiar technology in unfamiliar setups. To illustrate their stories participants had at their disposal a drawing notebook each, pens of various types and colours, scissors, and empty cards to possibly add functions.

After a 20 minutes break during which participants relaxed and chatted, random groups of three were formed. As a first group exercise, each participant should display and explain his/her story to the other two group members, who would discuss it briefly. Then they should collaborate to create a common story to be later performed in front of the other groups, inspired by the three personal ones. They were allowed to discard or add elements to the story, but were encouraged to keep as many of the technological functions as they could. Finally, the room was rearranged and a scenic space created, on which each group acted out their mini-play, each lasting about five minutes.

Results

Analysing the data collected during this workshop consisted in two parts. Firstly, studying the answers from the first individual exercise related to the relationship between participants and mobile phone/TV. Secondly, tracking the evolution and possible modifications of the individually selected functions and their potential inclusion in the mini-stories and mini-plays.

Personal relationship with TV and mobile phones

When asked about their anticipated emotions if TV and mobile phones were not accessible to them anymore,

participants reacted differently for both devices. While the imagined loss of television left the participants largely neutral, despite mild sadness and surprise, the idea of not having a mobile phone anymore provoked great sadness and mild anger.

The analysis of the selected adjectives reveals further discrepancy between the perception of mobile phones and TV. The top five adjectives associated with each device are:

- **Television**: Passive (75%), Loud (50%), Exciting (42%), Public (42%), and Lazy (42%)
- **Mobile phone**: Convenient (92%), Personal (84%), Private (67%), Small (50%), and Active (42%)

If in general these findings were to be expected, it confirms nevertheless current general opinion about what TV and mobile are about in a heavily connected society with ubiquitous media access: Namely the passive and shared consumption of TV content, contrasting with the discrete, active use of the mobile phone that is always carried around. Additionally, the difference in amplitude of the replies is worth noticing. Similarly to the previous exercise, participants reacted more strongly about the mobile phone characteristics than they did for the TV ones. This indicates a strong relationship (personal and private) with mobile phones, compared to a more distant connection (due to its public and loudness features) with TV.

Technological functions, mini-stories and mini-plays

Each participant identified functions s/he considers essential for mobile phones and televisions. Then they all created mini-stories around these functions. Finally these mini-stories inspired the groups of 3 participants in creating and acting out a mini-play. These mini-plays thus include some of the functions previously put forward by each participant. Tracking down how the functions have been used and/or modified throughout this creative process not only provides a better understanding of how important they are for users individually and as a group, but also informs about the group dynamics during such an activity.

In average each participant thought about a little less than 5 functions to be essential for both devices. The 56 functions named can be categorized into the following eight clusters based on their similarity: Access to information, Specific use, Communication, Design + specification, Entertainment + relaxation, Secondary function, Music + sound, and Others (unspecific, etc.). Surprisingly, even within the clusters, the functions cited are little redundant, and instead tend to cover various aspects of the same issues.

When creating their individual mini-stories, participants used most of the functions they identified as essential, discarding only 13% of them. Three quarters of the functions kept were then used unmodified in the mini-stories, while the rest was modified to better fit the story. At the end of the group work however, only a third of the original functions were kept untouched, the rest of the 32 remaining functions being modified during either of the exercises. Additionally, if participants only used the functions they generated in their individual mini-stories, 15% of those used in the group mini-plays were new ones, created to fit the purpose of the plays. These observations illustrate the participant willingness to reach group consensus, when merging their ideas together, contrasting with their intent to use all the elements they have at their disposal when creating their own stories. Examples of mini-stories are given in Figure 5.

Regarding the content of the stories, the degree of realism evolved between individual stories and group plays. If all individual mini-stories are highly realistic in terms of environmental settings and how the technology is put into use, the group mini-plays were much more surreal, especially with regard to the scene setups. Furthermore the groups used the context cards in different ways: Three groups reused 67%, 83% and 100% of them, while the last group only used one card unmodified to fit the story, while half of the other cards could only be somehow considered implicitly in the play. Extracts of the four groups mini-plays are displayed in Figure 6.

DISCUSSION
The following topics emerged while evaluating the data collected through the three studies. They aim at informing HCI researchers interested in adopting drawing and/or drama workshops to investigate UX with technology.

Personal Matters
It seems that drawing facilitates the expression of personal matters. In both Japan and Denmark, intimate stories were depicted in the drawing-only workshops. We argue that these stories would take longer to collect through verbal

interviews, as the act of drawing provides both a personal sphere to reflect in (centred on the paper sheet), and time to think and organize one's thoughts. It is further argued that drawing provides an opportunity for reflecting on one's behaviour, which opens for further discussions with the drawer. For instance both Japanese and Danish participants realized that they were sometimes using two phones at the same time and that could be considered strange.

Ubiquitous Mobile Phones
Cultural factors should be considered when asking people to remember a remarkable event related to a specific device. Some participants in both Japan and Denmark (two countries with a high rate of always-on users) expressed their difficulty to think about such a memory related to mobile phones. In fact they considered the device to be so embedded in their everyday life that finding an extraordinary event linked to it was hard. The very strong personal character of mobile phones was also noticeable in all case studies: Participants reacted more strongly when inquired about phones than about televisions.

Japanese vs. Danish Drawings
For what concerns the memory-based drawings (CS1 and CS2), in general Danish drawings were more ambiguous and harder to interpret on their own than the Japanese ones. For instance it was easy to determine whether a Japanese memory was associated with positive, negative or neutral feelings. On the contrary drawings collected in Denmark were ambiguous and could only be guessed. In both countries most memories related to mobile phones referred to the use or misuse of the device by the participant alone. However when remembering an event related to TV, Japanese participants referred mostly to the TV content, while Danes focused on the device more frequently. Japanese also visibly experienced these events either alone or with family members, while Danes were more ambiguous on the matter. Regarding the story-based drawings (CS3), all but one of the stories were easily understood without further insight from the drawer.

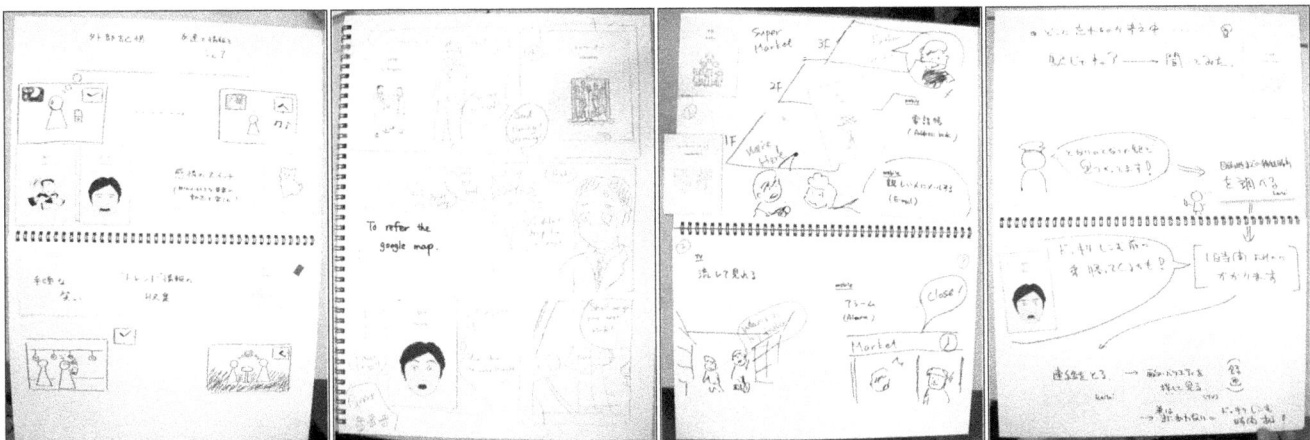

Figure 4. Extracts from individual mini-stories created by four participants.

Figure 5. Extracts of the mini-plays acted by the four groups.

Acquaintance among Participants

Even though the participants produced the drawings (including as mini-stories) on their own, the presence of colleagues, friends or strangers around might influence productivity and the level of attention to details. However, the drawings collected during the three case studies seem to indicate no such effect. It could even be argued that both familiar and unfamiliar social surroundings may positively influence how people draw. In a familiar social setting, one might want to impress or amuse friends, and when surrounded by strangers, one might want to appear assiduous. In both cases, the attention given to the drawings might be high. Nevertheless, consistency bias may occur in case of participants exchanging heavily during the study.

When grouped together to perform a collective creative activity, it is important that participants feel comfortable enough to share their ideas and voice comments toward other's ideas. This can be achieved by either selecting participants who know each other prior to the workshop, or by creating an atmosphere supporting constructive group creativity. These strategies were applied in the case studies presented in this paper as follows. In the three case studies participants knew each other beforehand. Additionally, CS1 participants' attitude was oriented toward creativity as part of the event they were involved in (a project seminar involving group reflective activities). In CS2, participants' reflective potential was triggered as part of the learning process they were engaged in (a course in UXD). As for CS3, an icebreaking game invited participant to think creatively from the onset of the workshop, and a general playful atmosphere was later maintained by the facilitators. These have been proven successful strategies to encourage participation. The level and way to establish playfulness need however to be adapted to the cultural and social characteristics of the participants, in order not to appear brusque, inappropriate or irrelevant.

Interpreting Results

Analysing qualitative data such as drawing and theatre plays can be challenging. Based on the literature and the experience gathered while conducting the activities documented in this paper, a few guidelines concerning result analysis are discussed in the following paragraphs.

Participants might respond negatively at first when asked to draw, as they might not feel comfortable about their drawing abilities. "*But I can't draw...*" was a typical

reaction during the three case studies. It is essential to make clear that the "quality" of the drawing for this activity lies not in its artistic value, but rather in its ability to convey an idea, to express a memory, to illustrate a setup or a fact, etc. Moreover it is necessary to stress that the drawings are not judged in any way, they are merely a support for expression. Encouraging participants to use stick figures and words helps fight their possible discomfort or reticence. After this first barrier is overcome and participants completed their drawings, self-critiques disappeared and only a cheerful mood and the joy of having participated in a playful activity remained.

Similarly, the guidelines for the mini-plays created in the third case study were loose and encouraged the groups to be creative. In fact, the frame of the stories was implicitly defined by the previous activities conducted in the workshop, and as a result all groups stayed within the scope of the workshop theme. They used the opportunity to express themselves and this led to discovering potential use cases of technology in unconventional situations.

Being aware of the events unfolding at the time of the study is also important as they might influence participants involved in a creative group activity: The largest the event the higher the probability of impacting the group's creation. This phenomenon was particularly visible in the third case study, which took place in Japan less than two weeks after the March 11, 2011 disaster in the Tohoku region, which greatly affected the whole country. Especially the group plays reflected the difficult time, as all involved a dramatic plot and three out of the four plays explicitly included the massive wave of earthquakes that were still shaking the country at the time of the workshop. Individual exercises focusing on personal experiences such as the two first case studies and the first exercises in the third case study were not impacted by such event. They specifically focused on personal experiences and therefore referred to events from a relatively distant past.

Comparison to quantitative results

After performing the activities related so far in this paper, an online survey was conducted among 116 Danes and 102 Japanese to investigate various aspects of their everyday experience with TVs and mobile phones. Some differences between the two populations are reported to further argue for the need to consider cultural factors when conducting UX research. The survey mostly aimed at exploring interest and behaviors related to second screen activities, however these issues will not be discussed here as they are irrelevant to this paper. Instead, we shall focus on the more generic UX aspects with mobile phones and television also reported in the survey and overlapping with the topics explored though the drawing- and drama-based workshops. In that regard, the survey respondents were asked to:

- name the most important features they consider when buying a new mobile phone
- describe what they like and dislike about their mobile phone and television (separately)
- express their expected feelings if they had no longer access to their mobile phone and television (separately)

Important buying factors are comparable in both countries: features (such as camera, calendar, and music player), design and price are the top three criterion influencing device acquisition. The features cited are secondary functions of the mobile phone, which were already found important for workshop participants (in CS3); although to a lesser extent than the primary, communicative, functions. The importance of these primary and secondary functions was confirmed by what respondents reported liking and disliking about their mobile phone, as functions such as calling and accessing Internet were frequently mentioned. This is also coherent with previous findings: The importance of mobile phone functions in the perception of the device has been previously established for Japanese and North Europeans (Swedes) in [2].

Then, respondents were asked to select the emotions that best match their expected feelings in case they could not use their mobile phone any longer. They could choose among Ekman et al.'s six basic emotions (this time including disgust and fear, as well as the possibility to freely name any other emotion). Both Danes and Japanese chose sadness as the dominant emotion they would most likely experience if they were suddenly deprived of mobile phone, confirming the results obtained in CS3.

Then they were asked to imagine that they had no longer access to their television. As previously, sadness was mostly chosen in Japan and Denmark. However, an especially large number of respondents (34% of Danes and 48% of Japanese) found that none of the six basic emotions suggested represented well their expected feeling in this situation. A potential explanation is actually the lack of reaction that would experience the respondents with no longer TV access, as further indicated by the additional emotions freely cited by participants. Indeed, indifference was frequently mentioned explicitly, which aligns with the results collected in CS3.

Finally, respondents described what they like and dislike about their television. Answers collected in Denmark differed visibly from those collected in Japan. The two predominant sources of positive feedback in Denmark are the content and the purpose of watching TV (catching up with news and being entertained). This matches the two

functions mostly cited during CS3. In Japan however, the TV's performances are the main source of satisfaction with television, followed by content and purpose. The two populations also differ in the features they dislike about TV: It is considered a time waster by Danes, and the content available is a source of dissatisfaction for them. Japanese complain mostly about the content available and the specifications of their TV set. Often TV is appreciated for its relaxing or informative purpose but watchers tend to get caught up and keep on watching even though they lose interest in the programme, leading to frustration. When comparing these findings with those extracted from the drama workshop, the Danish survey respondents agree with the Japanese workshop participants in the general functions they appreciate the TV for, while the Japanese survey respondents pointed out more specific topics.

CONCLUSION

This paper documented three case studies utilizing drawing and a drama workshop to investigate personal relationships with television and mobile technology, as well as to generate possible scenarios for such technology in a creative approach. To the extent of the knowledge acquired while conducting the two first case studies and during their analysis, drawing as a stand-alone technique and as part of a drama workshop seems a valuable technique for acquiring qualitative insights on the user experience with technology. The following statements have been verified and summarize the findings of the experiment so far:

1. Drawing helps create a relaxed and comfortable atmosphere in which test participants are willing to express personal matters,
2. The absence of boundaries in drawings further encourages participants to reveal personal aspects of their lives,
3. Responses are influenced by the experimental setup,
4. Analyzing drawings should start by focusing on the primary data (directly relevant to the topic), before possibly including secondary data to broaden the perspective,
5. Drawings should be used in triangulation with other research methods.

The final case study further acknowledged the benefits of drawings when integrated in a drama workshop. It also verified the usefulness of engaging participants in theatre-based activities for visualizing UX with technology. This was successfully investigated in the case of a workshop encompassing self-reflection on personal experience and scenario elicitation in group, conducted in a cultural environment where verbal communication was a challenge.

These findings however need to be further investigated, combined with additional user experience evaluations as suggested in the literature and compared to other inquiry methods in order to assess the performance of drawings as an HCI research tool. A first step in that direction has been documented in the paper, comparing the qualitative results collected through the aforementioned activities to those emerging from an online cross-cultural survey. The outcome of preliminary comparisons between the approaches demonstrates the benefits of applying both qualitative and quantitative inquiry methods when exploring user experience with technology. Indeed in the present case, not only the qualitative findings re-emerged from the survey and thus further strengthened them, but the two strategies also generated a richer pool of results from which future research questions emerged. In particular, conducting these studies in two distinct cultural settings led to the identification of common traits and singularities, which would be worth investigating further.

ACKNOWLEDGMENTS

The author thanks Professor Mizukoshi for his kind support at the University of Tokyo, as well as all participants who voluntarily challenged their drawing and acting skills and shared personal stories for the purpose of this study.

REFERENCES

[1] Anning, A. & Ring, K. (2004), *Making sense of children's drawings*, Open University Press.

[2] Baron, N. S. (2009), 'Three Words about Mobile Phones: Cross-Cultural Findings from Sweden, the US, Italy, Japan, and Korea', in *Proceedings of the COST Action 298 Conference, "The Good, the Bad, and the Challenging: The User and the Future of Information and Communication Technologies'*.

[3] Beebe, J. (2001), *Rapid assessment process: an introduction*, AltaMira Press.

[4] Ekman, P., Friesen, W. V. and Ellsworth, P. (1972), *Emotion in the human face: Guidelines for research and an integration of findings*. Pergamon Press.

[5] Ekman, P. (1989), 'The argument and evidence about universals in facial expressions of emotion', in *Handbook of social psychophysiology* 58, Lawrence Erlbaum, 342--353.

[6] Guillemin, M. (2004), 'Understanding Illness: Using Drawings as a Research Method', *Qualitative Health Research* 14(2), 272--289.

[7] Haseman, B. C. (2006), 'A manifesto for performative research', Media International Australia Incorporating Culture and Policy: quarterly journal of media research and resources(118), 98--106.

[8] Hasuike, K., Tamaru, E. and Tozaki, M. (2006) 'Creating prototypes of prospective user activities and interactions through acting by design team and users', in *Proceedings of the 3rd International Conference on Enactive Interfaces (Enactive)*, 149-150.

[9] Jacucci, C.; Jacucci, G.; Wagner, I. & Psik, T. (2005), 'A manifesto for the performative development of ubiquitous media', in *Proceedings of the 4th decennial conference on Critical computing: Between sense and sensibility*, ACM, New York, NY, USA, pp. 19--28.

[10] Kearney, K. S. & Hyle, A. E. (2004), 'Drawing out emotions: the use of participant-produced drawings in qualitative inquiry', *Qualitative Research* 4(3), 361--382.

[11] McCarthy, J. & Galvão, K. (2004), *Enacting participatory development: theatre-based techniques*, Earthscan.

[12] Mehto, K.; Kantola, V.; Tiitta, S. & Kankainen, T. (2006), 'Interacting with user data - Theory and examples of drama and dramaturgy as methods of exploration and evaluation in user-centered design', *Interacting with Computers* **18**, 977--995.

[13] Millen, D. R. (2000), 'Rapid ethnography: time deepening strategies for HCI field research', in *Proceedings of the 3rd conference on Designing interactive systems: processes, practices, methods, and techniques*, ACM, New York, NY, USA, pp. 280--286.

[14] Mills, J. E. (2010), 'Why We Draw: An Exploration Into How and Why Drawing Works', Master's thesis, Virginia Polytechnic Institute and State University.

[15] Newell, A. F.; Carmichael, A.; Morgan, M. & Dickinson, A. (2006), 'The use of theatre in requirements gathering and usability studies', *Interacting with Computers* **18**, 996--1011.

[16] Roam, D. (2009), *The Back of the Napkin (Expanded Edition): Solving Problems and Selling Ideas with Pictures*, Penguin Group US.

[17] Seland, G. (2006), 'System designer assessments of role play as a design method: a qualitative study', in *Proceedings of the 4th Nordic conference on Human-computer interaction: Changing roles*, ACM, New York, NY, USA, pp. 222--231.

[18] Sova, R. & Sova, D. H. (2006), 'Storyboards: a Dynamic Storytelling Tool', in *Proceedings of the 2006 UPA conference on Usability through Storytelling*.

[19] Theodor, J. (2010), 'The Creative Method and Systems v2 – a toolkit for the age of ideas', http://jasontheodor.com/.

[20] Tiitta, S.; Mehto, K.; Kankainen, T. & Kantola, V. (2005), 'Drama and user-centered methods in design', in Coleman, R. and Macdonald, A. (ed.), *Proceedings of Include 2005: International conference on inclusive design*.

[21] Vavoula, G. and Sharples, M. (2007) Future technology workshop: A collaborative method for the design of new learning technologies and activities, *International Journal of Computer-Supported Collaborative Learning* 2, Springer, 393-419.

[22] Voy, S. K. L.; Pedersen, W. C.; Reitz, J. M.; Brauch, A. A.; Luxenberg, T. M. & Nofsinger, C. C. (2001), 'Children's Drawings', *School Psychology International* 22(1), 53--63.

[23] Yardley-Matwiejczuk, K. (1997), *Role play: theory and practice*, Sage Publications.

[24] Yuen, F. C. (2004), '"It was fun… I liked drawing my thoughts": Using drawings as a part of the focus group process with children', *Journal of Leisure Research* 36(4).

Effects of Trust on Group Buying Websites in China

Na Chen

Institution of Human Factors & Ergonomics
Room 524A, Shunde Building, Tsinghua
University, Beijing, China 100084
chenn4@163.com

Pei-Luen Patrick Rau

Institution of Human Factors & Ergonomics
Room 524A, Shunde Building, Tsinghua
University, Beijing, China 100084
rpl@mails.tsinghua.edu.cn

ABSTRACT

The research aimed to investigate 1) the factors influencing Chinese customers' trust and purchasing probability of group buying websites; 2) the differences of trust on B2C and group buying websites; and 3) whether the Theory of Reasoned Action and Gefen's summarization of trust antecedents applicable for Chinese group buying websites.

The study consisted of three phases: 1) a pre-questionnaire about general trust on B2C and group buying websites; 2) an in-lab experiment following by a post-questionnaire after each trust situation; 3) a short open interview.

According to the results, 1) Cognition-Based Antecedent trust is the most important factor influencing Chinese customers' trusts and purchasing probabilities of both B2C and group buying websites. 2) Participants show significantly lower general Trust Beliefs and Trust Intends on group buying websites. However, under the same trust situation, participants show significantly higher purchasing probabilities on group buying websites. 3) The Theory of Reasoned Action and Gefen's summarization of trust antecedents are not applicable for current Chinese group buying. Some implications for group buying websites were discussed.

Author Keywords

group buying website; B2C website; trust antecedent; trust belief and trust intend.

ACM Classification Keywords

H.1.2. User/Machine Systems: Human factors.J.4 Social and Behavioral Sciences: Economics and Psychology.

General Terms

Economics, Human Factors, Performance.

INTRODUCTION

In Jan. 9, 2012, Lingtuan, a Chinese large group buying platform website, released one public online report "2011 national station census data report of group buying websites".

The report indicates that 2011 national transaction volume of group buying websites reaches 21.632 billion RMB, which is surprisingly 8 times of 2010. Since August 2011, the size of Chinese market has been the global largest one, bigger than North American (Lingtuan, 2012).

The report of Lingtuan also indicated that by the end of 2011, 1968 group buying websites have shut down and quitted the competitive market, taking up 1/3 of the nationwide websites (Lingtuan, 2012). As early as in December 2011, one online article of Reuters (www.reuters.com) pointed that Chinese group buying websites were facing a trust crisis (Lee, 2011). Even Gaopeng, the Chinese version of Groupon in America (www.groupon.com), was reported to sell fake watches. Therefore, studies of customers' trust on Chinese group buying websites are necessary to understand their perception of group buying and inner motivations to purchase on the websites. Because of the short history, few studies about group buying are available.

Group buying is a typical business model of e-commerce. It provides a platform for firms to sell products or service online. The most attractive and competitive feature of group buying is cheapness. The cheapness is based on large sales volumes in a short time. The online group buying price is lower than the actual price, always by 30% ~ 50% discounts, even by 90% discount in China. Customers should place orders within a certain period of time, one or several days. Cheapness attracts a large amount of orders. Firms earn money through small profits but large sale volume and they can expand the famousness. The world's earliest group buying website is Groupon, which started in November 2008. The field of China started in 2009 and experienced a fast development in 2010 and 2011. Since last year, the field has been facing a serious trust crisis.

Trust plays an important role in e-commerce (Handy, 1995). Most researches indicated that trust can reduce the perceived uncertainty in commerce (Gefen, 2000; Gefen, Karahanna & Straub, 2003; Javanpaa, 2000). In business, only when trust exists, it is possible that buyers and sellers are willing to maintain long-term relationships (Dasgupta, 1988). Reichheld and Schefter thought trust was even more important than price while the controlling and rule system was imperfect (Reichheld and Schefter, 2000), like today's Chinese group buying market.

The transaction in other commerce is built on the gradual interaction between each other (Gefen, 2000). E-commerce takes Internet as the media. Social Presence Theory indicates that people's sense of social presence is relative low with computer-mediated communication (Short, Williams & Christie, 1976). They will have low sense of immersion in e-commerce, so as that they have low probability to build trust and purchase. Hence, the built of trust is harder with computer-mediated communication.

The researches about conceptualization of trust can be divided into two categories. In the first category, researchers consider trust as a multidimensional collection based on context (Bulter, 1991; Gefen, 2002; Kumar et al., 1995). In particular, trust is a group of beliefs, i.e. integrity, benevolence and ability (Doney & Cannon, 1997; Gefen, Karahanna & Straub, 2003; McKnight, Choudhury & Kacmar, 2002). In the second category, researchers consider trust as a whole. Trust is a general belief that other members and groups are credible (Gefen, 2000; Hosmer, 1995). This study takes the conceptualization in of the first category.

Gefen, Karahanna and Straub summarized that trust was influenced by five trust antecedents, e.g. Personality-Based Antecedent, Knowledge-Based Antecedent, Cognition-Based Antecedent, Calculative-Based Antecedent, and Institution-Based Antecedent (Gefen, Karahanna & Straub, 2003). Cognition-Based Trust Antecedent is based on the first impression rather than through experiential personal interactions (Brewer and Silver, 1978; Meyerson et al. 1996; Gefen, Karahanna & Straub, 2003). In contrast, Knowledge-Based Trust Antecedent is the familiarity based on the experience with what, who, how and when of what is happening (Gefen, Karahanna & Straub, 2003; Gefen, 2004), which can reduce social uncertainty through the increased understanding (Luhmann, 1979; Gefen, Karahanna & Straub, 2003). Calculative-Based Trust is built through rational assessments of the costs and benefits of other groups in the relationship (Buckley and Casson, 1988; Coleman, 1990; Dasgupta, 1988; Gefen, Karahanna & Straub, 2003; Lewicki & Bunker, 1995; Shapiro et al., 1992; Willianson, 1993). Institution-Based Trust Antecedent is the sense of security from guarantees, safety networks, or other impersonal structures inherent in a specific context (Gefen, Karahanna & Straub, 2003; Shapiro, 1987; Zucker, 1986). There are two types of Institution-Based Trust, i.e. Structure Assurance (Baier, 1986; Lewis and Weigert 1985) and Situational Normality (McKnight, Cummings & Chervany, 1998; Shapiro 1987; Zucker 1986). Personality-Based Trust is the tendency whether to believe in others (Farris et al. 1973; Mayer et al. 1995; McKnight, Cummings & Chervany, 1998; McKnight, Choudhury & Kacmar, 2000; Rotter 1971). There are three types of Personality-Based Trust, i.e. Trust Proposition, Humanity Loyalty (Gefen, 2000; McKnight, Cummings & Chervany, 1998), and Trust Stance (McKnight, Choudhury & Kacmar, 2002).

The Theory of Reasoned Action by Fishbein and Azen defines that trust antecedents determine Trust Beliefs, and then Trust Beliefs determine Trust Intends (Fishbein & Azen,

1975), which finally implicates purchasing behaviors in e-commerce (Gefen, 2000). This research takes the trust framework to investigate 1) the influences factors on trust of Chinese customers on group buying websites; 2) the differences between trusts on B2C and group buying websites; and 3) whether the trust framework applicable for Chinese group buying websites.

METHODOLOGY

Trust questionnaire

The study used Xu's trust questionnaire (Xu, 2011). The complete trust questionnaire is shown in Appendix I.

Because the websites provided to participants are unfamiliar to them, the questionnaire did not include questions about Knowledge-Based Antecedent.

Table 1 shows the numbers of questions of trust antecedents' scale and their sub-scales. For brief introduction, the abbreviations of some terms are used in the following paper. Table 1 also includes Trust Beliefs and Trust Intends scales.

All the questions were tested through Likert 7-point scale.

Tasks

The study consisted of three phases, a pre-questionnaire, an in-lab experiment, and a short open interview.

Scale (sub-scale) of trust antecedents	No. of questions	Abbreviation
Personality-Based Antecedent		PER
Trust Proposition	2	TP
Humanity Loyalty	2	HL
Trust Stance	2	TS
Cognition-Based Antecedent	2	COG
Calculative-Based Antecedent	3	CAL
Institution-Based Antecedent		INS
Structure Assurance	3	SA
Situational Normality	3	SN
Trust Beliefs	5	Belief
Trust Intends	3	Intend

Table 1. Trust questions and abbreviations.

The pre-questionnaire aims to investigate the participants' general trust on B2C and group buying websites. This questionnaire also tests the demographic information and group buying experience.

The experiment aims to investigate the participants' trust and purchasing probability of eight specific websites (four are B2C websites and four are group buying websites). Each website stood for one kind of trust situation. During the experiment, each participant purchased specific items from the websites. Before purchasing, the participants were provided a description of the purchasing goal and the trust situation of the website. The description is introduced detailed in part of "**Trust situation**".

For each website, participants had three steps to do, 1) browsing the website; 2) searching for the specific items; 3) deciding whether to purchase. Browsing the website was to strengthen the participants' perception and understand of the trust situation. In this step, experimenter had some guidance for the participants. After searching for the specific items, if the participant decided to purchase, he/she should implement purchasing behaviors. In this step, the participant could choose whether to provide private information to the website, e.g. email and cell phone number.

After purchasing on each website, participants should complete a post-questionnaire about the trust on the website. The post-questionnaire was similar to the pre-questionnaire, except for Personality-Based Antecedent scale.

After the experiment, participants should have a short open interview about their behaviors and thinking about group buying. The interview provided supplement for the analysis.

Variables
There were six independent variables in the study, i.e. four trust antecedents, gender and website kinds. Personality-Based Antecedent was defined as the intrinsic property of participants, which will not change with different websites. The study just considered the influences of other three trust antecedents and their interactions. Considering the participants' workload, the study used 2^{3-1} (=4) factorial design. Each participant should implement four purchasing for B2C and four purchasing for group buying websites. Table 2 shows the treatment for trust situations. Each trust antecedent has two levels, high and low.

There are subjective and objective dependent variables in the study. The subjective variable is the scores of Trust Beliefs and Trust Intends scale. The objective variable is the purchasing probability of each website.

Trust situation

Trust antecedent	Trust situation			
	1	2	3	4
COG	+	+	-	-
CAL	+	-	+	-
INS	+	-	-	+

Table 2. Treatment of antecedents for each trust situation.

To control the trust antecedents in each trust situation, the experimenter provided one paragraph description of the task goal and trust situation.

The task goals are:

"You are a university student in Beijing. Christmas is coming, so you want to purchase a mini humidifier (double meal) for your girl-/boy- friend in the B2C web (group buying web)."

Antecedents	B2C	Group buying
COG	Good/bad reputation	Good/bad reputation
CAL	Whether support cash on delivery	Whether support return service
INS	Whether be embodied in CNNIC trusted site list	Whether be embodied in CNNIC trusted site list

Table 3. Treatment description.

The goal products of B2C and group buying websites were different, mini humidifiers for B2C and double meals for group buying. There are three reasons for the setting.

1) Appropriate items reflect actual demands

According to literature review and researcher's experience, customers tend to purchase service, especially meals and dinning, from group buying websites. They tend to purchase products from B2C websites, like electronic products and books. The appropriate items for each website kind can reflect customers' actual demand and trust.

2) The prices are similar

The prices of mini humidifiers on all the specific B2C websites are from 100 to 200 RMB, and the prices of double meals are generally around 100 RMB. The prices of the two kinds of items are similar, so as to reduce the influence of price difference on website kinds.

3) The numbers of alternatives are similar

The numbers of mini humidifiers on the selected B2C websites are around 50, and the numbers of double meals on the selected group buying websites are about from 30 to 50. The numbers of alternatives are similar, so as to reduce the influences of numbers of alternatives.

To avoid the influences of price and traffic (especially for double meals), the participants are told that

"The item is considered as new year benefit, which is provided by lab. And because 'you' are a Beijing student and your family has a car, there is no traffic problem."

Then, the participants are provided the description of trust situation, which control the levels of variables. The following paragraph is an example.

"Youle is a B2C website, which has a good reputation among customers. But the website does not support cash on delivery, and the website are not embodied in CNNIC trusted site list."

"Good reputation" stands for the high level of Cognition-Based Antecedent. "Does not support cash on delivery" stands for the low level of Calculative-Based Antecedent. On a website which support cash on delivery, customers can avoid the risk of private information credit card theft. And the quality uncertainty is reduced. "Be not embodied in CNNIC trusted site list" stands for the low level of Institution-Based Antecedent. CNNIC is short for China Internet Network Information Center, which is set up by the Chinese government and functions as the national Internet information center. Table 3 shows the description of each trust antecedent for B2C and group buying websites.

The study designs three measures to ensure the participants understanding the trust situations.

1) Provide some comments of the websites through Baidu for the participants – Cognition-Based Antecedent.

2) Ask participants some questions, like "do you usually use cash on delivery" – Calculative-Based Antecedent.

3) Explain "CNNIC trusted site list" and guides the participant find whether the website has the pattern of the CNNIC – Institution-Based Antecedent.

Website
Based on the trust situations, the study selected four B2C websites and four group buying websites. To avoid the influence of website designs, all the websites were selected in accordance to several large e-commerce websites, e.g. Jingdong, Dangdang, Meituan, 58tuan and so on. After the experiment, participants are also asked "Whether you think the website design is any strange or different from websites you usually use". To avoid the influences of participants' experience and other unexpected influences, all the selected websites are medium-scaled and the top 20 famous websites are excluded.

Participants
Previous researches indicated that younger people are the major customers of group buying websites (Wu, 2010). Young people are expected to be more willing to accept new technologies and services and they are the major user groups of group buying. Hence, the research recruited 12 students from Tsinghua University as the participants. all the participants should have certain experience of using group buying websites. The numbers of male and female participants are balanced, so as to reduce the gender influence and to investigate the differences between male and female group buying customers.

DATA ANALYSIS

Participants' information and experience of group buying websites
Twelve subjects participated in the experiment. All participants were come from Tsinghua University, aging from 20 to 25 years old. The numbers of male and female participants were equal to balance the gender influence. Four participants are undergraduates, six are master students, and two are PhD students.

The participants' experience of group buying is shown in Table 4. The first time of most of participants to use group buying was in 2011. Over the past six months, they browse group buying websites 1~5 times per week. But they purchase on the websites only once per month or less.

Analysis of pre-questionnaires about general trust on B2C and group buying websites
The pre-questionnaire consisted of 6 scales, i.e. PER, COG, CAL, INS, Beliefs and Intends. PER scale consisted of three sub-scales, i.e. TP, HL, and TS. INS scale consisted of two sub-scales, i.e. SA and SN.

Objects	Level	Frequency
Time of first use	Before 2010	1
	First half of 2010	6
	Second half of 2010	5
Browsing frequency	Every day	1
	3~5 times per week	5
	1~2 times per week	5
	Less than once per week	1
Purchasing frequency	Once per week or more	1
	2~3 times per month	2
	Once per month	5
	Twice per month or less	4

Table 4. Participants' group buying experience.

Except for PER scale, other scales were tested twice for each participant, for the general trust of B2C websites and for the general trust of group buying websites.

Reliability analysis
The reliability tests are shown in Table 5. Considering the numbers of questions for the each sub-scale are small, the Cronbach's Alpha will be relatively smaller, so the value of 0.6 is accepted. SN and Intends of B2C, and SN of group buying are still smaller than 0.6. This may result from the small sample size. For the consistency and completeness of the questionnaire, the study remains the three sub-scales.

Scale	Sub-scale	Cronbach's Appha	
		B2C	Group Buying
COG		0.828	0.883
CAL		0.676	0.837
INS	SA	0.635	0.709
	SN	0.548	0.436
Trust	Belief	0.631	0.752
	Intend	0.292	0.728
PER	TP	0.719	-
	HL	0.877	-
	TS	0.873	-

Table 7. Reliability test of pre-questionnaire scales.

Variance homogeneity test
The results of normality test of the pre-questionnaires indicated that the significance values of all the sub-scales are higher than 0.30, which means the sub-scales satisfy variance homogeneity. Parametric statistics tools can be used.

Variable	B2C		Group buying		F	Sig.
	Mean	SD	Mean	SD		
Belief	5.02	0.54	4.37	0.76	5.844	0.024
Intend	5.75	0.59	4.53	1.26	9.283	0.006

Table 8. Differences of general trusts between B2C and group buying websites.

Factors influencing general trust on B2C and group buying websites
Stepwise regressions were used to investigate the influence factors on general trust (Beliefs and Intends) of B2C and group buying websites.

Trust	Dependent variable	Std. Coef.	t	Sig.
Belief	(Constant)		1.984	0.083
	COG	1.183	8.614	0.000
	HL (of PER)	0.268	2.554	0.034
	SA (of INS)	-0.330	-2.361	0.046
Intend	(Constant)		3.570	0.006
	COG	0.894	7.568	0.000
	TS (of PER)	-0.398	-3.368	0.008

Table 6. Factors influencing general trust on group buying websites.

The results are shown in Table 6 and Table 7. COG is significant for both Beliefs and Intends on group buying websites, and significant for Beliefs on B2C websites. PER and INS have no significant influences on Beliefs and

Trust	Dependent variable	Std. Coef.	t	Sig.
Belief	(Constant)		2.024	0.056
	COG	0.850	7.883	0.000
	HL (of PER)	0.243	2.251	0.035
Intend	(Constant)		1.698	0.128
	CAL	0.516	5.182	0.001
	TS (of PER)	-0.778	-7.701	0.000
	SN (of INS)	0.578	5.287	0.001

Table 7. Factors influencing general trust on B2C websites.

Intends. Only different sub-scales of PER and INS show significance.

Hence, the trust framework is not applicable for general trust of B2C and group buying websites, because 1) not all trust antecedents have significant influence on trust; 2) Trust Beliefs cannot determine Trust Intends and there are other factors to influence Trust Intends.

Differences between general trusts on B2C and group buying websites
ANOVA was used to analyze the differences between general trusts on B2C and group buying websites, as shown in Table 8. The general Trust Beliefs and Trust Intends of on B2C websites are significantly higher than group buying websites.

Analysis of experiment about trust and purchasing probability under specific trust situations
Reliability test of post-questionnaire scales
All the Cronbach's Alpha values of scales are larger than 0.70, which indicated the questionnaire could be considered internally consistent.

Variance homogeneity test
One-Sample Kolmogorov Test was used to investigate the normality of the variables. All the significance values are higher than 0.05, which means the sub-scales satisfy variance homogeneity. Parametric statistics tools can be used.

The variable of purchasing probability does not satisfy normality and variance homogeneity. The significance is 0.000. This variable needs nonparametric statistics tools to analyze.

Influence factors on trust
MANOVA is used to investigate the influence factors on trust (Beliefs and Intends), as shown in Table 9. The main effects of website kind, COG and CAL are significant. For Beliefs, the main effects of website kind, COG, CAL and PER are significant.

Variable	Belief		Intend	
	F	Sig.	F	Sig.
Website	8.776	0.004	6.873	0.010
COG	53.791	0.000	48.580	0.000
CAL	4.408	0.039	7.560	0.007
PER	2.749	0.013	-	-

Table 9. Factors influencing trust under specific trust situations.

Considering only group buying websites, COG is significant for Beliefs and Intends, as shown in Table 10. CAL is significant for Intends.

Objects	Belief		Intend	
	F	Sig.	F	Sig.
COG	34.612	0.000	4.727	0.036
CAL	-	-	27.607	0.000

Table 10. Factors influencing trust on group buying websites under specific trust situations.

Difference between trusts on B2C and group buying websites

The main effect of website kind is significant for trusts as in Table 9, which indicates that there are significant differences between trusts on B2C and group buying websites.

The results of ANOVA indicated that only under Trust Situation 1, the Trust Beliefs of group buying website is significantly higher than B2C websites, as shown in Table 11.

Variable – Trust situation	B2C		Group buying		F	Sig.
	Mean	SD	Mean	SD		
Belief-1	5.13	0.71	5.70	0.63	4.313	0.050
Intend-1	5.31	0.89	5.81	0.75	2.219	0.151
Belief-2	0.77	0.22	0.92	0.26	1.837	0.189
Intend-2	1.35	0.39	1.27	0.37	2.423	0.134
Belief-3	0.89	0.26	0.70	0.20	1.378	0.253
Intend-3	1.07	0.31	1.19	0.34	2.854	0.105
Belief-4	0.83	0.24	0.62	0.18	1.007	0.327
Intend-4	0.95	0.27	0.95	0.27	0.186	0.671

Table 11. Differences of trust between B2C and group buying websites.

Influence factors on purchasing probability

Because the variable of purchasing is a 0-1 binary variable, binary logistic regression can be used to analyze the influences of trust antecedents, website kinds and gender on purchasing probability.

Based on the results of regression, Cox & Snell R Square is 0.465 and Nagelkerke R Square is 0.623. Considering the small sample size, the fitting of the regression model is accepted.

The model is shown in Table 12. There is significant difference between purchasing probabilities of B2C and group buying websites. Besides, COG and CAL have significant influences. The significant influence variables on Trust Intends and purchasing probability are the same. There is no significant difference between male and female participants. And Institution-Based Antecedent also is not significant, which is consistent with the results of interview.

Model	B	S.E.	Wald	Sig.	Exp(B)
Website	2.041	0.670	9.278	0.002	7.698
COG	3.554	0.787	20.373	0.000	34.963
CAL	2.866	0.759	14.258	0.000	17.565
Constant	-4.239	1.861	5.187	0.023	0.014

Table 12. Factors influencing purchasing probability.

Considering only group buying websites, no trust antecedents were significant. Then, take Beliefs and Intends as the independent variables. Only Intends has significant influence on purchasing probability (sig. is 0.021).

Difference between purchasing probabilities of B2C and group buying websites

According to Table 13, the purchasing probabilities of group buying websites are higher than those of B2C websites under each trust situation. The results are in consistent with the differences of trust above. Especially, all participants purchased double meals from the group buying website under Trust Situation 1, and no participants purchased mini humidifiers from the B2C website under Trust Situation 4.

Trust situation	B2C		Group buying		Ratio of B2C/group buying
	Mean	SD	Mean	SD	
1	0.92	0.29	1.00	0.00	0.92
2	0.25	0.45	0.58	0.52	0.43
3	0.08	0.29	0.50	0.52	0.16
4	0.00	0.00	0.17	0.39	0.00
Total	0.31	0.47	0.56	0.50	0.55

Table 13. Descriptive statistics of purchasing probability.

RESULTS AND DISCUSSIONS

The significant influence factors on trust and purchasing probability of group buying websites

For group buying websites, Cognition-Based Antecedent plays most important roles in general trust and trusts on specific websites, as shown in Table 6 and Table 10. Besides, Calculative-Based Antecedent is significant for Trust Intends and purchasing probability under specific trust situations, as shown in Table 9. Humanity Loyalty (of Personality-Based Antecedent) and Structure Assurance (of Institution-Based Antecedent) are significant only for general Trust Beliefs of group buying websites, and Trust Stance (of Personality-Based Antecedent) is significant only for Trust Intends, as shown in Table 6. However, no trust antecedents have significant influence on purchasing probability of group buying websites.

The results show that cognition (it means the reputation in the experiment) of websites is the most important factor for group buying websites.

Cognition-Based Antecedent (it is reputation and reliability in the experiment) is the most important factor for group buying. Calculative-Based Antecedent has only significant influence on Trust Intends under specific trust situations. It is the last phase of trust, which directly determines purchasing. For a new business model, like group buying, customers rely highly on the reputation, rather than calculating the real benefits. Based on the results of interview, friends' recommendations are the determinate factor whether participants trust on a website. Institution-Based Antecedent plays a less important role in the study. Based on the interview with participants, they all highly distrusted on Chinese supervisory system and institution on e-commerce. The distrust can be easily associated with the social trust crisis in China, which beyond this study.

For purchasing probability of group buying websites, only Trust Intends show significant influence. The relationship between Trust Intends and Trust Beliefs in the model cannot be reflected in the study. The relationship is not insufficient and unconvincing. Some other factors also have influence on Trust Intends.

Differences of B2C and group buying websites
The general Trust Beliefs and Trust Intends of B2C websites are significantly higher than group buying websites, as shown in Table 8. However, under the same trust situation, they have no significant differences, as shown in Table 11. Furthermore, the purchasing probabilities of group buying websites are much higher than B2C websites, as shown in Table 13. Under Trust Situation 1 (the best situation), all participants purchased on group buying websites, but some participants did not purchase on B2C websites. Under Trust Situation 2 and 3, the purchasing probabilities of B2C websites are less than half of group buying websites. Under Trust Situation 4, no participants purchased on B2C websites, but still two participants purchased on group buying websites.

The differences of psychological demands, purchasing items, and development phases of the two website kinds can be the incentives.

1)　The differences of psychological demands

B2C websites have longer history, and more mature markets and institution. Their customers have more relational consumption behaviors. With the development of B2C websites, there becomes a large amount of loyal customers. They consider purchasing on B2C websites as a regular and general behavior, like purchasing in super markets. On the contrary, customers usually purchase on group buying websites with the demand of "purchase cheap". Hence, they are willing to take more risk and the purchasing probabilities are higher. However, group buying is still a new business model, so the general trust is still lower than B2C websites.

2)　The difference of purchasing items

Participants were asked to purchase mini humidifiers from B2C websites and double meals from group buying websites. There are two differences between the items in the study.

Firstly, mini humidifiers are a kind of physical commodity, while double meals are a kind of service. The service consumption of Chinese customer has not been matured, so the acceptance criterions are relatively lower, which promotes higher purchases.

Secondly, mini humidifiers should be used for a period of time, at least one winter. A double meal will be consumed for just once. Based on the results of interview, even though the quality of the meal was low, most participants still thought just one-time consumption was accepted. They considered it as "a fall into a pit, a gain in your wit". However, a low-quality humidifier will bring them a lot of matters, so they performed more relational.

3)　The differences of development phases

The field of group buying in China started just form about 2009 and experiences a fast development in 2010. Since the second half year of 2011, the field of group buying is facing a trust crisis. When the development of the field is not yet mature, there are plenty of low-quality websites with bad reputation. Some cheat behaviors happened. The behaviors have negative impact on the overall field of group buying websites and lower customers' trust and impression. B2C websites have ever experienced this development phase. After years of development, B2C websites are gradually recovering from such a negative impression. Hence, the general trust of group buying websites is significantly lower than B2C websites.

Browsing frequencies are much higher than purchasing frequencies
Based on the results of interview and questionnaires, for group buying websites, the frequencies between browsing and purchasing are largely different. The browsing frequency is several times per week, but the purchasing frequency is once per month or less, as shown in Table 4. The entertainment and items' renewal speeds on group buying websites may be the incentives.

1)　The entertainment of group buying websites

"Browsing group buying websites" seems to be an entertainment, which can satisfy customers' demand of "pursuing cheap". Hence, customers regularly browse those websites for fun. However, when they actually purchase, they still can keep rational consumption to some degree. As the development of the market of group buying websites, the difference will be smaller.

2)　The renewal speed of items on group buying websites

The items on group buying websites are changed every day. Customers always have new alternatives to select from. So they are willing to pay more time on searching for preferred items, which results in high browsing frequency. However, the overall number of alternatives on group buying websites is still much lower than B2C websites. On Jingdong (a typical and successful B2C website), there are hundreds of thousands of items, while even the largest group buying websites do not have more than 500 of items. Hence, the purchase frequencies of group buying are much lower than browsing frequencies.

Gender has no significant influence on trust and purchasing probability

Some previous researches indicated (Wu, 2010) that young females are the major consumer groups of group buying websites. However, in this research with balanced gender ratio (6 females and 6 males), there is no any significant differences between male and female participants. Some incentives promote females to get touch with group buying, so as that they have more chances to purchase on group buying websites.

1) Communication characteristics

Communication characteristics of female customers can be one of the incentive factors. They have stronger willing to exchange the opinions of shopping online or offline. Hence, females have more channels and chances to get in touch with group buying.

2) Working field characteristics

Working field characteristics of female customers can be another incentive factors. More females are engaged in service industry, like sales, hotel and restaurant fields. Their working fields are more familiar to group buying field, which sells service more.

The Theory of Reasoned Action and Gefen's summarization of trust antecedents are not applicable for current Chinese e-commerce, especially for group buying

In sum, the Theory of Reasoned Action (trust antecedents determine trust beliefs, so as to determine trust intends), is not applicable for current Chinese B2C and group buying websites.

We test four trust antecedents in the study, i.e. Cognition-Based, Calculative-Based, Institution-Based and Personality-Based Antecedent. For general Trust Beliefs and Trust Intends on B2C and group buying websites, PER, CAL and INS are all not significant, as shown in Table 6 and Table 7. Only their sub-scales show differently significant influences.

As the definition of trust, trust has two phases, Trust Beliefs and Trust Intends. Based on analysis, there is significant influence of Trust Beliefs on Trust Intends. However, Trust Beliefs cannot predict purchasing probability, as shown in part "**Influence factors on purchasing probability**". Some other factors together with Trust Beliefs influence Trust Intends, so as determine purchase behaviors.

Implications for group buying websites

Based on the results, reputation is the most important factor for group buying. Increase the reputation becomes the major chance for group buying websites to survive in the trust crisis.

Although Calculative-Based Antecedent and Institution Antecedent trust are not so significant for both B2C and group buying websites, some of their sub-scales show significance. Websites owners and managers should not ignore these factors. Some other factors beyond the trust framework also have influences on final purchasing behaviors, which need further researches.

It seems that providing one-time consumption of service is still the major development direction, if the field of group buying does not have larger trust improvement or changes of business models, Customers have more interests and are willing to have a try, so as that the outstanding ones among the group buying websites may cultivate customers' loyalty.

CONCLUSIONS

The research aimed to investigate 1) the factors influencing Chinese customers' trust and purchasing probability of group buying websites; 2) the differences of trust on B2C and group buying websites; and 3) whether the Theory of Reasoned Action and Gefen's summarization of trust antecedents applicable for Chinese group buying websites.

The study consisted of three phases. The first phase was a pre-questionnaire about general trust on B2C and group buying websites. The second phase was an in-lab experiment following by a post-questionnaire after each trust situation. The third phase was a short open interview.

According to the results, 1) Cognition-Based Antecedent trust is the most important factor influencing Chinese customers' trusts and purchasing probabilities of both B2C and group buying websites. 2) Participants show significantly lower general Trust Beliefs and Trust Intends on group buying websites. However, under the same trust situation, participants show significantly higher purchasing probabilities on group buying websites. 3) The Theory of Reasoned Action and Gefen's summarization of trust antecedents are not applicable for current Chinese group buying. Not all trust antecedents are significant for Trust Beliefs and Trust Intends and no trust antecedents are significant for purchasing probability. Trust beliefs has no significant influence on purchasing behaviors.

Some implications for group buying websites were discussed.

REFERENCES

1. Baier, A. "Trust and Antitrust," Ethics (96), 1986, pp. 231-260.

2. Brewer, M. B., and Silver, M. "Ingroup Bias as a Function of Task Characteristics," European Journal of Social Psychology (8), 1978, pp. 393-400.

3. Buckley, P. J., and Casson, M. "A Theory of Co-operation in International Business," in Cooperative Strategies in International Business, F. J. Contractor and P. Lorange (eds.), Lexington Books, Lexington, MA, 1988, pp. 31-53.

4. Butler, John K. Toward understanding and measuring conditions of trust: Evolution of a condition of trust inventory. Journal of Management, Vol. 17, 1991, pp. 643-63

5. Coleman, J. S. Foundations of Social Theory, Harvard University Press, Cambridge, MA, 1990.

6. Dasgupta, P. "Trust as a Commodity," in Trust, D. G. Gambetta (ed.), Basil Blackwell, New York, 1988, pp. 49-72.

7. Doney, P. M., and Cannon, J. P. "An Examination of the Nature of Trust in Buyer-Seller Relationships," Journal of Marketing, Vol. 61, 1997, pp. 35-51.

8. Farris, G., Senner, E., and Butterfield, D. "Trust, Culture, and Organizational Behavior," Indus- trial Relations (12), 1973, pp. 144-157.

9. Fishbein, M., and Ajzen, I. Belief, Attitude, Intention and Behavior: An Introduction to Theory and Research, Addison-Wesley Publishing Company, Reading, MA, 1975.

10. Gefen, D. "Customer Loyalty in E-Commerce," Journal of the Association for Information Systems, Vol. 3, 2002, pp. 27-51.

11. Gefen, D., Straub, D. W. "Consumer trust in B2C e-Commerce and the importance of social presence: experiments in e-Products and e-Services," Omega, Vol. 32, 2004, pp. 407-424.

12. Gefen, D. "E-Commerce: The Role of Familiarity and Trust," Omega, Vol. 28, 6, 2000, pp. 725-37.

13. Gefen, D., Karahanna, E. and Straub, D. W. "Trust and TAM in Online Shopping: An Integrated Model" MIS Quarterly, Vol. 27, 1, 2003, pp. 51-90.

14. Handy, C. Trust and the virtual organization. Harvard Business Review, Vol. 73, 3, 1995, 40-50.

15. Hosmer, L. T. "Trust: the Connecting Link between Organizational Theory and Philosophical Ethics," Academy of Management Review, Vol. 20, 2, 1995, pp. 379-403.

16. Jarvenpaa, S. L., Tractinsky, N., and Vitale, M. "Consumer Trust in an Internet Store," Information Technology and Management(1), 2000, pp.45-71.

17. Kumar, N., Scheer, L. K., and Steenkamp, J.-B. E. M. "The Effects of Supplier Fairness on Vulnerable Resellers," Journal of Marketing Research, Vol. 17, 1995, pp. 54-65.

18. Lee, Melanie. "Chinese group buying websites are facing failure," Retrieved January 10, 2012, from http://cn.reuters.com/article/techMediaTelcoNews/idCNSB125601020111201.

19. Lewicki, R. J., and Bunker, B. B. "Trust in Rela-tionships: A Model of Trust Development and Decline," in Conflict, Cooperation and Justice, B. B. Bunker and J. Z. Rubin (ed.s), Jossey- Bass, San Francisco, 1995, pp. 133-173.

20. Lewis, J. D., and Weigert, A. "Trust as a Social Reality," Social Forces (63:4), June 1985, pp. 967-985.

21. Liangtuan. "2011 national station census data report of group buying websites," Retrieved January 10, 2012, from http://zixun.lingtuan.com/article-15899-1.html.

22. Luhmann, N. Trust and Power, John Wiley & Sons, Chichester, England, 1979.

23. McKnight, D. H., Choudhury, V., and Kacmar, C. "Trust in E-Commerce Vendors: A Two-Stage Model," Proceedings of the 21st International Conference on Information Systems, W. Orlikowski, S. Ang, P. Weill, H. Krcmar, and J. I. DeGross (eds), Brisbane, Australia, 2000, pp. 532-536.

24. McKnight, D. Harrison, Choudhury, V., Kacmar, C., "Developing and Validating Trust Measures for E-Commerce: An Integrative Typology," Information Systems Research, 2002, Vol. 13, 2002, pp. 334-359.

25. McKnight, D. H., Cummings, L. L., and Chervany, N. L. "Initial Trust Formation in New Organizational Relationships," Academy of Management Review Vol. 23, 3, 1998, pp. 472-490.

26. Meyerson, D., Weick, K. E., and Kramer, R. M. "Swift Trust and Temporary Groups," in Trust in Organizations: Frontiers of Theory and Research, R. M. Kramer and T. R. Tyler (eds.), Sage Publications, Thousand Oaks, CA, 1996, pp. 166-195.

27. Reichheld, F. F., and Schefter, P. "E-Loyalty: Your Secret Weapon on the Web," Harvard Business Review Vol. 78, 4, 2000, pp. 105-113.

28. Rotter, J. B. "Generalized Expectancies for Interpersonal Trust," American Psychologist (26), May 1971, pp. 443-450.

29. Shapiro, D. L., Sheppard, B. H., and Cheraskin, L. "Business on a Handshake," Negotiation Journal (3), 1992, pp. 365-377.

30. Shapiro, S. P. "The Social Control of Impersonal Trust," American Journal of Sociology (93), 1987, pp. 623-658.

31. Short, J., Williams, E., & Christie, B. The social psychology of telecommunications, John Wiley, London, England, 1976.

32. Williamson, O. E. "Calculativeness, Trust, and Economic Organization," Journal of Law and Economics (34), 1993, pp. 453-502.

33. Wu, C. C. (2010). A Study of the Effect of Consumer's Internet Group Buy Motivation, Internet Involvement and Product Involvement on Leisure Experience-An Example of Websites for Group Buy.

34. Xu, C.L. "The Influence of cultural factors in America, Japan, and China On Trust in E-Commerce," Tsinghua University, Beijing, China, 2010.

35. Zucker, L. G. "Production of Trust: Institutional Sources of Economic Structure, 1840-1920," in Research in Organizational Behavior (Volume 8), B. M. Staw and L. L. Cummings (eds.), JAI Press, Greenwich, CT, 1986, pp. 53-111.

APPENDIX I TRUST SCALE

The following 25 questions aim to test the trust antecedents and trust level on e-commerce.

Trust Proposition of Personality-Based Antecedent

1. I generally trust other people

2. I tend to count upon other people

Humanity Loyalty of Personality-Based Antecedent

3. I generally have faith in humanity

4. I feel that people are generally reliable

Trust Stance of Personality-Based Antecedent

5. I usually trust people until they give me a reason not to trust them.

6. My typical approach is to trust new acquaintances until they prove I should not trust them

Cognition-Based Antecedent

7. Online vendors receive good professional review.

8. Online vendors are large companies.

Calculative-Based Antecedent

9. Online vendors have nothing to gain by being dishonest in their interactions with me.

10. Online vendors have nothing to gain by not caring about me.

11. Online vendors have nothing to gain by not being knowledgeable when helping me.

Structure Assurance of Institution-Based Antecedent

12. I feel safe conducting business with online vendors because I accessed their sites through well-known, reputable portals.

13. I feel safe conducting business with online vendors because legal structures adequately protect me.

14. I feel safe conducting business with online vendors because my friends recommend them.

Situational Normality of Institution-Based Antecedent

15. I feel good about how things go when I do purchasing or other activities in the Website of online vendors.

16. The steps required searching for and order goods are typical of other similar Web sites.

17. The information requested of me at the Websites of online vendors is the type of information most similar type Web sites request

Trust Beliefs

18. Online vendors are trustworthy.

19. I trust stores keeps my best interests in mind

20. Based on my experience with online vendors in the past, I know they are honest.

21. Based on my experience with online vendors in the past, I know they provide good service.

22. Based on my experience with online vendors in the past, I know they are competent and effective in providing satisfactory service.

Trust Intends

23. I would use online vendors to inquire information about the goods they sell.

24. I would purchase from online vendors.

25. I am likely to provide online vendors with the information they need to better serve my needs.

Estimation of Conversational Activation Level during Video Chat using Turn-taking Information.

Yurie Moriya
Tokyo University of Agriculture and Technology
2-24-16 Nakacho, Koganei, Tokyo
50011646135@st.tuat.ac.jp

Takahiro Tanaka
Tokyo University of Agriculture and Technology
2-24-16 Nakacho, Koganei, Tokyo
takat@cc.tuat.ac.jp

Toshimitu Miyajima
Tokyo University of Agriculture and Technology
2-24-16 Nakacho, Koganei, Tokyo
tomiyaji@cc.tuat.ac.jp

Kinya Fujita
Tokyo University of Agriculture and Technology
2-24-16 Nakacho, Koganei, Tokyo
kfujita@cc.tuat.ac.jp

ABSTRACT

In this paper, we discuss the feasibility of estimating the activation level of a conversation by using phonetic and turn-taking features. First, we recorded the voices of conversations of six three-person groups at three different activation levels. Then, we calculated the phonetic and turn-taking features, and analyzed the correlation between the features and the activity level. The analysis revealed that response latency, overlap rate, and speech rate correlate with the activation levels and they are less sensitive to individual deviation. Then, we formulated multiple regression equations, and examined the estimation accuracy using the analyzed data of the six three-person groups. The results demonstrated the feasibility to estimate activation level at approximately 18% root-mean-square error (RMSE).

Author Keywords

Conversational activation; estimation; phonetic feature; speech information processing.

ACM Classification Keywords

H.5.2. User Interface: Theory and methods

INTRODUCTION

The growth of high-speed broadband networks facilitates the development and spread of various remote communication systems, such as instant messaging tools, micro-blogs, and video chat systems. A video chat system provides an easy-to-use remote communication function that includes images of the users. However, privacy-sensitive users might be unwilling to display their own images. Furthermore, there is a risk of an unintentional leak of personal information from the background image. On the other hand, avatar-based communication systems, such as Second Life [18], are utilized for casual remote communication. The use of an avatar, as the surrogate of the user, allows the user to avoid unintentional transmission of personal information. However, the conventional avatars lack the ability to express nonverbal information, such as a gaze, facial expressions, and gestures. Vargas noted that 65% of the message is communicated via nonverbal channels [20]. Mehrabian reported the roles of facial expression, phonetic information, and verbal information are 55%, 38%, and 7%, respectively, if contradictory information is expressed via verbal and nonverbal information [9]. Therefore, the expression of adequate nonverbal information is needed for smooth and natural avatar-mediated communication. However, the nonverbal information is manually controlled in most of the avatar communication systems.

The manual control of all nonverbal information, such as gaze and gesture, is cumbersome and increases the user task load. Therefore, the automatic control methods of nonverbal information have been studied. Interactor, developed by Watanabe et al., revealed that the automatic control of nods and gestures using the vocal information of the speaker facilitates the conversation [22]. Miyajima and Fujita also proposed methods to control the gaze, facial expressions, and gestures of avatars based on phonetic features, and experimentally examined the effects of these features on communication [10]. In natural communication, the magnitude and velocity of gestures are thought to change with the level of enthusiasm in conversation. Therefore, it is expected that automatically controlling the magnitude and velocity of gestures to reflect the conversational activation level produces a more natural impression and facilitates communication. Saeki et al. studied a unified control algorithm used to control the multiple nonverbal information based on the activation level [17]. However, methods to estimate conversational activation levels have not been established.

Maeda et al. proposed a method to estimate the activation level based on gestures such as hand motions [7]. The proposed method was expected to work well with a camera-compatible environment; however, the use of a camera limits

Table 1. Relationship between emotions and phonetic features (summary of preceding studies).

	emotion				
	anger	joy	dislike	sad	laxation
pitch	high	high	low	low	low
intensity	high	high	low	low	-
utterance rate	very fast	fast	fast	slow	-
cadence	-	appear	-	-	disappear

the possibilities for the usage of the proposed method. On the other hand, voice is essentially required information for voice-based chatting and is less restrictive in terms of system setup. Therefore, we experimentally discuss the feasibility of automatically estimating the activation level during natural conversation based only on vocal information.

It is known that prosodic information of the voice reflects emotions [14]. Turn-taking features are also known to change to reflect emotions [13]. Therefore, we studied the relationship between the phonetic and turn-taking features and the activation level in conversation among groups of three subjects. The results indicated the correlation between the activation level and the response latency, and the overlap rate and the speech rate. Therefore, the off-line estimation of the activation level was also examined on the basis of these three indicators. It demonstrated the feasibility of activation level estimation that is robust against individual differences and environmental variations. The contribution of this study to CHI is to demonstrate the feasibility of calibration-free conversational activation level estimation. It is expected to allow voice communication systems, as well as avatar chat systems to control their functions and reflect the activation level of the users.

RELATED STUDIES

Activation Level and Phonetic and Turn-taking Features

Numbers of studies have pointed out the change of conversational voice features due to emotional variations. For example, intensity, pitch, and utterance rates are higher when speakers are angry or joyful [1, 12]. On the other hand, these three features are lower when the speakers are sad [12], and intensity and pitch are lower [12] and utterance rate is higher [3] when speakers are expressing dislike. In addition, the previous studies indicated a higher pitch and a strong cadence when speakers are joyful, and a lower pitch and a decrease of cadence when the speakers are relaxed [11]. The changes of prosody due to emotional variations are summarized in Table 1. As the emotions during the conversation stabilize or change gradually without a strong prompt, the emotion is expected to induce automatically detectable changes in a conversational voice.

A circumplex model of affect, proposed by Russel, represents emotions by using two dimensions of pleasure-displeasure and sleep-arousal[15]. In this circumplex model, anger and joy are considered as higher arousal level emotions. On the other hand, the arousal levels of dislike and sadness are considered as low. When we define the conversational activation level as the enthusiasm in the conversation, it is consid-

ered to be proportional to the arousal level in the circumplex model. Therefore, the activation level is expected to induce the observable effects in the conversational voice, and the estimation of activation level based on phonological information would be possible.

In addition to the prosodic changes, turn-taking features were also researched [16]. It has been pointed out that the overlap frequency of utterances also increases along with the activation level [13]. It has also been reported that turn-taking latency, which is the interval after one speaker finishes speaking and the other starts speaking, decreases in the case of an affirmative or an approval response [6]. Therefore, in the conversations in which the speakers expressed joy, the response latency could be a good indicator of the activation level. In addition, motion synchronization among the speakers was also indicated in continuous conversation, and prosodic synchrony occurred, especially in groups of women [13].

Avatar Control using an Estimated Activation Level

If the duration and speed of the avatar behavior, such as gesture and facial expression, are appropriately controlled in conjunction with the conversational activation level, avatar communication might be more natural. Therefore, we defined the degree of conversational activity as enthusiasm of the speakers during the conversation, and studied the automatic control algorithms of avatar behavior according to the activation level [17]. Sejima et al. reported that conversational impressions are improved by controlling the avatar behavior based on the estimated conversational activation level that is a weighted moving average of overlap frequency [19].

If the real-time estimation of the activation level from the conversational voice is possible, the automatic control of the avatar behavior would be feasible. The activation-based control will allow avatars to behave more naturally. However, a certain amount of conversational voice is required for accurate estimation. It causes an estimation delay from several seconds to several minutes. This delay issue is discussed in the discussion section.

The activation levels of the participants are individually different. The speaker's activation level is supposed to be reflected by the voice features. On the other hand, the listening participant, who say nothing, would also be influenced by the general mood of the group and might feel his ore her own activation level. Therefore, a parameter is required to describe the conversational mood of the entire group. Thus, in this study, with the objective of controlling an avatar to reflect the activation level of not only a speaker but also the group, we assume two activation levels: a group activation level and a personal activation level.

EXPERIMENTS

Methods

We conducted video chat experiments among groups of three subjects under three different conditions, and recorded the conversation voices. In principle, avatar-mediated communication has limited nonverbal expression functions compared to face-to-face or video communication, even with automatic control mechanisms. Therefore, to limit the nonverbal communication channel, we limited the viewing range of the camera, which allowed the users to watch only the face and chest images of their partners. There were 18 subjects (nine male and nine female) in their twenties. The conversation groups were three three-male groups and three three-female groups. Each conversational group consisted of participants of the same gender who were acquainted with each other to minimize the influence of factors other than the test activity and to let the groups raise their activation level more easily.

We attempted to control the activation level of each conversation as low, medium, or high by imposing different constraints on the topics during the experiment. There were no other constraints, which allowed participants to converse naturally. The duration of the experiments was 15 minutes for each condition; 45 minutes in total. The sequence of the conditions was randomized to avoid order effect. After the conversation during each condition, the participants were required to evaluate the subjective activation level using a linear scale from 0 to 100. The participants scored their own personal activation level as well as the entire group's activation level, for the beginning, middle, and final parts of the conversation, as well as for the entire conversational period.

Experimental Conditions
To control the conversational activity at each of the three levels, we imposed several conditions on the talking topics for discussion. Before the experiments, topics related to news and social issues were collected as conversational topic candidates. Then, we interviewed the subjects to determine their interest and amount of knowledge of each topic. According to the answers from the interview, the topics for discussion were selected as follows:

- L-condition, envisaged low activity: We requested the subjects to seriously discuss topics related to news, in which all three subjects were least interested and had least knowledge. The conversation about other topics was strictly prohibited.

- M-condition, envisaged middle activity: We requested the subjects to discuss topics related to social issues of which they had some knowledge but little interest. The conversation about other topics was strictly prohibited.

- H-condition, envisaged high activity: We imposed no limitations on the topics for discussion. To help the participants choose discussion topics, the results of the survey questionnaire about the hobbies of each subject was disclosed to all the subjects. Furthermore, the subjects were instructed to enjoy the conversation.

During the L-condition, subjects had very little knowledge and interest for the discussion topic. The expected activation level was low because the subjects had difficulty in broadening the conversation. On the other hand, in H-conditions, there was no limitation on the topics, and the speakers were allowed to talk about their favorite topics. Therefore, the activation level was higher. In M-conditions, the subjects were able to broaden the conversation, because they had some

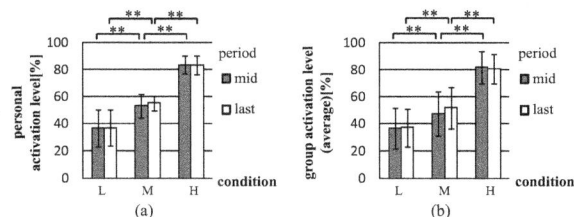

Figure 1. Evaluation of subjective activation level. (a) personal activation level, (b) group activation level (error bars represent standard deviations)

knowledge about the topics. However they had less interest about the topics than during the H-condition. Therefore, the expected activation level was between the L and H conditions.

Summary of Experimental Results
To confirm that the activation levels were controlled as designed, we calculated the averages of the subjective activation levels. The results are shown in Figure 1. The data for the first five minutes of each discussion was excluded from the analysis because we observed that a similar conversation concerning what to speak about occurred in each condition independent of the imposed topics. The significant differences in each pair of conditions were observed in multiple comparisons, after the confirmation of the significant difference in variance analysis ($p<0.01$). The results indicated that the conversations could be controlled at three levels by imposing limitations on the discussion topics.

ANALYSIS OF THE RELATIONSHIP BETWEEN THE ACTIVATION LEVEL AND VOICE FEATURES
In this study, we analyzed 10 features in conformity with previous studies. The analyzed features that reflect the prosody are average sound pressure, average pitch, sound pressure variation, pitch variation, utterance rate, utterance length and synchrony of sound pressure. In addition, we analyzed the average of response latency, overlap rate, and speech rate features that reflect the structures of conversations. The features were experimentally examined as activation level indicators for automatic estimation.

Methods of Voice Features Calculation
We used the application software, Praat [2], for analysis, similar to the preceding studies [23]. The calculation interval of sound pressure and pitch was set to 30 ms. To calculate the turn-taking features, we clipped out the vocal durations by applying the experimentally determined threshold, which was five times the white noise level and one tenth of the average sound pressure. Because short silences among utterances are caused by sound fluctuation and breathing, we interpolated short silences similar to the manner in the preceding study [21]. In this study, the silent durations less than 0.3 s were interpolated. After the interpolation of the temporal silence, the utterances longer than 0.1 s were regarded as the actual utterances and others were regarded as noise. The calculation method for each feature is described as follows:

- Average sound pressure: The sound pressure levels, sampled at 30 ms intervals, were normalized from 0 to 1, by dividing by the maximum value for each speaker. Average sound pressure was calculated every 5 minutes.

- Average pitch: Average pitch was calculated every 5 minutes after the normalization.

- Sound pressure variation: Variation in sound pressure is expected to be larger in tonic utterances. Therefore, the standard deviation of the sound pressures for the utterances was calculated and normalized by the average value.

- Variation coefficient of pitch: Pitch also has a great variation during tonic utterances. The standard deviations of pitch for the utterance interval was calculated and normalized.

- Utterance rate: To calculate the rate of utterances, it was necessary to detect each syllable and count the number of the syllables. In this study, the syllables were approximated to the duration between the two troughs of the sound pressures [8]. The rate of utterance was approximated as the average of the duration of each syllable.

- Utterance length: The utterance duration for a sentence decreases as the speaking speed increases. Consequently, the utterance length is likely to change in reflection of the change of speaking speed. Therefore, the length of each utterance, which was clipped out as described previously, was calculated by subtracting the start time of the utterance from the end time.

- Sound synchrony: The cases, that showed a positive correlation among the three speakers in sound pressure, pitch, utterance rate, or utterance length were regarded as the synchrony of the subjects, as similarly regarded by previous studies [13]. The rate of the correlative utterances was calculated as the synchronic trend feature. Linear interpolation was applied to the non-utterance durations, similar to methods used in previous studies. The rate of positive correlation coefficients for each 50 utterances was calculated as the measure of synchrony.

- Overlap rate: In enthusiastic conversations, more speech overlaps occurred, such as laughing. Therefore, we determined the overlaps by detecting when subject began speaking while another person was speaking. Furthermore, the rate of the overlaps was calculated to eliminate the effect of the total number of the utterances [6].

- Average response latency: After the detection of the turn-taking, the intervals were calculated between the end of the utterance of the first speaker and the beginning of the utterance of the next speaker. The intervals are regarded as the response latency of the latter speaker. The response latency takes a negative value when overlap occurs. In enthusiastic conversations, the faster turn-taking rhythm was presumed to shorten the response latency.

However, turn-taking did not occur in the utterances that completely overlapped another utterance, such as laughter or back-channel feedback. Therefore, we eliminated the cases in which the lately-begun utterance ended before the end of the turn-holding utterance. The latencies were calculated only for the cases without complete overlaps, which means turn-taking occurred.

- Speech rate: The personal speech rate was calculated as the rate of the utterance duration for which the system detected the utterance of the subject during the entire experiment.

Results of Analysis

The averages of the features of each speaker and each group for the last 10-minute periods of the conversations are shown in Figures 2 and 3. The speech rate of a group was defined as the rate of non-silent state time, during which at least one of the three participants is speaking. The group features, other than the speech rate, are the average values of the three subjects. Synchrony was not observed for both utterance rate and utterance length, but similar synchrony was observed for sound pressure and pitch. Therefore, we show only the results of the sound pressure. The groups were composed as follows:

- Group G1: Speakers a, b, and c

- Group G2: Speakers d, e, and f

- Group G3: Speakers g, h, and i

- Group G4: Speakers j, k, and l

- Group G5: Speakers m, n, and o

- Group G6: Speakers p, q, and r

Speakers a-i were male, and speakers j-r were female.

As a result of the analysis, similar to the previous studies, at a high activation level, the averages of the normalized sound pressures, the averages of the normalized pitches, the overlap rate, and the speech rate showed increasing tendencies, and decreasing tendencies were observed in the response latencies. On the other hand, the variations of sound pressure and pitch, the speaking rate, and the utterance length did not show significant correlation with the activation level. The synchrony was observed in only the female groups, similar to results reported in the previous study [13]. The Kruskal-Wallis test showed significant differences in five features: the average of normalized sound pressure and pitch, overlap rate, the average of response latency, and speech rate.

Depending on the activation level, an increase or a decrease was observed in the averages of normalized sound pressure and pitch, the overlap rate, the average response latency, and the speech rate for most of the subjects. However, the sound pressure and the pitch also showed larger individual differences even after the normalization. On the other hand, the overlap rate and the speech rate showed relatively smaller differences among the groups. The average response latency decreased to 0 s at a high activation level for most of the subjects, and both the group differences and the individual differences were smaller.

The changes of three turn-taking features related to the conversation structure of G1 are exceptionally smaller at a high activation level. The difference of the activation level between L and H-conditions was approximately 50% for the five other groups; however, it was 20% for G1. In other words, it is considered that the subjects in G1 were less excited compared to those in other groups during the H-condition. This result might be due to the less effectiveness of topics control in G1.

Selection of Indicators for Estimation

Out of the analyzed features, the averages of the normalized sound pressure and the pitch, the overlap rate, the speech rate, and the average response latency showed tendencies to increase or decrease depending on the activation level. They showed good correlation with the activation level. The sound pressure and pitch showed larger individual differences even after the normalization. In addition, they also were affected by factors in the system environment, for example, microphone sensitivity. Therefore, the features must be calibrated before using them to control avatars, which could be a potential disadvantage for practical usage. On the other hand, the overlap rate, the average response latency, and the speech rate, which relate to the conversational structure, showed fewer individual and group differences during the H-condition. Because these three features are calculated on the basis of the relationship between time and utterance, they are not affected by the system environment or by the phonetic individual differences. Therefore, the estimation of the activation level without calibration is expected to be feasible.

We discuss the feasibility to estimate personal and group activation levels by using three features as an indicator: overlap rate, the average of response latency, and speech rate, as discussed in the following sections.

ESTIMATION

Examination of Estimation Equation

Relationship between the Activation Level and Conversational Indicators

To discuss the feasibility of estimating the activation levels using overlap rate, average response latency, and speech rate, we analyzed the correlation between each indicator and the subjective activation level. The scatter plots of the average values of the three indicators during the middle and the final conversational periods versus the subjective activation level of each speaker or each group are shown in Figure 4. Because of the individual variability of the subjective scale, the averages of the three speakers were utilized as the group activation levels, which was the subjectively scored activation level of the entire group. Furthermore, exceptionally long latencies were observed in some situations, for example, when the topics of discussion were exhausted. They reflect the state of the group, but are different from the conversational rhythm. Therefore, we eliminated the longer latencies using an experimentally decided threshold of 5 s. The averages were calculated after the exceptional values were eliminated. Table 2 shows the Pearson product-moment correlation coefficients between each indicator and activation level. The decorrelation test indicated significant correlation between the activation level and all indicators (p<0.05).

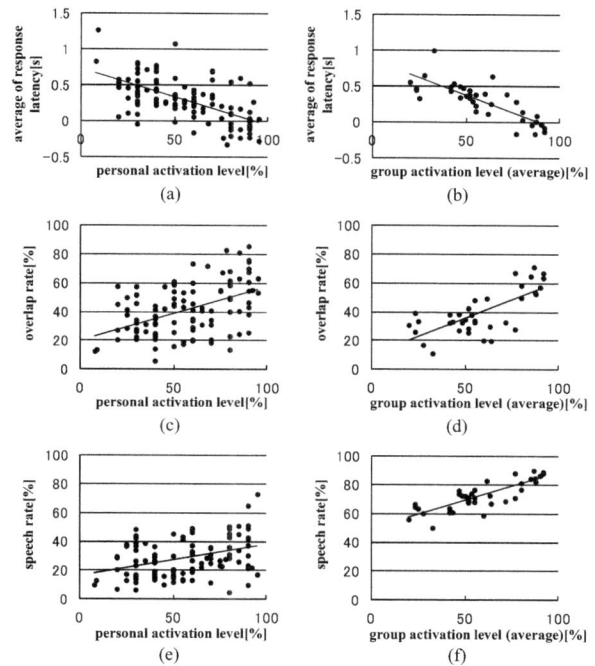

Figure 4. Scatter plots of activation levels and turn-taking features. (a,b) averages of response latency, (c,d) overlap rates, and (e,f) speech rates

The personal activation level, as seen in the scatter plot, showed a strong correlation with the average response latency. Moderate correlations were observed in the overlap rate and the speech rate, even their variability was relatively larger. The variabilities for the groups were smaller than those for the persons for all three indicators, and they showed a stronger correlation. In summary, there is some difference in accuracy, but the feasibility to estimate the activation levels of individuals and groups by using the three conversational indicators was demonstrated.

Determination of the Estimation Equation

The correlation has been confirmed between the activation level and each of the three indicators. The use of larger numbers of indicators is expected to improve the estimation robustness against the variation of the conversational patterns. Therefore, we performed multiple regression analyses using all three indicators and obtained multiple regression equations as estimation equations. The estimation equations for personal and group activation levels are shown as Equations 1 and 2, respectively.

Table 2. Correlation coefficients between activation levels and turn-taking features.

	overlap rate	average of response latency	speech rate
personal	0.48	−0.60	0.37
group	0.72	−0.79	0.82

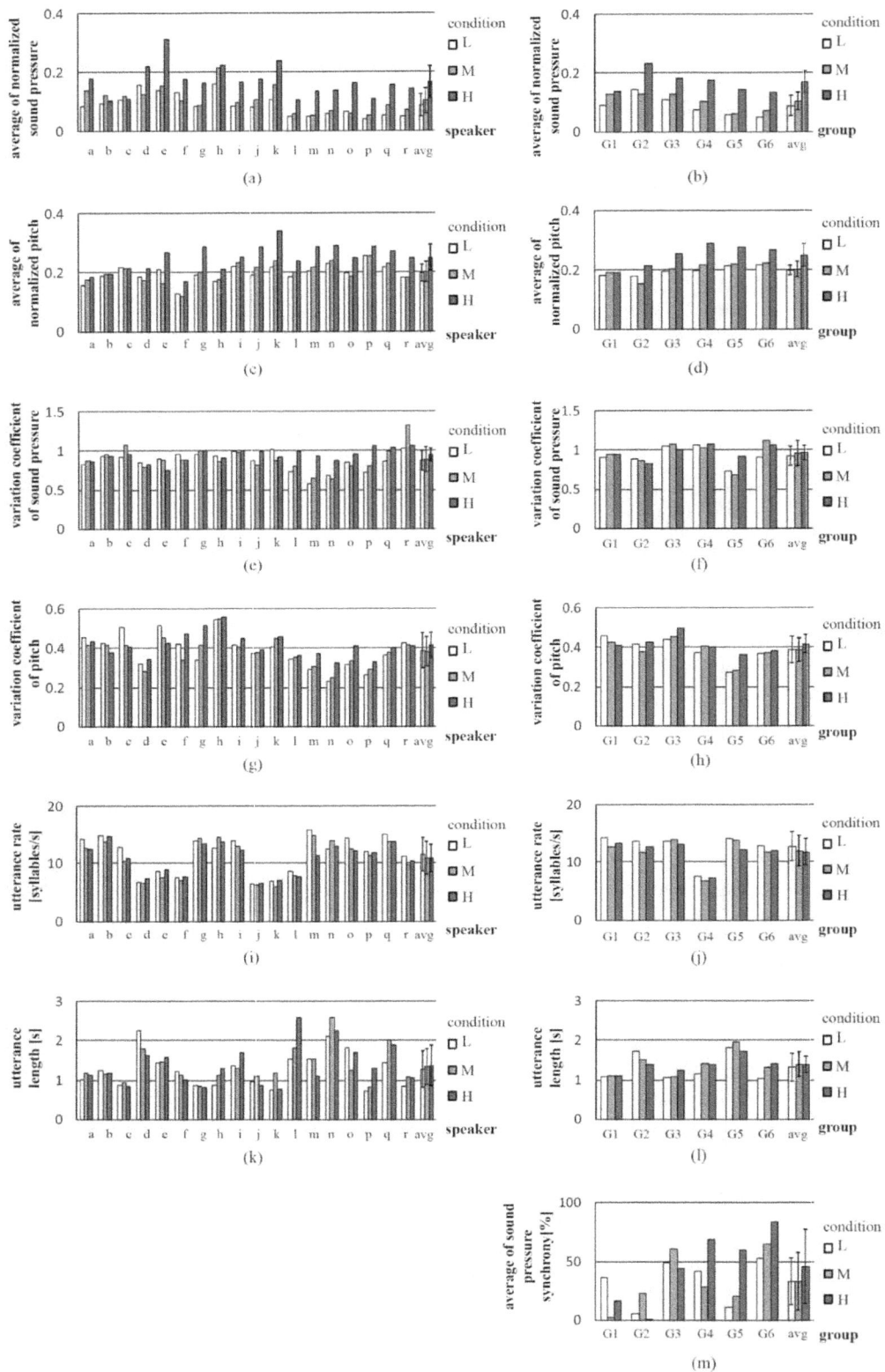

Figure 2. Results of phonetic feature analysis. (a,b) averages of normalized sound pressure, (c,d) averages of normalized pitch, (e,f) variation coefficients of sound pressure, (g,h) variation coefficients of pitch, (i,j) utterance rates, (k,l) utterance lengths, and (m) averages of normalized sound pressure synchrony

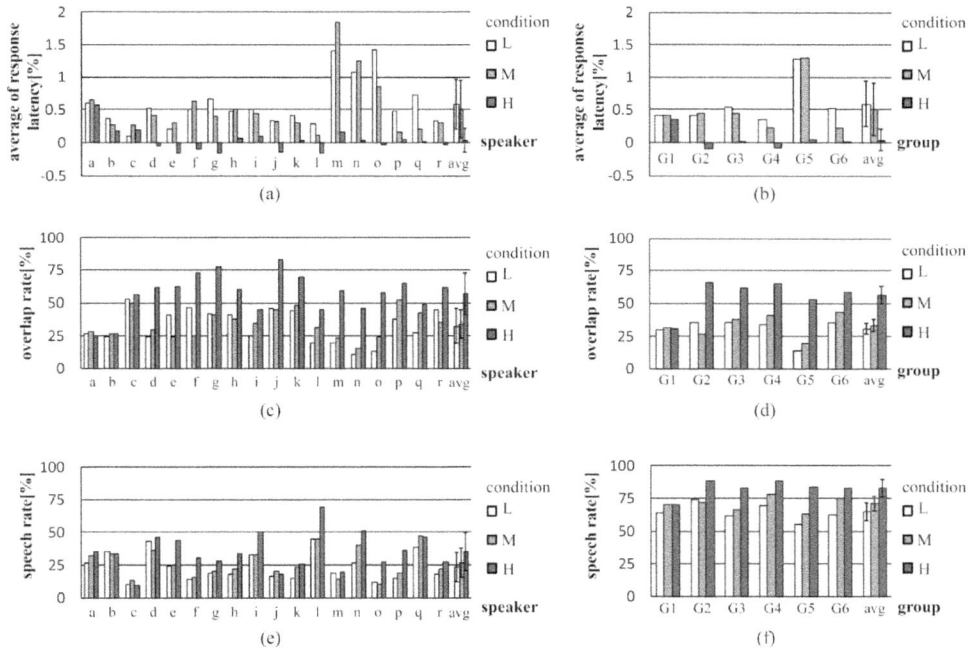

Figure 3. Results of turn-taking feature analysis. (a,b) averages of response latency, (c,d) overlap rates, and (e,f) speech rates

personal activation level

$$
\begin{aligned}
= \quad & 0.276 * \text{overlap rate}[\%] \\
& -27.2 * \text{avg. of response latency}[\text{s}] \\
& +0.423 * \text{speech rate}[\%] + 41.1
\end{aligned} \tag{1}
$$

group activation level

$$
\begin{aligned}
= \quad & 0.363 * \text{overlap rate}[\%] \\
& -33.8 * \text{avg. of response latency}[\text{s}] \\
& +1.44 * \text{speech rate}[\%] - 22.0
\end{aligned} \tag{2}
$$

Estimation Experiment

To verify the estimation capability, we performed off-line estimations of the personal and group activation levels of the analyzed conversational data of all six groups using Equations 1 and 2. The selected three indicators during the middle and final periods were utilized for estimation. The estimated values below zero and over 100 were limited to zero and 100. The root-mean-square errors (RMSE) of the estimated activation levels and the correlation coefficients between the subjective evaluation activation levels and estimated values are shown in Table 3.

The RMSE for personal and group activation levels were 18% and 12%. respectively. The estimation error for group activation levels was less than that for personal activation levels, but strong correlations were obtained in both cases. Therefore, in summary, the activation level estimation is highly feasible using conversational indicators without individual or group calibration.

DISCUSSIONS

Estimation Accuracy

In this study, the accuracy for the group activation level was high compared to that for personal activation level because of the following reasons: The subjective scales of persons essentially have individual variation. The effect of the individual variation was reduced in the group activation level evaluation because the scores of three subjects were averaged, while the personal activation level is the score of a person. Furthermore, the personal activation level indicator, such as overlap rate or average latency, tended to show a larger variance coefficient, especially for the relatively silent speakers, because the number of their utterances was small. In contrast, compensatory behaviors were observed in the groups. For example, participants sometimes intentionally spoke to avoid the awkward continuance of silence. This kind of behavior reduces the variance coefficient of the group speech rate. Therefore, a more robust estimation would be generally possible for group activation levels compared to the personal activation levels, similar to the proposed results.

To improve the accuracy, methods to reduce the individual differences are required, such as automatic calibration of the indicators or automatic setting of parameters as determined by machine learning. However, the deviation of the indicator might be also affected by dynamic factors, such as mood or

Table 3. RMSE and correlation coefficients for analyzed data set.

	RMSE	Correlation
personal	18%	0.60
group	12%	0.83

the subject's role in the conversation, as well as individual difference. The effectiveness of the parameter setting needs to be evaluated before applying it in various cases. In this study, we did not utilize sound pressure and pitch, because of larger individual differences. However, they could be candidates for activation level estimation parameters after additional processing to reduce the individual differences. The group activation level might be utilized for the improvement of the accuracy of the personal activation level. For example, the summation of the relative change of the personal activation level as an offset and the group activation level as a baseline might be effective for the persons whose activation level tends to be underestimated.

In this study, no mixed-gender group was studied to minimize the influence of the factors other than activity and to let the groups raise the activation level more easily. The turn-taking indicators, which were used for estimation, showed less gender difference compared to personal or group differences as seen in Figure 3. The mixture of gender might make conversation difficult in some situations. In these cases, the speech rates of the participants would become unbalanced, as seen in G4 in Figure 3. However, the estimated values of G4 were comparable to the other groups. Therefore, it is expected that the estimation of a mixed-gender group's activation level is feasible.

Control of Avatar Activation Level
In this study, each subject subjectively evaluated his or her own activation level. However, the self-judged activation level of a person does not necessarily correspond to the activation level evaluated by another person. For example, the activation level will be estimated to be lower than the self-judged level in the subjects whose voice and conversational behavior show less change even during enthusiastic conversations. The activation level, which is subjectively evaluated by another person, is likely to be lower as well as the automatically estimated value. Therefore, the use of the estimated activation level to control avatars might improve the degree of coincidence between the avatar behavior and the impression induced by the voice. The appropriateness of the automatically estimated activation level needs to be discussed by applying the estimated values to avatar behavior.

The activation levels were estimated on the basis of the subjects' voices during a five-minute conversation. The use of voice for a longer duration imposes a time-delay to the behavioral change of the avatar. The proposed method will adequately reflect the gradual change of the mood in calm conversations. On the other hand, the avatars might not adequately behave during sudden changes in activity level caused by a joke or other factors. However, the shortening of the estimation duration will seriously affect the estimation accuracy. The temporal activation usually disappears during a shorter term. Therefore, the activation level appears to be modeled better by a temporal component and a continuous component. The proposed method appears suitable for the continuous component estimation. The supposed method for using a temporal component is the usage of the initial sound pressure of a responsive utterance, which was utilized for the control of an avatar's smile level [10].

LIMITATIONS
In this study, the experiments were carried out in groups of three people of the same gender. Therefore, the effects of the gender mixture and the number of the participants still need to be studied. A video chat system was used instead of an avatar voice chat system. However, the voice-driven automatic control of nonverbal expressions might affect the turn-taking behaviors of the users. It would be necessary to perform the experiments with an avatar voice chat system. Furthermore, the current study utilized voice data of five-minute intervals for estimation. It theoretically produces a delay in estimation. However, the shortening of the data for the estimation will increase estimation error, which was 18% in this study. The detection of a momentary change of the activation level is the next challenge.

CONCLUSIONS
In this study, we examined the relationship between the conversational activation level and the phonetic and turn-taking features, which were calculated from the voice recordings of the conversations in groups of three persons each. The response latency, the overlap rate and the speech rate showed strong correlation with both the personal and group activation levels. The off-line estimation was performed using a multiple regression equation on the basis of the three indicators. The feasibility of automatically estimating the activation level was demonstrated. The future work is to develop the real-time estimation algorithm and the application to avatar control.

ACKNOWLEDGEMENTS
This work was partly supported by the MEXT Fund for Promoting Research on Symbiotic Information Technology and JSPS KAKENHI.

REFERENCES
1. Bezooyen, R, V.: Characteristics and Recognizability of Vocal Expressions of Emotion, Foris Pubns USA (1984).

2. Boersma, P., and Weenink, D.: Praat: doing phonetics by computer (Version 5.2.21) [Computer program]. Retrieved from http://www.praat.org/.

3. Coleman, R, F., and Williams, R.: Identification of emotional states using perceptual and acoustic analyses, Transcripts of the 8th Symposium on Care of the Professional Voice, The Voice Foundation Vol. 1, pp. 77-83 (1979).

4. Hartmann, B., Mancini, M., and Pelachaud, C.: Implementing Expressive Gesture Synthesis for Embodied Conversational Agents; Gesture Workshop 2005: pp.188-199 (2005).

5. Kato, Y., Kato, S., and Akahori, K.: Effects of emotional cues transmitted in e-mail communication on the emotions experienced by senders and receivers, Computers in Human Behavior, Vol. 23, No. 4, pp.1894-1905 (2007).

6. Kawahara, T., Kawashima, H., Hirayama, T., and Matuyama, R.: "Automated Information Concierge" based on Proactive Dialog and Information Retrieval, Magazine of the Information Processing Society of Japan, Vol. 49, No. 8, pp. 912-918 (2008).

7. Maeda, T., Takashima, K., Kajimura, Y., Yamaguchi, N., Kitamura, Y., Kishino, F., Masda, N., Daibo, I., and Hayashi, Y.: A study of nonverbal cues and atmosphere in three-person conversation (in Japanese), IEICE Technical Report, Vol. 109, No. 457, pp.73-78 (2010).

8. Maeran, O., Piuri, V., and Storti, G. G.: Speech recognition through phoneme segmentation and neural classification, Instrumentation and Measurement Technology Conference, 1997. IMTC/97. Proceedings. "Sensing, Processing, Networking" IEEE, Vol. 2, pp. 1215-1220 (1997).

9. Mehrabian, A.: Nonverbal communication. Aldine-Atherton, Chicago, Illinois (1972).

10. Miyajima, T., Fujita, K.: Control of avatar's facial expression using fundamental frequency and sound pressure in multi-user voice chat system (in Japanese), Trans. Human Interface Society, Vol. 9, No. 4, pp. 503-512 (2007).

11. Moriyama, T., Saito, H., and Ozawa, S.: Evaluation of the Relation between Emotional Concepts and Emotional Parameters in Speech (in Japanese), Trans. IEICE, Vol. J82-DII, No. 4, pp. 703-711 (1999).

12. Murray, I. R., Arnott, J. L.: Toward the simulation of emotion in synthetic speech: A review of the literature on human vocal emotion, J. Acoust. Soc. Am, Vol. 93, No. 2, pp. 1097-1108 (1993).

13. Nishimura, R., Kitaoka, N., and Nakagawa, S.: Analysis of Factors to Make Prosodic Change in Spoken Dialog (in Japanese), Journal of the Phonetic Society of Japan, Vol. 13, No. 3, pp. 66-84 (2009).

14. Nwe, T. L., and Foo, S. W.: Speech emotion recognition using hidden Markov models, Speech Communication, Vol. 41, pp.603-623 (2003).

15. Russell, J. A.: A circumplex model of affect, Journal of Personality and Social Psychology, Vol. 39, pp.1161-1178 (1980).

16. Sacks, H., Schegloff, E., and Jefferson, G.: A Simplest Systematics for the Organization of Turn-Taking for Conversation, Language, Vol. 50, No. 4, pp. 696-765 (1974).

17. Saeki, Y., Tanaka, T. and Fujita, K.: Unified Control of Avatar's Motion Based on Conversation Activity (in Japanese), Correspondences on Human Interface, Vol. 11, No. 2, pp. 71-74 (2009).

18. Second Life Official Site. http://secondlife.com/.

19. Sejima, Y., Ishii, Y., and Watanabe, T.: A Virtual Audience System for Enhancing Embodied Interaction Based on Conversational Activity, Lecture Notes in Computer Science, Vol. 6772, pp. 180-189 (2011).

20. Vargas, F. M.: Louder than words − An Introduction to Nonverbal Communication, Iowa State University Press (1987).

21. Murakami, I., Katou, H., and Watanabe, T.: Patient-Nurse Communication Support System by Using Speech-Driven Embodied Characters Called InterActors (in Japanese), Proceedings of 67th National Convention of IPSJ, pp. 25-26 (2005).

22. Watanabe, T., Okubo, M., Nakashige, M., and Danbara, R.: InterActor: Speech-Driven Embodied Interactive Actor, International Journal of Human-Computer Interaction, Vol. 17, No. 1, pp. 43-60 (2004).

23. Werker, J. F., Pons, F., Dietrich, C., Kaiikawa, S., Fais, L., Amano, S.: Infant-directed speech supports phonetic category learning in English and Japanese, Cognition, Vol. 103, Issue 1, pp. 147-162 (2007).

User-defined Surface+Motion Gestures for 3D Manipulation of Objects at a Distance through a Mobile Device

Hai-Ning Liang[1,2], Cary Williams[2], Myron Semegen[3], Wolfgang Stuerzlinger[4], Pourang Irani[2]

[1] Dept. of Computer Science and Software Engineering
Xi'an Jiatong-Liverpool University, Suzhou, China
haining.liang@xjtlu.edu.cn

[2] Dept. of Computer Science
University of Manitoba, Winnipeg, Canada
umwill22@cc.umanitoba.ca, {haining, irani}@cs.umanitoba.ca

[3] Virtual Reality Centre
Industrial Technology Centre, Winnipeg, Canada
msemegen@itc.mb.ca

[4] Department of Computer Science and Engineering
York University, Toronto, Canada
wolfgang@cse.yorku.ca

ABSTRACT

One form of input for interacting with large shared surfaces is through mobile devices. These personal devices provide interactive displays as well as numerous sensors to effectuate gestures for input. We examine the possibility of using surface and motion gestures on mobile devices for interacting with 3D objects on large surfaces. If effective use of such devices is possible over large displays, then users can collaborate and carry out complex 3D manipulation tasks, which are not trivial to do. In an attempt to generate design guidelines for this type of interaction, we conducted a guessability study with a dual-surface concept device, which provides users access to information through both its front and back. We elicited a set of end-user surface- and motion-based gestures. Based on our results, we demonstrate reasonably good agreement between gestures for choice of sensory (i.e. tilt), multi-touch and dual-surface input. In this paper we report the results of the guessability study and the design of the gesture-based interface for 3D manipulation.

Author Keywords

Motion gestures; surface gestures; input devices; interaction techniques; multi-display environments; mobile devices; 3D visualizations; collaboration interfaces.

ACM Classification Keywords

H.5.2. Information and interfaces and presentation: User Interfaces. Input devices and strategies.

INTRODUCTION

Large displays are becoming more widespread and frequently used in the collaborative analysis and exploration of 3D visualizations. Manipulating 3D visualizations on large displays is not trivial, but present many challenges to designers [5,6,7,18,32]. Researchers have investigated the use

of mobile devices to interact with objects located on distant-shared displays [2,19,20]. However, there is little research on how mobile devices can be used to carry out 3D interactions with objects at a distance. Malik et al. [17] suggest that interacting at a distance using mouse-based input is inefficient when compared to gestural interaction. Aside from being more natural, gesture-based interactions can be learned by observing other users.

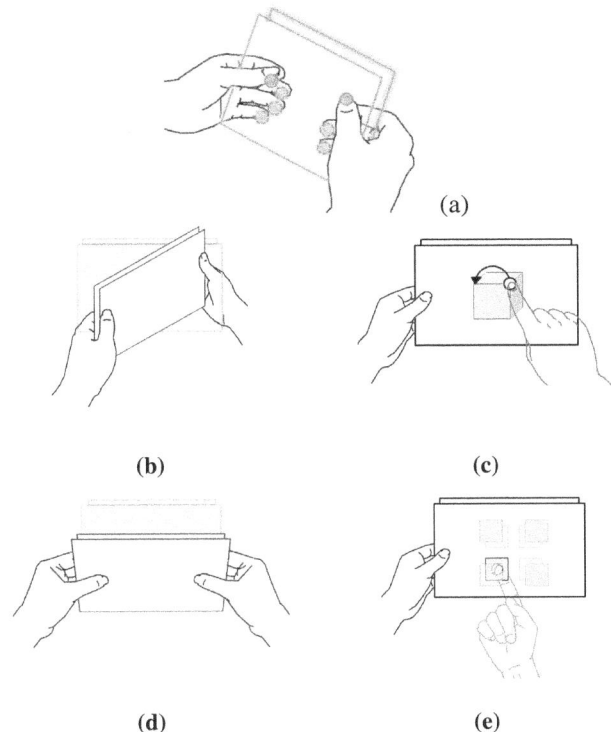

Figure 1. The dual-surface bimanual touch- and motion-enabled concept device (a); different ways of making gestures with the device: (b) rotating along the y-axis (motion-based gesture); (c) rotating along the x-axis (motion-based gesture); (d) rotating along the z-axis through the front-side (surface-based gesture); (e) interacting with a occluded objects through the back-side (surface-based gesture)

Most mobile devices now come with a touch-enabled display which can detect gestures on its surface (i.e., *surface* gestures); furthermore, these devices usually incorporate highly sophisticated sensors (e.g., accelerometers, gyroscope, and orientation registers) which can recognize a variety of motions (i.e., *motion gestures*). The combination of these input capabilities enables users to express a rich set of gestural language for enhanced interaction with the mobile devices themselves [26] but also with other types of systems, such as a tabletop or wall display [2,19].

In this work, we develop a set of gestures that are easy to learn and use for 3D manipulations of distant objects via a mobile device. Gestures can be surface-based (e.g., sliding of a finger on the touch-sensitive display) and/or motion-based (e.g., shaking the device). Wobbrock et al. [39], proposed a set of *surface gestures* for tabletop systems, using a participatory approach to elicit a set of user-defined gestures. They subsequently showed that the user-specified set was easier for users to master [22]. Ruiz et al. [26] followed Wobbrock and Morris' approach and developed a user-defined set of *motion gestures* to operate mobile phones (e.g., answering a call, hanging up, etc.).

Inspired by the work of Wobbrock et al. and Ruiz et al., we developed a user-defined gesture set. We targeted 3D manipulations performed at a distance and integrated both surface and motion types of gestures—an area with little development. In this work, we addressed two research questions: (1) if users have access to more input degrees-of-freedom (multi-touch, dual-touch, and tilt), will they actually make use and benefit from them?; (2) do users have consensus as to what kinds of surface and motion gestures are natural for 3D manipulations via a mobile device? To answer these questions, we developed an experimental prototype (see Figure 1) which enables surface gestures through both the back and front sides of a tablet and can sense multiple, simultaneous finger movements. The device also detects changes in orientation, allowing users to express commands using motion. The combination of dual-surface input with simultaneous motion input can allow users varied ways of expressing gestures.

In the following sections we describe in more detail the background of our work, our experimental setup and our findings. We also elaborate on a design and a preliminary study of a potential interface for 3D manipulation.

RELATED WORK
Our work builds upon prior research on back- and front-side two-handed (or dual-surface bimanual) interaction, user-defined gestures, interaction at a distance with mobile devices, multi-display environments, and 3D interaction.

Dual-surface and bimanual interaction
The prototype (see Figure 1) used to elicit user-preferred gestures was influenced by research on back- and front-of-device, two-handed (bimanual), and dual-surface interaction.

Back-of-device interaction has been explored for mobile devices, particularly for mobile phones [1,28,29,36,41]. This type of interaction allows users to use the back-side of a device as an additional input space. RearType [28], for example, enable users to perform text-entry activities by placing a key pad on the back. HybridTouch [31] and Yang et al's prototype [41] have a trackpad mounted on the back of the PDA to enable gesture-based commands for tasks such as scrolling and steering, while Wobbrock et al. [40] suggest that such a trackpad will let users perform gestures to input unistroke alphabet letters.

Some back-of-device input enabled prototypes emphasize the use of one hand, while others require users to use both hands—i.e., in a bimanual mode. One of the benefits of bimanual interaction is the division of labor to perform simultaneous tasks. For example, Silfverberg et al.'s prototype [29] has two trackpads on the back, one for each hand, so that one hand can be delegated to zooming and the other hand to panning actions. Similarly, users need two hands to input text from a keyboard placed on the back-side in RearType [28].

Bimanual interaction is also common when interacting through the front of touch-enabled mobile devices. Touch Projector [2], a system that enables users to interact with remote screens through their mobile devices, require users to employ both hands, one for aiming at and selecting a distant device (e.g., a wall display or tabletop) and the other for manipulating objects. Researchers have claimed that two-handed interaction is more efficient, cognitively less demanding, and more aligned with natural practices than its one-handed counterpart [2,13,36].

Researchers have experimented using both sides of a device to enable input—hence, *dual-surface* input [36,41]. Yang et al. [41] have showed that *one-handed* operations can be enhanced with synchronized interactions using the back and front of a mobile device in target selection and steering tasks. Similarly, for *bimanual* operations, Wigdor et al. [36], using their *LucidTouch* dual-surface prototype, have demonstrated that users found favorable the additional dimension of back-side input because, among other things, it enabled them to interact using all of their fingers. Our dual-surface prototype was inspired by such systems that enable back-side input.

Surface and motion gestures
Aside from touch-enabled displays, current mobile devices come with other sensors which can detect motion and orientation changes. Given these capabilities, Ruiz et al. [26] have categorized gestures that these mobile devices can perform into two groups: (1) *surface* gestures and (2) *motion* gestures.

Surface gestures are carried out on the touch-enabled screen and are primarily two-dimensional. These gestures have frequently been studied in multi-touch tabletop systems (e.g., [8,10,22,39]). Morris et al. [20], from an evaluation of a multi-user photo application, have identified a classification, or 'design space,' for collaborative gestures with seven axes: symmetry, parallelism, proxemics distance, additivity, identity-awareness, number of users, and number of devices. For single tabletop users, Wobbrock et al. [38] present a taxonomy of gestures and a set of user-specified gestures derived from observing how 20 users would perform gestures for varied tasks. Surface gestures on mobile devices have also been a theme of intense study. Bragdon et al. [3] have found that, in the presence of distractors, gestures offer better performance and also reduced attentional load. Techniques, such as Gesture Avatar [16] and Gesture Search [14], show that gestures can support fast, easy target selection and data access. Gestures can also increase the usability and accessibility of mobile devices to blind people [12].

Motion gestures, on the other hand, are performed by translating or rotating the device in 3D space. These gestures have been studied for different tasks, such as to input text [10,23,34], to validate users' identity [15] and to navigate an information space [25]. Because of its wide availability, tilt has been often explored more than other types of motions. Current mobile devices allow for a rich set of motions. Ruiz et al. [26] provide a taxonomy of motion gestures, which has two main dimensions: *gesture mapping* and *physical characteristics*. Gesture mapping refers to the manner by which users map gestures to device commands and depends on the *nature*, *context* and *temporal* aspects of the motion. Physical characteristics, on the other hand, deal with the nature of the gestures themselves: the *kinetic impulse* of the motion, along what *dimension* or axes the motion occurs, and how *complex* the motion is. Ruiz et al.'s taxonomy was formulated based on a guessability study, similar to Wobbrock et al.'s study [39]. From the study, they also developed a user-inspired set of motion gestures.

To the best of our knowledge, there has not been any published research examining surface and motion gestures for dual-surface mobile devices in the content of manipulating 3D objects from a distance.

Interaction at a distance

Interaction at a distance occurs due to the unavailability of touch and unreachability of certain regions of a display. Large displays are affected by these issues, as users and the display could be separated at various distances [34]. One solution that has been proposed is to bring the content closer to the user by coupling a hand-held mobile device to the large display [2,19,20,]. Given that mobile devices also have a display, they can show a scaled-down version of the complete version shown in the large display, or as Stoakley et al. [30] would have called it a *'world in miniature'*. The coupling between the two displays can bring several benefits. It allows users to be more mobile, especially in the case of tabletops, because they do not need to touch the table surface during interaction. In addition, it supports *direct and indirect input*. Users can manipulate the content by

interacting through the small device and see the effects on the large display (i.e., *indirect input*) or they can interact with the small device and observe what happens to the content on the small device itself (i.e., *direct input*). Furthermore, the small device can provide some *'personal'* or *'private'* viewing and input space only to one user—something often not available or not possible to have on large displays.

3D manipulation on 2D surfaces

Manipulating 3D object on multi-touch surfaces is non-trivial and different solutions have been proposed [4,7,8,9,18,33,37]. Davidson and Han [4] have suggested that objects' movement in the z-axis could be achieved using pressure. With Hancock et al.'s technique, Shallow-Depth [7], users can perform rotation and translation movements with a single finger, but 3D operations (such as rolling and pitch) will require two different touches, one for selecting the object and the other for gesturing. Another technique, Sticky Tools [8,33], need the users to first define a rotational axis using two fingers and then using a third finger to do rotation motions. The movement along the z-axis in both Shallow-Depth and Sticky Tools involves using a pinching gesture. Studies show that both techniques could be learned; however, they cannot be considered *'natural'* [9]. Hilliges et al. [9] and Reisman et al. [24] suggest that a more natural way of manipulating 3D objects in multi-touch surfaces is to simulate how people interact with physical objects—for example, by allowing these objects to be 'picked up' off the surface. However, understanding how the technique works is not easy because of ambiguity issues.

These proposed solutions could be categorized into two groups. The first concerns providing users with more degrees-of-freedom (e.g., [8]), while the second with offering users interactions that are natural (e.g., [9,24]). Our work is inspired by both these groups. We use a prototype which allows for a large number of degrees-of-freedom and types of input mechanisms so that we can assess whether and how they are used; and, we also develop natural interactions through a user-elicitation study with our prototype.

User-elicitation studies

A common approach to conceptualizing new interaction techniques is through *user-elicitation*, an important component of *participatory* design [27]. User-elicitation or *guessability* studies have been used by Wobbrock et al. [39] to develop their set of *surface gestures for tabletops* and by Ruiz et al. [26] to inform the design of their set of *motion gestures for smartphones*. The idea underlying a guessability study [38] is to observe what actions users will follow given the effect of a gesture (i.e., asking users to provide the *cause* for the *effect*); then, from observations across a group of users, find whether there are patterns and consensus about how a gesture is performed. In line with Wobbrock et al. and Ruiz et al., we have also developed a user-defined surface and motion gesture set by employing a user-elicitation guessability study, which we describe next.

DEVELOPING A USER-DEFINED GESTURE SET FOR A DUAL-SURFACE AND MOTION INPUT DEVICE

Our primary goal was to elicit user-defined gestures using our bimanual dual-surface tablet device (see Figure 1). The secondary goal was to identify which of the following sensory input users would employ most: (1) *Front-side* multi-touch surface; (2) *Back-side* multi-touch surface; (3) *Gyroscope* (for orientation); and/or (4) *Accelerometer* (for tilt).

Participants and apparatus

We recruited 12 participants (10 male) from a local university between the ages of 22 to 35. All participants had some experience with touch-based mobile devices.

Our experimental prototype was a dual-surface device created by putting back-to-back two Acer Iconia tablets running Android OS. The prototype had a 10.1" multi-touch surface on the front and back and connected through a wireless network. Each tablet supported up to ten touches simultaneously and came with an accelerometer and gyroscope. Users could perform *surface* gestures by moving (sliding) one finger or a set of fingers; whereas *motion* gestures were performed through rotating (rolling, pitching, or yawing) the dual-surface device. The device allowed immediate visual feedback of all users' touches on the front surface of the device

Task

Participants were asked to design and perform a gesture (surface, motion, or a hybrid of the two) via the dual-surface device (a *cause*) that they could potential use to carry out the task (an *effect*). There were 14 different tasks (see Table 1). We asked participants to do a gesture twice and explain why they chose the gesture. Participants were not told of the difference between surface and motion gesture, but only asked to perform a gesture that they feel comfortable doing.

Procedure

Each participant was asked to define a set of gestures for the above listed 14 different 3D manipulations using the dual-surface device. Participants were then handed the device so that they could get a feel for it; they began the experiment when ready.

The 14 manipulations were graphically demonstrated via 3D animations on the front display of the device. After an animation was run once, the researcher would explain the task for clarity. The animation could be replayed as many times as needed. The participant was then asked to create a gesture to effectuate the effect seen in the animation. This could be with whichever sensory input they wanted and in whatever manner they wished. While creating their gesture, the participant was asked to think aloud. Afterward s/he was asked to sketch or write a short description of the gesture on paper. This process was repeated for all 14 manipulation animations.

3D Manipulation Tasks	
Manipulation	Animation Descriptions
Rotation	
About *X* Axis	Rotate the cube so that the **top face** is facing **forward**
About *Y* Axis	Rotate the cube so that the **left face** is facing **forward**
About *Z* Axis	Rotate the cube so that the **top-right** corner becomes the **top-left** corner
Translation	
Along *X* Axis	Move the **red** cube **beside** the **blue** cube (i.e., red cube left side of blue cube)
Along *Y* Axis	Move the **red** cube **on top** of the **blue** cube
Along *Z* Axis	Move or push the **red** cube **back** towards the **blue** cube
Stretch	
Along *X* Axis	Stretch the cube **horizontally** to the **right**
Along *Y* Axis	Stretch the cube **vertically up**
Along *Z* Axis	Stretch the cube by **pulling** the cube **forwards**
Plane Slicing	
XZ plane	Cut the cube into an **upper and lower** portion
YZ plane	Cut the cube into an **left and right** portion
XY pane	Cut the cube into an **front and back** portion
Selection	
2D	Select the cube in the **top-left** corner
3D	Select the cube in the **back bottom-left** corner, hidden behind the front bottom left cube

Table 1. The 3D tasks given to participants by category.

Results

From the collected gestures, we were able to create a set of gestures that seemed natural to users. We grouped identical gestures for each task, and the largest group was chosen as the user-defined gesture for the task. The set composed of the largest group for each task represents the *user-defined gesture set*. We then calculated an agreement score [38,39,26] for each task using the group size. The score reflects in one number the degree of consensus among participants. The formula for calculating the agreement scores is:

$$A_t = \sum_{P_i} \left(\frac{P_i}{P_t} \right)^2$$

where t is a task in the set for all tasks T; P_t is the set of proposed gestures for t; and P_i is a subset of identical gestures from P_t. the range for A_t is between 0 and 1 inclusive. As an example let us assume that for a task, four participants gave each a gesture, but only two are very similar. Then, the agreement score for that task would be calculated according to Figure 2.

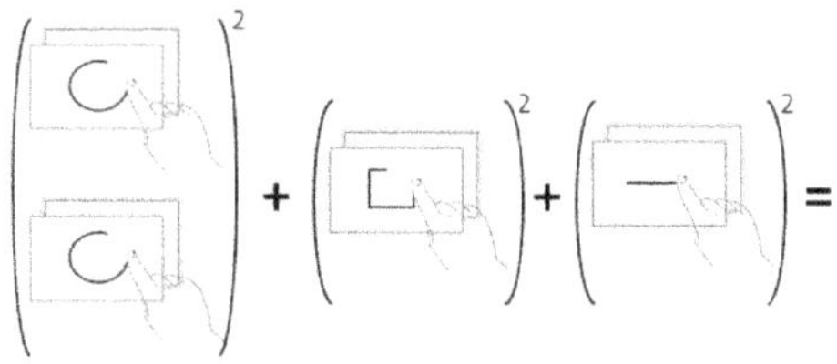

$$A_t = (2/4)^2 + (1/4)^2 + (1/4)^2 = 0.375$$

Figure 2. Example of an agreement score calculation for a task.

Figure 3 shows the agreement scores for the gesture set, ordered in descending order. The highlighted square shows the gestures with relatively high agreement scores. The scores involving the Z Axis are located at the lower end, indicating a lower consensus. Figure 4 (next page) shows the resulting 3D gestures from the user study and obtained from the agreement scores.

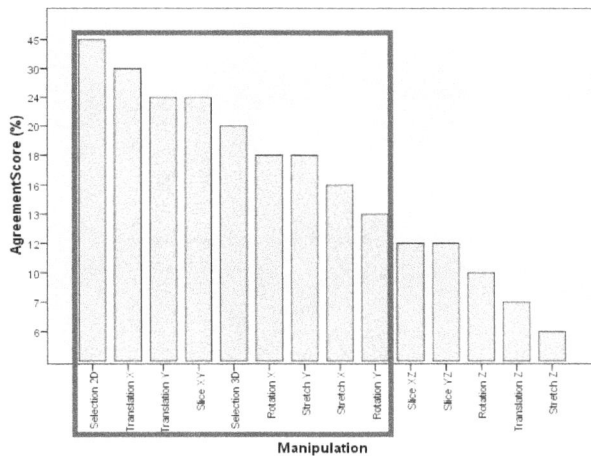

Figure 3. Agreement scores for all tasks sorted in descending order.

Figure 5 shows the user-defined gestures grouped by the sensory input used. Participants were allowed to use compound gestures. For example, to move an object along the Z Axis, some participants asked if they could rotate the entire scene and then perform a gesture along the X or Y axes to obtain the same result. The yellow cells correspond to inter-

actions with equal agreement scores for a given input method. The front-side surface seems to be most frequently used input modality, followed by both tilt and orientation+front surface, and finally by back-side surface.

	Rotation X	Rotation Y	Rotation Z	Translation X	Translation Y	Translation Z	Stretching X	Stretching Y	Stretching Z	Slicing XZ	Slicing YZ	Slicing XY	Selection 2D	Selection 3D
Front Surface				X	X	X		X	X		X	X		X	
Back Surface														X
Tilt	X	X			X									
Orientation + Front S.					X			X			X			

Note:
⬜ Equal Agreement Scores

Figure 5. Gestures grouped by sensory input.

Discussion

From Figure 3, we observe that the agreement scores are high for tasks related to the X and Y axes, unlike the scores for tasks in the Z Axis. This shows that gestures along the Z Axis are difficult to perform. We observed that if a participant could not think of a gesture for manipulating the 3D object along the Z Axis, they would ask if the scene could be rotated in order to perform the manipulation using a gesture along the X and Y axes.

Figure 5 appears to suggest that participants preferred using *surface* gestures over *motion* gestures. However, Figure 4 indicates that participants also made use of motion gestures, especially for rotation tasks and tasks dealing with the Z Axis. During the study, we observed that most participants did not like to make large movements with the dual-surface device to create gestures. This shows that, although participants can make use of motion gestures, there seemed to be some hesitation, perhaps due to their unfamiliarity with motion gestures or maybe because the relatively large size of the device made it more difficult to perform motions with it.

From figures 4 and 5, we can see that most gestures were carried out on the front-side of the dual-surface device. That is, the front-side was the *main* input space. Figure 5 shows that the back-side was not used frequently. The few gestures that were performed on the back were unique among participants, and they therefore produced low agreement scores (see Figure 3).

There is one observation that the figures 3-5 do not show and that is that participants would touch (or begin to make a gesture from certain regions on or around the object (in our case a cube) to perform interactions. For example, to stretch along the X Axis, many participants would usually begin by touching the midpoint of the object's left and right edges. The same pattern was found for other tasks, especially those with high agreement scores (see Figure 6 for other tasks).

Rotation

About X Axis
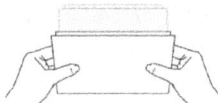
Flick forward then back

About Y Axis
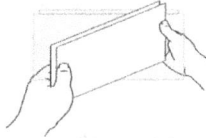
Flick left side forward then back

About Z Axis
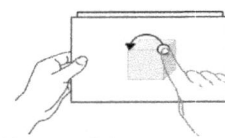
Move top-left corner to top-left

Translation

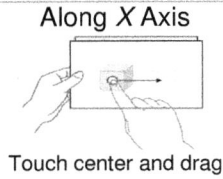

Along X Axis
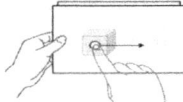
Touch center and drag

Along Y Axis
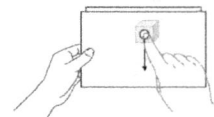
Touch center and drag

Along Z Axis
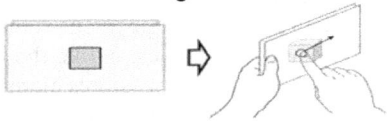
Rotate device to alter view, then touch and drag

OR

Along Z Axis

Rotate object, then touch center and drag

Stretch

Along X Axis
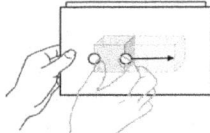
Anchor one edge and pull the other edge

Along Y Axis
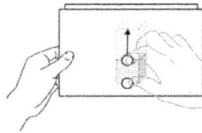
Anchor one edge and pull the other edge

Along Z Axis
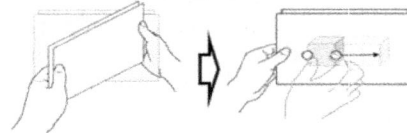
Rotate object, then anchor one edge and pull the other edge

Plane slicing

XZ Plane
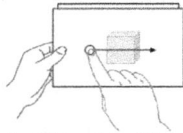
Start off the object the slice through

YZ Plane
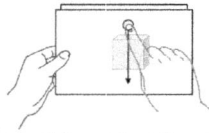
Start off the object the slice through

XY Plane
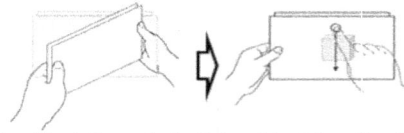
Rotate object, then start off the object the slice through

Selection

2D
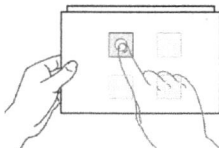
Tap object on front surface

3D
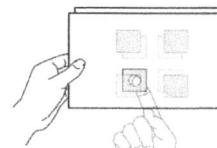
Tap object from back surface

Figure 4. Resulting user-defined gesture set.

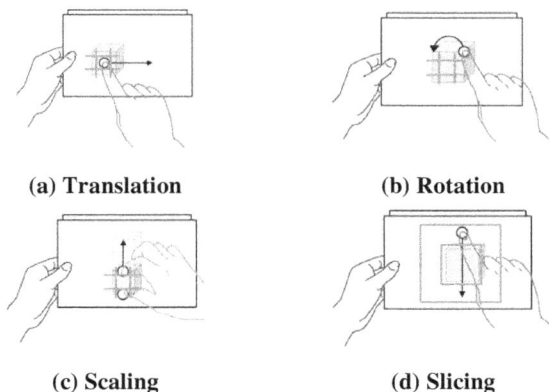

(a) Translation   (b) Rotation

(c) Scaling   (d) Slicing

Figure 6. Specific manipulation regions for four tasks.

SQUAREGRIDS: AN INTERFACE FOR 3D MANIPULATION THROUGH GESTURES

From the above experiment, we observed that (1) participants preferred to perform actions on the *front-side* of the dual-surface device; (2) they preferred to enact *surface* gestures along the X and Y axes; and (3) they touched specific regions (or 'hotspots') on virtual objects when performing gestures. These findings led us to modify our experimental device and design a new interface for 3D manipulation, SquareGrids (Figure 7).

Figure 7. SquareGrids: A potential interface for 3D manipulations of distant objects.

SquareGrids used a single-sided multi-touch tablet with a accelerometer and gyroscope. Based on the gesture-input mappings obtained from the first experiment, the touch surface and the accelerometer were used as the primary input mechanisms. In addition, a new graphical interface was developed for the tablet based on the hotspots touched by users when manipulating objects.

The interface was partitioned into 3 major regions, *on-object*, *off-object* and *environment* manipulations (Figure 8). The center of the interface consisted of a 3×3 grid representing the nine regions (or hotspots) that map to the 3D object designated for *on-object* interactions (Region 1 in Figure 9). The middle region (Region 2; area contained

within the orange box but outside of the 3×3 grid) was an area designated for *off-object* interactions. A combination of *off-* and *on-object* interactions could be defined. For instance, most participants preferred to start the plane slicing gesture just outside the 3D object's boundaries then slice through the object (see Figure 4 plane slicing). Outside the orange box was a region for *environment* interactions (Region 3). If gestures were performed in this region, a user can manipulate the entire 3D scene (e.g., changing the camera's point of view).

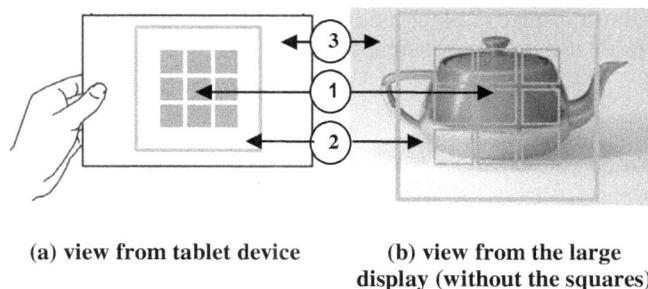

(a) view from tablet device   (b) view from the large display (without the squares)

Figure 8. Mapping of the three main regions (for (1) *on-object*, (2) *off-object*, (3) *environment* manipulations) of the SqureGrids interface (a) to a 3D object displayed on other screen (b).

Each region and their subdivision were assigned an ID (see Figure 9a). As users drag their fingers across the regions of the interface to perform a gesture, a sequence of numbers would be generated. For instance, the gesture in Figure 9b would generate the number sequences 2, -1, 0. As the gesture is being performed, the gesture recognition engine then checks the number sequence against a set of predefined gesture sequences. Once the engine recognizes the gesture, the correct 3D transformation is invoked. The gesture would continue until the user stopped the gesture motion.

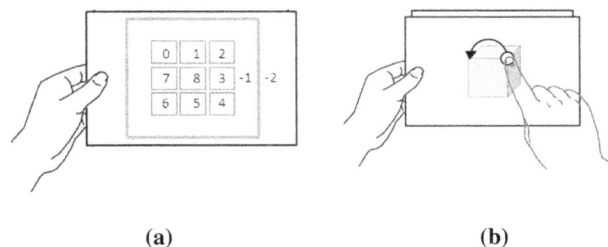

(a)   (b)

Figure 9. (a) assignment of ID numbers to reach region; (b) a user performing a gesture with sequence 2, -1, 0.

User evaluation of SquareGrids

A preliminary usability study was conducted to assess the performance of new interface against the traditional mouse for 3D manipulations.

Participants, apparatus, and task

Six male participants between the ages of 23 and 35 were recruited from a local university to participate in this study.

All participants used computers on a daily basis and are familiar with touch-based mobile devices.

To conduct this experiment we used a desktop computer (with 1.86 GHz Core 2 Duo running Windows XP) with a regular USB mouse and connected to a 24" LCD monitor. In addition, we had a laptop (with 2.0 GHz Dual Core and an Intel GMA running Windows XP) connected to another 24" LCD monitor which was linked to the mobile device prototype via a wireless network.

The task was to manipulate a solid red block by rotating, scaling and/or slicing it so that it would match in size a semi-transparent block and then dock the solid red block inside the semi-transparent block (Figure 10).

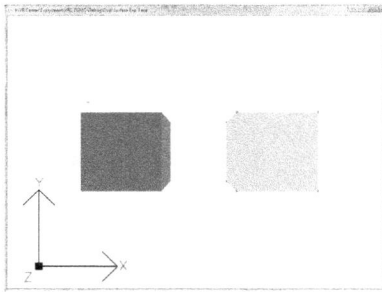

Figure 10. The 3D manipulation task: (1) match the left solid to the right solid in terms of size; (2) move the left solid inside the right solid

Conditions and procedure
This study compared two interfaces: *Mouse* (GUI-based interactions) and *Tablet* (with *SquareGrids*). In the Mouse condition participants interacted with a toolbar to select the manipulation mode and handles on the 3D object to interact with it. In the Tablet condition, participants interact with the 3D object via SquareGrids.

Each trial consisted of these tasks: *Rotation*, *Scaling* or *Plane Slicing* of the 3D object, followed by *Translation* of the object to dock it inside the semitransparent solid.

We first explain how each of the two interfaces would work and then gave participants practice trials (3 for Translation; 3 for Rotate+Translate; 3 for Scale+Translate; and 3 for Slice+Translate). In the actual experiment, participant repeated the same type of tasks, but these were slightly more complicated. The experiment lasted an hour.

We used a within-subject design. The independent variables were *Interface* (*Mouse* and *Tablet*) and *Task Type*. The order of the presentation of the interface was counterbalanced using a Latin Square design.

Results
Results indicated that participants completed the manipulation and docking tasks faster with the traditional mouse and GUI. These results could be partly due to the fact that most

users were familiar with this type of interface because of frequent use.

However, participants commented that they enjoyed using the tablet interface more than the mouse interface and could see themselves using the interface in future applications. One interesting observation was that participants only needed to look at the user-defined gesture set (from Experiment 1) once or twice at the initial stages of the study. That is, the Tablet interface was easy to learn and use. This was supported by participants' comments (e.g., "the interface was intuitive to use.").

DISCUSSION
Implications for user interfaces
A few implications can be derived from this work. First, more modalities may not be better. As our study results suggest, despite the availability of sensors which can detect motion (both tilt and rotation), users have difficulty performing these types of actions. The size of our device could have affected users in making motion-based gestures, and a smaller device (e.g., a smartphone) would perhaps lend itself better in supporting motions. Therefore, when dealing with tablets of 10.1" or greater in size, designers should minimize the use of motion gestures. Second, although research has shown that the back-side could enrich users' interactive experiences, our results show that users, given the choice of using the front-side, will try to minimize their use of the back-side. Such is the case despite the fact that the back-side would have enabled them to use several fingers simultaneously, potentially facilitating concurrent operations. As such, designers should perhaps maximize the use of the front-side. Third, we observed that even using the front-side, users would barely rely on multiple fingers to issue gestures. This observation indicates that users may have difficulty employing multiple touches at once, and therefore designers should be careful when designing gestures based on multi-finger operations using a 10.1" handheld tablet.

Limitations and future work
We conducted our guessability study with a mobile device of one size only. This may have influenced the types of gestures participants would make. A future line of exploration is to assess whether we can obtain the same or similar set of gestures with devices of smaller sizes, perhaps between 3.5 to 5" (the range of sizes of smartphones).

In addition, our guessability study was performed mainly with one object being displayed. We cannot be certain that we will obtain the same results if we have more than one 3D object on the screen. For instance, if objects are dense or the view shows 2 objects side-by-side, a swipe may instead affect more than one object, an operation which may not be desired. Only further research can help us come to a more definite conclusion.

Finally, related to the previous point, selection of an occluded object required participants to know in advance where the object was hidden and that there was only one object hidden by the occluding object. If there were more than one hidden object, we may not have arrived at such high agreement scores for selection operations in 3D selection. However, only further research will be able to tell us how different the gestures across users could be for these selection tasks.

SUMMARY

In this paper, we describe a guessability study to elicit a set of user-defined surface and motion gestures for a mobile device to support 3D manipulations of distant objects. The results show that there is a broad agreement in user gestures to carry out actions dealing with the X and Y axes, whereas there is a wide disagreement of those actions concerning the Z Axis. In addition, our observations indicate that users would likely prefer to use the front-side of a device than its back-side to perform gestures. Furthermore, observations suggest that users may be more readily able to use surface gestures than motion gestures. Finally, we provide a potential interface derived from our observations and describe a user study with the device. Our results suggest that the interface could be easy to learn and use and enables the performance of 3D tasks with a simple interface.

ACKNOWLEDGMENTS

We thank the participants for their time. We would also like to thank the reviewers for their comments and suggestions which have helped to improve the quality of the paper. We acknowledge NSERC and the Virtual Reality Centre for partially funding this project.

REFERENCES

1. Baudisch, P. and Chu, G. (2009). Back-of-device Interaction allows creating very small touch devices. CHI'09. pp. 1923 - 1932.

2. Boring, S., Baur, D., Butz, A., Gustafson, S., and Baudisch, P. (2010). Touch Projector: Mobile Interaction Through Video. CHI'10, pp. 2287-2296.

3. Bragdon, A., Nelson, E., Li, Y., and Hinckley, K. (2011). Experimental Analysis of Touch-Screen Gesture Designs in Mobile Environments. CHI'11, pp. 403-412.

4. Davidson, P. L. and Han, J. Y. (2008). Extending 2D object arrangement with pressure-sensitive layering cues. UIST'08, pp. 87-90.

5. Grossman, T., Balakrishnan, R., Kurtenbach, G., Fitzmaurice, G.W., Khan, A., and Buxton, W. (2001). Interaction techniques for 3D modeling on large displays. I3DG'01, pp. 17-23.

6. Grossman, T. and Wigdor, D. (2007). Going Deeper: a Taxonomy of 3D on the Tabletop. Proc. IEEE International Workshop on Horizontal Interactive Human-Computer Systems, pp. 137-144.

7. Hancock, M., Carpendale, S., and Cockburn, A. (2007). Shallow-depth 3d interaction: design and evaluation of one-, two- and three-touch techniques. CHI'07, pp. 1147-1156.

8. Hancock, M., ten Cate, T. and Carpendale, S. (2009). Sticky Tools: Full 6DOF Force-Based Interaction for Multi-Touch Tables. ITS'09, pp. 145-152.

9. Hilliges, O., Izadi, S., Wilson, A. D., Hodges, S., Garcia-Mendoza, A., and But, A. (2009). Interactions in the Air: Adding Further Depth to Interactive Tabletops. UIST'09, pp. 139-147.

10. Hinrichs, U. and Carpendale, S. (2011). Gestures in the Wild: Studying Multi-Touch GestureSequences on Interactive Tabletop Exhibits. CHI '11, pp. 3023-3032.

11. Jones, E., Alexander, J., Andreou, A., Irani, P., and Subramanian, S. (2010). GesText: Accelerometer-Based Gestural Text-Entry Systems. CHI '10, pp. 2173-2182.

12. Kane, S.K., Bigham, J.P. and Wobbrock, J.O. (2008). Slide Rule: Making mobile touch screens accessible to blind people using multi-touch interaction techniques. ASSETS '08, pp. 73-80.

13. Kin, K., Hartmann, B., and Agrawala, M. (2011). Two-handed marking menus for multitouch devices. ACM Trans on CHI, 18(3), 1-23.

14. Li, Y. (2010). Gesture Search: A Tool for Fast Mobile Data Access. UIST'10, pp. 87-96.

15. Liu, J., Zhong, L., Wickramasuriya, J., and Vasudevan, V. (2009). User evaluation of lightweight user authentication with a single tri-axis accelerometer. MobileHCI '09, pp. 1-10.

16. Lu, H. and Li, Y. (2011). Gesture Avatar: A Technique for Operating Mobile User Interfaces Using Gestures. CHI'11, pp. 207-216.

17. Malik, S., Ranjan, A., and Balakrishnan, R. (2005). Interacting with large displays from a distance with vision-tracked multi-finger gestural input. UIST'05 pp. 43-52.

18. Martinet, A., Casiez, G., and Grisoni, L. (2010). The effect of DOF separation in 3D manipulation tasks with multi-touch displays. VRST '10, pp. 111-118.

19. McAdam, C & Brewster, S. (2011). Using mobile phones to interact with tabletop computers. ITS'11, p. 232-241.

20. McCallum, D.C. and Irani, P. (2009). ARC-Pad: absolute+relative cursor positioning for large displays with a mobile touchscreen. UIST '09, pp. 153-156.

21. Morris, M.R., Huang, A., Paepcke, A., and Winograd, T. (2006). Cooperative Gestures: Multi-User Gestural Interactions for Co-located Groupware. CHI'06, pp. 1201-1210.

22. Morris, M.R., Wobbrock, J., and Wilson, A. (2010). Understanding Users' Preferences for Surface Gestures. GI'10, pp. 261-268.

23. Partridge, K., Chatterjee, S., Sazawal, V., Borriello, G., and Want, R. (2002). TiltType: accelerometer-supported text entry for very small devices. UIST '02, pp. 201-204.

24. Reisman, J.L., Davidson, P.L., and Han, J.Y. (2009). A screen-space formulation for 2D and 3D direct manipulation. UIST '09, pp. 69-78.

25. Rekimoto, J. (1996) Tilting operations for small screen interfaces. UIST '96, pp. 167-168.

26. Ruiz, J., Li, Y., and Lank. E. (2011). User-Defined Motion Gestures for Mobile Interaction. CHI'11, pp. 197-206.

27. Schuler, D. (1993). Participatory design: principles and practices. L. Erlbaum Associates, Hillsdale N.J., 1993

28. Scott, J., Izadi, S., Rezai, L. S., Ruszkowski, D., Bi, X., and Balakrishnan, R. (2010). RearType: Text Entry Using Keys on the Back of a Device. MobileHCI'10. pp. 171-180.

29. Silfverberg, M., Korhonen, P., and MacKenzie,I.S. (2006). Zoomig and panning content on a display screen. United States patent 7075513, July 11, 2006.

30. Stoakley, R., Conway, M.J., and Pausch, R. (1995). Virtual reality on a WIM: interactive worlds in miniature. CHI'95, pp. 265-272.

31. Sugimoto, M. and Hiroki, K. (2006). HybridTouch: an intuitive manipulation technique for pdas using their front and rear surfaces. Extended Abstracts of MobileHCI'06. pp. 137-140.

32. Valkov, D., Steinicke, F., Bruder, G., and Hinrichs, K.H. (2011). 2D Touching of 3D Stereoscopic Objects. CHI'11, pp. 1353-1362.

33. Vlaming, L., Collins, C., Hancock, M., Nacenta, M., Isenberg, T. and Carpendale, S. (2012). Integrating 2D mouse emulation with 3D manipulation for visualizations on a multi-touch table. ITS'10, pp. 221-230.

34. Vogel, D. and Balakrishnan, R. (2004). Interactive public ambient displays: transitioning from implicit to explicit, public to personal, interaction with multiple users. UIST'04 , pp. 137-146.

35. Wigdor, D. and Balakrishnan, R. (2003). TiltText: Using tilt for text input to mobile phones. UIST '03, pp. 81-90.

36. Wigdor, D., Forlines, C., Baudisch, P., Barnwell, J., and Shen, C. (2007). LucidTouch: A See-through Mobile Device. UIST'07. pp. 269-278.

37. Wilson, A., Izadi, S., Hilliges, O., Garcia-Mendoza, A., and Kirk, D. (2008). Bringing physics to the surface. UIST'08, pp. 67-76.

38. Wobbrock, J.O., Aung, H.H., Rothrock, B., and Myers, B.A. (2005). Maximizing the guessability of symbolic input. CHI '05 Extended Abstracts, 1869.

39. Wobbrock, J.O., Morris, M.R. and Wilson, A.D. (2009). User-defined gestures for surface computing. CHI'09, pp. 1083-1092.

40. Wobbrock, J. O., Myers, B. A., and Aung, H. H. (2008). The performance of hand postures in front- and back-of-device interaction for mobile computing. IJHCS. v66 (12), pp. 857-875.

41. Yang, X. D., Mak, E., Irani, P., and Bischof, W. F. (2009). Dual-Surface Input: Augmenting One-Handed Interaction with Coordinated Front and Behind-the-Screen Input. MobileHCI'09. pp. 1-10.

An Exploration of Interaction Styles in Mobile Devices for Navigating 3D Environments

Hai-Ning Liang[1,2], James Trenchard[2], Myron Semegen[3], Pourang Irani[2]

[1] Dept. of Computer Science and Software Engineering
Xi'an Jiatong-Liverpool University, Suzhou, China
haining.liang@xjtlu.edu.cn

[2] Dept. of Computer Science
University of Manitoba, Winnipeg, Canada
umtrench@cc.umanitoba.ca, {haining, irani}@cs.umanitoba

[3] Virtual Reality Centre
Industrial Technology Centre, Winnipeg, Canada
msemegen@itc.mb.ca

ABSTRACT

Large displays are becoming more ubiquitous, but often only present passive information to passerby (e.g., about the 3D layouts and maps of buildings). To improve users' experience, museums and similar places could have a system where users would be able to interactively navigate maps of these public, large buildings to browse quickly what is available and plan their trips so that they are efficient and more enjoyable. Personal touch-based mobile devices can be used effectively as input devices, allowing for opportunistic and serendipitous user interaction. In this paper, we explore the coupling of mobile devices to large displays. We present three interaction styles that enable users to navigate in 3D environments and describe the result of a usability study with the three styles. The results of our study indicate that users prefer a combination of two styles, one supporting discrete, precise motions and the other fluid, continuous movements.

Author Keywords

Large displays; 3D navigation; mobile devices; interaction techniques; virtual environments.

ACM Classification Keywords

H.5.2. Information interfaces and presentation (e.g., HCI): User Interfaces – *input devices and strategies; interaction styles*.

General Terms

Design, Experimentation, Human Factors.

INTRODUCTION

Large displays are becoming more ubiquitous and can be seen in many public venues such as museums, libraries, malls, and airports. In parallel, smartphones are also becoming de facto pervasive personal devices [3]. On the

one hand, we have large displays which are often broadcasters of passive information to passersby; and, on the other hand, we have smartphones which now come with highly sophisticated sensing capabilities (e.g., a multi-touch display, accelerometer, and other orientation registers). The combination of large displays and mobile devices, one to output information and the other to input commands, can be an ideal 'marriage' [14] that enables spontaneous, opportunistic, and serendipitous interaction [2,4,6].

In this work, we explore the coupling of large displays and mobile devices to support the navigation within 3D virtual environments. In particular, we aim to explore what types of interaction styles designed for a touch-enabled mobile (a smartphone) are more conducive to enhanced 3D navigation. This work is motivated by research in *large displays, navigation in 3D environments* and *use of mobile phones as input devices*, which we review briefly next.

Interacting with public large displays

In the context of large displays, input technologies and interaction techniques remain one of the biggest challenges [9]. Direct touch and using device-free gestures are two common ways of allowing interaction with large displays [11,16]. Direct touch, however, is not scalable given that some displays are beyond users' reach, may be unsanitary, and cannot extend to multiple users; while gestures (and also speech) may not be feasible in audibly and visually noisy public environments [2].

Navigating 3D environments in large displays

Spatial navigation is concerned with the movement (or change in the viewports) that occurs within a simulation of a 3D physical environment (e.g., museum or library) [10]. While spatial navigation is well studied in traditional desktop environments [5], its study in large displays is more recent [15]. Tan et al. [15], from a series of studies involving users in navigating 3D spaces, reported several advantages of using large displays as compared to smaller, desktop size screens. Two main advantages were that users had a greater sense of immersion and that they developed better cognitive maps of the virtual worlds, both of these subsequently led users to perform better in their navigation tasks in 3D (also supported by Bakdash et al. [1]).

In their experiments of 3D navigation tasks, researchers have often relied on the use of devices such a mouse and keyboard; a gaming joystick; or motion-tracked wands [1,13,15]. In a public setting, the use of these devices could bring forth issues about physical security, sanitation, and maintenance [2].

Coupling of mobile devices with large displays

The use of mobile devices to interact with large displays has been touted as a possible candidate to meet most, if not all, of Ballagas et al.'s concerns, including portability, sanitation, physical security, and social acceptability [2]. Researchers have introduced a variety of techniques (e.g., see [4,6,8,12]). Despite this, there seems to be lack of research about the use of touch-enabled mobile devices to support the navigation in 3D environments. Most recently, Du et al. [7] have proposed the use of the tilt and touch capabilities of a mobile to enable 3D interaction, but their research does not provide any comparative assessment of specific interaction styles or techniques that users prefer and that designers and researchers can develop further.

In this work we aim to investigate how well three different interaction styles, derived from input devices and techniques familiar to users, perform in supporting users' navigation in 3D spaces and which of these styles users prefer.

INTERACTION STYLES

We implemented three interaction styles in a touch-enabled mobile device (an iPod) based on techniques and devices familiar to users of desktop computers and mobile phones (Figure 1).

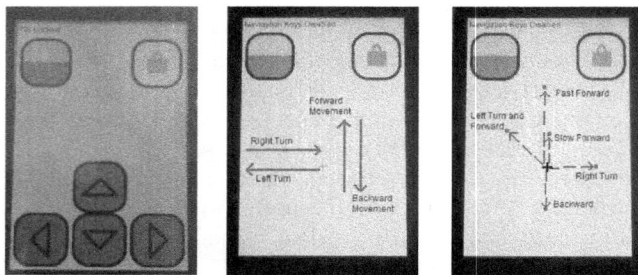

Figure 1. Screenshots of the three interaction styles on the iPod (L-R: Discretized button-based, Momentum gesture-based, and Continuous motion-based)

Discretized button-based (DB) control

This style is the baseline interaction technique and attempts to emulate how the arrows of a standard keyboard work to support 3D movement—quite common in earlier computer games requiring 3D navigation. Four arrow keys are displayed on the touch screen: up, down, left, and right (see Figure 1, left). The up and down buttons controlled forward and backward navigation, while the left and right buttons would turn the main viewpoint.

Momentum gesture-based (MG) control

This second style (see Figure 1, middle) is similar to the flicked gestures commonly used in touch-based mobile devices. The speed of the gesture controls the initial momentum and direction of movement, which slows down and comes to a full stop over time. Users are able to navigate in forward and backward directions by flicking their finger in the corresponding direction. While engaged in forward or backward movement, this interface will not allow users to turn left or right. When there is no movement, left and right flicks allow turning the viewpoint. In this way, users can move forward or backward at a faster speed, but still able to make small movements when precision is required (e.g., turning and walking slowly).

Continuous motion-based (CM) control

The CM control style (see Figure 1, right) is derived from how video game joysticks work. When the screen is touched the camera will move in that direction relative to the center of the touch screen. This simulates operations applied to a joystick, as if, for example, it is being pushed in the direction. CM provides continuous navigational movements so that users will not have to lift their finger off the screen when navigating. This style is also used in portable gaming devices with touch-enabled displays (e.g., iPod and Samsung's Galaxy).

All three styles allowed changing the upward-downward viewpoints by tilting the iPod (e.g., to look at the ceiling and floor). The tilt control is implemented using the accelerometer from the device.

USABILITY STUDY

Goal

The purpose of this experiment was to assess the suitability of using a touch-enabled mobile device to navigate 3D environments in large displays. In particular, we wanted to compare the performance of the three interaction styles described earlier.

Apparatus

The experiment was performed on a large, room-size rear-projection display (7.26×3.03m with a resolution of 2560×1024 pixels). The input was from an iPod Touch device ($110 \times 61.8 \times 8.5$mm, with a 3.5-inch display and 480×320 pixels resolution). The iPod was connected wirelessly to a workstation (HP wx9400, with 4 dual-core processors and 8 GB of RAM).

Participants and tasks

The experiment involved 15 participants (13 males) who were recruited from a local university. Participants had access to a mobile phone device, used a desktop or laptop computer daily, and were familiar with touch-based devices.

Participants were asked to navigate a 3D virtual environment (Figure 2) displayed on the large rear-projected display using the iPod. The environment was based on a family house with multiple floors and rooms. To make their navigation purposeful, they were tasked to locate a set of 24 targets placed in different locations in the environment. These targets would disappear once located. To speed up the search and to make certain all targets would be found, participants were told where the next target would be in the form of a directional arrow.

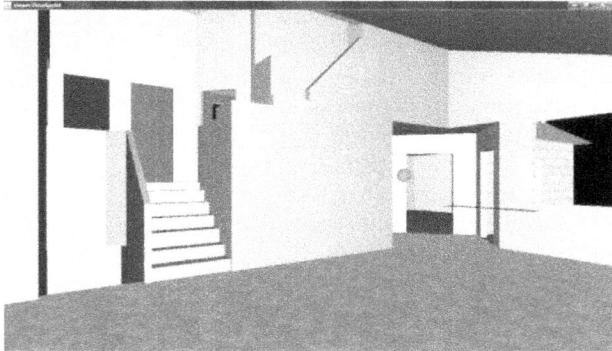

Figure 2. Screenshot of the displayed 3D environment with a target located in the middle.

Design and procedure

The study followed a within-participants design. Participants performed three trials, one per interaction style. For each trial, participants would need to follow the same path and locate 24 targets along the path. The order of the presentation of the styles was counterbalanced using a Latin square approach.

At the beginning of each trial, participants were told how the style would work, and given some time (3-5 minutes) to do a warm-up practice session navigating through a small area of the 3D environment. Upon completion of the practice session and once participants indicated that they were comfortable with the style, they would proceed to the actual trial.

The experiment collected data about the time participants would need to finish a trial. In addition, at the end of the study, participants completed a questionnaire which asked them to compare the three interaction styles based on how easy it was to learn each style, the speed of navigation, the overall usability of each style, and other subjective data.

Results

Completion time

As shown in the boxplots in Figure 3, the overall mean completion times for both DB and CM conditions were similar and faster than the MG condition.

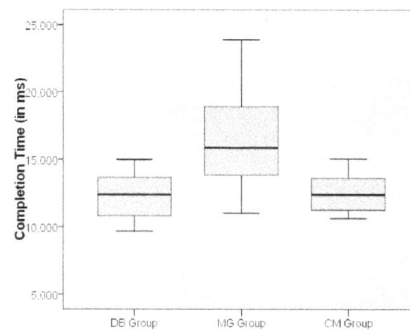

Figure 3. Boxplots of the mean completion times for all conditions.

A repeated-measures ANOVA was performed on the completion time data, followed by a Tukey LSD *post hoc* test (with Bonferroni corrections). Since Mauchly's test indicated that the assumption of sphericity had been violated ($\chi^2(2)=6.73$, $p<0.05$), degrees of freedom were corrected using Greenhouse estimate of sphericity ($\varepsilon=.71$). The results showed that the *Interaction Style* had a significant effect on the completion time ($F_{1.4, 19.9}=18.69$, $p<0.001$). *Post hoc* tests indicated that both DB and CM groups completed the trials significantly faster than MG group ($p<0.05$). The tests showed an insignificant difference between the DB and CM groups.

Participant preferences

We also analyzed the data collected from the post-study questionnaire. Participants were asked to rate (with 1 being low and 5 high) the level of frustration, speed of navigation, ease of learning, and the overall usability of each style. Friedman's ANOVA tests were performed on the data with follow-up pairwise Wilcoxon signed-ranked tests (with Bonferroni corrections) (see Table 1 for a summary of the results). Results indicated that there was a significant difference in the perceived level of frustration ($\chi^2(2, N=15)=10.39$, $p<0.05$), with significant difference between DB and MG groups (DB *Mdn*= 1, CM *Mdn*=2, MG *Mdn*=4, $z=-2.61$, $p<0.05$), but not between DB and CM groups ($z=-1.53$, $p>0.05$) and MG and CM groups ($z=-1.73$, $p>0.05$). Similarly, test results suggested that there was a significant difference in the perceived speed at which participants were able to navigate the 3D environment ($\chi^2(2, N=15)=10.72$, $p<0.05$), with significant difference between DB and CM groups and MG and CM groups (MG *Mdn*=2, DB *Mdn*=3, CM *Mdn*=4, $z=-2.86$, $p<0.05$), but not between DB and MG groups ($z=-1.042$, $p>0.05$). Likewise, results showed that there was significant difference in participants' perception of how easy it was to learn each style ($\chi^2(2, N=15)=13.45$, $p<0.05$), with *post hoc* tests pointing to a significant difference between DB and MG groups (DB *Mdn*=5, MG, CM *Mdn*=3, $z=-2.73$, $p<0.05$) and DB and CM groups ($z=-2.61$, $p<0.05$), but not between MG and CM groups ($z=-1.12$, $p>0.05$). Finally, there was a significance difference in the perceived overall usability of the styles ($\chi^2(2,

$N=15)=14.44$, $p<0.05$), with further *post hoc* tests indicating that there was significant difference only between DB and MG (DB *Mdn*=5, CM *Mdn*=4, MG *Mdn*=3, $z=-3.09$, $p<0.05$), but not between DB and CM groups ($z=-2.14$, $p>0.05$) groups and MG and CM groups ($z=-2.32$, $p>0.05$).

Mean values	Frustration	Speed	Learning	Usability
DB *Mdn*	1	3	5	5
MG *Mdn*	4	2	3	3
CM *Mdn*	2	4	3	4
Results from the statistics tests ($\sqrt{}$ = significant; Ø = nonsignificant)				
DB & MG	√	Ø	√	√
DB & CM	Ø	√	√	Ø
MG & CM	Ø	√	Ø	Ø

Table 1. Summary of statistical analysis of data about participants' preferences.

Discussion

Broadly speaking, this study adds to the existing research about the usefulness of coupling private mobile devices with large displays. More specifically, the results show that out of the three styles, *MG* seems to be the least suitable for controlling navigational movements and change of viewpoints in 3D environments. Tasks completion times is the longest for MG, while participants have had the highest level of frustration with it. Comments made by participants indicated that MG did not allow the proper level of *'sensitivity'* and resulted in the constant break in the *'flow'* of movements. Participants may have referred to that fact that once a command was issued (i.e., by flicking the finger on the screen), they would lose control until the movement came to a halt, after which they would able to issue the next command. The frequent stop-move cycles made the navigation process slow, hence the significantly more time participants spent on the trials. Although participants said that the style was very *'intuitive'* and *'very easy'* to learn, it was *'not easy to use'*. Particularly, participants had difficulties knowing how far they would walk for each flick command, making them to guess often. All these factors contributed to making the style the least usable.

Both *DB* and *CM* styles received positive comments from participants, and had similar performances in task completion. *DB* was the most *'intuitive'* style. Most participants commented that it was very easy and quick to learn how to use it. We noted that one negative aspect of DB in a touch-based device was the lack of haptic feedback. One participant commented that *'Buttons were good and basic... but on a touch screen device it is hard to know which button is pushed without looking.'* Having to switch back and forth between the device screen and the large display would have created visual discontinuities, which could have increased participants' cognitive load and affected negatively their performance. Other participants noted that, although DB was somewhat slow, it was great for moving within small, confined spaces. That is, DB allowed a high degree of control and precision. Despite some issues, DB was rated the least frustrated to use, easiest to learn, and most usable.

CM was the most interesting style. Some participants liked it very much. For example, one commented that *'The continuous motion method was great for its speed and was almost as accurate as the button presses.'* While some participants found CM *'easy to control'* and *'intuitive to learn and use'*, others found it *'difficult'* (*'because I needed to track my current position exactly'*), and *'frustrating'* (*'because you can't feel where the center is and the bounds'*). In general, from our observations, participants had some difficulty at the beginning. However, once they had become familiar with it, they appreciated it. For example, one participant said *'[C]ontinuous motion was a little hard to control but [I] caught on quick, and it was faster [than the other two],'* while another suggested that *'[C]ontinuous motion felt fastest at longer motions'*, and *'I liked continuous best because you could move while turning'*.

Given the above findings, a *DB-CM* hybrid style might be a suitable style and could be preferred by users. Each style would complement the other, helping each other to mitigate its less desirable features. DB has been deemed the most intuitive, easiest to learn and use, and most precise, but it could be slow and tedious for moving large continuous spaces. On the other hand, CM was considered as the fastest and the most natural, but it had some initial learning curve. A hybrid interface would enable users to choose how and when to use the different features of the two techniques.

CONCLUSIONS AND FUTURE WORK

In this paper, we explore the use of touch-enabled mobile devices to interact with large displays. In particular, we compare three different interaction styles for mobile devices to support the navigation of 3D environments in large displays. The results of a study show that the design of the interaction style is important, and that a hybrid style which combines discrete and continuous gesture motions represents a potential and feasible solution.

In the future, we would like to extend this research and conduct further studies with users in naturalistic settings and with larger 3D virtual environments. Results from such studies will inform us of users' acceptability of the usage of their mobile devices to navigate these environments in actual public settings. In addition, it would be interesting to explore how to support collaborative interaction among several users employing their mobile devices at the same time for one large public display in crowded environments.

ACKNOWLEDGMENTS

We thank the participants for their time. We would also like to thank the reviewers for their comments and suggestions which have helped to improve the quality of the paper. We acknowledge NSERC and the Virtual Reality Centre for partially funding this project.

REFERENCES

1. Bakdash, J.Z., Augustyn, J.S., and Proffitt, D.R. (2006). Large displays enhance spatial knowledge of a virtual environment. *APGV'06*, pp. 56-173.

2. Ballagas, R., Rohs, M, Sheridan, J., and Borchers, J. (2004). BYOD: Bring your own device. *UbiComp'04*.

3. Ballagas, R., Rohs, M, Sheridan, J., and Borchers, J. (2006). The Smart Phone: a ubiquitous input device. *Pervasive Computing*, 5(1), pp. 70-77.

4. Boring, S., Altendorfer, M., Broll, G., Hilliges, O., and Butz, A. (2007). Shoot & copy: phonecam-based information transfer from public displays onto mobile phones. *Mobility '07*, pp. 24-31.

5. Chen, C. (2004). *Information visualization: Beyond the horizon*. Springer.

6. Dearman, D. and Truong, K.N. (2009). BlueTone: a framework for interacting with public displays using dual-tone multi-frequency through Bluetooth. *Ubicomp '09*, pp. 97-100.

7. Du, Y., Ren, H., Pan, G., & Li, S. (2011). Tilt & touch: mobile phone for 3D interaction. *UbiComp'11*, pp. 485-486.

8. Jeon, S., Hwang, J., Kim, G.J., and Billinghurst, M. (2010). Interaction with large ubiquitous displays using camera-equipped mobile phones. *Per Ubiquit Comput*, 14, pp. 83-94.

9. Kurtenbach, G. and Fitzmaurice, G. (2005). Applications of large displays. *IEEE Computer Graphics and Applications*, (July/August), pp. 22-23.

10. Liang, H-N and Sedig, K. (2009). Characterizing navigation in interactive learning environments. *Interactive Learning Environments*, 17(1). pp. 53-75.

11. Malik, S., Ranjan, A., and Balakrishnan, R. (2005). Interacting with large displays from a distance with vision-tracked multi-finger gestural input. *UIST'05*, pp. 43-52.

12. McCallum, D.C. and Irani, P. (2009). ARC-Pad: absolute+relative cursor positioning for large displays with a mobile touchscreen. *UIST'09*.

13. Ni, T., Bowman, D.A., and Chen, J. (2006). Increased Display Size and Resolution Improve Task Performance in Information-Rich Virtual Environments. *GI'06*, pp. 139-146.

14. Pering, T., Ballagas, R., and Want, R. (2005). Spontaneous marriages of mobile devices and interactive spaces. *Communications of the ACM*, 48(9), pp. 53-59.

15. Tan, D.S., Gergle, D., Scupelli, P., and Pausch, R. (2006). Physically Large Displays Improve Performance on Spatial Tasks. ACM Trans. HCI, 13(1), pp.71-99.

16. Vogel, D. and Balakrishnan, R. (2004). Interactive public ambient displays: transitioning from implicit to explicit, public to personal, interaction with multiple users. *UIST '04*, pp. 137-146.

Author Index

www.ingramcontent.com/pod-product-compliance
Lightning Source LLC
Chambersburg PA
CBHW080916220326

41598CB00034B/5589